AF864103

# Florida Basic Recruit Training Program:

# LAW ENFORCEMENT

## VOLUME 1

## Disclaimer

Florida BRT Curriculum Volume 1

ISBN 13: 978-1-58152-836-7
ISBN 10: 1-58152-836-1

FDLE makes a sincere effort to ensure accuracy and quality of its published materials; however, no warranty, expressed or implied, is provided. FDLE disclaims any responsibility or liability for any direct or indirect damages resulting from the use of the information in this course or products described in it.

Mention of any product does not constitute an endorsement by FDLE of that product. All referenced persons, places, or situations are intended to be fictional, unless otherwise stated. Any resemblance to real persons, places, or situations is coincidental.

The training in this course is provided to familiarize students with issues that may involve high liability and/or high stress. FDLE urges students to ensure that their practices are correct in accordance with their agencies' policies and procedures. Employing agencies are solely responsible for guiding their employees' actions in actual situations.

Designed by Kessler Creative
Cover art by Saeedeh Posey, FDLE
Published by Copley Custom Textbooks, an imprint of XanEdu Publishing, Inc., 138 Great Road, Acton, Massachusetts 07120.

# TABLE OF CONTENTS

Florida CMS Basic Recruit Training Program: Law Enforcement, Volume 1

## Chapter 1 Introduction to Law Enforcement



## Chapter 2 Legal

## Chapter 3 Communications



## Chapter 4 Human Issues

## Chapter 6 Patrol 2



## Chapter 7 Crime Scene Investigations

# PREFACE

The mission of the Florida Criminal Justice Standards and Training Commission is to ensure that all citizens of Florida are served by criminal justice officers who are ethical, qualified, and well-trained. The Commission certifies officers who complete a Florida Basic Recruit Training Program and gain sworn employment through a Florida criminal justice agency, or who are diversely qualified through experience and training and who meet minimum employment standards.

As staff for the Commission, the Florida Department of Law Enforcement (FDLE) Professionalism Program is responsible for establishing and maintaining officer training programs. Criminal Justice officer training is conducted at 41 Commission-certified training schools housed in Florida criminal justice agencies, community colleges, and vocational technical schools. By statute, entrance into the basic recruit training programs for law enforcement, correctional, and correctional probation officers is limited to those who have passed a basic skills examination and assessment instrument, which is based on a job task analysis in accordance with §943.17(g), F.S. The same job analysis process is used to develop job related training and performance standards for basic recruit training. Hundreds of officers, citizens, and instructors have participated in the development of the officer job analysis and training curricula.

In 2001, the FDLE Professionalism Program established the Curriculum Maintenance System (CMS) to ensure that officer training remains job-related, valid, and up-to-date. Through CMS, basic recruit training curricula is reviewed and revised on an annual basis and further ensures that basic recruit graduates are prepared for sworn employment with state or local criminal justice agencies in Florida.

# CHAPTER 1

## Introduction to Law Enforcement



Law enforcement officers have the authority to enforce laws and maintain civil order. This responsibility must never be taken lightly. Officers must always act within the boundaries of their authority and uphold the recognized standards of their profession's code of ethics. This chapter provides an overview of the law enforcement training program and the requirements for students to become sworn officers, gives students instruction on basic criminal justice values and ethics, defines sexual harassment and ways to avoid compromising interactions with other officers and the public, and emphasizes the command structure within a criminal justice agency. Students will also receive a basic understanding of the structure and components of the criminal justice system.

# LESSON 1 | Officer Training Program Overview

**OBJECTIVES**

**IN028.1.** Identify the requirements for successful completion of and graduation from the Basic Recruit Training Program.

**IN028.2.** Identify the role of the Criminal Justice Standards and Training Commission established by the Florida Statutes.

**IN028.2.C.** Identify the requirements for certification according to the Florida Statutes.

**IN028.2.D.** Identify the reasons the Criminal Justice Standards and Training Commission may take action against an officer's certification.

**IN028.2.D.3.** Identify the penalties that may be imposed in the officer discipline process.

Every person who enters this training program has one goal in mind: to become a sworn law enforcement officer in the state of Florida. Florida Statute §943.10(1) provides the following definition:

> "Law enforcement officer" means any person who is elected, appointed, or employed full time by any municipality or the state or any political subdivision thereof; who is vested with authority to bear arms and make arrests; and whose primary responsibility is the prevention and detection of crime or the enforcement of the penal, criminal, traffic, or highway laws of the state. This definition includes all certified supervisory and command personnel whose duties include, in whole or in part, the supervision, training, guidance, and management responsibilities of full-time law enforcement officers, part-time law enforcement officers, or auxiliary law enforcement officers but does not include support personnel.

New recruits have questions about the process of becoming a Florida law enforcement officer. This section attempts to answer those questions by exploring the requirements for officer training and certification.

The Florida Statutes and rules under the Florida Administrative Code (FAC) enacted by the Criminal Justice Standards and Training Commission (CJSTC) provide the requirements and standards for the training and certification process of Florida criminal justice officers. Ultimately, each recruit is responsible for his or her own success in this academy. Recruits must adhere strictly to these requirements and follow the academy rules and regulations. The Florida CMS Law Enforcement Basic Recruit Training Program has been approved, and this training academy has been certified according to the guidelines set by law and the CJSTC rules.

To successfully complete this basic recruit training program, recruits must achieve a passing score on each of the written end-of-course examinations. Recruits must also demonstrate proficiency skills in the DUI Traffic Stops course and in the high liability courses (vehicle operations, first aid, firearms, and defensive tactics) and participate in the CJSTC Physical Fitness Program. See Rules 11B-35.001 and 11B-35.0024, FAC. *(IN028.1.)*

## Criminal Justice Standards and Training Commission

The Criminal Justice Standards and Training Commission was created to oversee the certification, employment, training, and conduct of Florida law enforcement, correctional, and correctional probation officers *(IN028.2.)*. The Commission meets quarterly and has as its purpose "to ensure that the citizens of the state of Florida are served by the most qualified, well-trained, competent and ethical criminal justice officers in the nation."

In pursuit of these goals, the Commission is committed to delivering quality standards and training and increasing the professionalism of officers throughout the state.

The Commission is composed of 19 members:

- Attorney General (or a designee)
- Secretary of the Department of Corrections (or a designee)
- Director of the Division of Florida Highway Patrol
- 16 members appointed by the Governor:
  - three sheriffs
  - three police chiefs
  - five law enforcement officers
  - two correctional officers
  - one training center director
  - one county corrections administrator
  - one state resident who does not fall into any of the previous categories

## Primary Responsibilities of the Commission

Florida Statute §943.12 explains the Commission's duties as follows:

- establish uniform minimum standards for the employment and training of full-time, part-time, and auxiliary law enforcement, correctional, and correctional probation officers
- establish and maintain officer training programs, curricula requirements, and certification of training schools and training school instructors
- certify officers who complete a Florida Basic Recruit Training Program or who are diversely qualified through experience and training and who meet minimum employment standards
- review and administer appropriate administrative sanctions in instances when an officer, instructor, or training school is found to be in violation of Florida Statutes and Commission standards
- promulgate rules and procedures to administer the requirements of Section §943.085–943.255, F.S.
- conduct studies of compensation, education, and training for correctional, correctional probation, and law enforcement disciplines
- maintain a central repository of records of all certified criminal justice officers
- develop, maintain, and administer the State Officer Certification Examination for criminal justice officers

The Criminal Justice Professionalism Program (CJPP) is statutorily created within the Florida Department of Law Enforcement (FDLE) to support and assist the Commission in the execution, administration, implementation, and evaluation of its powers, duties, and functions.

### *Officer Certification*

Section 943.13, Florida Statutes, sets the minimum requirements and standards a person must meet before becoming certified as an officer. An officer must

- be at least 19 years of age
- be a citizen of the United States
- be a high school graduate or its equivalent
- have processed fingerprints on file with the employing agency
- have passed a physical examination by a licensed physician based on specifications established by the Commission
- have a good moral character, as determined by a background investigation under procedures established by the Commission
- submit an affidavit attesting to compliance (a signed document agreeing to abide by all Commission rules)
- have satisfactorily completed a Commission-approved course of basic recruit training
- have satisfactorily passed a state examination in the respective specialty
- not have been convicted of any felony or of a misdemeanor which involves perjury or a false statement, regardless of withholding of adjudication or suspended sentence
- not have received a dishonorable discharge from any of the Armed Forces of the United States

A recruit has four years from the starting date of the basic recruit training to complete the certification process. In order to become ***certified*** (sworn) as a law enforcement officer, a person must do all of the following:

- meet all the minimum requirements and standards
- complete the approved basic recruit training
- pass the State Officer Certification Examination
- become actively employed with a law enforcement agency in an auxiliary, a part-time, or a full-time sworn officer position

Simply completing the basic recruit training and passing the certification exam does not mean that a person is certified.

For example, if Rob Recruit begins basic recruit training on July 1, 2008, he must meet all the minimum requirements and standards, complete the approved basic recruit training, pass the State Officer Certification Examination, and become actively employed with a law enforcement agency as a sworn officer by June 30, 2012.

If Rob Recruit does not meet all these requirements by June 30, 2012, he will have to repeat the basic recruit training, at which time a new four-year period begins. *(IN028.2.C.)*

## *State Officer Certification Examination*

Upon completion of a basic recruit training program, an individual must pass the State Officer Certification Examination (SOCE) to become certified as a law enforcement officer. An applicant must pass the SOCE within three attempts.

The Commission publishes an annual SOCE schedule with 3–5 exam administrations per month in various cities around the state.

Individuals must apply to take the SOCE and pay the exam fee prior to the application deadline date established for each administration.

Information concerning the SOCE can be found in the Applicant Information Handbook available at criminal justice training academies or online at http://www.fdle.state.fl.us. Other information on the web site includes SOCE schedules, registration information, exam topics, and example questions.

## *Officer Compliance*

When a recruit is being hired by a law enforcement agency, the agency will conduct a thorough background investigation to determine his or her moral character prior to employment with the agency. If a recruit has entered the academy prior to employment, the recruit is subject to the same moral character requirements as active certified officers and may be denied certification by the Commission if evidence indicates noncompliance with these standards.

## *Disciplinary Action*

In addition to certifying criminal justice officers, the Commission has the authority to take disciplinary action on an officer's certification if the officer fails to maintain the required standards of conduct.

The Commission may take action against an officer's certification if the officer does the following:

- pleads *nolo contendere*, pleads guilty, or is found guilty of any felony
- pleads *nolo contendere*, pleads guilty, or is found guilty of a misdemeanor involving perjury or false statement
- fails to maintain good moral character as defined by the Florida Statutes and Florida Administrative Code (CJSTC Rule 11B-27, FAC)
- commits any act constituting a felony offense, regardless of criminal prosecution
- commits any act constituting any of a specified group of serious misdemeanor offenses, regardless of criminal prosecution
- commits any principal, accessory, attempt, solicitation, or conspiracy, pursuant to Chapter 777, Florida Statutes, where there would have been a felony offense had the crime been committed or completed
- commits any act in any jurisdiction other than the state of Florida, which if committed in the state of Florida, would constitute a felony, any of the specified serious misdemeanors, or a violation of Chapter 777, Florida Statutes
- tests positive for controlled substances by a urine or blood test, in accordance with the requirements for testing reliability and integrity set forth in Rule 11B-27.00225, FAC
- is found guilty of excessive use of force under color of authority under Rule 11B-27.0011(4)(c)1., FAC
- engages in sexual harassment involving physical contact or misuse of official position
- misuses the official position, as defined by Section 112.313(6), Florida Statutes
- engages in sex while on duty
- has unprofessional relationships with an inmate, detainee, probationer, parolee, or community controlee; has written or oral communication that is intended to facilitate conduct which is

## Section Vocabulary

*certified*

prohibited by Commission rule; engages in any physical contact not required in the performance of official duties that is normally associated with the demonstration of affection or sexual misconduct as defined in section 944.35(3), Florida Statutes

- makes false statements during the employment process
- subverts or attempts to subvert the officer certification examination process pursuant to Rule 11B-30.009(3), FAC
- subverts or attempts to subvert the CJSTC-approved training examination process or an employing agency's promotional examination process pursuant to, but not limited to, acts described in Rule 11B-27.0011(4)(c)9., FAC *(IN028.2.D.)*

Officers can read more about the disciplinary process in Rule 11B-27.0011(4)(a-d), FAC.

The Commission may take disciplinary action against an officer's certification in keeping with an established set of penalty guidelines. The penalties include written reprimand, probation of up to two years (with or without mandatory retraining or counseling, if applicable), suspension of up to two years (with or without mandatory retraining or counseling, if applicable), and revocation of certification.

Under Florida Law, the Commission must revoke an officer's certification if he or she is convicted, pleads guilty or *nolo contendere*, or is found guilty of any felony offense, regardless of withholding of adjudication or suspension of sentence. In this case, the Commission has no discretion; the penalty is revocation. See §943.1395(6), F.S. When the Commission revokes an officer's certification, the officer can no longer work as a certified officer in the state of Florida. *(IN028.2.D.3.)*

While these guidelines are specific to sworn officers, it is important to remember that the Commission and the academy expect officers to adhere to the standards of conduct during basic recruit training. Violation may result in the denial of officer certification.

Because of the nature of the job, law enforcement officers are held to the highest standard. The knowledge and skills that will be learned in this basic recruit training program will prepare future officers for a rewarding and satisfying career in the criminal justice profession. Upon a person's entering this profession, the Commission, the training academy, and the employing agency are devoted to ensuring he or she is fully trained and ready to assume the duties of a Florida law enforcement officer.

# LESSON 2 | Criminal Justice Values and Ethics

## Environmental Influences on Ethical Problem Solving

Many environmental factors affect how individuals solve problems and whether or not they do so in an ethical manner. Some officers come from families that emphasize strong values, while others are taught that everything is acceptable as long as they are not caught. Still other individuals grow up in violent neighborhoods, possibly exposed to inappropriate activities. The influence of family members and peers can greatly affect how officers solve problems. Values instilled during childhood can affect an officer's decisions in adulthood.

An officer's past is by no means the only thing that influences his or her current problem-solving abilities. Co-workers can influence the way officers respond to a problem by their attitudes alone, whether they are positive and upbeat or cynical and negative. The way officers view their roles and the roles of their co-workers can also have a large impact on their actions.

Home life is especially important—it can affect everything from an officer's view of the world to behavior and decision making. A good support system in place at home can give an officer confidence in his or her opinions. Honestly communicating expectations and working out differences enhance an officer's ability to communicate with others.

An officer's time in the academy can also influence how he or she responds to situations both in and outside the criminal justice field. Instructors should display professionalism and act as mentors and role models, extending respect and courtesy to all members of the academy. Students should take advantage of the fact that instructors are experts in their fields.

Criminal justice professionals may face unique situations regarding the citizens they are sworn to protect and serve. Some people within the communities that officers patrol voice or show negative feelings toward law enforcement that might encourage officers to respond unprofessionally.

An officer's job is filled with stress. If not properly managed, stress may affect how officers respond to their duties and could lead to unprofessional conduct.

**OBJECTIVES**

**IN002.1.C.1.** Define *values.*

**IN002.1.C.2.** Define *personal values.*

**IN002.1.B.** Define *ethics.*

**IN002.1.A.** Define *ethical principles.*

**IN002.1.** Identify ethical behavior.

**IN002.2.** Identify unethical behavior.

**IN002.2.D.** Define *bribery.*

**IN002.2.C.** Define *perjury.*

**IN002.2.F.** Identify misuse of position of authority.

**IN002.2.E.** Define *conflict of interest.*

**IN002.2.B.** Define *gratuity.*

**IN002.1.D.1.** Define *professionalism.*

**IN002.1.C.** Describe the relationship between ethics, personal values, and professionalism.

**IN002.3.** Identify ethical standards of conduct based on the Law Enforcement Code of Ethics.

**IN002.5.A.1.** Identify an ethical decision making tool.

## Officer Discipline

Ethical violations can result in disciplinary action up to and including decertification by the CJSTC. The most frequent violations by criminal justice officers include giving false statements, DUI, unprofessional relationships, perjury, larceny, official misconduct, sexual offenses, domestic violence, assault, and battery.

# Values and Ethics

***Values*** are principles, standards, or qualities considered worthwhile or desirable. They are core beliefs or desires that guide or motivate attitudes and actions. They also define the things we prize most. Therefore, they provide the basis for ranking those things we want in a way that elevates some over others. Thus, values determine how people behave in certain situations. *(IN002.1.C.1.)*

***Personal values*** are an individual's convictions about what is right and wrong, based on religious beliefs, cultural roots, family background, personal experiences, laws, organizational values, professional norms, and political habits. The personal values that a student brings to the academy shape his or her behavior. These are not the best values for making ethical decisions—not because they lack importance, but because they are not universal. Examples of personal values include attitudes about work, courage, honesty, fairness, friendship, trustworthiness, respect, responsibility, compassion, service, self-discipline, caring, and citizenship. *(IN002.1.C.2.)*

***Ethics*** is a standard of conduct based on moral duties and virtues that are derived from the principles of right and wrong. Ethics indicate how a person should behave *(IN002.1.B.)*. ***Ethical principles*** are rules of conduct derived from ethical values. These values may give rise to many principles in the form of specific "do's and don'ts." Honesty is an important ethical value. Some of the characteristics associated with honesty include truthfulness and fairness *(IN002.1.A.)*. ***Ethical behavior*** is principled, value-based decision making, practiced daily.

Ethical behavior in law enforcement includes treating all persons with courtesy and fairness, refusing to accept or offer gratuities, preserving evidence, giving true and impartial testimony, obeying all laws and regulations, protecting the civil rights of all citizens, and respecting confidential and privileged communication. *(IN002.1.)*

# Unethical Behavior

There are types of behavior that society considers unethical; laws make certain unethical behavior criminal. Some unethical behavior that law enforcement officers should be on guard against includes engaging in bribery, committing perjury, and misusing their position or authority. Officers should also be wary of divulging privileged communication, engaging in situations that present a conflict of interest, and accepting inappropriate gratuities. *(IN002.2.)*

***Bribery*** is defined in F.S. §838.015 as follows:

> . . . corruptly to give, offer, or promise to any public servant, or, if a public servant, corruptly to request, solicit, accept, or agree to accept for himself or herself or another, any pecuniary or other benefit not authorized by law with an intent or purpose to influence the performance of any act or omission which the person believes to be, or the public servant represents as being, within the official discretion of a public servant, in violation of a public duty, or in performance of a public duty. *(IN002.2.D.)*

***Perjury*** may be defined as a false statement made under oath which the person making the statement does not believe to be true. Criminal violations differ depending on the situation in which an individual commits perjury. For example, in official proceedings, perjury is considered a felony of the third degree; in unofficial proceedings, perjury is considered a misdemeanor of the first degree. *(IN002.2.C.)*

### *Misuse of Position of Authority*

Section 112.313(6), F.S. states the following:

> No public officer, employee of an agency, or local government attorney shall corruptly use or attempt to use his or her official position or any property or resource which may be within his or her trust, or perform his or her official duties, to secure a special privilege, benefit, or exemption for himself, herself, or others. *(IN002.2.F.)*

## Privileged Communication

A law enforcement officer spends a great deal of time collecting information. Privacy, trust, and loyalty are important issues when people volunteer information or act as informers. Certain types of communication between people are protected or privileged, which may include communication resulting from protected relationships, such as that between attorney and client. Officers should record statements that bear on an incident, even if they may appear to be protected. The decision about whether the information is protected will be made later.

New officers should use discretion when divulging job-related information in unofficial situations. They should not gossip or socially discuss cases with friends, relatives, the public, or others. Doing so may jeopardize ongoing departmental investigations and result in serious consequences for the officer and his or her department. If an officer divulges privileged information for non-law enforcement purposes, he or she could face agency and CJSTC disciplinary action.

## Conflict of Interest

For the public to maintain its faith in the integrity and impartiality of law enforcement officers and their departments, officers must avoid taking or influencing official actions that could conflict with their responsibilities. There are several prohibitions describing the standards of conduct related to a ***conflict of interest***. For instance, an officer must, unless required by law or policy, refrain from becoming involved in official matters, influencing actions of other officers in official matters, or influencing an officer's immediate family, relatives, or persons with whom the officer has or has had a significant personal, business, or employment relationship. *(IN002.2.E.)*

In addition, an officer must not engage in any off-duty employment if the position compromises or would reasonably tend to compromise the officer's ability to impartially perform his or her official duties.

A ***gratuity*** is anything of value intended to benefit the giver more than the receiver; it is something given to a person because of that person's position or authority. This is an ethical issue law enforcement officers face. Whenever a situation involving a gratuity arises, an officer should ask and respond ethically to the following questions: "Does this person want something from me?" "Would I be offered this if I were not a law enforcement officer?" "What is expected in return?" *(IN002.2.B.)*

## Professionalism

***Professionalism*** is behavior that demonstrates good character and is marked by pride in self and career. Examples of these characteristics include service, integrity, respect, quality, fairness, honesty, courage, compassion, moral/ethical leadership, trustworthiness, and common sense. *(IN002.1.D.1.)*

Ethics, personal values, and professionalism are inseparably intertwined, and each element is essential in a law enforcement officer's personal and professional life. *(IN002.1.C.)*

## Ethics Codes

Some national law enforcement organizations have established general codes of ethics for law enforcement officers. Agencies generally adopt one of these codes or create a code that is specific to each agency and its mission. Furthermore, section 112.313, Florida Statutes, specifies certain standards of conduct for public officers. Other sections of the statutes set forth the punishment for violating ethical standards.

### *Sections of Florida Statutes Related to Ethical Conduct and Violations*

| | |
|---|---|
| **F.S. §92.525** | Perjury by false written declaration. |
| **F.S. §837.012** | Perjury when not in an official proceeding. |
| **F.S. §837.02** | Perjury in official proceedings. |
| **F.S. §837.021** | Perjury by contradictory statements. |
| **F.S. §837.05** | False reports to law enforcement authorities. |
| **F.S. §837.06** | False official statements. |
| **F.S. §838.015** | Bribery. |
| **F.S. §838.016** | Unlawful compensation or reward for official behavior. |
| **F.S. §839.20** | Refusal to execute criminal process. |
| **F.S. §839.26** | Misuse of confidential information. |
| **F.S. §914.14** | Witnesses accepting bribes. |

The Law Enforcement Code of Ethics provides specific principles by which the law enforcement officer operates with respect to ethical values and expectations. The Law Enforcement Oath of Honor provides officers with a shorter version of these same ethical values that can be better anchored into officers' long-term memories for easy recall when they are confronted with ethical dilemmas and stressful situations.

Officers should become familiar with the laws related to ethical conduct, the Code of Ethics, and the Oath of Honor, and conduct themselves by these principles. *(IN002.3.)*

## Law Enforcement Code of Ethics

As a law enforcement officer, my fundamental duty is to serve the community; to safeguard lives and property; to protect the innocent against deception, the weak against oppression or intimidation, and the peaceful against violence or disorder; and to respect the constitutional rights of all to liberty, equality, and justice.

I will keep my private life unsullied as an example to all and will behave in a manner that does not bring discredit to me or to my agency. I will maintain courageous calm in the face of danger, scorn, or ridicule; develop self-restraint; and be constantly mindful of the welfare of others. Honest in thought and deed both in my personal and official life, I will be exemplary in obeying the law and the regulations of my department. Whatever I see or hear of a confidential nature or that is confided to me in my official capacity will be kept ever secret unless revelation is necessary in the performance of my duty.

I will never act officiously or permit personal feelings, prejudices, political beliefs, aspirations, animosities, or friendships to influence my decisions. With no compromise for crime and with relentless prosecution of criminals, I will enforce the law courteously and appropriately without fear or favor, malice or ill-will, never employing unnecessary force or violence and never accepting gratuities.

I recognize the badge of my office as a symbol of public faith, and I accept it as a public trust to be held so long as I am true to the ethics of police service. I will never engage in acts of corruption or bribery, nor will I condone such acts by other police officers. I will cooperate with all legally authorized agencies and their representatives in the pursuit of justice.

I know that I alone am responsible for my own standard of professional performance and will take every reasonable opportunity to enhance and improve my level of knowledge and competence.

I will constantly strive to achieve these objectives and ideals, dedicating myself before God to my chosen profession . . . law enforcement.

*Source: International Association of Chiefs of Police at www.theiacp.org (as of 8-11-08)*

## Law Enforcement Oath of Honor

On my honor, I will never betray my badge, my integrity, my character, or the public trust.

I will always have the courage to hold myself and others accountable for our actions.

I will always uphold the constitution, my community, and the agency I serve.

*Source: International Association of Chiefs of Police at www.theiacp.org (as of 7-10-09)*

The Critical Thinking Test is an assessment tool that can assist officers in making decisions when faced with difficult ethical situations. It guides the officer through a series of questions encouraging the officer to think through what he or she plans to do and analyzing alternative actions that can accomplish the goal.

## Ethical Decision Making

1. Is my action legal?

   If no, stop! What action should I take?

   If yes, ask the next question.

2. Will the result of my action be good?

   If no, stop!

   If yes, ask the next question.

**Section Vocabulary**

*bribery*

*conflict of interest*

*ethics*

*ethical behavior*

*ethical principles*

*gratuity*

*perjury*

*personal values*

*professionalism*

*values*

3. Will what I plan to do actually work?

   If no, stop!

   If yes, ask the next question.

4. Is there a less harmful alternative?

   If yes, stop and use the less harmful alternative!

   If no, ask the next question.

5. Does it undermine some equal or more important value?

   If yes, stop!

   If no, go ahead with the decision.

6. Does a good end ever justify a bad means?

   No!

7. Will I be able to justify my action if my decision is made public?

   If no, stop!

   If yes, go ahead with the decision. *(IN002.5.A.1.)*

# LESSON 3 | Sexual Harassment

## Laws Related to Sexual Harassment

Every employee has a right to work in an environment free of sexual harassment and hostile conditions. Respecting others is an important aspect of ethical behavior and professionalism. Sexual harassment can also be a career killer. According to the federal Civil Rights Act of 1964, Title VII, it is unlawful for employers to discriminate in the workplace. Sexual harassment is a form of discrimination. Courts have held employers responsible for acts of sexual harassment by their employees in the workplace. See 42 U.S.C. Sec.200e-4(a). Florida has incorporated the federal laws related to sexual harassment in Florida Statute §110.1221 and Rule 60L-36.004, FAC. *(IN030.7.A.4.)*

***Discrimination*** is the action(s) a person takes to deprive another individual or group of a right because of prejudice involving color, national origin, race, religion, or sex. Discrimination may manifest itself through a form of harassment. *(IN030.7.A.)*

**OBJECTIVES**

**IN030.7.A.4.** Identify the relationship between sexual harassment and discrimination as stated in federal law.

**IN030.7.A.** Define *discrimination*.

**IN030.7.A.3.** Define *sexual harassment.*

**IN030.7.** Give examples of sexual harassment.

**IN030.7.A.2.** Define *quid pro quo*.

**IN030.7.A.1.** Define *hostile work environment.*

**IN030.7.A.5.** Identify appropriate responses to sexual harassment.

**IN030.2.** Identify possible consequences to the officer as a result of inappropriate behavior in the workplace.

**IN030.2.B.** Identify agency liability as a result of an officer's sexual harassment.

## Harassment in the Workplace

Where harassment occurs, working conditions may become hostile. Examples of harassment in the workplace may include providing less support or on-the-job training to persons of a particular group or denying an employee a deserved promotion or necessary training because of the employee's age or gender. Assigning menial or demeaning tasks regularly or exclusively to a person because of characteristics such as national origin, race, or age is another form of workplace harassment, as is using those characteristics to place people in jobs that provide no opportunity for progression, recognition, or increased responsibility. Another example of workplace harassment is keeping critical information purposely from a person because of race, age, sexual preference, or other characteristics. As a result, that person looks unprepared and uninformed to those who have influence.

***Sexual harassment*** is defined as unwelcome sexual advances, requests for sexual favors, and other verbal or physical conduct of a sexual nature. *(IN030.7.A.3.)*

The courts have held that intent is not a factor in determining what constitutes sexual harassment. Rather, they focus on the impact of the conduct. "I didn't mean anything by it" has no relevance to a determination of whether sexual harassment occurred. See *Burlington Industries v. Ellerth*, 524 U.S. 742 (1998).

Courts use the reasonable person legal standard to determine if behavior constitutes sexual harassment. It is not what message the party intended to give, but whether a reasonable person in the same circumstances as the complainant would find the behavior offensive.

Some examples of sexual harassment behavior include verbal, nonverbal, and physical actions. Verbal actions can include sexual compliments, pressure for dates, or ridicule with a harsh sexual message. Nonverbal actions can include facial gestures, displaying nude pictures, or suggestive body language. Physical actions may include touching and brushing against another, hugging and patting, or horseplay.

The harasser or the victim may be a woman or a man. The victim does not have to be of the opposite sex. The harasser could be the victim's supervisor, an employee supervised by the victim, a supervisor or manager in another area, a co-worker, or even a nonemployee. The victim can also be a third party affected by the offensive conduct. For example, someone is offended by overhearing lewd banter between consenting parties. The third party may make a complaint against the people engaging in the lewd conversation. *(IN030.7.)*

Harassment occurs when submission to or rejection of such conduct by a person is the basis for making career or employment decisions affecting that person, and the purpose or effect of such conduct is to unreasonably interfere with a person's performance or create an intimidating, hostile, or offensive working environment.

In the work environment, sexual harassment may manifest itself in two forms. ***Quid pro quo*** is a Latin term that means "something for something in return". An example of *quid pro quo* harassment is when a supervisor demands sexual favors from an employee in return for allowing that employee to continue to work. The employee believes that any complaint will result in job loss *(IN030.7.A.2.)*. A ***hostile work environment*** is an office culture where lewd jokes or other offensive habits are acceptable. For example, explicit photographs and posters are displayed in a coffee break room. An employee may not complain for fear of negative consequences.

In *Meritor Savings Bank v. Vinson*, 477 U.S. 57 (1986), the United States Supreme Court recognized that sexual harassment violates the Civil Rights Act of 1964 Title VII and that sexual harassment can create a hostile or abusive work environment. The court further established the standards for analyzing whether conduct was unlawful and when an employer would be liable.

A workplace environment that allows sex-based discussions, humor, banter, posters, etc., promotes a hostile work environment. It is becoming increasingly difficult to define the workplace. Court cases have created a very wide definition of where people do work. The building where one works is certainly one workplace, but depending upon the circumstances and the context of an employee's behavior, the workplace can also be defined as business trips to conferences, seminars, or meetings; the courthouse, state attorney's office, or other agency requiring an officer's attendance in an official capacity; or an officer's patrol car. A business, private residence, school, or any other location where an officer responds to a call for assistance may also be considered a workplace, as are lunches, other meals, or work-related social gatherings. Anywhere an officer functions as a representative of his or her agency, including off-duty security details, is considered a part of the workplace. Additionally, any place an officer goes in uniform could be defined as a workplace by the court. *(IN030.7.A.1.)*

## Responses to Sexual Harassment

When harassment occurs, the person being offended has several options. For example, he or she can inform the offender that the behavior is unwelcome. Personally discussing the offense with the parties involved may resolve the issue without further action. The offended individual should always first review the situation to make sure he or she correctly perceived the harassment. Then, the person offended can plan a response and practice what to say. Tone of voice should be considered, and the offended individual should speak professionally, not blaming or being judgmental but asserting the position that he or she resents being sexually harassed. The person being harassed must make it clear that he or she wants the words and behavior to stop. The offended should also prepare for resistance and possible repercussions.

Additionally, those being harassed should review and follow the agency's discrimination policies and procedures for filing a complaint. Agencies have trained staff members who act as resources for sexual harassment complaints, procedures, and training. The behavior should be reported to a supervisor or member of management, either informally or formally, as policy dictates. The offended individual should also file a formal complaint.

The Equal Employment Opportunity Commission (EEOC) is the governmental agency that enforces compliance with the Civil Rights Act (Title VII). The harassed party has the right to file a complaint with the EEOC or consult with an attorney. *Note:* An agency may file a complaint on another person's behalf in order to protect the victim's identity. If the conduct becomes criminal, the affected party may make a report to the appropriate law enforcement agency. *(IN030.7.A.5.)*

**Section Vocabulary**

*discrimination*

*hostile work environment*

*quid pro quo*

*sexual harassment*

## Consequences of Sexual Harassment

An officer who participates in sexual harassment may be held liable with serious consequences. The officer's agency may impose internal disciplinary action such as mandatory retraining, leave without pay, loss of rank, and even discharge. The CJSTC could revoke the officer's certification. If a lawsuit is filed, the courts may impose monetary damages. In a criminal case such as stalking, battery, assault, or official misconduct, an officer could face imprisonment. *(IN030.2.)*

Harassment that goes unaddressed at the agency level may result in fines or administrative penalties. In addition, an agency that tolerates a hostile work environment may lose good employees. Harassment may also result in lawsuits and judgments against the agency and its management. Employees or supervisors creating or allowing a "sexually hostile atmosphere" to develop at the workplace can lead the courts to hold governmental agencies liable. See *Faragher v. City of Boca Raton*, 524 U.S. 775 (1998). *(IN030.2.B.)*

## Preventing Sexual Harassment

Like all acts of discrimination, sexual harassment is not always easy to define. Education is the key to understanding and preventing sexual harassment. The government and private industry lose hundreds of millions of dollars each year in legal damage awards due to harassment that could have been avoided through early intervention. To prevent personal and agency liability, officers should follow the law and agency policy. Treating people with respect is a must; harassment is the opposite of respectful behavior. Officers should also avoid engaging in behavior that could be misinterpreted. They should act professionally, remembering that the community views officers as members of law enforcement even when they are off duty. Any inappropriate behavior should be reported as soon as it occurs to prevent escalation.

# LESSON 4 | Criminal Justice System and Components

**OBJECTIVES**

**IN017.1.** Identify the major components of the Criminal Justice System.

**IN017.1.A.1.** Identify the responsibility of law enforcement.

**IN017.1.A.2.** Identify the responsibility of the court system.

**IN017.1.A.3.** Identify the responsibility of corrections.

**IN017.1.B.** Describe the levels of law enforcement.

**IN017.1.B.1.** Give examples of federal law enforcement agencies.

**IN017.1.B.2.** Give examples of state law enforcement agencies.

**IN017.1.B.3.** Give examples of county law enforcement agencies.

**IN017.1.B.4.** Give examples of municipal law enforcement agencies.

**IN017.1.C.** Identify the levels of the U.S. court system.

**IN017.1.D.** Identify the levels of the state court system.

**IN017.1.E.** Identify the major components of the court system.

**IN017.1.F.** Describe the components of the corrections system.

## Structure of the Criminal Justice System

A law enforcement officer is a small piece of a large, complex system known as the Criminal Justice System. Law enforcement officers play an important role in the Criminal Justice System and interact on a regular basis with other parts of the system. An officer's ability to interact effectively within the system directly affects the officer's job performance.

***Criminal justice*** refers to the structure, functions, and decision-making processes of those agencies that deal with the management and control of crime and criminal offenders. The three main components of the criminal justice system include law enforcement, the court system, and corrections. *(IN017.1.)*

***Law enforcement*** is the part of the system responsible for the enforcement of and maintaining civil order *(IN017.1.A.1.)*. The ***court system*** is the part of the system responsible for the interpretation of laws *(IN017.1.A.2.)*. ***Corrections*** is the part of the system responsible for enforcing punishment as defined by the court system. *(IN017.1.A.3.)*

There are four levels of law enforcement agencies within the United States: federal (U.S. government agencies), state, county, and local or municipal. Federal law enforcement agencies enforce federal laws across state lines and within the state. State law enforcement agencies are responsible for enforcing state laws within the state. The job of county law enforcement agencies is to enforce county ordinances and state laws within the county. Traditionally, they also handle unincorporated areas, the county jail, and civil processing. Municipal or local law enforcement agencies enforce the ordinances of the municipality as well as state laws within the jurisdiction of the agency. *(IN017.1.B.)*

The single largest segment of American law enforcement is found at the local level and comprises over 75 percent of total sworn personnel. There are over 17,000 different law enforcement agencies in this country. Florida has more than 17,000 municipal police officers and more than 18,000 deputy sheriffs. Each level is responsible for enforcing the laws in its jurisdiction.

### *Examples of Federal Law Enforcement Agencies*

*Note:* This list does not include all federal law enforcement agencies.

#### *The Department of Justice*

**Federal Bureau of Investigation (FBI):** The mission of the FBI is to uphold the law through the investigation of violations of federal criminal law; to protect the United States from foreign intelligence and terrorist activities; to provide leadership and law enforcement assistance to federal, state, local, and international agencies; and to perform these responsibilities in a manner that is responsive to the needs of the public and faithful to the Constitution of the United States.

**Drug Enforcement Administration (DEA):** The mission of the Drug Enforcement Administration is to enforce the controlled substances laws and regulations of the United States and to recommend and support nonenforcement programs aimed at reducing the availability of illicit controlled substances on the domestic and international markets.

**The Bureau of Alcohol, Tobacco, Firearms and Explosives:** ATF enforces federal laws and regulations relating to alcohol and tobacco products, firearms and explosives, and acts of arson.

**United States Marshals Service:** The mission of the United States Marshals Service is to protect the federal courts and ensure the effective operation of the judicial system. The Marshals Service is responsible for providing protection for the federal judiciary, transporting federal prisoners, protecting endangered federal witnesses, managing assets seized from criminal enterprises, and pursuing and arresting federal fugitives.

## *The Department of Homeland Security*

**United States Secret Service:** The Secret Service is charged with protecting the President and Vice President of the United States and their immediate families, the President-elect and Vice President-elect and their immediate families, former Presidents and their wives, the widows of former Presidents until death or remarriage, minor children of a former President until they reach 16 years of age, and visiting heads of foreign states or foreign governments and their spouses traveling with them. The Secret Service is also charged with the detection and arrest of any person committing any offense against the laws of the United States relating to coins, currency, stamps, government bonds, checks, credit/debit card fraud, computer fraud, false identification crimes, and other obligations or securities of the United States.

**U.S. Customs and Border Protection (CBP):** The Customs and Border Protection safeguards and protects the sanctity of the U.S. borders.

**Coast Guard:** The United States Coast Guard is the nation's leading maritime law enforcement agency and has broad, multi-faceted jurisdictional authority. The operational law enforcement mission is directed primarily in the areas of boating safety, drug interdiction, live marine resources, alien migrant interdiction, and responding to vessel incidents involving violent acts or other criminal activity.

**U.S. Immigration and Customs Enforcement (ICE):** Immigration and Customs Enforcement handles all issues related to the United States' immigration laws (i.e., Immigration and Nationality Act and other related provisions of the United States Code) including violations, enforcement, terrorist financing, money laundering, smuggling, intellectual property rights, protective services for federal agencies, customs intelligence, etc.

## *The Department of Treasury*

**Internal Revenue Service (IRS):** The IRS serves the American public by investigating potential criminal violations of the Internal Revenue Code and related financial crimes in a manner that fosters confidence in the tax system and compliance with the law.

**Financial Crimes Enforcement Network (FinCEN)**: FinCEN supports law enforcement investigative efforts and fosters interagency and global cooperation against domestic and international financial crimes.

**United States Postal Inspectors**: The mission of the U.S. Postal Inspection Service is to protect the U.S. Postal Service, its employees, and its customers from criminal attack and to protect the nation's mail system from criminal misuse. *(IN017.B.1.)*

## Examples of Florida State Law Enforcement Agencies

*Note:* This list does not include all state law enforcement agencies.

**Florida Department of Law Enforcement (FDLE):** The mission of FDLE is to provide services in partnership with local, state, and federal criminal justice agencies to prevent, investigate, and solve crimes by granting investigative, forensic, and protective services in several key investigative focus areas: major drug crime, violent crime, child predator cybercrime, public integrity, fraud/economic crime, and domestic security. In addition, FDLE supports the Criminal Justice Standards and Training Commission in the establishment and oversight of criminal justice officers, standards, and training.

**Florida Highway Patrol (FHP), Department of Highway Safety and Motor Vehicles:** The FHP promotes a safe driving environment through proactive law enforcement, public education and safety awareness. These practices and FHP's values of courtesy, service, and protection help the FHP reduce the number and severity of traffic crashes in Florida, preserving and protecting human life and property. The Florida Highway Patrol Commercial Vehicle Enforcement office (FHP/CVE) performs safety inspections on commercial vehicles and enforces traffic laws with a focus on commercial motor vehicle violations as well as passenger vehicle interactions with large trucks.

**Florida Fish and Wildlife Conservation Commission (FWC):** The FWC Division of Law Enforcement is charged with the vital responsibility of providing wildlife and marine law enforcement services along more than 8,400 miles of Florida's saltwater coastline and 37 million acres of land and fresh water. The FWC may also enforce federal wildlife laws.

**Florida Department of Environmental Protection (DEP):** The Department of Environmental Protection is responsible for statewide environmental resource law enforcement and for providing basic law enforcement services to the state parks, greenways, and trails. Activities include environmental education and enforcement; investigation of environmental resource crimes such as abandoned drums and waste tires and illegal dredge and fill activities; and responding to natural disasters, civil unrest, hazardous material incidents, and oil spills which threaten the environment.

**Division of Alcoholic Beverages and Tobacco (ABT), Department of Business and Professional Regulation:** The Bureau of Law Enforcement is responsible for the management of ABT's law enforcement and investigation programs. These responsibilities include conducting license discipline investigations; providing guidance, direction, and leadership to licensees; conducting criminal investigations pursuant to alcohol and tobacco laws and statutes; and determining the need for using extraordinary emergency suspension powers when a business licensed by ABT has become an immediate danger to the health, safety, and welfare of Florida's citizens.

**Department of Agriculture and Consumer Services:** The Office of Agricultural Law Enforcement (AgLaw) inspects all agricultural products that pass across the borders of Florida. These include food products, aquacultural and agricultural products, livestock, and plant materials. AgLaw is also involved in investigations of consumer fraud, especially in the areas of telemarketing and vehicle repair. It investigates criminal cases concerning the theft of farm equipment and livestock. AgLaw investigators participate in control and investigation of any criminal activities that occur in state forests.

**Florida Department of Financial Services:**

*State Fire Marshal:* The Bureau of Fire and Arson Investigations is the law enforcement branch of the Division of State Fire Marshal. It investigates possible criminal activities related to fire.

*Division of Insurance Fraud:* This division investigates possible criminal activities related to the insurance industries (life, health, title, worker's compensation).

**Office of Attorney General:**

*Medicaid Fraud Control Unit:* This unit investigates fraud committed by health care providers and the abuse, neglect, and exploitation of the elderly, ill, and disabled residents of healthcare facilities.

*Economic Crimes:* This division is responsible for investigating all multi-circuit violations of the Florida Deceptive and Unfair Trade Practices Act and works with the Federal Trade Commission in the investigation of national companies. *(IN017.B.2.)*

## Examples of County Law Enforcement Agencies

*Note:* This list does not include all county law enforcement agencies.

**Sheriff's Office:** County law enforcement agencies in Florida are composed mainly of Sheriff's Offices/Departments. In Florida, the primary role of the Sheriff's Office is law enforcement. Sheriffs in the state of Florida are elected in countywide elections. Traditionally, these agencies are responsible for law enforcement in the unincorporated areas of the county, the county jail, and civil processing. Civil processing involves law enforcement's assistance to the court system, which can include serving subpoenas, enforcing eviction notices, and providing court bailiffs. *(IN017.B.3.)*

## Examples of Municipal Law Enforcement Agencies

*Note:* This list does not include all municipal law enforcement agencies.

**Police Departments:** The local police department is responsible for enforcing the laws and ordinances within its municipality.

**Public Safety Departments:** Some Florida municipalities have Public Safety Departments combining police, fire, and emergency medical services. *(IN017.B.4.)*

# The Court System

The court system in the United States includes federal, state, county, and local courts. The President appoints federal judges, while state judges in Florida are elected or appointed by the Governor. The federal courts are the highest courts in the U.S. and generally take precedence over the state courts.

There are courts of general jurisdiction and limited jurisdiction. ***Jurisdiction*** means the types of cases in which the court can make decisions. Federal courts only hear cases that are violations of federal laws, including constitutional violations. State courts hear cases involving violation of state law. Courts of limited jurisdiction only decide a limited set of case types.

## United States Federal Court System

**Supreme Court of the United States:** The U.S. Supreme Court is the highest court in the United States and the chief authority in the judicial branch, which is one of three branches of the U.S. federal government. The Supreme Court hears appeals from decisions of lower federal courts and state supreme courts, and it resolves issues of constitutional and federal law. It stands as the ultimate authority in constitutional interpretation, and its decisions can be changed only by a constitutional amendment. The Supreme Court's most important responsibility is to decide cases that raise questions of constitutional interpretation. The court decides if a law or government action violates the Constitution. This power, known as judicial review, enables the court to invalidate both federal and state laws when they conflict with its interpretation of the Constitution.

**Courts of Appeal:** Formerly known as the Circuit Courts of Appeals, these courts make decisions on appeals from lower federal courts which are subject to review in the U.S. Supreme Court.

**United States District Courts:** District courts are the federal trial courts presided over by U.S. district judges, who are assisted by magistrates. The magistrates are appointed by the district judges and are responsible for issuing warrants, presiding over some civil cases, misdemeanor trials, petty cases, preliminary hearings, and making pretrial motions.

The scope of the federal judiciary system includes all federal codes (criminal, civil, and administrative) in all 50 states, U.S. territories, and the District of Columbia. *(IN017.1.C.)*

## Florida State Court System

The state court system in Florida is made up of four levels:

**Florida Supreme Court:** The highest court in the state of Florida is the Florida Supreme Court, consisting of seven justices who are appointed by the Governor. The Supreme Court hears cases including final orders imposing death sentences and appeals from lower state courts.

**Florida District Courts of Appeal (DCA):** The five District Courts of Appeal decide appeals from circuit courts in most criminal and civil cases.

**Florida Circuit Courts:** The 20 circuit courts handle the following:

- domestic relations cases such as dissolution of marriage (divorce), guardianship, and juvenile delinquency
- major criminal offenses (felonies) which can result in imprisonment in a state correctional institution
- probate matters, such as the processing of wills and settling of the estates of deceased persons
- civil cases involving amounts greater than $15,000
- Baker Act and Marchman cases

- issuance of search and arrest warrants within the circuit
- appeals from county court judgments, except when a state statute or provision of the state constitution is held invalid

**Florida County Courts:** The 67 county courts have limited jurisdiction and handle:

- minor criminal offenses (misdemeanors), which provide a maximum sentence of one year or less in the county jail
- county and municipal ordinance violations, including traffic infractions (some counties use hearing officers for these cases.)
- civil cases involving amounts of $15,000 or less and small claims disputes (less than $5,000)
- issuance of search and arrest warrants within the county *(IN017.1.D.)*

## Major Components of the Court

To function properly, the court system requires many persons acting in designated roles:

**Judge:** The judge is authorized to decide questions of law brought before the court and preside over the courtroom.

**Prosecutor:** The prosecutor is responsible for presenting the government's case. Each court has its own prosecutor. In federal court, the U.S. Attorney's Office serves this function. Each federal district has its own U.S. Attorney and Assistant U.S. Attorneys. In our state court system, the prosecuting office is the Office of the State Attorney. Each judicial circuit has its own State Attorney and Assistant State Attorneys. The State Attorney is responsible for filing formal charges in criminal cases.

**Defense Attorney:** The defense attorney is responsible for representing the defendant's case. In Florida, defendants are represented either by an attorney whom they have hired, a public defender who is appointed by the court, or in certain circumstances, themselves.

**Clerk of the Court:** Each county elects a clerk of the court who is responsible for maintaining files and official records and issuing subpoenas. Deputy clerks are appointed to assist judges in court paperwork and proceedings.

**Court Administrator:** The court administrator is responsible for the day-to-day administration of a court system. Responsibilities can include arranging facilities and scheduling and facilitating the interaction of the court system with the other components of the criminal justice system.

**Jury:** A jury is a group of citizens that determines questions of fact in a trial. Their responsibilities may differ depending on the particular case. A jury is not always required for a court to hear a case. In a nonjury or bench trial, the judge hears the case and renders a verdict.

**Bailiff:** A bailiff or a court deputy generally is a sworn law enforcement officer who is responsible for security in the courtroom.

**Court Reporter:** The court reporter is responsible for making a record of the proceedings. (Not all court proceedings are recorded.) Some proceedings may have voice or video recordings; others have written transcripts or merely notes from a court clerk. *(IN017.1.E.)*

## Section Vocabulary

*community control*

*corrections*

*court system*

*criminal justice*

*jurisdiction*

*law enforcement*

*parole*

*probation*

# Corrections

A general overview of the corrections systems in Florida includes the following components:

**Prisons (federal and state):** Prisons are correctional institutions maintained by the federal and state governments for the confinement of convicted felons.

**County Jails:** County jails are used for booking and temporary detention of defendants awaiting trial or disposition on federal or state charges and of convicted offenders sentenced to short-term detention (a year or less).

**County and Municipal Holding Facilities:** These facilities provide a place for detainees while booking procedures are completed or until they can be transported to a county jail.

**Treatment and Evaluation Centers:** These facilities are designed to meet the special needs of particular offenders. Treatment centers deal with alcohol/drug abusers or mentally ill offenders. Evaluation centers are the first stop when entering the prison system. In addition to general processing procedures, various tests (e.g., medical, education aptitude) are performed at these facilities.

**Probation, Parole, and Community Control:** Probation, parole, and community control are part of a community-based correctional system. Its purpose is to supervise the enforcement of specific restrictions on individuals who may have received a suspended sentence after conviction or may be on parole. ***Probation*** is a sentence placing a person under the supervision of a probation officer for a specified length of time instead of confinement. Individuals who violate their probation may be returned to the system to serve their original sentence. ***Parole*** is the release of an inmate from a correctional institution prior to the conclusion of the inmate's court-imposed sentence. Under supervision, the inmate serves the remainder of his or her sentence in compliance with the specific terms of the release agreement. Individuals who violate their release agreement may be returned to the institution. ***Community control*** (house arrest) is a form of closely monitored community supervision and is more restrictive than probation or parole.

**Juvenile Assessment/Detention Center:** Juvenile suspects are taken to a center for processing and possible pretrial detention. Officers should check their agencies' policies and procedures for the proper detainment center for juvenile suspects in their district. *(IN017.1.F.)*

# LESSON 5 | Chain of Command

## Organizational Structure

**OBJECTIVES**

**IN016.1.A.** Identify the purpose of organizational structure within a criminal justice agency.

**IN016.1.** Identify the organizational and command structure of a typical criminal justice agency.

**IN016.3.A.3.** Define *chain of command.*

**IN016.3.A.1.** Identify why chain of command within a criminal justice agency should be followed.

**IN016.1.B.** Identify how chain of command facilitates communication within the organization.

**IN016.2.B.** Define *delegation of authority.*

In order to function properly and provide prompt service to the community, all law enforcement agencies must be organized with specific goals and objectives. Organizations function properly because they have good organizational structure and follow an organizational communication system. The purpose of having an organizational structure is to create a working relationship that encourages communication between each employee and the chief executive officer.

An organization is defined as a group of two or more people who cooperate to accomplish an objective or multiple objectives. The mission statement, goals, and objectives are organizational statements that describe the intended results of the organization's work.

The structure found in most law enforcement agencies is both historical and practical. In almost every organization, subordinates report to superiors *(IN016.1.A.)*. This is called a hierarchy. An organizational chart is a visual representation of the hierarchy.

Rank structure is used to delineate between the different levels within the organization. In law enforcement agencies, this rank structure might be as follows:

- Sheriff or Chief of Police
- Undersheriff or Chief Deputy, Deputy Chief of Police
- Colonels
- Majors
- Captains
- Lieutenants
- Sergeants
- Corporals
- Deputies or Officers *(IN016.1.)*

***Chain of command*** is the order of authority within an organization. It provides the linkage of authority and responsibility that joins one level of an organization to another. *(IN016.3.A.3.)*

Most organizations use the chain of command as a means of communicating and decision making. A chief or sheriff cannot answer all the questions that all subordinates might have on any given day. Most workers go to their immediate supervisor for information and assistance.

Command is sometimes a held position. For example, the head of a Special Weapons and Tactics (SWAT) team could be an experienced officer or an officer with rank.

Command is usually given to the most experienced officer, one who has extensive background in a specific area of law enforcement (e.g., vice, drugs, explosives, or even white-collar crimes).

Following a chain of command facilitates coordination, reduces confusion, and enhances the efficiency of the organization. *(IN016.3.A.1.)*

The failure to follow orders from superiors in the chain of command is known as ***insubordination***, a very serious offense. Because agencies do have the legal authority to vary from their own policies, even an order that appears to constitute a violation of policy must be followed. If it is later shown that the order was improper, responsibility will rest with the supervisor who issued the order, not the subordinate who followed the order. An order known to be illegal, however, must not be carried out. An officer refusing to follow an order must be absolutely certain of the law involved and will be subject to charges of insubordination if he or she is wrong.

All employees should strive to operate within the chain of command and keep their immediate supervisor informed of their activities. Violations of the chain of command can result in miscommunication of important information and data, thus damaging the relationship between officer and immediate supervisor. Confusion will result, and there may be a lack of coordination within the unit. In some situations such as those in the field, an officer's direct supervisor will not be available to answer an important question. This is when the academy training comes into play, and officers must make decisions to the best of their ability, knowledge, and training.

## Communication

There must be uniform channels for communication within the organizational structure to facilitate the accomplishment of objectives. These channels must include both vertical and lateral communications within the structure.

***Vertical communication*** is a term for information from the chief executive officer that flows down through the supervision levels to the lowest levels of the organization. Equally important is the information that also flows in reverse, from the lowest levels to the highest.

***Lateral communication*** is that which travels across a level of the organization to employees on the same level within the chain of command. Sometimes, information must be processed at all levels and then channeled to the individual or individuals responsible for accomplishing a specific objective.

In a law enforcement agency, structural levels are identified through the rank held at a particular level within the organization. In most agencies, officers with rank such as lieutenant, captain, and higher are usually regarded as command level.

The structure of an organization is defined as how the employees are grouped to perform the work of the organization. There are usually units (patrol, investigations, parking), and within these units are sub-units. In investigations, there may be sub-units on vice, homicide, child abuse, burglary, and assault and battery. *(IN016.1.B.)*

## Delegation of Authority

Whether it is the chief of police, the sheriff, or the agency director, the consequences of everything that happens within the organization ultimately rest on one person. To effectively manage an organization, the person in command needs to assign decision-making authority to those under his or her command. This granting of power by the person with authority to another person is called ***delegation of authority***. *(IN016.2.B.)*

On each level of the chain of command, there is a distribution of authority and responsibility. Knowing who has the authority to make decisions and who has the responsibility for the follow-through is the foundation of an effective organization.

**Section Vocabulary**

***chain of command***

***delegation of authority***

***insubordination***

***lateral communication***

***vertical communication***

# CHAPTER 2

## Legal



To act properly and effectively as law enforcement officers without infringing on citizens' rights, students must have an understanding of federal, state, and local laws. Students should also become familiar with case law and how it interprets and further explains enacted laws. Officers' duties include a variety of responsibilities, such as answering citizen calls, patrolling, determining violations of law, making arrests, using force, and conducting investigations, all of which require a foundational knowledge of the law and the ability to apply that law to specific incidents. This chapter will provide a solid legal foundation from which students may function as law enforcement officers.

# UNIT 1 | INTRODUCTION TO LAW

## LESSON 1 | Evolution of Laws

**OBJECTIVES**

**IN001.2.A.** Describe the history of the American legal system.

**IN001.1.A.** Identify types of law in America.

**IN001.1.A.1.** Define *constitutional law.*

**IN001.1.A.4.** Define *statutory law.*

**IN001.1.A.6.** Define *ordinance.*

**IN001.1.A.2.** Define *criminal law.*

**IN001.1.A.5.** Define *case law.*

**IN001.1.A.3.** Define *civil law.*

### Legal System

Law is a form of social control or a method of encouraging people to behave in a certain way. Other forms of social control include morality and religion. Religious concepts such as sin are often the basis for criminal law. In a simple society, written laws are unnecessary. The behavior of the inhabitants is controlled by more primitive means such as violence or removal from the community.

As societies became more complicated, written laws were necessary to maintain order. The rules of the society, which developed naturally, were codified by being written down. This natural development of law is sometimes referred to as common law. The American legal system is based primarily on English common law. *(IN001.2.A.)*

In addition to maintaining order, laws also serve to protect ownership of property, regulate certain businesses, and raise revenue.

### Types of Law in America

There are several types of law that govern the way we live in the United States including constitutional law, statutory law, ordinances, criminal law, case law, and civil law *(IN001.1.A.)*. ***Constitutional law*** defines the form of government we as Americans have established for ourselves; the Constitution defines our representational government and its three-branch structure (executive, legislative, and judicial) *(IN001.1.A.1.)*. Through constitutional law, we can identify the powers and limitations of each branch. Additionally, constitutional law consists of standards set forth in the Constitution and of court decisions or interpretations of the Constitution handed down by U.S. District and Supreme Courts.

The state of Florida has its own state constitution that generally parallels the U.S. Constitution. This means that the Florida Constitution affords Florida's citizens the same level of rights or greater than they derive from the federal Constitution.

***Statutory law*** is written and enacted by Congress, state legislatures, or local governing authorities in response to a perceived need to clarify the function of government. Statutory law includes civil, criminal, administrative, and regulatory laws. *(IN001.1.A.4.)*

Statutes enacted by a municipal (city) or county government are known as ***ordinances*** *(IN001.1.A.6.)*. Local governments create ordinances which regulate matters of narrow application such as curfews for minors, restrictions on the hours when alcohol may be sold, or parking regulations. Ordinances apply only within the jurisdiction of the governmental entity that enacted them. Some ordinance violations are criminal, while others are civil infractions. These laws cannot conflict with state or federal law, including case law.

Within statutory law, some provisions define unacceptable behaviors and government prosecution of those who commit them. These statutes are called ***criminal law*** and must clearly describe the unacceptable behavior and set a punishment for it. *(IN001.1.A.2.)*

The body of law formed by the decisions of the court system (the judicial branch) is called ***case law***. These court-imposed decisions are based on the court's interpretation of constitutional provisions, and they clarify the meaning of a statute or rule as applied to a specific set of facts. *(IN001.1.A.5.)*

***Civil law*** pertains to legal action a person takes to resolve a private dispute with another person *(IN001.1.A.3.)*. The courts provide a forum for the parties to resolve disputes through legal action. In civil lawsuits, the person filing the lawsuit must have a recognized cause of action. A cause of action is to a civil case what a criminal statute is to a criminal case. In many situations, crime victims also have causes of action that allow them to sue the perpetrators of the crimes. Sometimes, law enforcement's actions in enforcing a law can generate a civil lawsuit.

**Section Vocabulary**

***case law***

***civil law***

***constitutional law***

***criminal law***

***ordinance***

***statutory law***

## UNIT 1 | INTRODUCTION TO LAW

## LESSON 2 | Focus on Constitutional Law

### Basic Concepts of the U.S. Constitution

Law enforcement officers are required to abide by the limitations that the Constitution sets and the case law decisions that interpret those limitations. Certain amendments are particularly relevant to law enforcement. The Constitution protects individuals from governmental abuse of power and defines law enforcement's authority to act. *(IN001.2.C.)*

In any situation, an officer must be able to determine how to follow the law. According to the U.S. Constitution, all people stand equal before the law and therefore share certain rights. These rights, such as freedom of speech, protection against unreasonable searches and seizures, and prohibition of cruel and unusual punishment, are described in the first ten amendments to the Constitution, which are known as the Bill of Rights *(IN001.2.F.)*. Although many of these amendments focus on the courts and the legislature, some, such as the Fourth, Fifth, and Sixth Amendments, focus on law enforcement activities.

**OBJECTIVES**

**IN001.2.C.** Explain the importance of the U.S. Constitution to law enforcement officers.

**IN001.2.F.** Identify the Bill of Rights.

**IN001.2.B.** Identify basic concepts incorporated in the U.S. Constitution.

**IN001.2.D.** State the purpose of the Articles of the Constitution.

**IN001.3.A.** Explain the supremacy of the U.S. Constitution.

**N001.2.E.** State the purpose of the Amendments to the Constitution.

**IN001.2.G.1.** Identify the key aspects of the First Amendment.

**IN001.2.G.2.** Identify the key aspects of the Second Amendment.

**IN001.2.G.3.** Identify the key aspects of the Fourth Amendment.

**IN001.2.G.4.** Identify the key aspects of the Fifth Amendment.

**IN001.2.G.5.** Identify the key aspects of the Sixth Amendment.

**IN001.2.G.6.** Identify the key aspects of the Eighth Amendment.

**IN001.3.B.** Identify the key aspects of the Fourteenth Amendment.

**IN001.3.D.** Describe how case law directs a law enforcement officer's actions.

The purpose of government is to secure and protect these rights. The government is the agent of the people, not their master, and a law enforcement officer represents the law. The U.S. Constitution sets parameters within which the government operates and establishes laws. The decisions of the U.S. Supreme Court and other appeals courts resolve issues or conflicts which arise under the Constitution. *(IN001.2.B.)*

## The Articles of the Constitution

The Articles of the Constitution form the Constitution's main body. Their purpose is to form a contract between the people of the United States and the United States government that spells out the responsibilities and authority of the three branches of government. *(IN001.2.D.)*

The supremacy clause is a significant idea incorporated into the Constitution by the founding fathers. Set forth in Article VI, the supremacy clause states that when laws conflict, federal law generally overrules state and local law. State law can be more restrictive than federal law, but it cannot undermine the federal standard. *(IN001.3.A.)*

## The Amendments to the Constitution

The Amendments to the Constitution affect law enforcement officers more than any other part of the Constitution. Their purpose is to ensure that individual rights are not infringed upon by the government. *(IN001.2.E.)*

### *The Bill of Rights*

The First, Second, Fourth, Fifth, Sixth, and Eighth Amendments are of particular importance to law enforcement, as they concern issues of officer liability.

The First Amendment protects freedom of speech, press, peaceful assembly, and religion. Examples of law enforcement activities that may be affected by the First Amendment include arrests for disorderly conduct and seizure of press materials such as cameras, tapes, and writing material. *(IN001.2.G.1.)*

The Second Amendment guarantees the right to bear arms. Chapter 790 of the Florida Statutes sets forth the guidelines regarding firearms in the state of Florida. *(IN001.2.G.2.)*

The Fourth Amendment prohibits unreasonable search and seizure and generally requires a warrant signed by an independent magistrate (judge). Law enforcement activities affected by the Fourth Amendment include law enforcement's entry into homes, vehicles, luggage, purses, or other places where a person has a reasonable expectation of privacy, including his or her person, and interference with people's right to possess and maintain control over their property. Law enforcement stops and arrests, including the use of force on persons, are considered seizures and must meet the reasonableness requirement. *(IN001.2.G.3.)*

The Fifth Amendment is best known for prohibiting compelled self-incrimination. It also requires grand jury indictment for capital crimes and prohibits double jeopardy and deprivation of life, liberty, or property without due process of law. Law enforcement activities affected by the Fifth Amendment include interviewing and arresting suspects or taking other illegal law enforcement action in violation of due process. *(IN001.2.G.4.)*

The Sixth Amendment guarantees the right to a speedy and public trial, counsel, an impartial jury, to be informed of the nature of the charges, and to confront witnesses. Law enforcement activities affected by the Sixth Amendment are related to making contact with a suspect who is represented by counsel. *(IN001.2.G.5.)*

The Eighth Amendment prohibits excessive bails and fines and cruel and unusual punishment. Other than making a bond recommendation or request to the judge, a law enforcement officer has little to do with fines or punishment. *(IN001.2.G.6.)*

The Bill of Rights was originally intended to restrict actions of the federal government only. The Fourteenth Amendment expanded the application of the Bill of Rights to state and local governments as well. This was done by the ***due process clause*** of the Fourteenth Amendment:

> No state shall make or enforce any law which shall abridge the privileges and immunities of citizens of the United States; nor shall any State deprive any person of life, liberty or property, without due process of law; nor deny any person within its jurisdiction of the equal protection of the laws.

The Fifth Amendment also contains a due process clause but is limited only to the actions of the federal government. Simply put, the due process clauses of the Fifth and Fourteenth Amendments require the government to be fair when taking away someone's life, liberty, or property. *(IN001.3.B.)*

**Section Vocabulary**

*due process clause*

## Keeping Current in the Law

The rules under which law enforcement officers operate are constantly changing based upon revisions in statutes and the case law interpreting those statutes. Each officer is responsible for keeping current with these changes.

There are a variety of sources available to help officers stay current, including police magazines, training bulletins, and official web sites, such as the Florida Department of Law Enforcement, Florida Attorney General, and Florida Supreme Court. Officers should avoid obtaining legal knowledge from unofficial sources such as newspapers, television, unofficial web sites, and word of mouth.

Violating case law holdings may have the same consequences as violating statutory law. When an officer violates these principles, he or she may risk exclusion of evidence at trial, case dismissal, administrative discipline, civil liability, and criminal prosecution. *(IN001.3.D.)*

# UNIT 1 | INTRODUCTION TO LAW

## LESSON 3 | Classification of Offenses

**OBJECTIVES**

**IN023.2.B.** Define *offense.*

**IN023.2.** Identify the classification and category of a criminal offense.

**IN023.1.A.** Identify the relevant facts for use in classifying a criminal or noncriminal offense.

**IN023.2.B.2.** Define *felony.*

**IN023.2.C.** Identify the levels of felony offenses.

**IN023.2.B.3.** Define *misdemeanor.*

**IN023.2.D.** Identify the levels of misdemeanor offenses.

**IN023.2.B.4.** Define *noncriminal violation.*

**IN023.2.B.5.** Identify municipal/county ordinance violation.

### Categories and Classes of Offenses

The term ***offense*** broadly describes acts that are punishable under Florida law *(IN023.2.B.)*. Criminal offenses are punishable by incarceration and classified as either felony or misdemeanor *(IN023.2.)*. Noncriminal offenses, or civil infractions, are punishable by monetary fines or something other than incarceration. An example of a noncriminal offense is a traffic violation such as failure to yield the right of way. *(IN023.1.A.)*

A ***felony*** is any crime committed for which the maximum penalty is death or incarceration in a state correctional facility for more than one year. See §775.08(1), F.S. *(IN023.2.B.2.)*

Felonies are classified based on the severity of the offense's maximum or minimum penalty. Each of the five felony classes is defined by the penalty and/or fine associated with it. Most penalties are defined in §775.082(3); and most fines are set forth in §775.083(1). A capital felony is the highest class of felony. The penalty for offenses in this class is death or life imprisonment in a state correctional facility without the possibility of parole. For example, first-degree murder described in §782.04(1), F.S. is a capital felony and the only capital felony for which the state may impose the penalty of death. All other capital felonies require the state to impose a life sentence without the possibility of parole. An example is sexual battery on a child under 12 years old by a person 18 years or older. See §794.011(2)(a), F.S.

A life felony has varying penalties, including up to life imprisonment in a state correctional facility, a fine of up to $15,000, or both. The penalty may vary depending on when the crime was committed and the type of crime committed. In addition, some crimes classified as a first-degree felony, such as kidnapping or rape, may be reclassified as a life felony, if the crime was committed with the use of a weapon or firearm. See §775.087, F.S.

A first-degree felony carries a maximum penalty of 30 years in a state correctional facility, a fine of up to $10,000, or both. However, certain first-degree felonies specifically carry a maximum penalty of life imprisonment in a state correctional facility. For example, kidnapping is a first-degree felony punishable by life imprisonment. See §787.01(2), F.S.

A second-degree felony is punishable by a maximum of 15 years in a state correctional facility, a fine of up to $10,000, or both. Aggravated Battery is an example of a second-degree felony. See §784.045, F.S.

A third-degree felony carries a maximum penalty of five years in a state correctional facility, a fine of up to $5,000, or both. For example, Aggravated Assault is a third-degree felony. See §784.021, F.S.

Penalties of imprisonment may be extended for defendants who have been classified as violent career criminals, habitual felony offenders, or habitual violent felony offenders under the provision in §775.084, F.S.

In most criminal offenses, the penalty classification for the particular offense is stated within the relevant section of law. However, for a few offenses, the classification and penalty are specified in a separate section within the same statutory chapter. Some crimes may be reclassified to the next higher degree when certain factors are present. Examples of such reclassifications include the following:

- violent offenses committed against law enforcement officers, correctional officers, State Attorneys, Assistant State Attorneys, and judges
- wearing a mask, hood, etc. to conceal identity while committing a felony or misdemeanor
- wearing a bulletproof vest while committing certain offenses
- evidencing prejudice while committing a crime (hate crimes)
- possessing a weapon while committing a crime
- unlawful taking, possessing, or using of a law enforcement officer's firearm during the commission of a crime
- committing a misdemeanor or felony that facilitated or furthered an act of terrorism

Similarly, some offenses may be reclassified based on certain factors. For example, attempting most crimes is a degree lower than the completion of the offense. So, attempted robbery is a third-degree felony, but completing the crime is a second-degree felony. *(IN023.2.C.)*

A ***misdemeanor*** is any criminal offense with a maximum incarceration penalty in a county jail up to one year. See §775.08(2), F.S. *(IN023.2.B.3.)*. Misdemeanors are divided based on the maximum penalty and/or fine associated with the offense. See §775.081(2) and §775.083(1), F.S. A first-degree misdemeanor carries a maximum penalty of one year in a county jail, a fine of $1,000, or both. Battery is a first-degree misdemeanor. See §784.03(1), F.S. A second-degree misdemeanor carries a maximum penalty of 60 days in a county jail, a fine of $500, or both. An example of a second-degree misdemeanor is criminal mischief involving property damage totaling less than $200. See §806.13(1)(a) and (b)1., F.S. *(IN023.2.D.)*

An offense for which the only penalty may be a fine, forfeiture, or other civil penalty is a ***noncriminal violation***, also known as a civil infraction. According to §775.08(3) F.S., a "noncriminal violation does not constitute a crime, and conviction for a noncriminal violation shall not give rise to any legal disability based on a criminal offense." *(IN023.2.B.4.)*

## Ordinance Violations

Municipalities or counties may enact ordinances or local regulations for the protection and well-being of its citizens and property. Local ordinances apply only to the geographical area of the county or city that enacted them. Most ordinance violations are not criminal in nature. Certain ordinances may prohibit acts that are also crimes by statute. When in conflict, state/federal statutes take precedence over local ordinances.

## Section Vocabulary

*felony*

*misdemeanor*

*noncriminal violation*

*offense*

The maximum penalty for violating a local criminal ordinance is a fine of $500 or incarceration in a county jail for a period of up to 60 days. *(IN023.2.B.5.)*

| | | | |
|---|---|---|---|
| **Criminal Offense** | **Felony** | **Capital felony** | **Death or life imprisonment in a state correctional facility without possible parole** |
| | | **Life felony** | **Life imprisonment, $15,000 fine, or both** |
| | | **Felony 1st degree** | **30 years and, in some cases, life imprisonment, $10,000 fine, or both** |
| | | **Felony 2nd degree** | **15 years imprisonment, $10,000 fine, or both** |
| | | **Felony 3rd degree** | **5 years imprisonment, $5,000 fine, or both** |
| **Criminal Offense** | **Misdemeanor** (does not include noncriminal traffic violations or infractions) | **Misdemeanor 1st degree** | **Imprisonment in a county correctional facility for up to 1 year, $1,000 fine, or both** |
| | | **Misdemeanor 2nd degree** | **Imprisonment of up to 60 days, $500 fine, or both** |
| **Noncriminal Offense/ Civil Violation** | **Infraction/ violation** | | **$500 fine, forfeiture, or other civil penalty. According to §775.08(3), F.S., *noncriminal* shall not mean any conviction for any violation of any municipal or county ordinance.** |
| **Municipal/ County Ordinance Violation** | **Civil/criminal** | | **Civil penalty of up to $500 or imprisonment of up to 60 days, or both** |

Classification of offenses

*Figure 2-1*

# UNIT 2 | LEGAL CONCEPTS

## LESSON 1 | Standards of Legal Justification

### Reason to Act

The U.S. Constitution guarantees a right of privacy—a "right to be left alone"—to all citizens who do not break the law. This right, guaranteed by the Fourth Amendment, separates the United States from totalitarian dictatorships in which people can be stopped at random, forced to produce identity cards, and searched, often simply because they disagree with the government. Everyone, citizen and alien alike within U.S. borders, is entitled to walk and drive the streets and highways and move about in public places free from police interference as long as they obey the law.

There is no right to be left alone for people who violate the law. The Constitution does not object to their being searched, seized, and punished for their crimes. But what about the situations in between the two ends of the spectrum? The greater the restriction on a person's liberty or freedom, the more justification an officer must have. The law recognizes four standards of legal justification, usually listed from least to most liberty restrictions: mere suspicion, reasonable suspicion, probable cause, and proof beyond a reasonable doubt. *(IN027.2.)*

### Mere Suspicion/Consensual Encounters

Not every police-citizen encounter is a seizure under the Fourth Amendment. A ***consensual encounter*** occurs when an officer comes into voluntary contact with a citizen under circumstances in which a reasonable person would feel free to disregard the police and go about his or her business. It involves no coercion, no detention, and therefore is no Fourth Amendment seizure *(IN027.2.C.2.)*. The Constitution doesn't prohibit officers from approaching pedestrians or motorists and engaging them in conversation by asking them if they are willing to answer questions, questioning them if they are willing to listen, or offering voluntary answers to such questions as evidence in any criminal prosecution. See *Florida v. Royer*, 460 U.S. 491 (1983) *(IN027.2.C.3.)*. In determining whether an encounter was consensual, the court will look at all of the circumstances surrounding the encounter. Questions the court will ask include the following:

- Was the individual physically stopped or restrained by the officer?
- Was the individual restricted from leaving at any time during the encounter?
- Was the individual's freedom of movement restricted in any way? For example, did the officer's vehicle block the subject's vehicle and prevent the subject from leaving?
- Was the officer doing more than asking questions? Any demands made by the officer can turn an encounter into a stop.

**OBJECTIVES**

**IN027.2.** Identify the four standards of legal justification common to law enforcement.

**IN027.2.C.2.** Define *consensual encounter.*

**IN027.2.C.3.** Identify the actions a law enforcement officer may take during a consensual encounter.

**IN027.2.C.1.** Define *mere suspicion.*

**IN027.2.B.1.** Define *reasonable suspicion.*

**IN027.1.E.1.** Identify the actions a law enforcement officer may take based upon reasonable suspicion.

**IN027.1.E.5.** Define *pretext stop.*

**IN027.2.A.** Define *probable cause.*

**IN027.2.A.1.** Identify the totality of circumstances test.

**IN027.2.D.** Explain ways that probable cause is developed.

**IN027.2.E.** Identify sources of probable cause.

**IN027.2.E.3.** Explain photo arrays as a source of probable cause.

**IN027.2.E.1.** Explain lineups as a source of probable cause.

**IN027.2.E.2.** Explain show-ups as a source of probable cause.

**IN027.2.H.** Define *proof beyond a reasonable doubt.*

If the answers to any of these questions are "yes," then the officer's contact with the citizen will be deemed a stop rather than an encounter. A consensual encounter may be based on mere suspicion or no suspicion at all.

***Mere suspicion*** is sometimes described as a hunch or gut feeling based on law enforcement training and knowledge *(IN027.2.C.1.)*. Detaining a person or searching him or her, however, requires more than mere suspicion. Examples of mere suspicion that might cause an officer to initiate a consensual encounter with a person include the following:

- a person wearing a heavy winter coat in the middle of summer with the temperature in the mid 90s
- a dirty car with a clean vehicle tag
- a person dressed in all black walking in a residential neighborhood at 3:00 a.m.
- a person pulling a lawnmower in a residential neighborhood at 11:30 p.m.

The certainty that a particular person committed a crime can range from 0 percent to 100 percent, depending on the evidence available, and that range can fluctuate as additional facts become known and circumstances unfold. For example, a complainant may report facts to the responding officer with unwavering confidence. Additional witnesses, however, may report different facts, so the certainty of the complainant's statement will be reduced in the officer's mind. On the other hand, if subsequent witnesses confirm the complainant's report, the officer's certainty of what happened increases. The least amount of certainty is mere suspicion while the greatest is proof beyond a reasonable doubt.

As the certainty level rises, the Fourth Amendment permits the officer to infringe more on a suspect's right to be left alone; the officer may detain the suspect or frisk him or her during an investigative stop or arrest the person and search and seize his or her property.

Law enforcement officers must develop a keen awareness of the legal justification levels at each point during a criminal investigation. An officer must be prepared to articulate or explain in court his or her actions and the legal justification for them.

## Reasonable Suspicion

The next level above consensual encounters involves investigative or *Terry* stops, so called because of the U.S. Supreme Court case *Terry v. Ohio*, 392 U.S. 1 (1968). The Florida Legislature incorporated the *Terry* stop guidelines into the Florida Stop and Frisk Law, F.S. §901.151. Under the Stop and Frisk law, an ***investigative stop*** may be made only if the officer has reasonable suspicion that the person stopped was committing, is committing, or is about to commit a law violation.

***Reasonable suspicion*** is the standard of justification needed to support a legal *Terry* stop or investigative detention. Reasonable suspicion is sometimes called "articulable suspicion" or "founded suspicion." All three terms simply mean that an officer can articulate, or put into words, facts that support a suspicion that the person stopped was involved in a law violation. The facts and circumstances must support the suspicion that a person committed a crime, is committing a crime, or is about to commit a crime. *(IN027.2.B.1.)*

Reasonable suspicion, as well as probable cause required for arrests, may be established through a number of sources such as personal observation, information from fellow officers, information from third parties such as informants, and BOLOs (Be On the Look Out). A BOLO is a description of the suspect, the suspect's name, and any additional information that would help apprehend the suspect.

An officer's personal observations are formed by his or her training and experience and may include the following:

- subject's nervousness
- subject's running or trying to evade the officer
- subject is in a known high-crime area
- time and location of the encounter/stop
- subject's unusual dress or actions
- perceived smells or sounds

None of the above alone justifies a stop. "An individual's presence in an area of expected criminal activity, standing alone, is not enough to support a reasonable, particularized suspicion that the person is committing a crime... But officers are not required to ignore the relevant characteristics of a location in determining whether the circumstances are sufficiently suspicious to warrant further investigation." See *Illinois v. Wardlow*, 528 U.S. 119, 124 (2000).

As noted in the section on Search and Seizure, if the officer has reasonable suspicion that the detained person is armed and a danger to the officer or others, the officer may frisk the person for weapons. The Florida Stop and Frisk Law states that such a frisk can be conducted only upon probable cause. However, case law has interpreted probable cause in that context to mean reasonable suspicion.

The duration of a *Terry* stop is limited to the time reasonably necessary to accomplish the purpose of the stop. An investigative detention may become an arrest even if the officer does not initially intend to make the arrest. Questioning that prolongs the detention but is not justified by the purpose of the investigative stop is unreasonable under the Fourth Amendment. During the stop, the officer may not require the person to move from the location of the stop or its immediate vicinity. Doing so would turn the stop into an arrest. Whether someone is under arrest is a subjective inquiry from the arrestee's perspective.

An officer may lawfully use force during an investigative stop if he or she reasonably believes it protects his or her safety or the public's safety. Handcuffs may be used if reasonably necessary, but the officer must be able to articulate the reasons that force or restraints were necessary. *(IN027.1.E.1.)*

## Pretext Stops

Sometimes, an officer may suspect that evidence of criminal activity is in a vehicle, but the officer won't have enough information for reasonable suspicion to make a stop. However, if the driver of the vehicle commits a traffic infraction, or if the vehicle shows evidence of an equipment violation such as a broken taillight, the officer may stop the vehicle on that basis. Such stops are sometimes called ***pretext stops*** because the officer stops the vehicle due to equipment violation but really wants to investigate other, more serious criminal activity. Pretext stops were formerly considered a violation of the Fourth Amendment. However, the U.S. Supreme Court, in *Whren v. U.S.*, 517 U.S. 806 (1996), said that the courts are not required to consider an officer's motive for stopping a vehicle as long as the officer had an objective basis for the stop. Because of *Whren*, pretext stops do not violate the Fourth Amendment. Thus, a detective who suspects that a vehicle contains drugs can stop the driver for failing to signal for a turn. This stop is valid even if the detective is not assigned to traffic patrol and does not normally stop drivers who fail to signal for turns. *(IN027.1.E.5.)*

# Probable Cause

The standard of justification required to make an arrest or conduct a search is probable cause. Because probable cause justifies greater invasions into a person's privacy, it is a stricter standard than reasonable suspicion. ***Probable cause*** is a fair probability or reasonable grounds to believe that a crime was committed, based on the totality of circumstances *(IN027.2.A.)*. The U.S. Supreme Court asserts the following information about probable cause:

> Probable cause exists where facts and circumstances within the arresting officer's knowledge and of which they had reasonably trustworthy information, are sufficient in themselves to warrant a man of reasonable caution in the belief that an offense has been or is being committed . . . we deal with probabilities. They are the factual and practical considerations of everyday life on which reasonable and prudent men, not legal technicians, act. *Draper v. U.S.*, 358 U.S. 307 (1959)

> Probable cause is a fluid concept—turning on the assessment of probabilities in particular factual contexts—not readily, or even usefully, reduced to a neat set of legal rules. *Illinois v. Gates*, 462 U.S. 213, 232 (1983)

Examples of probable cause include a computer hit confirming that a vehicle is stolen, victim and witness sworn statements, and the odor of marijuana coming from inside a car.

## *Developing Probable Cause*

The difference between reasonable suspicion and probable cause is the amount and quality of information available to the officer concerning the commission of a crime by a particular suspect or that evidence of a crime is present in a place to be searched. In deciding whether the reasonable suspicion or probable cause standards have been met, courts review all factors known to the officer at the time of the incident. This is known as the ***totality of circumstances*** test. *(IN027.2.A.1.)*

To establish probable cause and subsequently make an arrest or conduct a search, an officer may rely on many types of information and evidence. The officer is not limited by the rules of evidence used in criminal trials. For example, a prosecutor cannot relate hearsay statements and anonymous tips to a jury for the purpose of determining guilt. However, an officer can use this information to justify probable cause or reasonable suspicion. With specific limited exceptions, the rules of evidence allow defendants in a criminal trial to prevent spouses from testifying against each other. But officers do not have to ignore information a spouse provides. In fact, an officer can use that information in the affidavit of a search warrant to obtain evidence that can be used in court to convict. The jury hears only evidence found as a result of the warrant. Jurors do not hear about the officer's conversation with the spouse.

Information used to formulate reasonable suspicion and probable cause must be specific. Descriptions should be detailed enough to make identification possible; the description "a blue van" may not be specific enough to describe a turquoise 2007 Dodge Caravan. *(IN027.2.D.)*

## *Sources of Probable Cause Information*

Sources of information used to establish probable cause or reasonable suspicion must be those that the court recognizes as reliable. The courts deem several sources as reasonable for officers to rely on: the fellow officer rule, a citizen informant, corroborated (verified) anonymous tips, reliable and credible confidential information, lineups, and show-ups.

The ***fellow officer rule*** involves relying on the collective knowledge of other officers in taking law enforcement action. An example would be making an investigative stop based on a BOLO:

> Under the 'fellow-officer' rule, law enforcement officials cooperating in an investigation are entitled to rely upon each other's knowledge of facts when forming the conclusion that a suspect has committed or is committing a crime. *United States v. Meade*, 110 F.3d 190, 193-94 (1st Cir. 1997)

Information from a third party such as a citizen informant may also be used by an officer in developing reasonable suspicion for an investigative stop or probable cause. If the source is an anonymous tipster, however, the information must have some indication of reliability and must be corroborated before the officer may rely upon it to take law enforcement action. For example, if an anonymous call comes in that a white male wearing jeans and a tie-dyed t-shirt is selling drugs from an older yellow VW van at the intersection of Main Street and Elm Avenue, the information is so specific that it appears to be reliable. The officer can corroborate the information when he arrives at the intersection. If the anonymous call was that a guy in jeans and a t-shirt was selling drugs "down the street," that information is too vague to be reliable or corroborated.

Information from a confidential informant may be used to establish probable cause for an arrest or a search only if the information has been substantiated as credible and reliable. Information can be substantiated if the informant has given reliable information in the past or if it is independently corroborated. *(IN027.2.E.)*

Probable cause may also be based on identifications from photo arrays and live lineups. The ***photo array*** is a presentation to a victim or witness of a series of photographs in a nonsuggestive manner for the purpose of identification of a suspect. A photo array generally consists of a minimum of six photographs that have similar backgrounds and portray persons of similar physical characteristics including age, race, hair color and length, and facial hair. Officers must guard against any action, whether in the selection of photos or through a comment, gesture, or body language, that might be interpreted as suggesting to the witness which photo should be identified. Such actions will result in suppression of the photo identification as evidence. *(IN027.2.E.3.)*

A ***live lineup*** is the presentation of a number of individuals, which may include a known suspect, to a victim or witness in a nonsuggestive manner for the purpose of identification. This type of lineup is rarely used in investigations but is commonly seen on television programs and in movies. *(IN027.2.E.1.)*

A ***show-up*** occurs when a law enforcement officer locates a suspect a short time after the commission of an offense and attempts to get a one-on-one identification in the field by a victim or witness *(IN027.2.E.2.)*. The witness should be transported to the location of the suspect. Generally speaking, the less time that passes between the crime and the show-up, the greater the likelihood that the witness will be able to identify or eliminate a person as a suspect. This method of identification is inherently suggestive and should be used with caution.

## Proof Beyond a Reasonable Doubt

Before a person may be found guilty of a crime and sentenced, the prosecution must present evidence sufficient to prove guilt of each element of the crime beyond a reasonable doubt. In Florida criminal trials, judges read to the jury the following instruction explaining ***proof beyond a reasonable doubt***:

## Section Vocabulary

*consensual encounter*

*fellow officer rule*

*investigative stop (Terry stop)*

*live lineup*

*mere suspicion*

*photo array*

*pretext stops*

*probable cause*

*proof beyond a reasonable doubt*

*reasonable suspicion*

*show-up*

*totality of circumstances*

> A reasonable doubt is not a mere possible doubt, a speculative, imaginary, or forced doubt. Such a doubt must not influence you to return a verdict of not guilty if you have an abiding conviction of guilt. On the other hand, if, after carefully considering, comparing, and weighing all the evidence, there is not an abiding conviction of guilt, or, if, having a conviction, it is one which is not stable but one which wavers and vacillates, then the charge is not proved beyond a reasonable doubt, and you must find the defendant not guilty because the doubt is reasonable. (Florida Standard Criminal Jury Instruction 3.7)

Although probable cause may exist that a person committed a crime, without further evidence, the state may not be able to prove the case beyond a reasonable doubt, and the case may not be filed by the prosecutor. *(IN027.2.H.)*

Different standards of proof are used in civil and administrative cases in Florida. The burden of proof in civil cases is "the greater weight (preponderance) of the evidence." In administrative proceedings, the burden of proof is "clear and convincing evidence." Each of these is a lesser standard than proof beyond a reasonable doubt.

# UNIT 2 | LEGAL CONCEPTS

## LESSON 2 | Search and Seizure

**OBJECTIVES**

**IN027.1.A.** Describe the constitutional guarantees related to search and seizure.

**IN027.1.A.1.** Define *search.*

**IN027.1.A.2.** Define *seizure.*

**IN027.1.A.3.** Define *search warrant.*

**IN027.1.C.** Identify the legal requirements of a search warrant.

**IN027.1.H.** Define the *exclusionary rule.*

**IN027.1.G.** Define the Good Faith Doctrine.

**IN027.4.** Identify the exceptions to the search warrant requirement.

**IN027.4.A.** Identify the abandoned property exception to the search warrant requirement.

**IN027.4.B.** Identify the open fields doctrine as an exception to the search warrant requirement.

**IN027.4.C.** Identify the plain view exception to the search warrant requirement.

**IN027.4.E.** Identify the probable cause search of a conveyance exception to the search warrant requirement.

**IN027.4.F.** Identify the exigent circumstances exception to the search warrant requirement.

**IN027.4.G.** Identify a *Terry* frisk as an exception to the search warrant requirement.

**IN027.4.H.** Identify the plain feel doctrine as an exception to the search warrant requirement.

### Fourth Amendment Guarantees

The purpose of the Fourth Amendment of the Constitution is to protect people from governmental intrusion in areas where they have a reasonable expectation of privacy. It prohibits searches and seizures unless they are conducted with probable cause and under reasonable circumstances. *(IN027.1.A.)*

A ***search*** occurs when the government intrudes into a place where a person has a reasonable expectation of privacy *(IN027.1.A.1.).* A ***seizure*** occurs when the government affects a person's right to have or control his or her property, usually by physically taking it. *(IN027.1.A.2.)*

#### *Search Warrants*

The Fourth Amendment generally requires officers to obtain a search warrant before intruding into a place where the individual has a reasonable expectation of privacy. While there are numerous exceptions to the search warrant requirement, officers should always first consider whether obtaining a search warrant is possible and practical.

A ***search warrant*** is a court order that authorizes law enforcement to conduct a search and seizure *(IN027.1.A.3.).* The search warrant must be directed to a person or agency with specific jurisdiction over the location of the search. The affiant may be anyone, but the person serving the warrant must have jurisdiction over the place chosen for service.

In order to be deemed valid, a search warrant must meet a number of legal requirements. First, it must be authorized and signed by a neutral magistrate or judge. The warrant must be based on an affidavit that states sufficient facts to establish probable cause that evidence of a crime will be found in the place to be searched. The basis of the information in the affidavit must come from reliable sources. For example, an unnamed or confidential informant may be the source of probable cause only if the officer swearing to the affidavit can attest that the informant has given reliable information in the past.

The existence of probable cause will be determined based on the totality of the circumstances. Courts will also consider how recent the information supporting the probable cause is and how likely it is that the contraband or evidence is still at the location to be searched.

The search warrant must particularly describe the person or place to be searched and the items to be seized. The detailed description in the search warrant is a crucial element, designed to prevent an intrusion into the wrong location. The description must include

**IN027.4.K.** Explain the legal application of U.S. Supreme Court decision of *Arizona v. Gant*, as it relates to searches incident to arrest.

**IN027.4.D.** Identify the search incident to arrest exception to the search warrant requirement.

**IN027.4.J.** Identify the consent exception to the search warrant requirement.

**IN027.4.I.** Identify the vehicle inventory exception to the search warrant requirement.

**IN027.2.C.8.** Identify the importance of regulatory searches.

**IN027.1.D.** Define the proper scope of a search.

**IN027.1.B.** Identify items that may be seized after a lawful search.

**IN027.1.I.** Describe the Florida Contraband Forfeiture Act.

directions to the place to be searched beginning from a known landmark, such as an intersection. The search warrant is valid only for the specific location it describes; it must also describe in detail the person or items to be seized. Officers must connect the seized items to criminal activity. For example, courts do not normally accept the general description "drugs" or "illegal controlled substances." They require law enforcement to name the specific drugs they expect to find. *(IN027.1.C.)*

## The Exclusionary Rule

The Supreme Court has ruled that evidence obtained by the government in violation of the Constitution cannot be used as evidence in court. This is known as the ***exclusionary rule***. Its purpose is to discourage officers from violating citizens' constitutional rights during criminal investigations. *(IN027.1.H.)*

## The Good Faith Doctrine

The Good Faith Doctrine applies to an officer's actions in conducting a search pursuant to a search warrant. If officers execute a search warrant they believe to be valid and a court later determines the warrant to have a legal error, any seized evidence may still be admitted. *(IN027.1.G.)*

## Exceptions to Search Warrant Requirements

Under the Fourth Amendment, a search or seizure may be defined as the government intruding where a person has a reasonable expectation of privacy (REP). The three elements that comprise a Fourth Amendment "search" are thus **Government + Intrusion + REP.** If any element is missing, the activity is not a search, and the Fourth Amendment is not implicated. For example, if a person walks into his neighbor's garage, finds evidence of a crime, and calls the police, the evidence can be used because the government was not involved in the search. If an officer sees a dead body on the backseat of a vehicle he stopped for speeding, he can seize it and use all evidence obtained because seeing the body was not an intrusion. If a suspect drops a bag containing controlled substances when an officer approaches him, the officer can seize the bag and use it as evidence because the suspect abandoned his REP in the bag when he dropped it. In each of the above examples, one of the elements of a Fourth Amendment search is missing. If all three elements are present, however, the Fourth Amendment does apply. If the action by the officer is a search, and the officer does not have a search warrant, he or she must determine if one of the ten exceptions to the search warrant requirement applies. Five of the exceptions require probable cause, and five do not. *(IN027.4.)*

*Note:* Two search types that are often considered exceptions to the search warrant requirement are not technically searches because the person does not have a reasonable expectation of privacy in the place to be searched. Those are searches of abandoned property and open fields. An example of abandoned property is the contents of a trash can which have been put out by the curb for pickup. The owner of the trash has abandoned any expectation of privacy in the trash, so officers may seize it and search through it without a warrant *(IN027.4.A.)*. Open fields are areas of someone's property where there is no reasonable expectation of privacy. The Supreme Court has made a distinction between the ***curtilage*** (the enclosed space of ground and outbuildings immediately surrounding a structure) of someone's home and an open field. Whether particular property is an open field or curtilage depends upon the steps the occupant has taken to create an expectation of privacy and its common use. Fenced and posted fields are given a higher degree of constitutional protection than areas that do not have such improvements. *(IN027.4.B.)*

The law presumes that a search without a warrant is invalid; however, there are a number of exceptions, five of which require probable cause:

1. plain view
2. mobile conveyance
3. destruction of evidence
4. fresh pursuit
5. emergency scene

## 1. Plain View (probable cause required)

Any contraband an officer can see can be seized without a warrant as long as three conditions are met: (1) the officer is lawfully present in the place where he or she sees the item, (2) the item is in plain sight, and (3) the officer has probable cause to believe the item is contraband or crime evidence.

First, the officer must lawfully be positioned where he or she can see the contraband. An officer responding to a domestic dispute who sees bags of cocaine sitting on the dining room table inside the residence can seize the cocaine because the officer has answered a call for assistance. However, if the officer creeps up to a house and peeks in the window in order to see, he or she is not lawfully present in the place where the cocaine is seen, and the seized drugs would be excluded from evidence.

Second, the seized item must be in plain sight. The officer may not move a blanket, for example, to see what is underneath. Use of a flashlight is permitted, but any movement of the item will likely invalidate the search.

Third, the criminal nature of the seized item must be immediately apparent. An officer must know instantly that the item is contraband. In *Sawyer v. State*, 842 So.2d 310 (Fla. 5th DCA 2003), a police officer saw a white pill on the console of a car and, thinking it was ecstasy, seized it. Testing proved the officer was correct. However, the court said that the pill's nature as an illegal drug was not immediately apparent upon first sight, so the evidence was suppressed. *(IN027.4.C.)*

## 2. Mobile Conveyance (probable cause required)

Because vehicles and other mobile conveyances are easily moved and have a reduced expectation of privacy because they must be licensed, registered, and insured, they may be searched without a warrant. Probable cause is required for a mobile conveyance search, however. This is sometimes called the *Carroll* Doctrine, so named for the case of *Carroll v. U.S.* which was decided by the U.S. Supreme Court in 1925. See *Carroll v. U.S.*, 267 U.S. 132 (1925).

A mobile conveyance search may be conducted without a warrant even if there was time to get a warrant. The scope of a search under the *Carroll* Doctrine extends to the entire vehicle and to all containers where the evidence could reasonably be found. If the facts and circumstances provide probable cause that the trunk contains contraband, the officer may only search the trunk. If it applies only to the glove compartment, the officer may only search the glove compartment. For example, a canine alert on a car's trunk gives the officer probable cause to search the trunk. Similarly, if an officer smells burning marijuana during a traffic stop, he or she may search the passenger compartment of the car as well as its occupants.

A mobile conveyance search does not have to occur at the same time as the stop. Courts have held that it is not a search to use a certified police K-9 to detect odors of controlled substances by walking the dog around the exterior of the car. *(IN027.4.E.)*

## 3. Destruction of Evidence (probable cause required)

Destruction of evidence is one of the exigent circumstances that permit search and seizure without a warrant. ***Exigent circumstances*** are certain emergencies such as evidence destruction, an emergency scene, or fresh pursuit that justify a warrantless entry. If an officer has probable cause to believe that contraband or evidence is in immediate danger of being destroyed, the officer does not need to obtain a search warrant before seizing the contraband or evidence. The law is clear, however, that the officer cannot create the exigent circumstance to justify a warrantless entry. See *Hornblower v. State*, 351 So.2d 716 (Fla. 1977). So, an officer may not knock loudly at a house where he or she has a hunch drugs are being held and announce, "Police officer," and then enter the house because he or she thinks the residents may be trying to destroy drugs inside. The officer must have probable cause to believe the drugs are inside and in immediate danger of destruction before this exception will apply.

## 4. Fresh Pursuit (probable cause required)

To enter a residence or other private place while chasing a suspect generally requires (1) probable cause that the suspect committed a serious crime, (2) immediate or continuous pursuit of the suspect, and (3) probable cause that the suspect is in the premises that is being entered without a warrant. Any contraband or evidence in plain view found in the place entered in fresh pursuit will not be subject to suppression because of failure to obtain a search warrant.

## 5. Emergency Scene (probable cause required)

The emergency scene exception involves a situation in which officers may make a warrantless entry in order to ensure their own safety or that of the public. For this exception to apply, the officer must have probable cause to believe that someone is in immediate danger. Deputies who found a four-year old wandering naked outside an apartment complex in the middle of a cold night were justified in entering an apartment where the door was ajar because they had probable cause to believe that the child's parents might be injured or ill and in need of emergency care. See *Riggs v. State*, 918 So.2d 274 (Fla. 2005).

Officers must remember that there is no general crime scene or murder scene exception to the Fourth Amendment warrant requirement. Although officers responding to a homicide scene may conduct a protective sweep to make sure there are no more victims and that the assailant is gone, to search a crime scene further will require a warrant or a valid exception. *(IN027.4.F.)*

Five additional search warrant exceptions require less than probable cause:

1. stop and frisk
2. incident to arrest
3. consent
4. inventory
5. administrative searches

## *1. Stop and Frisk (probable cause not required)*

In *Terry v. Ohio*, 392 U.S. 1 (1968), the United States Supreme Court ruled that a law enforcement officer may search the exterior clothing of someone lawfully detained if the officer has reasonable suspicion to believe that the person is armed. A frisk or pat down is not a full search, but is simply patting down outer clothing for weapons. Note: Florida's Stop and Frisk law, Florida Statute §901.151 requires probable cause before such a weapons pat down is permitted. Case law, however, has held that in this context the term probable cause means reasonable suspicion.

A *Terry* stop is justified if an officer has reasonable suspicion to believe that the person is committing, has committed, or is about to commit a criminal offense. The detention can last no longer than what is necessary for the officer to either confirm or dispel that suspicion. The suspect cannot be transported away from the immediate vicinity of the detention location. A pat down is justified if the officer also has reasonable suspicion that the person stopped possesses a weapon. An officer must be able to articulate his or her reasons for believing the subject possessed a weapon or the pat down will violate the Fourth Amendment. The two elements necessary for a lawful pat down or frisk are (1) the subject is lawfully detained, and (2) the officer has reasonable suspicion to believe that the subject possesses a dangerous weapon.

The scope of the frisk is limited to a pat down of outer clothing, containers, and property being carried by the subject. A frisk is not restricted to the body of the subject. Even the passenger compartment of an automobile may be frisked based on a reasonable belief that an occupant of the vehicle is armed and dangerous. Further search will be justified only if the officer detects something readily apparent to be a weapon or immediately apparent to be contraband. If an illegal weapon or evidence of a crime is discovered during the detention, the officer may make an arrest as appropriate. *(IN027.4.G.)*

An officer who conducts a valid stop and frisk as described above, and in the process feels an item he or she readily recognizes as contraband, may seize that contraband. Known as the plain touch/feel doctrine, this rule allows the officer to seize the contraband even if it does not feel like a weapon. Plain touch/feel does not permit any manipulation or groping of the object in an effort to identify it as contraband. The officer must be able to articulate that, based upon his or her training and experience, he or she immediately recognized the item as contraband. See *Minnesota v. Dickerson*, 508 U.S. 366 (1993). *(IN027.4.H.)*

## *2. Incident to Arrest (probable cause not required)*

When a person is lawfully arrested and taken into custody, he or she may be searched without a warrant. Such a search incident to arrest is reasonable under the Fourth Amendment. The Supreme Court has noted "two historical rationales for the search incident to arrest exception: (1) the need to disarm the suspect in order to take him or her into custody, and (2) the need to preserve evidence for later use at trial." See *United States v. Robinson*, 414 U.S. 218 (1973).

A search incident to arrest may only be conducted when two requirements have been met. First, there must have been a lawful custodial arrest. Second, the search must be "substantially contemporaneous" or at the same time with the arrest. For example, a search done ten minutes after an arrest will generally be valid, but one conducted an hour after the arrest will likely be invalid. This exception has two purposes: officer safety—to locate weapons and prevent escape—and preservation of evidence.

A search incident to arrest may not be conducted unless there is a custodial arrest. An officer may not search incident to issuing a traffic citation or a notice to appear. There must be a physical, custodial arrest.

The scope of a search incident to arrest is the arrestee's person and the areas "within the immediate control of the arrestee" at the time of the arrest. See *Chimel v. California*, 395 U.S. 752 (1969). However, a search incident to arrest may also include a vehicle in which the arrested person was a passenger just before the arrest. See *Thornton v. U.S.*, 541 U.S. 615 (2004).

Under *New York v. Belton*, 453 U.S. 454 (1981), the scope of a vehicle search incident to arrest includes the entire passenger compartment, and all containers located therein, locked or unlocked. The trunk of a sedan is not considered part of the passenger compartment, but the rear area of a van or SUV is included in the search area. *Arizona v. Gant*, 556 U.S. 332, 129 S.Ct. 1710 (2009), has further refined the scope of searches incident to arrest involving vehicles. Officers may search the passenger compartment of a vehicle incident to the arrest of an occupant only when the arrestee is unsecured and the passenger compartment is within reaching distance of the arrestee or if it is "reasonable" to believe the vehicle contains evidence of the crime for which the subject was arrested *(IN027.4.K.)*. Officers should document the facts and circumstances on which they relied for decisions regarding a search and be prepared to articulate those reasons at a deposition or hearing.

A search incident to arrest may include a strip search only under certain circumstances. Officers should consult F.S. §901.211 and individual agency policy for details. *(IN027.4.D.)*

### 3. Consent (probable cause not required)

Consent searches do not require probable cause, reasonable suspicion, or even mere suspicion. An officer may ask anyone for consent to search. If the consent is knowing and voluntary and the person giving consent has authority to do so, then the search is valid, and any evidence obtained can be used in court. Many times people who hide contraband will consent to an officer's request to search thinking that because they consented, the officer will assume they are not hiding anything and will not complete the search. The burden is on the prosecution to prove that consent was valid. Consent should be obtained in writing if possible, though verbal consent is sufficient.

Voluntary means the consent is unequivocal, specific, and intelligently given and more than mere acquiescence in the face of a claim of lawful authority. In other words, a reasonable person under the circumstances would feel that he or she could refuse the request for consent to search. Officers do not need to advise people that they have a right to refuse.

Under limited circumstances, consent to search may be implied. Examples are searches of airline passengers, searches of patrons attending sporting events, and searches of visitors to courthouses or other government buildings. Except for such limited situations, courts will not generally approve of warrantless searches based on implied consent.

Third party consent to search may be valid if the third party has mutual access and control over the area to be searched. A search may not be done by consent of one co-tenant if another co-tenant is present and objects to the search. See *Georgia v. Randolph*, 547 U.S. 103 (2006). Unless he or she is the owner, a vehicle's passenger may not consent to the search of the driver's vehicle.

In cases involving juveniles, the consent of a parent or guardian will generally overrule objection by the child. A child may provide consent for a warrantless entry to a parent's home if the child shares the home with the parent and the parent is not physically present to grant or deny consent.

Consent may be withdrawn at any time during the search and once withdrawn, officers must stop searching immediately. The scope of consent can be limited as well. For example, a driver may consent to the search of the vehicle's passenger compartment but not the trunk. Of course, if an officer develops probable cause to search at any time, the withdrawal of consent will be meaningless. *(IN027.4.J.)*

### *4. Inventory (probable cause not required)*

Inventory searches are not designed to search for evidence but to protect the arrested person's property and to protect the officer from accusations of theft. An inventory is a written list of all valuable property in a vehicle. When the driver of a vehicle is arrested, the arresting officer must make sure the vehicle is properly secured. Three options are available. First, the vehicle may be lawfully parked, locked, and left at the scene of the arrest if that can be done safely. Because of the risk of theft or damage, this option should seldom be chosen. Second, the vehicle may be turned over to a friend or family member of the arrested person if such a person is available. Third, the vehicle may be impounded. Officers will generally use the third option unless a passenger in the vehicle may lawfully take possession of the vehicle. An inventory search is appropriate only if the vehicle is impounded.

To be valid, inventory searches require a written department policy that spells out when and how the inventory search must be done. The search must occur at about the same time as the impoundment of the vehicle, and it must be done in compliance with the written department policy. Any evidence or contraband found during a valid inventory search may be used against the defendant in court. *(IN027.4.I.)*

### *5. Administrative Searches (probable cause not required)*

Administrative searches generally do not require a warrant due to the setting or special conditions. Searches of this type include students, public schools, people in government offices, government property (such as desks, lockers, and vehicles), persons engaged in certain businesses or licensed activities, and persons on probation or parole. Administrative searches generally do not require warrants because they are for administrative or regulatory purposes and usually are not conducted by law enforcement personnel. Because certain industries are heavily regulated, their expectation of privacy is reduced. Other examples of administrative searches are fire marshal or OSHA inspections of businesses, probationer searches, building inspections, and restaurant inspections. Agency policy will dictate the extent to which officers may be involved in assisting with such searches. *(IN027.2.C.8.)*

## Scope of Searches

The scope of constitutional searches is limited to the items being searched. Once the items are found, the search must stop. An officer who conducts a probable cause search of a vehicle for a stolen gun and finds the gun in the glove box must stop searching unless there is probable cause to search for other specific items. The nature of the search should be based on the item the officer expects to find. For example, if an officer has probable cause to search a home for stolen refrigerators, searching drawers, clothing, and under the bed is unreasonable because a refrigerator cannot fit in those places. *(IN027.1.D.)*

**Section Vocabulary**

*curtilage*

*exclusionary rule*

*exigent circumstances*

*forfeiture*

*search*

*search warrant*

*seizure*

### *Items That May Be Legally Searched For and Seized*

Whether conducting a search using a warrant or acting under a legally recognized exception, case law and statutes allow officers to search for these items:

- dangerous weapons
- fruits of the crime—things a criminal receives as a result of committing a crime
- instruments of the crime—things a criminal uses to commit a crime
- contraband—an illegal possession due to the nature of the item, the amount, the person, or the type of activity for which the item is being used
- evidence relevant to proving the commission of a felony
- items defined by statute (Ch. 933, F.S.—Search and Inspection Warrants)
- suspects *(IN027.1.B.)*

## Florida Contraband Forfeiture Act

Florida Statute §932.701 gives law enforcement agencies the authority to seize and forfeit certain property known as contraband articles. Contraband articles include items which are illegal to possess, items used in the commission of a felony, and items purchased with the profits of felonious activity. ***Forfeiture*** is a civil proceeding wherein the law enforcement agency asks the court to transfer ownership of the property from the defendant to the government. The government may then sell the property at auction or use the property for law enforcement purposes. For example, the law enforcement agency seizes the car of a drug dealer. After the forfeiture proceeding, the car is used for the Drug Abuse Resistance Education (DARE) program. *(IN027.1.I.)*

Because forfeiture deprives a person of interest of his or her property, courts closely scrutinize law enforcement officers' actions and motives in seizing their property as contraband. The Fourth Amendment guards against not only unreasonable searches but also unreasonable seizures. Officers must use great care in applying principles of constitutional search and seizure law before seizing property under the Florida Contraband Forfeiture Act. Illegal pretextual stops, reliance upon drug-courier profiles, or racial or ethnic profiling must never be any part of the basis for a contraband seizure. These topics are discussed in greater detail elsewhere in this curriculum.

Officers must remember that the purpose of seizure and forfeiture of contraband is never to obtain revenue, but to further the law enforcement purposes of public safety, the safety of law enforcement officers, or the investigation and prosecution of criminal activity. Florida has established mandatory guidelines for seizure and forfeiture of contraband. Officers should be familiar with these guidelines and their department's forfeiture policies.

# UNIT 2 | LEGAL CONCEPTS

## LESSON 3 | Laws of Arrest

**OBJECTIVES**

**LE395.7.** Identify the authority of a law enforcement officer under Florida law to make an arrest.

**LE395.7.A.** Define *arrest.*

**LE395.7.B.** Identify the two types of arrest under Florida Law.

**LE395.7.B.1.** Define *arrest warrant.*

**LE395.7.B.2.** Identify the four situations under which a Florida law enforcement officer is authorized to make a warrantless arrest.

**LE395.8.** Identify the exceptions to the misdemeanor arrest requirements.

**LE395.7.C.** Define *notice to appear.*

**LE395.7.D.** Explain the concept of fresh pursuit.

**LE395.7.D.1.** Identify jurisdictional issues related to an arrest in fresh pursuit.

### Authority to Arrest

Chapter 901, Florida Statutes, gives law enforcement officers the authority to make arrests *(LE395.7.)*. An ***arrest*** is defined as depriving a person of his or her liberty by legal authority *(LE395.7.A.)*. There are two types of arrest under Florida law: arrest with a warrant, F.S. §901.02, and arrest without a warrant, F.S. §901.15. *(LE395.7.B.)*

An ***arrest warrant*** is a court order authorizing law enforcement to take the individual named on the warrant into custody to answer for charges specified in the warrant *(LE395.7.B.1.)*. An arrest warrant may be obtained only upon a showing of probable cause contained in an affidavit.

Florida Statute §901.19 authorizes law enforcement officers to enter the residence of the wanted felon in order to make an arrest. In order to enter a third party's residence to arrest a subject named in an arrest warrant, officers must obtain a search warrant or articulate the basis for an applicable search warrant exception.

### Warrantless Arrests

A law enforcement officer may make a probable cause arrest without a warrant under the following circumstances:

1. The person has committed a felony or misdemeanor or violated a county or municipal ordinance in the presence of the officer.
2. A felony has been committed outside of the officer's presence, but the officer has probable cause to believe the person committed it.
3. A warrant for arrest has been issued and is being held by another law enforcement officer or agency.
4. The general rule is that an officer may not make an arrest for a misdemeanor which does not occur in his or her presence. The Florida Statutes contain numerous exceptions to this rule, including the following: *(LE395.7.B.2.)*
   - Carrying a Firearm in Violation of an Injunction (F.S. §790.233)
   - Battery (F.S. §784.03)
   - Act of Retail Theft (F.S. §812.015)
   - Traffic Offenses Related to Crash Investigation (F.S. §316.645 and §318.17)
   - Carrying a Concealed Weapon (F.S. §790.02)
   - Disorderly Conduct on Premises of Establishment (F.S. §509.143)
   - Theft from a Dining or Lodging Establishment [F.S. §509.162(3)]
   - Trespass on School Grounds (F.S. §810.097)
   - Possession of Cannabis <20 grams [F.S. §893.13(6)(b)]

- Stalking (F.S. §784.048)
- Transit Fare Evasion [F.S. §812.015(4)]
- Contributing to the Delinquency/Dependency of a Minor (F.S. §827.04)
- Criminal Mischief (F.S. §806.13)
- Trespass on Certain Properties (F.S. §810.08)
- Act of Domestic Violence (F.S. §741.28)
- Violation of Injunction for Protection (F.S. §741.31 and §784.047) *(LE395.8.)*

## Notice to Appear

After an officer has developed probable cause, he or she has three choices: terminate the encounter, issue a notice to appear, or physically take the suspect into custody.

According to Florida Rule of Criminal Procedure 3.125, a ***notice to appear*** is a written order that may be issued by a law enforcement officer in lieu of physical arrest requiring a person accused of violating the law to appear in court at a specified date and time. It may only be used under limited circumstances for misdemeanor offenses, municipal or county ordinance violations, and criminal traffic violations. The officer advises the defendant of the charges and releases him or her at the scene provided that he or she signs the notice and promises to appear in court. *(LE395.7.C.)*

According to the Florida Rules of Criminal Procedure 3.125, an officer may issue a notice to appear except in the following circumstances:

1. The accused fails or refuses to sufficiently identify him- or herself or supply the required information;
2. The accused refuses to sign the notice to appear;
3. The officer has reason to believe that the continued liberty of the accused constitutes an unreasonable risk of bodily injury to the accused or others;
4. The accused has no ties with the jurisdiction reasonably sufficient to assure his or her appearance, or there is substantial risk that the accused will refuse to respond to the notice;
5. The officer has any suspicion that the accused may be wanted in any jurisdiction; or
6. The accused has previously failed to respond to a notice or a summons or has violated the conditions of any pretrial release program.

The Rules of Criminal Procedure provide a Notice to Appear form. Most agencies provide their own form, based on the standard form, which may be combined with the arrest affidavit.

## Fresh Pursuit

***Fresh pursuit*** is a legal doctrine that permits a law enforcement officer to make an arrest of a fleeing suspect who crosses jurisdictional lines. It is an exception to the general rule that a Florida officer's arrest powers are limited to the jurisdiction of the agency that employs the officer. Fresh pursuit does not necessarily mean high-speed pursuit. It may be very brief and undramatic. *(LE395.7.D.)*

The fresh pursuit statute in F.S. §901.25 removed a barrier that allowed criminals to escape to the next county or otherwise beyond the officer's jurisdiction. There are a number of statutory and case law conditions and procedures that must be followed by officers pursuing a suspect into another jurisdiction.

The offense must have occurred within the pursuing officer's jurisdictional boundaries. If a criminal offense was committed for which a probable cause arrest may be made, the officer may leave his or her jurisdiction to arrest the suspect. The pursuit must be continuous and uninterrupted; however, the pursuing officer does not need to be in constant visual contact before making the arrest. The commission of the offense and the pursuit of the suspect must be closely related in time. When the arrest occurs in another jurisdiction, the arresting officer must notify the officer in charge of that jurisdiction and must take the suspect before a trial judge in the county where the arrest occurred. *(LE395.7.D.1.)*

Officers must follow their agency policy regarding fresh pursuit, which may be more restrictive than state law.

**Section Vocabulary**

*arrest*

*arrest warrant*

*fresh pursuit*

*notice to appear*

# UNIT 2 | LEGAL CONCEPTS

## LESSON 4 | Laws of Interrogation

### *Miranda* Decision

Until the *Miranda* case, the law presumed that people knew their Constitutional rights. The *Miranda* decision put the burden of explaining Fifth and Sixth Amendment rights on the law enforcement officer. Failure to inform a person of these Constitutional rights during a custodial interrogation may result in an admission or confession not being allowed in court. *(IN001.3.D.1.)*

In 1966, the United States Supreme Court decided the landmark case of *Miranda v. Arizona*, 384 U.S. 436, 86 S.Ct. 1602 (1966). ). The decision affected law enforcement throughout the United States. In *Miranda*, the Court decided that whenever a law enforcement officer questions a suspect in custody, the officer must advise the person of certain Constitutional rights. These rights include the right to remain silent and the right to have an attorney present when being questioned by law enforcement. If the officer fails to follow the rules set forth in *Miranda*, any statement or admission obtained from the interview cannot be used in court. *(IN008.3.A.5.)*

There are four elements to the *Miranda* decision: custody, interrogation, understanding, and free and voluntary waiving of rights. The *Miranda* requirements are necessary whenever the law enforcement officer conducts a custodial interrogation. *(IN008.3.E.2.)*

**OBJECTIVES**

**IN001.3.D.1.** Explain the importance of the *Miranda* decision to law enforcement.

**IN008.3.A.5.** Identify the key aspects of the *Miranda* decision.

**IN008.3.E.2.** Identify when *Miranda* warnings are required.

**IN008.3.E.3.** Identify the concept of custody as related to the *Miranda* decision.

**IN008.3.E.6.** Identify the concept of interrogation as related to the *Miranda* decision.

**LE142.9.A.** Describe how law enforcement should advise *Miranda* warnings.

**LE142.9.B.** Identify the importance of a waiver of *Miranda* warnings.

**LE142.9.B.2.** Identify the importance of having an advice of rights form signed.

**LE149.9.C.** Explain the significance of an invocation of rights.

**IN008.4.C.** Identify restrictions on police interview tactics.

## Custody

***Custody*** means the suspect is deprived of freedom in a significant way. Generally, interviews at the scene or field sobriety exercises are not considered custody. Handcuffing the subject or otherwise restricting his or her movement so that he or she is not free to leave is considered custody. In deciding whether a person is in custody for purpose of *Miranda*, courts ask two questions: first, what were the facts and circumstances surrounding the interrogation, and second, given those circumstances, would a reasonable person have felt he or she was not at liberty to terminate the interrogation and leave. See *Thomas v. Keohane*, 516 U.S. 99, 112 (1995). If, from all of the circumstances, it appears that the subject was not free to terminate the interview and leave, and a reasonable person in the subject's place would have believed that he or she was not free to leave, then the subject was in custody and *Miranda* warnings were required. See *Stansbury v. California*, 511 U.S. 318 (1994). The most common custody situations involve subjects who are physically placed under arrest.

Officers must be careful not to create a police-dominated environment for a ***noncustodial interview***, an interview in which the person is not under arrest and a reasonable person would believe that he or she is free to leave at any time during the interview.

In *Ramirez v. State*, 739 So.2d 568 (1999), the court ruled that "The determination of whether a reasonable person in the suspect's position would consider himself in custody for purposes of *Miranda* requires consideration of the manner in which the police summoned the suspect for questioning; the purpose, place, and manner of interrogation; the extent to which the suspect is confronted with evidence of his guilt; whether the suspect is informed that he is free to leave the place of questioning." *(IN008.3.E.3.)*

## Interrogation

The interrogation element of *Miranda* is satisfied whenever a law enforcement officer is questioning a suspect about criminal activity. The interrogation element is also satisfied when the officer's actions amount to the functional equivalent of interrogation.

The elements of interrogation include questioning initiated by law enforcement that is directly or indirectly intended to elicit an incriminating response. See *Rhode Island v. Innis*, 446 U.S. 291 (1980), and *Brewer v. Williams*, 430 U.S. 387 (1977).

Often, a suspect who is in custody will voluntarily give information even when not solicited through questioning. These statements, known as spontaneous statements, will be admissible even if an officer does not advise the suspect of the *Miranda* rights. The officer may allow the suspect to continue talking but may not ask the suspect any questions without giving *Miranda* warnings. *(IN008.3.E.6.)*

# Giving *Miranda* Warnings

Officers are only required to provide a suspect with *Miranda* warnings when the elements of custodial interrogation have been satisfied. Once the *Miranda* warnings are required, the rights should be read one at a time from an agency-provided *Miranda* card. Although the law does not require that *Miranda* warnings be given identically every time, officers should get in the habit of always reading from a *Miranda* card. Not only will this guarantee that none of the rights are forgotten or mixed up, it can also enhance the officer's courtroom testimony. Defense attorneys can do little with an officer who testifies that he or she always reads *Miranda* from the card. *(LE142.9.A.)*

## *Miranda Cards*

Officers usually are issued a *Miranda* card (illustrated below) to use when reading the *Miranda* rights to a subject.

| *Miranda* Warning | Acknowledgment of Rights |
|---|---|
| **1. You have the right to remain silent.**<br>**2. Anything you say can and will be used against you in court.**<br>**3. You have the right to call or obtain an attorney at this time and have one present now or at any time during questioning.**<br>**4. If you cannot afford an attorney and you want one before or at any time during questioning, one will be provided for you.**<br>**5. If you decide to answer questions now, you have the right to stop answering at any time during questioning.** | *After the warning and in order to secure a waiver, the following questions should be asked and an affirmative reply secured to questions (1) and (3). If the individual has previously asked for an attorney, no valid waiver may be obtained, unless he or she initiated the conversation.*<br>**1. Do you understand each of these rights I have explained to you?**<br>**2. Have you previously requested any law enforcement officer to allow you to speak to an attorney?**<br>**3. Having these rights in mind, do you wish to talk to us now?** |

*Miranda* warning & acknowledgment of rights *Figure 2-2*

## *Understanding*

The officer must ensure that the defendant understands his or her rights, taking into account the defendant's age, national origin, education, circumstances of the advising of rights, mental condition, and whether or not the defendant is under the influence of an intoxicating substance.

## *Waiver of Rights*

Once the suspect has been advised of his or her *Miranda* rights, a waiver is required before questioning may commence. The waiver ensures that the suspect understands his or her rights and will speak with the officer. A written waiver is preferred but not essential. A waiver can be verbal or even implied. The waiver of rights

**Section Vocabulary**

*custody*

*noncustodial interview*

must be freely and voluntarily given. An officer may not make any promises or coerce the defendant in order to obtain a confession. *(LE142.9.B.)*

*Note:* Special rules apply for the questioning of juveniles. Officers should be particularly cautious when interviewing a juvenile suspect. See J.D.B. v. North Carolina, 564 U.S. __ (2011).

### Advice of Rights Forms

In addition to a *Miranda* card, agencies may provide their officers with an Advice of Rights form. Officers should refer to their local agency's policies and procedures regarding the use of either the *Miranda* card or the Advice of Rights form. The Advice of Rights form, when signed by the person receiving rights, greatly aids in proving those rights were validly given and understood by that person. It may protect an officer's case by helping to ensure the admissibility of evidence generated as a result of statements made by that person. It may also help the officer avoid liability for failure to follow policy. *(LE142.9.B.2.)*

## Invocation of Rights

If the suspect makes a clear and unequivocal request to invoke any of his or her rights under *Miranda*, all questioning must cease immediately. Officers should remember that there are several rights included in the *Miranda* warnings. If the suspect invokes only his or her right to remain silent, the officer may re-initiate the interview after a significant lapse of time. On the other hand, if the suspect requests an attorney, no further questioning is allowed unless the suspect's attorney is present.

The right to counsel contained in the *Miranda* warnings is not crime-specific. Therefore, an officer may not question the suspect about a burglary even though the suspect was arrested on completely unrelated charges. *(LE149.9.C.)*

## Police Interview Tactics

Florida law gives officers a substantial amount of discretion in conducting interviews and interrogations. While officers are allowed to be deceptive to a point, there are limitations on what an officer may say during the interview. Some things officers are not allowed to do include making threats, promising leniency, and creating physical evidence for use during the interview. These examples are considered gross deception, which when used will result in the suppression of any admissions or confessions obtained during the interview. Such tactics may also result in administrative discipline and civil liability for the officer and the agency. *(IN008.4.C.)*

# UNIT 3 | SUBSTANTIVE CRIMINAL LAW

## LESSON 1 | Criminal Intent

**OBJECTIVES**

**IN023.5.** Explain how to determine if a crime has been committed.

**IN023.3.B.1.** Define *intent.*

**IN023.3.C.** Identify the four categories of criminal intent.

**IN023.3.C.2.** Define *general intent.*

**IN023.3.C.3.** Define *specific intent.*

**IN023.3.C.4.** Define *transferred intent.*

**IN023.3.C.1.** Define *criminal negligence.*

### Proving a Criminal Offense

To determine if a crime has occurred, an officer must determine whether elements of a criminal act are present. The officer must have probable cause to believe that a crime has been committed (***corpus delicti*** or "body of the offense") and that the person to be charged committed the crime.

Generally, to prove that a crime has been committed, it must be shown that a criminal statute specifically prohibits the alleged act or omission and that the person committing the act or omission did so knowingly or intentionally. *(IN023.5.)*

In most cases, a criminal offense requires an offender to take some physical action or act toward committing the criminal offense. Mere thoughts do not constitute criminal liability. However, a person may also commit a criminal act by failing to act, that is, by omission. To base criminal liability on failure to act, it must first be found that the person had a legal duty to act and not simply a moral duty.

To determine whether a statute specifically prohibits an alleged act or omission or to determine the requisite intent to commit the crime, an officer needs to determine what specific acts or facts must be present before an offender can be charged with a crime.

### Intent

For an offender to be guilty of a criminal offense, the offense must be defined so that the offender engages in specific conduct or intentionally produces a specified result. ***Intent*** is defined as purposely doing what the law declares to be a crime, whether the person's purpose was to commit the crime or to meet its outcome. *(IN023.3.B.1.)*

#### *Categories of Criminal Intent*

Under criminal law principles, there are four basic classifications of intent: general, specific, transferred, and criminal negligence. *(IN023.3.C.)*

***General intent*** defines most criminal offenses, which require some forbidden act by the offender. To qualify as an act, the offender's bodily movement must be voluntary. Therefore, to some extent, all crimes requiring an act also require at least the offender's intention to make the bodily movement, which becomes the act to commit the criminal offense. For example, resisting a law enforcement officer with violence is a general intent crime. *(IN023.3.C.2.)*

***Specific intent*** requires more than reasonable expectation of the result. Specific intent designates a special mental element of intention to cause a particular result, which is required over and above any mental state required for the offender to commit the act.

## Section Vocabulary

*corpus delicti*

*criminal negligence*

*culpable negligence*

*general intent*

*intent*

*specific intent*

*transferred intent*

A specific intent crime will list in the statute the specific elements which must be met. For example, burglary is a specific intent crime. *(IN023.3.C.3.)*

***Transferred intent*** is present when an intentional act harms an unintended second victim. For example, a person intending to illegally shoot one victim unintentionally misses and strikes a second victim. *(IN023.3.C.4.)*

For criminal liability to exist based on an offender's act, there must also be a causal relationship between the offender's act and the resulting harm. The offender's conduct must cause the result. In other words, but for the offender's conduct, the result would not have occurred. It is not enough for an offender to act and expect a specified result; the result must follow the offender's act. The crime ultimately charged must bear some causal relationship to the actions of the defendant. Situations involving transferred intent are complex, and officers generally should seek legal or supervisory advice prior to determining what crime, if any, will be charged based upon a theory of transferred intent. The causal relationship between the offender's act and the resulting harm may also be specifically permitted by law. This principle is known as a legal defense or legal justification.

The fourth category of intent, sometimes referred to as ***criminal negligence*** or recklessness, imposes criminal liability on a defendant when he or she did not intend for his or her behavior to cause the resulting harm at all *(IN023.3.C.1.)*. Simple negligence cannot give rise to criminal charges; it is only when that negligence is gross or flagrant that it reaches the level of criminal responsibility called culpable negligence. ***Culpable negligence*** is consciously doing an act that the person knew or should have known was likely to cause injury. An example of this fourth category of intent is vehicular homicide.

# UNIT 3 | SUBSTANTIVE CRIMINAL LAW

## LESSON 2 | Elements of Crimes

Officers must be familiar with the elements of specific crimes in order to be able to recognize a violation of a statute, apply the statute to an incident, write a report and affidavit, and testify effectively in court. The following crimes listed are the most common crimes that officers will encounter (other than traffic offenses).

**Elements of Theft**, F.S. §812.014, Misdemeanor/Felony
The State must prove the following elements to convict a suspect of theft:

1. The offender knowingly and unlawfully obtained or used or endeavored to obtain or use the property of another.
2. The offender did so with intent, either temporarily or permanently, to deprive victim of his or her right to the property or any benefit from it with the intent to deprive the victim of its use, or appropriate the property of the victim to his or her own use or to the use of any person not entitled to it. *(IN023.3.A.1.)*

**Elements of Retail Theft**, F.S. §812.015(1), Misdemeanor/Felony *(IN023.3.A.2.)*
The State must prove the following elements to convict a suspect of retail theft:

1. The offender knowingly did the following:
   a. took possession of or carried away merchandise
   b. altered or removed a label or price tag from merchandise
   c. transferred merchandise from one container to another
   d. removed a shopping cart from a merchant's premises
2. The offender intended to deprive the merchant of the possession, use, benefit, or full retail value of the merchandise or shopping cart.

The theft statute details many different classifications of offenses and penalties. Theft crimes are initially divided between grand theft and petit theft. If the property stolen is valued at less than $300, the offender commits the first degree misdemeanor of petit theft. If the property is valued at $100 or more but less than $300, and is taken from a dwelling or the curtilage thereof, it is a felony of the third degree. If the property stolen is valued at over $300, the offender commits the felony of Grand Theft. See F.S. Chapter 812 for details.

*Note:* A person who commits petit theft and who has been previously convicted of any theft commits a misdemeanor of the first degree. A person who commits petit theft and who has been previously convicted two or more times of petit theft commits a felony of the third degree. Regardless of its value, sometimes a felony is determined by the type of property stolen:

**OBJECTIVES**

**IN023.3.A.1.** List the elements of the crime of Theft.

**IN023.3.A.2.** List the elements of the crime of Retail Theft.

**IN023.3.A.3.** List the elements of the crime of Robbery.

**IN023.3.A.4.** List the elements of the crime of Burglary.

**IN023.3.A.5.** List the elements of the crime of Trespass in structure or conveyance.

**N023.3.A.6.** List the elements of the crime of Trespass on property.

**IN023.3.A.7.** List the elements of the crime of Loitering and Prowling.

**IN023.3.A.8.** List the elements of the crime of Assault.

**IN023.3.A.9.** List the elements of the crime of Aggravated Assault.

**IN023.3.A.10.** List the elements of the crime of Assault on a Law Enforcement Officer.

**IN023.3.A.11.** List the elements of the crime of Battery.

**IN023.3.A.12.** List the elements of the crime of Felony Battery.

**IN023.3.A.13.** List the elements of the crime of Aggravated Battery.

**IN023.3.A.14.** List the elements of the crime of Battery on a Law Enforcement Officer.

**LE061c.6.A.** Define *domestic violence* from the Florida Statutes.

**IN023.3.A.15.** List the elements of the various levels of Homicide.

**IN023.3.A.16.** List the elements of the crime of Disorderly Conduct.

**IN023.3.A.17.** List the elements of the crime of Disorderly Intoxication.

**IN023.3.A.33.** List the elements of the crime of Open House Party.

**IN023.3.A.34.** List the elements of the crime of Selling or Giving Alcoholic Beverages to a Person Under the Age of 21.

**IN023.3.A.35.** List the elements of the crime of Possession of Alcoholic Beverage by a Person Under the Age of 21.

**IN023.3.A.36.** List the elements of the crime of Possession of Tobacco Products by a Person Under 18 Years of Age.

**IN023.3.A.37.** List the elements of the crime of Selling, Delivering, Bartering, Furnishing, or Giving Tobacco Products to Persons Under 18 Years of Age.

**IN023.3.A.18.** List the elements of the crime of Sale and/or Delivery of Controlled Substance with intent.

**IN023.3.A.19.** List the elements of the crime of Possession of Controlled Substance.

**IN023.3.A.20.** List the elements of the crime of Possession of Drug Paraphernalia.

**IN023.3.A.21.** List the elements of the crime of Resisting an Officer without Violence.

**IN023.3.A.22.** List the elements of the crime of Resisting an Officer with Violence.

**IN023.3.A.23.** List the elements of the crime of Stalking.

- will or other testamentary instrument
- firearm
- motor vehicle
- any commercially farmed animal
- an aquaculture species raised at a permitted aquaculture facility
- fire extinguisher
- 2,000 pieces of citrus fruit
- property from a posted construction site
- any stop sign
- property, funds, or assets from a person 65 years of age or older
- anhydrous ammonia

**Elements of Robbery**, F.S. §812.13, Felony *(IN023.3.A.3.)*
The State must prove the following four elements to convict a suspect of robbery:

1. The offender took the money or property from the victim or custody of the victim.
2. Force, violence, assault, or putting in fear of violence was used in the course of the taking.
3. The property taken was of some value.
4. The taking was with the intent to permanently or temporarily deprive the victim of his or her right to the property or any benefit from it.

The difference between theft and robbery involves the use of force or threat of force against a person.

**Elements of Robbery by Sudden Snatching**, F.S. §812.131, Felony (See Criminal Jury Instructions or Florida Statutes.)

**Elements of Carjacking**, F.S. §812.133, Felony First Degree (See Criminal Jury Instructions or Florida Statutes.)

**Elements of Home Invasion Robbery**, F.S. §812.135, Felony First Degree (See Criminal Jury Instructions or Florida Statutes.)

**Elements of Burglary**, F.S. §810.02, Felony *(IN023.3.A.4.)*
The State must prove the following elements to convict a suspect of burglary:

1. The offender entered and/or remained in a structure or conveyance owned by or in the possession of the victim.
2. The offender did not have the permission or consent of the victim, or anyone authorized to act for the victim, to enter and/or remain in the structure or conveyance at the time.
3. At the time of entering and/or remaining in the structure or conveyance, the offender had a fully formed, conscious intent to commit the crime that is listed in the charge.

A burglary involves an entry into some place without permission to enter in order to commit a crime therein. Burglary can be charged in addition to the underlying crime such as theft or assault. Burglary involving assault, battery, a weapon, an explosive device, or entering into a dwelling, occupied structure, or conveyance carries a greater penalty (F.S. §810.02).

**Elements of Possession of Burglary Tools**, F.S. §810.06, Felony (See Criminal Jury Instructions or Florida Statutes.)

**Elements of Trespass—In Structure or Conveyance**, F.S. §810.08, Misdemeanor/Felony *(IN023.3.A.5.)*
The State must prove the following elements to convict a suspect of trespassing in a structure/conveyance:

1. The offender willfully entered or remained in structure or conveyance alleged, or having been authorized, licensed, or invited to enter or remain in structure or conveyance alleged, willfully refused to depart after having been warned by owner or lessee or person authorized by the owner or lessee alleged to depart.
2. The structure or conveyance alleged was in the lawful possession of person alleged.
3. The offender's entering or remaining in the property was without the permission, expressed or implied, of the person alleged or any other person authorized to give that permission.

***Structure*** means any building of any kind, either temporary or permanent, which has a roof over it, and the enclosed space of ground and outbuildings immediately surrounding that structure.

***Conveyance*** means any motor vehicle, ship, vessel, railroad car, trailer, aircraft, or sleeping car; to enter a conveyance includes taking apart any portion of the conveyance.

For the explanation of "authority," see Criminal Jury Instructions.

**Elements of Trespass—On Property Other than a Structure or Conveyance**, F.S. §810.09, Misdemeanor/Felony *(IN023.3.A.6.)*
The State must prove the following elements to convict a suspect of trespassing on other property:

1. The offender willfully entered or remained in property alleged.
2. The property was owned by or in the lawful possession of person alleged.
3. Notice not to enter upon or remain in that property had been given by actual communication to the offender or via posting, fencing, or cultivation of the property.
4. The offender's entering or remaining in the property was without permission, expressed or implied, of person alleged or any other person authorized to give that permission.

For the explanation of "authority," see Criminal Jury Instructions.

For the definitions of "posted," "cultivated," or "fenced land," see Criminal Jury Instructions.

**IN023.3.A.24.** List the elements of the crime of Sexual Battery.

**IN023.3.A.25.** List the elements of the crime of Carrying Concealed Weapon.

**IN023.3.A.26.** List the elements of the crime of Criminal Mischief.

**IN023.3.A.39.** List the elements of the crime of Forgery.

**IN023.3.A.40.** List the elements of the crime of Uttering a Forged Instrument.

**IN023.3.A.41.** List the elements of the crime of Giving a Worthless Check.

**IN023.3.A.27.** Define the various crimes of Elderly Abuse.

**IN023.3.A.28.** List the elements of the crime of Child Abuse.

**IN023.3.A.29.** List the elements of the crime of Kidnapping.

**IN023.3.A.30.** List the elements of the crime of False Imprisonment.

**IN023.3.A.31.** List the elements of the crime of Luring and Enticing a Child.

**IN023.3.A.38.** List the elements of the crime of Human Trafficking.

**IN023.3.A.42.** List the elements of the crime of Human Smuggling.

Although trespass is generally a misdemeanor, certain aggravating facts can enhance the offense to a felony. See F.S. §810.08-.09.

**Elements of Loitering or Prowling**, F.S. §856.021, Misdemeanor Second Degree *(IN023.3.A.7.)*
The State must prove the following elements to convict a suspect of loitering or prowling:

1. The offender loitered or prowled in a place at a time or in a manner not usual for law-abiding individuals.
2. Such loitering and prowling was under circumstances that warranted justifiable and reasonable alarm or immediate concern for the safety of persons or property in the vicinity.

For the explanation of the circumstances, see Criminal Jury Instructions.

**Elements of Assault**, F.S. §784.011, Misdemeanor Second Degree *(IN023.3.A.8.)*
The State must prove the following elements to convict a suspect for assault:

1. The offender intentionally and unlawfully threatened, either by word or act, to do violence to the victim.
2. At the time, the offender appeared to have the ability to carry out the threat.
3. The act of the offender created in the mind of the victim a well-founded fear that the violence was about to take place.

**Elements of Aggravated Assault**, F.S. §784.021, Felony Third Degree *(IN023.3.A.9.)*
The State must prove the following elements to convict a suspect of aggravated assault:

1. The offender intentionally and unlawfully threatened, either by word or act, to do violence to the victim.
2. At the time, the offender appeared to have the ability to carry out the threat.
3. The act of the offender created in the mind of the victim a well-founded fear that the violence was about to take place.
4. The assault was made with a deadly weapon without the intent to kill, or the assault was made with the intent to commit a felony.

**Elements of Assault on Law Enforcement Officer or Firefighter** (or certain other specified officers, agents, medical providers, or employees), F.S. §784.07(2)(a), Misdemeanor *(IN023.3.A.10.)*
The State must prove the following elements to convict a suspect of this type of assault:

1. The offender intentionally and unlawfully threatened, either by word or act, to do violence to the victim.
2. At the time, the offender appeared to have the ability to carry out the threat.
3. The act of the offender created in the mind of the victim a well-founded fear that the violence was about to take place.
4. The victim was at the time a law enforcement officer, firefighter, emergency medical care provider, law enforcement explorer, public transit employee or agent, or other specified officer.
5. The offender knew the victim was a law enforcement officer, firefighter, emergency medical care provider, law enforcement explorer, public transit employee or agent, or other specified officer.
6. At the time of the assault, the victim was engaged in the lawful performance of his duties.

**Elements of Aggravated Assault on Law Enforcement Officer or Firefighter** (or certain other specified officers, agents, medical providers, or employees), F.S. §784.07(2)(c), Felony (See Criminal Jury Instructions or Florida Statutes.)

**Elements of Battery**, F.S. §784.03, Misdemeanor/Felony *(IN023.3.A.11.)*
The State must prove one of the following elements to convict a suspect of battery:

1. The offender actually and intentionally touched or struck the victim against the victim's will.
2. The offender intentionally caused bodily harm to the victim.

*Note:* A person who has one prior conviction for Battery, Aggravated Battery, or Felony Battery and commits a second or subsequent Battery commits a felony of the third degree.

**Elements of Felony Battery**, F.S. §784.041, Felony Third Degree *(IN023.3.A.12.)*
The State must prove the following elements to convict a suspect of felony battery:

1. The offender actually and intentionally touched or struck the victim against the victim's will.
2. The offender caused the victim great bodily harm, permanent disability, or permanent disfigurement.

**Elements of Aggravated Battery**, F.S. §784.045, Felony Second Degree *(IN023.3.A.13.)*
The State must prove the following elements to convict a suspect of aggravated battery:

1. The offender intentionally touched or struck the victim against his or her will or caused bodily harm to the victim.
2. The offender in committing the battery
   a. intentionally or knowingly caused great bodily harm, permanent disability, or permanent disfigurement to the victim, or
   b. used a deadly weapon, or
   c. knew or should have known that the victim was pregnant

**Elements of Battery on Law Enforcement Officer or Firefighter** (or certain other specified officers, agents, medical providers, or employees), F.S. §784.07(2)(b), Misdemeanor/Felony *(IN023.3.A.14.)*

The State must prove the following elements to convict a suspect of battery on an officer:

1. The offender intentionally touched or struck the victim against his or her will or caused bodily harm to the victim.
2. The victim was a law enforcement officer or a firefighter (or other specified person).
3. The offender knew the victim was a law enforcement officer or a firefighter (or other specified person).
4. The victim was engaged in the lawful performance of his or her duties when the battery was committed.

**Elements of Aggravated Battery on Law Enforcement Officer or Firefighter** (or certain other specified officers, agents, medical providers, or employees), F.S. §784.07(2)(d), Felony (See Criminal Jury Instructions or Florida Statutes.)

**Domestic Violence**

Pursuant to section 741.28(2), Florida Statutes, ***domestic violence*** means:

> any assault, aggravated assault, battery, aggravated battery, sexual assault, sexual battery, stalking, aggravated stalking, kidnapping, false imprisonment, or any criminal offense resulting in physical injury or death of one family or household member by another *(LE061c.6.A.)*

Section 741.28(3), Florida Statutes, defines ***family or household member*** as:

> Spouses, former spouses, persons related by blood or marriage, persons who are residing together as if a family, or who have resided together in the past as if a family, and persons who are parents of a child in common regardless of whether they have been married. With the exception of persons who have a child in common, the family or household members must be currently residing together or have in the past resided together in the same single dwelling unit.

There is not a specific charge of domestic violence. The actual crime would generally be one of the aforementioned with enhancement added to the charge, i.e., battery (domestic violence) or aggravated battery (domestic violence). Domestic violence will be discussed in more detail in Criminal Investigations.

**Homicide** *(IN023.3.A.15.)*

See Criminal Jury Instructions or Chapter 782, Florida Statutes, for more information, including the specific elements of each offense, and additional offenses.

**Elements of Murder—First Degree**, F.S. §782.04(1)(a)1., Capital Felony

**Elements of Murder—Second Degree**, F.S. §782.04(2), Felony

**Elements of Felony Murder—First Degree**, F.S. §782.04(1)(a)2. & 3., Capital Felony

**Elements of Felony Murder—Second Degree**, F.S. §782.04(3), Felony

**Elements of Felony Murder—Third Degree**, F.S. §782.04(4), Felony

**Elements of Manslaughter**, F.S. §782.07, Felony

**Elements of Vehicular Homicide**, F.S. §782.071, Felony

**Elements of DUI Manslaughter**, F.S. §316.193(3)(c)3., Felony

**Elements of Disorderly Conduct/Breach of Peace**, F.S. §877.03, Misdemeanor Second Degree *(IN023.3.A.16.)*

The State must prove one of the following elements to convict a suspect of disorderly conduct:

1. The act was of a nature to corrupt the public morals.
2. The act outraged the sense of public decency.
3. The act affected the peace and quiet of persons who witnessed it.
4. The person charged engaged in brawling or fighting.
5. The person charged engaged in any such conduct as to constitute a breach of peace or disorderly conduct.

**Elements of Disorderly Intoxication**, F.S. §856.011, Misdemeanor Second Degree *(IN023.3.A.17.)*
The State must prove one of the following elements to convict a suspect of disorderly intoxication:

1. The offender was intoxicated and endangered the safety of another person or property; or
2. The offender was intoxicated or drank any alcoholic beverage in a public place or in or upon a public conveyance and caused a public disturbance.

For the definition of "intoxication" and optional definitions, see Criminal Jury Instructions.

**Elements of Open House Party**, F.S. §856.015, Misdemeanor Second Degree *(IN023.3.A.33.)*
The State must prove the following elements to convict a suspect of open house party:

1. An adult was in control of the residence.
2. The adult knowingly allows a social gathering.
3. The possession or consumption of alcoholic beverages or controlled substances by one or more minors occurs during the gathering.

*Note:* A person who violates subsection (2) a second or subsequent time commits a misdemeanor of the first degree. Additionally, if a violation of subsection (2) causes or contributes to causing serious bodily injury or death to the minor, or if the minor causes or contributes to causing serious bodily injury or death to another as a result of the minor's consumption of alcohol or drugs at the open house party, the violation is a misdemeanor of the first degree.

**Elements of Selling or Giving Alcoholic Beverages to a Person Under the Age of 21**, F.S. §562.11, Misdemeanor Second Degree *(IN023.3.A.34.)*
The State must prove the following elements:

1. The defendant sold, gave, or served
2. an alcoholic beverage
3. to a person under the age of 21.

**Elements of Possession of Alcoholic Beverage by a Person Under the Age of 21**, F.S. §562.111, Misdemeanor Second Degree *(IN023.3.A.35.)*
The State must prove the following elements:

1. The defendant is under 21.
2. The defendant is in possession of or consuming an alcoholic beverage.

**Elements of Possession of Tobacco Products by a Person Under 18 Years of Age**, F.S. §569.11, Noncriminal Infraction *(IN023.3.A.36.)*
The State must prove the following elements:

1. The defendant is under 18.
2. The defendant has in his or her possession a tobacco product.

**Elements of Selling, Delivering, Bartering, Furnishing, or Giving Tobacco Products to Persons Under 18 Years of Age**, F.S. §569.101, Misdemeanor Second Degree *(IN023.3.A.37.)*
The State must prove the following elements:

1. The defendant sold, delivered, bartered, furnished, or gave
2. to a person under 18
3. any tobacco product.

**Elements of Drug Offenses—Sale, Purchase, Manufacture, Delivery, or Possession with Intent**, F.S. §893.13(1)(a), Felony *(IN023.3.A.18.)*
The State must prove the following elements to convict a suspect of a drug offense:

1. The offender sold, purchased, manufactured, delivered, or possessed with intent to sell, purchase, manufacture, or deliver a certain substance.
2. The substance was the specific substance alleged.
3. The offender had knowledge of the presence of the substance.

Certain drugs and chemical substances are by law known as controlled substances. "Specific substance alleged" is a controlled substance.

**Elements of Drug Abuse—Sale, Purchase, Manufacture, Delivery, or Possession within 1,000 feet of a School**, F.S. §893.13(1)(c), (d), (e), and (h), Felony (See Criminal Jury Instructions or Florida Statutes.)

**Elements of Drug Abuse—Possession**, F.S. §893.13(6)(a), Felony Third Degree and F.S. §893.13(6)(b), Misdemeanor* *(IN023.3.A.19.)*
The State must prove the following elements to convict a suspect of drug possession:

1. The offender possessed a certain substance.
2. The substance was the specific substance alleged.
3. The offender had knowledge of the presence of the substance.
   * for possession of marijuana less than 20 grams or possession of 3 grams or less of a controlled substance described in s. 893.03(1)(c)46.-50.

**Elements of Use or Possession of Drug Paraphernalia**, F.S. §893.147(1), Misdemeanor First Degree *(IN023.3.A.20.)*
The State must prove the following elements to convict a suspect of use/possession of drug paraphernalia:

1. The offender used or had in his or her possession with intent to use drug paraphernalia.
2. The offender had knowledge of the presence of the drug paraphernalia.

For the definition of "paraphernalia," see Criminal Jury Instructions or Florida Statutes.

**Elements of Resisting Officer without Violence**, F.S. §843.02, Misdemeanor First Degree *(IN023.3.A.21.)*
The State must prove the following elements to convict a suspect of resisting an officer without violence:

1. The offender resisted, obstructed, or opposed the victim (officer).
2. At the time, the victim (officer) was engaged in the execution of legal process or the lawful execution of a legal duty.
3. At the time, the victim was an officer.

**Elements of Resisting Officer with Violence**, F.S. §843.01, Felony Third Degree *(IN023.3.A.22.)*
The State must prove the following elements to convict a suspect of resisting an officer with violence:

1. The offender knowingly and willfully resisted, obstructed, or opposed the victim (officer) by offering to do him or her violence or by doing violence to him or her.
2. At the time, the victim (officer) was engaged in the execution of legal process or lawful execution of a legal duty.
3. At the time, the victim was an officer.

**Elements of Stalking**, F.S. §784.048(2), Misdemeanor First Degree *(IN023.3.A.23.)*
The State must prove that the offender willfully, maliciously, and repeatedly followed, harassed, or cyber-stalked the victim to achieve a conviction.

***Harass*** means to engage in a course of conduct directed at a specific person that causes substantial emotional distress in such person and serves no legitimate purpose.

***Cyber-stalk*** means to engage in a course of conduct to communicate or cause to be communicated, words, images, or language by or through the use of electronic mail or electronic communication, directed at a specific person, causing substantial emotional distress to that person, and serving no legitimate purpose.

**Elements of Aggravated Stalking**, F.S. §784.048(3), §784.048(4), and §784.048(5), Felony Third Degree (See Criminal Jury Instructions or Florida Statutes.)

**Elements of Sexual Battery—Victim Less Than 12 Years of Age**, F.S. §794.011(2), Capital Felony (See Criminal Jury Instructions or Florida Statutes.)

**Elements of Sexual Battery—Person 12 Years of Age or Older**, F.S. §794.011(5), Felony Second Degree *(IN023.3.A.24.)*
The State must prove the following elements to convict a suspect of this type of battery:

1. The victim was 12 years of age or older.
2. The offender committed an act upon or with the victim in which the sexual organ of the offender or victim penetrated or had union with the anus, vagina, or mouth of the victim or the offender, or the offender committed an act upon the victim in which the anus or vagina of the victim was penetrated by an object.
3. The act was committed without the consent of the victim.

    ***Consent*** means intelligent, knowing, and voluntary consent and does not include coerced submission.

    ***Sexual battery*** means oral, anal, or vaginal penetration by, or union with, the sexual organ of another or the anal or vaginal penetration of another by any other object… F.S. §794.011(1)(h)

**Elements of Exposure of Sexual Organs**, F.S. §800.03, Misdemeanor First Degree (See Criminal Jury Instructions or Florida Statutes.)

**Elements of Lewd or Lascivious Offenses**, F.S. §800.02, §800.03, and §800.04 (See Criminal Jury Instructions or Florida Statutes.)

**Elements of Carrying Concealed Weapon**, F.S. §790.01, Misdemeanor/Felony *(IN023.3.A.25.)*
The State must prove the following elements to convict a suspect of carrying a concealed weapon:

1. The defendant knowingly carried on or about his or her person the weapon alleged.
2. The weapon alleged was concealed from the ordinary sight of another person.

For the definitions of "weapon," "electric weapon," "device," or "firearm," see Criminal Jury Instructions or Florida Statutes.

**Elements of Criminal Mischief**, F.S. §806.13, Misdemeanor/Felony* *(IN023.3.A.26.)*
The State must prove the following elements to convict a suspect of criminal mischief:

1. The offender injured or damaged property.
2. The property belonged to someone else.
3. The injury or damage was done willfully and maliciously.

For the definitions of "willfully" and "maliciously," see Criminal Jury Instructions or Florida Statutes.

*Misdemeanor value of loss is less than $1,000. Felony value is $1,000 or more.

**Elements of Fraudulent Use of Credit Card**, F.S. §817.61, Misdemeanor/Felony
There are no Criminal Jury Instructions for these violations. Refer to Florida Statutes.

**Elements of Criminal Use of Personal Identification Information (Identity Theft)** F.S. §817.568, Felony
There are no Criminal Jury Instructions for these violations. Refer to Florida Statutes.

Personal identification information is listed in subsections (1)(f). The elements of the crime are specified in (2)(a).

**Elements of Forgery**, F.S. §831.01, Felony *(IN023.3.A.39.)*
The State must prove the following elements to convict a suspect of forgery:

1. The offender falsely made, altered, forged or counterfeited a document (specified in statute).
2. The offender intended to injure or defraud some person or firm.

It is not necessary that the defendant intended to use the document or to profit him- or herself from its use. It is sufficient if he or she intended that some person would use it to injure or defraud.

**Elements of Uttering a Forged Instrument**, F.S. §831.02, Felony *(IN023.3.A.40.)*
The State must prove the following elements to convict a suspect of uttering a forged instrument:

1. The offender passed or offered to pass as true a document (specified in statute).
2. The offender knew the document to be false, altered, forged, or counterfeited.
3. The offender intended to injure or defraud some person or firm.

**Elements of Giving a Worthless Check**, F.S. §832.05, Misdemeanor/Felony* *(IN023.3.A.41.)*
The State must prove the following elements to convict a suspect of uttering a worthless check:

1. The offender drew, made, uttered, issued or delivered the check admitted in evidence.
2. When the offender did so, there was not sufficient money on deposit in the bank to pay the check.
3. The offender knew when he wrote the check that he did not have sufficient money on deposit with the bank.

4. The offender knew he had no arrangement or understanding with the bank for the payment of the check when it was presented.
5. The check was in the amount of __________.*

Even if all these elements are proved, the offender is not guilty if any of the following three defenses is proved:

1. The payee or holder knew that the offender's funds and credit at the bank at the time the check was given were insufficient to pay the check; or
2. The payee or holder had good reason to believe that the offender's funds and credit at the bank at the time the check was given were insufficient to pay the check; or
3. The check was post-dated.

*Misdemeanor is less than $150. Felony is $150 or more.

**Elder Abuse** *(IN023.3.A.27.)*
There are no Criminal Jury Instructions for these violations. Refer to Florida Statutes for the specific elements of the offenses.

| | |
|---|---|
| **F.S. §825.101** | Definitions |
| **F.S. §825.102** | Abuse |
| **F.S. §825.103** | Exploitation |

**Elements of Child Abuse**, F.S. §827.03, Felony *(IN023.3.A.28.)*
The State must prove the following elements to convict a suspect of child abuse:

1. The defendant committed at least one of the following:
   a. intentionally inflicted physical or mental injury upon the victim
   b. committed an intentional act that could reasonably be expected to result in physical or mental injury to the victim
   c. actively encouraged another person to commit an act that results in or could reasonably have been expected to result in physical or mental injury to the victim
2. The victim is under the age of 18.

For definitions of "child," "neglect of child," and "child abandonment," see F.S. §827.03.

*Note:* Leaving a newborn infant at a hospital, emergency medical services station, or fire station without intent to return does not constitute a crime. See F.S. §827.035.

**Elements of Kidnapping**, F.S. §787.01, Felony *(IN023.3.A.29.)*
The State must prove the following elements to convict a suspect of kidnapping:

1. The defendant forcibly or secretly or by threat confined, abducted, or imprisoned the victim against his or her will.
2. The defendant had no lawful authority.
3. The defendant acted with intent to
   a. hold for ransom or reward or as a shield or hostage, or
   b. commit or facilitate commission of (applicable felony), or

c. inflict bodily harm upon or to terrorize the victim or another person, or

d. interfere with the performance of any governmental or political function

In order to be kidnapping, the confinement, abduction, or imprisonment:

a. must not be slight, inconsequential, or merely incidental to the felony,

b. must not be of the kind inherent in the nature of the felony, and

c. must have some significance independent of the felony in that it makes the felony substantially easier of commission or substantially lessens the risk of detection

Confinement of a child under the age of 13 is against the child's will if such confinement is without the consent of the parent or legal guardian.

**Elements of False Imprisonment**, F.S. §787.02, Felony *(IN023.3.A.30.)*
The State must prove the following elements to convict a suspect of false imprisonment:

1. The defendant forcibly or secretly or by threat confined, abducted, or imprisoned the victim against his or her will.
2. The defendant had no lawful authority.

Confinement of a child under the age of 13 is against the child's will if such confinement is without the consent of the parent or legal guardian.

**Elements of Luring or Enticing a Child**, F.S. §787.025, Misdemeanor/Felony *(IN023.3.A.31.)*
The State must prove the following elements to convict a suspect of luring or enticing a child:

A person 18 years of age or older (misdemeanor)

1. intentionally lures or entices, or
2. attempts to lure or entice,
3. a child under the age of 12
4. into a structure, dwelling, or conveyance for other than a lawful purpose

A person 18 years of age or older who, having been previously convicted of a misdemeanor violation of luring and enticing, (felony)

1. intentionally lures or entices, or
2. attempts to lure or entice,
3. a child under the age of 12
4. into a structure, dwelling, or conveyance for other than a lawful purpose

A person 18 years of age or older who, having been previously convicted of a violation of F.S. Chapter 794, §800.04, or §847.0135(5) or a violation of similar law of another jurisdiction, (felony)

1. intentionally lures or entices, or
2. attempts to lure or entice,
3. a child under the age of 12
4. into a structure, dwelling, or conveyance for other than a lawful purpose

**Elements of Human Trafficking**, F.S. §787.06(3)(a), Felony Second Degree *(IN023.3.A.38.)*

The State must prove one of the following elements to convict a suspect of human trafficking:

1. The defendant engaged or attempted to engage in human trafficking with the intent or knowledge that the trafficked person would be subjected to forced labor or services, or
2. The defendant benefited financially by receiving anything of value from participation in a venture that subjected a person to forced labor or services.

***Human trafficking*** means transporting, soliciting, recruiting, harboring, providing, or obtaining another person for transport. See F.S. §787.06(2)(c)

**Elements of Human Smuggling,** F.S. §787.07, Misdemeanor First Degree *(IN023.3.A.42.)*

The State must prove one of the following elements to convict a suspect of human smuggling:

1. The defendant transported into this state a person from another country who does not have authorization to enter the United States legally.
2. The defendant knew or should have known that the person does not have authorization to enter the United States legally.

**Section Vocabulary**

***consent***

***conveyance***

***cyber-stalk***

***domestic violence***

***family or household member***

***harass***

***human trafficking***

***sexual battery***

***structure***

# UNIT 3 | SUBSTANTIVE CRIMINAL LAW

## LESSON 3 | Levels of Criminal Involvement

**OBJECTIVES**

**IN026.1.** Identify all persons related to an incident involving a crime.

**IN026.1.A.** Define *witness.*

**IN026.1.B.** Define *victim.*

**IN026.1.C.** Define *suspected perpetrator.*

**IN026.2.** Identify the criteria for criminal responsibility.

**IN026.2.A.** Define *principal in the first degree.*

**IN026.2.B.** Define *accessory after the fact.*

**IN026.2.C.** Define *attempt.*

**IN026.2.D.** Define *solicitation.*

**IN026.2.E.** Define *conspiracy.*

### Identifying Persons Involved in an Incident

Investigating officers must determine the identity of persons involved in an incident, including witnesses, victims, and suspected perpetrators of crime. Officers must also determine what each person knows about the incident and whether a person participated in the commission of the crime, was a victim, or merely witnessed it. Officers make initial determinations by questioning persons, observing physical evidence at the scene, and reviewing documentation related to the incident. *(IN026.1.)*

A ***witness*** is any person who has information about some element of the crime or about evidence or documents related to the crime *(IN026.1.A.)*. A witness may have heard statements or observed events before, during, or after the crime. A witness may have information about a piece of physical evidence associated with the crime or knowledge of some document related to the crime.

A ***victim*** is a witness who suffers an injury as a result of a crime *(IN026.1.B.)*. The injury may involve physical harm, loss of money, loss of property, or damage to property. The victim of a crime such as an aggravated battery has a physical injury. The victim of fraud has an injury in the form of lost money. The victim of criminal mischief may have an injury in the form of property damage.

Not all crimes have an identifiable victim. For example, the crime of unlawful possession of a controlled substance has no specific victim. In victimless crimes, the victim is the state of Florida.

Florida Statute §960.001 provides that a victim has the right "to be informed, present, and to be heard, when relevant, at all crucial stages of a criminal or juvenile proceeding…" In some cases, the victim also has the right to be notified if the suspect is released from jail.

A ***suspected perpetrator***, or ***suspect***, is the person believed to have committed a crime *(IN026.1.C.)*. An officer may identify a suspected perpetrator directly by observing that person commit the crime, indirectly through statements or observations that witnesses provide, through the suspect's own statements, or by learning of the person's identity based on evidence collected while investigating the crime.

A person may directly commit a criminal violation by contributing to a crime in some other, more limited capacity. The way in which a person participated in the crime determines a person's criminal responsibility. *(IN026.2.)*

Section 777.011, F.S. defines ***principal in the first degree***. If the defendant helped another person or persons commit or attempt to commit a crime, the defendant is a principal and must be treated as if he or she had done all the things the other person or persons did if the defendant had a conscious intent that the criminal act be done; and the defendant did some act or said some word which was intended to and which did incite, cause, encourage, assist, or advise the other person or persons to actually commit or attempt to commit the crime. To be a principal in the first degree, a person does not have to be present when the crime is actually committed or attempted. *(IN026.2.A.)*

An ***accessory*** is defined as a person who aids or contributes in the commission or concealment of a crime. Section 777.03, F.S., defines ***accessory after the fact***, which is an offense with all the following elements: (1) An offender commits a felony. (2) After the felony, another person maintains or assists the offender. (3) While giving assistance, the person knows that the offender committed the felony. (4) The person assists with the intent of helping the offender avoid or escape detection, arrest, trial, or punishment. *(IN026.2.B.)*

If the offender is related to the person by blood or marriage as husband, wife, parent, grandparent, child, grandchild, brother, or sister, the offender cannot be charged with accessory after the fact. However, this exception does not apply to certain crimes, for example, those involving the victimization of children.

## Criminal Attempt

Florida Statute §777.04(1) describes the conditions for charging a person with attempt. ***Attempt*** is an offense when either the person did some act toward committing the crime that went beyond just thinking or talking about it; or the person would have committed the crime except that someone or something prevented him or her from doing so, or the person failed *(IN026.2.C.)*. However, it is not an attempt if a person abandons the attempt to commit the offense or otherwise prevents the commission of the crime. Circumstances must show that the person completely and voluntarily gave up his or her criminal purpose.

Voluntary abandonment is not a defense to a crime when the suspect decides not to pursue the crime because of unforeseen difficulties in completing the crime or when detection of the criminal activity is imminent.

The seriousness of the crime that the person attempted to commit establishes the penalty for attempt. Generally, attempt is punishable at the level of offense just below the degree of crime that the offender attempted to commit. For example, if the person attempts to commit a crime that is a third-degree felony, the attempt is a first-degree misdemeanor.

## Solicitation

The crime of ***solicitation*** is best defined in the Criminal Jury Instructions as follows:

**Elements of Solicitation**, F.S. §777.04(2) *(IN026.2.D.)*
The State must prove the following elements to convict a suspect of solicitation:

1. The offender solicited a person to commit a certain offense.
2. During solicitation, the offender commanded, encouraged, hired, or requested the other person to engage in specific conduct which would constitute the commission of the offense or attempt to commit the offense.

**Section Vocabulary**

*accessory*

*accessory after the fact*

*attempt*

*conspiracy*

*principal in the first degree*

*solicitation*

*suspect*

*suspected perpetrator*

*victim*

*witness*

The seriousness of the crime that the offender solicited sets the penalty for solicitation. Generally, punishment for solicitation is the level of offense just below the degree of crime that the offender committed.

## Conspiracy

The crime of ***conspiracy*** is best defined in the Criminal Jury Instructions as follows:

**Elements of Conspiracy**, F.S. §777.04(3.) *(IN026.2.E.)*
The State must prove the following elements to convict a suspect of conspiracy:

1. The intent of the offender was that the offense (object of conspiracy) would be committed.
2. In order to carry out the intent, the offender agreed, conspired, combined, or confederated with the person(s) alleged to cause (object of conspiracy) to be committed either by them, or one of them, or by some other person.

It is not necessary that agreement, conspiracy, combination, or confederation to commit (object of conspiracy) be expressed in any particular words or that words pass between the conspirators. It is not necessary that the defendant do any act in furtherance of the offense conspired.

Conspiracy requires two or more parties with a criminal intent; therefore, if one of the two conspiring parties is a law enforcement officer or agent, then a conspiracy does not exist. It is a defense to the charge of criminal conspiracy that a person, after conspiring with one or more persons to commit a crime, convinced another not to do so or in some other way prevented commission of the crime.

For more information, officers should refer to the Florida Criminal Jury Instructions and *Mickenberg v. State*, 640 So.2d 1210 (Fla. 2nd DCA 1994) regarding two or more persons to conspire.

# UNIT 3 | SUBSTANTIVE CRIMINAL LAW

## LESSON 4 | Legal Defenses to Criminal Responsibility

Officers should be aware of potential legal defenses that suspects may raise in court. Throughout an investigation, an officer should anticipate these defenses and be prepared to rebut them with evidence to the contrary. However, an officer has a responsibility to investigate and notify the state attorney of any evidence that may point to the suspect's innocence. This type of evidence is known as exculpatory evidence.

The most common legal defenses include the following:

- alibi
- mistake or ignorance of fact
- intoxication
- duress or coercion
- justifiable use of force
- self-defense
- defense of property
- entrapment
- insanity
- mental incompetence
- statute of limitations
- consent *(IN023.4.A.)*

An ***alibi*** is a suspect or defendant's claim that he or she was not present when the alleged act was committed. Officers need to follow up on any claim of an alibi in the investigation of a crime. *(IN023.4.A.1.)*

***Mistake or ignorance of fact*** is a legal defense that is used when the accused does not possess the mental state required to commit a criminal offense because of a reasonably mistaken belief about the facts relating to the circumstances. It is not to be confused with diminished mental capacity or insanity. A defendant who does not have the intent necessary to commit the crime cannot be convicted *(IN023.4.A.2.)*. For example, a woman picks up someone else's luggage at the airport that is identical to hers. There was no criminal intent to steal; it was a mistake. She is not guilty of theft if she returns the luggage.

There is a special exception to this legal defense for controlled substances. Possession of a controlled substance presumes knowledge of the illicit nature of the substance, and the person in possession is therefore presumed guilty. Ignorance of the law—when a person believes that his or her conduct does not violate the law—is generally not recognized as a defense to criminal liability.

**OBJECTIVES**

**IN023.4.A.** Identify the legal defenses of criminal responsibility.

**IN023.4.A.1.** Define *alibi* as a legal defense of criminal responsibility.

**IN023.4.A.2.** Define *mistake or ignorance of fact* as a legal defense of criminal responsibility.

**IN023.4.A.3.** Define *intoxication* as a legal defense of criminal responsibility.

**IN023.4.A.4.** Define *duress or coercion* as a legal defense of criminal responsibility.

**IN023.4.A.5.** Define *justifiable use of force* as a legal defense of criminal responsibility.

**IN023.4.A.10.** Define *self-defense* as a legal defense of criminal responsibility.

**IN023.4.A.11.** Define defense of others as a legal defense of criminal responsibility.

**IN023.4.A.12.** Define *defense of property* as a legal defense of criminal responsibility.

**IN023.4.A.6.** Define *entrapment* as a legal defense of criminal responsibility.

**IN023.4.A.7.** Define *insanity* as a legal defense of criminal responsibility.

**IN023.4.A.8.** Define *mental incompetence* as a legal defense of criminal responsibility.

**IN023.4.A.9.** Define *statute of limitations* as a legal defense of criminal responsibility.

**IIN023.4.A.13.** Define *consent* as a legal defense of criminal responsibility.

***Intoxication*** is a legal defense in limited circumstances when it negates an essential element of the crime, such as the ability to form criminal intent in the commission of certain offenses *(IN023.4.A.3.)*. The defendant may argue the same defense as insanity. Intoxication is not a defense for offenses such as DUI and disorderly intoxication (in which being intoxicated is an element of the crime) or when an individual argues that he or she would not have committed the crime if sober. Usually, intoxication as a defense occurs when a person is so intoxicated as to be incapable of forming the necessary intent for the crime.

Criminal law recognizes two types of intoxication. A person who is voluntarily intoxicated is aware of ingesting the intoxicant, either alcohol or a controlled substance. Involuntary intoxication occurs when an individual is unaware of ingesting the intoxicant, is tricked into ingesting it, or is following doctor's orders.

A person who faces a threat from another and commits a criminal act in response may have the legal defense of ***duress*** or ***coercion***. This defense requires that the person committing the act must reasonably believe that the only way to avoid death or great bodily harm to self or a third party is to commit the crime. The person under duress is faced with the choice between the lesser of two evils and chooses to commit the lesser criminal act to avoid the threatened greater criminal act *(IN023.4.A.4.)*. Duress is never a defense to an intentional homicide or the killing of an innocent third party.

A person may legally use force to defend against the use of force by another. Chapter 776, F.S. defines ***justifiable use of force*** in Florida. *(IN023.4.A.5.)*

***Self-defense*** is a common legal term that describes the justifiable use of force that is necessary to protect oneself *(IN023.4.A.10.)*. This same legal term also describes the justifiable use of force necessary for the defense of others. *(IN023.4.A.11.)*

***Defense of property*** is a common legal term describing a person's authority to take reasonable steps, including the use of force (except deadly force) to the extent that a person reasonably believes is necessary to protect his or her possessions from trespass or theft or to terminate these acts *(IN023.4.A.12.)*. For example, a man armed with a gun breaks into John's home. John shoots the man. Florida law justifies the action John took to protect himself and his family. In situations like this, state law authorizes individuals to commit acts that usually would lead to criminal liability, but only when their use of force is justified.

***Entrapment*** occurs when a law enforcement officer uses undue persuasion or fraudulent means to induce a person to commit a crime he or she would not have otherwise committed. Entrapment can be used as a legal defense in these cases. In order to use the defense of entrapment, the defendant must admit that he or she committed the crime *(IN023.4.A.6.)*. Section 777.201, F.S. provides elements of entrapment.

***Insanity*** is defined legally as any mental disorder so severe that it prevents a person from having legal capacity and excuses the person from criminal or civil responsibility.

When using an insanity defense, the accused alleges that he or she suffered from a mental disorder at the time the crime was committed and that the disorder caused the commission of the crime. *(IN023.4.A.7.)*

In the state of Florida, courts follow the *M'Naughten rule*, which states

> A person is not criminally responsible if, at the time of the alleged crime, the defendant, by reason of a mental disease or defect, (1) does not know of the nature or consequences of his or her act; or (2) is unable to distinguish right from wrong. *Wheeler v. State*, 344 So.2d 244 (Fla. 1977)

If the defense cannot show insanity at the time the crime occurred, it cannot use the insanity defense.

The legal defense of ***mental incompetence*** recognizes that a criminal defendant will be judged on his or her present ability to assist counsel by participating in the criminal defense. A person deemed mentally incompetent at the time of trial cannot legally stand trial or testify. It is possible for a person to regain competence, at which time the person would be required to stand trial for the crimes charged. *(IN023.4.A.8.)*

The legal principle of the ***statute of limitations*** bars the state from prosecuting an individual after a certain period of time has elapsed since the criminal act occurred *(IN023.4.A.9.)*. Section 775.15, F.S. contains the general statute of limitations for criminal offenses. Prosecution may begin at any time after the commission of a capital offense, a life felony, or a felony that resulted in death. Prosecution must begin within four years after the commission of a felony of the first degree and within three years after the commission of any other felony. Prosecution must begin within two years after the commission of a misdemeanor of the first degree and within one year after the commission of a misdemeanor of the second degree or a noncriminal offense. Florida law also provides several exceptions to the statute of limitations. Most are in F.S. §775.15.

***Consent*** is a possible excuse against civil or criminal liability. Defendants who use this defense argue they should not be held liable because the acts in question were committed with the victim's consent and permission *(IN023.4.A.13.)*. Generally, if there is consent, there is no crime.

An exception would be that a minor cannot consent to a sex act. An example of consent is when a person plays football, that person consents to battery by another player. However, if a fan in the stands throws a soda can at a player, that act is considered battery.

Victims who, because of age, mental illness, or intoxication, are not legally capable of reasonable judgment may not give consent.

## Section Vocabulary

***alibi***

***consent***

***defense of property***

***duress or coercion***

***entrapment***

***insanity***

***intoxication***

***justifiable use of force***

***mental incompetence***

***mistake or ignorance of fact***

***self-defense***

***statute of limitations***

UNIT 3 | SUBSTANTIVE CRIMINAL LAW

# LESSON 5 | Evidence Rules and Concepts

**OBJECTIVES**

**LE089b.5.A.** Identify the location of basic concepts and rules of evidence.

**LE089b.5.A.1.** Define *evidence.*

**LE089b.5.A.2.** Define *direct evidence.*

**LE089b.5.A.3.** Define *indirect* or *circumstantial evidence.*

**LE089b.5.A.4.** Identify the three primary categories of evidence.

**LE089b.5.A.5.** Define *fruits of a crime.*

**LE089b.5.A.6.** Define *instrumentalities* of a crime.

**LE089b.5.A.7.** Define *contraband.*

**LE089b.5.A.8.** Identify the three basic reasons why evidence is offered in court.

**LE089b.5.A.9.** Define *admissibility of evidence.*

**LE089b.5.A.10.** Identify the three primary reasons for evidence rules.

**LE089b.5.A.11.** Identify the general rules for excluding evidence.

**LE089b.5.A.12.** Define *hearsay evidence.*

**LE089b.5.A.13.** Identify four specific requirements that officers must be aware of to ensure admissibility of evidence.

**LE089b.5.A.14.** Identify the types of privileged communication protected under Chapter 90, F.S.

## Types of Evidence

The Florida Evidence Code, found in Chapter 90 of the Florida statutes, provides the basic concepts and rules of evidence that may be used in a criminal or civil proceeding *(LE089b.5.A.)*. ***Evidence*** is anything that tends to prove or disprove the existence of a fact *(LE089b.5.A.1.)*. There is a legal distinction between evidence and proof. Evidence is information that is allowed in court, while proof is the effect produced by that information.

There are two primary types of evidence: direct and indirect. ***Direct evidence*** is that which proves a fact without an inference or presumption and which, if true in itself, conclusively establishes that fact. Examples of direct evidence that someone was speeding would be the admission by the driver that he was speeding, speed measurement device results, and testimony from eyewitnesses to the speeding. *(LE089b.5.A.2.)*

***Circumstantial*** or ***indirect evidence*** requires an inference or presumption to establish a fact. An example of circumstantial evidence is eyewitness testimony that the defendant entered the victim's home around the time of the crime. It requires the judge or jury to infer from the evidence that the defendant committed the crime. Contrary to the speeches given by criminal defense lawyers on television, most criminal cases are often based primarily on circumstantial evidence. *(LE089b.5.A.3.)*

Evidence presented in court can be placed into one of three primary categories: testimonial, documentary, or physical. ***Testimonial evidence*** is witness statements tending to prove or disprove facts about the case. It includes the testimonies of law enforcement officers, experts, and other witnesses. ***Documentary evidence*** is anything written or printed which is offered to prove or disprove facts pertaining to the case. It includes bank records, medical records, or a certified copy of a subject's driving history.

***Physical*** or ***real evidence*** refers to actual objects which may be offered to prove facts about a case. Examples include items such as drugs, a gun, clothing, or money. This evidence is crucial for the prosecutor because it gives the jury something to touch and take back to the jury room while they conduct deliberations. *(LE089b.5.A.4.)*

The physical objects introduced as evidence can either be fruits of a crime, instrumentalities of a crime, or contraband. ***Fruits of a crime*** are the objects obtained by the defendant as a result of committing the crime *(LE089b.5.A.5.)*. An example is money stolen by a bank robber. ***Instrumentalities*** are the items used by the defendant to commit the crime. The crowbar used by a burglar to gain entry into the building is an instrumentality of the crime *(LE089b.5.A.6.)*. ***Contraband*** is anything that is illegal to possess. Illegal drugs are the most common example of contraband. *(LE089b.5.A.7.)*

Evidence is offered in court for three basic reasons. First, evidence is offered to prove or disprove a crime. Most of the evidence seized by a law enforcement officer is used to prove that the defendant committed the crime. Fingerprints, photographs, physical evidence, and eyewitness testimony collected by law enforcement are typically offered to prove that the defendant committed the crime. The defendant may offer evidence, such as an alibi witness, in an attempt to disprove his or her responsibility for the crime.

Evidence is also offered in court to support or undermine other evidence. For example, a chemist may be called as an expert witness in a drug case to support the fact that the substance in question was actually an illegal drug.

Finally, evidence is offered in court to help determine an appropriate sentence. Florida law allows for enhanced sentencing of certain defendants based upon their criminal history. Documentary evidence in the form of certified prior convictions may be used to support the argument for an enhanced sentence. *(LE089b.5.A.8.)*

## Admissibility of Evidence

Once an officer understands why evidence is collected and introduced, he or she must understand the rules of admissibility. ***Admissibility of evidence*** refers to the legal requirements that must be met before a jury is allowed to see or hear about the evidence *(LE089b.5.A.9.)*. The rules of evidence are in place for at least three primary reasons: to protect the defendant's constitutional rights, to protect jurors from being misled or confused, and to expedite the trial. *(LE089b.5.A.10.)*

Sometimes evidence is excluded from trial. There are several reasons for excluding evidence. Evidence may be excluded because it was obtained in violation of the defendant's constitutional rights. The law provides rules that guide how law enforcement officers must act. The exclusionary rule is actually a rule of evidence that prohibits use of evidence obtained by law enforcement in violation of the rules. The reason for the rule is to reduce violations of the Constitution by law enforcement; for instance, there is no benefit to the case by conducting an illegal search if the jury will never hear about the evidence collected.

Some evidence is excluded to avoid undue prejudice against the defendant, such as his or her prior criminal history. This rule exists so a jury does not convict the defendant because of his or her past crimes. A legal conviction must be based on evidence that the defendant committed the crime charged. Evidence may also be excluded to prohibit jury consideration of unreliable evidence. The reliability of evidence is critical to its admissibility. The laws of evidence ensure reliability by allowing only experts to give opinions, excluding hearsay evidence, and requiring officers to follow certain rules with respect to the collection and preservation of evidence. *(LE089b.5.A.11.)*

***Hearsay*** is a statement other than one made by the declarant while testifying at the trial or hearing, offered in evidence to prove the truth of the matter asserted *(LE089b.5.A.12.)*. Hearsay testimony is excluded if its reliability cannot be tested by cross-examination. However, there are more than 20 exceptions to the hearsay rule. Some of the more common hearsay examples include spontaneous statements, F.S. §90.803(1); excited utterances, F.S. §90.803(2); and statements against interest, F.S. §90.804(2)(c). The court determines the admissibility of each of these types of statements.

The admissibility of evidence also depends upon the manner in which the officer collected and preserved the evidence. There are four specific requirements that ensure admissibility. The evidence must be relevant to the

## Section Vocabulary

*admissibility of evidence*

*circumstantial or indirect evidence*

*contraband*

*direct evidence*

*documentary evidence*

*evidence*

*fruits of a crime*

*hearsay*

*instrumentalities*

*physical or real evidence*

*testimonial evidence*

case, obtained legally, and preserved properly. The chain of custody must also be preserved. *(LE089b.5.A.13.)*

The Florida Evidence Code recognizes that the need to protect communications within certain relationships is more important than the admissibility of evidence obtained from those communications. The privileged communications protected under sections 90.501 - 90.510, F.S. include the following:

- lawyer–client
- journalist–source
- husband–wife
- psychotherapist–patient
- accountant–client
- clergy–penitent
- sexual assault counselor–victim
- domestic violence advocate–victim

*Note:* Each of these privileges may be waived by voluntary disclosure in accordance with F.S. §90.507.

Florida law also recognizes privileges with respect to the disclosure of certain information:

- Automobile accident: F.S. §316.066(7)
- Trade secrets: F.S. §90.506
- Reports of child abuse or neglect: F.S. §39.202 *(LE089b.5.A.14.)*

# UNIT 3 | SUBSTANTIVE CRIMINAL LAW

## LESSON 6 | Drafting Probable Cause Affidavits

### The Probable Cause Affidavit

One of the most important skills a law enforcement officer must develop is the ability to write legally sufficient probable cause affidavits for arrests. A ***probable cause affidavit***—also called an arrest affidavit—is a sworn, written statement by a law enforcement officer establishing certain facts and circumstances to justify an arrest *(LE395.2.A.)*. This document is used by the judge to determine if there was sufficient probable cause to detain the individual. The assistant state attorney may also review the document to decide whether to file formal charges for the alleged crime. An officer should remember that the probable cause affidavit is an officer's statement of the facts made under oath and may be used by the defense attorney in preparing the defense. *(LE395.2.B.)*

**OBJECTIVES**

**LE395.2.A.** Define *probable cause affidavit.*

**LE395.2.B.** Identify the purpose of a probable cause affidavit.

**LE395.2.C.** Identify the elements of a probable cause affidavit.

**LE395.2.D.** Identify any supplemental information that may be used with a probable cause affidavit.

There are several minimum requirements for an arrest affidavit. First, it must contain a narrative of the offense stating facts sufficient to show probable cause as to each and every element of the charged offense. Some of the facts in the affidavit may include the following:

- date
- time
- place
- reason for the contact and/or seizure
- if and why a search occurred
- name and address of all parties present (including names of superior officers present)
- name, address, identifying information, and description of the accused
- any statement of the accused
- name of victim (State law protects the public release of the identification of sexual assault victims.)
- city or county where offense occurred
- offense charged
- correct Florida Statute number or county or municipal ordinance
- any other information necessary to establish probable cause

In addition, the arresting officer must swear or affirm that the information contained in the probable cause affidavit is true and then sign the document. The notary public, deputy clerk of court, or another officer who administered the oath to the arresting officer must also sign as required and affix an official seal. *(LE395.2.C.)*

**Section Vocabulary**

*probable cause affidavit*

Supplemental information is often attached to the probable cause affidavit. This information may include names and addresses of essential witnesses, witness statements, or a list of tangible evidence seized *(LE395.2.D.)*. Probable cause affidavits vary in format and style among agencies and judicial circuits.

## Guidelines for Writing a Probable Cause Affidavit

When writing probable cause affidavits, an officer must write legibly, use the appropriate form designated by the officer's agency or jurisdiction, and ensure that the offense occurred within the officer's jurisdiction. The officer must also check the Florida Statutes or the Criminal Jury Instructions to review the elements of the offense for which probable cause is to be established. Personal identification information of the suspect is required on the form. The officer should review witness statements, offense and supplemental reports, and collected evidence before writing the affidavit narrative.

This narrative is not a duplicate of the offense report, nor is it a statement of all evidence against the suspect. The officer should review the narrative for completeness and accuracy and correct any grammatical or typographical errors before swearing to the truthfulness of the affidavit. Finally, the officer must follow department policy for approval and submission of paperwork.

# UNIT 4 | USE OF FORCE

## LESSON 1 | Use of Force

### Objective Reasonableness

Law enforcement officers have been granted certain powers through statutes and case law. Many of these powers include an authorization to use physical force. It is the duty of the individual officer to determine the appropriate level of force based upon the facts and circumstances of each situation.

The Fourth Amendment governs police contact with individuals by protecting people from unreasonable search and seizure by the government. When a law enforcement officer decides to detain, arrest, or use any level of force against an individual, the officer's actions will be scrutinized through the reasonableness test of the Fourth Amendment.

In *Graham v. Conner*, 490 U.S. 386 (1989), the United States Supreme Court held that all law enforcement use of force cases are to be judged by an objective reasonableness standard based upon the Fourth Amendment. The use of force is to be judged from the perspective of a reasonable officer under the same circumstances without the benefit of hindsight. The Court clearly considered that officers are often required to make split-second, sometimes deadly decisions, in circumstances that are "tense, uncertain, and rapidly evolving." The Court concluded that the objective reasonableness test is not a precise or clear rule but requires careful review of the facts and circumstances of each case, including the severity of the crime, whether the suspect posed an immediate threat to the safety of officers or others, and whether the suspect was actively resisting arrest or attempting to evade arrest by flight. *(IN029.3.)*

The objective reasonableness test requires the officer to answer two questions about the level of force used in any situation: Was the action reasonable and necessary, and was the amount of force applied reasonable and necessary? *(IN029.3.A.)*

Officers are faced with use of force decisions in three main circumstances. Each of these is governed by both case law interpreting the U.S. Constitution and Chapter 776 of the Florida Statutes: the arrest or detention of a suspect, to prevent escape or return an individual to custody, and to defend oneself or another. *(IN029.1.)*

### *Use of Force in Arrest and Detention, F.S. §776.05*

A law enforcement officer is justified in the use of force when the officer reasonably believes it to be necessary to defend him- or herself or another person from bodily harm while making the arrest *(IN029.1.A.)*, when it is necessary for retaking felons who have escaped *(IN029.1.A.4.)*, and when it is necessary in arresting felons fleeing from justice.

**OBJECTIVES**

**IN029.3.** Identify the factors used in the objective reasonableness standard.

**IN029.3.A.** Identify the questions an officer will have to answer in any use of force situation.

**IN029.1.** Identify the circumstances under which law enforcement officers are faced with use of force decisions.

**IN029.1.A.** Identify the law authorizing law enforcement officers' use of force in making arrests.

**IN029.1.A.4.** Identify that a law enforcement officer may use force to apprehend escaped inmates.

**IN029.1.B.4.** Identify when an officer may use deadly force to apprehend a fleeing felon.

**IN029.1.B.1.** Define *deadly force* pursuant to Florida law.

**IN029.1.A.6.** Identify when a law enforcement officer may use force during an investigative detention.

**IN029.1.A.3.** Identify when a law enforcement officer may use force to prevent an arrested person from escaping custody.

**IN029.1.B.5.** Identify when individuals may use deadly force in self-defense or in defense of others.

**IN029.1.A.1.** Describe the *no retreat law.*

**IN029.1.A.5.** Identify when individuals may use force in the protection of their property.

The statute further explains the three conditions required before an officer may use deadly force in stopping a fleeing felon: when deadly force is necessary to prevent the suspect from escaping; when a warning has been given when feasible; and when the officer reasonably believes that the fleeing felon poses a threat of death or serious physical harm to the officer or others or that the fleeing felon has committed a crime involving the infliction or threatened infliction of serious physical harm to another person. *(IN029.1.B.4.)*

In *Tennessee v. Garner*, 471 U.S. 1 (1985), the United States Supreme Court struck down a Tennessee law which allowed law enforcement officers to use whatever force was necessary to stop fleeing felons. Using the objective reasonableness standard, the court found the statute unconstitutional and set forth the guidelines for using deadly force now found in F.S. §776.05(3). Case law has further established that a law enforcement officer is not required to use alternative methods short of deadly force to resolve a deadly force situation. The only question that will be asked is whether the decision to use deadly force was reasonable. Florida law defines ***deadly force*** as any force that is likely to cause death or great bodily harm under F.S. §776.06 *(IN029.1.B.1.)*. The most common deadly force incidents involve the use of a firearm. The statute further establishes that shooting at a fleeing motor vehicle constitutes deadly force.

Law enforcement officers are also authorized to use reasonable and necessary force to effect an investigative detention (*Terry* stop). The Florida courts have recognized that officers may draw their weapons when conducting an investigative detention when they reasonably believe that the use of weapons is necessary to protect themselves or prevent a suspect's ability to flee *(IN029.1.A.6.)*. See *State v. Hendrex*, 865 So.2d 531 (Fla. 2nd DCA 2003), review denied 879 So.2d 621 (Fla. 2004). The court stated, "the fact that the investigative stop was effected at gunpoint did not convert the stop to an arrest."

## Use of Force to Prevent Escape, F.S. §776.07

The statute authorizes law enforcement officers to use reasonable and necessary force in order to prevent the escape of an arrested person. The use of deadly force under this circumstance would be analyzed under the factors set forth in *Tennessee v. Garner* and contained in F.S. §776.05(3). Furthermore, the statute authorizes law enforcement and corrections officers to use deadly force to prevent the escape of an inmate from a penal institution (prison or county jail). *(IN029.1.A.3.)*

## Use of Force in Defense of Person, F.S. §776.012 and F.S. §776.013

These two Florida statutes work in conjunction to allow all individuals, including but not limited to law enforcement officers, to use reasonable and necessary force to defend themselves when faced with the imminent threat of unlawful force. The statutes allow an individual to use deadly force under two circumstances: if the individual has reason to believe that deadly force is necessary to prevent imminent death or great bodily harm to him- or herself or another person or to prevent the commission of a forcible felony as defined in F.S.§776.08. *(IN029.1.B.5.)*

Florida Statute §776.013 further explains that a person is presumed to be in imminent fear of death or great bodily harm when there is an unlawful and forceful entering of a dwelling or occupied vehicle. This statute, sometimes referred to as the ***no retreat law***, also establishes that an individual has "no duty to retreat" when faced with imminent harm, "has the right to stand his or her ground," and may "meet force with force, including deadly force when he reasonably believes it is necessary to do so to prevent death or great bodily harm." *(IN029.1.A.1.)*

Florida law enforcement officers should also be aware that an individual may use reasonable and necessary force, not including deadly force, to protect property. Florida Statute §776.031 authorizes the use of force to protect one's property and the property of an immediate family member or other person whose property the person has a duty to protect. *(IN029.1.A.5.)*

**Section Vocabulary**

*deadly force*

*no retreat law*

# UNIT 5 | CIVIL AND CRIMINAL LIABILITY

## LESSON 1 | Civil and Criminal Liability

### Types of Liability

**OBJECTIVES**

**IN025.1.B.** Define *civil liability.*

**IN025.1.B.5.** Define *tort.*

**IN025.5.A.** Identify examples of intentional torts.

**IN025.1.B.2.** Define *negligence.*

**IN025.3.** Identify the elements of negligence.

**IN025.4.A.** Identify the two major categories of damages.

**IN025.1.B.3.** Define *compensatory damages.*

**IN025.1.B.4.** Define *punitive damages.*

**IN025.1.C.** Define *civil rights violations.*

A career as a law enforcement officer is exciting and full of challenges. It provides opportunities to make a difference in people's lives. However, liability issues are inherent in the job. These issues arise when an officer improperly performs a job task or does not perform a job task that he or she reasonably should have performed. If an officer does not fully understand and limit situations that give rise to liability, the potential for harm to both the employing agency and the officer is great. Officers can suffer severe consequences including job loss, assessment of devastating monetary awards, or even a prison sentence if found liable of criminal wrongdoing.

The most recognized types of liability are criminal and civil. They are not mutually exclusive; an officer can be prosecuted criminally and civilly for the same act. For example, an officer can be tried for murder (criminal liability) and sued by the decedent's family for wrongful death (civil liability). In such cases, criminal charges are addressed first. Acquittal in a criminal case does not necessarily preclude civil liability, as the O.J. Simpson case demonstrated.

***Criminal liability*** occurs when an officer is found guilty of committing a crime and is sentenced to incarceration or other penalties. ***Civil liability*** is responsibility for a wrongful act or an omission that injures a person or property and most often involves

**IN025.1.A.** Identify how an officer may be subject to criminal liability.

**IN001.3.G.** Define *color of law.*

**IN025.4.** Identify the impact on an officer who is found civilly or criminally liable.

**IN025.2.** Identify the types of agency liability.

**IN025.2.A.** Define *direct liability.*

**IN025.2.B.** Define *vicarious liability.*

**IN025.5.** Identify situations when an officer may be subject to civil or criminal liability.

**IN025.6.** Identify the types of legal defenses available if an officer is faced with potential civil or criminal liability.

**IN025.6.C.1.** Identify the effect of the Sovereign Immunity Law, Section 768.28, Florida Statutes, in state civil actions.

**IN025.6.A.5.** Define *acting within the scope of employment.*

**IN025.6.C.2.** Identify the key aspects of Chapter 111 of the Florida Statutes.

**IN025.6.C.3.** Explain the concept of qualified immunity.

negligence *(IN025.1.B.)*. Penalties for civil liability are normally payment of money damages to the victim or the victim's heirs.

## Torts

In criminal law, an improper act is called a ***crime***, while in civil law an improper act is called a ***tort***. A tort is a civil wrong in which the action or inaction of a person or entity violates the rights of another person or entity. *(IN025.1.B.5.)*

Torts may be intentional, such as battery or false imprisonment, or unintentional, such as negligence. The difference is intent. Very seldom does a person deliberately crash his or her vehicle into another person's vehicle; usually it is an accident. If the at-fault driver was speeding or looking at a cell phone rather than the road, he or she could be sued for the unintentional tort of negligence. Battery is a deliberate act, so it is an intentional tort. Causing someone's death, called wrongful death in tort law, may result from a deliberate act such as shooting a gun into the air during a New Year's celebration. It may also result from an unintentional accident such as driving carelessly. Liability may result from either one.

Many crimes can also be torts when a case is brought in civil court *(IN025.5.A.)*. Some examples of crimes and their corresponding intentional torts under Florida law are as follows:

| CRIME | TORT |
|---|---|
| Battery | Battery |
| Theft | Conversion |
| False Imprisonment | False Arrest |
| Homicide | Wrongful Death |

Crimes vs. torts *Figure 2-3*

## Negligence

A common definition of ***negligence*** is failure to use due or reasonable care in a situation that results in harm to another *(IN025.1.B.2.)*.

For example, an officer is looking at the screen on her in-car computer while driving her patrol car. She doesn't see the traffic has stopped and rear-ends the car in front of her. Since the officer breached her duty to act with reasonable care, she and/or her agency could be held liable for the damages caused by the crash.

Another example of negligence would be an off-duty officer who leaves his loaded weapon on the kitchen counter in reach of his 10-year old son. The son takes his father's weapon to show a neighborhood friend and accidently fires the pistol, killing the friend. The officer could be held liable for the accidental death of the child because of his negligence.

## Elements of Negligence

To convict a defendant of a crime, the state must prove in criminal court that he or she committed all elements of a particular offense. In a civil negligence action, the plaintiff must prove a different set of elements to find the defendant negligent. The elements of negligence are (1) a duty to act with care, (2) breach of the duty to act, (3) causation or proximate cause, and (4) damages. *(IN025.3.)*

A duty is usually created by statute or contract. Duties may be general or specific. For instance, everyone who drives a vehicle in the state of Florida has a general duty to do so using reasonable care. An officer who is hired to direct traffic at an intersection has a specific duty to the people relying on that officer as they pass through the intersection.

The second element of negligence is a breach of duty. A breach is a failure of some kind. The term ***breach of duty*** means that the defendant unreasonably failed in the duty he or she was obligated to perform. A breach of duty is generally proved by evidence that the defendant violated a law or accepted practices, such as a departmental policy or rule. A duty may be breached by not taking action when a reasonable officer should have taken action. For example, if an officer decides to wait for EMS instead of performing CPR on an injured person who is not breathing, and the person dies or suffers brain damage from lack of oxygen, the officer may be held liable for those consequences because he or she breached his or her duty of care.

The third element of negligence is proximate cause, which means that the breach caused the harm. ***Proximate cause*** is the legal phrase for the link between the breach of duty and the harm caused (damages). In deciding proximate cause, the judge and jury will have to determine if the harmful event was a foreseeable outcome of the defendant's act or failure to act.

The final element of negligence is damages. There are two main categories of damages: compensatory and punitive *(IN025.4.A.)*. All four elements must be proven in a negligence action to recover damages. If any of the four elements is missing, the defendant cannot be found negligent. Each element is like the leg of a chair; if one leg is gone, the chair will collapse.

### Compensatory Damages

***Compensatory damages*** are designed to compensate for the actual property damage, harm, or injury the plaintiff suffers *(IN025.1.B.3.)*. Compensatory damages may include general, special, or nominal damages. General damages are those presumed to result from the defendant's actions. They include awards for pain and suffering, discomfort, humiliation, fright, and emotional distress. Special damages are those actually caused by the injury. They are available to the plaintiff for lost earnings, medical expenses, destruction of personal property, and attorney's fees. Nominal damages are damages in name only; they are awarded when the jury believes the plaintiff's rights were violated, but there is insufficient proof of measurable financial harm.

### *Punitive Damages*

***Punitive damages*** are damages awarded in addition to actual damages when the defendant acted with recklessness, malice, or deceit. They are intended to punish the defendant for his or her act and to warn others from doing the same act. Punitive damages can be very high. *(IN025.1.B.4.)*

# Civil Rights

A ***civil rights violation*** is an unlawful interference with the fundamental rights of another person, such as the rights to due process and equal protection under the law *(IN025.1.C.)*. Officers' use of force is often the basis for civil rights lawsuits. Law enforcement officers who violate someone's civil rights may be subject to civil liability and even criminal prosecution.

## *Criminal Violations of Civil Rights*

Being a law enforcement officer does not give a person the right to commit acts that violate the law. Violating the law results in criminal liability. For example, if an officer commits an act that violates state or local law, the State Attorney may bring charges against him or her. If the officer commits an act that violates federal law, the U.S. Attorney's Office may file criminal charges. *(IN025.1.A.)*

18 U.S.C. Section 242, prohibits anyone acting under color of law from intentionally depriving another person of a constitutional or other civil right. Penalties for doing so range from imprisonment for one year to life and may even include the death penalty, depending upon the circumstances of the crime and the resulting injury.

> Whoever, under color of any law, statute, ordinance, regulation, or custom, willfully subjects any person in any State, Territory, Commonwealth, Possession, or District to the deprivation of any rights, privileges, or immunities secured or protected by the Constitution or laws of the United States, or to different punishments, pains, or penalties, on account of such person being an alien, or by reason of his color, or race, than are prescribed for the punishment of citizens, shall be fined under this title or imprisoned not more than one year, or both; and if bodily injury results from the acts committed in violation of this section or if such acts include the use, attempted use, or threatened use of a dangerous weapon, explosives, or fire, shall be fined under this title or imprisoned not more than ten years, or both; and if death results from the acts committed in violation of this section or if such acts include kidnapping or an attempt to kidnap, aggravated sexual abuse, or an attempt to commit aggravated sexual abuse, or an attempt to kill, shall be fined under this title, or imprisoned for any term of years or for life, or both, or may be sentenced to death.

When an officer acts or purports to act in the performance of official duties under any law, ordinance, or regulation, he or she is acting under ***color of law*** *(IN001.3.G.)*. An officer's illegal act that causes injury or other serious consequences to a person may result in an FBI investigation to determine if the officer violated federal law. For example, a suspect's death due to a police beating will result in a federal investigation, whether or not the local law enforcement agency or State Attorney's Office fully investigates the incident.

The Fifth Amendment's double jeopardy bar does not prohibit criminal prosecution for civil rights violations even after acquittal of state criminal charges because the state and federal governments are two separate and distinct sovereigns. Each government operates its own criminal court system under its own set of laws. For example, an officer charged with aggravated battery for beating a suspect who resisted arrest may be acquitted of all state charges. After the acquittal, the federal government may indict the officer for criminal civil rights violations for the same incident. A state crime and a federal civil rights violation are different offenses even though they may arise from the same facts.

### *Civil Violations of Federal Civil Rights*

In addition to criminal prosecution, an officer who violates an individual's civil rights may be subject to civil liability in federal court. 42 U.S.C. §1983 is the most common federal statutory basis used to sue law enforcement officers. The provisions of an action for civil rights violations are similar to the criminal provisions contained in 18 U.S.C. §242. Before imposing liability, both sections require proof that the officer acted under the authority of his or her agency and intentionally violated a clearly established constitutional or civil right of the victim. Negligence does not give rise to a §1983 action under federal law. Officers who violate the civil rights of others may also be subject to discipline by the Criminal Justice Standards and Training Commission and their employing agency.

## Effects of Liability on Officers

Being found criminally or civilly liable for actions taken while doing law enforcement work can result in consequences to an officer that range from minor to catastrophic. It can cost an officer his or her freedom and result in financial ruin. Although it may result in nothing more than a reprimand or brief suspension from work, a criminal conviction can lead to loss of employment and decertification as an officer. Financial ruin can result if the court orders an officer to pay punitive damages. Under state law, the officer's employing agency cannot pay the punitive damages; they must be paid by the individual officer. *(IN025.4.)*

## Agency Liability

In a civil suit, the officer may not be the only defendant. Most suits also name the employing agency, its chief or sheriff, or other governmental officials because in most cases, the officer acted within the scope and course of his or her authority. A plaintiff will sue the employing agency because it normally has more money than the individual officer. If the plaintiff proves at trial that the officer committed a tort or violated civil rights as part of his or her duties, the employing agency is likely to be liable for damages through direct or vicarious liability. *(IN025.2.)*

***Direct liability*** arises in cases in which the officer committed an intentional or a negligent tort in violation of the employing agency's orders or policies *(IN025.2.A.)*. An example is an officer's illegal use of force in arresting a suspect. The agency's liability is based on action it took or failed to take regarding the officer's alleged policy violation. Direct liability may result from negligent hiring of a problem employee, negligent assignment of duties to a person who is not able to perform them, negligent retention of a problem employee, or failure to adequately train an employee.

***Vicarious liability*** occurs when one person or entity is held liable for the negligent actions of another person even though the first person or entity was not directly responsible for the injury *(IN025.2.B)*. In law enforcement, an officer's agency is often vicariously liable for damages caused by the officer's actions. For example, an agency may be required to pay damages if an officer is guilty of sexual harassment even though the agency did not know of the harassment when it occurred. If it is shown that neither the employing agency nor the supervisor is responsible for an employee's improper act, then neither vicarious nor direct liability applies to the agency.

# Acts That Lead to Civil Liability

The most common types of civil liability are related to arrests, searches, use of force, administration of first aid, and operation of vehicles. The same unlawful acts that result in civil liability may also subject the officer to criminal charges.

An unlawful arrest occurs when an officer takes someone into custody without probable cause. Unlawful arrest is an intentional tort. If an officer makes an arrest without probable cause, he or she may be liable for false imprisonment of the arrestee or violating the arrestee's civil rights.

An unlawful search is a search or seizure performed without probable cause or reasonable suspicion. This sometimes happens inadvertently, for example, when a suspect is arrested on an outstanding warrant that is no longer valid. This can happen when the warrant has been served on the defendant but not cleared or removed from the computer system. This civil violation is based on an unlawful seizure of the person because the arrest was not supported by probable cause. Because the officer acted under the color of law, the suspect can file a federal civil rights lawsuit under Title 42, §1983, U.S. Code. This emphasizes the importance of confirming the validity of a warrant before making an arrest.

An officer's excessive use of force against a suspect can lead to civil and criminal liability. An officer may only use the amount of force that is reasonable and necessary under the circumstances.

Negligently driving a vehicle and causing damage to another vehicle or property will likely lead to civil liability. If an officer's negligent actions amount to recklessness, the officer may also be subject to criminal charges like vehicular homicide under F.S. §782.071.

An officer who fails to provide appropriate first aid to someone who needs immediate medical assistance may face civil liability. The term ***omission*** means neglecting to perform what the law or duty requires. Officers may be liable not only for performing required actions improperly but also for failing to perform actions required of them. *(IN025.5.)*

# Protecting Officers Against Liability

There are federal and state laws that protect officers against civil and criminal liability and provide legal defenses, including sovereign immunity, F.S. Chapter 111, qualified immunity, good faith, reasonable manner, justified acts, and emergency doctrine. *(IN025.6.)*

## *Sovereign Immunity*

***Sovereign immunity*** is derived from the common law idea that the king and his agents can do no wrong. The concept has been applied to state and local government agencies, including law enforcement. The sovereign immunity law—F.S. §768.28—is a limited waiver of this immunity.

The sovereign immunity law provides one of the most important protections for governmental employees and law enforcement agencies. It includes a list of circumstances and requirements that must be met before the state, a county, a municipality, or a law enforcement agency or any of its employees can be sued in a state tort action. It also protects individual officers and government employees from personal liability and from being named as a defendant in a state civil lawsuit. This means that unless an officer or employee acts or fails to act with willful or wanton disregard of someone's rights or property, the officer or employee must be dismissed from a state civil tort action. *(IN025.6.C.1.)*

Because the sovereign immunity law covers only state tort actions, it does not protect officers and employees named in federal civil rights actions. However, before a plaintiff can prevail in such a case, he or she must show more than mere negligence on the part of the officer or employee.

## *Chapter 111, Florida Statutes*

Chapter 111, Florida Statutes, protects employees, including officers, charged with civil and criminal actions, provided those actions occurred within the scope and course of the employees' employment. ***Acting within the scope of employment*** refers to the range of reasonable and foreseeable activities that an employee does while carrying out the employer's business *(IN025.6.A.5.)*. If an employee acts outside the scope of employment, the employee may be held individually liable.

In order to ensure that their actions are within the scope and course of their employment, officers should avoid willfully or wantonly infringing on others' rights. Chapter 111 contains the following provisions:

- The employing agency may, but is not required to, reimburse legal costs for its employees who have been sued or charged with a crime.
- The employing agency may provide legal counsel for its employees who are sued in either state tort actions or federal noncriminal civil rights actions.

*Note:* An employing agency may opt not to defend an employee in a civil case, even if the action arose from within the scope of employment. However, if the employee prevails, the agency must reimburse court costs and reasonable attorney's fees. The employing agency may pay any final judgment, including damages, costs, and attorney's fees, arising from a complaint for damages or injury that resulted from any act or omission of the employee in a civil or civil rights lawsuit. *(IN025.6.C.2.)*

If the action is for an alleged civil rights violation under 42 U.S.C. §1983 or a similar federal statute, payments for the full amount of the judgment may be made by the employing agency unless the final judgment states that the officer intentionally caused harm. This section also allows the employing agency to pay any pretrial settlement of any claim or litigation.

## *Qualified Immunity*

The defense of ***qualified immunity*** protects "government officials . . . from liability for civil damages insofar as their conduct does not violate clearly established statutory or constitutional rights of which a reasonable person would have known." See *Harlow v. Fitzgerald*, 457 U.S. 800, 818 (1982). *(IN025.6.C.3.)*

## *Acts Done in Good Faith*

To act in good faith, officers must be faithful to their duty and honestly intend to avoid taking undue advantage of others. Acts done in good faith are without malice, ill will, or the intent to unjustly harm anyone.

## *Acts Done in a Reasonable Manner*

Officers must act in a reasonable manner when responding to any law enforcement situation. Reasonableness involves acting professionally within the law and agency policies and procedures. It can range from having a reasonable belief that a person has committed an offense and arresting the person for that crime, to determining what type of first aid to perform, to knowing what level of force is needed in a given situation. Reasonableness is judged objectively (would a reasonable officer in the same situation have acted the same way).

**Section Vocabulary**

*acting within the scope of employment*

*breach of duty*

*civil liability*

*civil rights violation*

*color of law*

*compensatory damages*

*crime*

*criminal liability*

*direct liability*

*emergency doctrine*

*negligence*

*omission*

*proximate cause*

*punitive damages*

*qualified immunity*

*sovereign immunity*

*tort*

*vicarious liability*

### *Acts Justified Under the Law*

Some seemingly offensive police actions can be justified under the law. This occurs in situations where case law or statutory law provides a defense for an officer's actions. For example, Chapter 776, Florida Statutes, provides that an officer may use deadly force in self-defense or defense of another from a threat of death or serious physical injury. Other Florida laws permit officers to commit what would otherwise be illegal acts such as carrying concealed firearms, Chapter 790; use of force in riots, Chapter 870; and possession of controlled substances during a criminal investigation, Chapter 893.

### *Emergency Doctrine*

When sudden peril requires instinctive action, an officer is not required to use the same degree of care as when there is time to reflect. This is known as the ***emergency doctrine***. Of course, an officer is still required to use due care. Reckless disregard of others does not qualify as an appropriate response.

## Limiting Liability

Law enforcement agencies enact policies and procedures to help guide their sworn officers in performing their duties. These policies are carefully developed to ensure they comply with legal and ethical guidelines. Agency policies and procedures are developed and published for the officer's benefit. By following such policies, officers may avoid liability for acts done while on duty.

Attending required and optional training also helps officers stay informed of current law and police practices. Awareness of changes in legal and practice guidelines also helps officers avoid liability.

# UNIT 6 | RESPONSE TO CIVIL ISSUES

## LESSON 1 | Response to Civil Issues

### Landlord and Tenant Disputes

Law enforcement officers are sometimes called to disturbances arising from landlord and tenant disputes. It is important that officers faced with these situations have a general knowledge of what action, if any, they can take. The Florida Residential Landlord and Tenant Act, F.S. §83.40–83.682, governs most of the traditionally recognized rental arrangements for dwellings, such as those for apartments, town homes, duplexes, single-family housing units, and mobile home parks.

In tenancy situations covered by the law, the only way a landlord can legally recover possession of the leased residence without the consent of the tenant is to file an eviction proceeding in the county court where the residence is located pursuant to F.S. §83.59. If the landlord is successful, a writ of possession will be issued by the court to the sheriff, who is then authorized to evict the tenant and put the landlord in possession of the residence after a prescribed notice period. See F.S. §83.62. Officers should be aware that until legally evicted, a tenant has a right to enter the residence, and a landlord may not prevent entry by changing the locks. See F.S. §83.67(2).

Law enforcement officers may physically evict a tenant only pursuant to a writ of possession. Any action without a writ that causes the removal of a tenant, whether physically removing the tenant's belongings from the residence or suggesting to the tenant that failure to leave may result in arrest, is likely to be considered a wrongful eviction. *(LE061b.7.)*

There are three types of residential rental facilities where the Residential Landlord Tenant Act does not apply: public lodging establishments such as hotels and motels, F.S. §509.141; medical, geriatric, educational, counseling, religious, or similar residency facilities, F.S. §83.42(1); and recreational vehicle parks, F.S. §513.01. *(LE061b.7.1.)*

### Repossession of Property

When a creditor loans money to a borrower for the purchase of a vehicle, boat, or any other property, the creditor may obtain a security interest or lien against the property. The property is the collateral for the loan. If the borrower fails to pay the loan as agreed (called a default), the creditor is entitled to possession of the collateral. See F.S. §679.609(1).

When the creditor is entitled to possession of collateral after default, the creditor may go to court and obtain an order entitling the creditor to possession. This order is called a ***writ of replevin***. Florida law permits a creditor to take possession of the collateral after default without a court order, if that can be done without breach of the peace. See F.S. §679.609(2). This is called ***self-help repossession***.

**OBJECTIVES**

**LE061b.7.** Describe an officer's response to landlord-tenant disputes.

**LE061b.7.1.** Identify the three categories of residential or rental facilities.

**LE061b.8.** Describe an officer's response to repossessions of property.

**LE061b.9.** Describe an officer's response to the removal or towing of vehicles or vessels from private property.

**LE061b.10.** Describe an officer's response to recovering vehicles from tow yards.

**LE061b.11.** Describe an officer's response to motor vehicle repair disputes.

**LE061b.12.** Describe an officer's response to child custody disputes.

**LE061b.13.** Describe an officer's response to real property boundaries disputes.

**LE061b.14.** Describe an officer's response to a dispute over stolen property in the custody of a pawnbroker.

When an officer responds to a call involving self-help repossession of property, the officer's role is to keep the peace. The officer may not give legal advice to either the borrower or the person or company repossessing the property. *(LE061b.8.)*

Property subject to repossession may include a motor vehicle, mobile home, motorboat, aircraft, personal watercraft, all-terrain vehicle, farm equipment, industrial equipment, or any other property subject to a security interest or agricultural lien. See F.S. §493.6101(22), §679.609, and §679.1021(1). The most common type of property repossession is that of motor vehicles.

Vehicle repossession is usually done by a paid contractor hired by the creditor, although a creditor may repossess the property directly. The contractor is known as a recovery agent and must possess an employer's identification card and a Recovery Agent Class E or a Recovery Agent Intern Class EE license issued by the Florida Department of Agriculture and Consumer Services. A recovery agent is prohibited from carrying a firearm while on private property and in the course of repossession activities, even if the recovery agent possesses a license authorizing him or her to carry a firearm. See F.S. §493.6118(1)(u)9.

The recovery agent must notify the law enforcement agency having jurisdiction over the area where the vehicle is located within two hours after the repossession. See F.S. §493.6118.

A recovery agent may not enter the borrower's home or business without permission and generally may not open a gate or move aside a barrier. However, an agent can repossess a vehicle from a driveway or public street, provided the borrower makes no objection. If the borrower objects prior to the recovery agent taking possession of the vehicle, then the recovery agent must leave the property without the collateral. The recovery agent is free to attempt the repossession later, if it can be accomplished without a breach of the peace. In the repossession process, a recovery agent may not exert undue pressure on the borrower, such as the threat of force. Recovery agents also may not wear, present, or display a badge in the course of performing a repossession. See F.S. §493.6118(1)(u)11.

When there is an objection to the repossession of the property, the recovery agent may obtain a writ of replevin to recover property that is in the wrongful possession of another. The court order, which can only be served by the sheriff or a deputy sheriff, carries with it the authority to enter the property by force, if necessary, to make the recovery. In the absence of a writ of replevin, any breach of the peace stops a legal recovery by a recovery agent or the creditor.

When responding to a dispute or confrontation about a repossession occurring on public property, officers may have to determine whether the recovery agent has already taken possession of the vehicle. For example, if the vehicle has already been attached to the tow truck or the recovery agent is behind the steering wheel of the vehicle ready to drive away, the repossession has already occurred and the agent may be permitted to leave. However, if there is a dispute or confrontation regarding repossessing a vehicle still located on private property, this constitutes a breach of the peace, and the recovery agent cannot lawfully take the vehicle, even if the vehicle is already attached to the tow truck. The tow truck used by a recovery agent must have license numbers displayed on both sides in lettering not less than four inches high in a contrasting color to the background.

## Removal of Motor Vehicles from Private Property

Usually, law enforcement agencies have no jurisdiction concerning unwanted vehicles on private property. In such a situation, the complainant may call a tow truck, but the officer has no authority or jurisdiction to do so *(LE061b.9.)*. A person towing or removing a vehicle from the private property or a parking lot must surrender the vehicle when the owner offers payment of a reasonable service fee of not more than one-half the posted rate of the towing removal cost. The person or firm towing or removing the vehicle shall notify the appropriate law enforcement agency within 30 minutes after completion of such towing or removal. Noncompliance with statutory requirements and limitations could result in administrative and criminal penalties. See F.S. §715.07.

## Recovering Vehicles from Tow Yards

Officers may be called to a tow yard after a vehicle has been towed from private property. Disputes often arise when the owner of the vehicle has trouble getting the vehicle returned from the tow company. This situation is usually civil in nature and requires no police action. Sometimes, however, the vehicle owner claims that the vehicle was towed illegally or improperly, resulting in damage to the vehicle. If such a claim is made, officers need to refer to F.S. §715.07. If the vehicle was not towed properly, administrative and criminal penalties may apply. *(LE061b.10.)*

## Motor Vehicle Repair Disputes

Officers are sometimes dispatched to disturbances at automobile repair shops regarding disputes over repair costs. F.S. §559.917 permits the vehicle owner who refuses to pay the repair bill to take possession of the vehicle after posting a bond with the court clerk. After a bond is posted in the amount of the repair invoice, including storage fees, the clerk will issue a certificate directing the repair shop to release the vehicle to the owner. The repair shop's refusal to release the vehicle once the certificate is issued is a misdemeanor under F.S. §559.917(3). If the vehicle owner refuses to pay the repair cost and removes the vehicle from the repair shop without posting a bond, then the vehicle owner should be investigated for theft under F.S. §812.014. *(LE061b.11.)*

## Child Custody Disputes

An officer must consider several factors before taking law enforcement action in a child custody dispute. The mother of a child born out of wedlock is the natural guardian of the child and is entitled to primary residential care and custody of the child, unless a court order states otherwise, even if the father is known and acknowledges paternity.

When officers are called to a complaint regarding failure to return a child to the other parent at the designated time, officers should refer to their agency's policies and procedures for the appropriate action.

### *No Court Ordered Custody for Married or Unmarried Parents*

Officers may be called to the scene where one parent is alleging that the other parent is attempting to conceal the child from him or her or flee the jurisdiction with the child. Even without a court order determining custody, F.S. §787.03 makes such an action a third-degree felony.

If there is no court order determining custody and one parent attempts to leave with the child but is not fleeing the jurisdiction, the responding officer should talk to the parties and attempt to resolve the dispute. Generally that will be done by allowing the parent who has the child upon the officer's arrival to keep the child. Officers should encourage both parents to seek legal counsel and a court hearing to clarify visitation.

*Note:* F.S. §787.03 does not apply to a parent who is the victim of any act of domestic violence, believes that he or she is about to become a victim of an act of domestic violence, or believes that his or her action was necessary to preserve the child from danger to his or her welfare and seeks shelter from these acts or their possibility.

### Court Ordered Custody/Married or Unmarried Parents

If one of the parents has been awarded custody by a court order, and the other parent is attempting to conceal the child from the custodial parent or flee the jurisdiction with the child, such concealing or removal contrary to the court order is a felony of the third degree pursuant to F.S. §787.04.

### Child Custody Court Orders from Other States

An officer may not enforce a court order issued by another state or jurisdiction unless the court order has been domesticated and a break order has been issued by a court within the officer's jurisdiction. A domesticated order is evidenced by a signature of a judge in the local county.

### Conflicting Child Custody Court Orders from Different States

If one parent has a court order from one state and the other parent has a conflicting order issued from a local Florida court, the responding officer should refer both parents to the local family law court.

#### *Domestic Violence Injunctions*

The violation of a custody arrangement contained in a domestic violence injunction will generally remain a civil matter unless one of the provisions in F.S. §741.31 is violated. If the officer determines that the circumstances of the custody dispute are civil in nature, the officer should document the incident on the appropriate report and refer the parties to the local family law court in accordance with agency policies and procedures. *(LE061b.12)*

## Real Property Boundaries Disputes

Property disputes between neighbors are usually civil in nature. Officers should advise the parties to seek appropriate remedies in civil court. (*LE061b.13.)*

## Stolen Property in the Custody of Pawnbroker

Stolen property is often sold to pawnbrokers. The law provides the following from F.S. §539.001(16):

> When an appropriate law enforcement official has probable cause to believe that property in the possession of a pawnbroker is misappropriated, the official may place a written hold order on the property. The written hold order shall impose a holding period not to exceed 90 days unless extended by court order. The appropriate law enforcement official may rescind, in writing, any hold order. An appropriate law enforcement official may place only one hold order on property.
>
> While a hold order is in effect, the pawnbroker must upon request release the property subject to the hold order to the custody of the appropriate law enforcement official for use in a criminal investigation. The release of the property to the custody of the appropriate law enforcement official is not considered a waiver or release of the pawnbroker's property rights or interest in the property. Upon completion of the criminal proceeding, the property must be returned to the pawnbroker

> unless the court orders other disposition. When the additional disposition is ordered, the court shall additionally order the conveying customer to pay restitution to the pawnbroker in the amount received by the conveying customer for the property, together with reasonable attorney's fees and costs. *(LE061b.14.)*

For a claimant's procedure for recovery, see F.S. §539.001(15).

**Section Vocabulary**

*self-help repossession*

*writ of replevin*

# UNIT 7 | JUVENILE LAW

## LESSON 1 | Juvenile Law

**OBJECTIVES**

**IN023.6.A.3.** Define *child, juvenile,* or *youth.*

**LE461.6.** Describe the procedures for taking a juvenile into custody.

**LE026.14.B.** Identify the procedures for handling juvenile traffic offenders.

**LE461.3.C.** Define *juvenile sex offender.*

**IN006.4.** Identify the procedures for interrogating juveniles.

**LE461.6.B.** Identify the standards required for searching a juvenile's personal property at school.

### Children, Juveniles, and Youths

Florida Statute §985.03(6) defines ***child, juvenile***, or ***youth*** as follows:

> "Child" or "juvenile" or "youth" means any unmarried person under the age of 18 who has not been emancipated by order of the court and who has been found or alleged to be dependent, in need of services, or from a family in need of services; or any married or unmarried person who is charged with a violation of law occurring prior to the time that person reached the age of 18 years. *(IN023.6.A.3.)*

While the procedures for handling juveniles may be different, the crimes with which they are charged are the same as if committed by an adult. Children who commit crimes are considered to be delinquent. The purpose of the juvenile system is rehabilitation rather than punishment.

### Procedures for Taking a Juvenile into Custody

A law enforcement officer may take a child into custody pursuant to a court order or upon probable cause that the child committed a law violation. An officer has the authority to take a child into custody under the same circumstances and in the same manner as if the child were an adult. Upon arrival at the county jail, the officer must contact a representative of the Department of Juvenile Justice (DJJ) who will conduct an assessment to determine whether or not the child will be detained. If the DJJ representative determines that the child is to be detained, the arresting officer will transport the child to the appropriate juvenile detention facility. If it is determined that the child is not to be detained, the child may be released to a parent, guardian, legal custodian, or any responsible adult.

If the child's life or health is in such danger that he or she must be removed from his or her surroundings, the officer may take the child into protective custody. Likewise, if an officer reasonably believes a child has been abandoned, abused, or neglected, the officer may take that child into custody. In such situations, the child will normally be alleged to be dependent rather than delinquent. The officer should contact the Department of Children and Families at 800-96-ABUSE for immediate assistance. *(LE461.6.)*

Florida Statute §985.03(23) provides the following:

> "Family in need of services" means a family that has a child for whom there is no pending investigation into an allegation of abuse, neglect, or abandonment or no current supervision by the department or the Department of Children and Family Services for an adjudication of dependency or delinquency. The child must also have been referred to a law enforcement agency or the department for:
>
> (a) Running away from parents or legal custodians;
>
> (b) Persistently disobeying reasonable and lawful demands of parents or legal custodians, and being beyond their control; or
>
> (c) Habitual truancy from school.

Officers have no arrest authority for a child who is a runaway or a truant from school. However, if an officer believes a child is truant from school, the officer can pick the child up and deliver him or her back to the school system. If an officer believes a child is a runaway, the officer should take the child into protective custody and contact the parent or legal guardian of the child. If the parent or guardian is not available, the officer should contact the Department of Children and Families. This protective custody is not a criminal arrest.

A copy of the arrest report of any child 15 years of age or younger who is taken into custody for committing a delinquent act or any violation of law should be forwarded to the local service district office of the Department of Juvenile Justice. See F.S. §985.61(3).

## Juvenile Traffic Offenders

A juvenile traffic offender is a child who violates a provision of Chapter 316, Florida Statutes, or a local ordinance that supplements that chapter. The traffic court must transfer a juvenile charged with any felony traffic offense to the Juvenile Division of Circuit Court. In nonfelony cases, the traffic summons procedure should be followed if there are no serious circumstances involved.

In any of the above situations, the same procedures that apply to adults are to be utilized except that a child is not to be placed in any vehicle with an arrested adult unless the adult is involved in the same offense or transaction. *(LE026.14.B.)*

## Juvenile Sex Offenders

According to F.S. §39.01(7), a ***juvenile sex offender*** is a child 12 years of age or younger who is alleged to have committed a sexual battery as defined in F.S. Chapter 794, an act of prostitution in violation of F.S. Chapter 796, a lewd and lascivious act in violation of F.S. Chapter 800, an act of sexual performance by a child in violation of F.S. §827.071, or an act of obscenity in violation of F.S. §847.0133. A juvenile sex offender may also be a child under the age of 18 who is alleged to have committed any violation of the law or delinquent act involving juvenile sexual abuse.

F.S. §39.01(7) provides the following:

> Juvenile sexual abuse refers to any sexual behavior which occurs without consent, without equality, or as a result of coercion. Juvenile sexual offender behavior ranges from noncontact sexual behavior such as making obscene phone calls, exhibitionism, voyeurism, and the showing or taking of lewd photographs to varying degrees of direct sexual contact, such as frottage, fondling, digital penetration, rape, fellatio, sodomy, and various other sexually aggressive acts. *(LE461.3.C.)*

## Juvenile Interrogation Procedures

The standards for questioning a juvenile are the same as for adults. An officer is required to make a good faith effort to notify the parent, guardian, or legal custodian when the child is taken into custody as per F.S. §985.101(3). There is no statutory requirement for the parent's or guardian's consent before an officer may interview the child; however, officers should comply with department policy.

Officers should be aware that *Miranda* applies to juveniles and a waiver of those rights will be more closely scrutinized by the court. See *B.M.B. v. State*, 927 So.2d 219 (Fla. 2nd DCA 2006), *Lee v. State*, 2008 (WL 2694955, 1st DCA, July 12, 2008), and *State v. Roman*, 983 So.2d 731 (Fla. 3rd DCA 2008). Factors to be considered in determining a juvenile's understanding of his or her rights and the significance of waiving those rights include his or her age, marital status, education, intellectual level, and experience in the criminal justice system. Individual agency policies may be more restrictive regarding juvenile interrogation procedures.

Pursuant to *J.D.B. v. North Carolina*, 564 U.S.__ (2011), officers must be aware of whether a juvenile of the subject's age, education, background, and experience faced with the restriction of movement and associated indicia of arrest facing the subject would understand that he or she was under arrest. If the answer is yes, then the officer must give *Miranda* warnings to the subject juvenile. In order to ensure that the situation was clearly and accurately described to the subject juvenile, officers should document exactly what is said to the subject juvenile to indicate to him or her that he or she is under arrest or not under arrest. Officers would be wise also to document what the area layout is when they speak to the subject juvenile, the number of people present, where they stood in the area, and whether any doors/gates/entry ways were open or closed at the time they discussed arrest with the subject juvenile.

Juvenile interrogations may only last a reasonable length of time. Officers should consider and make adequate notes of the length of time the child is held before interrogation, any reasons for delay, and the number of breaks and rest periods given to the child. All juvenile interrogations should be videotaped. *(IN006.4.)*

**Section Vocabulary**

*child, juvenile, or youth*

*juvenile sex offender*

## Juvenile School Searches

The laws related to search and seizure apply to juveniles just as they do to adults. School officials may search a student's personal property when they have reasonable suspicion that the student is in possession of an illegal substance or object. They have broader authority to search students than do law enforcement officers. Such school searches may not be done at the direction or request of a law enforcement officer. See F.S. §1006.09(9); *M.E.J. v. State*, 805 So.2d 1093 (Fla. 2002); and *R.L. v. State*, 738 So.2d 507 (1999). *(LE461.6.B.)*

# CHAPTER 3

# Communications



Officers use various forms of communication: radios, telephones, computers, writing, and face to face conversation. Miscommunication often occurs and creates problems. This happens for different reasons: unclear expression, communication barriers, or dissimilar backgrounds. This chapter covers telecommunications, communications and interpersonal skills, human interaction issues, interviewing ideology, and report writing principles and mechanics.

# UNIT 1 | TELECOMMUNICATIONS

## LESSON 1 | Florida Crime Information Center/ National Crime Information Center

**OBJECTIVES**

**IN013.2.A.** Identify the acronyms FCIC and NCIC.

**IN013.2.** Determine what information is available through FCIC.

**IN013.2.A.1.** Identify the location of FCIC and NCIC.

**IN013.2.D.** Identify the relationship between FCIC and NCIC.

**IN013.2.B.** Identify the major assets of the FCIC.

**IN013.2.C.2.** Identify the national communication link available through FCIC.

**IN013.2.C.** Identify how information becomes available through FCIC.

**IN013.3.B.** Identify factors that will ensure officers' efficient and effective use of the FCIC system.

**LE005.6.B.** Identify the legal issues raised by the dissemination of confidential information for non-law enforcement purposes.

**IN013.3.A.** Identify what information to provide when requesting a check.

**IN013.1.** Identify how to obtain information related to desired check.

**IN013.4.** Identify how to submit information to dispatch.

**IN013.3.** Identify the policies for conducting a check.

Law enforcement officers will often have to obtain information quickly through their communications section. A system called the ***Florida Crime Information Center (FCIC)*** provides quick background information on persons and property. FCIC is connected to the ***National Crime Information Center (NCIC)*** *(IN013.2.A.)*. Information contained in the FCIC database includes but is not limited to the following: statewide information on persons and property, driver's license and registration information, wanted and missing persons, stolen guns, vehicles, and other property, and persons' status files and computerized criminal history. *(IN013.2.)*

Both systems are available 24 hours a day, seven days a week. FCIC is housed at the Florida Department of Law Enforcement (FDLE) in Tallahassee, Florida. NCIC is a system maintained by the Federal Bureau of Investigation (FBI) in Clarksburg, West Virginia *(IN013.2.A.1.)*. The NCIC system contains information from records of stolen, abandoned, and recovered property, and wanted and missing person files for all 50 states, Canada, the U.S. Virgin Islands, the Commonwealth of Puerto Rico, and the District of Columbia. The NCIC system makes Florida data available to all criminal justice agencies *(IN013.2.D.)*. Most information entered in FCIC is also recorded in NCIC. Agencies are encouraged to enter all warrants into both state and national systems for officer use and public safety.

These systems enable officers to gather criminal history or stolen property information so they can appropriately deal with many incidents *(IN013.2.B.)*. All information obtained from these systems is for criminal justice purposes only. Using it for noncriminal justice purposes is considered a misuse of the system and may result in serious consequences for the person responsible.

A major FCIC feature is that it connects to the National Law Enforcement Telecommunication System (NLETS), an international justice and public safety information sharing network. *(IN013.2.C.2.)*. A high-speed, nationwide message switching communications network, NLETS allows for interstate and interagency information exchange. NLETS has the capability to receive, store, and forward message traffic to and from its user agencies *(IN013.2.C.)*. It supports inquiries into out-of-state motor vehicle and driver's license files, criminal histories, and agency identification information.

The NLETS Hazardous Materials file provides users with online information about hazardous materials. Inquiries are run using the four-digit number normally found on the placard of a vehicle such as a railroad car or semi-trailer. The NLETS response to an inquiry contains a variety of information such as chemical name, personal safety precautions, general handling procedures, disposal methods, degree of hazard to public health, and availability of countermeasure materials. The U.S. Department of Transportation, Office of Hazardous Materials Safety supplies this information.

The Department of Highway Safety and Motor Vehicles (DHSMV) maintains records of vehicles or vessels/boats registered in Florida and driver license or Florida identification card information. Insurance information is also available through this system.

The Department of Health develops, maintains, and administers the 911 Public Safety Telecommunicator/Emergency 911 (formerly 911 Emergency Dispatcher) training program for certification and recertification purposes under F.S. §401.465.

The Department of Agriculture and Consumer Services (DOACS) maintains the Concealed Weapon Permit Files. Inquiries are made using a person's Social Security number or concealed weapon permit number. Information available includes name, date of birth, sex, race, license number, and expiration date.

## FCIC Information Sources

Using FCIC, law enforcement agencies may enter data about wanted and missing persons and stolen property. Only agencies that maintain a 24 hour a day, seven day a week operation are allowed to make entries into the FCIC/NCIC systems. Entered information includes stolen items, boats, guns, vehicles, securities, and missing persons records. The entering agency is responsible for the accuracy, timeliness, and completeness of the records entered.

A Computerized Criminal History (CCH) is created by the booking agency submitting fingerprints and arrest information for an arrested person. Before the record is created, information must first be processed and verified by fingerprint review at FDLE. Additional charges, arrests, dispositions, and other information will be added by the State Attorney's Office, Clerk of the Court, and Department of Corrections. CCH information constantly changes; when officers finish using retrieved information, they should destroy it by shredding or burning. When a CCH is disseminated to an authorized individual of another agency, a secondary dissemination log must be maintained for four years.

A record's reliability from FCIC depends on the agency's accuracy when entering the information. It is extremely important that the information included in arrest reports or on fingerprint cards is correct, from the spelling of suspects' names to the laws they violated.

## Using FCIC/NCIC

Due to the sensitive nature and sheer volume of information included in the FCIC/NCIC systems, officers must strictly follow policies when conducting a records check. System users must attend the Criminal Justice Information Services (CJIS) certification class and pass the certification exam. System users must also submit a state and national fingerprint-based background check within 30 days of employment or terminal assignment *(IN013.3.B.)*. Information obtained through FCIC/NCIC may be used only for criminal justice purposes, and the agency that enters the data is responsible for maintaining and removing it. The only exception is that registration and lien information may be given to towing companies per §713.78(4)(b), F.S. Computers accessing CJIS information must have adequate physical security to prevent unauthorized access.

**Section Vocabulary**

*FCIC/NCIC*

*hit*

Misuse of the FCIC/NCIC system can result in both disciplinary and legal action including termination of the officers involved. In addition, the agency involved could lose its certification as an FCIC terminal site *(LE005.6.B.)*. All FCIC/NCIC transactions are logged and can be electronically retrieved upon request. The logs can be used for criminal investigations, suspected system misuse, system compliance, public records requests, and administrative purposes.

## System Usage

Certain information is required for requesting a records check through FCIC/NCIC. This varies depending on the type of information an officer wants to receive from the system. When requesting information on a wanted or missing person, officers should provide all identification data available, such as name, race, sex, date of birth, physical features, approximate height and weight, etc. For vehicle or vessel identification information, an officer should provide the vessel name, manufacturer, license, tag/decal number, year of make, etc. For stolen property requests, the name, manufacturer, description of property, shape, etc., should be provided. *(IN013.3.A.)*

If the FCIC/NCIC database contains data that is the same as or similar to the information requested, a list of possible matches will be returned *(IN013.1.)*. Additional information may be needed to determine an exact match. An exact match, called a ***hit***, must be confirmed before an officer arrests a wanted person or recovers a missing person or stolen property. The hit confirmation process ensures that system information remains valid and is identical to the person or property of interest to the officer. The process prevents arrests based on outdated or invalid warrants. It also provides more details about the action the entering agency wants taken upon location of the person or property. For example, the entering agency can confirm if a wanted person will be extradited or what should be done if only part of an entered record has been recovered (e.g., a stolen vehicle entry where only the transmission was recovered).

When data must be entered into FCIC/NCIC, the officer must provide the original report and supplemental documentation to the person at the agency responsible for making such data entries *(IN013.4.)*. Some examples include cases involving missing or wanted persons, stolen property, or abandoned vehicles or vessels. Officers should follow agency policies for adding information to the systems or when conducting a database inquiry. *(IN013.3.)*

# UNIT 1 | TELECOMMUNICATIONS

## LESSON 2 | Using Mobile Data Terminals (MDT)

**OBJECTIVES**

**IN013.5** Determine the uses of the Mobile Data Terminal.

**Section Vocabulary**

*Mobile Data Terminal (MDT)*

A ***Mobile Data Terminal (MDT)*** is the laptop computer installed in a patrol vehicle. The terminal is used by the officer to access information regarding criminal records, driving history, and agency records as well as to write and submit electronic reports to the supervisor. The terminal also allows the officer to view calls for service that other patrol units are working on. Non-emergency calls for service are dispatched over the terminal to keep the radio channels open for critical events and crimes in progress. *(IN013.5.)*

The officer must remember that FCIC/NCIC rules forbid showing citizens any information displayed on the MDT computer screen. The officer should also note that any input in the MDT is recorded in a main computer.

One of the biggest problems with the MDT is the distraction it causes while an officer is driving and trying to read or input information in the MDT. To avoid causing a vehicle crash, the officer should never attempt to read or use the MDT while the patrol vehicle is in motion.

# UNIT 1 | TELECOMMUNICATIONS

## LESSON 3 | Radio Procedures, Equipment, and Codes

**OBJECTIVES**

**IN012.7.** Demonstrate proper use of a portable radio unit.

**IN012.1.** Locate radio equipment in a standard police vehicle.

**IN012.5.B.5.** Identify the duties of the public safety telecommunicator/ communications officer.

**IN012.2.** Identify primary components of a portable police radio.

**IN012.6.A.** Identify general radio procedures.

**IN012.5.** Speak into a police radio microphone using proper radio protocol.

**IN12.5.B.1.** Identify steps to take prior to voice transmissions.

**IN012.5.A.1.** Identify speech habits that affect clear communications when using a police radio.

**IN012.5.D.** Identify appropriate radio system use.

**IN012.5.C.** Identify communications privacy when using a mobile radio system.

**IN012.5.B.** Identify proper radio protocol.

**IN012.5.B.3.** Identify the basic radio codes.

**IN012.6.C.** Demonstrate proper preparation of radio messages.

**IN012.6.** Communicate essential information using a police radio.

### Using the Radio

Throughout their shifts, officers use radios to send and receive vital information, call for backup, or identify a suspect or wanted person *(IN012.7.)*. Proper knowledge and use of the radio is essential. The communications or dispatch center is the hub of contact with patrol officers. Transmitting calls, receiving calls for assistance from officers, broadcasting information about wanted and missing persons, checking records, and a multitude of other tasks comprise activities that the communications center handles daily to assist patrol officers.

Basic police radio communication generally relies on three types of equipment. First, the 911 dispatcher (also known as a public safety telecommunicator) uses the base station or the main unit to communicate with all officers. Second, officers use the patrol car radio, which is a small unit mounted in the patrol vehicle. Third, officers carry the portable radio on their belts or shoulders. The patrol car radio is usually under or affixed to the dashboard of the patrol car. In some patrol cars, radios are mounted on the vehicle transmission hump or in a metal rack designed for holding electronic equipment. In unmarked or undercover vehicles, the radio may be mounted under the seat or in the trunk. On police motorcycles, the radio is usually mounted in plain sight behind the handlebars. *(IN012.1.)*

### Communications Personnel

The 911 public safety telecommunicators/communications officers (formerly called 911 Emergency Dispatchers) are generally non-sworn personnel who operate the radio and telecommunications systems. They usually work in a centralized area with access to telephones and other resources needed to assist sworn officers. Their duties include, but are not limited to answering, receiving, transferring, and dispatching functions related to 911 calls; dispatching law enforcement officers, fire rescue services, emergency medical services, and other public safety services to the scene of an emergency; providing real-time information from federal, state, and local crime databases; or supervising or serving as the command officer to a person or persons having such duties and responsibilities. They also access the FCIC/NCIC systems to provide vital information to officers who request it *(IN012.5.B.5.)*. However, the term does not include administrative support personnel, including, but not limited to, those whose primary duties and responsibilities are in accounting, purchasing, legal, and personnel.

### Radio Features

There are many different brands, models, and types of radios for law enforcement use. Field training officers will explain the specific types of radios that different agencies may use. The basic police radio is generally fitted with at least three switches, levers, or buttons to control volume, squelch, and channel selection *(IN012.2.)*. The plug for the microphone is usually on the front or side of the radio, while power and antenna connections are usually at the rear of the radio case. Most patrol car radios have a channel light and on/off indicator light. Many also have a transmit indicator light.

**LE047.3.** Identify how to write a BOLO (Be On the Look Out) report of the person, property, or vehicle.

**IN012.6.B.** Identify essential information based on type of call.

**IN012.6.B.6.** Identify essential information for answering calls.

**IN012.6.B.2.** Identify essential information for checking in and out of unit.

## Radio Conduct and Procedures

The Federal Communications Commission (FCC) prohibits persons who use police radios, including communications center personnel and law enforcement officers, from:

- transmitting nonessential or excessive signals, messages, or communication
- using profane, indecent, or obscene language
- willfully damaging or permitting damage to radio apparatuses
- maliciously interfering with another unit's radio transmission
- making unidentified transmissions
- transmitting before the air is clear and interfering with other transmissions
- transmitting a call signal, letter, or numeral not assigned to the station or unit
- adjusting, repairing, or altering a radio transmitter (except by agency-authorized radio technicians)

An officer should plan messages before transmitting them. Though an officer will have to speak quickly in an emergency, the more planned the message is, the more coherent, capable, and professional the officer sounds. *(IN012.6.A.)*

Appropriate microphone techniques also help in making clear transmissions. The officer should speak directly into the microphone in an evenly modulated tone of voice *(IN012.5.)*. In stressful situations, an officer's voice may crack or become distorted or high-pitched because of the adrenaline rush. This can make the radio message difficult to understand, so officers should avoid displays of emotion. Before voice transmissions, officers should listen to make sure there is no other radio traffic and then depress and hold the transmit button for approximately one second before speaking *(IN012.5.B.1.)*. If an officer is uncertain that the channel is clear for all traffic, he or she should ask dispatch.

Some agencies use a phonetic alphabet or uniform codes; others prefer clear speech (plain English). Officers should refer to their agency policy concerning the radio language to use. An officer should also be aware that speech habits such as a trailing voice (diminishes in volume), the wrong rate of speech (too fast or too slow), or speaking in monotone or a soft or unclear (mumbling) voice may affect clear communications *(IN012.5.A.1.)*. If English is his or her second language, an officer should be careful not to revert to his or her first language in stressful situations.

Officers working high priority or felony calls may request that a radio channel be designated for emergency traffic only. Dispatch will then alert other officers not to transmit unless an emergency occurs. The dispatcher should be given time to acknowledge the call, and the officer should remember that dispatch performs multiple tasks. Because most communications centers are computerized, the dispatcher needs time to access the appropriate screen.

Officers should pay attention to transmissions from other units. An officer could be in the area of a unit requesting backup or closer to a call for service than another unit. Officers must also avoid arguments and sarcasm on the radio. If an officer has a problem with a dispatcher, he or she should contact the dispatcher's supervisor and not argue with the dispatcher over the air. Officers must be professional on the radio at all times and avoid humor and horseplay on the radio.

Officers should avoid using proper names in radio transmissions; rather, they should refer to themselves and other officers by agency-assigned identification numbers. Finally, all transmissions should be limited to law enforcement business. Appropriate radio system use includes the following:

- law enforcement-related messages to other agencies within the state or in another state
- driver's license status and driver history
- criminal records checks
- hazardous material queries
- aircraft, boat, and vehicle registration queries
- road condition and weather queries *(IN012.5.D.)*

In accordance with rules established by Florida's Secretary of State, all radio transmissions must be recorded and retained for 30 days. Some agencies may retain transmissions for a longer period of time. Criminal history details should only be transmitted by radio or cell phone when an officer's or the public's safety depends on it.

## Radio Privacy

An officer should expect no privacy in law enforcement radio transmissions *(IN012.5.C.)*. The only exceptions include special investigations units, such as Organized Crime Units, which use scrambled or encrypted channels that cannot be monitored.

Officers should also maintain proper volume levels on their portable radios. The public sometimes considers a loud police radio as an indication of a rude or pretentious officer. Volume should be kept at a level at which the officer can hear the radio but not so loud that it disrupts everyone nearby. Officers should display care and concern for the public. Using radio courtesy shows consideration and may lessen the distress or concern of an apprehensive citizen or witness. When in the presence of a suspect, officers can reduce the risks of exposure and danger by using appropriate codes. If possible, another officer should be asked to perform a records check, so the subject cannot hear the response.

## Radio Failure

If an officer experiences radio silence, he or she should switch to another channel to determine radio status. If radio contact is not available at all, the officer must immediately call his or her agency by a landline phone and report the communications difficulty. Officers should know their agency's operating procedures, general orders, or policy and procedure about what to do if the radio fails.

# Radio Protocol

***Radio protocol*** describes the procedures of properly constructing and transmitting messages. It also includes proper use of appropriate codes and signals, which varies among agencies and regions. *(IN012.5.B.)*

# Radio Codes

Radio codes and signals save airtime and convey precise and definite meanings. Radio codes also help maintain professionalism and uniform radio communications. There are four basic radio codes:

- ***Signals*** is a system of communication that uses the word "signal" to precede numbers
- ***Phonetic-alpha code*** system uses the letters of the English alphabet only. It identifies letters in voice communication
- ***Ten or numeric code*** system uses the number "10" to precede other numbers that represent specific activities; and
- ***Alphanumeric code*** system combines letters and numbers that may include officer call signs or auto tags. *(IN012.5.B.3.)*

Individual agencies might not use the codes reviewed in this textbook but will train their officers in the language they use. All officers will be expected to become proficient quickly in using a radio to communicate.

# Constructing the Message

Like any effective communication, a properly constructed radio message involves thinking in advance about what needs to be said. It also involves delivering accurate information in a clear, concise manner *(IN012.6.C.)*. Messages should follow this basic pattern: identification number, current location, reason for call, and information relative and essential to the situation *(IN012.6.)*. Officers should write out full descriptions of the person, property, or vehicle in question for BOLO (Be On the Look Out) reports before broadcasting them on the radio. *(LE047.3.)*

## *Officer-initiated Transmission*

If an officer encounters an emergency during patrol, the following information should be transmitted to dispatch:

- officer's identification number and location
- type of emergency (vehicle crash, fire, battery, etc.)
- other assistance needed (backup, ambulance, tow truck, etc.)
- description of suspect, if applicable
- description of suspect's vehicle, if applicable *(IN012.6.B.)*

In emergencies, the dispatcher may clear the channel for the responding officers to use during the call so they can communicate without competing for airtime.

### Transmitting Information About a Traffic Stop

When transmitting information about a traffic stop, the following essential information must be provided:

- officer's identification number
- officer's location and direction of travel
- tag number of vehicle for which information is being requested
- state that issued the tag and the year of issue, if possible
- vehicle color
- vehicle make, model, and year (If unknown, descriptions like "newer model" and "late 1990s" are acceptable.)
- number of vehicle occupants
- need for backup or other assistance as appropriate

Dispatchers state the time at the end of each transmission. One reason is to document on the radio the time of the transmission. Another is to tell the officer the transmission is complete.

### Transmitting a Description of a Person

When transmitting information about a person, an officer should provide the following:

- officer's identification number or call sign
- location
- full description of the person including race, gender, age, height and weight, clothing, hair color and length, and identifying characteristics such as scars, visible marks, or tattoos
- reason for the stop
- need for backup or other assistance as appropriate

## Receiving and Answering Calls

When an officer receives a call from dispatch, the officer must respond with his or her identification number and location and write down the information provided by the dispatcher, including the complainant's name and address *(IN012.6.B.6.)*. Nothing should be left to memory. The officer must advise dispatch upon his or her arrival at the call and note whether backup or any additional support or equipment is needed.

## Checking In and Out

When going on duty, an officer does not merely get in the patrol car and drive to an assigned area. He or she must check into service with dispatch when going on duty and out of service when the shift ends and the officer goes off duty. This allows dispatch to monitor the officer's location and ensure officer safety. When checking into service, the officer should provide his or her identification number (e.g., Two Charlie 104), the message in service (or 10-8), and the vehicle the officer drives (e.g., 9362). When checking out at the end of a shift, an officer should provide similar information and the message out of service (or 10-7). *(IN012.6.B.2.)*

## *Transmitting Information about a Vehicle Pursuit*

The information required for a vehicle pursuit is the same as that required for a traffic stop. If the attempted stop becomes a pursuit, the officer should keep dispatch informed of direction of travel and other descriptive information, such as street names, landmarks, and additional details about the fleeing suspect's vehicle. Remaining calm in such a situation may be difficult, however the dispatcher may have difficulty understanding if officers yell into the microphone or if different officers try to broadcast at the same time.

**Section Vocabulary**

*alphanumeric code*

*phonetic-alpha code*

*signals*

*radio protocol*

*ten or numeric code*

# UNIT 2 | COMMUNICATION AND INTERPERSONAL SKILLS

## LESSON 1 | Communication and Interpersonal Skills

***Communication*** involves the exchange of ideas or messages, verbally and nonverbally, through signals or writing. Communication is accomplished using common and accepted methods. These methods include spoken or written language, gestures, facial expressions, and body movements. Communication can happen simultaneously at multiple levels and in multiple ways. For example, a suspect may say one thing, but his or her body language may communicate something entirely different.

The purpose of interpersonal communication is to facilitate a primary function of interacting with others or to cause some kind of action *(IN004.1.)*. As officers gain experience in law enforcement, they will hone their ability to interpret simultaneous nonverbal and verbal communication. When interacting with individuals, suspects, victims, and witnesses, officers should always strive to match their verbal and nonverbal messages.

Terms used in describing the communication process include sender or source, message, receiver, and feedback *(IN004.3.A.)*. A ***sender*** transmits a message to a ***receiver***. The sender must transmit a message (a request, an order, a question, or a

**OBJECTIVES**

**IN004.1.** Identify the purpose of interpersonal communication.

**IN004.3.A.** Identify terms used in describing the process of communication.

**IN004.2.B.** Identify the elements that are essential to effective interpersonal communication.

**IN003.1.** Identify behaviors that convey courtesy.

**IN004.1.A.** Identify common forms of nonverbal communication.

**IN004.1.B.** Identify barriers that could hinder the communication process.

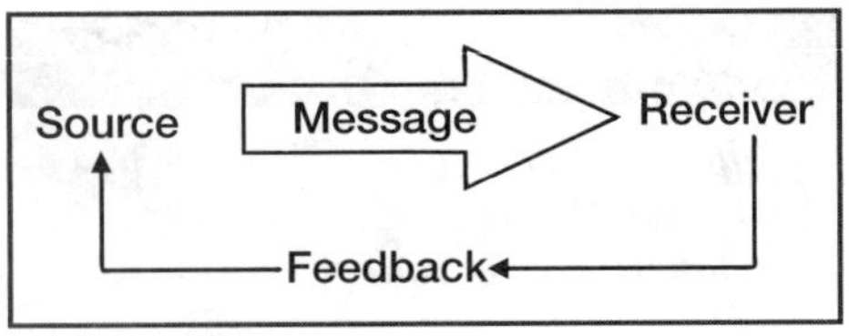


The communication process *Figure 3-1*

description) in a form that the receiver/listener understands. The receiver then acknowledges the message by providing feedback or responding. Interpersonal communication is cooperative in nature.

## Elements of Effective Interpersonal Communication

An effective communicator has several characteristics. First, the effective communicator recognizes his or her audience and modifies communication to fit the receiver. He or she uses short, commonly understood words and avoids slang, jargon, or obscure phrases that the listener may not understand. He or she keeps sentences brief and to the point. Short sentences minimize distraction, especially in stressful, confusing, or noisy situations. The effective communicator is explicit and uses specific terms; for example, saying "Stand next to the trunk of your car" is better than "Move over there where I can see you." The officer who communicates effectively also speaks in an appropriate tone of voice. How something is said is as important as what is said, and tone of voice and facial expressions greatly affect listeners.

In order to communicate effectively, officers must not allow emotions to color their words or actions. They must remain calm and show no anger, fear, or other negative emotions. Officers must be the calming presence and not allow their anger to worsen a situation. Hostility and rudeness have no place in an officer's relationship with the public. An officer does not gain public support by expressing irritation or frustration. Consequently, the officer should maintain a professional demeanor at all times. *(IN004.2.B.)*

## Listening

Listening takes practice and hard work and often requires much more energy than talking. A good listener concentrates on what is said, focusing on the words, ideas, and important data related to the subject and pays close attention to the speaker before evaluating his or her statement. Also, a good listener never imposes cultural biases on the speaker or the information, not relying on the assumptions and moral values normally used to assess information. Rather, he or she should remain open-minded and sincerely listen to the speaker.

## Projecting a Positive Self-Image

A person who feels comfortable expressing him- or herself generally projects a positive self-image. Officers should envision themselves as positive contributors to society and appreciate their own capabilities. An officer can increase self-confidence, self-image, and credibility through training, education, and experience in communication with others.

Appearance is the first nonverbal message an officer delivers upon arriving at a scene. Uniforms must be kept clean and pressed and shoes shined. In addition, officers should take care of their personal hygiene. Individual agency policies and procedures dictate guidelines concerning personal appearance.

***Command presence*** means the bearing of one who commands or influences others. A combination of training and self-confidence, command presence is an officer's most valuable nonverbal tool, and developing it is crucial for every officer. It includes appearance, demeanor, professional attitude, self-assurance, and professional poise.

## Courtesy

***Courtesy*** is demonstrated by showing consideration, respect, and cooperation when interacting with others. Courtesy and professionalism go hand in hand as officers interact with citizens and other law enforcement professionals. Officers should treat all persons with dignity, courtesy, and respect regardless of their race, gender, appearance, or behavior *(IN003.1.).* Maintaining a professional, courteous demeanor will help an officer respond appropriately to any situation.

## Nonverbal Communication

Nonverbal communication includes messages sent by posture, muscle tension, facial expression, and even how long it takes a person to respond to a question. Noticing differences between a subject's verbal and nonverbal communication is critical to effective interviewing.

Nonverbal communication in particular is subject to serious misinterpretation. One group may consider certain mannerisms and gestures to be appropriate, while another group may consider them extremely rude. If an agency has a large, diverse ethnic population, it is worthwhile for officers to do further research into nonverbal gestures that may be offensive within various ethnic communities.

People react to stressful situations in different ways. Arms folded across the chest or legs crossed may indicate deception or defensiveness. Sweating, rapid breathing, fidgeting, or blinking may indicate nervousness. Anger is sometimes demonstrated through clenched fists, pacing the floor, clamped teeth, or a clear unwillingness to communicate. When a person is nervous or withholds information, he or she may rock back and forth. An open body with arms down by the side or comfortably in the lap may indicate a receptive person who feels at ease with the officer and the situation. *(IN004.1.A.)*

Culture may influence how much eye contact is considered permissible. Certain cultures view eye contact as a sign of disrespect or aggression. Avoiding eye contact with an officer may also mean the person is shy, uneasy, shameful, fearful, or guilty. Looking directly at the officer may indicate that the person is truthful or challenging. If a person takes quick or cautious peeks at the officer, he or she may be seeking approval from the officer. The person may also be fearful and worried about giving too much information. The officer's eye contact can either intimidate the listener or indicate concern and openness.

Frowns may show displeasure, uneasiness, or confusion. Smiles may indicate pleasure, confusion, or failure to understand. A lack of obvious emotion may indicate shock, fear, not hearing or understanding, or sociopathy.

**Section Vocabulary**

*command presence*

*communication*

*courtesy*

*receiver*

*sender*

## Barriers to Communication

Communication efforts succeed when actual and potential barriers are recognized and addressed. Barriers include personal prejudices, stereotyping, and racial or ethnic slurs. Language differences, profane or derogatory language, and disrespectful or derogatory hand or body gestures can also serve as communication barriers. Distractions hinder good communication as well. *(IN004.1.B.)*

# UNIT 3 I HUMAN INTERACTION

## LESSON 1 I Professional Behavior in a Diverse Society

**OBJECTIVES**

**IN030.3.** Define *community.*

**IN030.3.A.** Identify an officer's response to community expectations.

**IN030.4.A.** Identify how an officer's responses can be influenced by his or her thoughts.

**IN030.1.A.2.** Define *self-talk.*

**IN030.1.** Describe techniques for self-control.

**IN030.13.** Define *self-knowledge.*

**IN030.4.A.3.** Identify emotional triggers that may influence an officer's behavior.

**IN030.18.** Identify ways to understand and provide feedback.

## Community Expectations and Officer Response

***Community*** refers to the people and locations comprising the neighborhoods, institutions, and workplace where an officer lives or works *(IN030.3.).* Law enforcement officers are important resources for making the community a more secure and protected area for the people. They serve by acting in a courteous, efficient, and accessible manner, and by treating all people impartially with consideration and compassion. The community expects officers to uphold the legal rights of citizens without bias. *(IN030.3.A.)*

Displaying professional behavior in dealing with community members is as important as demonstrating proficiency in firearms or defensive tactics. A slur or disparaging comment made by an officer can inflict emotional harm to the person who receives it. It can also undermine the officer's reputation and the law enforcement profession as a whole. Further, it can incite negative behavior that could escalate into a threatening situation.

## Citizens' Expectations and Officer Response

**IN030.17.** Define *stereotyping.*

**IN030.9.A.1.** Define *bias/prejudice.*

**IN030.14.** Define *perception.*

**IN030.15.** Define *assumption.*

**IN030.12.A.** Identify the impact different age groups may have on the community.

People from other countries may fear, distrust, or feel uncomfortable with the U.S. criminal justice system because they do not understand how the system works. As they become acclimated to the community, they begin to understand how local law enforcement agencies join the community in law enforcement efforts.

People's negative perceptions of law enforcement are frequent topics of community discussion. Citizens continue to refer to incidents of poor officer response that occurred many years ago. An unprofessional, inconsiderate officer's reaction to a situation can destroy goodwill that takes years to build. Surveys find that citizens complain about various unprofessional officer behaviors. These include inconsiderateness, humiliation, condescension, and rushing to judgment about situations before gathering all the facts. Citizens also complain about officers making assumptions about them based on their culture, religion, race, sex, age, sexual orientation, ethnicity, homeless status, or physical disability and then responding in an inappropriate, biased manner.

An officer must be particularly sensitive when dealing with crime victims and their families. The way an officer speaks to a sexual assault victim or family member of a deceased victim shows the responsibility the officer feels to the community. Community members expect professional responses to their requests.

Citizens who have had previous negative contact with law enforcement personnel may view officers unfavorably, and erasing such negative emotions and regaining and rebuilding trust is not easy. The public may refuse to work with law enforcement on neighborhood projects and campaigns, resulting in a lack of public respect, support, and cooperation during criminal investigations. One way an officer gains citizen support is to learn the geographical and social characteristics of the community he or she serves. Willingness to learn about different groups shows a sincere interest in public relations.

If an officer believes that he or she has negative biases, that officer should ask him- or her self, "Am I acting on biases and/or prejudice? Am I responding to this person differently than I would to a person of another race, sex, age, sexual orientation, religion, etc.?" *(IN030.4.A.).* If the answer to either question is "yes," then the officer should change his or her behavior in order to respond to situations fairly, professionally, and without bias.

The badge worn symbolizes trust and respect. An officer may be the only face of government some citizens ever see, interact with, and know. If law enforcement officers want to perform their duties in a professional manner and maintain a positive image, they must learn the skills of self-talk, self-control, active listening, self-assessment, and maintaining a positive attitude.

## Strategies of Self-talk

Officers constantly evaluate the world around them, a process usually referred to as self-talk. ***Self-talk*** is a continual internal monologue in which an individual narrates the events going on around him or her *(IN030.1.A.2.)*. Self-talk strategies for law enforcement professionals include thinking through a professional response by recalling skills and information learned during training and applying agency policy and procedures. Self-talk enables an officer to keep thoughts, verbal and nonverbal communications, and emotional responses in check and on track in order to assess a situation and complete a task. For example, if an officer finds him- or herself thinking in a manner that demeans a person or group, the officer should stop, re-evaluate those thoughts, and use positive self-talk to have respect for others in order to maintain a professional response.

Officers, now aware of their own perceptions, assumptions, and limitations, must also be aware that others have perceptions of them. When people curse officers and call them names, officers must remind themselves that those people are attacking the profession, not the individual officers. Self-talk can be used throughout the situation to help the officer behave professionally and not react to such comments.

## Attitude

An officer's beliefs and values help establish his or her attitudes and level of respect for a person, group, or event. With a positive attitude, an officer views him- or herself as a valuable member of society, asks appropriate questions, and stays a step ahead by planning possible responses to situations. Officers should be aware of their attitudes and values because they can shape expectations of what will happen in any situation.

## Self-control

It is important to remember that while interacting with the public, an officer might encounter people who react negatively to an officer's authority and not to the officer as a person. Self-control helps the officer remain strong even under emotional stressors. An officer should always be in control through appropriate use of professional attitude and behavior. When an officer finds him- or herself in a stressful situation, he or she should breathe smoothly, deeply, and evenly. He or she should balance his or her posture and acknowledge reality, saying to him- or herself, "This is real and I can handle it." *(IN030.1.)*

Officers should control their thoughts, emotions, and verbal and nonverbal communications. They must always maintain steadiness and speak calmly when facing frustrating situations. This awareness and demonstrated composure allows an officer to maintain professionalism.

## Self-knowledge

***Self-knowledge*** is an awareness of one's inner nature, feelings, abilities, and limitations *(IN030.13.)*. An officer should know his or her strengths and weaknesses as well as likes and dislikes. Assessing and overcoming weaknesses is extremely important in achieving self-control. Everyone has emotional triggers that stem from personal sensitivities and the traditions they value. These include maintaining a good name, self-respect, pride in heritage, and other personal beliefs. *(IN030.4.A.3.)*

An officer must be able to assess his or her trigger points and learn ways to control his or her emotions. Emotional triggers are officer safety issues. Officers should become aware of things that irritate them and exercise self-control over their own reactions.

## Evaluating Feedback from Others

The more an officer understands others' verbal and nonverbal cues (feedback), the greater his or her ability to communicate and choose appropriate words. Understanding the need to constantly evaluate attitude and exhibit verbal and nonverbal skills is important to an officer's job and safety. There are several ways to evaluate feedback. An officer can ask questions to determine if the person understands. The officer can observe facial expressions that show agreement or confusion or watch for gestures, such as shoulder shrugging.

An officer needs to attend to feedback in order to understand a subject. Possible questions an officer should ask him or herself in order to evaluate the situation include the following:

- What is the subject's body stance or position?
- What facial expressions is the interviewee making and do they indicate certain information?
- What is the position of the hands, arms, and legs?
- Is the subject reaching out for anything or anyone?
- Is the subject grabbing another person?
- Can the officer understand the subject?
- What is the tone, volume, and pitch of the subject's voice?
- What words are used?
- Does the feedback require a response?
- What response is appropriate for this situation? *(IN030.18.)*

## Unprofessional Behaviors to Avoid

***Stereotyping*** is a fixed and unvarying idea or opinion of a person, group, or subject *(IN030.17.)*. Labeling people, whether positively or negatively, may limit an officer's ability to obtain information or help a victim. Judging a person based on generalizations may cause valuable information and clues about the person to be lost, resulting in ignored situational context that could otherwise help save a life. Both positive and negative stereotypes hurt because they categorize people unfairly; they are therefore not acceptable practices. Officers should exhibit respect and integrity to all, irrespective of color, race, age, sex, religion, national origin, economic status, or physical and mental ability.

***Bias*** or ***prejudice*** is a strong belief or feeling about a person, group, or subject, whether positive or negative, that is formed without reviewing all available facts or information *(IN030.9.A.1.)*. Prejudices may grow from learned behavior and attitudes. Citizens or officers who act with prejudice may exhibit inappropriate behavior toward individuals or groups who represent a race, color, ancestry, ethnicity, religion, sexual orientation, national origin, homeless status, mental or physical disability, advanced age or other self-defining characteristic. This type of behavior may be destructive and can invite civil liability.

Discrimination is the negative behavior toward a person or group that is based on color, race, sex, age, religion, and/or ethnic and national origin. Discrimination occurs because people choose to act on their prejudice. Each person has the right to live and work free from discrimination and prejudices.

***Perception*** is the impression in a person's mind of an individual, a group of people, or events based on experiences, biases, beliefs, assumptions, and observations *(IN030.14.)*. People respond to situations based on their perceptions. An officer's beliefs, values, and life experiences influence the officer's behavior and view of others' behaviors. Perception also helps an officer develop and form personal opinions when communicating

**Section Vocabulary**

*assumption*

*bias/prejudice*

*community*

*perception*

*self-knowledge*

*self-talk*

*stereotyping*

with persons of different ages, genders, races, and physical and mental abilities. Likewise, others perceive an officer based on their life experiences, beliefs, and values.

An ***assumption*** is a notion, statement, or belief about a person, group, or event that may or may not be factual *(IN030.15.)*. It is also something considered as true or false without proof or demonstration. Assumptions are interpretations of what experience reveals, which may not always be accurate.

The following are examples of often false assumptions:

Young people are loud and noisy.

Young people are disrespectful to elders and authority.

Young people pose threats to officers.

Young people are violent, aggressive, and disrespectful.

Older people are gentle, peaceful, and respectful.

Older people pose no threat to officers.

Older people perform slowly and use antiquated methods.

Older people are conservative and cautious; they are not as effective as young people.

Using stereotypes, perceptions, and assumptions to judge people limits thought processes and may cause an officer to exclude vital information in an investigation. Limiting possibilities minimizes safety. Stereotypes, perceptions, and assumptions may cause an officer to act on emotions rather than plan a response. Responsive behavior requires an officer to think, plan a response, and act using verbal and nonverbal skills.

## Impact of Age Groups on the Community and Officer Response

While it is important not to judge people solely on identifying traits such as age, a large population of certain age groups do affect the type and volume of service calls. When determining how age affects the community and therefore law enforcement needs, officers should determine if the community is a college town or retirement area, is rural or urban, has theme parks and other attractions that draw vacationers and tourists, or sponsors events that attract large groups of people of the same age or with the same interest, such as Bike Week or spring break events. *(IN030.12.A.)*

# UNIT 4 I INTERVIEWING

## LESSON 1 I Preparing for the Interview

### Preparing for the Interview

Before asking the first question in an interview, officers must take certain steps to ensure that the interview will be successful. The pre-interview process includes determining whom to interview and when, the order of interviews, where to interview, what information to obtain, and how to record the interviews *(IN008.3.)*. An interviewer should obtain all pertinent information relating to the incident, compare it with other case information, and follow agency interview policy and procedures *(IN008.3.A.)*. Further, it is necessary to determine if *Miranda* warnings or the administration of an oath are needed. The U.S. Supreme Court case, *Maryland v. Shatzer*, 130 S.Ct. 1213 (2010), provides that there must be a 14-day break between the end of the initial custodial interview or interrogation of the subject and any resumption of interview or interrogation of that subject.

In preparing for an interview, an officer should check the interviewee's name through the FCIC/NCIC to determine if that individual is a wanted person. The officer should also review the initial findings of the crime scene investigation and then gather and review available background information on the interviewee.

Interviews should be conducted immediately or shortly after a crime in order to yield the most accurate and helpful information. However, if an officer does not have an opportunity to speak with a witness at the scene, the officer should schedule a post-scene interview with the person *(IN008.1.)*. The proper time to interview will be dependent upon various factors, including the physical and emotional condition of the interviewee. The officer should observe behavior patterns that can indicate the person's readiness for interview.

Officers can decide which people at a scene should be interviewed by asking some general questions and seeking information from anyone who knows something about the crime *(IN008.2.)*. The extent of a person's knowledge or involvement in the incident should be uncovered. Answers to general questions such as "Can you describe what happened?" can help identify potential interviewees. Interviewing all people with knowledge of an incident is important. If a particular person is not interviewed, the officer should explain reasons for not doing so in his or her report.

Generally, the people interviewed belong to one of five categories. A witness is one who personally perceived information through any of the five senses: sight, touch, taste, hearing, and smell. A suspect is a person thought to have committed an offense. A victim is a person or business against whom a crime was committed. A ***complainant*** is one who reports the crime. An ***informant*** is one who provides information confidentially and whose identity is normally not disclosed until required by law.

**OBJECTIVES**

**IN008.3.** List proper steps to prepare for an interview.

**IN008.3.A.** Identify the primary responsibilities of the interviewer.

**IN008.1.** Identify when to interview.

**IN008.2.** Identify whom to interview.

**IN008.3.C.** Identify the primary factors that influence the success of an interview.

**IN008.3.H.** Identify an appropriate location for an interview.

**LE142.6.** Identify the importance of allowing sufficient time for a thorough interview.

**IN008.3.F.** Identify factors that influence the order of interviews.

Factors that influence the success of an interview include isolation and privacy. The interviewer is responsible for creating a confidential atmosphere that will encourage honesty and forthrightness from the interviewee. Isolating the interviewee prevents outside influences; privacy helps build rapport and gain trust. A good physical and emotional comfort level is another factor that can influence the success of an interview. The interviewee's comfort will encourage cooperation. *(IN008.3.C.)*

The location of the interview is a factor that can determine success. Interviews may be conducted at the scene of the incident or in the officer's patrol vehicle. If available, the officer may choose to interview subjects at a location that has recording equipment available. Whatever location is chosen, it should be safe, out of the weather, and isolated as much as possible from the sight and hearing of other interviewees *(IN008.3.H.)*. Witnesses, victims, and suspects should be separated to discourage discussion or rehearsal of their stories.

Generally, interviews are conducted at the scene. In some situations, it is necessary to conduct an interview after leaving the scene of an incident. Many post-scene interviews take place after an injured individual is transported to a medical facility.

An officer should also schedule sufficient time for each interview. Interviews can be time-consuming, but the time will be well spent if the interviewer has planned and prepared *(LE142.6.)*. Phone contact is a means to screen potential interviewees (victims, witnesses, or informants) to determine whether a formal interview is necessary. Whenever possible, a person-to-person interview is preferable. An officer should talk to the people who can give the most information about the incident and record those statements along with names, phone numbers (home, work, cell), and addresses (home and work) for later use. The officer should personally obtain this information at the scene.

An officer should ask questions aimed at establishing the elements of a crime. Officers should avoid leading questions when interviewing. "And then she hit you with the bat, right?" is an example of a leading question. The interviewer should ask evenly spaced, nonthreatening, open-ended questions about the event. These questions usually require more than "yes" and "no" answers.

Open-ended questions that encourage conversation typically begin as follows:

*Who:* Who were you with? Who was involved? Who do you think did it? Who is the victim?

*What:* What happened? What did you see? What were the circumstances? What offense was committed?

*When:* When did you realize something was happening? When, in terms of date and time, did the incident occur?

*Where:* Where would you like to start? Where did the incident occur? (Here, the responding officer should establish whether the incident occurred in his or her jurisdiction.)

*Why:* Why did you call for help? Why did the incident happen?

*How:* How can I help you? How did the incident happen?

## Order of Interviews

Upon arrival at a scene, an officer should try to establish contact with the victim or the complainant. Generally, the complainant is the first person to be interviewed, but officer and scene safety factors may dictate otherwise. It is important to remember that the initial officer on the scene should render first aid before conducting any interviews. The officer should also be mindful of his or her safety relative to the scene. Once aid has been rendered and the scene has been secured, the officer shall determine the individuals to be interviewed and the order in which he or she will proceed. Normally, the initial responding officer should first seek the reporting person/victim to get information about the incident. If the victim is injured, an officer should attempt to get BOLO information from the victim while administering first aid. After all initial tasks are accomplished, the officer should seek other witnesses to the incident for interviews.

When conducting interviews, officer safety is of paramount importance. All interviewees should be checked for weapons and mental stability. If it is apparent that the interviewee is in shock or suffering trauma from the incident, then the interview should be conducted after the interviewee has stabilized.

Whether dealing with victims, witnesses, or subjects, the primary purpose is to gather information. Identifying attitudes of potential witnesses will help the officer decide the order in which to conduct the interviews *(IN008.3.F.)*. Three main types of interviewees that an officer will encounter are reluctant, hostile, or cooperative. The reluctant interviewee is unwilling to answer questions. The hostile interviewee is antagonistic or agitated, whereas the cooperative interviewee is willing to answer questions.

Officers encounter many different types of witnesses and interviewees during the course of their daily activities. The following are examples of the kinds of witnesses an officer may interview and the techniques an officer may use to interview them:

### *Angry or aggressive witnesses*

- Establish control of the interview.
- Maintain a neutral demeanor.
- Do not argue with the witness.
- Follow safety precautions, including checking for a weapon.
- Ask direct questions.
- Try to reduce the witness' stress and anxiety.

### *Cooperative witnesses*

- Establish rapport.
- Confirm the witness' observations and statements.
- Ask direct questions.
- Do not confuse or frustrate the witness.

### *Victim*

- Evaluate whether the victim is physically and mentally able to participate in the interview.
- Build trust and cooperation.

- Be aware of the victim's verbal and nonverbal cues.
- Prompt the witness with primary and follow-up questions.
- Maintain a relaxed and calm interview environment.

### *Other witnesses not directly involved with the incident*

- Listen carefully to the witness.
- Be polite, patient, and understanding.
- Encourage the witness to disclose information.

### *Suspect*

- Consider the safety of all concerned.
- Give *Miranda* warnings, when applicable.
- Do not stereotype, pre-judge, ridicule or bully the witness.
- Be honest and straightforward.

### *Talkative witnesses*

- Establish the purpose of the interview.
- Be patient.
- Ask closed-ended questions to redirect the witness back to the subject of the interview.

### *Reserved or reluctant witnesses*

- Establish rapport.
- State the purpose of the interview.
- Speak in a subdued tone of voice.

### *Uncooperative witnesses*

- Establish control of the interview.
- Keep your composure.
- Remind the witness of the penalties for withholding information.

### *Stressed witnesses*

- Establish rapport.
- State the purpose of the interview.
- Refer witness to professional counseling if appropriate.

### *Diversity (cultural, gender, race, ethnic)*

- Be aware of potential language barriers.
- Repeat and explain questions.

- Refrain from stereotyping.
- Be aware of the distinctive or unique verbal and nonverbal behaviors of witnesses who have a different race, ethnicity, gender, or culture than you.

**Section Vocabulary**

*complainant*

*informant*

## Common Signs of Deception

When interviewing, officers should always be alert to the body language of the interviewee. How a person acts or reacts to a question may suggest deception. Being familiar with certain body movements, gestures, and facial expressions may help an officer recognize an interviewee who conceals information or is deceitful.

Detecting deception is not easy. Indications of deception include various physiological and behavioral signs. Physiologically, increased perspiration, changes in skin color, dry mouth, increased pulse rate, or an observable change in breathing rate are signs of nervousness, stress, and possibly deception. Behavioral clues include nervous movements, pacing, an inability to sit still, refusing to look at the questioner, rehearsed answers, and inconsistent responses. Attempts to change the line of questioning, over-eagerness to help, too much or too little clarification, and a repeated insistence that simple questions are not understood are also behavioral signs of deception.

Effective interviewing and comprehensive investigation may help officers recognize deception or honesty. A truthful witness will exhibit confidence, make an obvious and sincere attempt to assist in the investigation, and offer a solid, sustainable alibi. Truthful but guilty people will give incriminating answers that prove true, express regret for involvement in the crime, and assert an awareness of evidence against them.

# UNIT 4 | INTERVIEWING

## LESSON 2 | Conducting the Interview

**OBJECTIVES**

**LE142.10.C.** Identify techniques that encourage a person to explain fully an action or activity.

**IN008.4.B.** Identify elements of the interview process.

**IN008.4.** Identify effective interview techniques.

**IN008.6.B.** Identify ways to ensure that the information obtained is suitable for submission to court.

**IN008.6.** Identify ways to evaluate the effectiveness of an interview.

During the interview, an officer must be alert at all times, keeping in mind the safety techniques learned in the academy. An officer should position him- or herself so that his or her firearm side is opposite the person being interviewed. When possible, an officer should avoid sitting or standing with his or her back to a door.

Effective interviewing techniques encourage an interviewee to explain a situation completely in his or her own words but do not influence the interviewee's responses. An officer should not suggest the right answers to an interviewee.

The initial stage of the interview is the warm-up. During this stage, the officer establishes rapport and builds understanding between the interviewee and him- or herself. The officer should introduce him- or herself and make sure the interviewee is physically and emotionally comfortable. The officer must take care to conceal personal feelings of animosity toward the interviewee based on prejudice, bias, or lifestyle choices. Next, the officer should explain what is going to be discussed during the interview and describe how the information will be collected and used and why it is important. The goal of an interview is the transfer of information; therefore officers should use simple language which can be easily understood.

During the primary interview stage, the officer tries to obtain the information needed about the case. The officer will ask a variety of open-ended questions designed to elicit as much information as possible. They are used to get the interviewee to describe something in his or her own words. Examples of open-ended questions include "What is your name?" and "Where were you when the accident occurred?" and "When did you hear the voices?" The interviewee is likely to answer questions like these in detail. Closed-ended questions elicit only "yes" or "no" answers. They are used to get specific answers or help the interviewee refocus. Examples include "Do you know where the suspect lives?" and "Were you in the room when the fight started?" Past performance questions solicit from the interviewee how he or she handled a situation in the past. These types of questions can uncover additional information about the history of a situation or determine a behavior pattern. An example would be "How had you reacted to the arguments of the couple next door in the past?" *(LE142.10.C.)*

The closing stage concludes the interview, and the officer should express appreciation to the interviewee for his or her time. The officer should request contact information from the interviewee in case additional questions come up in the future. The information collected in writing should be summarized by the officer and improvements for the next interview mentally noted. *(IN008.4.B.)*

## Basic Interview Techniques

Each officer should develop his or her own style of interviewing and apply those same interviewing skills to every interview. All officers should remember to use clear language and avoid police jargon when interviewing. Courtesy, consideration, and patience should be shown at all times. Interviewing officers should never suggest a conclusion or supply information to help a witness fill gaps in a story. An officer should also remember that just because an interviewee appears sincere does not mean he or she actually is.

**Section Vocabulary**

***minimal encouragers***

***mirroring***

***Mirroring*** is a technique in which the interviewer acts as if he or she is looking in a mirror and seeing him- or herself as the reflection of the interviewee. The interviewer assumes the interviewee's posture and repeats what the person is saying, only using a questioning tone to obtain clarification or a more detailed response.

***Minimal encouragers*** are brief statements which indicate that the officer hears what the person is saying and is inclined to hear more. Examples include "Okay," and "Go on," and "Then what?"

Proper language and tone of voice that parallels the interviewee's level of understanding and tone of voice convey the officer's willingness to listen and understand. However, officers should note that understanding does not necessarily mean agreement. It merely means that the officer comprehends what the person is trying to tell him or her.

Recall is enhanced by recreating the event stimuli, which can be both physical and psychological. The interviewee should be asked to think back to the original event, recalling the physical surroundings (time of day, workspace, and so on) as well as the emotional situation (rushed, bored, and so on). *(IN008.4.)*

There are a number of things an officer can do to evaluate the effectiveness of his or her interviewing skills. For instance, the officer can compare the results of an interview with the case paperwork and other completed interviews. The officer can also evaluate his or her approach, adjusting where necessary, and continue the investigation. If a written statement is obtained, the officer can read it before the interviewee signs it and make sure it can be read and understood; if not, it may be of little use at trial *(IN008.6.B.)*. Determining if the information is suitable for submission to court is another helpful method an officer can employ to evaluate his or her interviewing skills. If the who, what, when, where, why, and how of the incident can be answered, then most likely, the desired results were achieved *(IN008.6.)*. If an officer was not successful in obtaining the desired information, the officer should adjust the plan for follow-up interviews as necessary and continue working on the case.

# UNIT 4 | INTERVIEWING

## LESSON 3 | Documenting the Interview

**OBJECTIVES**

**IN008.5.A.** Identify ways to document the interview.

**IN010.2.** Identify the procedures to follow when taking notes.

There are three major methods for documenting an interview: taking notes, audio or video recording, and obtaining written statements *(IN008.5.A).* Documentation is important because it helps the interviewing officer remember important facts, complete the final investigative report, and prepare for deposition or trial. Documentation also helps other officers who become involved in the case.

Taking notes during an interview is necessary and must be done with great care. Usually, it is best to begin taking notes early in the interview. This is begun by writing names, addresses, date of birth, and other basic facts. This gets interviewees used to answering an officer's questions and seeing the officer write what they say. *(IN010.2.)*

Agency or local state attorney's policies should be followed if audio or video recording is used during the interview. Making a brief test recording before conducting the interview will ensure that the recording device is working properly. All recordings should be preserved as evidence.

Audio or video recording of interviews offers advantages and disadvantages. A recording can be beneficial because the entire conversation can be heard. Also, the interviewer's fairness can be readily evaluated. The disadvantages of recordings are that they may be subject to possible legal constraints, and some recorded words or descriptions may not be clear or may be subject to misinterpretation.

# UNIT 4 | INTERVIEWING

## LESSON 4 | Taking Statements

A ***statement*** is a permanent, verbal, or written record of a person's account of an incident or occurrence that may or may not be made under oath. Written statements may be taken from anyone who has information about any crime, incident, or occurrence. This may include, but is not limited to, witnesses, suspects, and victims. When to take a written statement often depends on circumstances or agency policy *(IN011.1.A.)*. Agency policies or the local State Attorney's Office should be consulted for the preferred procedure on locations, materials, equipment, and interpreters needed for the statement *(IN011.6.)*. Most jurisdictions require that a statement be sworn. Written statements must be notarized, and audio/video-recorded statements must be made under oath. These statements must be preserved as evidence in the case. *(IN011.1.C.)*

Information contained in witness statements may be used to complete a report, offer probable cause, file an affidavit, or obtain a warrant. The information may be admissible in court and could help to solve a crime or identify additional suspects or witnesses who have information about a crime, incident, or occurrence.

When asking an individual to provide a written statement, an officer must be sure to explain the reason(s) for the request and should be clear about what information (who, what, when, where, how, and why of the incident) is needed *(IN011.8.)*. However, the officer should never offer an opinion or interpretation of events. If the individual said something important but leaves it out of the written statement, that individual should be asked to include the information.

Multiple witnesses should be separated before being interviewed to prevent them from discussing the incident among themselves *(IN011.2.)*. To get the information needed, individuals should be questioned one at a time. General questions help to determine which persons should be asked to provide sworn statements. One of the best questions to begin with is, "Can you tell me what happened?" The officer should listen to the person's response before asking more questions *(IN011.10.)*. If the person has important information or facts regarding the incident, the officer should take a written statement. Statements are unnecessary from people who say they saw and heard nothing unless the officer believes that they are not being truthful.

Under certain circumstances, it may be impossible to take a statement. An officer should always document why there is not a statement from an individual. For example, an injured person who requires immediate medical attention probably cannot give a statement at the scene.

**OBJECTIVES**

**IN011.1.A.** Identify when statements should be obtained.

**IN011.6.** Identify appropriate location, materials, interpreters, and equipment for taking the statement.

**IN011.1.C.** Identify the basic procedures to follow when taking statements.

**IN011.8.** Identify reasons for requesting written, oral, or recorded statements from a participant, witness, or suspect.

**IN011.2.** Identify the importance of separating the interviewees.

**IN011.10.** Identify how to develop questions based on what the witness says.

**IN011.1.** Identify which person(s) should provide a statement.

**IN011.15.** Identify when an officer can notarize a statement according to Florida law.

**IN011.9.** Identify when it is necessary to administer an oath.

**IN011.13.** Identify the importance of interviewee's signature on written statements.

**IN011.4.** Identify whether the statements should be oral or written.

**IN011.7.A.** Identify the basic kinds of information needed in a statement.

**IN011.12.** Identify the importance of reviewing interviewee's statements for completeness.

**IN011.11.** Identify the action taken by any observing officer after a statement has been written for the witness.

**IN011.13.A.** Identify what to do if a person is unwilling to sign a statement.

**IN011.13.B.** Identify what to do if a person is unwilling to sign a statement.

**IN011.5.** Identify the appropriate method of recording a statement.

**IN008.5.** Document an interview.

# When and How to Give an Oath

After forming a mental picture of the sequence of events, the officer should identify from whom to get sworn statements *(IN011.1.)*. Depending on circumstances at the scene and the individual's willingness, the officer may take the sworn statement at the scene or contact the person later to arrange for a sworn statement.

Florida law, as per F.S. §117.10, provides law enforcement officers with the authority to administer oaths while performing their official duties. However, this does not certify an officer as a notary unless he or she has completed the normal appointment process *(IN011.15.)*. Officers should always administer an oath or affirmation for any sworn statement or affidavit when they want to commit the witness to his or her testimony. Sworn statements or affidavits are not admissible in court if the witness is also in court *(IN011.9.)*. An ***oath*** is a vow or pledge to tell the truth regarding an incident or occurrence. A person may object to taking an oath because of a religious or philosophical belief. Florida law allows that a person can make an affirmation instead of an oath. An ***affirmation*** is a solemn and formal declaration or assertion made in place of an oath.

It should be noted that the law does not certify law enforcement officers as notaries. They are not notaries unless they have completed the normal appointment process. As indicated, law enforcement officers have authority to administer oaths while performing their official duties.

When administering an oath, an officer should tell the interviewee of the need of a sworn, written statement and explain that the statement must be made under oath. The officer should also tell the interviewee that any false information about a material matter given in the statement may constitute perjury. The interviewee should also be told to raise his or her right hand. The law does not require raising the right hand; however, this well-known gesture may impress upon the individual the importance and seriousness of telling the truth. The officer administering the oath should ask the person, "Do you swear or affirm that the statement you are about to give is true and accurate to the best of your knowledge?"

In the event an officer is taking a written statement, the person should read the printed oath on the statement form and sign his or her name indicating the information contained is correct and factual *(IN011.13.)*. The wording usually reads, "Sworn to and subscribed before me this (date)." Next to or below the signature, the officer should note his or her profession and rank where applicable.

# Selecting a Location

Statements may be obtained in an office, in the field, or even in the officer's patrol car. The officer taking a statement should try to select a quiet area that provides privacy for the person giving the statement. A written statement is generally recognized as a better form of evidence than an oral statement or interview *(IN011.4.)*. If circumstances permit, the officer should obtain a written statement that is signed, dated, and witnessed. There are several methods of obtaining written statements.

## Option 1: Individual Writes Statement

The individual may handwrite the statement, though he or she should be advised to print clearly. It is the officer's responsibility to make sure that the individual's handwriting is legible. When writing a statement, an individual should describe, to the best of his or her recollection, every event, person, weapon, vehicle, and all property involved in the incident *(IN011.7.A.).* The officer should read the statement and compare its content with notes taken during the individual's first verbal report of the incident. If information is missing, the person should be asked to clarify that information in the statement. The officer must be careful not to put words in the person's mouth or insert personal interpretations.

## Option 2: Officer Writes Statement

The officer should administer the oath and ask questions or have the person relate the information in his or her own words while the officer writes down the statement. This is necessary if the witness does not read or write. The officer then should read the statement back to the witness, make any needed corrections, and ask the witness to date and sign the statement or make his or her mark *(IN011.12.).* Any observing officers should date and sign the statement as well *(IN011.11.).* At the beginning and the end of the written statement, the officer should note "Dictated by ____ and written by Officer ____."

A person who cannot speak English can write a statement in his or her own language. A translator may be needed; another law enforcement officer may serve as translator. Agency policy should be consulted regarding the use of a translator.

In some situations, a witness may be injured, sick, or incapacitated and unable to sign his or her name. The officer should write the reason the person cannot sign the statement and then sign it him- or herself *(IN011.13.A.).* If possible, any witnesses should be asked to sign the statement as well. If a person refuses to give a statement, it should be indicated as such in the officer's notes. If the person gives a statement but refuses to sign it, the officer should note, "refused to sign" *(IN011.13.B.).* Persons cannot be forced to provide statements; however, they can be served written subpoenas and be required to appear in court.

## Option 3: Audio Recordings

An officer may ask a witness to make an audio recording of the statement. On the recording, the officer must state his or her name and the names of others present, the day and date of the interview, the incident to be discussed, the case number, and the type of crime. The oath may then be administered.

Questioning begins the same way as it does for oral statements, or the person can be asked to narrate what happened in his or her own words. If beginning a new segment of the recording, the officer must once again document, as at the beginning of the statement, noting that this is a continuation of the statement given by the person and recording the date and time. An officer should pay attention to what the witness says during the course of this statement and ask that he or she clarify discrepancies or elaborate when necessary. At the end of the recording, the officer should say, "This now concludes the statement of ____, regarding incident _____, case number _____. The time now is _____." Agency policy will dictate the disposition of the recording.

## Option 4: Video Recordings

Due to facilities and equipment needs, officers normally use this method only in serious criminal cases where visual information about the scene or victim is needed. *(IN011.5.)*

**Section Vocabulary**

*affirmation*

*oath*

*statement*

## Interviewing Juveniles

Although interviewing juveniles is similar to questioning adults, basic differences exist. By properly applying interviewing techniques, law enforcement officers will be successful in obtaining the information to resolve investigations.

Parents have a right to talk to their children, if they so request, and the children have a right to talk to their parents, if they so request, before the child is questioned by law enforcement. Officers must be familiar with agency policies and procedures on parents' and children's access to each other during questioning.

All interviews with children who are victims or suspects should be recorded. The number of times a child may be interviewed is limited, and agency and local court policy should be consulted on this matter.

Be thoroughly familiar with agency policies on interviewing juveniles. The officer should carefully document how he or she or other officers communicate with the juvenile subject and whether or not a juvenile of similar education, experience, background, and age as the subject would understand the explanation as to whether or not the interview is custodial or non-custodial. Be sure to document exactly how the juvenile gives consent to be interviewed. If the juvenile is arrested, make sure that he or she is of sufficient age, experience, and education to understand that he or she is under arrest. Document whether the juvenile understands *Miranda* and understands what waiving his or her rights means. Courts will look closely at whether a suspect of the subject's age, education, experience, etc., would have understood the *Miranda* warning and what waiving his or her rights thereunder would mean. See *J.D.B. v. North Carolina*, 564 U.S. __ (2011).

A child may not be placed or transported in any law enforcement vehicle which at the same time contains an adult under arrest, unless the adult is alleged or believed to be involved in the same offense or transaction as the child. Whenever feasible, suspects should be transported separately to avoid collusion regarding their testimony.

## Incident Report

After completing an interview, the results should be documented in a report and properly filed *(IN008.5.)*. Proper filing depends on agency policy; most jurisdictions require that reports and other documents be forwarded to an administrative section for appropriate filing.

# UNIT 5 | REPORT WRITING

## LESSON 1 | Police Reports

**OBJECTIVES**

**IN009.1.A.** Define *report.*

**IN009.1.C.** Identify the purposes of a report.

**IN009.1.** Identify that agencies use a variety of different forms.

**IN009.1.C.1.** List the categories of operational reports.

**IN009.1.D.** Identify the potential readers of a police report.

**IN009.8.** Identify common proceedings in which a police report may be used.

A ***report*** is a written document prepared by a law enforcement officer that gives information about an event, situation, or person encountered by the officer *(IN009.1.A.).* Writing reports is a critical job function for all law enforcement officers. However, many officers find this important task difficult to accomplish. A report documents the facts of an incident. An officer will write some kind of report after completing nearly every assignment. Therefore, officers must become skilled in writing effective, clear, concise reports. A report reflects the writer's competency and professionalism not only in writing but also in all aspects of police work. *(IN009.1.C.)*

A well-written report is important because it results in better police work and more convictions, reduces legal liability for both the officer and the department, and saves the department time and expense. Law enforcement personnel frequently say, "If it isn't in the report, it did not happen." This underscores the point that report writing is one of the most important skills necessary for an officer's success. Most importantly, a criminal could go free and threaten the safety of the community as a result of a poor-quality report.

Once a report is submitted and approved, it becomes a permanent public record. The report must withstand the test of time because it may be used years after the incident occurred. Most agencies have procedures describing what forms are appropriate, who reviews reports, and how reports are stored. The officer should be familiar with agency forms and the pertinent information required to complete each one. *(IN009.1.)*

The primary officer prepares the offense-incident report. If the information pertains to a previously documented incident, the officer must prepare a supplemental report. The supplemental report should be attached to the primary officer's report. An officer's supervisor may be responsible for preparing certain reports following incidents such as officer use of force. Depending on agency policy, a community service officer may generate a number of criminal and noncriminal reports. Although officers write many types of reports, the focus here is operational reports. Operational reports are generally linked to three major categories: offense-incident reports, arrest affidavits, and supplemental or follow-up reports. *(IN009.1.C.1.)*

All reports are not written the same way. Before beginning a report, an officer should consider the circumstances and situation he or she is trying to document. A burglary report, for example, will have different information and may be in a different format than a found property report.

Other incidents that require reports include the following:

- all crimes
- use of force by an officer
- suicide
- natural death
- found property
- runaway juvenile
- traffic crashes (under certain circumstances) as required by law
- miscellaneous noncriminal or suspicious incidents
- additional or supplemental information

Reports serve specific purposes that include examining past events, keeping other law enforcement officers informed, continuing investigations, preparing court cases, coordinating law enforcement activities, planning future law enforcement services, and evaluating law enforcement officers' performance.

## Audience Considerations

Officers must analyze the potential audience and purpose of each report before writing it. The majority of people who read reports are not police officers. The readers will have varying life experiences, education levels, cultural backgrounds, and reasons for reading the report. To ensure the effectiveness of the report, the report writer must consider the audience, which may include:

- other officers
- supervisors
- defense attorneys and prosecutors
- judges
- city, county, or state officials
- reporters
- victims or their families
- suspects, defendants, or persons convicted of crimes
- citizens
- insurance companies *(IN009.1.D.)*

Each reader will develop an opinion about the author of the report based solely on the report's makeup. For example, prosecuting attorneys will make crucial decisions about the case based on what they read in the report, even if they have never met the officer who wrote it. On the other hand, defense attorneys will seek to exploit any weaknesses they see in a report, also making assumptions about the officer's competency.

The tone of the report is also important. It is a professional document and should be business-like and objective. The language must be universal; jargon, slang, and abbreviations should be avoided, and plain English should be used.

## *Purpose of a Report in Future Proceedings*

**Section Vocabulary**

*report*

Police reports become public records under Florida law and need to be retained long after the active case is completed. Statute and agency policy will dictate how long such reports must be retained. Apart from being public records, reports are typically used in many proceedings as an official representation of facts surrounding an incident. Some examples include:

- criminal case-filing
- depositions
- pretrial proceedings
- criminal trials
- victim restitution hearings
- civil proceedings
- appeals in criminal and civil cases
- probation and parole hearings
- internal affairs investigations
- workers' compensation cases
- research *(IN009.8.)*

# UNIT 5 | REPORT WRITING

## LESSON 2 | Recording the Facts

**OBJECTIVES**

**IN009.3.A.** Identify the basic steps of report writing.

**IN010.1.A.3.** Identify the purpose of note taking.

**IN010.1.** Identify the correct information to record in notes.

**IN011.7.B.** Identify the additional descriptions that may be required for proper identification.

**IN010.2.H.** Identify why it is important to alternate between listening and writing.

**IN010.2.D.** Identify the importance of using correct spelling and recording accurately all vital information in notes.

**IN010.2.F.** Identify common abbreviations to use in note taking.

The basic steps in report writing are recording the facts, organizing the facts, writing the report, and evaluating the report *(IN009.3.A.)*. An officer may need to remember facts about a particular call and cannot rely on memory alone. He or she must be sure to immediately record facts as they become available. Note taking is one of the ways to achieve this. Field notes are normally the primary documents an officer will use when writing operational reports *(IN010.1.A.3.)*. Additional sources may include written statements.

An officer's field notes will contain facts about specific events, interviews, information gathered from investigations, and information that might aid in future investigations. Field notes should include the basic facts:

- Where did the incident take place?
- When did the incident take place?
- Who was involved?
- What happened?
- How did it happen?
- Why did it happen? *(IN010.1.)*

*Where:* The location of an incident is generally one of the first pieces of information an officer obtains. The address or a description of where the incident occurred, or at least where the complainant is located, will be provided by the dispatcher. The officer should note the incident location in as much detail as possible. An example of this might be, "The incident occurred on State Road 33, approximately three miles east of Highway 99." Abbreviations may be used when taking actual notes but should be spelled out in any reports.

*When:* The "when" of an incident is simply the date and time the incident occurred. If an exact date cannot be established, the officer should define a range as closely as possible, such as "between Monday June 3 and Thursday June 6" rather than "unknown." The time of the incident can be critically important in establishing alibis given by suspects.

*Who:* The names of everyone who might have information about what happened should be recorded in the officer's notes. "Who" is more than a person's name but includes as much identifying information as possible: name, address, all phone numbers, date of birth (DOB) or age, employment information, race, and gender. It is important to note unique physical attributes that might help identify the person later such as scarring, body piercings, or tattoos. Any additional information such as height, weight, type of clothing, hair color and length, and unique mannerisms or speech patterns should also be included *(IN011.7.B.)*. The individual must be identified as a victim, witness, suspect, or other. Typically, officers annotate the individual's status in the case with a circled "v," "w," "s," or "o." An officer should document information he or she sees, hears or obtains from any person involved in an incident.

*What:* Included in "what" is information regarding the nature of the incident that occurred. Officers should also seek answers to the questions "to what" and "with what." For example, an officer could write, "The suspect committed criminal mischief to the victim's car with a sledgehammer." The descriptive information might also include identifiers specific to the theft, damage, or loss of particular items.

A detailed description of the property should include the type of property, identifying characteristics such as model number, year, etc., identifying marks or inscriptions, and estimated value. Descriptions of vehicles should include the type, make, model, style, exterior color of vehicle, interior color of vehicle, identification number, tag number, and any identifying marks such as scratches, decals, etc.

*How:* It is important to note the method used to carry out an incident: "how" it was done. This includes knowing what was used to commit it. Did someone hit the victim with his or her fist? Did someone use a knife to scratch graffiti into the side of a building? Did a vehicle knock over the mailbox? The answers to such questions should be written in the officer's notebook. Details about the method used as described in the "what" section should also be included.

Often, an officer can determine how something happened by observation. For example, in a burglary investigation, an officer might observe a doorjamb with fresh pry marks, which could indicate that a screwdriver was used to pry the door lock open. This type of information should be recorded in the notebook.

*Why:* The reason for an incident is sometimes called the motive or the "why." It may be a mystery during the initial investigation and may never be discovered. Different witnesses may attribute various motives based on their perspective. The officer should not jump to conclusions about motive based on the first or loudest witness. Often the motive forms part of the criminal intent for an offense. Proof of criminal intent is essential to obtaining a conviction. An officer should include in the field notes information about possible motives and evidence of intent.

Agency policy dictates which calls for service receive case numbers. An officer should call dispatch to request a case number and write the number in the field notes.

Notes should be written as soon as possible after collecting information. Sometimes, circumstances delay immediate note writing, but this should not happen often. The longer the officer delays in writing down what is observed or heard, the greater the chance that some of the information will not be accurately recalled.

Writing notes while interviewing a witness may result in an officer not hearing some of the witness's statement. The best practice is to listen and then ask the witness to pause while the officer writes down the information. The alternating method will permit officers to hear and record the most information from witnesses. *(IN010.2.H.)*

All names, addresses, and other relevant information should be correctly spelled and accurately recorded. If an officer is uncertain of a name's proper spelling, he or she should ask the witness to spell it. If the witness is not sure, then the officer should write the word phonetically and try to find the correct spelling later. Inaccurate information may result in the wrong person being arrested or in acquittal of a guilty person. *(IN010.2.D.)*

Using appropriate abbreviations can tremendously increase the note-taking speed. The following list gives examples of commonly accepted abbreviations that may be used:

| | |
|---|---|
| a.m. | morning |
| yr | year |
| hr | hour |
| v | victim |
| s | suspect |
| ph | phone |
| f | female |
| b | Black |
| a | Asian |
| DOB | date of birth |
| aka | also known as |
| p.m. | afternoon or evening |
| mo | month |
| min | minute |
| W | witness |
| mi | mile |
| yoa | years of age |
| m | male |
| w | White |
| nmi | no middle initial |
| tot | turned over to |
| tod | time of day *(IN010.2.F.)* |

When the first letters of the words "victim," "suspect," or "witness" are used as abbreviations, they should be circled to avoid confusion. Names for gender, ethnicity, and race are usually uppercase and separated by a slash: for instance, B/M (Black/male) or W/H/F (White/Hispanic/female).

# UNIT 5 | REPORT WRITING

## LESSON 3 | Organizing the Report

The officer must organize information obtained during the initial investigation of any case. This organization, or grouping of information, will make preparation of the report much easier and more efficient. When grouping information, it is advisable to start a new page for each new information source or subject. This may mean flipping notebook pages back and forth while writing, but the information will be easier to retrieve later.

**OBJECTIVES**

**IN010.2.I.** Identify how to organize notes.

**IN009.2.A.** Identify chronological ordering.

**IN009.2.B.** Identify categorical ordering.

**IN009.1.A.4.** Define *narrative.*

Notes can be organized in two ways: chronologically or by category. The most efficient way to organize notes is by grouping all information pertaining to or received from each individual *(IN010.2.I.)*. When using this system, the officer lists all victim information before witness or suspect information.

Organizing chronologically means sorting information by date and time from the first event to the last *(IN009.2.A.)*. Chronologically ordering information is especially useful when writing a narrative. Readers can readily tell what happened, when, and in what order.

Information may also be grouped by category such as witnesses, victims, suspects, weapons used, and crime elements *(IN009.2.B.)*. This type of ordering helps with filling in information on report forms, most of which group information by category. If notes are organized by category before a report is written, the risk of forgetting a piece of information is minimized. The practice is especially helpful for incidents that involve many witnesses or victims.

**Section Vocabulary**

***narrative***

The information collected from interviews, statements, and notes will next be transferred to the actual report. Before a report can be put into a narrative form, however, the officer must review and organize the information so that it best fits the purpose of the report.

## Reviewing Notes

Once an officer has gathered the applicable forms and organized the notes, he or she is ready to write the report. The first step is to review the field notes to make sure that all the specific facts are available. If pertinent facts are missing, the officer should obtain them. For example, if a victim's date of birth is missing, the officer should contact him or her to obtain it.

Report writing is much more than filling in the blanks on a preprinted form. The largest and most important part of most reports is the ***narrative***. A narrative can be defined as paragraphs containing specific details and pertinent information about an incident and the elements of the crime *(IN009.1.A.4.)*. Normally, narratives are written in a chronological sequence.

# UNIT 5 | REPORT WRITING

## LESSON 4 | Elements and Principles of Effective Report Writing

The report must be a complete representation of the facts that omits unnecessary verbiage and irrelevant material. A well-written report projects an image of professional competence.

**OBJECTIVES**

**IN009.3.B.** Identify the elements of report writing.

**IN009.4.A.4.** Identify which verb tense should be used in reports.

### Elements of an Effective Report

As the officer works on each step of report writing, he or she must keep in mind the following nine elements of an effective report. All reports must be as follows:

- factual
- clear
- concise
- complete
- accurate
- written in Standard English
- grammatically and structurally correct
- legible
- timely *(IN009.3.B.)*

### Factuality

A report must be factual. An officer must not intentionally alter any information about an incident. Doing so is considered falsifying a report and is a criminal offense.

Only the facts of the incident should be reported: where, when, who, what, how, and why; personal opinions, judgments, hunches, or guesses should never be included in a report. For example, consider this sentence in a report: "Sandra appeared upset." Different people might have different opinions of what appearing "upset" might mean. It would be best to state in the report, "Sandra's hands were shaking, and she was wiping tears from her face" and avoid drawing a conclusion about her emotional state.

An officer cannot merely write in a report that "The victim fears for her safety." A defense attorney might ask the officer why he or she believed the victim was afraid. Because the officer did not document what the victim said that indicated she feared for her safety, the officer might not be able to accurately testify about it.

A report should include the actions of all officers, witnesses, suspects, and victims involved in an incident. All sides of the story must be reported. Even if a witness's information is contradictory, each witness's account should be included. Officers should be careful, however, to avoid unnecessary or ambiguous information, as well as emotional, sarcastic, humorous, or opinionated content.

## Clarity

The report must be clear, allowing only one interpretation of the meaning of each sentence. This can be accomplished by using plain and straightforward language. Abbreviations may be used while taking notes; however, they should not be used in the narrative. It is acceptable to omit the race or gender of a person in the narrative when that information is documented in the victim/suspect/witness description boxes on the appropriate form.

When referring to an individual for the first time, an officer should give the individual's full name. In later references, the officer should be sure the individual is properly identified. Consistency helps prevent confusing the readers. For example, the first reference might be "Victim Jane Doe"; subsequent references would simply be "victim." Agency procedure should be followed for referring to victims, witnesses, or suspects in reports. If agency policy does not address this issue, the officer must comply with the requirements of the applicable State Attorney's Office.

## Conciseness, Completeness, and Accuracy

It is important to be concise and to the point, avoiding use of unnecessary words, but not being so brief that the report is inaccurate or incomplete.

It is important to review field notes to ensure that all pertinent information has been included. All the facts, whether favorable or unfavorable to anyone or anything, should be reported. The officer should remember that if it is not in the report, it did not happen.

To ensure accuracy, all relevant facts and specific details in the field notes must be included in the report. The facts must be correct as obtained through interviews and investigation.

## Use of Standard English

It is acceptable to use jargon, slang, and abbreviations when taking notes as long as the officer knows what it means. However, slang in report writing is not acceptable. Reports must be written in Standard English only. In many cases, the defense will try to discredit the investigating officer and the report is the officer's greatest strength or weakness.

***Jargon*** is the technical vocabulary of a particular profession that has meaning specific to people who work in that field. For example, AKA, DOA, or "smash and grab" are terms familiar to law enforcement officers but might be unfamiliar to civilians. ***Slang*** consists of informal, nonstandard words often characterized by regional or specific group usage. Examples might include "tight," "da bomb," "trippin'," and "my bad." Except when quoting witnesses, slang has no place in a police report. The terms "***improper***" or "***misused***" most often refer to words that are easily confused in use or spelling. Examples are words that sound the same but are spelled differently, such as "there/their/they're" or "to/too/two" and words that sound similar but have different meanings such as "accept/except."

Here are some examples of common jargon, slang, misused, and inappropriate words that have been used in law enforcement reports and their preferred alternatives. Many of these words may be familiar:

| Jargon | Better Wording |
|---|---|
| advised | told |
| altercation | fight |
| at this time | now |
| blue in color | blue |
| exited | left; got out |
| maintained surveillance | watched |
| noted | saw |
| notified | told |
| observed | saw |
| utilize | use |
| verbalized | said |

Jargon and its preferred alternative *Figure 3-2*

The following exercises are intended to help students practice replacing jargon with better words or phrases that have the same meaning and help students hone their proofreading abilities. These are skills that will be needed when editing reports.

*Correct the following exercises using Standard English grammar rules; make sure the exercise is free of jargon and slang.*

## Exercise 1

On March 3, 2008, at approximately 1500, this officer observed Jack Pollon proceed to operate a 1999 blue in color Oldsmobile bearing Florida license plate number FTS 134. this officer initiated a traffic stop on the vehicle after this officer observed it improperly backing into traffic. I asked Mr. Pollon for his registration and driver's license. He blew me off and ignored my request by stating he did not have to show me this information if he did not want to. I told him he needed to get his act together quickly and requested the pertinent information again. He again refused to comply with my request. I detected the strong odor of an alcoholic beverage. Mr. Pollon was asked by me if he had consumed any alcoholic beverages. He said yeah so I told him to get out of the car and he did. The field sobriety exercises were conducted by me. Mr. Pollon failed the field sobriety exercises. this officer placed him under arrest and transported him to the St. Johns' County criminal holding facility. The breath test was administered to him. The result was .10.

## *Exercise 2*

> On 16 Feb 08 at 1220 hours this officer responded to 2615 Airport Av Apt 65, Ponte Vedra Beach, reference a disturbance. Upon arrival, this officer scoped out what sounded like a loud verbal dispute emanating from within the home. Subsequently, this officer made contact with the owner of the dwelling, Doris Wardley, to assure the safety of anyone inside the apt. The defendant advised that her TV was on and that what this officer heard was a movie on TV. The defendant appeared confrontational and hostile to this officer's presence. The defendant told this officer to go cruise the block and dog out yo' buddy and attempted to shut the door in this officer's face with great force. this officer detected a strong odor that this officer recognized as marijuana coming from within the apt. this officer asked s1 if she had any illegal narcotics on her person. At stated time def provided a pack of rolling papers and a small baggie containing a green leafy substance from her right pant pocket. Such substance was tested using a dept issued kit. The examination results were presumptive positive for cannabis. Subj was placed under arrest and advised on her Mirandi Rights. Def was transported to the slammer by this officer.

Reports must be concise yet detailed. "I saw Charles Baker running northbound on 1st Street" is better than "I observed the defendant fleeing the scene in a northerly direction." If a witness, victim, or suspect uses jargon, slang, vulgar, inappropriate, or offensive language, report exactly what was said using quotation marks.

People could interpret the statement "Jim became uncooperative and belligerent" in different ways. The officer should have documented the actions of the suspect without adding personal interpretations of the suspect's actions. A better statement might have been, "Jim stood in front of me in a fighting stance. He pulled his right arm away from me when I attempted to handcuff him. Jim then said to me, 'I'm not going anywhere!'"

# Grammar, Structure, and Legibility

A report must contain proper spelling, grammar, and structure. When writing the report, the officer must also print clearly and legibly. Unless the officer's agency specifies otherwise, black or dark blue ink should be used for clear legibility and photocopy quality. Letters must be formed clearly and distinctly. In some cases, writing in all capital letters is a good alternative to bad penmanship, though agency instructions must be followed regarding their use. A perfectly written report is useless if no one can read it.

# Timeliness

The report should be completed as soon as possible after an incident occurs to avoid forgetting important details. If the report is prepared immediately, recalling important facts that were not recorded in the field notes will be easier.

The responding officer should be prepared to write the report and turn it in by the end of his or her assigned shift unless agency policy states otherwise. If further investigation is required, supplemental reports will be written and submitted as required. Some agencies allow officers to work overtime to complete reports; others do not. Late reports can hinder other operations, impede investigations, and delay prosecution preparations. If an officer takes too long writing a report, other officers may be forced to answer calls within his or her zone. This places a burden on the other officers and reduces the availability of law enforcement response. With practice and experience, an officer can complete accurate reports quickly and efficiently.

## Principles of Clear Report Writing

**Point of View:** Reports may be written in the first or third person, depending on agency policy.

first person: "I saw," "I spoke," "I arrived."

third person: "The officer saw," "The officer spoke," "The officer arrived."

**Voice:** Officers should write reports in active, rather than passive, voice. In active voice, the subject of the sentence acts: "Ann struck John with a frying pan." In passive voice, actions are done to the subject of the sentence: "John was struck with a frying pan by Ann." Use passive voice only when the actor is unknown or when the person acted on is more important than the person committing the action.

**Tense:** Law enforcement reports are about events that have already occurred, so they are always written in past tense *(IN009.4.A.4.)*. It is important to make sure that proper verb tenses are used. Writing in active voice does not mean that the writer must write in present tense. "Ann struck John with a frying pan" exemplifies active voice, past tense, and proper language for reports. "Ann strikes John with a frying pan," in contrast, is written in active voice and present tense, and is improper.

**Section Vocabulary**

***improper or misused words***

***jargon***

***slang***

# UNIT 5 | REPORT WRITING

## LESSON 5 | Content and Format

**OBJECTIVES**

**IN009.1.A.1.** Identify the differences between content and format.

**IN009.1.A.2.** Explain the importance of addressing all elements of a crime.

**IN009.1.A.3.** Identify the elements of the preferred method for structuring a report.

**IN009.1.A.5.** Identify the questions a report narrative must answer.

An effective report will have good content and will be written in the proper format. Content relates to the material aspects of the case: what happened, who was involved, etc. Format is the way this information is organized and presented in the report. *(IN009.1.A.1.)*

### Proper Identification of the Statute and Elements of the Crime

Officers must properly identify the correct name and number of the criminal statute violated. If the narrative accurately describes and outlines the elements of a crime, but it is not the crime listed as the classification on the offense report, the entire content of the report can be called into question. *(IN009.1.A.2.)*

### Introduction, Body, and Conclusion

To present a clear narrative, a report must contain an introduction, body, and conclusion. The opening usually includes the date, place, assignment and arrival time, the officer's name, the identity of the victim, suspect, or complainant, and the officer's first action. The body of the narrative is the detailed chronological account of the incident. This section includes the investigative actions taken by the officer and must address the elements of the crime. The closing explains how the incident was resolved or how the information obtained was handled, including any citations issued or arrests made with appropriate criminal charges documented. *(IN009.1.A.3.)*

Simply because a report typically contains three sections does not mean the officer should limit him- or herself to one paragraph per section. Often, the body of the report may contain two or more paragraphs, depending on the complexity of the case and the number of persons involved.

The content of the narrative should answer four key questions:

**1. Why was the officer there?**

Was the officer dispatched to a call at the location?

Was the officer flagged down while on patrol?

Did the officer see something occur while on patrol?

**2. What did the officer observe?**

What did the officer see, hear, smell, or feel?

What were the crime scene conditions?

What was the officer told by people at the scene?

Who else responded to the scene?

**3. What did the officer do?**

What investigative steps did the officer take?
What actions did the officer perform (CPR, Response to Resistance)?
Whom did the officer interview?
Whom did the officer notify about the situation?
Did the officer collect any evidence?

**4. What were the outcomes?**

What crimes were committed?
Did the officer arrest anyone?
What related documents were collected or disseminated?
Were any further actions or referrals required? *(IN009.1.A.5.)*

## UNIT 5 | REPORT WRITING

## LESSON 6 | Mechanics

Many people consider content (what the report says) to be more important than form (how it is written). However, grammar, punctuation, and spelling are equally important elements of a quality report. Even if the content reflects a good investigation, numerous mechanical errors will detract from the message and reflect poorly on the writer's competence.

**OBJECTIVES**

**IN009.4.A.1.** Define *sentence.*

**IN009.3.A.1.** Define *sentence fragment.*

**IN009.3.C.2.** Identify tools that can be used to reduce spelling errors.

**IN009.3.A.2.** Identify the rules of punctuation.

**IN009.3.C.1.** Identify the steps of evaluating a written report.

### Developing a Good Vocabulary

It is important for every officer's professional development to have a good vocabulary. As an officer encounters words and phrases that he or she may not know, he or she should take the time to find their meanings and proper usage. Improving his or her vocabulary will enable an officer to be more efficient in report writing and better able to accurately describe what he or she needs to document. An officer's writing will then be more concise and precise. An effective report should exhibit the writer's command of the language and be free of errors in sentence structure, grammar, and other writing mechanics.

### Proper Grammar

Grammar is defined as the rules and guidelines used by writers to make their messages clear and understandable to the reader. There are many grammatical rules in English.

Police officers should be aware of those rules recommended for use when writing reports. Recognizing the parts of speech and using them properly makes for streamlined and effective reports.

| Part of Speech | Description | Examples |
|---|---|---|
| **Noun** | Names, persons, places, things, actions, qualities, beliefs | The **officer** stopped the **car**.<br>The **subject** fled from the **officers**. |
| **Pronoun** | Acts as a substitute for a noun | **They** stopped the car.<br>**He** ran from **them**. |
| **Verb** | Expresses action, events, states of being | The officer **ran** after the subject.<br>The subject **was** fast. |
| **Adverb** | Describes, identifies, or quantifies a verb, adjective, or other adverb | The subject ran **quickly**.<br>He became **extremely** exhausted. |
| **Adjective** | Describes a noun or a pronoun | The **heavyset** man was the subject.<br>The **short** woman was also running. |
| **Preposition** | Links words and phrases and provides temporal, spatial, and logical relationships | The subject jumped **out** of the car, went **over** the retaining wall, and ran **into** the store. |
| **Conjunction** | Connects words with other words, clauses (parts of sentences), and ideas | Officer Russ **and** I approached the car.<br>I covered the car **while** he made contact with the subject. |

Parts of speech *Figure 3-3*

## Proper Sentence Structure

A ***sentence*** is a group of words that contains a subject (a noun) and a verb (action) and expresses a complete thought (*IN009.4.A.1.).* The subject and verb in each sentence must be consistent or "agree" in number. A singular subject must have a singular verb, and a plural subject must have a plural verb.

For example, "They are brothers" is correct since the subject "They" is more than one or plural and the verb "are" is also plural. "They is brothers" is incorrect because the singular verb "is" does not agree with the plural subject, "They." As noted previously, correct verb tenses must also be used. For example, an officer should write, "I saw the subject," not "I seen the subject," or "I see the subject."

Understanding the parts that make up a simple sentence will aid an officer in writing proper sentences. The *subject* of a sentence denotes what or who performs an action; the *verb* expresses action, existence, or state of being of the subject while the *object* conveys what or who is affected or receives the action of the verb.

| **John** | **hit** | **Monica.** |
|---|---|---|
| *subject* | *verb* | *object* |

Sentence structure *Figure 3-4*

A ***sentence fragment*** is a group of words that lacks a subject or verb or fails to express a complete thought *(IN009.3.A.1.).* Fragments such as "Witnessed a bank robbery in progress while on patrol" should be avoided. Because the sentence has no subject, it is unclear who witnessed the robbery. "The gun on the floor next to the body" should be "The gun was lying on the floor next to the body" or "I saw the gun lying on the floor next to the body." Officers should remember that incorrect grammar and sentence structure can affect the accuracy of a report and damage their credibility.

# Correct Spelling and Capitalization

Words in police reports should be spelled correctly. If using a computer to write a report, the officer should use the spell check feature. It is important to remember, however, that the spell check feature does not indicate whether the correct word has been used, only if a word has been misspelled. "The thief took there money" would not be flagged by spell check. Having another person proofread a report will help ensure that correct words have been used. If unsure of the spelling of a word, an officer should consider using a different word. Instead of "penitentiary," an officer might use "prison"; instead of "contusion," the officer could use "bruise." If an officer handwrites a report, he or she should use a dictionary. If carrying a dictionary is awkward, the officer should consider buying an electronic dictionary to use while on patrol. *(IN009.3.C.2.)*

Whichever method an officer chooses to check spellings, the officer should use it consistently during the entire evaluation process. Some agencies will recommend or require the use of all capital letters in reports. When not using all capitals, the following capitalization rules apply:

1. Capitalize names of persons, cities, states, and streets. "I spoke with the victim, Greg Alexander, at his house on 999 Monroe Street in Tallahassee, Florida."

2. Capitalize names of specific organizations and buildings.

   "The neighborhood meeting will be held at the city hall." (nonspecific)

   "The Oakbrook Neighborhood Association meeting will be held at the Tallahassee City Hall." (specific)

3. Capitalize days, months, and holidays. "Independence Day is on Saturday, July 4th."

4. Capitalize geographic locations.

   "She is from the South." (specific region or location)

   "I drove south on Monroe Street." (direction)

5. Capitalize titles of professionals only when names are used.

   "I stopped the chief's daughter for speeding." (chief not named)

   "I stopped Chief Smith's daughter for speeding." (chief named)

6. Capitalize brand names. "Mr. Jones reported that his Smith & Wesson revolver had been stolen."

## Proper Punctuation

Improper punctuation can result in confusing or even misleading reports. The comma is probably the most commonly misused punctuation mark. Commas are not inserted whenever the writer desires a pause. There are specific rules covering the use of commas:

1. Use a comma to separate two complete sentences joined by a coordinating conjunction (and, but, or, nor, for, yet, or so).

   "I met with the victim, and she gave me a statement." (correct)

   "I met with the victim and she gave me a statement." (incorrect)

   If the two complete sentences are not joined by a coordinating conjunction, use semicolon or period to separate them.

   "I met with the victim, she gave me a statement." (incorrect)

   "I met with the victim; she gave me a statement." (correct)

   "I met with the victim. She gave me a statement." (correct)

2. Use a comma after an introductory clause.

   "When the alarm sounded, the burglar ran from the store."

3. Use a comma to separate items in a series of three or more items.

   "The victim said his digital camera, television, DVD player, radio, and computer were stolen."

4. Use a comma to separate nonrestrictive (unimportant) phrases in a sentence. A phrase is a group of words that forms a grammatical unit, though not necessarily a complete sentence; it is considered nonrestrictive when no pertinent information is lost without it.

   "The fingerprints, which I found on the window, belong to the victim."

5. Use a comma between two or more adjectives that are not joined by "and" or "or" when they precede the noun.

   "The inmate used a small, metal object to cut his own arm."

6. Use a comma to introduce a quote.

   "When I arrested her, she said, 'I'm going to burn his house down when I get out.'"

7. Use a comma when writing dates and addresses.

   "The first robbery occurred on January 12, 2008, at 345 Monroe Street, Tallahassee, Florida." *(IN009.3.A.2.)*

Another misused punctuation mark is the apostrophe. An apostrophe is generally used to show possession or to create a contraction. Possession means that certain objects or qualities belong to a person or thing. A contraction is the result of combining two words; however, contractions should not be used in law enforcement reports. The following examples demonstrate proper apostrophe usage:

> "Officer Blair put the suspect's property in the trunk of the car before taking him to the jail."

> "An officer's size and skill are factors to consider in making a decision to use force."

Sometimes, a person's exact words may need to be used in an offense report. If using a direct quote, the officer should be sure to place quotation marks around the person's words. Quotation marks should not be used when paraphrasing a person's statement. For example, if the officer asked Keith Roberts whether an officer could search his car and Keith agreed, the officer should write in the report narrative: Keith Roberts said, "Go ahead and search." Because the officer is reporting Keith Robert's exact words, the officer must use quotation marks. However, if the officer states in the report, Keith Roberts gave me permission to search his car, quotation marks are not needed. Using a direct quote in this case documents that the officer received permission to make a lawful search of the vehicle.

## Evaluating the Report

Once the report has been written, it must be evaluated. The officer should take the time to carefully examine the content of the report. After looking at the entire report, the officer should correct any mechanical errors he or she has noticed. *(IN009.3.C.1.)*

During the evaluation, the officer should make sure that all pertinent facts from field notes are included and the information is correctly copied onto the appropriate report form in a complete, accurate, and organized manner. Replace unnecessarily passive sentences with active ones. The narrative should flow logically from one sentence to the next and should not be choppy. When possible, ask another officer to proofread the report before it is submitted.

### *Specific Steps in the Evaluation Process*

To review the report for content, officers should check to see if all content (the who, what, when, where, why, and how) is included and all elements of the crime are listed. All proper procedures must be documented, and BOLO notifications, case cards, victims/witness pamphlets, and DV information must be included.

To evaluate for errors, the following should be considered:

- **spelling:** Not only do all words need to be spelled correctly, but also the proper forms of words should be used.
- **grammar:** Verb tenses need to agree, and sentence structure should be correct. Whenever possible and proper, sentences should be written in active voice.
- **punctuation:** All possessives should be properly noted. All periods, commas, exclamation points, apostrophes, etc. should be included.
- **capitalization:** All appropriate words should be capitalized.

**Section Vocabulary**

*sentence*

*sentence fragment*

To analyze for clarity, officers should consider if the report flows properly and makes sense, and whether it is written in complete sentences. They should also check to see if any information needs to be added or subtracted and if the information will be clear to anyone who reads it. Necessary changes should be made and the report should be submitted in a timely fashion according to agency policy.

# CHAPTER 4

## Human Issues



Crisis intervention is a primary aspect of a law enforcement officer's job. Officers must know the different types of crisis situations that they could encounter when responding to a call. The correct response to a crisis may require providing appropriate management, intervention, and referral for individuals. Law enforcement officers must be able to recognize the issues specific to individuals in various situations involving a crisis in their life. People facing difficult and stressful problems may choose to use drugs, alcohol, or display dangerous behaviors, such as attempting to commit suicide. Individuals with physical and developmental disabilities, mental illness, or mental retardation may require special assistance. There are legal obligations when providing intervention, referral information, and transportation during a crisis situation.

# UNIT 1 | CRISIS INTERVENTION

## LESSON 1 | Responding to a Crisis Situation

**OBJECTIVES**

**IN007.2.B.2.** Identify types of crises.

**IN007.2.B.3.** Identify behaviors of persons in crisis.

**IN007.1.** Notify communications center on arrival.

**IN007.2.** Identify the need to position self safely according to officer safety techniques.

**IN007.4.A.2.** Identify techniques that may be used to stabilize the crisis situation.

**IN007.4**. Interview the person to identify the problem during a crisis situation.

**IN007.5.** Determine intervention options for handling a person during a crisis situation.

**IN007.7.A.** Identify if the person needs to be removed from a crisis situation.

**IN022.1.A.1.** Identify when referrals are required by Florida Statutes.

**IN007.6.** Identify services and agencies that are appropriate for an individual during a crisis situation.

**IN007.7.** Provide appropriate transportation or transport if the person needs to be removed from the situation.

**IN007.9.** Document incident in a report.

### The Role of Law Enforcement in Crisis Intervention

Crisis intervention is one of the most important duties of law enforcement officers. Without the help of law enforcement officers, a person in crisis might have no assistance. Each intervention, therefore, is important to the person in crisis, to his or her family, and to the community.

Officers are sworn to protect all citizens, and this obligation includes assisting with critical social issues, such as domestic disturbances. Law enforcement must respond to these incidents because employees of social service agencies are not trained to enter extreme crisis situations. Officers have the authority to act when other agencies cannot; as a result, law enforcement is often the first responder to individuals in crisis. During a crisis situation, officers have the duty to recognize and respond to persons in crisis; intervene safely, professionally, and effectively in a crisis; interact with community agencies to coordinate and resolve conflicts; and make referrals to appropriate agencies.

### Types of Crises

A ***crisis*** may be a situation or period that is very uncertain, difficult, or painful, especially when action must be taken to avoid complete disaster or breakdown. However, a crisis is also defined by the person's perception and response to the event. If the person sees the event as significant and threatening, has used all personal coping strategies without effect, and is unaware of or unable to pursue other alternatives, a state of crisis exists.

Crises can add stress to an individual's life or to an entire community. There are significant crises that nearly everyone may experience at some time: The death of a spouse or other loved one, a financial loss, termination from a job, separation from family and friends, or the beginning of retirement may create a crisis. *(IN007.2.B.2.)*

A crisis may be compounded by economic, personal, and social factors such as how the crisis affects a person's self-image and community standing, psychological factors, and physical factors. These factors are significant to the severity of the crisis and in determining how a person reacts to various situations.

For example, the severity of the crisis created by a job loss will depend on economic, personal, social, and psychological factors. The person may not have much in savings and slim prospects of finding another job before the next mortgage and car payments are due. The person may consider the job loss to be a personal insult to his or her professional ability or be embarrassed in front of family and friends.

On the other hand, loss of a job may not be an economic issue for someone who has savings and the prospect of finding another job soon.

## Behavioral Characteristics of Persons in Crisis

A person's sense of well-being can be disrupted during an emergency or other stressful event. If that well-being is not restored quickly, a crisis situation can result. The goal of crisis intervention is to provide assistance to the person in distress.

Some people in crisis may display behavioral characteristics including verbal anger, such as cursing, threats and shouting; and physical signs, such as a flushed face, heavy, rapid breathing, clenching and unclenching fists, pacing, pointing fingers, tightening the lips, clenching the teeth, or sweating. Others may appear calm. The effect of the crisis and stress may cause a diminished capacity for thinking and decision making. *(IN007.2.B.3.)*

## Stages of a Crisis

In the recognition stage, the person realizes he or she is unable to cope with the situation. Life is out of control, emotions are high, and reasoning ability is low. Emotions may range from anger to rage, from fear to panic, all leading to confusion.

In the attempted resolution stage, the person struggles to resolve the situation using methods that worked in previous situations. However, these methods may not work now. The person's failure to resolve the problem leads to the emotional blockage stage of crisis response. In this stage, the person is unable to solve the crisis and is overwhelmed by emotions. The individual cannot cope with the situation rationally. The inability to cope with the loss of problem-solving skills leads to diminished self-esteem. A downward cycle begins in which failure to cope lowers self-esteem, and lowered self-esteem interferes with ability to cope.

During the accommodations stage, the person in crisis is open to suggestion and is willing to try new options. He or she may begin to explain what the situation personally means and start to find answers. A solution is achieved at the resolution stage.

## Responding to the Call

Law enforcement officers receive crisis calls in various ways. Calls can be dispatched from the communications center or an officer may observe a crisis situation while on patrol. Crisis calls can even develop out of another call.

As with any call, the officer should notify the communications center upon arrival at the scene. The officer should get as much information as possible from the dispatcher (also known as a public safety telecommunicator) to help ensure safe arrival at the scene, such as the exact location and nature of the call, any weapons involved, the number of people involved, and the name of the person who called. If the officer observes changes at the location, it is important for him or her to update the communications center. *(IN007.1.)*

### *Entering the Scene*

A low-profile arrival will maximize officer safety and minimize officer vulnerability. There are certain techniques an officer should employ when initially assessing the scene. The officer should proceed as quickly and safely as is possible, and if emergency equipment (such as overhead lights and siren) is used, he or she should turn it off when nearing the scene. The officer should not drive by or park directly in front of the call location but should take note of double-parked vehicles and the number of people in the area. Officers should observe other signs of activity out of the ordinary. If not already dispatched backup should be requested. After assessing the situation, the officer should enter the scene safely and approach with due caution, look for cover and concealment, and survey entrances, exits, and grounds.

When entering a building to respond to a crisis call, officers should remember that someone could be lying in wait to ambush or kill them. Officers should stand to one side of the doorway to ensure safety, knock, and wait to be admitted. When someone answers the door, an officer should identify him- or herself and state the purpose for being there. The officer should visually assess the scene and note the number of people in the room, as well as the location of their hands and their expressions. The officer should also scan for hazards such as possible weapons, dangerous pets, or possible hiding places. The officer should position him- or herself in visual alignment with the door in case someone enters. *(IN007.2.)*

## Assessing the Crisis Situation

Immediately upon arrival, the officer should assess the subject's physical, intellectual, emotional, and risk status. The officer should determine if the person is sick or injured, is under the influence of drugs or alcohol, or has committed or been the victim of a crime.

Some crisis situations may involve a person who is disoriented, incoherent, unfocused, or behaving abnormally. The person may not respond to the officer or may appear to be "out of it." Such a person may be under the influence of drugs or alcohol or have a medical condition, and the officer should request additional assistance from EMS.

## Managing the Scene During a Crisis Situation

The officer must manage victims, witnesses, and suspects during a crisis situation. Depending on his or her personal attitude and behavior, the officer can defuse or escalate a situation. Crises may become more volatile if the officer injects his or her personal mood, bias, or prejudice. In helping to manage a crisis situation, the officer may use various techniques to stabilize and maintain control. While speaking with the people involved, the officer should maintain eye contact while maintaining awareness of proximity and officer safety issues. It is also essential to always know the location of a partner and backup. The goal is to restore or maintain order. People should be separated and removed from crowds if necessary. Any immediate threats should be dealt with first, before assisting any individuals.

The officer may need to calm the person in crisis or other individuals who are in conflict. Physically separating the disputing parties can reduce tension and calm the situation. Visual separation breaks eye contact between disputants and refocuses disputants' attention on the officer; it also restricts verbal insults and body language. When using visual separation, officers should maintain eye contact among themselves. An officer's body, a partition, or a doorway can be used for visual separation. Officers should avoid separating a hearing-impaired person from his or her interpreter. Asking disputants to be seated can reduce physical tension and calm a situation. Due to safety concerns, the officer should direct persons to specific seats. This reduces disputants' mobility and limits their access to weapons, exits, or other disputants.

When trying to calm an angry individual or defuse a situation, the officer should keep in mind the concepts of proximity and personal space. Each individual may have different boundaries regarding personal space, and some people may become uncooperative or violent if the officer stands too close to them. People prone to violence or abuse may require additional personal space.

Noise has the ability to energize and arouse anxiety. Officers should be aware that lowering the noise level reduces tension and physically relaxes people. In order to reduce the noise level, the officer should ask bystanders to leave, and request that disputants talk more quietly. Turning off other noise sources such as music systems and televisions will help calm the situation.

An officer should give calm, direct instructions to guide others to complete what he or she wants them to do. Quietly speaking may calm disputants by forcing them to focus on the officer instead of the problem. It may also reduce the noise level if someone is yelling. When the officer speaks softly, people will have to pay special attention to hear what is being said. *(IN007.4.A.2.)*

## Gathering Information About the Crisis Situation

When the officer arrives at a crisis scene, many people may be present. As a result, the person experiencing the crisis may not be immediately obvious. The officer can identify the person in crisis through observation and by asking questions. Information about the crisis and its cause will be gathered primarily through interviews by the officer with witnesses. During the interview with the person in crisis, the officer should empathize, but avoid minimizing the situation. The officer should ask appropriate questions to help identify the problem and determine the proper intervention.

After establishing rapport with the subject by expressing genuine interest and concern, the officer should ask one question at a time, using simple vocabulary and sentence structure. The officer should ask open-ended questions that encourage conversation and explanation, and avoid closed-ended questions, such as "How many pills did you take?" Closed-ended questions focus only on obtaining an answer to a specific question. Asking "Why?" should also be avoided because it may put a person on the defensive. The officer should attempt to ask questions to clear up any vagueness or inconsistencies and center on a specific part of the situation to gain a better understanding of the problem. *(IN007.4.)*

## Intervention During the Crisis

Officers may use any of several types of intervention options when responding to a crisis situation. It is important for officers to be familiar with the different types of intervention to better understand the legal impact and ramifications of their decisions. Examples of intervention options include relocating the person to a safe environment, taking the person into custody if he or she has committed an arrestable offense, initiating an involuntary treatment referral via the Baker or Marchman Acts if criteria exist, making a referral for services, and arranging for or providing transportation as necessary. *(IN007.5.)*

Some crisis situations will require an officer to move an individual from the crisis area to a safe environment. The officer must determine if the person can remain independent and care for him- or herself or if the person is a threat to him- or herself or others. In some situations, the officer may have evidence that someone has been abused. Signs of physical abuse may include cuts, scratches, burns, redness of the skin, or bruises. The officer must decide if the person or persons involved must be removed from the situation for their own safety. *(IN007.7.A.)*

Sometimes, a referral is required by law. In certain cases of abuse, the law mandates the removal of the endangered persons and custodial arrest of the abuser. Crisis situations that involve domestic violence, child abuse, disabled adult or elder abuse, and suicide risks all require a referral. Officers are legally required to contact the Department of Children and Families (DCF) for cases involving abuse. Florida Statutes require that law enforcement follow appropriate agency policy and procedures to assist DCF *(IN022.1.A.1.).* This may involve forced entry, emergency removal or emergency transportation of victims, and the enforcement of court orders.

## Available Referral Services

To make a referral, an officer must identify which services will help the individual in crisis. This information can generally be obtained during the interview and through observation. After identifying the need for referral, the officer should locate a service agency. Service agencies are designed to meet the needs of individuals in crisis and assist law enforcement with referrals. A community resource directory describes service agencies by geographic area, the types of services available, eligibility criteria, and the process for obtaining services.

The referral agency will attempt to remove the cause of the crisis, reduce the extent of the crisis, or give the person alternative assistance for future crises. For example, an elderly neighbor living alone may be a concern to others. A referral to the senior center could provide daytime activities, companionship, and daily meals. Referral sources cover a wide range of service types from employment to medical assistance. Officers should become familiar with the agencies and services available within their communities in order to provide appropriate referrals. *(IN007.6.)*

## Transportation During a Crisis Situation

In addition to making a referral for services, the law enforcement officer may have to transport a person to another location. Each law enforcement agency has a memorandum of understanding with each receiving facility within the law enforcement agency's jurisdiction that reflects a single set of protocols for the safe and secure transportation of the person and transfer of custody to a responsible person. If there is an abused person in need of shelter, the officer needs to arrange or provide for special transport.

DCF is responsible for the safe placement of abused and neglected children, the elderly, and disabled adults. After DCF is contacted in an abuse or neglect case, an agency representative will coordinate with law enforcement to have the victim transported to a safe location. The officer should transport an individual who is being involuntarily committed to a treatment facility, assuming the person requires no medical attention. Provided the officer is not required to stay at the scene, he or she should also transport an arrested person to jail.

If a crime has been committed and the officer takes the suspect to jail, the victim may need to be transported to another location. In such a case, the officer should contact victim services, or provide or arrange for transportation to the appropriate facility. *(IN007.7.)*

## Documenting a Crisis Situation

Like most incidents in which a law enforcement officer becomes involved, crises must be documented, at least in a general incident report. The officer's agency may also require additional specialized reports or forms. Reports should be as detailed as possible and include the victim's and subject's statements, actions, reactions, physical condition, and appearance. Additional information should include witness statements, known medications, weapons involved, and the disposition. *(IN007.9.)*

**Section Vocabulary**

*crisis*

# UNIT 2 | DISABILITY AWARENESS

## LESSON 1 | Responding to Persons with Disabilities

### Americans with Disability Act (ADA)

To understand the requirements regarding effective interactions with persons with disabilities, a law enforcement officer must understand the ***Americans with Disabilities Act (ADA).*** The ADA is a federal civil rights law that prohibits discrimination against people with disabilities and requires common places used by the public to provide an equal opportunity for access.

According to the ADA, an individual with a disability is a person who has a physical or mental impairment that substantially limits a major life activity, has a record of such impairment, or is regarded as having such impairment *(IN006.1.I.6.).* ***Impairment*** is defined as any mental or physiological condition that impedes the completion of daily tasks using traditional methods. Examples of impairments are blindness, severe breathing limitation, deafness, inability to use arms or legs, paranoia, or schizophrenia.

***Major life activities*** include caring for oneself, performing manual tasks, walking, seeing, hearing, speaking, breathing, learning, and working. Other major life activities include sitting, standing, lifting, and mental and emotional processes such as thinking, concentrating, and interacting with others. According to the ADA, a ***substantial limitation*** is a restriction of the manner, condition, or duration in which major life activities are performed compared to nonimpaired people.

**OBJECTIVES**

**IN006.1.I.6.** Define *disability* according to the Americans with Disabilities Act.

**IN006.1.I.** Identify common types of disabilities.

**IN006.1.** Identify guidelines for responding to an individual with disabilities.

**IN006.2.B.3.** Identify basic information about protecting the rights of individuals with disabilities.

The most common ADA disabilities that law enforcement officers encounter are mental retardation, mental illness, and hearing, speech, mobility, and vision impairments. *(IN006.1.I.)*

Title II of the ADA states that no qualified individual with a disability shall be discriminated against or excluded from participation in or sharing the benefits of the services, programs, employment, or activities of a public entity.

Since a law enforcement agency is a public entity that provides state or local government services, Title II has an impact on an officer's daily duties and responsibilities. Some examples of these duties include receiving and responding to citizen complaints; interviewing suspects, victims, and witnesses; arresting, booking, and holding suspects; providing emergency medical services; enforcing laws; and providing assistance to citizens.

The ADA does not in any way prevent an officer from enforcing laws, but it affects how law enforcement officers interact with persons with disabilities. In fact, the law requires that officers provide the same level of services and enforce the laws equally for people with or without disabilities. Officers must be able to recognize people with disabilities and know how to interact appropriately.

## Guidelines for Responding to Individuals with Disabilities

Officers should be sensitive and aware of people's differences while demonstrating respect for their limitations. Adults should be treated like adults and not subjected to condescending or patronizing attitudes. People should never be dismissed or disregarded simply because they have a disability. An officer should treat a person with a disability the same way he or she treats others. An officer should speak directly to the individual instead of through a third person, even if an interpreter is needed. The officer should speak in a normal tone of voice unless the person has a hearing impairment. In that case, the officer should speak clearly and distinctly and write notes if necessary. Officers should be patient because it may take extra time for a person with a disability to say, do, or show something. The officer should never physically assist an individual with a disability without talking to him or her first. Help should only be offered if the need seems obvious. If assistance is requested, the officer should follow the person's instructions.

Some people with disabilities use a service animal as described in Florida Statute §413.08, such as a dog trained to assist them with daily activities. A service animal for a person with a hearing or mobility impairment may or may not wear an identifying harness or vest. The person may have documentation showing that the animal is a service animal; however, no certification is required under the law. In the event the person with a disability is arrested, the officer must arrange care for the service animal. It is preferable to place the animal with a family member, a friend, or even a kennel rather than calling animal control. *(IN006.1.)*

## Protecting the Rights of Individuals with Disabilities

Individuals with disabilities have the same rights as everyone else. Law enforcement officers must make sure to protect these rights. Some individuals with disabilities may not understand the *Miranda* rights as they are usually explained. This is particularly likely if the person is in a stressful situation or has a disability that affects the ability to communicate. The officer should explain the *Miranda* rights in terms the subject can understand, keeping in mind that the subject's vocabulary and understanding of the concept of "rights" might be limited.

Whenever possible, an officer should ensure that someone who knows the individual, such as a relative, friend, attorney, or agency staff member is present, and the officer should videotape the interview. The officer should inform the State Attorney's Office and document the disability in the interview report. *(IN006.2.B.3.)*

**Section Vocabulary**

***Americans with Disabilities Act (ADA)***

***impairment***

***major life activities***

***substantial limitation***

## UNIT 2 | DISABILITY AWARENESS

## LESSON 2 | Mental Illness and Mental Retardation

***Mental illness*** is a thought disorder and comes in a variety of forms; it is a person's prominent behavior presented as odd or bizarre acts, which negatively impact the person's life (Section 394.455(18), F.S.) *(IN006.1.E.3.).* Mental illness is not directly related to intelligence and occurs in people of all intellectual abilities.

Mental illness is addressed in Chapter 394, F.S. It may be temporary and usually occurs in early adulthood (late teens, early 20s) or middle adulthood (late 30s, early 40s). It does not necessarily interfere with intellectual abilities but requires psychiatric evaluation. In contrast with mental retardation, mental illness may be cured, managed, or treated with counseling or medication.

**OBJECTIVES**

**IN006.1.E.3.** Define *mental illness.*

**IN006.1.E.** Identify some common symptoms of mental illness disorders.

**IN006.1.F.** Identify the possible reasons a person may experience the symptoms associated with mental illness.

**IN006.5.** Identify the rights of a person with a mental illness.

**IN007.5.A.** Identify Baker Act criteria according to Ch. 394, F.S.

**IN006.7.D.** Identify the basic duties of an officer when dealing with a person in a mental health crisis.

### Thought Disorders

A person with mental illness may have a thought, mood, or personality disorder. It is common for an individual to have a combination of disorders. People with a thought disorder, such as schizophrenia are sometimes unable to accurately perceive reality. This inability is called psychosis, and the person may be referred to as psychotic.

An officer might observe symptoms of a thought disorder by listening to what the person says and noticing that the person's thoughts seem disorganized and not logically connected. An officer might also notice that as the person talks, he or she reports

**LE018.4.B.** Transport a person with mental illness.

**IN006.1.G.5.** Define *mental retardation.*

**IN006.1.G.3.** Identify the differences between mental illness and mental retardation.

**IN006.1.G.** Identify the characteristics of a person with mental retardation.

**IN006.2.B.** Identify facts to consider when responding to persons with mental retardation.

**IN006.6.** Identify resources available to assist the officer when responding to a person with mental retardation.

hearing or seeing things that are not present or are unreal. These are called hallucinations and delusions.

A ***hallucination*** is a sensory experience in which a person can see, hear, smell, taste, or feel something that is not there. For example, a hallucinating individual may hear voices or claim that bugs are crawling under his or her skin. ***Delusion*** is a false belief that is firmly held in spite of obvious proof or evidence to the contrary. For example, a delusional individual could believe that he or she is someone famous or is being followed by the CIA.

## Mood Disorders

Major depression and bipolar disorder are two common examples of mood disorders. Major depression is different than the brief, situational depressive episodes most people commonly experience with the loss of a loved one, loss of a job, or financial loss. The term "major depression" refers to a clinically diagnosed mental illness. The symptoms an officer observes in an individual with major depression may be severe and could have lasted for several weeks. The officer may notice such symptoms as profound feelings of sadness, uncontrollable crying, inability to concentrate, suicidal thoughts, or problems sleeping and eating.

Alternating episodes of depression and mania are the hallmark of a mental illness known as bipolar disorder (formerly known as manic-depressive illness). Mania is the opposite of depression. A person in a manic episode feels charged up, high, or excitable. Usually, people with mania have previously experienced one or more episodes of major depression. An officer may observe the following symptoms in a person experiencing a manic episode: loud, quick, uninterrupted speech, "racing" thoughts, fidgeting, and hyperactivity. Such a person is easily distracted or may have an exaggerated sense of self, powers, and abilities.

Anxiety is another mood disorder. Anxiety can range from mild to debilitating. Some people with anxiety problems can have panic attacks that are so severe they mimic a heart attack. During a panic attack, the person will likely experience rapid heartbeat, chest discomfort, sweating, tension, trembling, choking, and a feeling that something terrible is about to happen. An officer may observe the following symptoms in a person experiencing an anxiety disorder: excessive nervousness, tension, apprehension, excessive fear or anticipation of imminent danger, ritualistic behavior such as excessive hand washing, or flashbacks.

## Personality Disorders

Some people have psychological problems that manifest in serious and persistent behaviors. A ***personality disorder*** is a deeply ingrained, non-psychotic, inflexible pattern of relating, perceiving, and behaving, serious enough to cause distress or impaired functioning. Depending on the specific disorder, an individual may display anxious, fearful, dramatic, emotional, or erratic behavior.

Two types of personality disorders are antisocial and borderline. A person with antisocial personality disorder, also known as psychopathic or sociopathic disorder, has a lifelong pattern of behavior that violates rules, social norms, and the rights of others. Individuals with this disorder also seem to lack the capacity for empathy, guilt, and remorse.

The hallmark of borderline personality disorder is instability. People with borderline personality disorder often experience rapid and intense mood changes, typically involving angry, erratic, and impulsive behavior and quickly changing feelings toward themselves and others. *(IN006.1.E.)*

## Considerations when Dealing with Individuals with Mental Illnesses

A person may exhibit symptoms generally associated with mental illness for many reasons. Some medical conditions and the effects of certain substances mimic mental illness symptoms. People with mental illness who stop taking their medications will also be symptomatic. Medications help people with mental illnesses manage their symptoms, much like insulin helps a diabetic person manage the symptoms of diabetes. When taken as prescribed, medications benefit persons experiencing symptoms of mental illness.

People stop taking their medications due to some of the following factors: They do not believe they need it, or they experience intolerable side effects that outweigh the benefits of the medication. They may also lack the money necessary to get the prescriptions filled, the transportation to get the medications, or the support of family and friends. Previous experiences may cause them to distrust the mental health system, or they may be misinformed about the benefits of the medication. Also, people may feel that the medication is somehow harmful.

Other mental illness symptoms may be part of a slow, deteriorating process, such as the dementia associated with Alzheimer's disease. When observing a person who displays symptoms commonly associated with mental illness, an officer should consider the possibility that the situation may in fact be a medical emergency. *(IN006.1.F.)*

When responding to a call or disturbance involving a person who may have a mental illness, an officer's concerns are the same as in any other situation. He or she should determine the nature of the environment, setting, or context of the situation, what has happened, and who is involved.

When working with individuals with mental illnesses, an officer should keep in mind that they have specific patient rights provided by Florida statute. According to Florida Statute §394.459, people with mental illnesses have the right to be treated with dignity; to receive treatment in a timely manner; to receive the least restrictive treatment available; to receive express and informed patient consent and treatment; to receive the care and custody of their personal effects unless access to them is deemed inappropriate; and to receive quality treatment. *(IN006.5.)*

Law enforcement officers have the following response options available when dealing with a person in a mental health crisis: release, voluntary examination, involuntary examination under the Baker or Marchman Acts, and arrest.

## Release

After responding to a situation, an officer may decide that an individual with a mental illness can be released into the community. How the person interacts with the officer and with other persons on the scene and other relevant information will help the officer determine if release is the appropriate course of action. In making a release determination, an officer should consider if the person has a residence or stable housing, has an established support system within the community, is actively experiencing symptoms that are severe or impair the ability to function, or if the subject satisfies the criteria for protective custody or involuntary treatment.

## Voluntary Examination

If an individual is willing to seek treatment, the officer should ask him or her to submit to a voluntary examination. A ***voluntary examination*** is the decision by an individual to seek psychiatric evaluation for symptoms that may be due to a mental illness. The individual must be competent, able to make a decision, and at least 18 years of age.

## Baker Act/Involuntary Examination

The ***Baker Act*** provides for emergency service and temporary detention for evaluation and voluntary or involuntary short-term community inpatient treatment, if necessary.

### *Criteria for a Baker Act/Involuntary Examination Response (Section 394.463, F.S.):*

A person may be taken to a receiving facility for involuntary examination if there is reason to believe that he or she has a mental illness and because of his or her mental illness the person:

1. has refused voluntary examination after he or she has received conscientious explanation and disclosure of the purpose of the examination; **or**
2. is unable to determine for him- or herself whether examination is necessary; **and**
3. without care or treatment, the person is likely to suffer from neglect or refuses to care for him- or herself; such neglect or refusal poses a real and present threat of substantial harm to his or her well-being; and it is not apparent that such harm may be avoided through the help of willing family members or friends or the provision of other services; **or**
4. there is a substantial likelihood that without care or treatment the person will cause serious bodily harm to him- or herself or others in the near future, as evidenced by recent behavior. *(IN007.5.A.)*

The subject must be examined within 72 hours of arrival upon admission to a receiving facility (§394.463(2)(f), (g), F.S.). If that examination does not determine that the person meets the criteria for involuntary treatment under §394.467, F.S., the person must be released unless he or she consents to voluntary treatment.

## Arrest

If probable cause exists, the officer may decide that arrest is the most appropriate intervention for a person with a mental illness. If the subject is arrested for a misdemeanor, the officer should transport the individual to an appropriate receiving facility. Misdemeanor criminal charges can also be handled by a Notice to Appear, referral to the state attorney for issuance of an arrest warrant, or another action according to department policy. When a person who satisfies Baker Act criteria is taken into custody for a felony offense, he or she should be transported to jail, unless emergency medical treatment is necessary. At booking, the officer must notify the detention supervisor of the arrestee's mental illness and document the Baker Act criteria on the arrest advisory. *(IN006.7.D.)*

## Transporting a Person with a Mental Illness

If the subject agrees to a voluntary examination, he or she can be transported to the medical facility by family, friends, or support agency personnel (such as a case manager), a group home worker, a mobile crisis team, or the officer. When transporting a person for involuntary examination under the Baker Act, in addition to the normal incident report, the officer must complete a form called the Report of Law Enforcement Officer Initiating Involuntary Examination, commonly referred to as a BA-52. The officer is required to cite specific criteria under Florida statutes that make the individual eligible for involuntary examination. *(LE018.4.B. )*

## Mental Retardation

***Mental retardation*** means significantly sub-average general intellectual functioning, existing concurrently with deficits in adaptive behavior that manifests before the age of 18 and can reasonably be expected to continue indefinitely *(IN006.1.G.5.)*. A mental disability resulting from a head injury or disease is not considered mental retardation unless the affected person is less than 18 years old. For example, a child under the age of 18 who suffers severe brain damage from a fall is considered to have mental retardation, even if the child was of normal intelligence before the fall.

Mental retardation is not mental illness. Mental retardation is a lifelong condition and is addressed in Chapter 393, F.S. It is characterized by slow intellectual development and requires developmental evaluation. Mental retardation cannot be cured, but the individual's capabilities and independence may be enhanced. *(IN006.1.G.3.)*

### *Characteristics of Mental Retardation*

There are four levels of mental retardation: mild, moderate, severe, and profound. The majority of individuals with mental retardation are at the mild level of retardation, which may not be easily identifiable. They may cover up their disabilities to appear "normal." At the mild mental retardation level, people can learn academic and prevocational skills with special training and normally live and work within their community. They might not understand long-range consequences or be able to make appropriate choices, but they do sometimes realize when they have done something wrong.

Individuals with moderate mental retardation might also cover up their disabilities to appear "normal." They can learn functional academic skills and may be able to perform semiskilled work under supervised conditions. They can be independent in familiar surroundings but may be easily frustrated by unfamiliar surroundings and circumstances. These individuals might also have trouble describing events in chronological order. They might not understand cause and effect, and while they may understand that they have done something wrong, they may not grasp the significance of their actions. Individuals with severe mental retardation have very slow motor development and communication skills. While they may be able to care for their personal needs and contribute to their own self-maintenance, they are usually under someone else's care or supervision. Often, they will be the victims of a criminal act committed by caretakers or family.

**Section Vocabulary**

*Baker Act*

*delusion*

*hallucination*

*mental illness*

*mental retardation*

*personality disorder*

*voluntary examination*

Persons with profound mental retardation require constant care and supervision. They have slow motor development and minimal language development but can learn basic self-care skills. Like individuals with severe mental retardation, they too are sometimes victimized by their caretakers or family. *(IN006.1.G.)*

## Communicating with Persons with Mental Retardation

An officer should be aware that individuals with mental retardation are no more violent than other members of the population. They might need additional time to respond to questions, should be asked questions phrased in easily understood language, and be given clear, simple instructions. An officer should not ask questions about possible reasons for someone's behavior and should explain unfamiliar terms such as "lawyer," "right," and "evidence."

Individuals with mental retardation may not be able to distinguish between abstract and concrete thought. They might not understand civil rights, court proceedings, or punishment. They might plead guilty to crimes they did not commit. An officer should watch such interviewees for clues because they may be easily intimidated, eager to please, and generally in agreement with authority. *(IN006.2.B)*

## Intervention and Services

Persons with mental retardation usually begin receiving services early in life. A valuable resource is the Association of Retarded Citizens (ARC), which has offices located throughout the state. The local ARC office may be located within the county or in a neighboring county. ARC provides information and support to individuals and agencies working with persons with mental retardation. *(IN006.6.)*

# UNIT 2 | DISABILITY AWARENESS

## LESSON 3 | Physical and Developmental Disabilities

### Communication Disabilities

The two major types of communication disabilities are hearing impairments and speech impairments. People with hearing and speech disabilities are entitled to the same rights as others without such impairments. This includes the right to be heard, even if that means bringing in an interpreter. People with communication disabilities may not be excluded or segregated from services, denied services, or treated differently. *(IN006.5.C.)*

A ***speech impairment*** is a physiological condition that causes difficulty in producing sound or understanding language, including reading and writing. Common examples of speech impairments include stuttering and slurring of words.

A ***hearing impairment*** refers to any degree of hearing loss. The two classifications of hearing loss are hard of hearing and deafness. A person who is ***hard of hearing*** may suffer a hearing loss but not to the extent that he or she must rely on visual communication. Hearing aids may not improve the person's ability to understand words but may just increase the ability to hear sound. ***Deafness*** is a hearing loss of such severity that the individual must rely on visual tools such as writing, gestures, and lip-reading to communicate. *(IN006.1.H.2.)*

### Communicating with Individuals with Hearing Impairments

A large majority of Florida cases involving defendants who are hearing impaired are dismissed because of events occurring **before** *Miranda* rights are explained. This emphasizes the importance of officers understanding the communication problems associated with hearing impairments.

People with hearing impairments are generally very attentive to their surroundings. Their eyes must see what their ears cannot hear. They rely on nonverbal communication, usually watching every facial expression and movement. People with hearing impairments often indicate that they cannot hear by gesturing. They point to their ears or mouths, shake their heads no, or make some other movement to indicate that they do not understand. ***Lip-reading*** is the ability to understand what is being said by watching the lips, facial expressions, and body language of the other speaker. Lip-reading is the least effective form of visual communication. *(IN006.1.H.)*

English is generally a second language for many persons who are hearing impaired. When communicating with an individual with a hearing impairment, an officer should speak directly to the person, face to face, not from the side or the back of the person. If an interpreter is being used, the officer should still speak directly to the individual with

**OBJECTIVES**

**IN006.5.C.** Identify the rights of a person with a communication disability.

**IN006.1.H.2.** Define *hearing impairment, hard of hearing,* and *deaf.*

**IN006.1.H.** Identify indications of a hearing impairment.

**IN006.7.C.** Identify how to communicate with a person with a hearing impairment.

**IN006.3.C.** Identify the limitations of *Miranda* rights when dealing with a person who is deaf.

**IN006.3.** Identify when an interpreter may be required.

**IN006.1.I.1.** Define *mobility impairments* according to the Americans with Disabilities Act (ADA).

**IN006.1.I.7.** Identify points to remember when dealing with an individual who is mobility impaired.

**IN006.1.J.3.** Define *blindness* and *partially sighted.*

**IN006.2.D.** Identify special considerations an officer should make when dealing with a victim, witness, or suspect of a crime with a visual impairment.

**IN006.1.L.1.** Identify characteristics of autism.

**IN006.1.L.** Identify how to correctly respond to a call involving an individual with autism.

the hearing impairment and not to the interpreter. If the officer has trouble understanding the person's speech, he or she should feel free to ask the person to repeat what was said. If that does not work, the officer might ask the individual to use a pen and paper. If using a pen and paper to communicate, the officer should make the questions brief and clear and be sure to understand the response. All written communication should be saved. A person with a hearing impairment may move quickly to obtain a pen and paper. On a traffic stop, this may be a sudden movement towards the glove compartment. Aids such as a computer word processor, a Telecommunications Device for the Deaf (TDD), or an assistive listening device (sound amplifier with headphones) may also be used to help with communication. It is important to remember that some persons with hearing impairments may have poor balance and/or slurred speech and therefore may appear to be intoxicated. *(IN006.7.C.)*

The *Miranda* Rights for the Deaf should be supplied in writing and conveyed by a sign-language interpreter to the suspect's level of understanding. A person who is deaf and has a limited understanding of the English language cannot knowingly waive his or her rights unless the warning is given in his or her language. *(IN006.3.C.)*

1. You have the right to remain silent; anything you say or write can and will be used against you in a court of law;
2. You have the right to contact an interpreter and a lawyer and to have them present while you are being questioned;
3. If you wish the services of an interpreter, one will be provided to you upon request;
4. If you cannot afford to hire a lawyer, one will be appointed by the court to represent you before questioning, if you wish one.

The ADA requires an officer to ensure effective communication with individuals who are hearing impaired. Whether that requires a qualified sign-language interpreter or other communication aid such as a TDD depends on the nature of the communication, the needs of the requesting individual, and agency policy. The ADA also requires that law enforcement give primary consideration to the individual's expressed choice of communication assistance. An interpreter may be required in situations such as interviews, interrogations, arrests, *Miranda* rights advisory, court appearances, and trials. *(IN006.3.)*

Generally speaking, an officer should not rely on family members or friends to provide sign language interpretation. The information received may be biased. The officer should also avoid using children as interpreters. They may be unable to understand certain concepts or lack the vocabulary to translate. In a domestic dispute, children may favor one parent over the other. A qualified ***sign-language interpreter*** is a person who can both receive and express information and interpret it effectively, accurately, and impartially. This definition recognizes that some types of communication require more sophisticated interpreting skills than others do. Consider videotaping all exchanges with a subject who is hearing impaired.

## Mobility Impairments

The ADA defines ***mobility impairment*** as a functional limitation that affects one or more of a person's limbs. People with mobility impairment may have limited use of one or more of their extremities for walking, grasping, or lifting objects. Their movement from place to place may require reliance on a variety of artificial means and devices that range from braces, canes, crutches, and walkers to regular and motorized wheelchairs. Some individuals have limited hand stamina that restricts their hand control and performance of certain movements. *(IN006.1.I.1.)*

There are some special considerations to keep in mind when communicating with individuals who have a mobility impairment. An officer should maintain good eye contact. When speaking to someone in a wheelchair, an officer should sit down to enable the individual and the officer to be at the same eye level, if it is safe to do so. The officer should not assume that a person who has a mobility impairment needs assistance. Some activities may appear to be difficult, but the person may not need or want help. As a point of safety, an officer should wear disposable gloves when searching a wheelchair. If the officer must transport a person with a mobility impairment, he or she must follow agency policy and procedure. *(IN006.1.I.7.)*

## Vision Impairments

Vision impairment refers to a loss or partial loss of vision. There are several types and degrees of visual impairments. People who have visual impairments, such as blindness or partial sight, meet the ADA definition of disability.

The types of vision impairments that an officer will encounter most often are blindness and partial sight. ***Blindness*** is a functional loss of vision. This definition applies both to people who cannot see at all (are unable to distinguish light from dark) and people who have some vision in one or both eyes. In fact, 80 to 90 percent of people who are blind or visually impaired have some vision. ***Partial sight*** is a visual impairment in which, after correction, objects still look dim or out of focus. People with partial sight may not see color well or at all or may lack peripheral vision, but they can still see and even read with magnifiers or other aids. *(IN006.1.J.3.)*

An officer should make special accommodations for suspects, victims, and witnesses who are visually impaired. When people cannot see, they may be afraid. The officer should reassure a crime victim that the assailant is no longer present. A person with a visual impairment who is arrested must be given large-print versions of any written documents that require the suspect's signature or have the documents read to him or her. A witness with a visual impairment may provide useful and reliable nonvisual observations. People deprived of one sense often develop their four other senses to make up for the loss. Their nonvisual observations may assist with investigations. *(IN006.2.D.)*

## Developmental Disabilities

***Autism*** is a developmental disability that occurs in early childhood and continues throughout adulthood, and which may result in difficulties with learning, communication, and social interaction. Autism operates on a continuum from mild to severe. An individual with autism may experience certain communication challenges. He or she may be nonverbal or have limited verbal skills, may not respond to commands or questions from strangers, may repeat words or phrases, and may have difficulty expressing his or her needs.

An individual with autism may display behaviors such as throwing tantrums or showing extreme distress for no apparent reason. They may flap their hands, rock themselves, or exhibit attachment to objects, and they may laugh, giggle, or ignore someone's presence. They may also avoid eye contact. Autism may cause an individual to be extremely sensitive to lights, sounds, and touch, but it may also cause them to appear insensitive to pain. It may also appear that they have no real fear of danger. *(IN006.1.L.1.)*

## Section Vocabulary

***autism***

***blindness***

***deafness***

***hard of hearing***

***hearing impairment***

***lip-reading***

***mobility impairment***

***partial sight***

***sign-language interpreter***

***speech impairment***

An individual with autism may experience certain limitations when interacting with law enforcement officers. For example, the person may not understand rights or warnings, may become anxious in new situations, may not understand the consequences of his or her actions, or may provide a false confession or misleading statement.

When responding to a call involving a person with autism, it is important to remember that each individual is unique and may act or react differently. Persons with autism may wander or be attracted to water sources, roadways, or dwellings. When responding to individuals with autism, officers should consider taking certain measures such as displaying calming body language and giving the individual extra personal space. Given time and space, the person may de-escalate his or her behavior. Officers should always exercise caution when restraining an individual with autism. They should be aware that persons with autism may have seizure disorders and low muscle tone. If restraining, officers should avoid positional asphyxia (inability to breathe caused by body placement), keep the airway clear, and turn the person on his or her side often. *(IN006.1.L.)* (Source: Debbaudt, Dennis. *Autism, Advocates, and Law Enforcement Professionals*)

# UNIT 3 I RESPONDING TO JUVENILES

## LESSON 1 I Responding to Juveniles

**OBJECTIVES**

**IN006.4.A.3.** Identify common characteristics of juvenile offenders.

**IN006.4.A.2.** Identify attributes of an officer who is effective in dealing with juveniles.

**IN006.4.A.** Identify actions that an officer may take when responding to a juvenile offender.

### Characteristics of Juvenile Offenders

Understanding the characteristics and issues associated with juveniles will assist an officer when dealing with a youthful offender. As with all people, young people differ in temperament and behavior. They may show a high degree of irresponsibility, little respect for authority, and unpredictable behavior patterns. Juveniles may also be manipulative and defiant when interacting with law enforcement.

Some juveniles' attitudes may be affected by prior unfavorable contacts with law enforcement. Many delinquent juveniles, also known as status offenders, come from broken or dysfunctional homes or from low-income families. An unstable home environment contributes greatly to behaviors such as bullying, violence, and aggression. Suicide is a leading cause of death among juveniles. Officers dealing with young people should be attentive to suicidal indicators such as depression, obsessive talk about death, or intentional self-injury. There is also a higher incidence of drug or alcohol involvement among youthful offenders. *(IN006.4.A.3.)*

### Responding to Juvenile Offenders

Each situation involving a juvenile is unique; some situations may require more patience and understanding, while others may require a firmer and more direct approach. A high degree of self-control, patience, flexibility, and understanding is necessary to work effectively with youth. The officer must be able to adapt to whatever situation arises with a juvenile from truancy, rebellion, or dangerous actions. Establishing positive working relationships with the youth of the area will help build community networks that will benefit the overall law enforcement effort. *(IN006.4.A.2.)*

An officer has a variety of options available when responding to juvenile offenders. Depending on the situation, an officer may issue a cursory warning or release the youth to parents or guardians with an explanation of the offense. It may be necessary to charge and then release the individual to a custodian. A suitable referral such as counseling, social services, or a juvenile crime prevention program could provide guidance for the juvenile and family. Available community resources may include the Juvenile Division of the local State Attorney's Office, the Runaway Switchboard at 1-800-RUNAWAY, or local counseling services.

Juveniles believed to be suffering from serious physical or mental conditions require prompt medical treatment. In the absence of EMS, officers may be called upon to transport such juveniles to a hospital, mental health service provider, or substance abuse or other treatment facility. The Baker Act and Marchman Act are applicable to juveniles as well as adults. Arrested juveniles who do not require medical or mental health treatment may be delivered to a Florida Department of Juvenile Justice (DJJ) Juvenile Assessment Center. The most desirable course of action is one that will be of greatest benefit to the juvenile and the community both now and in the future *(IN006.4.A.)*

# UNIT 4 | RESPONDING TO THE ELDERLY

## LESSON 1 | Responding to the Elderly

**OBJECTIVES**

**IN006.1.K.1.** Identify characteristics of the elderly population.

**IN006.1.K.** Identify physiological changes related to the aging process.

**IN006.1.K.2.** Identify ways to communicate with an elderly person.

**IN006.6.H.** Identify resources that may provide assistance to the elderly.

As Florida's elderly population increases, law enforcement officers will interact with older people more frequently than ever before and in a variety of settings. This increased interaction requires that officers become more aware of this group's special needs to ensure that older Floridians have the full protection of the law. Understanding the aging process and characteristics of the elderly population helps law enforcement officers relate to Florida's senior citizens in a positive and constructive manner.

Elderly people tend to be vulnerable to crime and neglect and are reluctant to report crimes committed against them. They often live in fear of crime. They commit only a small percentage of crimes—mostly misdemeanors. Generally, older people have a positive attitude toward law enforcement. Most members of the elderly population live at home, close to or with family members. A small percentage lives in nursing homes. Some elderly people require caregivers, and others who are chronically impaired require long-term care. Medical and personal services may be provided in hospitals, nursing homes, assisted living facilities, or a personal residence. Many elderly individuals receive assistance through federal or state programs, and more than one quarter of them have income below or just above the poverty level. *(IN006.1.K.1.)*

## Age-related Medical Conditions

Advancing age is not synonymous with disease and disability. Many older people are active and healthy throughout their lives. However, almost everyone who lives to a certain age experiences a number of normal physiological changes. In addition, the chances of developing certain medical conditions increase with age.

As people age, they may experience sensory impairment. Examples include changes in their eyesight, including a loss of visual acuity and a deterioration of depth, distance, and peripheral perception. In addition, hearing loss and the loss of the ability to tell where a sound originates may occur. These changes may limit a person's mobility, increase the likelihood of accidents, or lead to fear and isolation.

Older people may also experience a change in their sense of touch. Some older people suffer from neuropathy, a condition in which they cannot sense surface pain, and are therefore less likely to notice injuries. Yet, many elderly persons are more prone to rips, tears, and bruising from everyday activities. They are more likely to suffer loss of balance, which increases the risk of falls. Because older people often experience an increased sensitivity to changes in weather, officers should be aware that they are more susceptible to heat stroke, heat exhaustion, and hypothermia.

Another result of aging is the loss of muscle ability and strength, which makes performing daily tasks more difficult. Joints may stiffen due to arthritis, making movement extremely painful. Older people may also lose some cognitive ability, which is the ability to think, learn, and remember. They may experience slowness in thinking, finding the right words, or identifying objects. Officers should be patient when interviewing elderly people because it may take them longer than younger people to explain what they saw or experienced.

Some elderly people suffer from chronic medical conditions—such as dementia or Alzheimer's disease—that result in residual disabilities requiring long-term management or care. ***Dementia*** is an organic, progressive mental disorder characterized by loss of memory, impairment of judgment and abstract thinking, and changes in personality; the frequently used term "senile" has a negative connotation and should be avoided. These patients experience progressive declines in mental function. Overmedication or drug mixing may create a condition that resembles dementia. This is an important consideration for the responding officer to keep in mind. Elderly individuals may also experience a variety of mental illnesses, such as schizophrenia and depression. Other physical and emotional conditions that tend to affect the elderly more than other population groups include incontinence, bed sores, and dehydration.

The suicide rate among elderly people is significantly higher than that of the general population. Factors that place the elderly at risk for suicide include debilitating physical illnesses (often accompanied by severe pain), the death of a loved one, the loss of independence, and financial inadequacy. *(IN006.1.K.)*

## Guidelines for Communicating with the Elderly

As with any other citizen, the way an officer communicates with an elderly person affects that person's view of law enforcement. Just because a person is elderly does not mean he or she is simple minded. When communicating with an older person, the officer should always treat him or her with dignity, respect, and patience. The officer should speak directly to the person, establishing and maintaining eye contact, and should use a conversational tone, speaking loudly only if necessary. In addition, the officer should include the person in all discussions concerning his or her welfare and should adjust communication based on any disabilities or other limitations. *(IN006.1.K.2.)*

**Section Vocabulary**

*dementia*

## Available Resources

A variety of health and social services are available to assist older individuals and their families. These services include home-delivered meals, medical care, emotional support, financial management, and assistance with activities of daily living. The law enforcement officer should learn about organizations specific to assisting the elderly within the local community.

One important resource is the Florida Elder Help Line at 1-800-96-ELDER. It provides a wide range of information to help older citizens obtain specific local social services. Another resource is the Florida Abuse Registry Hotline at 1-800-96-ABUSE. This hotline is available 24-hours a day to take reports of suspected cases of abuse. *(IN006.6.H.)*

# UNIT 5 | RESPONDING TO SUICIDE

## LESSON 1 | Responding to Suicide

**OBJECTIVES**

**IN007.5.A.1.** Identify suicidality indicators.

**IN007.5.A.2.** Identify techniques for responding to an individual at risk for suicide.

### Indicators of Suicidality

There are a variety of indicators and observations an officer may use to assess an individual's risk for suicide. The officer should be aware of the suicidal person's behavior, which may range from calm to violent. When a person talks about committing suicide, attempts intentional self-injury, or sketches death-related drawings, it indicates his or her desperate situation.

Other clues that indicate the individual may be contemplating suicide include despair over the loss of a loved one, depression caused by life stressors, a lack of interest in daily activities, or hopelessness for the future. The person's change in behavior may lead to actions such as giving away personal belongings, lack of interest in eating, and dependence on drugs or alcohol. *(IN007.5.A.1.)*

### Responding to Individuals at Risk for Suicide

Responding to a situation in which an individual is suicidal requires an officer to remain aware of officer safety issues, while providing intervention for an individual in crisis. The officer should be aware that an existing suicidal situation may be aggravated through inappropriate handling of a troubled person. Upon arrival, the officer should assess the need for requesting backup or a crisis intervention team and remove any onlookers or potentially disruptive persons from the scene.

The officer must immediately determine if the subject has any weapons for use in a suicide attempt; weapons intended for suicide could be used against officers or members of the public as well. Separating the suicidal person from the weapons may prove difficult and dangerous. The officer should be aware that the person might initiate a sudden attack on others or him- or herself.

When responding to a call involving a suicidal person, a law enforcement officer can provide assistance through either intervention or referral. Communicating with a suicidal person is a vital part of the intervention process. The officer should try to establish contact and keep the person talking. The officer should carefully listen to what the person says and how he or she says it. Support, empathy, and interest can be shown by talking directly to the person without being judgmental. The officer should convey patience, self-assurance, and hope.

By carefully listening to the person, the officer will learn how serious and immediate the suicide threat is and possibly what method the person plans to use. The officer may also learn about the person's openness to available helpful resources.

A suicidal person needs to see a medical or mental health service provider as soon as possible. The officer should not leave the person alone. In cases where there is a high risk to the safety of the suicidal person, the officer may need to commit the person involuntarily, under the Baker Act, to a mental health facility. The receiving facility should be notified of the possible suicide risk. *(IN007.5.A.2.)*

## Available Resources

The National Suicide Prevention Lifeline is a service available to anyone and may be contacted at any time by calling 1-800-273-TALK (8255). Other community resources, friends, clergy, and relatives may also be available to assist a person contemplating suicide.

# UNIT 6 | SUBSTANCE ABUSERS

## LESSON 1 | Substance Abusers

**OBJECTIVES**

**IN006.2.A.1.** Define *substance use, substance abuse*, and *substance dependence.*

**IN006.1.A.2.** Identify some behavioral characteristics of substance abuse.

**IN006.1.A.3.** Identify some behavioral characteristics of substance dependence.

**IN006.1.A.4.** Identify some factors contributing to substance dependence.

**IN006.2.A.3.** Define terms that relate to substance use.

**IN006.1.B.4.** Identify symptoms of illness that resemble drug or alcohol use.

**IN007.5.B.** Identify Marchman Act criteria.

**IN006.6.A.** Identify the treatment options available to an officer when responding to a substance abuser.

### Substance Use

***Substance use*** is the use of a substance that alters physical or mental function: It can be legal or illegal, therapeutic or recreational, and can be done by sniffing, snorting, inhaling, swallowing, drinking, absorbing through the skin, smoking, or injecting the substance *(IN006.2.A.1.).* For example, substance use could include having a casual drink with friends, taking a prescribed drug according to label directions, or taking aspirin daily to prevent heart disease.

### Substance Abuse

***Substance abuse*** is the continued use of a substance, for nonmedical reasons, despite the knowledge that the substance causes adverse effects on an individual's social or occupational life and psychological or physical health *(IN006.2.A.1.).* Some examples of substance abuse include misusing prescribed medication, drinking 24 cans of beer in one night, sniffing or inhaling glue, using cocaine, or smoking marijuana. *(IN006.1.A.2.)*

### Substance Dependence

***Substance dependence*** is the compulsive use of substances to the point where the user has no effective choice but to continue use due to uncontrollable physical or psychological cravings for the substance *(IN006.2.A.1.).* The need to obtain and use the substance by any means necessary becomes the constant focus of a person's life. Substance dependence may also lead an individual to increase the dosage of the substance due to an increased tolerance *(IN006.1.A.3.).* Dependence can lead to devastating effects for the individual, his or her family, and society.

Some factors that can contribute to substance dependence include an addictive personality and the personal history of the dependent person. People sometimes are fearful of and wish to avoid life issues. Others, particularly the elderly, who may take many prescribed medicines throughout the day, may accidentally abuse medicine. The wide availability of drugs also contributes to dependence. *(IN006.1.A.4.)*

***Psychological dependence*** is the condition in which a person feels that he or she needs drugs in order to cope with problems, function better in life, or feel different, whether or not there is a physical addiction. ***Physical dependence*** is the condition in which the presence of a drug or alcohol is required to maintain normal functioning of the central nervous system. ***Addiction*** is a state of physical and/or psychological dependence on a substance. When use of the substance is discontinued, withdrawal symptoms occur.

***Withdrawal*** refers to the physical and mental symptoms that occur after chronic use of a drug is reduced or stopped. Symptoms vary depending on the drug, but can include agitation, confusion, cramps, sweating, and convulsions. ***Tolerance*** is a condition in which higher doses of a drug are required to produce the same effect as the initial use; this condition often leads to physical dependence. ***Detoxification*** is the process of allowing the body to rid itself of a drug while managing the symptoms of withdrawal and is often the first step in a drug treatment program. ***Overdose*** is the accidental or intentional use of a dangerously large amount of a substance. *(IN006.2.A.3.)*

## Illnesses that Mimic Substance Abuse

One of the most difficult challenges for an officer is recognizing the signs and symptoms of a substance abuser. Some illnesses and medical conditions have symptoms that mimic characteristics associated with substance abuse: A person in diabetic shock may stagger and appear drunk, and a diabetic coma may cause a person's breath to smell sweet like fruit. Epilepsy could cause a person to wander in a confused state and even become violent for brief periods. High blood pressure sometimes causes people to become temporarily irrational, and a head injury may cause confusion and belligerence. People suffering from a stroke may be dizzy and confused, vomit, or lose consciousness. Similar side effects are caused by carbon monoxide poisoning, which also causes general weakness. Parkinson's disease causes shaking, slurred speech, and the appearance of intoxication. Wernicke Syndrome causes sufferers to appear confused and have faulty muscular coordination or paralysis of the eye muscles. People with degenerative diseases such as Alzheimer's and dementia may stagger, act inappropriately, be forgetful, or wander aimlessly. Psychiatric disorders often cause people to behave unpredictably and experience sensory hallucinations such as sounds, physical sensations, or visions. *(IN006.1.B.4.)*

## Resources and Response

Treatment for substance abusers plays a vital role in reducing future drug use and criminal activity. In addition to local community resources, the Hal S. Marchman Act, drug courts, and ex parte court orders provide assistance for alcohol and substance abusers.

The ***Marchman Act*** (F.S. §397) provides substance abusers with access to emergency services and temporary detention for evaluation and treatment. The abuser may be voluntarily or involuntarily detained. The law enforcement officer should follow agency procedures when taking the person into custody and provide the appropriate documentation regarding the circumstances.

An involuntary commitment for alcohol or substance abuse under the Marchman Act may be used when the person is so impaired from substance abuse that he or she is unable to make a rational decision regarding the need for examination, lacks the ability to care for him- or herself, has threatened harm to him- or herself or others, or has actually harmed him- or herself or others. *(IN007.5.B.)*

Some jurisdictions offer treatment-based drug court programs as a choice for individuals whose criminal justice involvement is the result of substance abuse. In exchange for successfully completing its treatment program, the court may dismiss the original drug charge, reduce or set aside a sentence, propose a lesser penalty, or offer a combination of these.

Treatment-based drug court programs offer an opportunity for substance abusers to participate in an intensive, supervised program. The person must meet the requirements of the program or face sanctions for

## Section Vocabulary

*addiction*

*detoxification*

*Marchman Act*

*overdose*

*physical dependence*

*psychological dependence*

*substance abuse*

*substance dependence*

*substance use*

*tolerance*

*withdrawal*

noncompliance. Criteria for successful completion of the program include consecutive negative drug screens, a substance abuse assessment by a certified addictions counselor, and other coordinated strategies with ongoing judicial interaction.

An *ex parte* court order may be obtained by the filing of a petition by one party, without notice to any other party, stating that a person appears to meet the criteria for involuntary examination. The substance abuser's family members or other specified persons may petition the court for the abuser to be involuntarily evaluated. If the judge decides to issue an *ex parte* order, the individual is taken into custody and transported to a treatment facility designated by the judge. *(IN006.6.A.)*

# UNIT 6 | SUBSTANCE ABUSERS

## LESSON 2 | Substance Identification

### The Florida Comprehensive Drug Abuse Prevention and Control Act

The Florida Comprehensive Drug Abuse Prevention and Control Act, Chapter 893, F.S., places all substances regulated under existing federal law into one of five schedules. Schedule I is reserved for the most dangerous drugs and other substances that have no medical use. Schedule V is the classification for the least dangerous drugs.

A substance's schedule is based on medicinal value, harmfulness, and the potential for abuse and addiction. *(IN006.1.A.6.)*

See Figures 4-1 through 4-11 on the following pages for substance schedules.

**OBJECTIVES**

**IN006.1.A.6.** Identify the Florida statute that addresses the scheduling of substances.

**IN006.1.A.** Identify evidence of drug or alcohol usage.

**IN006.1.B.3.** Identify ways drugs or alcohol are taken.

**IN006.1.B.5.** Identify how fast an effect will typically occur for a specific type of drug (including alcohol).

**IN006.1.B.** Identify possible behavioral characteristics of individuals under the influence of drugs (including alcohol).

**IN006.1.B.1.** Identify physical signs and symptoms of individuals under the influence of drugs (including alcohol).

**IN006.1.B.6.** Identify the signs of individuals withdrawing from drugs (including alcohol).

| Type of Substance | Alcohol—Not Scheduled | |
|---|---|---|
| **Evidence of Use (IN006.1.A)** | Empty or open alcohol cans or bottles nearby<br><br>Smell of alcohol on clothes or breath<br><br>Glassy, bloodshot, and watery eyes | |
| **Appearance of Substance** | Almost always liquid (sometimes mixed with Jell-O)<br><br>Color ranges from clear to black<br><br>Common examples: beer, wine, vodka, whiskey, gin, rum, alcopop drinks | |
| **Method of Use (IN006.1.B.3.)** | Drinking is the primary way to use alcohol. Some severe alcoholics also use enemas. | |
| | **Orally** | **Enema** |
| **Onset of Effects (IN006.1.B.5.)** | 10–30 minutes | Immediate |
| **Duration of Effects** | 1–6 hours<br>(varies based upon amount consumed) | 1–6 hours<br>(varies based upon amount consumed) |
| | The onset and duration of the effects of alcohol depend on many factors, including weight, heredity, gender, tolerance level, if drinking is accompanied by food or mixer, the user's mood, and environment. | |
| **Behavioral Characteristics (IN006.1.B.)** | Sluggish behavior; extreme fatigue; thick, slurred speech; intoxication | |
| **Physical Signs and Symptoms (IN006.1.B.1.)** | Eyes cross when an object is brought close to user's face<br><br>Horizontal gaze nystagmus (HGN—a rapid involuntary oscillation or jerkiness of the eyes) usually present, glazed or bloodshot eyes, unsteady walk, slow reflexes, flaccid (limp or loose) muscles, impaired coordination and judgment, breath that smells strongly of alcohol | |
| **Withdrawal Symptoms (IN006.1.B.6)** | Insomnia, vomiting, anxiety, restlessness, convulsions | |

Alcohol *Figure 4-1*

| **Type of Substance** | **Cannabis (Marijuana)—Schedule I Drug** | | |
|---|---|---|---|
| **Evidence of Use (IN006.1.A)** | Strong smoke smell, often like a skunk<br>Odor of burnt hemp rope<br>Presence of seeds, plant material, and paraphernalia, including rolling papers, pipes, pipe cleaners, bongs (water pipes), scales, film canisters, plastic bags, and roach clips | | |
| **Appearance of Substance** | The three forms of cannabis are herbal, resin, and hash oil. | | |
| | **Herbal**<br>The most common form of cannabis is made from the plant's dried leaves and flowers. It looks like coarsely chopped, dried herbs used for cooking. Usually greenish-brown, it has a sweet herbal smell. | **Resin (Hashish)**<br>This form is made by compressing sap on the plant's leaves and stems into blocks. Varying in color from almost black to pale golden brown, some forms of resin are hard and brittle like charcoal, while others are as soft as licorice. | **Hash oil**<br>When dissolved in a solvent, filtered, and allowed to evaporate, cannabis resin leaves a thick oil. Varying in color from black to green, it smells strongly of rotting vegetables. |
| **Method of Use (IN006.1.B.3.)** | Typically cannabis leaves are dried, and then rolled into handmade joints similar to cigarettes. Leaves are also smoked loose in various-sized pipes or bongs (water pipes). Resin is usually heated with a lighter, crumbled, and mixed with tobacco in a hand-rolled cigarette. Hash oil is usually mixed with tobacco, or smeared on cigarette papers, and smoked.<br>Cannabis can also be added to food (cookies, brownies, or pasta, for example) and taken orally without loss of psychoactive effect. The food does not smell of marijuana, but herbal marijuana may be visible in the food. | | |
| | **Orally** | **Smoked** | |
| **Onset of Effects (IN006.1.B.5.)** | 30–45 minutes | 10–30 minutes | |
| **Duration of Effects** | 4–5 hours | 2–3 hours | |
| **Behavioral Characteristics (IN006.1.B.)** | Relaxed, disoriented, happy, euphoric, paranoid | | |
| **Physical Signs and Symptoms (IN006.1.B.1.)** | Increased appetite, anxiety and panic attacks, impaired coordination, fatigue, impaired judgment, possible psychosis, body tremors, reddening of the conjunctivae (whites of the eyes) | | |
| **Withdrawal Symptoms (IN006.1.B.6)** | Insomnia, nausea, decreased appetite, irritability, anxiety | | |

Marijuana

*Figure 4-2*

| Type of Substance | Cocaine/Crack (Type of CNS Stimulant)—Schedule II Drugs | | | |
|---|---|---|---|---|
| **Evidence of Use (IN006.1.A)** | Glass vials, bags, syringes, razor blades, long fingernails, scales, small hand mirrors, needle marks, white crystalline powder around nostrils, grinders for crushing cocaine, short straws and coffee stirrers for powder cocaine, aluminum cans (crack pipe), antennas (crack pipe), glass pipes (crack pipe), steel wool (screen device for crack pipe) | | | |
| **Appearance of Substance** | Most street cocaine is a white crystalline powder that looks like very fine salt. It is usually bought in a wrap containing 1g of powder.<br><br>Crack comes as crystals that look like small rocks. Some pieces look like grains of sand, although normally pieces can be as large as 2 cm across. Color varies from pale yellow or pink to white. Freebase crack is a fine white powder that looks a bit like powdered sugar. | | | |
| **Method of Use (IN006.1.B.3.)** | **Inhaled** | **Injected** | **Orally** | **Smoked** |
| **Onset of Effects (IN006.1.B.5.)** | 3–5 minutes | 5–10 seconds | 3–5 minutes | 5–10 seconds |
| **Duration of Effects** | 1–2 hours | 1–2 hours | 1–2 hours | 1–2 hours |
| **Behavioral Characteristics (IN006.1.B.)** | Agitation, excited state, exaggerated reflexes, euphoria, teeth grinding, increased alertness, body tremors, fast gait and speech, panic attacks | | | |
| **Physical Signs and Symptoms (IN006.1.B.1.)** | Loss of appetite, insomnia, high blood pressure, dilated pupils, increased perspiration (appears to be hot even in cool temperatures), increased heart rate, wild-looking eyes, talkative, nervousness, blistered and burned fingertips, red, runny eyes and nose, sniffing a lot | | | |
| **Withdrawal Symptoms (IN006.1.B.6)** | Increased body temperature, hallucinations, panic attacks, confusion, convulsions, cardiac arrest | | | |

Cocaine *Figure 4-3*

<table>
<tr><th>Type of Substance</th><th colspan="4">Narcotics (Narcotic Analgesics)—Schedule I, II, III, IV Drug (heroin, methadone, morphine, opium, paregoric, codeine, Demerol)</th></tr>
<tr><td>Evidence of Use (IN006.1.A)</td><td colspan="4">Hypodermic needles and syringes, lighters, aluminum foil, straws, aluminum bottle caps, spoons, tourniquets, razors, mirrors, plastic bags</td></tr>
<tr><td rowspan="4">Appearance of Substance</td><td colspan="4">Heroin comes in three forms: brown, china white, and pharmaceutical.</td></tr>
<tr><td>Brown<br>This crumbly, muddy-looking substance is smoked. Its color ranges from creamy white to dark coffee. The lighter the color, the higher the heroin content, which varies from 10 to 60 percent.</td><td colspan="2">China white<br>This form is smoked or injected. Its gray granules resemble instant coffee.</td><td>Pharmaceutical<br>This pure form of heroin is used for medical purposes.<br>It comes as a pure white powder, tablets, or vials of clear liquid. Note: Heroin has no approved medical usage in the U.S. (DEA)</td></tr>
<tr><td colspan="4">Methadone comes as tablets, oral concentrate, and vials of clear, injectable liquid. It is also found as brown, orange, or green, gummy, edible substances of varying strengths or as DTF, a mixture that comes in the same colors but is stronger.</td></tr>
<tr><td colspan="4">Other narcotic painkillers take a variety of forms; capsules, tablets, syrups, elixirs, solutions, and suppositories.</td></tr>
<tr><td>Method of Use (IN006.1.B.3.)</td><td>Inhaled<br>heroin</td><td>Injected<br>heroin, codeine, Demerol, morphine</td><td>Orally<br>morphine, paregoric, codeine, opium, Demerol, heroin, methadone</td><td>Smoked<br>opium, heroin</td></tr>
<tr><td>Onset of Effects (IN006.1.B.5.)</td><td>1–3 minutes</td><td>10–20 seconds</td><td>Varies</td><td>20–30 seconds</td></tr>
<tr><td>Duration of Effects</td><td>3–6 hours</td><td>3–6 hours</td><td>3–6 hours</td><td>3–6 hours</td></tr>
<tr><td>Behavioral Characteristics (IN006.1.B.)</td><td colspan="4">Clammy skin, slow movement, face scratching, restlessness, slow speech, “on the nod” (switching between a state of semi-consciousness to alert)</td></tr>
<tr><td>Physical Signs and Symptoms (IN006.1.B.1.)</td><td colspan="4">Drowsiness, respiratory depression, nausea, dry mouth, euphoria, clammy skin, convulsions, coma, depressed reflexes, pupils constricted to 2.9 mm or smaller</td></tr>
<tr><td>Withdrawal Symptoms (IN006.1.B.6.)</td><td colspan="4">Watery eyes, runny nose, yawning, loss of appetite, irritability, tremors, panic attacks, nausea, abdominal cramps, chills, sweating</td></tr>
</table>

Narcotics

*Figure 4-4*

| Type of Substance | Hallucinogens—Schedule I & II Drugs<br>PCP (phenylcyclohexyl piperidine hydrochloride) | |
|---|---|---|
| **Evidence of Use (IN006.1.A)** | Distinctive chemical odor resembling ether | |
| **Appearance of Substance** | The texture of powder PCP ranges from granular, like sugar, to loose powder to lumps. (The terms *crystals* and *powder* are interchangeable.) The liquid form is clear or yellow.<br>***Packaging:***<br>**Powder PCP**<br>The most common form of packaging is the hand-rolled cigarette or joint: 35–50 mg of PCP are sprinkled on vegetable matter (parsley, mint, oregano, or marijuana, for example) and then hand-rolled into a cigarette. Small PCP crystals should be visible when the cigarette is broken open. The powder is hermetically sealed in plastic, wrapped in aluminum foil, and placed in a tied corner of a plastic bag. | **Liquid PCP**<br>Because it is clear or yellow, liquid PCP can be disguised by adding color to it. It can be carried in eyedropper bottles, film canisters, glass or plastic vials, spice jars, plastic bags, tobacco pouches, tablets/capsules, syringe/needles, vanilla extract bottles, or similar containers. It can be sprayed, sprinkled, or soaked into a hand-rolled cigarette or joint. |
| **Method of Use (IN006.1.B.3.)** | **Orally** | **Smoked** |
| **Onset of Effects (IN006.1.B.5.)** | 30–60 minutes | 1–3 minutes |
| **Duration of Effects** | 4 hours | 1 hour |
| **Behavioral Characteristics (IN006.1.B.)** | Blank stare; disorientation; confusion; agitation; repetitive speech; initial lack of response but talkativeness later; sparse, slurred, and incoherent speech; possible violent and/or combative behavior; aggressive, self-destructive, bizarre behavior; feelings of weightlessness | |
| **Physical Signs and Symptoms (IN006.1.B.1.)** | Increased pain threshold, "super human" strength, generalized numbness, slurred speech, skin warm to the touch, incontinence, irritability, horizontal and vertical gaze nystagmus, poor concentration, appetite loss, anxiety, depression, hallucinations, difficulty reasoning, mimics alcohol intoxication<br>Large doses of PCP cause additional symptoms: moaning, groaning, inability to articulate, apparent wakefulness but lack of response to verbal stimuli, convulsions, coma, death | |
| **Withdrawal Symptoms (IN006.1.B.6.)** | No physical dependence. Psychological dependence is unknown. Tolerance can develop. | |

Hallucinogens - Schedule I & II *Figure 4-5*

| Type of Substance | Hallucinogens—Schedule I Drug<br>LSD (d-lysergic acid diethylamide) |
|---|---|
| **Evidence of Use (IN006.1.A)** | Plastic film canister, aluminum foil, plastic bag, liquid squeeze bottle (typically blue), pack of gum (one hit— a piece of blotter paper—is placed on an unwrapped stick of gum. The gum is rewrapped and replaced in the pack). |
| **Appearance of Substance** | Acid is a transparent crystal in its pure form. Typically, acid is sold in a liquid form. Acid is almost always soaked into small squares of blotting paper called tabs, blotters, or pieces. Tabs come in sheets of more than 100. Each tab is about 5 mm square and has a picture or design that varies according to fashion.<br><br>Microdots, small, colored pills impregnated with acid, are not as common as tabs. Only 2–3 mm across and available in different colors, they often contain high doses of acid. |
| **Method of Use (IN006.1.B.3.)**<br><br>**Onset of Effects (IN006.1.B.5.)**<br><br>**Duration of Effects** | **Orally, Absorbed Through the Skin**<br>(*Officer safety note:* LSD can be absorbed into the skin transdermally, so precaution should be taken when handling this drug)<br><br>30–90 minutes<br><br>12 hours |
| **Behavioral Characteristics (IN006.1.B.)** | Euphoria, expressiveness, relaxation, rapidly changing and exaggerated emotions, lowered emotional inhibitions, spontaneous laughing, crying, and smiling, altered perceptions of time, distance, size, movement, color, spatial arrangement, sound, touch, synesthesia (the transposition of the senses—sights may be transposed into odors, or sounds into sights, etc.) and own body image (the user might lose the ability to tell the difference between his or her body and the rest of the environment). |
| **Physical Signs and Symptoms (IN006.1.B.1.)** | Dilated pupils, rapid heart rate, flushed face, increased body temperature, heart rate, and blood pressure, flashbacks |
| **Withdrawal Symptoms (IN006.1.B.6.)** | No physical dependence. Psychological dependence is unknown. Tolerance can develop. |

Hallucinogens - Schedule I (LSD) *Figure 4-6*

| Type of Substance | Hallucinogens—Schedule I Drug<br>Ecstasy – "e", MDMA (N-methl-3-4 methylenedioxymethamphetamine)<br>Homologues – compounds of different chemicals:<br>• Bath Salts, MDPV (methylenedioxypyrovalerone)<br>• Synthetic Cannabis [Naphthalen-1-yl-(1-pentylindol-3-yl) methanone] | | | |
|---|---|---|---|---|
| **Evidence of Use (IN006.1.A)** | Nasal inhalers and decongestant rubs are the most common indicators of MDMA ecstasy use.<br>Blow pops, baby pacifiers, plastic bags, shampoo bottles for smuggling overseas, packs of candies that are the same size and consistency as MDMA pills.<br>Bath salts (MDVP) sold as Ivory wave, Bolivian Bath, Aura, Vanilla Sky; Herbal Incense or Smoking Blends sold as K2, Spice, Genie, or Zohai. (New names for these products are introduced constantly). | | | |
| **Appearance of Substance** | **MDMA powder** Color varies from bright white to tan to brown; same texture as cocaine<br>**MDMA pill** Aspirin-sized, various colors (often off-white); design stamped on front indicates name of pill. May have a line scored on the back | **MDMA wafer** Size of chewable vitamin C; off-white or tan color with visible dark specks<br>**MDMA capsule** Clear gelatin capsule filled with MDMA powder or small blue-and-white capsule (a smurf) | **MDMA bootleg pill** Aspirin-sized, various colors (often off-white); no markings on front or back<br>**MDPV— powder** Powder or granular substance identified as a bath salt, can be in small flat packet | |
| **Method of Use (IN006.1.B.3.)** | **Inhaled** | **Injected** | **Orally** | **Smoked** |
| **Onset of Effects (IN006.1.B.5.)** | 5–10 minutes | 10–20 seconds | 20–40 minutes | 20–30 seconds |
| **Duration of Effects** | 4–6 hours | 4–6 hours | 4–6 hours | 4–6 hours |
| **Behavioral Characteristics (IN006.1.B.)** | Teeth grinding, nervousness, dizziness, panic attacks, seizures, jaw thrusting, euphoria, biting of lips and inner mouth, skin scratching and rubbing, free-flowing conversations | | | |
| **Physical Signs and Symptoms (IN006.1.B.1.)** | No desire to eat or sleep until trip is over, abundant energy, constant movement, aggressive sexual behavior (dancing and flirting), hugging, physical touching, body massaging to intensify the high, scattered thought processes, profuse perspiration, body overheating, deep breathing, muscle cramping, rubbing of different textures to enjoy heightened sense of touch | | | |
| **Withdrawal Symptoms (IN006.1.B.6.)** | No physical dependence. Psychological dependence is unknown. Tolerance can develop. | | | |

Hallucinogens - Schedule I (Ecstasy, Bath Salts, Synthetic Cannabis) *Figure 4-7*

| Type of Substance | Hallucinogens—Schedule I Drugs<br>Psilocybin and Psilocin (Mushrooms), Mescaline (Peyote), Salvia divinorum & Salvinorin A |
|---|---|
| **Evidence of Use (IN006.1.A)** | No paraphernalia needed for dried mushrooms or Peyote cactus. Gelatin capsules used for synthetic Mescaline. Rolling papers or water pipe for Salvia divinorum & Salvinorin A |
| **Appearance of Substance** | **Mushrooms**<br>Light to dark brown dried mushrooms, some with long, thin stems and ball-shaped crowns.<br>**Mescaline**<br>Disc-shaped buttons cut from Peyote cactus; 2–3 inches in diameter, 1/2–1 inch thick (in natural form); brown-colored powder in a clear, gelatin capsule (synthetic form); manufactured substance is mescaline sulfate.<br>**Salvia divinorum & Salvinorin A**<br>Dried leaves light brown in color, covered with short hairs giving the leaves a velvety appearance in certain light. |
| **Method of Use (IN006.1.B.3.)**<br><br>**Onset of Effects (IN006.1.B.5.)**<br><br>**Duration of Effects** | **Mushrooms & Peyote Mescaline–Orally**<br>**Salvia divinorum & Salvinorin A is smoked or chewed**<br><br>**Mushrooms & Peyote Mescaline** 1–2 hours<br>**Salvia divinorum & Salvinorin A** 1-2 minutes<br>**Mushrooms & Peyote Mescaline** 6-10 hours<br>**Salvia divinorum & Salvinorin A** 15-20 minutes |
| **Behavioral Characteristics (IN006.1.B.)** | ***Mushrooms & Peyote Mescaline:*** Effects on users depend on their tolerance and the strength of the mushrooms. Users feel happy and euphoric; they may giggle and find everything hilarious. They feel detached from the world and on a different wavelength than everyone else. People become excited and engrossed in whatever they are doing. Some see and hear things that are not really there (hallucinate). For others, sounds and colors become distorted or intense, and things change shape (psychedelic effect). Users may lose track of time. If unprepared for the results of the drug, users often have panic attacks.<br>***Salvia divinorum & Salvinorin A:*** Effects on users may include uncontrollable laughter, unintelligible speech, past/childhood memories, overlapping realities, sensations of movement or disconnection from reality. |
| **Physical Signs and Symptoms (IN006.1.B.1.)** | Dilated pupils, sweating, garbled speech, disorientation |
| **Withdrawal Symptoms (IN006.1.B.6.)** | No physical dependence. Psychological dependence is unknown. Tolerance can develop. |

Hallucinogens - Schedule I (Mushrooms, Mescaline (Peyote), Salvia divinorum & Salvinorin A) *Figure 4-8*

| Type of Substance | Inhalants—Not Scheduled |
|---|---|
| **Evidence of Use (IN006.1.A)** | Odor of substance on clothing or breath; paint stains on clothing, fingertips, or around the nose or mouth |
| **Appearance of Substance** | Appearance is related to product used. For example, spray paints (silver and gold) have high toluene content.<br>Plastic bags containing chemically soaked rags<br>Nitrous oxide tanks and canisters, paint thinner, air freshener, gasoline, model cement, airplane glue, rubber cement, fingernail polish remover, whipped cream, insecticides, hairsprays, deodorants, glass chillers, frying pan lubricants (PAM), lighter fluid, spot remover, correction fluid, balloons, paper bags saturated with glue and rubber cement |
| **Method of Use (IN006.1.B.3.)** | **Inhaled fumes** |
| **Onset of Effects (IN006.1.B.5.)** | 2–4 seconds |
| **Duration of Effects** | 0.5–2 hours |
| **Behavioral Characteristics (IN006.1.B.)** | Sudden mood swings, defensiveness, impaired judgment, antisocial behavior, low academic achievement, juvenile delinquency, increased aggression, scattered thought process, lack of concentration, exaggerated feelings of well-being, euphoria, vigor and high spirits, followed or replaced by drowsiness and disordered perception |
| **Physical Signs and Symptoms (IN006.1.B.1.)** | Sneezing, coughing, runny nose, and other cold symptoms, horizontal gaze nystagmus, vertical gaze nystagmus, appetite and weight loss, poor coordination, slurred speech, red, glassy eyes, inflamed nose or nosebleeds, rash or sores around nose and mouth, odor of substance on breath, dilated pupils, sloppy dress, sudden lack of personal hygiene |
| **Withdrawal Symptoms (IN006.1.B.6)** | Increased body temperature, panic attacks, hallucinations, confusion, convulsions, cardiac arrest |

Inhalants *Figure 4-9*

<table>
<tr><th>Type of Substance</th><th colspan="5">Depressants (CNS Depressants)—Schedule I, II, III, IV Drugs<br>GHB (Gamma-hydroxybutyrate), barbiturates, sedatives, tranquilizers</th></tr>
<tr><td>Evidence of Use<br>(IN006.1.A)</td><td colspan="5">Packaging<br><br>Aluminum foil, plastic bag, child's blowing-bubble jar, capsule, water bottle, film canister, pills, hypodermic needles/syringes</td></tr>
<tr><td>Appearance of Substance</td><td colspan="5">GHB is usually sold in bottles that contain about 40 ml of liquid. Somewhat thicker than water. It may be in powder, tablet, or capsule form. Artificial flavorings and colorings are sometimes added to avoid detection.</td></tr>
<tr><td rowspan="2">Method of Use<br>(IN006.1.B.3.)</td><td colspan="2">Generic Depressants</td><td colspan="3">GHB</td></tr>
<tr><td>Injected</td><td>Orally</td><td>Inhaled</td><td>Injected</td><td>Orally</td></tr>
<tr><td>Onset of Effects<br>(IN006.1.B.5.)</td><td>10–20 minutes</td><td>30–45 minutes</td><td>10–20 minutes</td><td>10–20 minutes</td><td>10–20 minutes</td></tr>
<tr><td>Duration of Effects</td><td>4–8 hours</td><td>4–8 hours</td><td>1–3 hours</td><td>1–3 hours</td><td>1–3 hours</td></tr>
<tr><td>Behavioral Characteristics<br>(IN006.1.B.)</td><td colspan="5">Slurred speech, disorientation, long periods of sleep, drunken behavior with no alcohol odor, confused behavior<br><br>GHB<br>Anxiety, increased sexual pleasure, nausea, loss of muscle control, impaired judgment, loss of inhibition and coordination</td></tr>
<tr><td>Physical Signs and Symptoms<br>(IN006.1.B.1.)</td><td colspan="5">Staggering, slow heart and respiratory rates, confusion, lack of coordination, depression, muscular rigidity, horizontal gaze nystagmus, vertical gaze nystagmus, weak and rapid pulse, clammy skin, dilated pupils, lowered blood pressure<br><br>GHB<br>Euphoria, hallucinations, dizziness, horizontal gaze nystagmus, vertical gaze nystagmus, memory loss, deep sleep, slowed breathing and heart rates</td></tr>
<tr><td>Withdrawal Symptoms<br>(IN006.1.B.6)</td><td colspan="5">Anxiety, insomnia, tremors, delirium, convulsions, possible death</td></tr>
</table>

Depressants *Figure 4-10*

| Type of Substance | Methamphetamine (Type of CNS Stimulant)—Schedule II (Crank, Speed, Crystal, ICE, Glass, or Shards) | | | |
|---|---|---|---|---|
| **Evidence of Use (IN006.1.A)** | Red Devil Lye, coffee filters, Pseudophedrine (Sudafed), plastic tubing, glass bottles, empty milk jugs, solvents, strong chemical smell, steel wool (Brillo pads), hazardous chemicals, hydrochloric acid, phosphorous, iodine, ether, fingernail polish remover, kerosene, gasoline, rock/table salt, camera batteries, methanol, blacked out or boarded up windows | | | |
| **Appearance of Substance** | Beige or white powder, white crystalline rock, chalk | | | |
| **Method of Use (IN006.1.B.3.)** | **Inhaled** | **Injected** | **Orally** | **Smoked** |
| **Onset of Effects (IN006.1.B.5.)** | 1–30 seconds | 1–3 minutes | 20 minutes | 1–3 seconds |
| **Duration of Effects** | 2–4 hours | 2–4 hours | 2–4 hours | 2–4 hours |
| **Behavioral Characteristics (IN006.1.B.)** | Anxiety, body tremors, decreased appetite, dizziness, dry mouth, euphoria, excitability, grinding teeth, hallucinations, impaired awareness, increased alertness, insomnia, loss of coordination, restlessness, bizarre behavior, long intense trips, and psychosis | | | |
| **Physical Signs and Symptoms (IN006.1.B.1.)** | Headaches, sweating, chills, dilated pupils, elevated pulse, blood pressure, and body temperature, burn marks on fingers or lips and gums called "brands", lesions on skin called "drug bugs", dried and blistered condition on tongue called "White Tongue", dark carbon stains on teeth and gums | | | |
| **Withdrawal Symptoms (IN006.1.B.6.)** | Tremors, anxiety, panic attacks, psychotic reactions, depression, long periods of sleep, fatigue, intense hunger | | | |

Methamphetamine *Figure 4-11*

# CHAPTER 5

## Patrol 1



Most law enforcement officers will spend the majority of their time patrolling an assigned area. This chapter provides an overview of the law enforcement techniques and tactics officers use while on patrol. It focuses on Community Oriented Policing, officer safety and survival skills, and basic instruction on receiving a call, interacting with vehicles, and making an arrest.

# UNIT 1 | PROBLEM SOLVING

## LESSON 1 | Community Oriented Policing

**OBJECTIVES**

**IN018.1.A.1.** Identify Herman Goldstein's definition of Community Oriented Policing.

**IN018.1.B.** Identify the core components of Community Oriented Policing.

**IN018.1.B.3.** Identify the elements of problem solving as used in the SARA Model.

## Community Oriented Policing

Many regard Herman Goldstein as the father of Community Oriented Policing. He first developed and advanced the concept of Problem-Oriented Policing (POP) in 1979. With further refinement, his work became what is now called COP. Community Oriented Policing is an agency-wide philosophy promoting community partnerships to address the causes of crime and other community issues (Goldstein, 1990) *(IN018.1.A.1.)*. The goal of community policing is to examine issues that are characteristic of specific neighborhoods and collaborate with the community to combat these problems.

Community Oriented Policing has two core components: community partnerships and SARA model problem solving. Community partnerships increase understanding and trust between law enforcement agencies and community members. Possible community partners can include law enforcement representatives (elected, sworn, or civilian), governmental representatives (public housing, mental health agencies), and community representatives (local businesses, professional groups, neighborhood leaders).

These community partnerships are essential in developing the second component of Community Oriented Policing: problem solving. Community partnerships allow law enforcement agencies to develop long-term, proactive programs and strategies to address local problems. These relationships exist to inform law enforcement agencies about pertinent issues in the community, while establishing a rapport and understanding with the public about the agencies' methods to deter crime. *(IN018.1.B.)*

## SARA Model

Law enforcement agencies can practice the problem-solving component of COP by using the SARA Model. The SARA Model provides a tool for officers to proactively find solutions to community issues. The key elements in the SARA Model are as follows:

### *Scanning*

Officers should look for patterns in crimes, victims, or geographic locations. Scanning takes a broad, intensive view of a particular area or series of events to accurately describe community problems. Often, the descriptions can be stated as answers to the following questions:

- Have you identified a problem?
- How do you perceive the problem?
- How do those outside law enforcement perceive the problem?

- Does your perception differ from others' perceptions? If yes, how?
- How serious is the problem?
- Is the problem a law enforcement issue?

## *Analysis*

The analysis phase helps determine the cause of the problem by collecting information from various sources. An understanding of all components of a problem allows for the design of a custom-made response. Information should be gathered from everyone affected by the issue; law enforcement data should not be the only source of information. Officers must consider community perspectives and interpretations of the problem.

## *Response*

The response phase allows officers the opportunity to respond to the problem by working with citizens, businesses, and public agencies. The keys to Community Oriented Policing are the creative and long-term solutions resulting from thorough data collection and analysis that are put into practice during the response phase.

## *Assessment*

Generally, problem solving produces one of five beneficial results: the problem is eliminated; the problem is substantially reduced; the harm created by the problem is reduced; a better method of handling the problem is found, or the problem is found to be outside the realm of law enforcement.

The SARA model is a continuous cycle that reassesses and solves problems within the community. If the assessment process indicates the solution failed, the cycle continues until the problem is adequately resolved. Assessment may even indicate the presence of more than one problem or other partners who could assist in solving the issue. *(IN018.1.B.3.)*

# UNIT 1 | PROBLEM SOLVING

## LESSON 2 | SECURE

**OBJECTIVES**

**IN019.1.** Define *SECURE.*

**IN019.2.B.** Identify when to use the SECURE problem-solving model.

**IN019.1.A.** Identify the meaning of each letter in the acronym SECURE.

## SECURE: An Approach to Problem Solving in Law Enforcement

***SECURE*** stands for Safety, Ethics, Community, Understanding, Response, and Evaluation. It is a developmental tool that enhances problem-solving capabilities *(IN019.1.).* Whether responding to a crime in progress or making a public service call, an officer can review the SECURE model to ensure a safe, ethical, and effective response. It provides an approach to all situations, emphasizes law enforcement fundamentals (such as maintaining safety and serving the public interest), and provides a framework for responding effectively. It also allows for evaluation and long-term, problem-solving possibilities after the response is completed. *(IN019.2.B.)*

***Safety:*** In any law enforcement situation, officer safety is the leading concern. An officer cannot effectively assist the public if he or she is in danger. The techniques and procedures used should ensure the protection of the officer, public, and all persons involved such as victims, suspects, witnesses, or bystanders.

***Ethics:*** A great deal of authority accompanies law enforcement. Sworn officers have the authority to arrest individuals, use force to do so, and use deadly force if necessary. An officer must always consider ethics and use these powers within the limits of the law. Another aspect of ethics is how officers conduct themselves. They must treat all individuals with as much respect and consideration as the situation allows, regardless of the person's race, gender, or culture.

***Community:*** Community stands for the idea that officers serve the public. They serve the people directly involved in an incident, including the victim, complainant, neighbors, and in a broader sense, the entire community. Most agencies recognize that they can maximize their efforts by forming partnerships with community members.

***Understanding:*** An officer must gather and analyze information to understand a situation before proceeding. To understand a situation, an officer must determine the who, what, when, where, how, and why of the situation.

***Response:*** Response depends on the level of understanding and the options available. Once an officer understands the situation, he or she can decide on the best course of action. Gathering accurate information leads to a more informed decision and thus a better response.

***Evaluation:*** An officer must evaluate his or her actions to determine if the problem has been dealt with successfully. Officers can learn from their mistakes to prevent future errors. How evaluation is performed and the level of formality involved depends on agency policies, the significance of the problem, and the impact of not resolving the problem. The officer or supervisor may want to review officer performance to determine if the response could be improved. *(IN019.1.A.)*

**Section Vocabulary**

*SECURE*

# UNIT 2 | OFFICER SAFETY AND SURVIVAL

## LESSON 1 | Officer Safety

Every situation presents diverse safety concerns, which may include encounters with individuals, the use of makeshift weapons, and environments that restrict an officer's view or ability to communicate with dispatch. Each year, a majority of officer deaths and injuries occur due to lack of planning, lapsed training, carelessness, or overconfidence.

**OBJECTIVES**

**IN014.3.A.** Identify safety equipment that an officer can use to remain safe.

**IN014.1.A.** Identify factors that may lead to officers' deaths.

### Factors that Compromise Officer Safety

Experienced officers and recruits alike cannot assume a call is typical. They must react properly to each set of circumstances. Responding to a call without the appropriate mindset or attitude may cause an officer to drop his or her guard in a potentially life-threatening situation. The ability to remain alert and observe surroundings is key for a patrol officer. Officers should get a proper amount of rest in order to perform their jobs effectively.

While officers are expected to confront dangerous situations, they are not expected to rush into danger. Blind heroism may work on television, but in reality, it can endanger officers and others at the scene. Officers must rely on training, not emotional reactions, especially in stressful situations.

In order to handle the demands of dangerous situations, an officer must be in proper physical shape. An officer in poor shape endangers him- or herself, other officers, and the public. An officer's body is an important piece of equipment that must be maintained as regularly as a firearm or patrol vehicle.

An officer's ability to observe hazards and signs of criminal activity is an integral part of patrolling. Preoccupied officers can miss potential danger signs and cause injury or death to themselves, other officers, or civilians.

When an officer makes contact with anyone, he or she should always watch that person's hands. Hand position can give nonverbal cues about intent. Also, by watching an individual's hands, an officer can intercept a weapon before it is used.

Proper handcuffing is important for controlling suspects as well as providing protection for officers and the public. An officer should never assume, however, that a handcuffed suspect is no longer a threat.

Officers have an array of equipment including primary weapons, secondary weapons, flashlights, handcuffs, and subject control spray. Vehicles may have spotlights, takedown lights, a public address system, emergency lights, and sirens. If an officer does not use the proper equipment, he or she could be seriously injured or killed *(IN014.3.A.)*. Dirty, faulty, or improperly maintained equipment can cause injury or death. All equipment should be inspected on a regular basis and kept clean and in working order at all times.

Officers who fail to continuously train and maintain proficiency with equipment can cause serious injury or death to themselves or others. An officer might only fire his or her weapon once in a lifetime, but when that time comes, he or she must be fully prepared to use the firearm safely and effectively.

Officers are responsible for enhancing their ability to perform their duties. They should attend training programs and seek current information regarding up-to-date training. Coupled with real world experience, consistent training will help officers develop the mindset and attitude required to maintain officer and public safety. *(IN014.1.A.)*

# UNIT 2 | OFFICER SAFETY AND SURVIVAL

## LESSON 2 | Survival Skills

### Observational Skills and Techniques

***Observation*** is the act of noting what is presented to the senses by keeping in view, noticing, or giving attention to persons, things, or circumstances *(IN020.2.A.1.)*. Good observation skills are improved through practice, such as memorizing car descriptions or observing pedestrians and environmental details. When observing others, officers should note people's appearance, including height, weight, hair, clothing, or other distinguishing traits. An officer should also focus on indicators that situations are matters of police interest, including what is usual or unusual activity within a specific area. Officers should not be distracted by a few elements but observe the entire scene before making a judgment. *(IN020.2.A.)*

***Perception*** is organizing and attaching meaning to sensations so that they can be interpreted. Perception is the core of observation *(IN020.2.D.1)*. Perception is affected by various factors such as the observer's sex, race, environmental conditions, past experience, education, maturity, bias, mental and physical condition, and position or location. *(IN020.2.D.)*

### Using the Five Senses

Sight is often the starting point for officer action. Officers must be aware of various environmental and physical factors that can affect vision. Visual defects like nearsightedness (myopia) and farsightedness (hyperopia) can affect an officer's vision if he or she does not wear corrective lenses. Lighting from sources like streetlights or fluorescent lamps can distort color perception. Darkness can greatly affect vision. When entering a sparsely lit situation, an officer should allow time for his or her eyes to adjust. Dimly lit objects tend to blend into the background and are harder to distinguish. One technique for visually adapting to darkness is for an officer to stop briefly after entering a dark area to allow his or her eyes to adjust. *(IN020.2.C.1.)*

Hearing is used to identify elements such as voices, engines, and firearms. Factors such as traffic or noise from residences affect an officer's hearing. Sometimes, peripheral noises impair the ability to hear and thus prevent an officer from identifying indicators of a crime. Officers should always be conscious of environmental noises when responding to calls. *(IN020.2.C.3.)*

Officers use the sense of smell to identify dangerous substances by their odors. An officer may smell gasoline, petroleum products, natural gas, or gunpowder and determine that there is a potential threat. Many factors can affect an officer's sense of smell, such as an officer's health or weather conditions. Odors in an outside environment can mask other smells. Substances with strong odors like gasoline or

**OBJECTIVES**

**IN020.2.A.1.** Define *observation.*

**IN020.2.A.** Identify the role of memory in observation.

**IN020.2.D.1.** Define *perception.*

**IN020.2.D.** Identify factors that affect perception.

**IN020.2.C.1.** Identify factors affecting an officer's sight.

**IN020.2.C.3.** Identify factors affecting an officer's hearing.

**IN020.2.C.4.** Identify factors affecting an officer's sense of smell.

**IN020.2.C.6.** Identify factors affecting an officer's sense of touch.

**IN020.2.C.8.** Identify why discretion should be applied when using the sense of taste to identify a substance.

**IN014.2.A.** Identify basic survival tips that can help an officer respond safely.

**IN014.4.H.1.** Define *cover.*

**IN014.4.H.2.** Define *concealment.*

**IN014.4.** Identify officer safety procedures.

ether can temporarily deaden an officer's sense of smell. Some hazardous materials such as chlorine gas or ammonia may be harmful if smelled. *(IN020.2.C.4.)*

Officers may sometimes use touch to identify items during a search or pat down. Touch can also verify the presence of heat in tires and engines and determine if a vehicle has been driven recently. Touching walls or other surfaces can reveal heat that may indicate a fire. However, officers should be cautious about touching possible evidence or disturbing a crime scene. *(IN020.2.C.6.)*

An officer who tastes a hazardous substance such as a drug or poison to identify it can become very ill or die. Officers should never use taste to identify any unknown substance. *(IN020.2.C.8.)*

# Officer Survival

When observing a situation, an officer must choose a course of action. True survival readiness involves practical preparedness, firearm proficiency, and first aid skills. Acquiring and maintaining these skills can be accomplished through mental conditioning by understanding responses as they apply to different situations, practicing tactical preparedness, and by maintaining proper training and retraining. Under the stress of a physical attack, an officer will instinctively revert to his or her training. *(IN014.2.A.)*

## Cover and Concealment

***Cover*** protects officers from rounds being fired. Examples of cover include utility poles, automobiles, brick walls, dirt embankments, concrete, steel, and thick wood *(IN014.4.H.1.).* ***Concealment*** is an object or environment that provides camouflage for an officer but will not stop bullets *(IN014.4.H.2.).* Examples of concealment include shrubs, fences, display cases, and objects that keep an officer hidden but provide a position from which he or she can observe. It is preferable to use cover rather than concealment. When arriving at a scene, an officer should immediately identify cover and concealment areas in case a safe place is needed. Usually an officer selects and plans to use a cover/concealment area in order to observe activity.

## Safety Procedures

By studying, mentally rehearsing, and regularly practicing safety procedures, an officer can be prepared to maintain safety in difficult situations. The circumstances of a situation should dictate tactics. Officers should always be alert for indicators of danger and use their observational skills to analyze the scene and maximize distance from a potentially dangerous area.

There are several basic safety tips an officer must remember when on patrol. Tunnel vision, or the narrowing of the attention field due to stress caused by such elements as a vehicle pursuit, foot chase, armed confrontation, or other high stress situations, should be avoided. Tunnel vision causes an officer to focus on a specific object or an individual and ignore other potential hazards. In order to avoid tunnel vision, officers should observe their surroundings carefully.

Officers should always identify themselves as police officers and give direct commands, such as "Stop!" and "Don't move!" All commands should be delivered in an appropriate tone for the situation. Officers who believe a suspect is armed should coordinate with backup officers to use appropriate tactics to contact, control, and disarm the suspect. In addition, officers should visually assess their surroundings and note how many people are at the scene, and the position of their hands, and scan for hazards like weapons or items that may be used as weapons.

If an officer shoots a suspect, dispatch should be notified as soon as possible. Even after a suspect is shot, he or she may still be a threat. The officer should not rush to the injured suspect or put his or her weapons away. The officer should find cover and await the assistance of backup officers before approaching the suspect. If a suspect appears to submit, the officer should not assume he or she is sincere. The officer should watch the suspect for unusual actions, especially hand movements. The suspect should be handcuffed using standard handcuffing procedures, and medical assistance should be requested.

An officer should disarm a suspect before leaving cover. The suspect should be ordered to turn away from the officer, drop any weapons, and step away from them. If the weapon is a firearm, the suspect must be commanded to remove his or her finger from the trigger, slowly lay down the gun, and step away from it. Cover should never be left to take a weapon directly from a suspect.

While in a patrol vehicle, an officer may face attack from sniper fire, firebombs, rocks, or other missiles. If this occurs, the officer should accelerate away from the area, roll up windows, and turn off air conditioning to prevent chemicals from seeping into the vehicle. The vehicle should be abandoned if these actions do not eliminate the risk. If an officer is on foot and comes under sniper fire, he or she should seek immediate cover, call for assistance, and determine a safe approach for responding officers. *(IN014.4.)*

### Section Vocabulary

***concealment***

***cover***

***observation***

***perception***

# UNIT 2 | OFFICER SAFETY AND SURVIVAL

## LESSON 3 | Stress Management

**OBJECTIVES**

**IN015.1.A.2.** Define *stress.*

**IN015.1.A.1.** Define *fight or flight response.*

**IN015.1.** Identify types of stress.

**IN015.1.I.** Identify the causes of post-traumatic stress.

**IN015.1.B.1.** Define *stressors.*

**IN015.1.B.** Identify four categories of potential stressors.

**IN015.1.E.** Identify short-term and long-term stress responses.

**IN015.1.F.** Identify the most common warning signs of stress in an officer.

**IN015.3.** Identify techniques for reducing stress.

### Police Work and Stress

Officers respond to stressful situations such as domestic disputes, traffic accidents, and homicides. For victims, these may be once-in-a-lifetime incidents, but for officers, they may happen regularly. The capacity to cope with stress is vital to an officer's performance. Officers must be aware of the types of stress and how to prevent or minimize their effects.

### What is Stress?

***Stress*** is a physical or emotional reaction to an event or situation *(IN015.1.A.2.)*. Stress may come from a perceived or real threat or a physiological or psychological response to a demanding situation or change. Not all stress is negative. It can raise awareness of a potentially dangerous situation and prepare an officer to react. However, negative stress can slow reaction time, make the officer question his or her decisions, or cloud an officer's judgment. The normal reaction when facing a threat is the ***fight or flight response***, which is the body's preparation to either get far away from a dangerous situation or be physically prepared to face it head on. *(IN015.1.A.1.)*

### Types of Stress

The level of stress an officer feels in a given situation depends on his or her perspective and personality as well as the type of threat. There are four general stress levels. ***Acute stress*** is short-lived and similar to what people experience before taking a test or giving a speech. ***Chronic stress*** continues a long time, such as the stress of a difficult two-year training program. ***Cumulative stress*** results from a variety of sources over time. For example, an individual has domestic, financial, and career problems. These stresses could build on one another and an individual could experience cumulative stress. ***Delayed stress*** lies dormant for a period of time and then resurfaces. For example, an individual cares for a close relative during a long illness, ignoring the stress of the situation. Later, when a good friend becomes ill the individual experiences delayed stress. *(IN015.1.)*

***Post-traumatic stress disorder*** (PTSD) is a psychological reaction that occurs after one experiences a highly stressful event such as war, physical violence, or a natural disaster. Sufferers may display symptoms such as depression, anxiety, recurring nightmares, and flashbacks. Sometimes the sufferer is not the person threatened by the situation but someone who witnessed a violent car accident or whose family is a victim of a violent crime. Most agencies have programs that allow officers to anonymously access counseling services to address stress-related problems. *(IN015.1.I.)*

## Stressors

***Stressors*** are factors that may cause stress (IN015.1.B.1). They fall into four general categories: environmental, personal, self-induced, and work-related.

Environmental stressors involve elements of an officer's surroundings, such as the weather or high noise levels, that could add mental strain. Officers can also be physically affected. For example, moving from an air-conditioned patrol vehicle to a humid environment can be physically stressing.

Personal stressors depend on an individual's likes or dislikes. Factors that can contribute to personal stress include trauma related to injury or death, or to financial or family difficulties.

Self-induced stressors affect an individual's perception of situations and events. These stressors are very specific to the individual and include personal attitudes towards work, perceptions of others, and work-related goals.

Work-related stressors are elements of an officer's job that cause physical or emotional distress. Some are from forces outside the officer's agency. For example, officers may deal with ineffectual or delayed court procedures and court decisions restricting law enforcement powers. These stressors may also come from daily patrolling and may include the danger of patrolling, boredom contrasted with the need to be alert, and the responsibility for the safety and welfare of the public. *(IN015.1.B.)*

## Stress Reponses

Stress can affect an individual in many ways. Short-term stress responses include temporary increases in anxiety, tension, and irritability. Health-related stress responses may include headaches, blood pressure changes, and excessive eating. Job performance-related stress responses may include erratic work habits and decreased productivity. Domestic stress may cause relationship problems, displacement of anger towards family and friends, and withdrawal from domestic and social activities.

Long-term stress responses related to personality may include psychosis, chronic depression, or suicidal thoughts. Long-term stress responses related to health may include chronic disease, high blood pressure, ulcers, and coronary heart disease. Other health problems that could occur include asthma attacks, diabetes, alcoholism, and substance abuse. *(IN015.1.E.)*

## Signs of Stress

Officers should monitor themselves and fellow officers for warning signs of stress. These signs are often specific to an individual, but a few of the most common are sudden behavioral changes, erratic work habits, excessive accidents or injuries, fatigue, sleeping and eating disorders, excessive worry, excessive alcohol or drug use, and complaints from peers or citizens about negative interactions. *(IN015.1.F.)*

## Reducing Stress

Regular physical exercise is a good source of stress relief. Aerobic exercise such as running, swimming, or bicycling is one method of achieving physical fitness and stress relief. A healthy lifestyle decreases stress. Facets of a healthy lifestyle include getting seven to eight hours of sleep a night and avoiding excessive amounts of fat, sugar, caffeine, and alcohol. An extended vacation can also alleviate the effects of stress. The consequences of not monitoring emotional well-being affects officers' personal lives and their job performance. Poor job performance may lead to poor judgment, liability issues, absenteeism, and complaints. *(IN015.3.)*

**Section Vocabulary**

*acute stress*

*chronic stress*

*cumulative stress*

*delayed stress*

*fight or flight response*

*post-traumatic stress disorder*

*stress*

*stressors*

# UNIT 3 | PATROLLING THE ASSIGNED AREA

## LESSON 1 | Patrolling Techniques

**OBJECTIVES**

**LE022.5.A.1.** Identify patrol types.

**LE488.3.A.** Identify information obtained through roll call that may be useful when patrolling an assigned area.

**LE038a.1.** Identify the need to inspect and review duty equipment.

**LE047.1.** State how to identify a wanted person or vehicle when preparing a BOLO report.

**LE047.3.B.** Identify the appropriate descriptive details for a person, property, or vehicle when preparing a BOLO report.

### Patrol

Patrolling is the main activity officers perform daily. Its primary purpose is to maintain a public presence, enforce laws and ordinances, and deter crime. It also encompasses making proactive citizen and community contacts and providing information to citizens.

Reactive patrol is taking a responsive or after-the-fact role in dealing with crime. It requires immediate response to an incident, which increases the likelihood of catching the offender. This strategy is found in traditional policing in which officers are more likely to answer calls and take reports about recurring problems in their communities.

Proactive patrol discourages criminal activity through an officer's visibility. To make their presence known, officers must continuously travel through the patrol area and speak to people for short periods. Making one-on-one citizen contact provides interaction with the public while creating a network of potential information. *(LE022.5.A.1.)*

## Preparing to Patrol

***Roll call*** is a brief meeting attended before each shift. It gives an officer information about current issues to keep in mind while on patrol. Information shared at roll call comes from oral instruction from supervisors and the records and reports of officers from previous shifts. Some agencies distribute information via computer systems, radios, telephones, or other media. Officers should record all roll call information that may affect their shift, including addresses that require or request extra patrol, wanted and missing persons, stolen vehicles, stolen and lost vehicle tags, suspicious incidents, officer safety bulletins, and safety concerns. *(LE488.3.A.)*

**LE022.6.C.** Identify how to become familiar with the patrol area.

**LE022.8.C.** Identify the advantages of foot patrol.

**IN020.1.** Identify the importance of observing potential safety hazards.

The equipment used while on patrol is vital to safety and effectiveness. Because officers rely on these tools, they must routinely ensure each piece of equipment is in working order, fully equipped, and safely stored. Patrol vehicles should be checked to make sure elements such as emergency lights and tires are in good shape. If officers do not take equipment home, they must verify that preventative maintenance has been performed before going out on patrol. The functionality of emergency equipment like fire extinguishers, biohazard gear, and first aid kits must be verified regularly. An officer should never assume others have maintained equipment. *(LE038a.1.)*

## BOLO

***BOLO*** stands for "Be On the Look Out." A BOLO contains detailed information relating to situations. This information is dispersed by local, state, or national agencies and may include descriptions of a missing person, stolen vehicle, suspicious activity, or a specific area needing extra patrol attention. Because BOLOs can contain various types of information, they have no standard format or content. They may include printed information, photographs, verbal reports, electronic messaging, or internet postings. Officers should mentally note the major points of each BOLO. While patrolling their assigned area, officers should consult the current BOLO form if they encounter anything related to the information. They should also review information from previous BOLOs to keep the information fresh in their minds. Information from a BOLO should be kept for reference purposes until no longer needed.

If an officer is required to prepare a BOLO, he or she should relay all significant information to dispatch. Agency policies and procedures determine the method used to contact dispatch with this information. To prepare a BOLO, officers should identify information sources and verify all received information. If an officer has complete information on a suspect, such as name, description, and date of birth, the officer can run FCIC/NCIC for outstanding warrants and criminal history. *(LE047.1.)*

The BOLO should include the suspect's name and identifying information; location of the incident; reason for the BOLO; alleged violation or reason wanted; person, vehicle, or property description; and last known mode and direction of travel. Officers can include photographs in the BOLO. Possible sources of photographs are prior arrest photos, driver's license photographs, security videotapes, and photos obtained from family members *(LE047.3.B.)*. Officers should identify the personnel who will receive the photos and follow agency policy in consulting with other agencies or BOLOs.

## Becoming Familiar with the Patrol Area

One of the first things new patrol officers learn is the layout of their assigned area, district, or jurisdiction. The patrol area may remain the same or change daily depending upon factors related to staffing, call volume, and individual assignments. Usually, roadways or geographical entities such as rivers or railroad tracks serve as jurisdictional dividers. Before going on patrol, an officer must identify the boundaries of the assigned area. Learning major roadways, landmarks, crime hazards, community habits, and emergency medical treatment and mental health facility locations will help officers become familiar with the assigned area and enable them to respond quickly. An officer should always have a map with important landmarks and patrol areas highlighted. Throughout a shift, an officer's patrol status may change, and dispatch should be notified of the officer's status, availability, and location.

Repeated calls for service in a particular location may present an opportunity for the officer or agency to initiate crime-prevention programs and promote local civic meetings. An officer should identify groups such as the neighborhood watch, business owners, mail carriers, utility and sanitation workers, or anyone who walks or drives through the neighborhood on a regular basis. An officer should be aware of the community's resources such as shelters, social service agencies, or internal resources. *(LE022.6.C.)*

Knowledge of the patrol area allows officers to recognize suspicious activity while patrolling their assigned area. Suspicious activity is anything abnormal at a specific time of day in a particular area. However, it may not be criminal activity. Knowledge of the law and observational skills assist officers in determining whether the suspicious activity is a crime in progress. For example, a shop that opens at 9:00 A.M. is not open at 11:00 A.M: The owner may be on vacation, or a robbery may be in progress.

## Foot Patrol

An officer may also patrol on foot. While using a vehicle can allow an officer to cover larger areas, it can also isolate him or her from the public and divert his or her attention. The advantages of foot patrol include high visibility, greater accessibility to the community, and the ability to closely investigate community concerns and observe activity in specific areas.

While patrolling on foot during the day, officers should use sidewalks in order to be highly visible and observe surroundings more efficiently. At night, officers should keep close to buildings, which allows them to inspect interiors while concealed in shadows. They should vary their routine, occasionally retracing their steps or cutting through alleys in order to keep others from knowing their location. Usually the most effective patrolling is a combination of vehicle and foot patrol. This allows officers to cover a large area and closely observe specific areas. *(LE022.8.C.)*

## Safety Hazards

While patrolling, officers should identify and remove safety hazards. A safety hazard is anything that poses a threat to people who encounter it. For example, an officer observes a refrigerator with the door still attached on the side of the road. He or she should ensure the door is removed. This kind of proactive patrolling alleviates potential hazards and protects the community. *(IN020.1.)*

**Section Vocabulary**

*BOLO*

*roll call*

## UNIT 3 | PATROLLING THE ASSIGNED AREA

## LESSON 2 | Receiving the Call

### Receiving the Call

When receiving a call, an officer should evaluate the situation based on personal knowledge and information relayed by dispatch. Though incidents vary, officers use the same basic steps to receive a call. Once dispatch has notified an officer of a call, he or she should respond by giving identification and current location, and confirming that he or she will respond. *(LE022.10.)*

**OBJECTIVES**

**LE022.10.** Respond to calls for assistance while on patrol.

**LE022.10.B.** Notify dispatch of arrival at the scene when responding to a call.

**LE135b.1.B.1.** Identify basic officer safety techniques when arriving at the scene of a call.

**LE135b.1.C.** Identify assessment techniques when arriving at the scene of a call.

**LE049b.4.A.1.** Identify how to gather pertinent information from witnesses and complainants.

### Arriving at the Scene of the Call

To locate areas quickly, officers should keep current maps in their patrol vehicle. When selecting a route, they should identify the safest and quickest roads to the call. The most direct route may not be the quickest. Construction projects, street closings, or special events may present obstacles. Officers should always consider traffic, time of day, school zones, and congested areas before determining a route.

Prior to arriving at the scene, an officer should turn off emergency lights and sirens at an adequate distance from the scene and reduce speed. Depending on agency policies, officers can turn off the vehicle headlights at night in order to approach a scene without being detected. Officers should turn down the volume on radios and notify dispatch of their arrival by radio, cell phone, or computer to avoid excess noise. *(LE022.10.B.)*

An officer should collect as much information as possible about the call to make a preliminary assessment. He or she may need to determine if there have been other incidents at this location and their nature. As the officer approaches the location, all information, including reconfirmation of the call location, should be verified with dispatch.

Officers should use streets that run parallel to the location of the call in order to avoid driving past the address and alerting suspects to the officers' presence. Once an officer has arrived at the call, he or she should stop a short distance from the address and approach on foot. If other units are responding, officers should coordinate the direction from which each will arrive.

Upon arriving at the scene, officers should identify suspicious vehicles or people leaving the immediate area of the call. Writing down the tag number of any vehicle leaving the area and noting people moving about or forming a crowd can help identify potential suspects. Officers should be aware of parked cars with motors running and look for hidden suspects. An accomplice could be acting as a lookout or waiting in the area. If the call is a crime-in-progress, the officer should look for fleeing suspects.

A preliminary assessment of the immediate area should be done from the patrol car. Officers should check for obvious clues such as a vehicle parked in a lot normally empty at that time of day (or night) or the absence of a vehicle usually parked in a specific location. Any suspicious vehicles or persons should also be noted. Officers need to note the tag of any suspicious vehicle and run a registration and wanted check on the tag number.

## Officer Safety Techniques

When exiting the patrol vehicle, an officer should close the door gently and quietly. Keys and other loose objects should be placed in pockets or secured to reduce noise. *(LE135b.1.B.1.)*

Officers need to immediately identify areas that can be used for cover and concealment. The best tactical position should be taken and maintained, especially if the officer is waiting for backup. Once the cover or concealment position has been taken, officers should identify places such as rooftops and nearby vehicles where a suspect could be hiding. Officers should approach suspicious vehicles on foot and carefully check them for occupants. Touching the hood is a way to determine if the vehicle has been driven recently. *(LE135b.1.C.)*

Officers should get close to buildings by moving behind parked cars, fences, trashcans, or shrubbery. Walking in a low crouching position and taking an indirect route will help minimize the chances of being detected. Officers must constantly survey building entrances and surrounding areas to ensure their safety. When checking the exterior perimeter of a building, an officer should use caution in approaching corners, windows, and doors. Officers should remain conscious of animals, clotheslines, garbage cans, sprinkler heads, swimming pools, and other possible hazards.

When using a flashlight to examine the perimeter of a building, an officer must carry the flashlight in his or her non-weapon hand and hold it away from his or her body to avoid presenting a clear target. After shining the flashlight in an area, an officer should immediately move to a new position. An officer should be aware of other officers' presence and locations, making sure the light does not cast them in silhouette. Because a flashlight temporarily impairs night vision, an officer must know where to aim the light before turning it on to avoid blinding others.

When encountering a suspicious person, an officer should maintain a safe reactionary distance. An officer should always watch the person's hands and body language when talking with a suspicious person. An officer should watch for inconsistencies, such as a suspect claiming to have come from one direction but pointing in another. He or she should get identification from the suspect if possible and contact dispatch for a records check.

## Gathering Information

By assessing the scene and making initial contact with the victim or witness, an officer determines the type of complaint (civil, criminal, felony, misdemeanor). Next, the officer should identify how much time has passed since the incident occurred. If the officer determines the suspect is not in the area, the officer can contact and interview victims and witnesses.

When officers question a victim or complainant, they should ask for identification and personal information such as proper names, addresses, phone numbers, and other contact information. The victim or witness should describe what happened. An officer needs to ask follow-up questions to clarify his or her understanding of the incident. Good field notes of these accounts are important for constructing the report. The victim or witness should describe the suspect or positively identify the suspect later, which will help establish probable cause in the investigation.*(LE049b.4.A.1.)*

If victims or witnesses know the suspect, they may also know other information that can help locate that individual. The officer should ask such questions as where the suspect may have gone, where the suspect may live, where a suspect's friends may be, how the suspect generally behaves, or what kind of vehicle the suspect drives. The victim or witness may have personal knowledge of the suspect's physical, medical, mental, and emotional state and the suspect's ethnic or cultural background. The officer should record all information about the suspect. These facts may help the officer plan an approach and locate the suspect. If possible, the officer should obtain written statements, which add to probable cause for future arrest.

In cases where property is stolen or damaged, an officer needs to get a description of the property and an estimate of the lost value. Precise descriptions of stolen property are important for later identification and recovery. Serial numbers and owner-applied numbers should be recorded in the report. Unique distinguishing identifiers such as scratches or unique parts should also be noted to help identify the property if found. If applicable, information should be collected and entered into FCIC. Officers will prepare a written report of the facts with statements from the victims or witnesses. Also, the officer should determine where the property was stolen from, which will help define the type of crime and dictate what police actions may be taken. For example, if the case involves the theft of items from the front yard of a house, it is a theft rather than a burglary. There was no threat or force used, so it cannot be a robbery. If the items are worth over $300, the theft is a felony. If the suspect is found and enough probable cause exists, he or she can be arrested without a warrant. If an arrest is made, the officer will prepare an arrest affidavit and any other appropriate arrest paperwork.

# UNIT 3 | PATROLLING THE ASSIGNED AREA

## LESSON 3 | Approaching and Contacting the Suspect

**OBJECTIVES**

**LE100.2.** Determine the need for backup when approaching a suspect.

**LE100.3.** Evaluate the situation upon arriving at suspect's location.

**LE100.4.F.2.** Select appropriate officer safety techniques when approaching a suspect.

**LE100.7.** Obtain identification information from a suspect.

**LE101.5.** Check for outstanding warrants on a suspect.

**LE100.17.** Transport to appropriate facility if placing the suspect under arrest.

### Approaching the Suspect

When devising a plan for contacting a suspect, officers need to consider elements of their surroundings, such as areas of cover and factors that may affect sight and hearing. Officers should decide whether to contact the suspect immediately or wait for backup *(LE100.2.)*. When contacting a suspect, officers should select an appropriate contact and arrest area and identify possible hazards. When approaching a suspect, officers should consider the suspect's criminal history, behavior, and the possibility of him or her having weapons or items that could be used as weapons. Officers should also be mindful of the presence of other individuals and possible escape routes for the suspect. Another option for approaching a suspect is to contain the suspect by using additional units to establish a perimeter. *(LE100.3.)*

### Initiating the Stop and Establishing Communication with a Suspect

While moving toward a suspect, an officer should approach cautiously and keep visual contact with the person while scanning the surroundings. Officers should ensure they keep the appropriate distance between themselves and the suspect and stay alert to identify potential resistance or threats. Officers should watch the suspect's position and hand or foot movements and look for weapons or signs of weapons. If the officer believes the suspect poses a threat or may flee, he or she should handcuff the suspect immediately after initiating contact.

An additional consideration when approaching a suspect is officer safety. Contact and cover is an effective technique officers use to keep safe when approaching or confronting a suspect. It is a coordinated effort between a contact officer and a backup or cover officer(s). Each officer operates with a specific coordinated plan for approach.

Usually, the primary officer on the call is the ***contact officer***. This officer is responsible for directing the approach and handling all communication with the suspect, including commands and interviews. The backup officer is the ***cover officer***, who is strictly responsible for officer safety concerns at the scene, including observing interaction between the contact officer and the suspect and watching for outside factors such as hostile crowds, traffic, or escape routes. The primary officer should not assign the cover officer any duties other than maintaining officer safety. Additional officers share cover responsibilities and assist the contact officer as requested. *(LE100.4.F.2.)*

### Conducting the Stop

During a stop, officers should ask suspects for information such as name, date of birth, address, Social Security number, and legal identification cards. A suspect's identity should be verified by FCIC/NCIC and checked against the information that the suspect has provided *(LE100.7.)*. If a backup officer arrives, the officer should share all current information on the suspect. Officers should continue to seek information through interviewing and observing the suspect. If appropriate, the officer should establish a rapport with the suspect to create a noncustodial atmosphere, which can help with other investigative efforts like obtaining the suspect's consent for a search. If the interview becomes custodial, the officer must issue the *Miranda* warning, and the suspect must waive his or her constitutional rights for the interview to continue.

If the officer is certain the correct suspect has been detained, a show-up identification should be conducted if possible. Another unit should be asked to transport the victim and/or witness to the officer's location so that the victim remains safe and secure from the suspect. Then the victim/witness should be asked if the suspect is the person he or she saw committing the criminal offense.

**Section Vocabulary**

***contact officer***

***cover officer***

## Outstanding Warrants

If the FCIC/NCIC criminal history check reveals an unrelated outstanding warrant in the officer's jurisdiction, he or she has authority to arrest the suspect even if sufficient probable cause has not been developed for the current case being investigated. An officer can also arrest on a warrant issued by another jurisdiction in Florida, after dispatch confirms the warrant with the issuing agency *(LE101.5.)*. The officer should wait at the scene for confirmation if possible. If the agency issuing the warrant wants the suspect transferred back to that agency, the officer can make the arrest and transport the suspect to jail. The jail should hold the suspect in accordance with the transfer procedures of both agencies or jurisdictions involved.

If the warrant is an out-of-state warrant, the suspect is a "fugitive from justice" and must be arrested. The jail will hold the suspect in accordance with the state extradition procedures. If the issuing agency waives extradition or does not confirm within a reasonable time, the suspect must be released at the scene. The officer should follow agency policy regarding documentation of his or her actions. *(LE100.17.)*

## UNIT 3 | PATROLLING THE ASSIGNED AREA

# LESSON 4 | Making the Arrest and Transporting the Prisoner

**OBJECTIVES**

**LE100.8.** Identify how to communicate verbally and nonverbally that a suspect is being placed under arrest.

**LE044b.1.** Identify how to secure a prisoner to be escorted.

**LE043c.2.B.** Identify the appropriate method for loading a prisoner into a vehicle for transport.

**LE043c.3.A.** Identify potential issues that could occur during the transport of a prisoner.

**LE043c.6.C.** Identify the process upon arrival at the detention facility.

## Making a Physical Custody Arrest

Certain steps should be taken when making a physical custody arrest. Officers should inform the suspect that he or she is under arrest, the reason for the arrest, and whether the charge is a misdemeanor or felony. The suspect should be asked if he or she understands the charges. In accordance with agency policy, officers should properly handcuff the suspect before searching him or her for weapons or contraband. Using proper techniques, the officer should perform a custodial search. If custodial questioning is necessary, officers must issue the *Miranda* warning. *(LE100.8.)*

The officer should follow agency and jail policies and procedures to make the arrest, care for the arrestee's personal property, and make decisions regarding transport. Upon delivery to the jail, the suspect may qualify to be released on his or her own recognizance. The jail will process the suspect's paperwork.

## Escorting the Prisoner to the Patrol Vehicle

The first phase in the transport process is to escort the prisoner safely to the patrol vehicle. During transport, the officer must maintain physical control of the prisoner at all times. The officer should search the prisoner again before transporting, even though a full, detailed custodial search occurred upon arrest. If another officer did the first search, the transporting officer should perform another search. One officer should not assume that the other officer has searched properly. Proper search methods should be used in an external examination of the prisoner's clothing to identify hazardous objects or weapons. The officer should keep items removed during the search beyond the prisoner's reach until they can be secured in the patrol vehicle. *(LE044b.1.)*

## Loading and Transporting the Prisoner

Officers should maintain physical contact while placing the prisoner in the rear seat of the patrol vehicle and instruct or physically guide the prisoner as needed. The vehicle's interior should always be thoroughly searched prior to transporting a suspect. The arresting officer might encounter obstacles when loading a prisoner such as the prisoner's size, health or medical condition, or compliance level. If possible, adjustments should be made based on the agency's transport policies. Options might include requesting a larger transport vehicle or an ambulance, or adjusting the prisoner's position. If resistance is encountered during the loading and transporting of the prisoner, the officer should respond with the appropriate level of force, within agency policies or guidelines. *(LE043c.2.B.)*

Before transport begins, the officer should call dispatch and provide the current location, destination, and beginning vehicle mileage. If the officer cannot transport the prisoner immediately after loading, he or she should consider weather conditions. For example, a prisoner should not be left for long in a sealed vehicle on a hot day with no air conditioning.

If the prisoner is ill, the officer should notify dispatch of what he or she plans to do. The officer should follow the agency's policies and procedures if driving to a medical facility or ask EMS to come to his or her location. If the officer must take the prisoner to a medical facility, agency policies should be followed in accompanying a prisoner in the ambulance or following in the patrol vehicle. At the medical facility, the prisoner should be constantly observed until his or her release from the facility.

## Special Considerations

Transporting in a non-partitioned vehicle should be done only if no other options are available. If an officer must do so, he or she should refer to agency procedures. A second officer may ride next to the prisoner. When transporting a prisoner of the opposite gender, the officer should tell dispatch the destination and the vehicle's beginning and ending mileage. Officers should know whether their agency's policies require special procedures such as audio taping or videotaping the transport. These guidelines must be adhered to as they protect the officer and the agency from unfounded misconduct charges.

Dealing with juveniles in custody involves several important procedures. An officer cannot transport a juvenile in the same vehicle with an adult prisoner unless they are codefendants. Officers should know whether their agency's policies require special procedures such as audio taping or videotaping the transport of juveniles.

When transporting a prisoner with a physical, sensory, or language disability, transport procedures should be adjusted as needed without compromising officer safety. If a prisoner is physically disabled, the officer may need to handcuff that prisoner after he or she gets into the transport vehicle. In some cases, the officer may need to request an ambulance for transport. A prisoner with a sensory disability may require more help entering the transport vehicle. The officer may need to reassure a prisoner with language disabilities that he or she is working on ways to improve communication. The key is flexibility within the boundaries of personal safety and agency policies. *(LE043c.3.A.)*

## Arrival at the Detention Facility

The next phase of transport occurs after the officer arrives safely at the designated drop-off point. Upon arrival, the officer should communicate key information to dispatch such as identification number (call sign), location, arrival time, and ending vehicle mileage. He or she should then approach the appropriate drop-off point, announce his or her presence, and obtain clearance to enter. The officer should secure weapon(s) in a locked location such as the patrol vehicle's trunk, a weapons locker, or a lock box at the drop-off point. The officer's agency and/or the detention facility will specify acceptable locked locations.

The officer should gather personal property removed from the prisoner, and then safely remove the prisoner from the patrol vehicle. The officer must always maintain physical control of the prisoner during escort into the detention facility. Oral commands and physical direction should be used. The officer is responsible for the prisoner if there is a waiting period. Officers should remember that even though they are in a secure facility, the booking area can be a dangerous place. *(LE043c.6.C.)*

# UNIT 3 | PATROLLING THE ASSIGNED AREA

## LESSON 5 | Processing the Prisoner

**OBJECTIVES**

**LE101.3.** Identify documentation that must be completed when booking an arrested person.

**LE101.3.B.** Identify the specific information needed about the prisoner for booking purposes.

**LE101.3.C.** Identify appropriate communication adjustments to use with the prisoner.

**LE094.8.A.** Identify the detention procedures for a juvenile.

**LE101.6.** Explain that the suspect will be fingerprinted during the booking process.

**LE101.7.** Explain that the suspect will be photographed during the booking process.

### Entering the Detention Facility

After the officer arrives at the detention facility and secures his or her weapon(s), the officer must process the prisoner. Many agencies use booking or intake officers (law enforcement or correctional officers) at the county jail to perform some or all functions for the arresting officer. These facilities have their own policies and procedures, and officers must know and follow them.

The officer should inform the intake officer of the charges against the prisoner, any injuries the prisoner has, if the prisoner was contaminated with subject control spray, or if an electronic control device was used. The transporting officer needs to give the booking officer any personal property, not including contraband, removed from the prisoner and bagged at the scene. Then the transporting officer should transfer custody of the prisoner to the booking officer.

After the transfer, the booking officer processes the prisoner. The transporting officer may complete the ***arrest affidavit***; the charging document. The detention facility needs the arrest affidavit before the transporting officer leaves. *(LE101.3.)*

### Booking

Most agencies use booking or intake officers at the jail to book, fingerprint, and photograph prisoners. Before beginning, the booking officer performs another full, detailed search of the prisoner. Next, that officer should try to confirm the prisoner's biographical information by asking for verbal identification and then requesting legal identification. Photo identification such as a driver's license or immigration visa is preferred. If the prisoner cannot or will not provide identification, he or she should be processed as John Doe or Jane Doe. Important information such as medical conditions should then be obtained. If the prisoner has physical or mental illness(es) that require attention, appropriate facility personnel should be alerted. *(LE101.3.B.)*

The officer should make sure that the prisoner understands the charge(s) and determine his or her ability to do so. If the person does not understand, the officer may have to adjust the level of communication or contact an interpreter *(LE101.3.C.)*. During this part of intake, the transporting officer or the booking officer may ask dispatch or the warrants section to run a FCIC/NCIC check for the suspect's name and outstanding warrants.

The officer should inventory and describe in a written report all property belonging to and removed from the prisoner. The officer must itemize, tag, or otherwise properly identify all items taken. Different agencies and/or detention facilities can require different information. All items should be placed in a property container and secured in a designated depository. Taking accurate inventories and properly securing a prisoner's property protects an officer and the agency from theft charges and maintains the chain of custody for items that are evidence. A narrative report and a booking form or both, depending on the facility's procedures, should be completed as needed or required.

**Section Vocabulary**

*arrest affidavit*

## Processing a Juvenile

An officer may take juveniles to an adult jail or police lockup for temporary custody for no more than six hours or for the purpose of fingerprinting and photographing as long as the juvenile is out of the sight and hearing of adults. Most juveniles in adult jails or police lockups are awaiting transport to an appropriate facility and/or pre- or post-court holding. Exceptions apply to a juvenile charged with an adult felony or when the court previously dealt with the juvenile as an adult, and he or she is involved in the same criminal episode.

A juvenile cannot be released on his or her own recognizance when custody is terminated. An adult relative or a qualified adult or organization must take custody of the child from the officer and acknowledge the action by signing booking forms or charging documents. Parents should be notified within a reasonable time of their child's arrest. A detaining officer is responsible for a juvenile in the officer's custody who suffers from mental illness, medical abnormality, or effects of substance abuse. The responsibility is the officer's until parents, guardians, or a representative of the Department of Children and Family Services assumes responsibility. Specific agencies may have additional policies and procedures for processing a juvenile. *(LE094.8.A.)*

## Fingerprinting and Photographing the Prisoner

Fingerprinting creates a permanent physical record that law enforcement agencies use to identify a person alive or dead and compare with unknown prints *(LE101.6.)*. An officer should record all personal information about the prisoner, including name, race, sex, date of birth, Social Security number, criminal charges, and case number. Officers should remember that FCIC/NCIC derives criminal history data from fingerprint cards as well as arrest and correctional reports, so it is extremely important to complete them accurately and correctly. Photographs taken at booking provide a visual record of each suspect. Many facilities can access existing photos from prior bookings rather than taking new photographs. Officers should learn agency photographing procedures and the basic techniques of photographing prisoners. *(LE101.7.)*

## Completing Paperwork

If a video or audiotape system is used to document all or part of the contact, arrest, or transport, the tape becomes part of public record under Florida's public records law, F.S. Ch. 119. It must be kept in its original form for at least 30 days. An officer should learn his or her agency's policies and procedures for archiving tapes. When the paperwork is completed and filed, an officer should advise dispatch of the call's completion and final disposition. Mastering the skills of completing paperwork and documenting a call helps an officer to satisfactorily close calls by identifying the correct forms and writing reports that clearly and completely convey investigative facts. This mastery also helps other members of the judicial system do their jobs.

## UNIT 4 | PATROL FUNCTIONS

# LESSON 1 | Directing Traffic

**OBJECTIVES**

**LE298.1.** Identify the procedure for processing found property.

**IN006.1.J.4.** Identify traffic regulations to assist the blind.

**LE022.9.A.** Identify techniques for directing traffic.

**LE022.9.B.** Identify how to enforce parking citations and summons.

## Found Property

While patrolling, officers may handle found property given to them by citizens. Officers should inventory the item(s), complete a property/receipt form, and give items to the property clerk for storage. All necessary steps should be taken to identify the owner or determine if the item(s) are evidence of a crime. If the owner can be identified and the property is not evidence, the officer should attempt to return the property according to department procedures. *(LE298.1.)*

## Traffic Violations

One of the most common occurrences a patrol officer will deal with is traffic violations, which allow officers to interact with many individuals. Often, a simple traffic infraction can be the catalyst for arrest, evidentiary/contraband discoveries, or criminal case resolutions.

## Directing Traffic

Officers may be called to direct traffic for many reasons including roadway obstructions, traffic crashes, special events, utility repairs, or broken traffic signals. Whether it is day or night, officers should wear a reflective safety vest to ensure they are visible to motorists. Officers may use hand signals, whistles, a flashlight, direction wands, reflective vests and gloves, and a traffic control box when necessary; oral commands confuse drivers and are ineffective. Officers should try to give equal time to each side of traffic flow. At an intersection, officers should try to follow the traffic signal's preset pattern, making time for turning drivers as well as those traveling straight ahead. If traffic is heavier on one side, officers should give heavier traffic more time to flow through the intersection.

When encountering a traffic situation, an officer should safely park the patrol vehicle on the shoulder or another location that does not obstruct traffic. The officer should activate the vehicle's emergency lights to instruct motorists to slow down. Before getting out of the vehicle, officers should inform dispatch of their location. Depending on the volume of traffic and traffic patterns, officers may need to request additional help. The center of an intersection is usually the safest place to stand because the officer is most visible to motorists. If emergency vehicles are involved, officers must stop traffic, allow these vehicles access, and then ensure that traffic can go around or avoid the area where an emergency vehicle is parked.

When directing traffic from somewhere other than an intersection, an officer must find the safest possible area. An officer should avoid standing between two vehicles on the roadside, or directly in front of or behind a vehicle. The officer can be injured or killed if a motorist strikes the vehicle behind which the officer is standing. To get attention and direct vehicle movement, officers should make eye contact with drivers, use a whistle, and make crisp, clear hand movements.

An officer's job when directing traffic is to maintain safety for drivers and pedestrians. Officers should be especially aware of pedestrians who are totally or partially blind, guided by a dog, or carrying a white cane or a white cane tipped in red.

F.S. § 316.1301 states:

> Whenever a pedestrian is crossing, or attempting to cross, a public street or highway, guided by a dog guide or carrying in a raised or extended position a cane or walking stick which is white in color or white tipped with red, the driver of every vehicle approaching the intersection or place where the pedestrian is attempting to cross shall bring his or her vehicle to a full stop before arriving at such intersection or place of crossing and, before proceeding, shall take such precautions as may be necessary to avoid injuring such pedestrian. A person who is convicted of a violation of this subsection is guilty of a moving violation.

While a white tipped cane or guide dog are clues of a pedestrian's partial or total blindness, all pedestrians should be afforded the same rights when crossing a public street or highway. Officers should also be aware that it is unlawful for any person not partially or totally blind or otherwise incapacitated to carry a white cane in a raised or extended way. Any person convicted of such a violation is guilty of a misdemeanor of the second degree. *(IN006.1.J.4.)*

Directing traffic at night is difficult because of limited visibility and difficulty making eye contact with drivers. When directing traffic at night or in rainy weather, officers can improve their visibility by using a flashlight, direction wand, or signal wand. When using a flashlight direction wand, an officer should make bigger and slower motions because drivers may have difficulty interpreting short, sharp motions.

Roadway damage such as potholes, sunken or washed out areas, and broken pavement may require special attention. After inspecting the area, officers should inform dispatch of the damage, the location, and necessary actions. If the damage is severe enough to pose a danger to vehicle traffic, officers must direct traffic around the damage and request assistance from the appropriate department to respond and provide barricades or road signs. *(LE022.9.A.)*

## Parking Violations

An officer can only use a Uniform Traffic Citation (UTC) to enforce Florida statutes parking violations. The officer cannot issue a UTC to enforce a municipal or county parking ordinance. In that case, he or she would use a parking citation book or ordinance citation book issued by the municipality or county. If an officer's agency uses a parking summons in the enforcement of §316.1945, F.S., the officer can complete and attach that summons to the vehicle in violation. The statute specifies that officers must attach a citation, or parking summons, in a safe, conspicuous place (usually under the windshield wiper).

There are three ways to identify whether a driver violates F.S. §316.1945: F.S. §316.003 defines the terms ***stop*** **(52)**, ***stand*** **(49)**, and ***park*** **(27)**:

**Section Vocabulary**

*park*

*stand*

*stop*

**STOP OR STOPPING:** When prohibited, any halting, even momentarily, of a vehicle, whether occupied or not, except when necessary to avoid conflict with other traffic or to comply with the directions of a law enforcement officer or traffic control sign or signal.

**STAND OR STANDING:** The halting of a vehicle, whether occupied or not, otherwise than temporarily, for the purpose of, and while actually engaged in, receiving or discharging passengers, as may be permitted under this chapter.

**PARK OR PARKING:** The standing of a vehicle, whether occupied or not, otherwise than temporarily for the purpose of and while actually engaged in loading or unloading merchandise or passengers as may be permitted by law under this chapter.

Anyone who parks in a designated handicapped space must have the proper permit. Drivers who do not have permits and park in handicapped spaces violate F.S. §316.1955 and can be issued a citation. Any violation will not be dismissed for failure of the marking to comply as long as the parking space is in general compliance and clearly distinguishable as a designated accessible parking space for those with disabilities. *(LE022.9.B.)*

# UNIT 4 | PATROL FUNCTIONS

## LESSON 2 | Responding to Alarms and Building Searches

**OBJECTIVES**

**LE500.3.C.2.** Identify ways to park the patrol vehicle an appropriate distance from the scene when responding to an alarm call.

**LE500.1.A.** Identify types of alarm calls.

**LE089a.2.A.** Identify ways to establish a perimeter/search of the building or grounds.

**LE089a.8.** Identify the appropriate techniques for conducting a search of the building.

**LE089a.8.B.** Identify the different systematic search methods.

### Responding to Alarms

During the course of their patrol, officers may respond to various types of alarms. The type of business or location of the alarm may affect the response. A financial institution, pharmacy, medical facility, or veterinary office may demand a faster response. It is possible a crime involving drugs or large amounts of cash may be in progress.

Some agency policies stipulate that at least two officers must respond to alarm calls. Other agencies make a second officer available under certain circumstances or at the request of the initial responding officer. Officers should park their patrol vehicle an appropriate distance from the building. The location chosen depends on the situation. In a residential neighborhood, officers may park their vehicle a few houses from the actual address and then walk the rest of the way. If an officer drives past the address, he or she should keep driving and stop farther down the street or around the corner. *(LE500.3.C.2.)*

The alarm company may tell dispatch what type of alarm has gone off. As officers approach the scene, they or the dispatcher may be able to identify the alarm. The dispatcher may also know if the alarm is for a burglary or robbery. Whatever the alarm's type or purpose, officers should be aware of their surroundings and anticipate unknown risks. *(LE500.1.A.)*

### Establishing a Perimeter

A ***perimeter*** is the area surrounding an incident that may be cordoned off to prevent unauthorized personnel from leaving or entering. The perimeter's size depends on the situation. It may also include natural or manmade obstructions. *(LE089a.2.A.)*

### Building Searches

Once the exterior of the building is secure, an officer can search inside. The greatest threat in a building search is the possibility of a hiding suspect. A suspect in the building must always be considered armed and dangerous. Searching the interior of an unfamiliar building presents a dilemma; officers should conduct a thorough, methodical search but avoid complacently following a set routine, as this can lead to fatal results.

If possible, an officer should gain access to the property through a representative of the property. There are too many variables, problem areas, and areas of responsibility for one officer to control, so an officer must avoid searching alone and use a K-9 unit if available. When working with a partner, an officer must establish a plan to search and secure the building. They should decide what signals to use before fanning out. Officers should avoid moving next to each other. They should stay apart and position themselves so they can return fire without placing each other in crossfire.

When entering a building to secure it, an officer should draw his or her firearm and stand to the side of the door to avoid being an exposed target if someone inside opens the door. Usually, an officer and his or her partner are on either side of the door, one in a high or standing position and the other in a low crouching position. An officer should determine if a door opens in or out. Hinges on doors that open out are visible; hinges on doors that open in are not.

When an officer approaches a door that opens out, the officer and his or her partner must stay low at opposite sides of the door. One officer throws the door open towards his or her partner. The partner grabs the door and makes sure it stays open. If the door is at the end of a hallway with no room on either side, high and low positions should be utilized on the same side of the door. An officer should never enter a doorway too quickly. Instead, he or she should stop, look, and listen. If someone answers the door, that person should be visually checked for weapons.

If a door opens in, an officer should open the door slightly, step back, listen, then shove the door against the wall, waiting until the door strikes the wall before entering the room. If the door doesn't hit something hard, someone may be behind it. The primary officer should maintain visual contact and communicate with the backup officer. An officer should know what his or her partner is going to do. Hand signals can help both officers maintain a discreet advantage. At night, rapidly blinking flashlights or penlights may be an appropriate signal provided officers do not illuminate each other. If either officer faces an imminent threat, loud verbal commands should be given to identify officer purpose and authority. This will also alert an officer's partner to the situation and the threat. An officer should not assume that his or her partner sees and hears everything he or she does.

When entering a residence, an officer should systematically search for the suspect. He or she should establish an interior boundary or perimeter, keep track of searched rooms or areas and who searched them, and note lights going on or off. The officer must be aware of noise, especially from a television or radio, which might give away his or her position. When the officer feels it is safe, interior room lights should be turned on to help clear the building. *(LE089a.8.)*

## Tactics for Entering a Room

An officer should carefully look before entering a room. An officer needs to peer into a room from different heights as needed to see if a suspect is inside. An officer should not look into a room from the same level more than once and not expose his or her body. Another option for scanning a room is "cutting the pie" or "edging." Imagining that the room is a pie divided into portions, an officer should stand to one side of the door and scan as many parts of the room as possible. When an officer and his or her partner enter a room, they should move in low and fast, one behind the other. An officer's partner cuts the pie on his or her side of the door and searches as far as is practical.

Officers should always enter the room by using a crisscross or button hook technique. In the crisscross technique, officers stand on opposite sides of the doorway and rapidly enter, one after the other. They should go to opposite sides of the room, crossing in front of each other in an X pattern. In the buttonhook (wraparound) technique, an officer and a partner enter the room by hooking around the corner at the point of entry. They stand on opposite sides or on the same side of the door. One at a time, keeping their backs to the wall, they should wrap around the wall and into the room. Speed and fluid motion are important in this technique.

Once inside, officers should search the room using the leapfrog pattern; an officer's partner covers the officer and vice versa as each officer moves from place to place. It is important to stay together and search each room thoroughly before moving to the next. After searching each room, officers should secure the room by closing the door or keeping the room under observation if possible. If no obvious signs of damage are found or no crime was committed, control of the premises should be returned to the key holder. *(LE089a.8.B)*

**Section Vocabulary**

***perimeter***

# UNIT 4 | PATROL FUNCTIONS

## LESSON 3 | Interactions with Vehicles

**OBJECTIVES**

**LE001.3.A.** Determine how to identify pertinent information on an unattended, abandoned, or disabled vehicle.

**LE001.6.** Determine whether an unattended, abandoned, or disabled vehicle should be towed.

**LE002.8.B.** Identify when an officer is authorized to search an unattended, abandoned, or disabled vehicle.

**LE002.9.** Identify how to inventory an unattended, abandoned, or disabled vehicle.

**LE002.8.** Identify how to search an unattended, abandoned, or disabled vehicle.

**LE001.8.** Complete the appropriate report when conducting an inventory or search of an unattended, abandoned, or disabled vehicle.

**LE001.5.** Identify how to secure an unattended, abandoned, or disabled vehicle as evidence.

While patrolling, officers should look for vehicles blocking the roadway to avoid any traffic-related incidents and ensure public safety. Officers will also encounter vehicles stopped or parked in violation of state traffic laws. These encounters may involve a disabled vehicle stopped in an intersection or a roadway or an unoccupied vehicle left on the side of the road. These situations should be investigated and may result in identifying other criminal acts such as vehicle thefts and vehicle burglaries.

### Abandoned Property

An ***abandoned vehicle*** is a vehicle without a driver or person in charge of the vehicle. It could be a disabled vehicle, improperly parked vehicle, or a potential crime scene. When responding to an abandoned vehicle or property complaint, the initial concern is to identify public safety hazards. An officer may need to have the property removed from its original spot to alleviate danger.

Once safety concerns are satisfied, the officer should try to identify the owner. The most obvious sources of vehicle and owner information are the license tag and vehicle identification number (VIN). The VIN is a numbering system that meets governmental criteria to identify the vehicle. It is entered into the Florida Department of Highway Safety and Motor Vehicles (DHSMV) database to provide law enforcement with additional identification information. Because it is a unique number, the VIN is the confirming identifier for vehicles. Its most common locations are on the dashboard, in the bottom corner of the windshield on the driver's side, or on the driver's side doorjamb. The investigating patrol officer may also obtain information about the vehicle or owner from the complainant or people in the area. *(LE001.3.A.)*

### Towing Vehicles

In some cases, the abandoned, unattended, or disabled vehicle must be removed from its location. If so, the services of a wrecker company are needed. If the vehicle is evidence and needs to be held under the control of the investigating agency, a wrecker service would transport the vehicle to a preferred secure location. A vehicle inventory should be conducted and documented on the officer's agency's vehicle/inventory form. If the vehicle being removed is unattended, abandoned, or disabled, an officer will request a wrecker to transport the vehicle to the business' local lot. If the vehicle is disabled, and an owner or driver is present, he or she may request that a specific tow company respond. In this case, the owner will make arrangements with the company as to location and fees. *(LE001.6.)*

## Inventory

An inventory of a vehicle is a recognized exception to the Fourth Amendment search warrant requirement. An inventory is conducted to protect the vehicle and contents, safeguard the agency and others from danger, and protect officers and custodians against false claims of loss or damage. The inventory should document the vehicle's overall condition, such as mileage and damage, as well as contents and equipment like a radio, CD player, rims, and GPS units. An officer does not need probable cause to inventory a vehicle because the purpose of an inventory is to document items in or on a vehicle, not to search for evidence of a crime. Courts usually uphold the legality of an inventory when the agency has an established written policy regarding inventories and agency employees follow that policy. *(LE002.8.B.)*

After the decision is made to impound, the vehicle should be removed from the scene according to agency policy and procedure. Usually, agencies will provide inventory forms, which should include all items of value such as CDs, money, and jewelry. Often during inventories, officers will find contraband or evidence of a crime. Such items may include controlled substances, weapons, and burglary tools. Agency policies should be followed in reference to the recovery of evidence inside the vehicle *(LE002.9.).* Officers should remember that an inventory cannot be used as a pretext for a search for evidence in a criminal investigation.

## Exterior/Interior Vehicle Search

The authority to search a vehicle is based on probable cause, search incident to arrest, consent, or vehicle inventory. Whatever the purpose of the search, the method changes only slightly depending on the scope and purpose of the search. When searching the exterior and interior of a vehicle, an officer should ensure all areas are checked. The authority to search a vehicle's trunk is determined by the purpose of the search. When working through the search, an officer should avoid unnecessary damage to the vehicle.

Usually officers will search a vehicle using a specific pattern, which allows an officer to be consistent and thorough. All areas of the vehicle should be searched and re-searched. Gloves should be worn when searching to protect against discarded needles, weapons, or other hazards which could jeopardize officer safety. An officer must be cautious of suspicious buttons or switches in a vehicle, as they could activate explosives or chemical devices. If a vehicle is locked, agency policy will determine whether the officer conducts a visual search or calls a locksmith. *(LE002.8.)*

## Completing the Inventory Form

Many agencies simultaneously inventory while searching the vehicle. The officer should follow agency policy and procedure as related to the appropriate form or report for searching and inventorying a vehicle. While conducting the inventory, the officer should document, on the vehicle/property receipt form, the items inside and any damage to the vehicle. This ensures the entire process is documented. Agency policies may require completion of an incident report, which goes along with the inventory. Drugs, firearms, and other contraband should be removed from the vehicle, packaged, and taken back to the officer's agency. Agency policies may authorize the removal and inventory of valuables for impounding at the agency. The remaining agency forms should be submitted as agency policies require. *(LE001.8.)*

**Section Vocabulary**

*abandoned vehicle*

## Vehicles Involved in a Crime

If a vehicle is involved in a crime, the reporting/responding agency may send a crime scene technician to process the vehicle at its location or request that it be towed to the impound lot. If the originating agency sends someone to process the vehicle, the officer must immediately secure the vehicle as evidence. The vehicle should not be left unattended, and the officer should not touch it or allow anyone in or around it until the crime scene technicians arrive. The officer should treat it as a crime scene until it is processed by the crime scene technician or other responsible person. Agency policies should be followed regarding securing stolen vehicles as evidence. A secured storage facility will be used to maintain the chain of custody and ensure evidence is free from tampering. The officer should authorize a hold on the vehicle on the property/inventory form if it is evidence. *(LE001.5.)*

# CHAPTER 6

## Patrol 2



Officers must be prepared for many eventualities in the course of patrolling their assigned areas. This chapter provides an overview of law enforcement techniques and tactics focusing on ICS training, crowd control situations, gangs and extremist groups, HAZMAT situations, and bombs and explosives.

# UNIT 1 | INCIDENT COMMAND SYSTEM (ICS)

## LESSON 1 | Incident Command System (ICS)

The Incident Command System (ICS) is a standardized, on-scene, all-hazards incident management approach that allows for the integration of facilities, equipment, personnel, procedures, and communications operating within a common organizational structure.

The incident command chapter provided by the National Incident Management System (NIMS) is on the Federal Emergency Management Agency (FEMA) website. This course is taught through two units: Unit 1, IS-100.b Introduction to the Incident Command System and Unit 2, IS-700.a National Incident Management System (NIMS), An Introduction.

Recruits will use the NIMS website to access these units and pass an online evaluation.

# UNIT 2 | CROWD CONTROL

## LESSON 1 | Crowd Control

**OBJECTIVES**

**LE021a.1.C.** Identify the size and organization of a crowd.

**LE021a.1.C.1.** Identify officer safety considerations in a crowd control situation.

**LE021a.1.D.** Identify potential weapons in a crowd control situation.

**LE021b.4.C.1.** Utilize safe positioning and distancing when approaching crowds, demonstrators, or rioters.

**LE021a.1.A.1.** Identify the reason the group has gathered and what they want to achieve.

### Assessing the Crowd

Officers should be aware that the United States Constitution's First Amendment allows people to peaceably assemble. Officers should also be aware of Florida Statutes that apply to assemblies or groups. A few of these statutes that could aid an officer in crowd control situations include the following:

| | |
|---|---|
| **F.S. §877.03** | Breach of the Peace; Disorderly Conduct |
| **F.S. §870.02** | Unlawful Assemblies |
| **F.S. §870.01** | Affrays and Riots |
| **F.S. §856.011** | Disorderly Intoxication |

Individuals may gather as long as they cause no disturbance and act within the scope of state laws and city or county ordinances. An officer's duty is to determine if the demonstration or gathering is lawful based on state statutes.

Any large gathering has potential for danger and must be approached cautiously. Sheer numbers can be overwhelming for responding officers. The size and organization of a crowd influences whether an officer confronts it. The crowd's mood will also be a major factor in an officer's approach and gives insight to its possible reaction to law enforcement presence *(LE021a.1.C.)*. Though non-hostile crowds are more passive, officers should never become complacent when dealing with large groups as things can quickly change. Safety is an officer's main concern. *(LE021a.1.C.1.)*

As officers observe the crowd, they should identify weapons or objects that are potential weapons such as broken bottles and blunt edged objects *(LE021a.1.D.)*. Removing or arresting members of a large group is sometimes difficult because the anonymity of a crowd emboldens aggressive individuals. In large crowds, attacks can come from any direction, so officers should always have an exit strategy and prevent crowds from cornering them or limiting their ability to exit a scene *(LE021b.4.C.1.)*. A show of force or presence in numbers can be extremely persuasive in calming a crowd. In some situations, calling for assistance and waiting for backup before acting may be the safe and practical choice, especially if the situation looks like it could escalate.

**LE021a.4.B.1.** Identify the procedure for approaching and contacting the leader of crowds or demonstrations.

**LE021a.4.B.** Understand the importance of communicating with the group leaders to identify the problem or the disturbance.

# Identifying the Problem

Identifying why a group has assembled helps an officer better understand group goals and possible solutions for a peaceful dispersal. Officers can do this by looking for signs and symbols on clothing or listening to words or phrases yelled or chanted by the crowd. *(LE021a.1.A.1.)*

An important part of dispersing crowds and resolving group incidents is determining the leader or instigator. An officer can identify this person by observing how the crowd interacts. Whom does it rally behind? Who does all the talking? Who seems to stand out most, talking the loudest and prompting activity? Answers to these questions may point to the group leader. If the person responsible for the crowd has not been determined, the officer should attempt to do so by asking individuals in the crowd *(LE021a.4.B.1.)*. After identifying the leader or responsible person, officers should separate the individual from the crowd and interview him or her. Isolation allows an officer to speak to the leader without the support of the group. Good communication skills are essential in resolving conflicts involving many people *(LE021a.4.B.)*. An officer must speak in a professional manner to encourage cooperation. He or she should inform the leader of the reason for officer presence at the scene. The leader's willingness to cooperate is a major factor in subduing a threatening situation. Issuing a threat to arrest someone during initial contact may turn a peaceful event violent.

An officer should professionally request that the leader comply with laws and ordinances, if the group has violated any. Independent criminal violations may occur in a crowd, such as underage drinking or illegal narcotics usage. These violations must be addressed. An officer's primary responsibilities involve protecting life, restoring order, and maintaining the peace. If a violation of the law occurs, an officer should act swiftly to prevent further problems and use discretion when deciding on enforcement action. An officer can sometimes use the laws being violated as tools to dissuade individuals from becoming aggressive or hostile. If an officer expects to make a physical arrest, he or she should observe the crowd's actions, determine what law is violated, and identify the violator.

# UNIT 3 | CRIMINAL STREET GANGS AND EXTREMIST GROUPS

## LESSON 1 | Criminal Street Gangs and Extremist Groups

**OBJECTIVES**

**IN006.1.C.1.** Define *criminal street gang.*

**IN006.1.C.3.** Identify the importance of gang alliances.

**IN006.1.C.4.** Identify characteristics of Florida gang members.

**IN006.1.C.6.** Identify common motives for juvenile gang membership.

**IN006.1.C.7.** Identify common gang-related symbols, graffiti, colors, signs, and tattoos.

**IN006.1.D.** Identify the types of extremist groups.

**IN006.1.D.1.** Identify types of extremists known to be currently active in Florida.

### Gangs

One of the most dangerous population groups a law enforcement officer may encounter is a criminal street gang. Expansion of these groups and their violence and criminal activity has made gangs a national problem. The Florida Statutes defines a ***criminal street gang*** as follows:

> (1) a formal or informal ongoing organization, association, or group that has as one of its primary activities the commission of criminal or delinquent acts, and that consists of three or more persons who have a common name or common identifying signs, colors, or symbols and have two or more members who, individually or collectively, engage in or have engaged in a pattern of criminal street gang activity. F.S. §874.03. *(IN006.1.C.1.)*

What separates street gangs from other associations is criminal intent and organized criminal activity. Most Florida gangs are native to the state. However, a number of Florida gangs are influenced by or may have connections to gangs in other states. These relationships, called affiliations or alliances, are important to the overall growth and strength of local gangs because they bring together a diverse population with various levels of criminal experience and connections to gangs in other states. *(IN006.1.C.3.)*

### Gang Types

One type of gang with a growing national and worldwide membership is the outlaw motorcycle gang. Manufacturing and distributing methamphetamines is a major source of income for outlaw motorcycle gangs in most mainland states, including Florida. These gangs may promote their illegal activities by forming criminal alliances with independent methamphetamine cookers, street gangs, and organized crime groups.

Hundreds of gangs throughout the United States are associated by name under the Los Angeles based Bloods and Crips. However, not all gangs are affiliated with a larger, more well-known group. Hundreds of independent criminal street gangs have been identified from Pensacola to the Florida Keys. They operate in small rural towns, upper-middle-class neighborhoods, schools, and other areas.

The MS-13 gang, also known as the Mara Salvatrucha 13, is one of the most violently dangerous and well-organized gangs in the U.S. It has factions located throughout the United States and is unique in that it retains ties to its El Salvadoran counterparts. Many MS-13 members sport numerous tattoos on their bodies and faces and wear blue and white, the colors of the El Salvadoran flag. Their progressive increase in violent activities and careless disregard for the law (threats and attacks against law enforcement officials are common) has made them the most feared gang in the U.S.

As a result of drug trade and gang wars, many gang leaders and members end up in federal and state prisons. The Bloods and Crips can be found in various state and prison populations. In prison, a means of visual identification was established to provide protection for gang members.

## Characteristics of Gangs

Race and ethnicity play a prominent role in the makeup of associated gang members. In Florida, gangs are overwhelmingly populated by young males. The average age of gang members is between 13 and 23. Gang members are often products of child abuse or neglect and come from a disadvantaged socio-economic background. Often gang members are school dropouts, unemployed, and frequently in trouble with law enforcement. *(IN006.1.C.4.)*

The general structure of gangs can be broken down into four categories. Wannabes are potential members on the fringe of the gang. Not yet accepted, they experiment with the gang lifestyle. Associates are not officially gang members but are accepted to some degree. They participate on a limited basis in the gang's social and criminal activities. At this level, youths can become dangerous because they may be more willing to resort to violent behavior to gain acceptance. Regular members are initiated members who usually participate in the gang's social and criminal activities. They tend to back up hard-core members, who are members fully committed to gang life. Very influential in the gang, they are often leaders who determine the gang's activities and establish its level of violence.

## Why Juveniles Join Gangs

The prestige or power of being part of a gang is a motivating factor for many young people. The feeling of belonging or friendship may also entice a juvenile to join a gang. In addition, problems within the home or family may lead youth to look to a gang for a role model. For some, gangs provide a way to deal with social relationships and adjustment problems. Sometimes, joining a gang gives members a sense of identity *(IN006.1.C.6.)*. Peer pressure and intimidation from a dominant gang often influence juveniles, so juveniles may join gangs to protect themselves from outside sources. They feel more secure knowing other gang members will defend them against outsiders or take revenge for any action against them. Another enticement is the opportunity for financial gain. Children who grow up in poor neighborhoods are vulnerable to the influence of material consumption by gang members.

## Gang-related Symbols

Gang members use graffiti, tattoos, hand signs, and colors as nonverbal communication devices among themselves and with other gangs to identify themselves or other members and promote gang solidarity. These symbols and colors have special significance to a gang. Law enforcement officers should become familiar with gang symbols and/or activities in their patrol area. *(IN006.1.C.7.)*

Members may also express affiliation by wearing certain types of clothing, jewelry, bandannas, hats, and various haircuts and hairstyles. Because these symbols have very significant meanings to a gang, members go to great lengths to protect them from degradation by rival gangs, which is considered the ultimate humiliation. Violent altercations can occur when one gang disrespects a rival gang's symbols.

Graffiti is an initial indicator of gang presence in an area. Gangs often use graffiti to stake out or declare their presence in an area or state opposition to another gang. Closely monitoring it helps officers keep track of gang conflicts and can aid in developing a roster of members. If an officer finds graffiti in his or her patrol area, he or she should photograph it and report the information. Graffiti must be painted over or quickly removed. If not, others are likely to be encouraged to add graffiti of their own, and the effect will multiply. Some communities have paint-out programs as community service sentences. Recent laws increase penalties for creating graffiti and hold juvenile offenders' guardians liable.

Gang members use other forms of communication to acknowledge their presence and intentions. They use colors that have specific meanings to gang members and are part of a gang's ideology. Tattoos identify a member of a particular gang, make a statement, or honor a fallen gang member. Signals are made by forming letters or numbers with hands and fingers to communicate gang affiliation and to challenge rival gangs.

## Extremist Groups

An ***extremist group*** or terrorist group is a formal or informal association of individuals acting in concert or independently to advocate violence and the illegal disruption of the lawful activities of others. Extremist groups are either domestic or international. *(IN006.1.D.)*

Domestic terrorism is terrorist activity conducted by a group or by individuals who are U.S. citizens operating within the U.S. or its territories. Domestic extremist groups are divided into sub-groups depending on their motivations. Right-wing extremist groups believe in racial supremacy, and embrace anti-government and anti-regulatory beliefs. Left-wing groups generally profess a revolutionary socialist doctrine and view themselves as protectors of the people against capitalism and imperialism. These groups aim to change the United States by creating revolutionary movements.

International terrorism involves violent criminal acts intended to coerce or intimidate civilians or influence government policy. The primary objective of these groups is to plan and implement large-scale, high-profile, high-casualty attacks against U.S. citizens and interests as well as those of its allies worldwide. Lack of a formal structure makes identifying members difficult, although formalized terrorist organizations are autonomous and have their own personnel infrastructures, financial arrangements, and training facilities. These groups are divided into three sub-groups: International Islamic jihad movements, formalized terrorist organizations, and state-sponsored terrorist groups.

## Militias

Militias refuse to recognize the authority of municipal, state, and federal governments. They view law enforcement officers as representatives of the government, which they feel is controlled by people who cannot be trusted to preserve law and order. Therefore, militia members often train for preemptive attacks or ambushes by the government and are often arrested for weapons violations.

## Extremist Groups in Florida

Some extremist groups known to Florida law enforcement can be placed in these major categories: anti-abortion groups, militias, animal rights groups, racist (hate) groups, and international extremists. Currently about 70 domestic extremist groups are active in Florida. Many share similar agendas. Staying informed about their presence and activities in U.S. communities is a crucial law enforcement duty. *(IN006.1.D.1.)*

**Section Vocabulary**

*criminal street gang*

*extremist group*

# UNIT 4 | HAZMAT

## LESSON 1 | Preparation for Response

***Hazardous Material (HAZMAT)*** is any substance or material that when released may cause harm, serious injury, death to humans or animals, or harm the environment. An agency Emergency Response Plan (ERP) establishes safe and uniform guidelines for response to incidents involving hazardous material or weapons of mass destruction. Its goals are to protect the public and secure the scene while safeguarding responders. Officers should be familiar with agency ERPs to respond properly to HAZMAT situations. *(HZ001.3.)*

**OBJECTIVES**

**HZ001.3.** Identify the significance of having established local plans with regard to responding to hazardous materials emergencies.

**HZ001.2.** Identify the duty-to-act requirements that apply to public safety employees.

**HZ001.1.** Identify the role of the first responder at the awareness level.

Numerous laws, regulations, and standards influence an officer's actions at a hazardous materials incident. ***Standard of care*** is the level of competency expected or required during the performance of a service or a duty. It dictates that officers act appropriately when serving the public.

Decisions made by first responders during the first critical minutes of HAZMAT incidents greatly increase chances of survival. The agency's ERP and standard operating procedures (SOP) should contain procedures for emergencies. Public safety employees have a duty to act but the responders should not exceed the level of their training and equipment in responding to an incident *(HZ001.2.)*. The ***Emergency Response Guidebook (ERG)*** outlines the first responder's initial actions. The guidebook's purpose is to aid in the identification of materials, outline basic actions

## Section Vocabulary

*Emergency Response Guidebook (ERG)*

*Hazardous Material (HAZMAT)*

*standard of care*

for first responders, recommend areas of protective action, and give responders an initial safety plan.

# Modes of Operation

Responders to a hazardous materials incident conduct operations in two modes depending on individual training. Responders employ defensive modes when the level of training, available equipment, or degree of the incident prohibits further control of the incident. Responders may use the defensive mode, for example, while awaiting remote shut-off of a gas valve. An offensive mode places responders in close proximity to or in contact with the hazardous material or its vapors and gases. Therefore, responders take offensive action only after conducting a thorough risk vs. benefit analysis. Only properly trained and protected technician-level responders engage in offensive operations.

# Levels of Training

There are five levels of training for hazardous materials. A person at awareness level initiates the emergency response sequence and notifies authorities of the situation. The next level is operational. A person with operational training takes defensive action to contain the release and secure the area. An officer at the next level is a hazardous materials technician, who responds by taking offensive action to control a spill or leak. Some officers are hazardous materials specialists. The specialist has the expert knowledge to support the hazardous materials technician. The highest level is a hazardous materials incident commander. He or she assumes command of the incident above the level of the first responder because he or she is trained at the operational level and has received additional training in the methods needed to implement the employer's emergency response plan.

# Roles of First Responders at the Awareness Level

First responders at the awareness level have only four responsibilities or goals. The first is recognition/identification. Officers must recognize that an incident involves hazardous materials and, if possible, identify the materials. Both must be done without risk to the responder and the public. The second level is isolation, which is the ability to deny or restrict access to the involved area and remove uninjured and uncontaminated persons from that area. The third level is protection, which involves ensuring the safety of the officer and the public. If responders have proper training and equipment, protection may include using personal protective equipment and evacuating nearby occupancies. The fourth level is notification, in which the first responder informs the next level of response as defined in the employer's ERP. *(HZ001.1.)*

# UNIT 4 | HAZMAT

## LESSON 2 | Hazard Identification

**OBJECTIVES**

**HZ002.2.** Identify a hazardous material by class, name, or identification number.

### Occupancy and Location

Occupancy refers to a structure and its use; some examples are manufacturing facilities, storage facilities, retail establishments, and residences. Knowledge of an occupancy type allows an officer to anticipate what hazardous materials may be present. Location refers to an area and its use, for example, agricultural areas, industrial parks, business districts and residential neighborhoods. Details such as traffic patterns, time of day, inhabitants, and type of location may affect the first responder's reaction to a potential hazard. Illicit drug labs present unique dangers, such as chemical hazards and booby traps. Clues indicating a drug lab include unusual traffic at odd hours, heavy chemical odors, and fortification.

### Containers and Labels

Containers can be fixed, transportable, or portable. Fixed containers are permanent structures containing materials. Transportable containers are designed to transport materials safely. Portable containers are those that can be moved easily from location to location, such as portable propane tanks. The U.S. Department of Transportation (DOT) requires the use of labels and placards that identify the hazard class of a material. These appear on all four sides of a vehicle, railcar, or other large container and on individual packages of the material. Under special circumstances, DOT may not require placards. Exceptions may be affected by the class and quantity of material carried. Fixed facilities that store hazardous materials may also bear nonstandard or improper placards. However, the absence of a placard does not indicate the absence of hazardous materials.

### "Dangerous" Placard

Anything that holds two or more classes of hazardous materials must display the "DANGEROUS" placard and may use it instead of the specific placard for each class of material. The classification and amount of hazardous materials being transported restrict the use of this placard. Materials such as explosives and toxic gases cannot use the "DANGEROUS" placard.

### Hazardous Materials Listed by Class, Name, and Division

Below are examples of the most common classes of potentially hazardous materials.

**Class 1** refers to explosives. ***Explosives*** are materials or devices designed to release energy very rapidly. Emergency responders should consider all explosives to be extreme hazards when they are involved in or near a fire. Some examples of explosive materials are dynamite, black powder, and small arms ammunition.

**Class 2** contains gases. ***Gases*** are materials that are neither solid nor liquid at ordinary temperatures; they are contained under pressure. They may be flammable, non-flammable, poisonous, or corrosive. Some examples of potentially hazardous gases are acetylene, hydrogen, and anhydrous ammonia.

**Class 3** Flammable liquids (and Combustible liquids [U.S.]) These materials burn in the presence of an ignition source. Some examples are gasoline, diesel fuel, and acetone.

**Class 4** is composed of flammable solids, which are neither liquid nor gas materials and which burn in the presence of an ignition source. Some ignite spontaneously or in the presence of heat or friction. Others are dangerous when wet. Some examples are magnesium, sulfur, and calcium carbide.

**Class 5** incorporates oxidizing substances. They may yield oxygen and cause or heighten the combustion of other materials.

**Class 6** comprises toxic materials and infectious substances.

**Class 7** involves radioactive substances.

**Class 8** contains corrosive substances.

**Class 9** refers to miscellaneous dangerous goods. Not belonging to Classes 1–8, these hazardous materials are subject to DOT transportation regulations. Some examples are molten sulfur, PCBs (poly-chlorinated biphenyls), and hazardous waste.

## Shipping Papers and Facility Documents

Shipping papers itemize all hazardous materials during any mode of transport. The location of shipping papers depends on the mode of transportation. Generally, the person in charge of the vehicle or vessel has the papers. Law requires employers to maintain a Material Safety Data Sheet (MSDS) for any hazardous substance stored, manufactured, or used in the workplace. Facility documents may also include emergency response plans, action plans, and documents describing the materials present.

## Colors and Markings

Colors of placards and labels help identify a material's hazard classification. Company names and other unique markings may indicate the presence of hazardous materials. Familiarity with the users and suppliers of hazardous materials in the community can be helpful in a HAZMAT situation. The DOT has an identification numbering system to recognize hazardous materials in storage or transport.

## Using the Emergency Response Guidebook

The DOT has established the United Nations/North American (UN/NA) four-digit numbering system to identify materials. An officer can identify a material by finding the number on the orange panel on the container, placard, or shipping papers or packaging, and cross-referencing the ID numbers in the index of the DOT Emergency Response Guidebook (ERG). The officer may also find the name of the material on shipping papers or packaging, or may be able to ask the person responsible for the facility or vehicle containing the material.

## *NFPA 704 Diamonds*

The National Fire Protection Association (NFPA) has developed a standard facility marking system called the 704 system. Placed on structures or storage facilities' exteriors, this large symbol indicates products stored. The diamond-shaped symbol is divided into four segments that indicate the following risks:

- health (blue)
- flammability (red)
- reactivity (yellow)
- other (white)

In each area, a number from 0 to 4 indicates the material's relative hazard: a 0 indicates no hazard and a 4 indicates the highest hazard. The white area provides other information or any special hazards of the material.

## ***Identifying the Material by Name***

Accurate identification helps an officer to completely and accurately assess a situation. It is important that awareness-level responders not put themselves at risk in the process of identifying the material. To identify the material, officers may have to examine documents/shipping papers or conduct interviews with the transport driver or facility staff. Employees, vehicle drivers, and bystanders may be able to identify the product. If the officer cannot identify the material's specific name, he or she should make safety decisions as an awareness-level responder based on minimizing potential health hazards. The officer should rely on agency policies and procedures to avoid risk to persons and property. *(HZ002.2.)*

**Section Vocabulary**

*explosives*

*gases*

**UNIT 4 | HAZMAT**

# LESSON 3 | Taking Control

**OBJECTIVES**

**HZ003.1.** Identify actions to take to isolate the hazardous materials incident.

**HZ003.3.** Identify protective actions that can be taken in accordance with the Emergency Response Guidebook (ERG) in the event of a hazardous materials incident.

## Basic Protective Actions

Officers should always approach any potential HAZMAT situation with extreme caution. If an officer cannot approach from upwind, his or her next choice is crosswind. The main objectives are to isolate the area without entering it, keep people away from the scene, and ensure people are upwind and out of low-lying areas. *(HZ003.1.)*

An officer should prevent direct contamination by avoiding contact with the product, its gases and vapors, or smoke. He or she should also prevent secondary contamination resulting from contact with items or persons who have not been properly decontaminated. An officer should not allow anyone or anything to leave the area without evaluation for decontamination by qualified, properly protected personnel.

## Using the ERG

The Emergency Response Guidebook is composed of Public Safety and Emergency Response sections.

### *Public Safety*

The Public Safety section contains information on notification, protective clothing, and evacuation. The notification subsection identifies what officers must do immediately when called to a scene, such as activate agency emergency response plans and ensure help is on the way. Additional information can be gained from calling the emergency contact number on the shipping papers or the emergency response telephone numbers listed inside the guide's back cover. An officer should advise other responders of incident conditions, material(s) involved, amount of material, safe approach information, guide page to use, resources needed, and actions taken. The protective clothing subsection indicates when and if responders need specialized chemical protection. Protective clothing requires proper training to use. Most agencies do not furnish protective clothing to patrol officers.

After an officer isolates the immediate area, the next step is to evacuate or protect persons downwind or within the radius of the incident, depending on whether the material was spilled or involved in a fire. An officer should evacuate the area if the incident is going to last for an extended period or could potentially cause a fire or explosion. Since the evacuation process may be difficult (for example, due to dense population or the presence of a school or hospital) or expose people to greater hazards than remaining in the area would, an officer should rely on agency policy and instruction from supervisors before deciding to evacuate. The evacuation subsection also gives information about how far people should stay from a spill, also known as the

***protective action distance***. If the material's entry in the index is highlighted, the officer should consult the Table of Initial Isolation and Protective Action Distances.

Fire creates the potential for an explosion or a boiling liquid expanding vapor explosion (BLEVE). The ERG gives in-depth information about protective action distances. Recommendations depend on the spill's size, weather conditions, and time of day. Geographical conditions can also affect the distribution of any hazardous materials.

**Section Vocabulary**

*protective action distance*

## Emergency Response

This section has three subsections: Fire; Spill or Leak; and First Aid. The fire subsection provides guidelines to all levels of responders. Awareness-level responders must not attempt to extinguish a fire that involves hazardous materials. Normal fire extinguisher training is not sufficient to fight a fire that directly involves hazardous materials. Only properly trained and protected persons should attempt to fight such a fire. Operational-level personnel with the necessary protection and training can accomplish defensive fire attack. Technician-level personnel must conduct offensive fire attack.

Personnel engaged in controlling spills and leaks must have proper protection and training. Awareness-level responders are not usually trained in spill or leak control. Operational-level personnel can perform spill control if they avoid direct contact with the material and have proper protection. Operational-level responders can also activate remote shut-off. Technician-level responders can perform leak control.

The First Aid subsection outlines basic first aid for victims of exposure. Awareness-level responders with proper protection can come in direct contact with persons who present a significant risk of secondary contamination. An officer should therefore encourage contaminated, conscious victims to move to an isolated area and await medical assistance from properly trained and protected personnel. Untrained and unprotected personnel must not attempt to rescue victims who are unconscious because of exposure to hazardous materials. *(HZ003.3.)*

# UNIT 4 | HAZMAT

## LESSON 4 | Termination and Final Activities

**OBJECTIVES**

**HZ004.2.** Identify information that should be obtained during a hazardous materials incident debriefing.

**HZ004.1.** Identify actions to be taken during termination of a response to a hazardous materials incident.

### Termination Procedures

As awareness-level responders, officers should know what actions to take to terminate their involvement in an incident. Officers should always follow agency policies and procedure.

As responders terminate hazardous-materials incidents, agencies must meet Occupational Safety and Health Administration (OSHA) requirements. The intent of the OSHA requirements is to learn from mistakes and foster a continuing learning process that ultimately improves safety. During an incident debriefing, officers should identify operational weaknesses, document the termination process, and identify any need for post-exposure medical evaluations. *(HZ004.2.)*

During the on-scene debriefing process, officers should advise all responders of materials to which they may have been exposed, signs and symptoms of overexposure, and who to contact if they notice signs or symptoms of exposure. If exposure exceeds the published limits, it is necessary to send for medical evaluation. It is also necessary to identify operational strengths and weaknesses in the critique and after-action analysis phases. The employer identifies methods to correct weaknesses, implements the plan, and addresses training issues, if required. *(HZ004.1.)*

# UNIT 4 I HAZMAT

## LESSON 5 I Methamphetamine Laboratories (Meth Labs)

**OBJECTIVES**

**HZ005.1.A.** Identify how methamphetamine is consumed.

**HZ005.2.** Identify the various processes used to manufacture methamphetamine in clandestine laboratories.

**HZ005.3.** Identify the hazards associated with clandestine methamphetamine laboratories.

**HZ005.4.** Identify elements of immediate response protocol to an incident involving a clandestine methamphetamine laboratory.

### Manufacturing

A methamphetamine is an illegally manufactured, highly addictive stimulant. It can be injected, taken orally, or inhaled by smoking or snorting *(HZ005.1.A.)*. Methamphetamine is often manufactured in small, makeshift laboratories in rural areas and communities surrounding larger cities. Police departments and sheriff's offices often discover labs when serving arrest warrants or investigating other criminal activity.

Officers should follow safety guidelines when they encounter a methamphetamine lab. They should be aware of chemicals present during the manufacturing of methamphetamine and the equipment and stages involved in manufacturing it. Dangerous chemicals used in the manufacturing process can be kept in kitchens or cooking areas as well as stored throughout a residence. It is not unusual for meth labs to be mobile and located in a truck or trailer. Methamphetamine is manufactured by converting pseudoephedrine or ephedrine through a simple chemical process. Two common methods used are red phosphorous, the "Red P" method and anhydrous ammonia, the "Nazi" method. Commonly found paraphernalia used in the manufacture of meth are quart (mason) jars, beakers, two-liter bottles, and small gas cans with a hose. Also used in the manufacturing process are a heating source, blenders, coffee filters, and blister packs from nasal decongestant products. *(HZ005.2.)*

### Safety Hazards

Individuals involved in the manufacturing may pose a threat to the officer and community once discovered. If an officer suspects a lab is present, he or she should avoid inhaling fumes or having any contact with the chemicals, as they can cause explosions or oxygen depletion. In addition to being explosive, these chemicals are also highly corrosive. *(HZ005.3.)*

### Response Protocol

Decontamination protocol for a meth incident is the same as for any hazmat exposure. Officers should not touch anything or turn anything off or on. Any item may be booby-trapped. The occupants should be evacuated, and the officer should leave the premises immediately. The officer must not place anything in the patrol car prior to decontamination or allow the removal of any items from the site (due to possible contamination) *(HZ005.4.)*. It is necessary to establish a perimeter and follow agency policies and procedures for meth lab response. Officers should always err on the side of caution when they encounter a meth lab or suspected meth lab.

# UNIT 5 | BOMBS AND WEAPONS OF MASS DESTRUCTION

## LESSON 1 | Responding to a Bomb Threat

**OBJECTIVES**

**LE258.1.D.** Identify pertinent information concerning the possible bomb threat prior to arrival.

**LE258.5.B.2.** Identify the potential explosive device's location in relation and proximity to other potential threats.

**LE258.2.B.** Identify possible approaches to a location; select a safe and tactical approach.

**LE258.2.C.2.** Identify potential stopping areas which can provide protective cover from the force of an explosion.

**LE258.3.A.5.** Identify potential sites for the command post and staging areas.

**LE258.3.A.1.** Identify any signs that an explosion has occurred.

**LE258.1.C.** Identify complainant identity and location.

**LE163.1.B.1.** Identify sources of information about the building.

**LE258.3.D.** Identify factors in estimating the credibility of the threat.

### Basic Information When Responding to a Bomb Threat

When responding to a bomb threat, it is important to obtain as much information as possible from dispatch. This initial information guides an officer's actions upon arrival. Information collected should include the nature of the complaint, means of the threat and time it was received, alleged time of detonation, location of device, and threat recipient *(LE258.1.D.)*. If such information is not available from dispatch, an officer should obtain it by talking with witnesses or the complainant.

It is necessary to identify the nature of the complaint, which may be a threat, a suspected explosive device, an explosion, or a combination of these. Discovering how the threat was made is also important. Most are made by speaking to someone on a telephone. However, some are made by leaving a message on an answering machine, leaving a note at the scene, or sending a threat by letter, fax, or email. The officer should identify the time the threat was received. If the threat contained a phrase such as, "The bomb will go off one hour from now," the time of the call becomes very important and allows an officer to estimate the possible time of detonation, level of risk, and a deadline by which evacuations or searches must be completed.

A common policy or rule is to be out of a building at least 30 minutes before the alleged time of detonation and not return until at least 30 minutes after the alleged time of detonation. If a threat includes information about a location of an explosive device, this location should be noted when approaching the scene; it could assist in choosing an alternate route to the location and allow the officer to maximize his or her distance from the suspected explosive device. If the threat does not include the location of the device, the officer should attempt to obtain this information. In bomb threat situations, officers should always seek information beyond what is volunteered by complainants or witnesses.

### Location

If an officer is unfamiliar with the location of a threat, he or she should get directions or a map. Sometimes, the usual route may be unsafe or too congested. The first officer on the scene may suggest alternative routes for the fire department, EMS, or bomb squad. This route should be chosen based on information received from dispatch concerning the nature of the complaint.

An officer must also determine the device's location. Street maps, building layouts, or someone familiar with the area can help provide an accurate description of the location. If an officer can tell the bomb squad the exact location of the suspected device, the bomb squad can easily find it and predict possible damage caused by detonation. An officer must also determine and be able to describe as precisely as possible the item's location in relation to the layout of the building or area and its relation to potential hazards. Such hazards could include fuel storage tanks, stored chemicals, tanks of pressurized gas, steel rods, rolls of wire, or containers of bolts or nails *(LE258.5.B.2.)*. The bomb squad should be informed of any such additional hazards.

## Use of Radio and Transmitting Equipment

When approaching a possible bomb situation, an officer must decide whether to turn off radios and radio wave-transmitting devices. There is no universal agreement on whether to do this at or near a bomb threat scene. The purpose of this is to prevent accidental triggering or detonation of a bomb designed to be set off by radio waves. It is advisable to notify dispatch and supervisors just before arrival if an officer intends to turn off radios or other equipment that emits radio waves. If a phone is needed, officers should never use a cell phone or radio but use a "land line" phone. Civilians should also not use cell or cordless phones, two-way radios, or any electrical or electronic equipment in close proximity to a suspected explosive device or a suspected location.

## Approaching the Scene Safely and Tactically

Officers should avoid coming close to a device if its location is known and should choose a route that leads to a stopping point a safe distance from the danger *(LE258.2.B.)*. An officer should never park too close to the incident, or any suspicious item, or park in a manner which will impede additional units. The "300-foot-with-cover" rule for evacuations can also be used for parking a patrol vehicle. An officer can move in closer than 300 feet if there is a compelling reason and the risk is not great. The first officers on the scene often move in closer to confer with representatives of the building, interview witnesses, and further assess the situation. Once the officer has parked, he or she should maintain a safe location and distance from the threat. An officer should adjust distance and location if new information indicates the initial stopping point is too close. He or she should look for natural or man-made structures that might provide protective cover. *(LE258.2.C.2.)*

## Observations During Approach

The tactical approach and arrival to the site of a bomb threat directly affect the safety of officers and citizens. Officers should always check their position for secondary devices or suspicious packages, even if they are not the first responder. As an officer approaches the scene, he or she should note prominent features and approximate safe distances so specific directions may be given to other responding units. An officer should also recommend potential command sites to dispatch *(LE258.3.A.5.)*. Such sites share many of the characteristics of a good evacuation gathering area. When approaching the scene, it is also necessary to look for signs of hazardous materials. An officer might notice an unusual smell or irritation to his or her skin, eyes, or breathing passages. If this occurs, the officer should, if possible, move upwind and uphill from the hazard and seek medical attention.

If the officer approaches the scene and sees signs of an explosion, the situation has changed. Now there are new safety issues such as broken gas lines, weakened building structures, debris, and fires *(LE258.3.A.1.)*. The officer should immediately alert EMS and the fire department and request additional backup. He or she should also increase the perimeter distance to secure the possible crime scene. It is necessary to be aware of potential evidence in the area that cannot be immediately recognized and located. An officer should alert the bomb squad to investigate and provide recommendations.

## Interviewing People at the Scene

An officer must identify and locate the person who received the threat. Sometimes the recipient is the most important witness and should therefore be located and interviewed as soon as possible. The recipient should not be allowed to leave the scene, and the officer should keep track of him or her for further questioning by the bomb squad and investigators.

The officer should ask dispatch to contact the complainant, the owner/representative of the building or threatened area, or another knowledgeable person so that person can be interviewed *(LE258.1.C.).* That person should be asked to meet the officer at an agreed-upon place that is a safe distance from the building or area. An interviewee may know of new developments, such as finding a suspicious item. The first contact, however, may know little to nothing about the threat. This could occur if a threat was made to a location different than where the bomb has been placed, such as a media station or 911. Sources of additional information may include witnesses or persons with special knowledge about the threatened area. Any available physical evidence could also be a source of information.

Officers will likely talk with the threat site's owner or a representative shortly after arriving and throughout their stay at the scene. An officer should confer with this person as soon as possible about important issues including the officer's assessment of the situation, the owner's impression of the situation, the credibility of the threat, the level of risk, the advisability of an evacuation, the location's evacuation plan, the means of communication within the evacuation location, and the availability of building plans *(LE163.1.B.1.).* The owner/representative may have knowledge about the organization's history of bombings or threats. Exchanging information with the owner/representative helps an officer confirm what he or she may already know about the situation and learn additional information that may confirm a threat's credibility. Credibility will be the major issue in determining whether to search or evacuate. Besides providing information, the owner/representative must act in an official capacity in giving permission to search or evacuate.

If an officer's agency's policy authorizes him or her to assist in searching for explosive devices, the officer should inform the owner that officers will provide assistance but only with the aid of persons knowledgeable about the building's layout, contents, and occupants. An officer should advise the owner that he or she may decide to evacuate unless a device is found, in which case the officer will order a mandatory evacuation.

Information regarding entrances, exits, and any existing evacuation plans is critical when searching and evacuating a building and securing access, particularly if the building is large or complex. If the complainant or other first contacts cannot provide information about the building, it is necessary to obtain the names and locations of individuals who can, such as a custodian, security officer, or maintenance supervisor. The officer should ask questions about possible suspects (ex-employees, disgruntled employees, angry customers, expelled or suspended students, or employees who may be experiencing disputes with significant others) and find out who controls access to the building. The officer should also identify and interview anyone who might be familiar with the caller's threatening remarks or motivation.

If an officer responds to a situation in which the threat takes physical form, such as a letter or note, the item is evidence, and the officer should identify and interview the person in possession of it. For verbal threats, some agencies have procedures and arrangements with a local telephone company or cell phone companies for tracing phone calls.

# Estimating Credibility of Threat and Level of Risk

All threats and bomb situations must be treated as real until proven otherwise. An officer must estimate the credibility of the threat. This estimation will affect the officer's decisions to recommend a search or evacuation, participate in a search, notify the bomb squad, fire department, or EMS, or move the public farther from the threat.

Physical evidence may substantiate a threat's credibility and clarify the risk level involved for officers and others. Physical evidence could include a found device, a suspicious item, a threatening note or letter, a suspicious car, or suspicious circumstances, such as a door or window usually locked but found unlocked (or vice versa), signs of illegal entry, or items moved from their normal position. An officer should secure and protect any evidence. *(LE258.3.D.)*

Early in the investigation, it is also necessary to determine if there is a video security surveillance system. If video surveillance exists, the tapes must eventually be viewed, so they should be removed and preserved as potential evidence, especially if there is an evacuation. Officers must not allow surveillance tapes to be damaged or destroyed by an explosion.

# UNIT 5 | BOMBS AND WEAPONS OF MASS DESTRUCTION

## LESSON 2 | Searching the Building

**OBJECTIVES**

**LE258.4.A.** Identify the factors in deciding if a bomb search is advisable.

**LE258.5.C.** Identify the elements of a potential explosive device an officer should observe to give an accurate description to bomb technicians.

**LE258.5.A.1.** Identify what actions to avoid if a potential explosive device or suspicious item is found.

**LE258.5.A.6.** Identify the importance of leaving an area as soon as possible after identifying the type, description, and location of the suspected device or a potential explosive device.

**LE258.5.A.5.** Identify the importance of advising any fellow officers in the immediate area of a found explosive or suspicious device.

**LE258.5.A.8.** Identify the importance of advising any civilians in the immediate area of a found explosive or suspicious device.

**LE258.5.A.7.** Identify the importance of continued caution due to the possibility of a "secondary device."

### Deciding to Search

In a bomb threat situation, the advisability of a search depends on different factors, including the following:

- obtaining permission to search
- the level of risk for those conducting the search
- the possibility of threats in addition to a bomb
- agency policy on officers searching for explosives *(LE258.4.A.)*

### Level of Risk for Searchers

The level of risk might be too high to initiate a search. The information received in a threat or warning might indicate that the device is booby-trapped or could be triggered remotely by a bomber observing the scene from nearby. Such high risk factors weigh against conducting a search. In these situations, only special units or bomb squads should conduct a search. If the bomb is supposed to detonate soon, the search should be postponed. Everyone should remain at a safe distance outside the building until after the alleged time of detonation. After that time passes, an officer should re-evaluate the situation and determine if the search should begin. In some instances, an agency's procedure might mandate a waiting period before beginning a search. If an explosion occurs or occurred before the officer's arrival, then his or her responsibility is no longer to search for explosives. The officer should focus on the safety of others.

### Permission to Search

In most cases, the owner or person in charge must give permission to search his or her property. Exceptions include public buildings or private property that provides public access. The person in charge of a public access building cannot refuse entry. In most bomb threat cases, the owner is cooperative regarding a search. In an emergency, if the owner or another liable person cannot be located, an officer may conduct the search without consent.

### Types of Searches

In a covert search, members of management conduct a search without the knowledge or assistance of employees. This is the fastest type of search. However, covert searching is not thorough and is unsafe due to untrained personnel searching and uninformed employees left in the building.

In an overt search, members of management and employees conduct a search of their work areas. This method offers speed because the search is conducted by the people most familiar with the area. Overt searching can, however, be inefficient and dangerous if personnel are not trained.

## Searching

When planning a search, officers should use resources with valuable search information such as a person who has knowledge of the building layout, any existing search plan or search teams, and information contained in the threat or warning. A haphazard search, conducted without knowledge of the building's layout, particularly in a large or complex building, might mean some areas are searched more than once, while other areas are not searched at all. The most obvious area(s) to search are those mentioned in the threat, if any. If no device is found in the suspected places, the next area of concern would be the publicly accessible areas, including entranceways and foyers, lobbies, waiting areas, restrooms, cleaning and storage closets, and elevator shafts, including the top of the elevator.

If the public area search yields nothing, a decision needs to be made whether the entire building or area must be searched. A building's interior search should go from bottom to top, beginning with the basement areas and including utility rooms and areas with heating, cooling, electrical power, and telephone equipment.

The exterior search must include the exterior perimeter of the building and nearby surrounding areas and should be done first. If the building is situated next to a street, the search should begin at the edge of the street. An officer should look for any items that seem out of the ordinary and notice places where a device could be hidden. When searching internally or externally, the officer should make sure he or she conducts a thorough search because explosives can be located anywhere. An officer should also search any area that evacuees might use as an evacuation gathering point or that emergency responders might use as a staging area or command post. These areas are ideal locations for a secondary device.

## Identification of a Found Device

Officers are not expected to know and be able to identify all varieties of bombs, explosives, and military ordnances. Officers can assist bomb technicians by obtaining any information possible about a potential explosive device, if this can be done safely. This information usually consists of a reasonably accurate description of the suspected device. An officer should always view the device from a distance.

It is important to note the color, shape, and size of the device, as well as anything that might protrude from it and if the device is partially covered or inside a container. An officer should also observe any names, labels, placards, chemical symbols, or signs indicating the type of explosive *(LE258.5.C.).* Sometimes officers will not see the device, and the information will come from interviewing someone who has seen it. The more details obtained, the better the bomb team can perform its job. Most of the time, an officer will not see the bomb because it is concealed within its packaging. An officer should never attempt to open or even examine a suspected device or package. *(LE258.5.A.1.)*

## Suspicious Items

Sometimes a bomb is found not because of its appearance but because it is a suspicious item. Many bombs do not appear to be bombs at all. A bomb can be specifically constructed to resemble almost anything. If an item is found that seems suspicious, officers should ask an employee if the item belongs there. However, employees should never be allowed to handle suspicious items.

## Mail Bombs

Mail bombs are a special class of suspicious items. These could be delivered by the United States Postal Service, a delivery service such as FedEx, or by hand. Mail bombs can be difficult to detect. Some possible recognition points are envelopes or packages that are rigid, have excessive postage, are unevenly packed, or are packed with excessive securing material. Other factors include mail bearing incorrect titles, titles but no names, misspellings of common words, handwritten or poorly typed addresses, or restrictive markings such as "confidential" or "personal." Mail bombs may also bear oily stains or discoloration or have strange odors and protruding wires.

If officers or individuals at the location become suspicious of a mailed item, the item should not be handled and should be isolated by evacuating the area. The indicated sender, if known, should be contacted to verify the contents of the letter or package.

## Vehicle Bombs

A motor vehicle used as a bomb is referred to as a vehicle bomb. Vehicle bombs can be very powerful and dangerous. They are capable of carrying extremely large amounts of explosives. It is very difficult to bring 7,000 pounds of explosives into a building, but a small rental truck carrying that amount could detonate in front of a building, causing mass destruction to the structure and to humans.

A vehicle bomb may be present if a threat mentions it; if a vehicle is parked suspiciously close to the building or in a restricted parking area without a proper decal or sticker; if the car is unfamiliar to building occupants, seems to have a heavy load as indicated by riding low on its rear axle, or has a strange smell or leaks powder or liquid; if a witness says a driver or passenger exited the vehicle and left hurriedly; or if a bomb dog alerts officers the vehicle is a threat.

If officers suspect a vehicle might contain explosives, they should get a quick description of it, particularly its size. Then, they should evacuate the area around the vehicle and establish a perimeter. Evacuation distance from a vehicle should be much greater than evacuation distance from a building because the bomb is potentially very large and pieces of the vehicle can act as shrapnel. The evacuation distance depends on agency policy and the size of the vehicle.

## Suspicious Circumstances and Hiding Places

When approaching the scene, an officer should look for any suspicious items or activity that may indicate the presence of an explosive device or any place that could serve as a hiding location for such a device. Officers should take note of any vehicle that is parked unusually close to the building, abandoned luggage, gym bags, backpacks, buggies, strollers, or suspicious packages.

When the owner/representative of a building has approved the search, it is necessary to determine who will participate in the search, which areas will be searched first, and how the search will be conducted. The decision to search and the planning involved can take place within minutes of arrival. A search might be completed quickly, or it might take several hours. This depends on the building's size and the proficiency of the search teams. Above all, the search must be done systematically and with extreme caution. Knowing how to properly conduct an efficient and effective search can protect lives.

Searching systematically requires that an officer follow the search plan faithfully and that individual searchers use appropriate search methods and patterns. Divide and assign certain floors or rooms to various search teams.

Each team should place tape across the doorway of a room or area when it has been completely searched. On floor plans, an officer can check off rooms or areas after they are searched.

## External Triggering Devices

Some bombs explode when a person comes near them even if the device itself remains undisturbed. This could occur by several means. An unobservant searcher might not notice a thin or clear tripwire. Pressure switches could be placed under a rug, a doormat, or in soil in an outdoor situation. A wall light switch could be wired into the bomb's triggering circuit so it detonates when the light is switched on, or a device may be triggered by sensors that detect nearby motion or sound.

Officers can protect themselves against such booby-trapped detonation devices by being alert to the possibility of such devices, being observant, watching where they step, and not backing up without first looking behind them. Before entering a doorway, officers should lean through the door and look in all directions, above the door frame, and on both sides. They should also watch for trip wires, look for lumps or bulges in the carpet and rugs, and step over floor mats. Officers should not rush into any room or space. Officers should assume the worst and take extreme precautions, such as using binoculars to view the item from a distance.

## Finding an Explosive Device

If an explosive device is found, the room or area should be vacated as soon as possible, if not immediately. Generally, officers should take a brief look at the device, note any identifying numbers or markings, and leave the area immediately and carefully. *(LE258.5.A.6.)*

## Advising Others of a Found Hazard

Fellow officers in the immediate area must be advised of the found device and its location *(LE258.5.A.5.)*. However, officers should not use their radio to do this. Officers should alert any civilians who might be near or who have been assisting in the search. Immediately upon discovery of a potential explosive device, officers should advise civilians within earshot to safely and calmly depart. *(LE258.5.A.8.)*

## Being Aware of Possible Secondary Devices

Officers should never assume that because an explosive device has been found, it is the only planted explosive. In some bombing situations, the bomber has planted "secondary devices." These secondary bombs are intended to kill or injure first responders after they have found a device or after the explosion of the first bomb. The first bomb could be a decoy. The first device might be placed in a very obvious and visible location with the intention of convincing the officer the threat has been found and the danger is over. *(LE258.5.A.7.)*

# UNIT 5 | BOMBS AND WEAPONS OF MASS DESTRUCTION

## LESSON 3 | Evacuating the Building

**OBJECTIVES**

**LE258.3.A.4.** Identify potential evacuation areas in a bomb threat situation.

**LE059.6.A.** Identify where to establish the initial perimeter to protect the public during a bomb threat.

**LE259.2.B.** Confer with the owner, representative, or person in charge during an emergency situation requiring evacuation of a building or area.

**LE259.3.** Identify the factors in planning an evacuation of a building or area.

**LE259.3.D.** Identify means of communicating with occupants or residents of a building or area in an emergency situation.

An officer should look for safe locations as he or she assesses the scene. If evacuation becomes necessary, having distance and barriers will be the best safeguards against the effects of an explosion. To protect the public from an explosive device, a general safe distance for the initial perimeter is 300 feet with protective cover *(LE258.3.A.4.)*. This is a minimum evacuation distance and applies to situations in which the type or amount of explosive is unknown. Good protective cover might be unavailable. If this is the case, an officer should substantially increase the evacuation distance. If the type and the amount of the explosive is known, the recommended safe evacuation distance can be much greater than 300 feet *(LE059.6.A.)*. Occupants may already be evacuating upon officer arrival. If they gather too closely to the building or lack adequate protective cover, officers should direct them to move farther away. If circumstances allow, people should evacuate upwind (or at least crosswind).

### Officer Involvement in the Evacuation

If possible, before the officer arrives, he or she should determine the identity of the owner, manager, person in charge, or a representative of the owner with some authority. If the property is private, the owner or manager must make the decision to evacuate. It is necessary to confer with this person *(LE259.2.B.)*. A building is typically evacuated when a hazard is discovered. There are two types of evacuations when dealing with a bomb incident: partial evacuations and total evacuations. No evacuation might be used when the threat's credibility and the risk are low. A partial evacuation could be used in a location that has multiple buildings or facilities in which a specific building has been identified in the threat. If possible, people should move to the furthest point away from the search location or the suspicious item. A total evacuation should be used during incidents that have a moderate to high credibility and risk, and for which no specific area at the location was identified in the threat.

When a device or suspicious package is found, or an explosion occurs, the location becomes a crime scene. An officer has the legal authority to protect and secure a crime scene, and evacuation is one way to accomplish this. The officer must also contact the owner/representative or person in charge, inform him or her of the search results, and indicate the intention to evacuate.

An officer must determine the extent to which he or she will assist in planning and executing the evacuation. How extensively an officer participates depends on agency policy and procedures, how much officer assistance is wanted or required, and whether or not the owner/representative has conferred with his or her Emergency Action Plan (EAP) to determine evacuation procedures.

# Planning an Evacuation

When planning an evacuation, an officer must identify safety considerations, evacuee gathering points, and the best evacuation route(s). He or she must also determine the layout of the building or area to be evacuated, consider any existing evacuation plans, and identify a means of communication *(LE259.3.)*. Officers must also identify any safety considerations that might impact the evacuation. The primary consideration is to avoid the known or suspected location of the explosive device. This applies to both evacuation routes and evacuee gathering points. Officers should prioritize areas to be evacuated from most affected to least. They should consider special populations such as disabled, hospitalized, or elderly occupants who will require extra evacuation time and manpower.

Officers should establish a means (such as fire alarms) of communicating evacuation information to building occupants. However, fire alarms might cause additional problems; in a hotel, or other building where a fire drill is not expected, occupants could either panic or not take a fire alarm seriously. Many businesses, organizations, and government agencies have a single telephone system and can alert all employees by intercom or public address system. However, some large buildings contain several businesses that have separate phone systems. In such situations, the only alternative might be to proceed through the entire building, knocking on doors, alerting occupants, and directing them to evacuate by the specified routes to the established gathering points. *(LE259.3.D.)*

# Conducting the Evacuation

An officer should give evacuees minimal information to save time and prevent panic. People should be advised to move in a quick and orderly fashion and avoid elevators and areas that present a potential risk. They should be told exactly where to go after evacuating. They should not use cellular phones until they reach gathering points, and they should contact a supervisor or officer if they discover anything suspicious. If possible, the evacuation should be monitored to ensure that evacuees go to the right location and nobody is left behind. No one should be allowed to reenter the building after the evacuation is complete.

# UNIT 5 | BOMBS AND WEAPONS OF MASS DESTRUCTION

## LESSON 4 | Identifying Weapons of Mass Destruction

**OBJECTIVES**

**LE258.5.C.7.** Define weapons of mass destruction.

**LE258.4.C.** Identify the likely location for the use of CBRNE weapons.

**LE258.3.A.8.** List environmental indicators of exposure to biological agents.

**LE258.3.A.9.** Identify signs and symptoms for human exposure to biological agents.

**LE258.3.A.10.** Identify signs and symptoms for human exposure to nuclear agents.

**LE258.3.A.11.** List environmental indicators of exposure to nuclear agents.

**LE258.3.A.13.** List environmental indicators of exposure to chemical agents.

**LE258.3.A.12.** Identify signs and symptoms of human exposure to chemical agents.

The increase in terrorist activity has generated a need to prepare law enforcement officers to handle incidents involving weapons of mass destruction (WMD). Threats to the United States have been both internal and external. The domestic terrorism of the Oklahoma City Bombing in 1995 and the two international terrorist attacks on the World Trade Center in New York (in 1993 and 2001) have raised the awareness of terrorism.

## Weapons Of Mass Destruction

Florida State Statutes (in §790.166) define weapons of mass destruction as the

> Manufacture, possession, sale, delivery, display, use, or attempted or threatened use of a weapon of mass destruction or hoax weapon of mass destruction prohibited; definitions; penalties--
>
> (1) As used in this section, the term:
>
> (a) "Weapon of mass destruction" means:
>
> 1. Any device or object that is designed or intended to cause death or serious bodily injury to any human or animal, or severe emotional or mental harm to any human, through the release, dissemination, or impact of toxic or poisonous chemicals, or their precursors;
> 2. Any device or object involving a biological agent;
> 3. Any device or object that is designed or intended to release radiation or radioactivity at a level dangerous to human or animal life; or
> 4. Any biological agent, toxin, vector, or delivery system. *(LE258.5.C.7.)*

It is a first-degree felony to unlawfully manufacture, possess, sell, deliver, send, mail, display, use, threaten to use, attempt to use, conspire to use, or make readily accessible to others a "weapon of mass destruction" under F.S. §790.166. It is a violation of F.S. §790.166 and a second-degree felony to unlawfully manufacture, possess, sell, deliver, mail, send, display, use, threaten to use, attempt to use, conspire to use, or make readily accessible to others a "hoax weapon of mass destruction," which is a device or object that appears to be, or is falsely represented to be, an actual weapon of mass destruction. It is also a second-degree felony under F.S. §790.163 for a person to make a false report concerning the placing or planting of a weapon of mass destruction.

A WMD attack often focuses on heavily frequented locations or locations that greatly impact the population. Examples include airports, subways, schools, churches, government buildings, or large public gatherings such as fairs, festivals, or sporting events. *(LE258.4.C.)*

In order to make an appropriate response, officers must be able to identify chemical, biological, radiological and nuclear weapons and explosives. ***CBRNE*** is an acronym commonly used in reference to weapons of mass destruction and stands for

- Chemical
- Biological
- Radiological
- Nuclear
- Explosives

Officers must always be familiar with their patrol area and note any signs which might indicate a possible WMD threat. For example, officers should watch for strange chemical canisters or drums left abandoned in an empty field or ditch. Historically, terrorists conduct pre-operational surveillance before executing an attack. This surveillance can take many forms, such as videotaping a potential target location, sketching floor plans, taking still photographs of structural features, and taking notes on security force activity. Officers should observe potential WMD targets for any suspicious activities in their patrol area and observe suspicious vehicles. Many traffic stops and arrests for lesser crimes have led to the discovery of plans for developing and detonating a WMD.

## Types of WMD

WMD include weapons that could release biological contamination, toxic chemical agents, incendiary fires, and they also include conventional explosives. Each type of WMD is unique because of the scope of death and destruction, the insidious nature of the weapon, and the personal danger to first responders.

### *Biological*

Biological weapons contain living organisms and are unpredictable and uncontrollable when released. Biological agents can be dispersed through food and water supplies by using aerosols, liquid droplets, solid dispersion (such as powder), and by using common creatures like fleas, ticks, or other insects. With these weapons, exposure occurs well before the first signs and symptoms appear. The release might affect the entire police (and other first responder) infrastructure before the problem's nature is known. For example, the first victims of smallpox might become ill and unknowingly continue to work in public.

Aside from written or verbal threats, possible indicators of a biological attack include unusual numbers of sick or dying people or animals, an unusually high prevalence of respiratory involvement in diseases that typically cause a non-pulmonary syndrome, unexplained damage and ruin to crops and agricultural products, and abnormal swarms of insects. Other indicators can include an unscheduled or unusual distribution of sprayed material, casualty distribution aligned with wind direction, abandoned spray or dispersion devices, or the appearance of containers from laboratory or biological supply houses or biohazard cultures. *(LE258.3.A.8.)*

Many different biological agents could be used as potential weapons. Anthrax can be absorbed through the skin, by inhalation, and through the digestive system. Usually flu-like symptoms such as respiration problems, vomiting, and fever, occur seven days after exposure.

Smallpox is a contagious infectious disease that can be transmitted by prolonged face-to-face contact with an infected person, direct contact with infected bodily fluids, and direct contact with infected objects such as clothes. After an incubation period of seven to seventeen days, symptoms such as a pox-like rash, raised bumps, fever, muscle rigidity, shivering, malaise, headaches, and vomiting occur.

Ricin is a highly toxic poison found in seeds of the castor bean plant. Exposure to ricin can occur by ingestion and inhalation. When Ricin is ingested, symptoms begin within a few hours; they include abdominal pain, vomiting, and diarrhea. Within several days, sufferers experience severe dehydration, decreased urination, and decreased blood pressure. When the person inhaled Ricin, symptoms begin 18–24 hours after exposure and include fever, chest tightness, cough, nausea, and joint pain. Severe respiratory distress and death can occur in 36–72 hours.

Botulinum toxin is the single most poisonous substance. The man-made form, aerosolized botulinum toxin, is inhaled. All forms of botulism result from the absorption of the toxin through the digestive system, a wound, or the lungs and have the same symptoms, which include difficulty seeing, speaking, and swallowing, double vision, drooping eyelids, slurred speech, dry mouth, and muscle weakness. These symptoms occur within 12 to 80 hours of exposure. *(LE258.3.A.9.)*

## Nuclear

A ***nuclear weapon*** derives its destructive power from an uncontrolled nuclear reaction. Nuclear detonation energy is released through light, thermal energy, shock waves, blasts of wind, direct radiation, and fallout. Potential injuries include light damage to the eyes, burns to the skin, blast (pressure) injuries, being hit by propelled objects, radiation from the bomb ignition, and falling radioactive particles *(LE258.3.A.10.)*. There can be a radioactive component in a device but it does not necessarily make the device radioactive. Depending on the type, amount, or encasement of that component, it can be referred to as radiological (having a radioactive characteristic).

Nuclear facilities or transport vehicles used for nuclear materials might be targeted for attack for different reasons. Environmental indicators of a nuclear attack include damage to a facility or vehicle, the use of bombs, missiles, or other damaging objects, such as an airplane and the release of radioactive materials. *(LE258.3.A.11.)*

Dirty bombs are traditional bombs with radioactive materials loaded into the casing. They are not considered nuclear weapons because they do not contain the same explosive power, and their radiation is preloaded, whereas nuclear weapons create radioactivity upon detonation. There are several indicators of the presence of a dirty bomb. They require a casing and detonation mechanism, so these pieces may be present at the scene. Witnesses may give details of the event that do not seem to fit with the effects of explosive devices. For instance, they might say the bomb didn't blow anything up, but just blew apart. Radiation cannot be detected by the senses, but bomb squads and HAZMAT teams, as well as health officials, have equipment to detect the amount of radiation in the area.

## Incendiary Devices

Incendiary devices consist of a minimum of three components: the ignition source, the combustible filler material, and their housing/container. Common materials used are roadway flares, gasoline/motor oil, and light bulbs. These devices are very similar to explosive devices and can function in the same manner. They can be placed anywhere or thrown at the target. Officers should respond to potential incendiary events the same way they would respond to bomb situations and never touch, move, or disturb an incendiary device.

## *Chemical Weapons*

Chemical weapons can kill many people because a small amount of agent can be spread over a wide area. Physical destruction of property is minimal, but environmental contamination can be serious and prolonged and can include destruction of food crops, contamination of water sources, and the death and extinction of animals *(LE258.3.A.13.).* These weapons are relatively cheap, easy to produce, and may represent the greatest overall threat from the category of WMD.

Chemical (and biological) weapons present a danger that is much harder to identify than the conventional or nuclear detonation. Chemical weapons might release gases or aerosols that are only recognized upon exposure or shortly thereafter. When reports of numerous ill persons suffering breathing problems, blurry vision, and muscle contractions from an unidentifiable cause are received, officers should anticipate a threatening environment. *(LE258.3.A.12.)*

In addition to the physiological effects, an officer must be aware of the risks involved in responding to potential WMD situations. Officers might enter an unknown situation or a situation that at first does not appear to be WMD-related. They might enter a location in which physical structures are unstable or where the threat of a secondary device exists, or they might enter a situation in which people panic and look to officers for immediate relief.

**Section Vocabulary**

*CBRNE*

***nuclear weapon***

# UNIT 5 | BOMBS AND WEAPONS OF MASS DESTRUCTION

## LESSON 5 | Responding to Weapons of Mass Destruction

**OBJECTIVES**

**LE258.6.B.** Identify how to initiate actions to protect officers and others at a nuclear, biological, or chemical incident.

**LE258.3.A.14.** Identify evacuation measures during a CBRNE incident.

**LE258.3.A.15.** List notification and communication methods in the event of a nuclear, biological, or chemical threat.

### Basic Protection in WMD Incidents

An officer's first responsibility in a CBRNE situation is to protect him- or herself, others, and property. Officers should consider civilian safety by determining victims' mobility and the degree to which they have been exposed to materials. Are they ambulatory? Are they contaminated? After these questions are answered, emergency responders can decide whether to evacuate victims or protect them on-site.

As first responders called to investigate a report of suspected terrorist activity, officers should be prepared to encounter terrorists or criminals using weapons of mass destruction. For most incidents, officers are trained to quickly enter the scene and to help the victims as soon as possible. This traditional law enforcement response and rescue approach will not work for WMD incidents. Rushing into a chemical, biological, or explosive scene could result in the first responder's death or additional victims. Though every CBRNE incident is different, the same basic steps can be used for each. In an isolated area with no persons nearby, communication and notification can be done before securing the scene. However, if there is a threat to numerous people in the area, an officer may feel it is vital to secure the scene first and then contact dispatch with additional information for arriving units. *(LE258.6.B.)*

The officer should approach the incident cautiously from an upwind, uphill, and upstream position until he or she can safely identify and assess the CBRNE situation. The officer should stop a minimum of 300 feet from the incident scene. However, 500 to 1,000 feet might be needed. The ERG should be consulted for recommended shielding distances from blast zones and safe distances from chemical releases.

### Isolating an Area

Isolation is an important step in responding to a WMD incident. All persons should be instructed to move to an area upwind, uphill, and upstream from the contaminated area to a secure position set up for contaminated and uncontaminated persons. These areas are called Victim Collection Points and can be designated once a preliminary perimeter has been established. The Victim Collection Points allow EMTs to easily locate those who need medical treatment. *(LE258.3.A.14.)*

### Securing the Scene

Officers should secure the scene in order to isolate exposed victims and the contaminated area. The tactical considerations include monitoring entry to the scene, assuring public protection (evacuating or protecting an area), confining and containing all contaminated and exposed victims, determining if the scene is or can be made safe for operations, protecting the scene and any evidence, and coordinating with all agencies to provide security and control of perimeters.

Securing the scene should focus more on preventing entry to the scene itself than preventing the exit of victims. Attempting to stop panicked persons from leaving the site could place an officer in personal danger. Officers should avoid physical contact with possibly contaminated persons and direct those persons to a safe location where decontamination can occur.

The use of force to detain a contaminated person might be justified if officials suspect the person is involved in the attack. Potential witnesses should be strongly encouraged to remain in a safe area at the scene so investigators can question them. If they refuse, the officer should try to obtain their identity for the investigators. Also, any bystanders who might have information should be encouraged to stand in a safe place until law enforcement can interview them.

## Notification and Communication

If an officer is the first on the scene of a CBRNE incident, he or she should relay information to responding units. The officer's responsibilities might include notifying and updating other units as the incident develops, establishing the initial perimeter for responding units, and routinely communicating with dispatch as the incident unfolds. The officer may also need to tell dispatch about any unknown substances, the number of exposed victims, and, if known, what type of vehicle, container, or device is involved. The officer could also be responsible for setting up a temporary Incident Command Center and directing EMS to the contaminated and non-contaminated victims. Additionally, the officer should brief his or her supervisor on the situation and relinquish control to the supervisor or to the Incident Command director. *(LE258.3.A.15.)*

# CHAPTER 7

## Crime Scene Investigations



There is a sequence of steps to initiate upon arriving at an incident or crime scene to protect all parties, gather information to identify, separate, and interview subjects, and successfully complete the initial investigation. An officer must be aware of how to conduct a warrantless legal search of a crime scene, know different search patterns, and understand how to identify types of evidence that might be present at a scene based on the evaluation of the incident or type of crime. An officer must also know how to get help in searching the scene when necessary.

The single most significant part of the initial stage of a criminal investigation is processing the crime scene. An officer's first priority is to protect and preserve the scene to avoid contaminating evidence. Secondly, the officer must identify, protect, collect, preserve, and maintain the physical evidence, or the prosecution of the suspect may be in jeopardy.

# UNIT 1 I RESPONDING TO THE CRIME SCENE

## LESSON 1 I Initial Response

**OBJECTIVES**

**LE162.1.** Obtain information regarding the crime scene prior to arrival.

**LE162.3.** Determine if a crime or incident is life threatening.

**LE162.4.** Identify when to request medical assistance.

**LE089b.2.** Survey the scene.

**LE078.6.** Identify when to continue investigating or when to relinquish the crime scene.

An ***investigation*** occurs when an officer makes detailed and systematic inquiries or observations. This process begins upon the officer's arrival at the scene of a reported crime and usually ends with him or her filing the initial report or turning the matter over to a detective or investigator.

In responding to a potential crime scene, an officer will receive pertinent information regarding the incident from the 911 dispatch (also known as the public safety telecommunicator). This will identify the nature and location of the alleged crime as well as the complainant's name and relationship to the crime scene location. An officer may also learn from dispatch if someone is injured.

While driving to the scene, the officer should formulate some key questions to ask to help him or her assess the situation adequately:

- How many individuals are involved?
- What is the location?
- Are any weapons involved?
- Are additional services needed?
- Is special equipment needed?
- How many officers are necessary to safely contain or control the situation?
- Are any special concerns or dangers associated with the call?
- Has the complainant indicated the suspect's location? *(LE162.1.)*

An officer should begin taking field notes as he or she discovers the who, what, when, where, why, and how of the incident. This enables an officer to write a thorough report later. When gathering initial information about the call and arriving at the scene, safety is the highest concern. An officer should approach the scene in a way that will protect him- or herself, other officers, and the public. Specific concerns to consider for officer safety are the number of entrances and exits, suspects, bystanders, natural and man-made dangers, and the physical size of the scene.

Some common threats that may be present due to conditions at the scene include known weapons (firearms, knives, explosives), potential weapons (broken glass, stones, sticks, baseball bats, branches), and natural elements (fire, electricity, water hazards, rain). These factors affect the number of officers responding to a scene. Unnecessary people (officers, bystanders) on the scene can be counterproductive, increasing the possibility of contaminating evidence. *(LE162.3.)*

Any person on the scene should immediately be asked if the suspect is on or near the scene or if he or she knows if someone on the scene is armed. As soon as possible, the officer should determine whether any person at the scene has sustained injuries and the extent of those injuries. First-aid procedures should be applied and appropriate medical assistance should be requested through dispatch. *(LE162.4.)*

The first responding officer should make an initial determination regarding the type of crime committed and define the appropriate extent of the crime scene. Personal observations and statements from the victims, witnesses, and suspects should be used to learn the location of evidence. The officer should visually scan the crime scene using a systematic approach, trying to observe the total scene while determining where to establish the perimeter. The size of the crime scene depends on the type of crime, the type of evidence, and the location of evidence. Areas where blood spattered, dripped, or flowed, or where someone tracked through an area leaving footprints or handprints, must be included in the crime scene. Officers should look for the places where the crime or incident began and ended. When determining the extent of the crime scene, it is better to overestimate the perimeter. It is easier to adjust from a large scene to a smaller one than to expand to a larger scene as the investigation progresses. *(LE089b.2.)*

Agency policies and procedures will dictate how far the responding officer should continue investigating the incident before turning the scene over to specialized investigators. That determination will be made in part by the nature or severity of the crime or incident and available resources. Officers should consider jurisdiction issues, agreements with other agencies, and specific Florida Statutes. For example, FDLE handles incidents involving possible terrorist acts. *(LE078.6.)*

**Section Vocabulary**

***investigation***

# UNIT 1 | RESPONDING TO THE CRIME SCENE

## LESSON 2 | Identifying Victims, Witnesses, and Suspects

**OBJECTIVES**

**LE078.3.** Identify victims, witnesses, and suspects at a crime scene.

**LE162.9.** Secure victims, witnesses, and suspects.

**LE162.8.** Separate victims, witnesses, and suspects.

**LE054.3.** View injuries first-hand for evidence or testimony.

**LE162.10.** Brief the supervisor or other arriving personnel at the scene.

### Identify Persons on the Scene

At the scene of an incident, all parties involved, including complainants, victims, suspects, and witnesses, must be identified. A ***complainant*** is a person who alleges that a crime has been committed. A ***victim*** is a person harmed by a crime. A ***suspect*** is a person believed to have committed a crime or offense. A ***witness*** is a person who sees, knows, or vouches for something and makes a sworn statement about that information. The same person can belong to more than one category. For example, the victim may also be the complainant, or a person initially identified as a witness may become a suspect as the investigation progresses. *(LE078.3.)*

When establishing which people to interview at a crime scene, an officer should ask those present where they were and how they were involved in the incident. The officer should also determine the degree of direct or indirect involvement and the role each person played in the incident. The officer may not have the time or resources to interview all subjects at the scene, so he or she should determine who has the most information and knowledge of the incident. The victim or complainant who was present during the crime or offense should be asked to name any potential witnesses to the incident. In addition, witnesses should be asked if anyone else was involved and what their roles were. This will also help officers validate individuals' statements.

The officer should document in his or her field notes all witnesses, victims, complainants, and suspects present by name, date of birth, address, sex, race, and home and work telephone numbers. Vital witnesses should be asked to stay at the scene for further interviewing. Witnesses are often hesitant to get involved. They like to stay around for the excitement but will often try to leave or remain in the background when police attempt to ask them questions concerning their knowledge of the event.

The first step in preparing to interview victims, complainants, or witnesses at a crime scene is to determine to what extent the crime will be investigated. Is it a major crime? Does department policy require the officer to notify a supervisor or investigator? Larger agencies have investigators who will conduct all interviews in major cases. In smaller agencies, that responsibility may fall to the responding patrol officer. *(LE162.9.)*

### Keeping Witnesses Separated

Before beginning interviews, the officer must secure and separate all persons to be interviewed. It is extremely important to keep witnesses separated in crime scene investigations. The witnesses should not be allowed to talk among themselves in order to prevent them from discussing the incident and coordinating their accounts of what happened. Officers should place interviewees in separate places that are near the crime scene area but have no risk of contaminating evidence. Preferably, interviewees should be far enough apart that they cannot hear or see each other. If separate rooms are not available, witnesses can be isolated within one large room by being placed on opposite sides of the room with their backs to each other. The officer should ensure that there is enough distance between witnesses so that they cannot have physical contact with each other. Another possible controlled area is inside a patrol car, though because of space limitations, only one interviewee should be placed in each car. If necessary, another officer can stay with each witness to ensure control and safety until the primary officer can complete the interviews.

Separating witnesses helps each of them focus on what they saw or heard and maintains the integrity of their statements. Multiple witnesses who have viewed or experienced the same event never recall the same details. A witness overhearing another person describe the same event may be tempted, even unconsciously, to reiterate the other witness's version of the crime. Working together, they may come up with accounts that differ from the facts.

Some witnesses may try to intimidate others into giving officers false information. The interviewing officer should ensure that while giving statements, no victims or witnesses can be intimidated visually or verbally by anyone. If a suspect or another witness attempts to coerce or interfere with another witness's testimony, an officer may need to remove one or more subjects from the scene.

Some witnesses may have an unknown motive to mislead officers. They may want to help the suspect by diverting any possible evidence of involvement away from him or her. Witnesses who feel intimidated by an officer or others may say little or nothing so they can leave the scene quickly. Witnesses may also try to pass evidence, such as a weapon or contraband, to each other in order to hide it from officers.

Separation of family members during a crisis might make a bad situation even worse. In such cases, officers should use their best judgment in assessing whether separation is necessary. In a child abuse incident, for example, separation of certain family members from each other may be unavoidable.

All witnesses should be told not to discuss the incident until after they have all been interviewed. If an interviewee is suffering from physical or mental trauma, the officer should make a note to interview this person later when he or she has recovered. For safety reasons, officers must always maintain visual contact with witnesses, complainants, and suspects and always follow agency policy and procedures. *(LE162.8.)*

## Dealing with Injured Persons

When there are injured persons at the scene, responding officers have additional responsibilities such as providing first aid. If the victim does not require immediate first aid, the officer should ask direct, fundamental questions about how the victim sustained the injury, such as the following:

- Who hit you?
- What did the suspect use to hit you?
- When were you hit?
- Where were you hit?
- Where did you stand when hit?
- How were you hit?
- Why were you hit?

**Section Vocabulary**

*complainant*

*suspect*

*victim*

*witness*

The officer should view the victim's injuries and record detailed observations in field notes, keeping in mind these notes will be used to create reports and refresh the officer's recollection when testifying. The officer should note whether the information the victim provides appears to be consistent with the injuries and evidence at the scene. Specific information regarding the location, size, and type of injury is required. Photographs of injuries should be made as appropriate. If possible, when hospitalization is not required, an officer of the same gender as the victim should observe and photograph injuries to sexual organs. The officer should tell the victim that if bruising intensifies, further documentation may be required, and the victim should notify law enforcement. Officers must record the names of medical personnel who provide services to the victim because they may be called as witnesses. *(LE054.3.)*

An officer should share pertinent data with his or her supervisor or investigator to include the following:

- when the incident occurred
- how the incident occurred
- where the incident occurred
- all evidence gathered or specific items that are still the focus of a search
- descriptions of all property involved in the incident (obtained from complainants, victims, or witnesses who can identify the property)
- names and descriptions of victims, witnesses, and possible suspects
- description of the suspect's vehicle, if applicable and if known
- special concerns on the scene such as biohazards, a hostile crowd, at-large suspects, and severe injuries
- how the scene is being handled and protected
- scene's boundaries and protection
- plan for the continued investigation of the incident and the search for evidence
- identity of the public information officer who is communicating with the media (When dealing with the media or designating an assigned authorized spokesperson on the scene, the officer should refer to agency policy and procedure.) *(LE162.10.)*

# UNIT 2 | PROCESSING THE CRIME SCENE

## LESSON 1 | Protecting and Surveying the Crime Scene

**OBJECTIVES**

**LE089b.3.** Identify the requirements for obtaining a valid consent to search.

**LE162.11.** Continue to develop information while protecting the scene.

**LE162.5.** Determine the probable extent of the scene to secure as well as additional surrounding areas.

**LE089b.1.** Secure the scene.

**LE078.11.** Ensure physical evidence is preserved.

**LE089b.6.** Identify when to arrange for manpower and equipment, if required.

**LE162.7.** Identify requirements to effectively create a crime scene log.

### Officer Responsibilities in Managing a Crime Scene

The actions of the first responding officer on the scene have a significant impact on the success of an investigation. A protected, well-managed crime scene allows the production of credible evidence in court that can establish the guilt or innocence of a suspect.

When conducting an investigation, an officer should look for all sources of information about the crime. Evidence is anything that tends to prove or disprove an alleged fact. An officer will collect two kinds of evidence at crime scenes. Testimonial evidence is gathered from witnesses, while physical evidence consists of objects or things such as fingerprints, blood, or tire tracks. Testimonial evidence is generally less reliable than physical evidence because people perceive events differently, do not remember accurately, or lie. When physical evidence is correctly handled, preserved, maintained, and scientifically analyzed, it cannot give false results.

Prior to searching a potential crime scene, an officer should determine if the scene location is public or private property. ***Public property*** is designed for the use and enjoyment of the public and is open to the public. ***Private property*** belongs to an individual and is not open to the public. A person occupying private property has an expectation of privacy that may not be violated without a search warrant or a valid exception to the warrant requirement. Even though an area is a crime scene, a search warrant may still be needed. There is no crime scene exception to the Fourth Amendment search warrant requirement. *(LE089b.3.)*

### Crime Scene Perimeter

The type of crime committed will guide the officer in the types of evidence to expect at a scene. Certain types of evidence are typically associated with particular crimes. For example, at a burglary scene, an officer should look for evidence of illegal entry such as pry marks on a doorframe or broken windows. With experience and training, an officer will become skilled at detecting crimes and identifying relevant evidence.

The crime scene must be protected until it can be photographed and documented. Different crime scenes may require different methods of protecting the evidence they contain. An officer's recognition of threats to the evidence will determine the appropriate method of protection. For example, at an outside crime scene involving degradable, easily destroyed, biological, or trace evidence, officers must protect the evidence from weather elements such as rain, hail, lightning, or wind. However, the same evidence located inside a temperature-controlled house would not require the same level of protection. Once the nature of the scene and type of crime being investigated are determined, an officer can decide how best to protect the scene. *(LE162.11.)*

Crime scene perimeters should be larger rather than smaller. It is easier to reduce the size of a perimeter than to enlarge it. A larger crime scene also helps keep crowds back if citizens gather. Once a survey of the area is completed, a supervisor or investigator assigned to the case may decide to adjust the original boundaries or perimeter of the crime scene based on the size and type of the structure or property to be searched. *(LE162.5.)*

An officer should first attempt to locate and identify the point of the suspect's entry to and exit from the crime scene. This can be done by visually inspecting the scene and reviewing field notes and statements from victims or witnesses. Evidence of entry or exit might include broken glass or pry marks around doorways. An officer should also identify the most distant pieces of evidence. Boundaries should be established for the crime scene and guarded against unnecessary entrance by cordoning off the area with crime scene barrier tape.

Officers must always be aware of potential threats to the crime scene area. Alert officers help protect the scene and the evidence it contains from unnecessary intrusion or handling. Curious, unauthorized people can damage, contaminate, or destroy evidence at a scene, and should not be allowed to enter the secured crime scene area. Officer safety can also be jeopardized by the entry of unauthorized people into a scene. To prevent intrusion by anyone who knowingly or unknowingly approaches the crime scene perimeter, an officer should use verbal commands and directions. Persons should be instructed to move behind the crime scene tape and advised that refusal may result in arrest. Officers have the authority to arrest any individual who crosses an area marked by crime scene tape after having been warned. *(LE089b.1.)*

Once the crime scene perimeter is established, an officer must not allow unauthorized removal or alteration of any evidence. If evidence is contaminated or altered in any way, the crime scene officer must document the incident in a contamination list or crime scene log. Information about the original condition of the evidence and the events leading to its damage or destruction should be included. *(LE078.11.)*

The size and type of search dictates the number and type of personnel or resources needed for crime scene processing. Agency policy, procedures, and available resources will also factor in how to proceed. Larger agencies have specialized crime scene units that can process the scene and collect evidence. Other agencies require responding officers to process scenes or in serious cases may call for outside assistance, such as FDLE's crime scene personnel. The responding officer's supervisor will make the decision to request crime scene or investigative assistance. *(LE089b.6.)*

## Crime Scene Log

The primary officer or investigator will designate one point of access to the crime scene and assign an officer to maintain a crime scene log at that location. If more than one point of access is designated, an officer must be assigned to each location. All officers should be notified of and required to use the access point. The officer posted at the crime scene access point must document in the crime scene log the entry and exit of all persons to the scene. The log should include the name, rank, and agency of each person entering or leaving the scene, the date and time of the person's entry or exit, and the reason the person was at the scene. The list provides proof of security and validates the evidence collected. It is important to keep a list of all officers involved at the crime scene and keep track of their movements. However, officers not assigned to the crime scene are not given access just because they are law enforcement officers. The supervisor or investigator will usually coordinate duties such as evidence collection, scene perimeter securing, and other assignments. They will also assign shifts for officers, taking weather and staffing limitations into consideration. *(LE162.7.)*

**Section Vocabulary**

*private property*

*public property*

# UNIT 2 | PROCESSING THE CRIME SCENE

## LESSON 2 | Evidence Handling Procedures

**OBJECTIVES**

**LE089b.5.** List the types of evidence that may be found at a crime scene.

**LE089b.7.** Conduct a search for evidence.

**LE078.7.** Identify search procedures to be conducted.

**LE089b.9.** Determine if evidence can be properly collected by the officer or if a crime scene unit should collect evidence.

**LE110.7.** Demonstrate the ability to dust, lift, and document latent prints.

**LE109.9.** Define *patent*, *plastic*, and *elimination prints*.

Dr. Edmond Locard (1877–1966), a pioneer in forensic science, formulated the fundamental principle of forensic science: "Every contact leaves a trace." Referred to as Locard's Exchange Principle, this contends that everyone who enters a crime scene will both bring something into and take something from it. The job of a crime scene analyst is to determine what evidence at the scene belongs to the criminal and not to the victims or witnesses. An officer can begin this determination by talking to witnesses about the evidence at the scene. At any crime scene, the victim and the suspect usually leave or take away some sort of evidence.

A few examples of evidence that might be found and collected at a crime scene are fingerprints, shoe prints, blood, fibers, hair, tool marks, paint scratches, broken glass, body fluids, controlled substances, electronics equipment and computers, firearms, broken or damaged materials, tire tracks, documents, and bones. An officer should try to identify possible sources of evidence found at a crime scene. For example, if a substance appears to be blood, he or she should identify whether anyone at the scene had a bleeding injury. If the victim was not injured, the perpetrator might have been. Some evidence will be unidentifiable to the responding patrol officer; the crime scene unit or laboratory can assist in identifying, comparing, and interpreting such evidence. Some surfaces may contain contaminants that require expert processing. Based on the type of

**LE089b.10.** Follow evidence collection procedures when collecting evidence.

**LE078.12.** Ensure the chain of custody is protected.

crime committed and the kind of evidence consistent with the crime, an officer should be able to identify the type and category of each item of evidence. *(LE089b.5.)*

## Searching for Evidence

When searching a scene for evidence, an officer should use a systematic approach or established pattern. The type of crime scene will help dictate the type of search pattern. Officers should study the whole scene first, keeping in mind that the relationships of the items' positions may be important. *(LE089b.7.)*

Officers will use one or more of the following search patterns:

- ***spiral search pattern***: usually used outside by one person. The searcher begins at a certain point and walks in increasingly larger circles to the outermost boundary of the search area.
- ***strip/line search pattern***: usually used outside by several people. The search area is divided into lanes that are searched by one or more people in both directions until the entire area has been examined.
- ***grid search pattern***: often used indoors; a variation of the strip/line search pattern. It overlaps a series of lanes in a cross pattern, making the search more methodical and thorough.
- ***zone/quadrant search pattern***: used outdoors or for an area that is large. The area should be divided into four different sections and searched using one of the patterns above.
- ***pie/wheel search pattern***: entails dividing the area into a number of pie-shaped sections, which are usually searched using the strip/line search pattern. This method should be used for extremely large search areas. *(LE078.7.)*

Officers should never handle evidence with their bare hands. Personal protective equipment (PPE) must be used whenever evidence is handled or collected. PPE will protect the evidence from contamination and protect the officer from exposure to dangerous substances. At times, an officer may need booties, facemasks, goggles, aprons, and other protective clothing or gear, depending on the type of evidence being collected. Officer safety and evidence preservation requires the utmost care.

There are special considerations for handling specific types of evidence based on the type of evidence. For example, wet evidence, such as items soaked with body fluids or living plant material, must either be air-dried, packaged in breathable containers such as paper bags, or both. If packaged improperly, wet items will deteriorate to a point where they have no evidentiary value. Proper tools, equipment, and appropriate containers and packaging help prevent contamination and degradation issues for each particular type of evidence. An officer must pay particular attention to the proper collection of evidence. Agency policies and procedures will dictate specific evidence-handling procedures. *(LE089b.9.)*

| Trace Evidence | Biological Evidence DNA | Impression Evidence | Firearms Evidence | Electronic Evidence | Chemistry or Toxicological Evidence | Questioned Documents Evidence |
|---|---|---|---|---|---|---|
| hairs | blood | fingerprints | weapons | computers | blood alcohol levels, drugs, poisons, etc. | checks |
| fibers, clothing | semen | tire tracks | projectiles | cell phones | | bank statements |
| paint chips, transfer evidence | saliva | footwear impressions | gunshot residue | PDA | | address books |
| glass | bones | footprints | cartridge cases | thumb drives | | wire transfers |
| wood | teeth | bite marks | tool marks | external hard drives | | credit cards |
| soil, dirt | body tissues | tool marks | database information | CDs, DVDs, VHS tapes | | phone bills |
| | hair | | | digital cameras | | photographs or cameras |
| | DNA | | | answering machines, digital recording devices | | photo copies |

Trace evidence chart

*Figure 7-1*

## Trace Evidence

Microanalysis is the process of microscopically analyzing trace evidence, such as paint, glass, and cloth fibers, to determine a possible source or origin. Microanalysis is also used to analyze, identify, and compare other materials such as textile fibers, plastics, duct tape, lamp filaments, and fractured, torn, or cut items.

A transfer of fibers between the clothes of the victim and the assailant sometimes takes place. Fibers can come from clothing, carpet, rope, automobile carpeting, upholstery, and other common articles. Fiber analysis can reveal the manufacturer and other information about the source item. The relationship of fiber evidence to the victim, suspect, or the crime scene is crucial evidence in many cases. Broken windows, torn screens, or other sharp edges may snag fibers during a subject's entry into or exit from a building. Inside a vehicle that is part of a crime scene, an officer should examine the seat belts, airbag, steering wheel, and other components for fibers. Holding a flashlight to create side light and using a magnifying glass may help an officer to spot fiber evidence.

Comparing and matching fragments from a broken piece of glass can establish a common origin and relationship between the victim, the suspect, and the crime scene. The crime laboratory can analyze the glass pieces and compare characteristics such as color, density, and thickness, as well as type of glass (tempered window, non-tempered, headlight, bottle), to match and identify its origin. In addition, if a suspect or victim is near a piece of glass when it breaks, the person's body, shoes, and clothing may become contaminated with glass fragments. The direction of force or the sequence of glass breakage can determine on which side of the glass the suspect stood, thus establishing the suspect's entry or exit path.

Paint transfer can be useful evidence in solving crimes such as a hit-and-run crash. Samples may show that paint at the scene and on the suspect's vehicle came from a common source. Tools used to gain illegal entry into buildings and safes can leave paint residue. Sometimes, soil from the crime scene attaches to a suspect or victim's clothing, shoes, tires, or other objects, and the person transports it to another location.

## Biological Evidence

Biological evidence left at crime scenes may contain DNA. These specimens could be blood, saliva, urine, semen, perspiration, vaginal secretions, feces, or vomit. These are usually found at murder, aggravated battery, sexual assault, hit-and-run, and burglary scenes. The biological specimens most often encountered include blood, seminal fluid, or saliva. Crime laboratory experts in serology can identify these body fluids and, if needed, conduct further testing using DNA analysis. For blood evidence, the laboratory will determine through chemical testing whether blood is possibly present and if it is of human origin. Blood type and DNA identification is also possible with a sufficient blood sample. Sexual assault cases may require an examination of semen. Other pieces of evidence that may contain saliva and require examination are cigarette butts, drinking straws, soda and beer cans, masks, bottles, etc. Bite marks may also contain saliva.

Blood evidence may include blood pooled on the floor, a wet or dried stain on upholstery or carpet, or a sample collected from the victim or the suspect after the incident. The direction of blood spray or spatter can be analyzed by experts to determine the type of weapon, direction of attack, and relative size of the attacker.

Teeth can be used in some cases for identification and evidence. In the event an officer discovers human skeletal remains, a supervisor should be contacted so that agency policy and procedures can be followed in processing the scene. Because of the nature of the evidence, a medical examiner or a trained forensic specialist should see the bones at the site as they are discovered.

## Impression Evidence

Working edges of tools leave distinct marks on surfaces. An officer should never try to fit a suspect's tool into a mark. The entire damaged surface may need to be collected and submitted to the laboratory for comparison with the suspect's tool. Comparing fracture sites of two or more parts of a broken, torn, or cut object and determining whether they were once whole can provide strong evidence in court. An officer should not attempt to reconstruct the items or to process latent prints from the pieces before submitting them. If it is not possible to submit the entire damaged surface as evidence, agency policy and procedures should be followed for proper processing.

Footwear impressions and tire tracks are individualizing evidence because they can link a suspect to a crime by matching an impression at the scene with an object in the suspect's possession. Such impressions can be found in mud, soil, or other pliable material. Surface footwear impressions or tire prints can remain on wood, tile, paper, or paint, or in dust, blood, or grease.

Teeth can provide dental evidence in the form of bite mark impressions that can lead to the identity of the suspect. There is a high likelihood of saliva being present in bite marks. Bite marks should be photographed and documented according to agency policy and procedure as soon as possible.

***Latent prints*** are among the most valuable types of physical evidence and one of the most common types of evidence an officer will recover at crime scenes. Although generally invisible to the naked eye, latent prints result from body residues left behind when the friction ridges of the hands or feet make contact with a surface. All objects at a crime scene should be considered possible sources of fingerprints. When collecting evidence, an officer should wear gloves to prevent leaving his or her own latent prints. Care should be taken to avoid smudging or smearing existing latent prints when handling and packaging evidence. By examining the submitted evidence, the latent prints section of the laboratory may be able to determine the presence of latent prints and determine if they are identifiable.

The most common way to process latent fingerprints is by dusting with one of several types of powder, which develops the print and makes it visible. Fine brushes are used to apply dust to the surface on which an officer suspects prints have been left. Found prints are lifted from the original surface with clear or frosted tape, which is then attached to a small note card. An officer should follow these guidelines when dusting for and lifting latent prints:

1. Wear latex gloves to avoid contaminating the area with your own fingerprints. Be careful not to wipe possible prints off the surface.
2. Hold a flashlight at an angle, and look for obvious signs of a latent print.
3. Once you have a target area, take your brush, and lightly dab into the powder.
4. Tap and twirl the excess powder off the brush in the jar of powder. Use it sparingly because it tends to get on everything. It is better to use too little than too much.
5. Lightly brush from side to side, or swirl the brush on the target area. If the powder adhered to the print is too thick, brush off the excess powder with a clean brush and adjust the amount of powder.
6. When a print is found, apply the tape in the following manner:
   a. Place a suitable fingerprint card on a flat surface nearby so it is ready for the print you lift with the tape.
   b. Turn under the end of the lifting tape to form a tab.
   c. Extend the tape to a distance long enough to cover the print.
   d. Place the rolled end of the tape just above the latent print, but keep it off the print.
   e. Make sure that you do not trap foreign matter or air bubbles under the tape.
   f. Smooth from the tabbed end of the tape back toward the rolled end or vice versa. Use your finger, pen, or another object to smooth out the tape and release any trapped air. It is the same basic process as putting a decal on a window. With time and practice, you will develop your own technique for applying the tape.
7. Slowly lift the tape containing the developed prints from both ends, being careful not to touch the tape to another surface. Before lifting the tape, consider removing your latex gloves. Sometimes the lifting tape sticks to the gloves, making it awkward to lift the developed print.

8. Carefully place the tape on the fingerprint card in the same way that you placed the tape over the latent print. Place the print in the designated place on the correct side of the card.

9. On the back of the fingerprint print card, record the date, case number, the location within the crime scene where you retrieved the fingerprint, and any other information your department policy requires. Be careful not to damage the print.

10. Follow your agency policy and procedures to submit print evidence.

Most agencies provide officers with a basic latent fingerprint kit that includes latex gloves, black and light gray powder, a brush, tape, and cards. Before lifting latent prints, officers should refer to their agency policy and procedures regarding the available equipment and familiarize themselves with that equipment. If they are authorized to lift prints, they should have an adequate supply of materials on hand and be trained in how to use them. Lifting latent prints is a basic skill of law enforcement, and the ability to lift a latent print directly relates to an officer's attention to detail. Lifting a print is often a "one shot" opportunity and should be treated as such. Specially trained crime scene and laboratory personnel use numerous other methods for processing latent prints in a controlled environment. *(LE110.7.)*

***Patent prints*** are transferred from the friction ridges on fingers by a foreign substance (not a body residue), like blood, paint, or dirt, and are readily visible. ***Plastic prints*** are molded or imbedded fingerprints created by touching an impressionable surface such as wet paint or mud and are easily seen. An officer should follow agency policy and procedures regarding photographing visible prints and determining the best method to collect and preserve the evidence. ***Elimination prints*** allow fingerprint analysts to distinguish between prints belonging to the victim or witnesses and possible suspects. Inked fingerprints must be taken from innocent parties who may have been at the crime scene in order to eliminate their prints from the scene. *(LE109.9.)*

## Firearms Evidence

The firearms section of a laboratory examines firearms for function and safety. Analysts can examine fired bullets, cartridge cases, and shotgun shells to determine if the suspect's weapon fired them. They examine bullets recovered from a crime scene to identify the make and type of weapon involved. An analyst may also examine the crime scene for the presence of gunpowder and shot pellet spread to determine firing distance. Tool marks, after-market modifications, and serial number restoration can also be identified by the analyst.

When officers recover firearms or ammunition, they should follow agency policy and procedures for handling the evidence. Officers should always properly secure the weapon or ammunition. If the weapon or ammunition is part of the crime scene, officers should avoid evidence contamination. If a wooden object or other material contains an embedded bullet, officers should not attempt to remove it. If other weapons are found, officers should follow agency policy and procedures for evidence recovery.

## Electronic Evidence

Computers are commonly found at crime scenes and can often store vital evidence. Types of computer equipment and media may include personal computers, network systems, personal digital assistants (PDAs), removable disks, tapes, digital cameras, and other data storage media. An officer who encounters electronic evidence must not touch any part of the equipment to avoid possible damage to it. Computer evidence recovery is a complex task that requires highly specialized training. An officer should follow agency policy and procedure for computer evidence recovery.

## Chemical or Toxicological Evidence

The crime laboratory's chemistry section analyzes substances submitted to the laboratory to determine the presence or absence of any controlled substance as listed under Florida Statute §893.03. Analysts prepare reports of their findings and often testify in court regarding the results of their analyses.

The toxicology section of a laboratory analyzes samples of blood and urine to detect alcohol and other impairing drugs or chemicals. In any criminal investigation in which a question arises about alcohol or drug use on the part of the suspect or the victim, an analysis by the toxicology section of a laboratory may be performed. Such cases usually result from investigations of DUI, sexual assault, and death. Toxicology also analyzes alcoholic beverages for suspected chemicals.

An officer should be able to identify a wide variety of controlled substances and drug paraphernalia by sight or smell. In some cases, an officer may field test a substance before collecting and packaging it as evidence. When collecting drug paraphernalia, an officer should package sharp objects such as needles or syringes in puncture-proof packages clearly labeled with the words WARNING: SHARPS. Personal protective equipment is essential for an officer who encounters any chemical or biological substances. Specialized assistance in such cases may be needed and should be called in accordance with agency policies and procedures.

**Section Vocabulary**

*chain of custody*

*elimination prints*

*grid search pattern*

*latent prints*

*patent prints*

*pie/wheel search pattern*

*plastic prints*

*spiral search pattern*

*strip/line search pattern*

*zone/quadrant search pattern*

## Questioned Documents Evidence

A document is anything containing a mark to convey a message. An officer must carefully handle all documents found in a crime scene to preserve their condition. Document analysts use a variety of scientific methods to examine documents for alterations, obliterations, handwriting analysis, indentations, ink comparisons, and machine impressions. This analysis may answer questions about the document's authorship and authenticity.

Currency is sometimes analyzed by document experts. An officer who finds money at a crime scene should follow agency policy and procedures for handling it as evidence. When handling money taken from crime scenes or seized from suspects, an officer should be very careful to avoid any appearance of impropriety. *(LE089b.10.)*

## Chain of Custody

When an officer recovers evidence of any kind, a chain of custody of that evidence is begun. The ***chain of custody*** is documentation of everyone who handled the evidence as well as when, why, and what changes, if any, were made to it. A chain of custody documentation also proves that the evidence submitted in court is the same evidence that was collected at the crime scene. An officer should follow agency policy and procedure regarding documenting the chain of custody to help eliminate ethical and legal concerns about the handling and preservation of evidence. Florida Statute §918.13 states that to alter, destroy, conceal, or remove any record, document, or thing with the purpose to impair its verity or availability in such proceeding or investigation is a felony. *(LE078.12)*

# UNIT 2 | PROCESSING THE CRIME SCENE

## LESSON 3 | Documenting the Crime Scene

**OBJECTIVES**

**LE089b.12.** Document activities at a crime scene.

**LE114.4.** Identify the elements of effective crime scene photography.

### Sketching the Crime Scene

Crime scene sketches are a means of documentation that aid in the reconstruction, explanation, and permanent recording of an incident. Sketches can show relative positions (spatial relationships) of objects within the crime scene that are not readily seen in photographs. They can be used to document where evidence was recovered within the crime scene. An officer can use crime scene sketches during interviews with witnesses, victims, and suspects to correlate testimony. A crime scene sketch supplements an officer's field notes and photographs and helps with report writing. These sketches are usually admissible in court.

Items used to construct a sketch include a blank sheet of paper or graph paper, pen or pencil, tape measure, and template or ruler. The sketching officer's name and rank, the case number, location, and type of crime should be included in the sketch information. Additional information to include is compass direction, relevant items of physical evidence along with the location of such items indicated by measurements from at least two fixed points or other methods, and a legend of the symbols used to identify objects or points of interest on the sketch. Measurements, or a scale of the diagram, are also important information. Sketches should include the statement "not to scale" unless the officer is prepared to testify that every item is precisely drawn to scale on the sketch.

An officer should draw an initial sketch at the crime scene with enough detail to stand alone and include measurements for use in preparing a more formal sketch. The most common method of sketching is using the ***bird's-eye-view*** or downward observation perspective. ***Triangulation*** is the most common method of surveying (measuring and documenting) objects within the crime scene. The method measures objects from at least two fixed points forming a triangle.

The sketch should show, room by room, the size and relationship of entrances, exits, and contents. Officers should record each relevant item, including evidence. If an officer leaves something out of a sketch, such as a window, piece of furniture, or light fixture, he or she must be prepared to explain the omission at the deposition or trial. *(LE089b.12.)*

### Photographing the Crime Scene

Photographing the crime scene allows the court and jury to obtain an accurate understanding of how it looked on the day the officer responded. Photographing perishable, fragile, and transitory evidence ensures its documentation. Photos and videos provide a visual record that may be stored indefinitely and is readily available when needed.

Photographing should take place before any detailed investigation begins. The photographing officer should include his or her name, the case number, time, and date in order to identify all photographs. When photographing specific items such as blood drops, weapons, or tire marks, an officer should place an identifier with the evidence to establish the original positions for photographing and sketching. An identifier is a label used to illustrate size and provide scale and other valuable information relevant to the scene. Most agencies provide cards with a ruler printed on them. Other examples of identifiers are pens, *Miranda* cards, dollar bills or coins, or rulers. An officer will need to be able to testify that the photographs are a true and accurate representation of the scene as it appeared when the pictures were taken. All objects pictured must be material or relevant to the scene. Officers should avoid including bystanders or pets in crime scene photographs. *(LE114.4.)*

**Section Vocabulary**

***bird's eye view***

***triangulation***

# CHAPTER 8

## Criminal Investigations



An officer's first step in investigating any crime against a person is to determine if there are any injuries, provide first aid, and summon medical assistance if needed. The second step is to determine whether a crime has occurred and the type of crime. If no crime has occurred, the officer should provide assistance and complete the necessary reports as required by agency policy and procedure. If a crime has occurred, the officer should determine the type of crime and call for assistance, depending on the severity of the crime or injuries. Witnesses must be located, identified, and separated and the offender identified and arrested if he or she is on the scene. If the offender has fled, the officer should put out a Be On the Look Out (BOLO). Detailed information about what happened should be obtained from the victim and any witnesses.

Often, law enforcement officers think the arrest is the end of their role in a criminal case. However, the arrest is only a suspect's entrance into the criminal justice system; officers remain an integral part of the prosecution process until the case is resolved through entry of a plea or a conviction or acquittal after trial.

# UNIT 1 | CRIMES AGAINST PERSONS

## LESSON 1 | Assault, Battery, and Domestic Violence

**OBJECTIVES**

**LE053.9.** Describe when to issue a victim's rights brochure.

**LE061a.6.** Describe the elements of a pro-arrest policy in a domestic violence situation.

**LE061a.10.** Define dating violence.

**LE054.4.** Identify when to photograph injuries resulting from a domestic violence situation.

**LE061a.8.** Describe the circumstances under which an officer would make an arrest in a domestic violence situation.

**LE061a.7.** Describe a possible course of action an officer could suggest to parties in a domestic violence situation in which arrest is not a viable option.

**LE061a.12.** Describe the paperwork necessary to complete a domestic violence call.

### Victim's Rights Brochures

The victim of any crime shall be provided a victim's rights information card or brochure that contains essential information concerning the rights of the victim and services available to the victim as per §960.001, F.S. If the situation is a domestic violence situation, the officer should present the "Notice of Legal Rights and Remedies for Victims of Domestic Violence, Dating Violence, Repeat Violence, Sexual Violence" brochure as per §741.29, F.S. The victim must sign a receipt for the domestic violence brochure, which the officer will place in the incident report. If the situation involves a sexual battery, the officer should present the "Sexual Battery—Victim's Rights and Services" brochure from the Florida Council Against Sexual Violence, as per Florida Statutes §794.052. *(LE053.9.)*

### Domestic Violence

It may surprise many new law enforcement officers in Florida that domestic violence is not a criminal charge. When a person is arrested as the result of a domestic violence incident, the actual charge will be from a related statute such as those prohibiting assault, battery, and sexual battery.

Simple assault is the intentional, unlawful threat by word or act to do violence to another person, coupled with an apparent ability to do so, or doing some act that creates a well-founded fear in the other person that such violence is imminent. Simple assault is a misdemeanor but is elevated to aggravated assault, which is a felony, if a deadly weapon is used without intent to kill or if the assault is committed with intent to commit a felony.

Simple battery is also a misdemeanor and is actually and intentionally touching or striking another person against his or her will or intentionally causing bodily harm to another person. If the battery causes great bodily harm, permanent disability, or permanent disfigurement, but the defendant did not intend such a result, the defendant will be charged with felony battery. If a battery is committed with a deadly weapon or if the defendant intentionally causes great bodily harm, permanent disability, or permanent disfigurement, the defendant will be charged with aggravated battery.

In ***domestic violence*** cases, the underlying charge normally is battery, aggravated battery, or sexual battery. Such charges are classified as domestic violence because of the relationship between the perpetrator and the victim. Florida Statute Section 741.28 defines domestic violence as "any assault, aggravated assault, battery, aggravated battery, sexual assault, sexual battery, stalking, aggravated stalking, kidnapping, false imprisonment, or any criminal offense resulting in physical injury or death of one family or household member by another family or household member."

If, after thorough investigation, an officer develops probable cause that a domestic violence crime was committed and the suspect is present, an arrest should usually be made *(LE061.a.6.)*. Most employing agencies have pro-arrest policies that make arrest mandatory if probable cause exists. Whenever a law enforcement officer determines probable cause exists that an act of domestic violence has been committed within the jurisdiction, the officer may arrest the person or persons suspected of its commission, and charge such person or persons with the appropriate crime. The decision to arrest and charge shall not require consent of the victim or consideration of the relationship of the parties.

Usually, the victim and suspect are the only persons present at the scene of a domestic violence incident and therefore have all of the information to provide an officer. Sometimes, obtaining the details of the incident from the victim and suspect is almost impossible. If either or both refuse to provide adequate information about the incident, an officer should turn to witnesses who were in the room during the incident. If no witnesses were in the room at that time, persons closest to the action should be contacted to obtain more information. If children are present, an officer may obtain additional information from them if they witnessed the incident. An officer may need to contact the Department of Children and Families if he or she determines that the home is not safe for the children or if a decision is made to arrest both combatants.

Often, an officer will end up charging people directly or indirectly associated with domestic violence incidents with disorderly intoxication. An officer should refer to Florida Statute §856.011 in such cases.

## Dating Violence

Dating violence is violence between individuals who have or have had a continuing and significant relationship of a romantic or intimate nature. The existence of such a relationship shall be determined based on the following:

- The existence of the relationship within the past 6 months
- The relationship is characterized by the expectation of affection or sexual involvement
- The frequency and type of interaction must occur over time and on a continuous basis during the course of the relationship

This term does not include violence in a casual acquaintanceship or violence between individuals who only have engaged in ordinary socialization in a business or social context. The investigation of dating violence is similar to domestic violence as per statute, §784.046 (11–16), F.S. *(LE061a.10.)*

## Documentation

Physical evidence is very important in domestic and dating violence investigations and an officer should photograph and document it carefully. It may be necessary for an officer to return in 24–48 hours to take additional pictures of the victim to fully document any bruising. Physical evidence can help solve a case involving uncooperative witnesses. The consent or cooperation of the victim is not required before an arrest can be made in a domestic violence incident. Evidence can also help to corroborate the accounts of witnesses or participants. *(LE054.4.)*

## Determine the Primary Aggressor

An officer should evaluate each party's statements separately to determine whether there is probable cause for arrest. If probable cause exists to believe that two or more persons have committed a misdemeanor or felony or if two or more persons make complaints, an officer should try to determine the primary aggressor. Determining who the primary aggressor is can be done by analyzing the totality of the circumstances of the incident. By comparing all information obtained and then looking for inconsistencies and untruths, an officer should be able to identify the primary aggressor in almost all incidents that involve two or more combatants.

Except in rare circumstances, an officer should arrest only the primary aggressor and not a person who acted reasonably to protect or defend him- or herself or another family or household member from domestic violence. If only one person lodged a complaint, the incident did not involve mutual combatants.

An officer should use the following factors to help identify the primary aggressor and make an arrest:

- Compare physical evidence to statements.
- Compare injuries to statements.
- Consider evidence or patterns of assault and coercion; include physical, sexual, and psychological abuse.
- Compare the victim, witness, and suspect's statements.
- Assess the verbal and nonverbal communication of involved parties.
- Consider the emotional state, relative size, and fearfulness of involved parties.
- Consider violent physical acts such as the following:

  Who damaged property?

  Who injured animals?

  Who ripped the phone from the wall?

  Does the injury fit the story of the person who claims self-defense? Typical defensive wounds include bruising or cuts on outer forearms, back, backs of legs, palms, or inside fingers or fingertips. *(LE061a.8.)*

## Child Custody Court Orders

An officer may not enforce a court order issued by another state or jurisdiction unless the court order is domesticated by a court within the officer's jurisdiction. The officer should contact his or her supervisor when confronted with this kind of situation and should follow agency policy and procedure.

Occasionally, an officer may be faced with a child custody situation in which one parent has a court order from Florida or another state and the other parent has a conflicting order issued from a different state or even a different country. The Florida order will not necessarily be the proper and enforceable one. Such cases involve application of the "Uniform Child Custody Jurisdiction and Enforcement Act" and can be legally complex. Responding officers should not attempt to determine which order is enforceable, but should maintain the status quo, contact a supervisor, and follow agency policy and procedure when dealing with such situations.

## Course of Action

After arresting the suspect, an officer should tell the victim the reason for the arrest and where the suspect will be taken. A suspect who is arrested for an act of domestic or dating violence must remain in custody until brought before the court for a bail determination. This prevents the offender from immediately returning to the household or reinitiating contact with the victim, and gives the victim time to obtain a restraining order or injunction for protection without the suspect's interference. Additionally, it provides the victim time to seek help and possibly a safe place to stay. When determining bail, the court will consider the safety of the victim, children in the home, and any other person who may be in danger if the court releases the defendant. Before the court releases the offender, the officer should notify and advise the victim of safety precautions he or she may take.

When probable cause for arrest does not exist, an officer should advise involved parties. When all persons involved in the incident are calm enough to be reasonable, they should be brought within hearing distance and the officer should explain the options available to the family unit:

- Obtain counseling.
- Act on information provided on handouts covering domestic and dating violence and injunctions.
- Seek assistance from social service agencies the officer refers them to.
- In order to keep the peace, one party leaves. The officer can coordinate the change by arranging for transportation or safe haven.

For example, an officer could ask participants to sit at their dining room table. The primary officer provides participants with information about alternatives and social services available in their community. The backup or cover officer takes a position of cover and observation. *(LE061a.7.)*

## Injunctions

Injunction for Protection Against Domestic Violence is for persons who meet the statutory definition of family or household member. According to Florida Statute §741.28(3), family or household member

> "means spouses, former spouses, persons related by blood or marriage, persons who are presently residing together as if a family or who have resided together in the past as if a family, and persons who are parents of a child in common regardless of whether they have been married. With the exception of persons who have a child in common, the family or household members must be currently residing or have in the past resided together in the same single dwelling unit."

An Injunction for Protection Against Repeat Violence pursuant to § 784.046, F.S. is for persons who do not meet the statutory definition of family or household member, but who have been victims of at least two incidents of violence or stalking by the alleged abuser within the last six months.

An Injunction for Protection Against Dating Violence is for persons who have or have had a continuing and significant relationship of a romantic or intimate nature. According to § 784.046(1)(d), F.S., "the existence of such a relationship shall be determined based on whether the person was in a dating relationship that existed within the past six months. The expectation of affection or sexual involvement between the parties characterized the nature of the relationship. The frequency and type of interaction between the parties involved in the relationship must have included that the persons have been involved over time and on a continuous basis during the course of the relationship."

**Section Vocabulary**

*domestic violence*

An officer should inform the victim that he or she could go to the courthouse and file for the appropriate injunction. The victim must complete an affidavit, explaining why she or he needs the protection. All forms can be obtained for free from the clerk of court. A judge reviews the affidavit and grants or denies the request. The victim is not assessed filing fees for an injunction. Although an injunction is a civil action, it has criminal implications that are enforceable by law. Law enforcement honors injunctions from another state or country (foreign), and can advise a victim to notify the local clerk of the court to re-issue the injunction in Florida if the victim is now residing in Florida.

The violation by the respondent of a custody arrangement outlined in an injunction will generally remain a civil matter unless one of the provisions in § 741.31, F.S. is violated. If an officer determines that the circumstances of the custody dispute are civil in nature, he or she should maintain the status quo and document the incident on the appropriate report.

If an officer does not make an arrest in a domestic violence incident, he or she is required to document the incident, as stated in § 741.29, F.S., indicating in a full report why the officer made no arrest. In doing so, the officer assumes, as does his or her agency, a certain amount of liability should the parties reengage in violence and injury occur. *(LE061a.12.)*

The final step involved in a domestic violence situation requires the officer to present the victim with a victim's rights brochure as per § 960.001, F.S and the "Notice of Legal Rights and Remedies for Victims of Domestic Violence, Dating Violence, Repeat Violence, Sexual Violence" brochure as per § 741.29, F.S. The victim must sign a receipt for the brochure, which the officer will place in the incident report. Section 741.29, F.S. states that no law enforcement officer can be held liable in any civil action for an arrest based on probable cause, enforcement of a court order, or service of process in good faith arising from an alleged incident of domestic violence.

# UNIT 1 | CRIMES AGAINST PERSONS

## LESSON 2 | Child Abuse

### Elements of Child Abuse and Neglect

***Child abuse*** is the intentional act resulting in or the intentional infliction of physical or mental injury upon a child. Child abuse also involves the active encouragement of any person to commit any act that results in physical or mental injury to a child. According to § 827.03, F.S., "a person who knowingly or willfully abuses a child without causing great bodily harm, permanent disability, or permanent disfigurement to the child commits a felony of the third degree..."

***Aggravated child abuse*** is a first-degree felony that occurs when a person either commits aggravated battery on a child; tortures, maliciously punishes, or cages a child; or knowingly or willfully abuses a child and in so doing causes great bodily harm, permanent disability, or permanent disfigurement to the child. Florida Statute defines ***maliciously*** as wrongfully, intentionally, and without legal justification or excuse. Maliciousness may be established by circumstances from which one could conclude that a reasonable parent would not have engaged in the damaging acts toward the child for any valid reason and the primary purpose of the acts was to cause the victim unjustifiable pain or injury.

***Child neglect*** occurs when a caregiver omits or fails to provide a child with the care, supervision, and services necessary to maintain the child's physical and mental health. This includes, but is not limited to, food, nutrition, clothing, shelter, supervision, medicine, and medical services that a prudent person would consider essential for the well-being of the child. Child neglect can be a caregiver's failure to make a reasonable effort to protect a child from abuse, neglect, or exploitation by another person. Neglect of a child may be repeated conduct or a single incident or omission that results in serious physical or mental injury or a substantial risk of death to a child. A person who willfully or by culpable negligence neglects a child, causing great bodily harm, permanent disability, or permanent disfigurement to the child commits a second-degree felony. The same neglect without great bodily harm, permanent disability, or permanent disfigurement resulting to the child is a third-degree felony.

Child abuse or neglect may include the following:

- inflicting or allowing physical, mental, or emotional injury
- committing or allowing sexual battery, or lewd and lascivious acts
- allowing, encouraging, or forcing the sexual exploitation of a child
- abandoning a child
- exposing a child to an illegal controlled substance

**OBJECTIVES**

**LE052.1.** Escort a DCF child protection team investigator to the scene of an abused or neglected child.

**LE051.3.** Conduct an initial investigation alleging child abuse or neglect.

**LE052.2.** Initiate contact with the parent(s) or guardian(s) of the child.

**LE052.5.** Apply state and local judicial procedures regarding the interviewing of juveniles.

**LE051.1.** Initiate contact with a victim of child abuse or neglect.

**LE051.2.** Identify when to provide first aid or obtain medical attention for a child abuse or neglect victim.

**LE051.6.** Identify what to include in field notes regarding child abuse or neglect situations.

**LE052.6.** Assist DCF in removing an abused or neglected child.

**LE051.11.** Identify child abuse and neglect reporting requirements.

- using mechanical devices, unreasonable restraint, or extended periods of isolation to control a child
- engaging in violent behavior that demonstrates a wanton disregard for the presence of a child and could reasonably result in serious injury to the child
- negligently failing to protect a child from inflicted physical, mental, or sexual injury caused by acts of another
- allowing a child's sibling to die because of abuse or neglect

Behaviors that can indicate child abuse are when the child does the following:

- fears remaining at home, or returning to the home
- is wary of adult contact
- startles easily
- appears overly affectionate (inappropriate) or withdrawn
- acts violently or aggressively
- cries uncontrollably
- exhibits inappropriate sexual behavior

Certain parental behaviors can indicate an environment of abuse, such as the presence of stressful relationships, acute tension in the home, unreasonable discipline, unrealistic expectations, and impulsive behaviors.

Evidence of physical abuse may be easy to identify because of its threatening appearance. Although less apparent visually, child neglect can be as harmful as child abuse. Signs of neglect in the home can be the absence of necessities such as food, water, and heat. Victims can have bedsores, skin disorders, rashes, untreated injuries, or medical problems. There may be signs of mismanaging health and medication such as empty, unmarked, and outdated prescription bottles. The child may exhibit poor personal hygiene, including soiled clothing, matted or lice-infested hair, odors, dirty nails or skin, and the presence of feces. If the child's size is inconsistent with his or her age, this may indicate malnutrition and hunger. Fragile skin, dry, sore mouth, apathy, lack of energy, and mental confusion can indicate dehydration. A pallid complexion and sunken eyes or cheeks can indicate dehydration and malnutrition. An officer may discover the lack of clean bedding or clothing, or the child wearing clothing inappropriate for the weather. Hazards in the home can include exposed wires and roach infestation. Infants can have a bald spot on the back of their heads that indicates neglect.

## Surrendered Infants

A parent neither commits child neglect nor contributes to a child's dependency if he or she leaves a newborn infant at a hospital, emergency medical services station, or fire station, or brings a newborn infant to an emergency room with the intent to leave the infant and not return. Section 383.50 and §827.035, F.S. defines a newborn infant as a child whom a licensed physician reasonably believes to be approximately seven days old or younger. Law enforcement cannot initiate a criminal investigation just because a parent leaves a newborn infant at a hospital, unless there is actual or suspected child abuse or neglect.

# Initial Response

The officer may become aware of suspected child abuse or neglect during the course of a separate investigation, by direct contact with a citizen in the community, or through 911 dispatch (also known as the public safety telecommunicator). Officers should keep in mind the reporter or complainant of the abuse may have valuable information to aid the investigation. Conversely, the complainant may have a negative agenda. The reporter or complainant may be a family member, estranged spouse, DCF representative, school official, neighbor, medical worker, or any other person who encounters the child. To prevent the suspect from seeking retribution, an officer needs to keep the reporter's identity confidential.

The majority of the time, an officer's response to dispatch will be to meet with or escort a representative from the DCF to the scene. The DCF representative will conduct a social services investigation. The officer's job will be to conduct a criminal investigation. Due to the hostile nature of these types of calls, the unarmed civilian social worker from the DCF is at some risk. One of the officer's responsibilities is to provide security while the civilian conducts his or her social services investigation. *(LE052.1.)*

Investigating child abuse can be a very difficult task for law enforcement. Officers must overcome many barriers, such as defensive parents who fear that an officer will remove their child from home or children who fear their parents or fear that an officer will remove them from their home. An officer's feelings about child abuse and child discipline can interfere with his or her judgment during a child abuse incident. An officer should maintain a professional, fair, and impartial attitude while conducting a child abuse investigation. Officers should be aware of and document relevant information about visible injuries, the living environment, and the demeanor of involved parties. The scene should be secured to avoid destruction of or tampering with evidence. After a preliminary interview and assessment of the scene, officers should decide the appropriate actions to take to continue the investigation and ensure the child's safety.

An officer's responsibilities include conducting an initial investigation to determine if a crime has occurred, and if so, which crime. If a crime has occurred, the officer should document it and take appropriate action. Child abuse investigations are time sensitive. Upon arrival, the officer should survey the scene for evidence of alleged child abuse or neglect. If an officer cannot establish where the incident occurred, he or she must treat the entire area as a crime scene. When searching the home for children, the officer may learn that an individual is hiding a child. *(LE051.3.)*

While securing the scene, the officer should identify all parties and their relationships to one another, including parents, caregivers, or guardians. Preliminary questions should be asked to identify victims, witnesses, and suspects and to determine allegations made by the complainant. When the officer has identifying information, he or she should contact dispatch, and ask for wants/warrants checks and criminal histories of household members and others involved. *(LE052.2.)*

# Initial Interviews

Prior to conducting any interview with a victim of child abuse, the officer should contact his or her supervisor and take appropriate action. Often an investigator or a very experienced patrol officer conducts this interview. Sometimes a child protective investigator and a law enforcement officer jointly conduct the interview.

**There is a statutory limit on the number of interviews conducted with a child victim.**

The officer should refer to local agreements or agency policy on interviewing procedures. In addition, the chief judge in the officer's judicial district, acting under § 914.16, F.S., has set guidelines and limits on interviewing child abuse or sexual abuse victims who are under 16 years old. The limits also apply to persons with mental retardation. The purpose of the limitations is to protect the victim from psychological damage caused by repeated questioning about a traumatic incident. *(LE052.5.)*

The officer or detective should conduct a thorough interview and plan to share statements with DCF at the appropriate time during the criminal process. However, when the officer or detective and DCF child protective investigator are conducting a joint interview, the decision about who interviews should be tactical rather than legal or jurisdictional. Who has the best chance of eliciting needed information from the child in a manner that makes the information admissible as evidence in court? Before the interview, the officer must learn the victim's age. Knowing this helps the officer prepare for the interview and use language and word questions so a child of that age understands. An officer should consider what he or she knows about the child's mental capacity. A 10-year-old child with a mental disability may understand less than other children of the same age.

If an officer initiates contact with the child, and the parent or guardian refuses to let that officer interview the child, the officer should determine if the child is in immediate danger. If the child is in immediate danger, the officer should remove the child from the scene, and notify his or her supervisor. *(LE051.1.)*

If the child is not in immediate danger that warrants removal from the scene, the officer should determine the relationship between the suspect and victim for purposes of protecting the child from further abuse and then physically separate the child and suspect. The officer should make sure that the child and the suspect cannot see or hear each other. This prevents the suspect from using eye contact or body language to intimidate or coerce the child.

Without seeking details, the officer should find out from the victim what happened, observe any injuries to the victim or other household members, and immediately determine whether anyone needs medical treatment. There may be victims of domestic violence or other evidence of criminal offenses in the household. Officers should look for signs of physical abuse such as suspicious bruises, welts, burns, fractures, lacerations, and abrasions. Whenever possible, an officer of the same sex should examine the injured person. This is particularly important if an officer must remove or open clothing to examine injuries. *(LE051.2.)*

If there are pets or animals present, look for signs of animal abuse, such as malnourishment, mange, or mistreatment. Often if there is child abuse in the home, animal abuse is also present.

The officer should document excited utterances or spontaneous statements made by the victim, suspect, witnesses, and other children present, noting their exact words in quotation marks, their emotional state, and indicating the approximate time the statement is made after the incident has occurred. Such statements may be admissible as excited utterances, an exception to the hearsay rule. *(LE051.6.)*

A child protective investigator will determine when the child should be placed in protective custody. The law authorizes child protective investigators to remove children from a caretaker's custody and control without a custody order. If this occurs, the responding officer must help the investigator lawfully execute the investigator's duties. This responsibility includes ensuring the personal safety of all involved. Law enforcement agencies and DCF representatives must be familiar with interagency agreements about joint investigations. *(LE052.6.)*

## Reporting Requirements

Individuals who are legally required to report child abuse, abandonment, or neglect are physicians, medical examiners, nurses, hospital personnel, mental health professionals, spiritual healers, school personnel, social workers, day care workers, foster care, residential or institutional workers, law enforcement officers, and judges.

If the incident seems to involve a criminal violation or if there is concern about the child's safety and well-being, the officer is required by Florida Statute §39.201 to contact the DCF Abuse Hot Line at 1-800-96-ABUSE.

The officer should determine whether to continue or end the investigation if no criminal violation is apparent. Terminating the criminal investigation does not prevent an officer from contacting the DCF Abuse Hotline at 1-800-96-ABUSE if he or she still has concerns for a child's safety and well-being. A child protection investigation is separate from a criminal investigation. DCF can conduct its investigation with or without a criminal investigation. *(LE051.11.)*

**Section Vocabulary**

***aggravated child abuse***

***child abuse***

***child neglect***

***maliciously***

## UNIT 1 | CRIMES AGAINST PERSONS

# LESSON 3 | Disabled Adult and Elder Abuse

**OBJECTIVES**

**LE154.2.** Verify that a person is being threatened or victimized when responding to an alleged disabled adult or elder abuse situation.

**LE154.1.** Respond to a disabled adult or elderly person being victimized.

**LE154.3.** Develop a plan of action to immediately remove the threat to the victim of disabled adult or elder abuse.

**LE154.4.** Take action as required to protect the disabled adult or elder person from threatened abuse.

***Abuse of a disabled adult or elderly person*** is any willful or threatened act by a caregiver that significantly impairs or is likely to impair a vulnerable adult's physical, mental, or emotional health. Section 825.101, F.S. defines ***caregiver*** as

> "a person who has been entrusted with or has assumed responsibility for the care or the property of a disabled adult or elderly person; includes, but is not limited to, relatives, court-appointed or voluntary guardians, adult household members, neighbors, health care providers, and employees and volunteers of facilities."

A ***disabled adult*** is a person 18 years of age or older who suffers from a condition of physical or mental incapacitation due to a developmental disability, organic brain damage or mental illness, or who has one or more physical or mental limitations that restrict the person's ability to perform the normal activities of daily living.

An ***elderly person*** is a person 60 years of age or older who is suffering from the infirmities of aging as manifested by advanced age or organic brain damage or other physical, mental, sensory, or emotional dysfunction to the extent that the ability of the person to provide adequately for the person's own care or protection is impaired.

According to §415.102 (27), F.S., the *Adult Protective Services Act* defines a ***vulnerable adult*** (disabled adult or elderly person) as a person 18 years of age or older whose ability to perform the normal activities of daily living or to provide for his or her own care or protection is impaired due to a mental, emotional, sensory, long-term physical, or developmental disability or dysfunction, brain damage, or the infirmities of aging.

***Exploitation of a disabled adult or elderly person*** transpires when someone knowingly, by deception or intimidation, obtains or uses a disabled adult's or elderly person's funds, assets or property. The suspect's intent must be to deprive the person of the use, benefit, or possession of the funds, assets, or property, or to benefit someone other than the disabled adult or elderly person temporarily or permanently.

## Initial Response

A young officer may not easily relate to Florida's disabled or elderly citizens, a group that has become one of the largest populations in this state. More and more, officers will come to the aid of our elderly and disabled population. It is imperative that an officer treats the elderly or disabled with the same care, concern, and enthusiasm that he or she treats any other victim of abuse.

Many disabled adults and elderly persons in this state are in need of protective services. These services support disabled adults and elderly persons' rights. These are the same rights that other citizens have. These services also protect them from abuse, neglect, and exploitation. Florida Statute Chapter 825 deals with the abuse, neglect, and exploitation of elderly persons and disabled adults. It establishes protective services programs for all disabled adults and elderly persons who need them.

An officer may become aware of suspected abuse or neglect of a disabled adult or elderly person during the course of a separate investigation, through direct contact with a citizen in the community, or through dispatch. The officer should keep in mind that the reporter or complainant might have valuable information to aid the investigation; conversely, the complainant may have a negative agenda. The reporter or complainant may be a family member, caregiver, a DCF representative, neighbor, medical worker, or any other person who encounters the adult. To prevent the suspect from seeking retribution, the officer should keep the reporter's identity confidential.

## Initial Observations

If a victim has serious, life-threatening injuries, the officer should begin first aid treatment. If the victim is stable and needs no medical attention, however, he or she should isolate and interview the victim, witnesses, and complainant.

The officer should observe firsthand the living conditions of the disabled adult or elderly person by asking to see his or her living area, bedroom, or sleeping area. The officer should also ask to see and speak with the disabled adult or elderly person. The officer should observe the person's hygiene and note if it looks as if someone is taking care of the individual. How does he or she smell? Is the smell of urine or feces present on the person or in the room? Is there a smell of rotting food? In addition, the officer should check whether there is appropriate food in the kitchen and refrigerator. The officer should try to determine if the disabled adult or elderly person has special needs that are unmet.

If the disabled adult or elderly person takes medication, the officer should try to determine if that medicine affects comprehension or awareness. The officer should ask what prescriptions the individual takes or look around the house to find prescription bottles. The person may wear a medical alert bracelet or necklace or have a membership card for a support group, which are useful tools in determining a person's medical or mental state.

Signs of abuse or exploitation may not be obvious. The disabled adult or elderly person's surroundings might be hygienic, but the caregiver might not let the person leave the room. The officer may observe varying levels of neglect. It may be recent or long-standing. When evaluating neglect situations, it is important to reserve judgment about people's lives and lifestyle choices. Impoverished families often lack amenities and necessities. Hygiene and cleanliness standards also vary. However, the officer may have cause for concern when the caregiver withholds needed care or items from a disabled adult or elderly person or if that person endures undue hardships, or his or her health and safety are in jeopardy. *(LE154.2.)*

The caregiver may become increasingly frustrated as the disabled adult or elderly person becomes more financially, emotionally, or physically dependent. Increased frustration can lead to abuse. Sometimes a caregiver has had a lifelong relationship with the individual he or she supports. An abuser may see the relationship as unequal or unfair and resent the disabled adult or elderly person. This is particularly true if the caregiver's expectations of the disabled adult or elderly person's abilities are unrealistic. The caregiver might be diverting the disabled adult or elderly person's pension or Social Security funds for his or her own financial gain. Officers should look for the influence of drugs, alcohol, or mental illness on the caregiver. Such circumstances require an officer's insightful investigation.

**Section Vocabulary**

*abuse of a disabled adult or elderly person*

*caregiver*

*disabled adult*

*elderly person*

*exploitation of a disabled adult or elderly person*

*disabled adult*

*vulnerable adult*

When an officer responds to an incident involving any kind of abuse or exploitation of a disabled adult or elderly person, he or she should be prepared to take action to protect the victim or person threatened. The officer must recognize the victim's reactions and respond accordingly. Loud or argumentative reactions can signal impending violence. Crying or laughing may express the victim's relief that an officer has finally arrived. Quiet or regressive behavior may indicate suffering. The officer should take extra time to be sensitive to the victim's needs; observe carefully, speak simply, and have patience. Elderly persons tend to be trusting and thus vulnerable to crime and victimization. *(LE154.1.)*

Abused or neglected disabled adults or elderly persons may have some, all, or none of the following normal or trauma reactions: embarrassment that they allowed the victimization, fear that abuse may escalate, irrational anger, confusion, and denial.

When an officer learns of a case of abuse, neglect, or exploitation of a disabled adult or elderly person, he or she should consider the criminal conduct a public concern, not merely a private family matter. The officer should immediately remove the threat to the victim. If a crime has occurred, the officer must identify the statute violated. *(LE154.3.)*

Florida Statutes mandate that any person, including any state, county, or municipal criminal justice employee or law enforcement officer who knows, or has reasonable cause to suspect, that a disabled adult or elderly person is abused, neglected or exploited must immediately report such knowledge or suspicion to the DCF Abuse Hot Line at 1-800-96-ABUSE. Services provided are on a voluntary basis unless it is determined that the individual in need of services is mentally incapable of providing consent, as provided in § 415.105, F.S. *(LE154.4.)*

# UNIT 1 | CRIMES AGAINST PERSONS

## LESSON 4 | Death and Homicide

## Circumstances Involving the Death of a Human Being

Before the officer can determine what information and evidence to look for, he or she needs to recognize the possible circumstances and categories of the death of a human. There are three broad categories of causes of death: natural, accidental, and criminal. Criminal includes suicides. Although the cause of death may not be immediately apparent, in many cases the officer will be able to determine if the death was the result of an accident, natural causes, or criminal wrongdoing.

### *Child Deaths/SUID (Sudden Unexpected Infant Death)/SIDS (Sudden Infant Death Syndrome)*

Sudden Infant Death Syndrome or crib death is the sudden unexpected death of an apparently healthy infant, usually less than one year of age that remains unexplained even after a complete medical history, death scene investigation, and postmortem examination. SIDS is one of several causes of SUID. However, SIDS, unlike the other SUID causes, is a diagnosis of exclusion; when all other possibilities have been ruled out. If there is a determined cause of death, it is **not** a SIDS incident.

Actions or conditions that may cause illness, injury, or death that are not SIDS-related include child abuse and neglect, immunizations, contagious diseases, heredity, overheating, suffocation, and vomiting. A greater number of male infants die from SIDS than do females (a 3-to-2 ratio). The greatest number of deaths takes place in the fall, winter, and early spring. SIDS occurs in all socioeconomic, racial, and ethnic groups.

Circumstances surrounding the death of an infant are usually similar in each SIDS case. The infant is usually healthy before death, but occasionally there is evidence of a mild upper respiratory infection or recent physical stress. SIDS usually occurs when an infant is asleep or assumed to be asleep. Parents or caregivers may have placed the infant in a bed or crib for a nap and returned to find the infant not breathing or apparently dead. This may occur 10–20 minutes or up to several hours after the parent places the child in bed. Parents or caregivers may have placed the infant in a crib for a nap and returned to find the infant face down with blankets covering its head, wedged into the corner of the crib. Parents or caregivers report not hearing any signs of a struggle, even though they were within hearing distance at all times.

In most cases the infant's skin is altered (mottled, blue, or gray), which may give the appearance of bruising. There may be frothy, blood-tinged mucus draining from the infant's mouth or nostrils. The position of the infant is crucial to the investigation.

**OBJECTIVES**

**LE124.3.** Conduct an initial assessment of a criminal, accidental, or natural cause of death.

**LE124.2.** Assess the situation prior to approaching a dead body.

**LE124.5.** Identify the indications of death.

**LE124.7.** Preserve any evidence on or near the body.

**LE124.11.** Identify when to contact the Medical Examiner's office.

**LE124.10.** Identify when to contact the doctor of the deceased.

**LE124.6.** Obtain medical confirmation of a recent death.

**LE096.6.** Notify a victim's family of death.

Parents or caregivers often move infants from their deceased position in an attempt to resuscitate. This can cause confusion and difficulty in obtaining information that the Medical Examiner will need to determine what caused or contributed to the infant's death. The officer should pay close attention to the area surrounding the infant. What are the personal habits of the parents or caregiver? Does anyone smoke cigarettes or other tobacco products? Are there signs of illicit drug use or manufacture? Are there signs that the infant ingested alcohol?

The officer should interview the person that last saw the infant alive and the person who found the infant dead, asking about the infant's exact position and anything observed or heard.

An officer who is the primary or responding officer to a SUID/SIDS death should follow his or her agency policy and procedure for an incident involving the death of an infant. The officer should explain to the parents or caregivers his or her agency's responsibility to perform a complete investigation. The officer should be prepared for the parents' or family's responses, keeping in mind that they are in shock, distraught, and most likely confused. The officer may need to repeat information several times.

This is a serious investigation; however, an officer should try to understand the family's level of grief when experiencing this type of loss. Different cultures respond in different ways to death. Some families are very vocal in their grief, while others may appear unemotional and reserved. The officer should not jump to any conclusions about the way the family is reacting to the tragedy based on his or her own cultural background.

The officer should be aware of his or her own emotional reaction. Understand that these extremely challenging scenes can be difficult to experience. This stress is often part of an officer's job. The officer should remain professionally distant and not take on grief that does not belong to him or her. Some stress indicators the officer may experience include anger, recurring dreams, physical illness, depression, changes in eating and sleeping patterns, mood swings, and concentration problems.

## Responding to the Scene

After arriving at a scene involving a dead person, the officer should begin collecting information to make an initial assessment regarding the circumstances of the person's death. The officer should always approach the scene as a crime scene and consider it a homicide crime scene until the information he or she gathers consistently points to elements of a death by natural causes or accident. *(LE124.3.)*

The officer should scan the area surrounding the possible dead body for potential hazards or evidence by performing a 360 degree visual sweep of the perimeter. The best path to the body should be determined so as not to destroy or contaminate possible evidence. Officers should remember to apply universal precautions and use personal protection equipment when approaching the body. *(LE124.2.)*

There are several ways to determine if a person is dead. One method is to look for signs of breathing. The chest or abdominal area will not move if the person is dead. When the vital functions of the body cease, body temperature will adjust to that of the surrounding environment. The medical examiner may be able to determine the approximate time of death based on the rate of temperature loss and the temperature of the area where the officer finds the body. Skin may be pale, waxy, and translucent; the fingernails may be pale. The eyes may have become milky or cloudy, and the eyelids may remain open if they were open at the time of death.

The officer should look for signs of rigor mortis and lividity. Rigor mortis is a stiffening of the body that first appears one to six hours after death. Full rigor mortis is set six to 24 hours after death, begins to disappear within 12 to 36 hours, and is completely gone 36 to 60 hours after death. Lividity is caused by the pooling and settling of blood within the body because of gravity. Rigor mortis and lividity can help determine time of death, position of the body at death, whether the body was moved after death, and in some cases, the manner of death. Lividity is noticeable within 30 minutes and fixed 12 hours after death. Once lividity is fixed, the blood remains pooled around the white pressure points where the weight of the body was resting on the surface at the time of death. If a body was moved after death (postmortem), it may indicate foul play.

While observing the body, the officer should look for obvious signs of trauma, such as the presence of blood, cuts, gashes, or bruising. The officer should look for an obvious fatal injury, such as a bullet hole in the head or chest, and notify his or her supervisor or detectives of any signs of trauma or obvious fatal injury. *(LE124.5.)*

During this initial assessment, the officer should try to determine whether the death was from criminal, accidental, or natural causes by identifying observable evidence. Any evidence on or near the body should be preserved as the officer secures the crime scene. The officer should remember to document the names of persons on the scene and any changes made to the scene. If the officer is in a public location, he or she should place a visual barrier between the body and the public without cross contaminating any evidence. The officer should then notify specialized units and the medical examiner and wait for their arrival. *(LE124.7.)*

## Notifying the Medical Examiner (ME)

When any person dies in Florida by criminal violence, accident, suicide, or through any suspicious or unusual circumstance, the Medical Examiner (ME) must be notified, as stated in § 406.11, F.S. The officer should not disturb the body until authorized by the ME, pursuant to multi-agency agreements. *(LE124.11.)*

If there are no signs of foul play or trauma, the officer should contact the deceased person's physician and inform him or her of the death. If an officer finds prescription bottles at the scene while examining the personal effects of the deceased person, he or she should examine the bottles for the doctor's name. This information will enable the officer to contact the doctor or his or her medical staff for notification of the death. The officer may also be able to obtain an explanation of the medicinal use of the medication. *(LE124.10.)*

If a doctor refuses to sign a death certificate, the officer should immediately contact the ME and inform him or her of the findings. The medical examiner or the deceased's physician must confirm a death. *(LE124.6.)*

## Notifying the Next of Kin or Relatives

The officer should obtain the name, address, and telephone number of the deceased person's next of kin. Clergy can help an officer make the required notification to the next of kin. If an officer can determine the deceased person's religious preference, the officer should try to locate his or her clergy or another clergy of the same faith to assist in the notification. A victim advocate may prove very helpful when an officer must notify a family member of the death of a loved one.

After the officer has identified the location of relatives, he or she should go to the location, if feasible. When an officer responds in person with clergy, a victim's advocate, or interpreter, the officer should request a backup officer. Normally this is a non-confrontational situation. Nevertheless, always use officer safety techniques.

If the next of kin live in the same city as the deceased person, the officer should notify them in person. Although it is acceptable to notify local next of kin by phone, this is the least preferred method. The officer should not phone unless there is no other option. If the officer must notify the next of kin by telephone, he or she should call as soon as possible.

The officer should be aware of the human diversity issues involved in handling this delicate situation. Before attempting to deliver a death notification, the officer should try to identify any language or cultural barriers.

In some cases, the relatives may live in another state or town and the officer is not able to go to their home to deliver the message. The officer should contact the local law enforcement agency in that area and request that one of their officers deliver the message for the originating agency. The officer can obtain that agency's telephone number by contacting dispatch.

When the officer makes contact with the next of kin, it is his or her responsibility to answer their questions concerning the deceased person's location and the circumstances surrounding the death if the officer knows the answers and if the investigation permits. This will assist the family in dealing with its loss. If the investigation does not permit an officer to provide answers about the circumstances surrounding the death, the officer should explain this to the family. Agency policy and procedure should be followed regarding death notifications.

## *Recommended Procedures for Delivering Death Notifications*

(An excerpt adapted from *Law Enforcement and Victim Sensitivity* (1996) by Major Frank LeBlanc of the Broward County Sheriff's Office)

### *Goals of a Death Notification*

to make a clear statement that the death has occurred

to allow time for the venting of feelings

to obtain medical help, if needed

to guide the bereaved if they go into shock

to provide guidance in managing details

to assist in notifying significant others

to make referrals for follow-up support services

### *Recommended Procedures*

Be absolutely certain of the identity of the deceased.

Get as much medical information as possible.

Go in person; do not call, if possible.

Take someone with you, such as a Victim Advocate, clergy, another relative, or neighbor.

Talk about your reactions on the way.

Present credentials and ask to come in.

Sit down and ask them to sit down.

Inform simply and directly and with compassion.

Do not discount feelings—theirs or yours.

Join the survivors in their grief; however, do not become overwhelmed by it.

Answer all questions honestly.

Offer to make calls.

Talk to the media only after discussion with the family (if necessary).

Do not leave survivors alone.

Give your contact information.

Describe the procedure for identifying the deceased and provide transportation to the morgue, if necessary.

Call the next day, as follow-up, and ask to visit again.

Let the survivors know that you care.

Communicate in time, in person, in pairs, in simple language, and with compassion.

## *What Not to Say*

I know how you feel.

Time heals all wounds.

You will get over this.

You must go on with your life.

He did not know what hit him.

You can always find someone worse off than yourself.

You must focus on your precious memories.

It is better to have loved and lost than never to have loved at all.

**Unhealthy Expectations:**

You must be strong for your wife/husband/children/parents.

You must get hold of yourself.

**God Clichés:**

It must have been his/her time.

Someday you will understand why.

It was actually a blessing, because ____________.

God must have needed her/him more than you did.

God never gives us more than we can handle.

Only the good die young.

**Disempowering Statements:**

You do not need to know that.

What you do not know will not hurt you.

I cannot tell you that.

### What to Say

It is harder than most people think.

Most who have gone through this react similarly to what you are experiencing.

If I were in your situation, I would feel very ________________ too.

I will check back with you tomorrow to see if I can do anything more for you.

### Survivor Needs during Death Notification

Venting of emotions

Restoration of control

Calm, reassuring authority

Preparation and prediction *(LE096.6.)*

# UNIT 1 | CRIMES AGAINST PERSONS

## LESSON 5 | Human Trafficking

**OBJECTIVES**

**LE601.2.** Differentiate between human trafficking and smuggling.

**LE601.3.** Identify the nature and scope of the human trafficking problem.

**LE601.4.** List related international criminal enterprises that lend themselves to involvement in human trafficking.

**LE601.5.** Apply the Trafficking Victims Protection Act (TVPA) of 2000.

**LE601.6.** Apply the Florida Statutes related to human trafficking offenses.

**LE601.7.** Identify the immigration issues of human trafficking victims.

**LE601.8.** Identify human trafficking indicators that can be present.

## Smuggling and Trafficking

Human trafficking is a multi-billion dollar global problem that is present in and affects the United States. The U.S. is, for the most part, a destination country for traffickers. Recent estimates indicate thousands of people are trafficked into the U.S. annually, and there are ongoing human trafficking investigations in almost every state.

Victims are often foreign-born and speak little to no English. They are often very poor, disadvantaged, and vulnerable for a variety of reasons that make them easy prey for traffickers who will kidnap them outright or entice them with false promises of a better life and work. In Florida, Domestic Child Sex Trafficking (DCST) is the single most underreported, under-identified, and severe form of trafficking. Traffickers use promises of love, money, and glamour to lure runaways into prostitution. This occurs at rest stops, migrant farms, construction sites, bars, restaurants, hotels, private homes, sweatshops, the back seats of taxis, or anywhere that will accommodate a child and adult. Trafficked children may be advertised on popular social networking sites.

Despite the term, human trafficking is a crime phenomenon about people being held in a condition of compelled service, not about the movement of people. "Trafficking victims" are people who cannot leave captors without risking punishment or retaliation. The term "trafficking" comes from the intentional agreements to curtail the international trade in slaves, but movement and trade are not required. Human trafficking is a form of modern day slavery that involves holding people (including minors) in compelled service for commercial sex trade or otherwise legitimate labor. Victims may be from other countries or originate from within our borders. Traffickers use force, fraud, or coercion to control their victims. Human trafficking crimes can involve multiple violations of various other state and federal laws and regulations.

**LE601.9.** Identify key information to investigate during the initial conversation with the victim of human trafficking.

**LE601.10.** Identify considerations for human trafficking victim rescue and restoration.

**LE601.11.** Identify the community's role in recognizing and reporting human trafficking.

Force is physical violence that may include beatings, rapes, shootings, or physical confinement. Fraud includes false or deceptive offers of employment, marriage, or a better life. Coercion involves threats of serious harm to the victim, the victim's family, or another person, document confiscation, and abuse or threatened abuse of the legal system, such as the threat of deportation.

The difference between smuggling and human trafficking is that ***trafficking*** is an offense against a person for the purposes of subjection to involuntary servitude, peonage, debt bondage, slavery, or commercial sex. Traffickers maintain ongoing control over the victim. Trafficking is often a financially based business that exploits cheap labor. ***Smuggling*** is an offense against the integrity of the United States borders. It is transportation based, whereas trafficking is exploitation based. Smuggling is typically a short-term "business relationship" and may be a part of a human trafficking scheme whereas trafficking is a long-term, ongoing captivity and subjugation of victims. *(LE601.2.)*

Two threshold questions will help determine if a person is a victim of human trafficking. First, was the person recruited, transported, or held in the service of another for labor or commercial sex acts? Second, was the victim's service obtained or maintained through force, threats, psychological manipulation, or confiscation of legal documents?

## Scope of the Problem

The United States Department of State estimates that every year 800,000 to 2 million people are trafficked worldwide; rough estimates indicate that 18,000 to 20,000 such victims are brought into the United States annually. The FBI is currently investigating cases in every US state. According to international watchdog groups, up to 27 million people are in slavery worldwide.

Human trafficking is a lucrative business, with an estimated $13+ billion in profits each year and reputed ties to organized crime. Unlike drugs and arms traffickers, human traffickers continue to exploit their victims after the initial point of sale. Human trafficking has the potential to become the business of choice for criminal syndicates around the world. Human trafficking has a global economic base. There is a constant source of hopeful, vulnerable immigrants. The promise of a better life, or the "American Dream," lures victims into trafficking situations. Economically desperate victims and market demand for cheap labor fuel human trafficking, as brokers rush to provide compliant labor forces. Our culture's insatiable appetite for sex also fuels the human trafficking flow, and pimps use brutality against young boys and girls to meet the demand for commercial sex.

Florida's growing immigrant population, the state's need for low-skilled labor, and the presence of foreign, criminal syndicates have led to an increasing number of human trafficking cases involving the exploitation of immigrants—especially immigrant women. Not all victims have been immigrants; however, many teenage runaways (or kidnapping victims) who are U.S. citizens become human trafficking victims. Other cases have arisen where substance-addicted homeless persons were trafficked for labor. Cases in Florida typify what investigators nationwide are finding: while immigrants are often the victims, traffickers may exploit anyone who is vulnerable.

## Tampa Bay "Treasure Island" Sex Trafficking Case (Ongoing, 2009)

Pimps exploited numerous women who were U.S. citizens for forced prostitution and dancing in a number of Tampa's strip clubs. When they were not exploiting the women for commercial sex, the pimps allegedly held them in virtual slavery in a luxury waterfront home where the pimps resided. While being held at the home, the women had their clothes, credit cards, identification documents, and money confiscated by the pimps. The women were also subjected to extreme physical violence and emotional abuse that law enforcement investigators described as the equivalent of torture.

## Boca Raton Filipino Labor Trafficking Case (Ongoing, 2009)

Over 50 workers from the Philippines were brought to Boca Raton by Filipino natives Sophia Manuel and her husband Alfonso Baldonado. Owners of two employment-leasing companies called "Quality Staffing Services Corporation" and "DAR Workforce Solutions USA," Manuel and Baldonado promised the workers free housing and full-time jobs in food service at a Boca Raton country club. Recruiters in the Philippines showed workers pictures of upscale Florida homes, beautifully manicured lawns, and scenes from Disney World. Upon their arrival, a very different world awaited the migrants. They instead found part-time jobs paying $6.67 an hour, and as many as 30 of them were forced to live in a three bedroom house in Boca Raton. Their passports were confiscated, and they were threatened with deportation if they complained. Money was routinely deducted from their earnings to supposedly cover the costs of uniforms, transportation, and visa renewals. After the weekly wage deductions by Manuel and Baldonado, none of the workers earned a federal minimum wage.

## Tallahassee and Clearwater Melchor & Monsalve Sex Trafficking Case (2008)

A woman in an upscale Tallahassee neighborhood was startled by two young Guatemalan women knocking frantically on her back window and crying out in Spanish for help. This Good Samaritan neighbor discovered that the young women were fleeing a sex trafficker—Colombian national Jorge Melchor—who had held them in a "safe house" in the same neighborhood, since their arrival two days earlier. Each of the preceding evenings, the women had been driven to trailers and apartments on the outskirts of Tallahassee where they had been forced to engage in multiple sex acts as part of a larger prostitution scheme. Taken to a hospital and the Tallahassee police station, the women's accounts of their ordeal led Florida law enforcement agents to a two year, multi-jurisdictional investigation that eventually dismantled an international sex trafficking ring.

## *Miami Paulin Labor Trafficking Case (2008)*

Maude Paulin was a Haitian immigrant and a middle school teacher who lived in the south Miami community of Cutler Bay. She came from a successful family in Haiti that had run an orphanage for many years in a mountain village. A young Haitian girl ("Anna") was taken by Paulin's parents from her biological mother at the age of five and kept for seven years at the orphanage run by Paulin's family. When the young girl reached the age of twelve, Paulin's mother, Evelyn Theodore, removed the girl from the orphanage and brought her to the family home in Haiti to live and work as a house servant there. In 1999, the family then smuggled Anna into the United States where she was kept as a house slave for another six years in Paulin's Cutler Bay home. *(LE601.3.)*

## Trafficking Victims

Trafficking victims are often "invisible." Many are undocumented aliens and fear United States authorities. Traffickers exploit this fear. U.S. citizens can also be exploited by these criminal organizations, which seek out and prey on vulnerabilities. Victims may be physically isolated or guarded; others are held through psychological coercion. Many victims do not speak English and have no idea where they are in the United States. Victims face tremendous cultural and economic barriers and often do not realize that they are victims or that they have rights under United States law. Victims can be minors, mentally challenged, or caught in the throes of an addiction. There are many industries where an officer can find trafficked victims including:

- prostitution
- massage parlors
- exotic dancing
- pornography
- agricultural work
- landscape work
- domestic work and child care
- factory work
- begging/street peddling
- restaurant work
- construction work
- carnival work
- hotel housekeeping
- criminal activities
- day labor
- nail salons

## Trafficker Typology

Traffickers may or may not be members of the victim's ethnic or national community and may be in the United States legally, maintaining close contact with their country of origin. They may be fluent in English as well as their native language and have greater social or political status in their home country than their victims. People who traffic humans often also smuggle drugs and guns and are involved in money laundering, extortion, and various other criminal activities. Traffickers often have established international smuggling routes that involve "mom-and-pop" family operations through an extended family that operates on both sides of the border.

Traffickers can also be part of a legal, independently owned business, such as contractors, agents, and subcontractors who provide laborers for agricultural work, construction work, restaurants, janitorial services, diplomatic staff, and foreign executives. Other professionals may arrive in the U.S. with "servants" or have servants on staff. Recruiters for traffickers may be female, and are sometimes neighbors, friends, or relatives of the victim.

Traffickers can be members of an international organized criminal syndicate and often have "diversified criminal portfolios." Related international criminal enterprises, such as smuggling, transportation, and harboring of illegal immigrants, child pornography, child prostitution, and sex tourism lend themselves to involvement in human trafficking. *(LE601.4.)*

## Federal and Florida Human Trafficking Laws

The 13th Amendment to the United States Constitution provides that neither slavery nor involuntary servitude shall exist on United States soil.

In 2000, Congress passed the Trafficking Victims Protection Act (TVPA) to update traditional slavery laws and combat trafficking in persons. Since that time, several agencies of the United States Department of Justice, Homeland Security, and Health and Human Services, along with a number of state and local agencies, have mounted significant efforts to address this problem. The TVPA was created to combat trafficking in persons, to ensure just and effective punishment of traffickers, and to protect their victims. The TVPA defines severe forms of human trafficking in persons as sex trafficking in which a commercial sex act is induced by force, fraud, or coercion, or sex trafficking of a minor, and recruitment, harboring, transportation, provision or obtaining of a person for forced labor or services through the use of force, fraud, or coercion. This supplements traditional slavery law, which requires that the coercion used involve physical violence. Under the TVPA, a servitude case can involve psychological coercion or confiscation of the victims' documents.

## Human Trafficking Offenses

**Forced Labor or Services is defined in18 U.S.C. 1589,**—providing or obtaining the labor or services (farm, construction, domestic, striptease) of a person through threats of serious harm to that person or another, any scheme, plan or pattern that places the victim in fear of serious harm, or the abuse or threatened abuse of the legal process, such as threats of deportation.

**Sex Trafficking is defined in 18 U.S.C. 1591,**—the recruitment, harboring, transportation, provision, or obtaining of a person through force, fraud, or coercion, for the purpose of a commercial sex act, or in which the person induced to perform such an act is under 18 years of age. When a minor is trafficked for a commercial sex act, there is no need to prove force, fraud, or coercion (although one of these elements may be present).

Traffickers can be liable whether they actually engage in the trafficking act of recruiting, enticing, harboring, transporting, providing, or obtaining a person for commercial sex or they merely benefit financially from knowingly participating in a venture that does so.

## TVPA Legal Changes

The TVPA is a victim-centered law. It ensures trafficking victims, even if they are living in the United States illegally, to be viewed as victims of crime. The law no longer treats them as aliens, but as victims of a crime with rights. Under federal law, trafficking victims can be U.S. citizens or legal or illegal immigrants. This is a crime about exploitation, not movement, or immigration. The TVPA creates programs to assist victims, including immigration remedies.

While prior laws, many that date back to the Civil War, are still in place, the TVPA brought some very important additions and modifications. Physical force is no longer a required element; showing psychological coercion now suffices. It enables trafficking victims to obtain medical care, witness protection, housing assistance, and other social services. Trafficking victims can attain temporary legal immigration status and civil remedies for financial detriment they have suffered if they are willing to cooperate with law enforcement.

Several well-established legal rules still apply. For instance, the fact that a person consented to be smuggled into the United States illegally does not preclude him or her from becoming a trafficking victim. The fact that a victim may have initially consented to perform an illegal act (prostitution) is not a defense to the subsequent use of force, fraud, or coercion. Things that a victim hears about other workers suffering are admissible to show a "climate of fear" in which they were held. *(LE601.5.)*

## Florida Law

Florida law is similar to federal law and is codified in § 787.06, F.S. All Florida human trafficking crimes are Racketeer Influenced and Corrupt Organization (RICO) offenses according to Chapter 895, F.S. Section 796.03, F.S. prohibits procuring persons under the age of 18 for prostitution and can be used to address trafficking minors. *(LE601.6.)*

## Immigration Issues

An understanding of specific immigration terms will assist the officer when he or she encounters a trafficking victim from another country. An alien is any person who is not a United States citizen. An illegal alien is a foreign national who entered the United States without inspection at a border crossing or airport, with fraudulent documents, or legally as a nonimmigrant, but then violated that status and remained without authority.

## Role of Immigration Officials: Immigration and Customs Enforcement (ICE)

The Immigration and Customs Enforcement (ICE) agency enforces United States laws, including federal immigration laws and regulations. ICE investigates smuggling, trafficking, fraud, money laundering, and narcotics trafficking cases as well as domestic and international criminal activities occurring on or facilitated by the internet and performs computer forensics examinations. ICE can determine the true immigration status of victims, witnesses, and offenders and can aid in the detection of travel and identity document fraud.

ICE can conduct investigations outside the United States through ICE foreign attachés and liaison with foreign government officials and agencies and provides domestic and international training. There are over 60 ICE attaché offices throughout the world.

ICE can provide temporary immigration relief to victims through "continued presence" and certification for "T Visas." Continued Presence (CP) is a federal law enforcement tool that provides temporary victim and witness relief during an investigation and prosecution, is good for one year, and is renewable. T-Visa is relief that can lead to permanent residency and allows a victim to remain in the United States legally for four years. To qualify for a T-visa, an alien must demonstrate that he or she is or has been a victim of a severe form of human trafficking. The victim must be physically present in the United States, have complied with reasonable requests by law enforcement to assist in the investigations and/or prosecution of traffickers (if the victim is 15 or older), and would suffer "extreme and unusual hardship" if removed or deported back to the victim's home country.

Conferring legal status on victims takes a humanitarian approach instead of treating the victims like criminals, and it makes the victims available as witnesses, rather than in pre-TVPA days when victims faced deportation. This is because "human trafficking," by its definition, is about compelled service. Because a victim of this crime is a slave in the United States, Congress has chosen to protect these crime victims by allowing them to stay in America. *(LE601.7.)*

## Investigating Human Trafficking

Many factors might suggest the presence of victims of human trafficking; no set combination or minimum number of indicators automatically lead to a human trafficking case. While any one of the items alone is not enough to indicate a trafficking case, it is enough to warrant further investigation. The first officer on the scene is in a key position to identify potential human trafficking cases on routine calls for service. These calls can be domestic violence calls, disputes and fights, assaults/sexual batteries (minor victims), concerned citizen calls, anonymous callers on the tips hotline, and petty or retail theft (suspect may very well be a victim of human trafficking).

The officer should be familiar with the terrain of his or her area, the community, its social networks, and local confidential informants. The officer should have knowledge of the problem areas in his or her community and the identities of the "troublemakers." An officer should know who will give information, and he or she should have access to local informants who have their "ears to the ground."

## Human Trafficking Indicators

Officers often overlook possible evidence of human trafficking crimes during a routine traffic stop or domestic violence call. Alertness to the indicators discussed below can help officers rescue trafficking victims. At a minimum, an officer should look more closely at a situation he or she thinks might involve human trafficking.

Living and working conditions for human trafficking victims are usually atypical. Victims live on or near work premises, reside in overcrowded living spaces, are restricted or have controlled communications, and are moved frequently by traffickers. Often there are locks on the outside of windows and doors. Victims may lack personal items or possessions, cell phones (may be an exception), calling cards, and financial records. They often lack individual transportation, knowledge about how to get around in the community, and legal and travel documents because someone else has taken possession of them.

Types of evidence that may be present at a human trafficking crime scene include the following:

- money wire transfer receipts
- phone records

- pay stubs
- medical condition of the victim
- legal or fraudulent identification
- legal or fraudulent immigration documents
- weapons
- medical records
- photographs
- cell phones
- computers
- codebooks

Personal and physical indicators can include injuries from beatings or weapons, including old injuries, signs of torture (cigarette burns), brands or scarring indicating ownership, and signs of malnourishment. Victims may be fearful of discussing their living or working situations.

Victims may state they "owe" someone money for getting them into the United States or have ongoing debt at a "company" store; the only store they are allowed to shop at. Often a third party, or one person, insists on interpreting for an entire group or an individual.

Signs indicating human trafficking in labor camps or sweatshops may include security intended to keep victims confined or self-contained camps with barbed wire angled in, bars on windows, bouncers, guards, and guard dogs, and excessive amounts of garbage.

Signs indicating a brothel situation that might involve sex trafficking can include large amounts of cash and condoms, a customer logbook, and a receipt book (trick book). Sparsely furnished rooms may contain only luggage, travel photographs, alcohol, lubricant, paper towels, and tokens (cards, marbles, bobby pins, and condom wrappers). Men come and go frequently, and there are used twin mattresses stacked up outside of the residence. *(LE601.8.)*

## Investigative "Conversation"

In addition to these indicators, there are other things to look for to help identify human trafficking victims. These include information or issues about the victim's employment situation, personal safety, social networks, and immigration status. It is important to obtain this information through conversations rather than formal interviews. The best way to communicate with these victims is to hold a casual, relaxed conversation with them. Officers should be sensitive to the fact that the police in the victim's home country may be corrupt or involved in criminal activity.

An officer who hovers over the victim with his or her badge and gun can be intimidating. If the officer attempts to conduct a "police interview" or conduct a "checklist interview," the victims may be reluctant to speak openly and candidly, and the officer will not make any progress. This is a good time for the officer to draw on his or her skills and department expertise in interviewing child victims of sexual abuse, as the interviewing techniques are similar.

The officer should allow the victim to set the length and pace and watch for nonverbal cues. He or she should not make promises or video tape or audiotape initial conversations. The officer should be patient with both the victim and the victim advocate, if one is present. The officer should separate the victim from his or her trafficker prior to questioning, and convey a sense of safety, bringing the victim to an area of safety, away from the location the officer encountered the victim. The officer should avoid placing the victim in the patrol car, if possible.

A trusted interpreter can make the difference between an officer discovering a trafficking case and rescuing victims, or being misguided by someone. Considerations when using an interpreter include his or her availability on the crime scene, as well as to testify in court, and if the interpreter can be trusted. The officer should be aware of possible traps such as on-scene interpreters affiliated with traffickers, possible bias of interpreters, or prior relationships between the victim and the interpreter. Officers should bear in mind that interpreters have regional dialect variations and cultural and gender beliefs.

The officer should look at the assumed victim while talking and avoid looking at the interpreter. Rapport is possible, even through an interpreter. The conversation should begin with the following questions:

- What is your name?
- Do you have any identification documents? If not, who has your documents?
- Where were you born? Who do you live with now?
- When was the last time you talked to your family?
- Do you go to church?
- Where do you work? How do you get back and forth to work? How many days a week do you work? How long are you at work? Who pays you?
- Where do you go shopping? Do you go by yourself or with friends?
- What was your favorite thing to do when you were living in your native country? Are you able to do that here in the United States?
- Did anyone tell you what to tell me?

The officer should avoid using the term "immigration status" when talking with the victim. The officer should obtain any identification and immigration documents later in the interview, in a low-key manner, without making the victim feel as though the officer is investigating him or her as opposed to the traffickers. Additional questions the officer might ask, using a relaxed, conversational format to obtain information that helps identify trafficking victims, fall into four categories:

1. **immigration status** (Avoid using this term.)
    - How did you come to the United States?
    - When did you come to the United States?
    - Why did you come to the United States?
    - What is your date of birth and place of birth?
    - What are your parents' names?

**2. employment** (Use simplified terms.)

- Did you come to the United States for a specific job or purpose?
- What did someone promise you to come here?
- Are you doing different work than you expected?
- Does your employer provide housing, food, clothes, or uniforms?
- Do you have to have sex as part of your job? Did you want to?
- Does your employer hold wages back from your pay?
- Did anyone make you do anything you were not comfortable doing? Could you refuse?
- Did you ever see someone punished for not working? Were you? How?
- Could people choose to pay their debt another way, not just by working it off? Did the debt grow?
- Did anyone try to leave before they paid off their debt? What did the bosses do? How did that make you feel?
- Do you feel you could just go work somewhere else?

**3. safety and/or coercion** (Stress victim and the victim's family safety.)

- Has anyone threatened your family?
- What would happen to you if you left your job?
- Have you been hurt physically?
- Has someone deprived you of food, water, sleep, medical care, or withheld any other necessities from you?

**4. social networks** (Traffickers do not have to be physically with victims to control them.)

- Are you able to buy clothes or food on your own?
- Can you come and go by yourself? Does someone have to go with you to the store? *(LE601.9.)*

After "scratching the surface," the officer may determine that what is before him or her is a severe human trafficking incident. At this point, the officer will have to consider many things. Unlike other crimes such as drug trafficking, human trafficking cases require that an officer consider the timing of taking down the suspect and organization and the complexity of rescuing the victims. It is critical that an officer weigh his or her options. An officer can use questions to think through this complex problem, including:

- Is the victim you have identified in immediate danger?
- Are there still workers at the jobsite or brothel?
- What do you know about how the suspects treat their victims?
- What are the ages of the potential victims?
- Will an immediate rescue preclude the chance of rescuing others later?
- Will an immediate rescue result in the arrest of minor players as opposed to the dismantling of an organization?

Once the officer has identified a victim, he or she must have a plan in place that includes keeping the victim out of harm's way. Victims have a variety of needs, and it takes many different agencies to provide the services or resources needed to assist them and investigate and prosecute the case. Agencies involved in combating human trafficking include law enforcement agencies, prosecution offices, victim services organizations and charities, Non-Governmental Organizations (NGOs), and legal services organizations. Each has different roles and responsibilities, and collectively can make a comprehensive effort in working human trafficking cases and provide a victim-centered approach to the investigation.

## Victim-Centered Approach to Human Trafficking

There are unique issues surrounding human trafficking victims that differ from other crime victims. It is critical that officers recognize and approach human trafficking cases from a victim-centered perspective. The officer's ability to employ this approach effectively is critical. A victim-centered approach is exactly that; the victim is the center of the investigation and can make or break the case. The strength of the case, in large part, will depend on the victim. In addition, since the violation of the victim's rights is the heart of the crime, the officer should take special care to rehabilitate the victim and not re-victimize him or her as he or she goes through the justice system.

Human trafficking victims often provide the information and testimony that become evidence in the case. In order to show existence of force, fraud, or coercion, the officer will have to depend on the victim. In evidence-based investigations, cases proceed as if the victim will not testify; however, in human trafficking investigations, the victim has a much greater role.

## Victim Issues

Victims of human trafficking often suffer from serious physical and psychological trauma. Meeting their needs requires law enforcement and service providers to be aware of a victim's culture, able to communicate in his or her language if the victim does not speak English, and be versed in trauma and its impact on victims.

Dealing with trafficking victims requires patience because victims may not identify themselves as victims, speak English, or understand the concept of compelled service or slavery. They are likely to lie or use rehearsed stories initially. Cultural or religious background may deter victims from telling the full story. The victim's story may change over the course of the interview or investigation.

Victims may exhibit "Stockholm syndrome," or behavior favorable toward or empathic to their captors. They may also be behaviorally dependent on the trafficker and unaware of their rights.

Victims may be reluctant to speak to someone wearing a gun, badge, or uniform because they are culturally conditioned to fear law enforcement. They may exhibit hostility towards the law enforcement officer. Victims may resist communicating with an officer, not because of who the officer really is, but because of what someone said that officer is. These victims have gone through terrible ordeals, and an officer is possibly their first contact with law enforcement in the United States.

An officer should give victims a choice of speaking with a male or female investigator, if possible. Victims may not want their family to know of their circumstances. Safety of the victim's family in the home country is an important consideration.

Victim service providers can provide a communication bridge, often the only avenue to obtain critical evidence from the victim. Human trafficking victims require different services than other crime victims, not only in type of service but also in duration of service. This is a joint effort; the scope and intensity of such cases mandate that a team environment prevail.

## Collaborative Approach

This approach requires collaboration between law enforcement and victim service providers. Probably more than any other crime, to solve or prosecute human trafficking cases requires the assistance of victim service providers. Law enforcement cannot promise benefits to victims; however, they must endorse the application for assistance, so they have to be involved in the case, hand-in-hand with victim service providers.

Victim service providers are Non-Governmental Organizations (NGOs) such as immigrant advocacy groups, human rights groups, crime victim-advocacy groups, faith-based community organizations, domestic violence shelters, rape crisis centers, and child advocacy centers. Governmental organizations that can assist in human trafficking investigations are the Federal Bureau of Investigation (FBI), Immigration and Customs Enforcement (ICE), United States Attorney's Offices, the Department of Justice (DOJ), and the Florida Department of Law Enforcement (FDLE).

The officer should involve victim services or NGOs as soon as possible, even when there is only a slight indication of victimization. NGOs can assist in a human trafficking case by building trust between the victim and law enforcement, and advising victims of benefits, immigration options, and family stabilization issues. They can help the victim navigate through the maze of services, forms, and organizations, which can be a daunting challenge for anyone.

## Interagency Cooperation

The nature and scope of human trafficking dictate a high degree of interagency cooperation. The strengths of the local and state agency combined with NGOs and federal agencies can provide a formalized, collaborative approach to increase the jurisdiction's ability to combat human trafficking effectively and successfully. NGOs can help the officer win the case by serving as an intermediary, collaborating with law enforcement on victim safety, and assisting in witness preparation. They can help restore dignity to the victim by helping the victim gain new employment and facilitating victim access to pre-certified and certified services.

Local and state agencies can assist in the investigation by conducting spontaneous undercover operations and having ready access to local intelligence, facilities, and equipment in the community.

The FBI, a key investigative agency at the federal level, can provide document analysis, surveillance teams, computer evidence recovery and analysis, and overseas investigations. They can assist with multi-jurisdictional cases, federal jurisdiction, grand jury, continued presence application, and victim and witness assistance.

ICE, another key investigative agency at the federal level, responsible for immigration-related activities, can provide document analysis, surveillance teams, computer evidence recovery and analysis, and overseas investigations. They can assist with multi-jurisdictional cases, federal jurisdiction, grand jury, continued presence application, and victim and witness assistance. ICE specializes in immigration status review, border interdiction, and domestic and international training.

Many of the services victims require are included as rights under the TVPA. Human trafficking victims have the right to rescue and removal to appropriate shelter or housing—not being detained in facilities inappropriate to their status as crime victims—and medical care, including physical and psychological treatment. They have the right to information about their rights as victims, translation services, legal representation, and mandatory restitution. Human trafficking victims have the right to social assistance and economic self-sufficiency, including job counseling, skills training and education, immigration assistance, assistance returning to their country of origin and privacy and safety under the Victim and Witness Protection Act. (LE601.10.)

## Working with the Community to Prevent Human Trafficking

Over time, local law enforcement, because of its role in the community, should develop subject-matter expertise in the forms of human trafficking present in their community. However, communities can serve as intermediaries in detecting human trafficking and ensuring delivery of services to victims of human trafficking.

The people in the community act as "eyes and ears" to what is happening. They see and hear things that law enforcement does not. They may witness human trafficking but not identify it as such. The community may see human trafficking, know about it, or possibly suspect something is not right with an individual or a situation long before it comes to the attention of law enforcement. The better informed the community is about what human trafficking is, who the victims are, and what resources victims need, the better position law enforcement will be in addressing the problem.

Victims' needs are many, and a single agency is unable to provide all the various services required. The community must be a part of the effort. Collaboration among governmental agencies and NGOs is critical to ensure needed services are available and provided. Local communities are essential in creating coalitions that can serve as intermediaries in detecting human trafficking and ensuring delivery of services to victims of human trafficking.

## Building Awareness

Officers should begin with research to accumulate information about the problem and responses to human trafficking crimes on a global, national, and local level. Building community awareness creates a base of information that begins efforts with intermediaries and promotes general community outreach.

Communities have many intermediaries who may encounter victims of trafficking and bring a situation or a victim to an officer's attention. Types of intermediaries in the community can be advocacy groups such as immigrant, labor, sexual assault, and domestic violence victim advocates. Homeless shelters, food banks, and faith-based and ethnic organizations can encounter victims. Other intermediaries are health care providers, walk-in health clinics, hospitals, and mutual assistance associations. The health and labor department, schools, code enforcement, the fire marshal, utilities, alcohol-licensing agency, and building inspectors can encounter victims.

Human trafficking often looks initially like other traditional crimes. Intermediaries may not identify a situation as human trafficking, but will instead identify a situation that may not be right. Types of situations an officer may overlook as human trafficking incidents can be when a person visits a local clinic for medical reasons, but is not allowed time alone with the physician; a large migrant population exists in a community, but the children or the workers do not attend the local public school; or a domestic employee is rarely seen outside of the employer's home.

## Developing Intermediaries

Officers should begin with those persons most likely to have contact with victims. Then, officers should make contact with and inform community members how they can be part of the solution to the problem. Many victims have escaped or been rescued at large discount stores, grocery stores, convenience stores, or gas stations. Some of these organizations have also helped by providing benefits for the victims. Groups in the community that can prevent human trafficking by reporting victims are the intermediaries the officer has developed within his or her community. Local non-profit organizations and coalitions can provide food, shelter, and emergency medical care (some examples are Catholic Charities, Salvation Army, and Florida Coalition Against Human Trafficking). Immigrant advocacy groups can provide free legal representation and victim advocate offices from state and federal government can provide benefits to victims of crime.

More time is needed to help victims of trafficking and to affect the necessary outreach and communication to providers and other key contacts for victims of trafficking. Because service providers and law enforcement are often the first contact with victims, they must be informed and able to identify and assist victims of trafficking. Collaboration among key service providers, law enforcement, and many others at the local level is crucial. The need for a collaborative approach across all sectors and levels of law enforcement, prosecution, and victim services is most important. *(LE601.11.)*

**Section Vocabulary**

*smuggling*

*trafficking*

# UNIT 1 I CRIMES AGAINST PERSONS

## LESSON 6 I Kidnapping and False Imprisonment

**OBJECTIVES**

**LE155.1.** Identify the difference between kidnapping, false imprisonment, and interference with custody.

**Section Vocabulary**

***interference with custody***

### Kidnapping

Kidnapping, as stated in §787.01. F.S., is

> "forcibly, secretly, or by threat confining, abducting, or imprisoning another person against his or her will."

Kidnapping occurs without lawful authority and with intent to hold for ransom or reward, hold as hostage or shield, facilitate commission of a felony, interfere with governmental or political function, or confine a child under 13 without the consent of the custodial parent.

### False Imprisonment

False imprisonment, as stated in §787.02, F.S., is

> "forcibly, by threat, or secretly confining, abducting, imprisoning, or restraining another person without lawful authority and against his or her will" with any purpose other than those referred to in kidnapping.

Generally speaking, kidnapping requires movement of the victim by the offender. The difference between kidnapping and false imprisonment can be illustrated in a domestic violence call. A suspect who forces the victim to stay at home may be guilty of false imprisonment. If the suspect forces the victim into a car to travel to another location where the suspect holds the victim against his or her will, the appropriate charge would be kidnapping.

### Interference with Custody

***Interference with custody*** as stated in §787.03, F.S. means that a person who, without lawful authority, knowingly or recklessly takes or entices any child under the age of 18 years from the custody of its parent, guardian, or other lawful custodian, is guilty of a third-degree felony.

Concealing or removing minors from the state with full knowledge of a court order is also a third-degree felony pursuant to Florida Statute §787.04. The person in violation must have knowledge of the court order or receive notice of the pending proceeding. However, it is a defense if the person reasonably believes that his or her action was necessary to protect the minor from child abuse. *(LE155.1.)*

# UNIT 1 | CRIMES AGAINST PERSONS

## LESSON 7 | Missing and Endangered Persons

### Initial Response

When dispatched to a call regarding a missing person, an officer should do the following:

1. Respond promptly to the scene of the report of a missing person.
2. Consider activating patrol-vehicle-mounted video camera when approaching the scene to record vehicles, people, and anything else of note for later investigative review.
3. Interview the person who made the initial report.
4. Confirm that the person is in fact missing. *(LE049a.2.)*
5. If a child is missing, verify the child's custody status.
6. Identify the circumstances of the disappearance.
7. Determine who last saw the missing person, when and where.
8. Interview the individual(s) who last had contact with the missing person.
9. Identify the person's zone of safety for his or her age, developmental, physical, and mental state. *(LE049a.5.)*
10. Make an initial determination of the type of incident.
11. Obtain a description of the missing person including photograph(s) and videotapes. *(LE049a.4.)*
12. Obtain a description of the suspected abductor(s) and other pertinent information.
13. Evaluate whether the circumstances of the child's disappearance meet AMBER Alert criteria and other immediate community notification protocol. Discuss plan activation with supervisor.
14. Provide detailed descriptive information to communications unit for broadcast updates.
15. Identify and interview everyone at the scene separately.
16. Continue to keep communications unit apprised of all appropriate developing information for broadcast updates.
17. Obtain and note permission to conduct a thorough search of the missing person's home. Extend the search to surrounding areas including vehicles and other places of concealment. Determine if surveillance or security cameras in the vicinity may have captured information about the disappearance. *(LE049a.9.)*
18. Secure and safeguard the area as a potential crime scene.

**OBJECTIVES**

**LE049a.2.** Identify the cause of the search in the case of a missing person.

**LE049a.5.** Identify possible physical or psychological problems of a missing person.

**LE049a.4.** Obtain descriptive data of missing person, including a photo, if available.

**LE049a.9.** Conduct an initial search of the scene of a missing person situation.

**LE049a.8.** Identify areas to be searched in a missing person situation.

**LE049a.6.** Notify supervisor of location and search assignment.

**LE049a.10.** Provide necessary medical care to a rescued missing person.

**LE049a.3.** Apply federal and state law in a missing person situation.

**LE174.6.** Identify additional resources to locate the missing person.

**LE049a.12.** Document a missing person incident and record into NCIC/FCIC.

19. Record if the missing person has access to an online computer, cellular telephone, and pager.
20. Review sex-offender registries to determine if any such individuals live, work, or associate within the area of the child's disappearance.
21. Determine the correct National Crime Information Center (NCIC) Missing Person File category and ensure entry within 2 hours of the report.
22. Prepare necessary reports and complete appropriate forms.

The initial search should include buildings and areas where someone last saw the missing, lost, or endangered person. The officer should do this to make sure the person is not inside the residence, especially when he or she is searching for children. The officer should use a scent-discriminating dog, preferably a bloodhound, to search the residence and the area around it. If the person is not in the building, the officer should set up a perimeter. *(LE049a.8.)*

The officer should use knowledge of how far the missing person could travel based on his or her physical condition and where he or she was seen last to determine the scope of the search. The officer should secure the area where someone last saw the person, and control entry and exit points if the situation seems to be a criminal abduction or if foul play is suspected. The officer should notify his or her supervisor of any need for additional back-up units. *(LE049a.6.)*

The officer should evaluate the contents and appearance of the missing person's room, home, car, and other personal spaces. Then, he or she should inspect the room with the caregiver to learn if personal items are missing. Hairbrushes, drinking glasses, toys, and other items should be seized and protected. They are valuable sources of fingerprints, DNA, and scent. Diaries, remote controls, CDs, computers, and computer discs should also be secured. They may contain useful information.

After questioning the complainant, the officer should determine whom else to interview. Family members, friends, business associates, teachers, visitors, and workers who regularly or periodically come to the home should be considered. The officer should identify and seek all witnesses, associates, and acquaintances. The officer should contact dispatch with the information he or she has gathered in the interviews and ask dispatch to run a record check on the missing person. An officer should know about sexual offenders and predators living in his or her patrol area. Section 856.022 F.S. prohibits a sexual offender from loitering or prowling within a specific distance of places where children are congregating. Agency policy should be followed when making contact with a sex offender.

If an officer finds the missing person alive, he or she must make sure the person receives necessary medical attention. If the victim does not need medical treatment, the officer should follow reunification preocedures to ensure the child or adult is brought to a safe environment. *(LE049a.10.)*

## Child Trafficking/Runaway Children

Children who run away are missing, and at considerable risk of falling prey to heinous crimes. Child trafficking is a problem in Florida. Victims of child trafficking may come from troubled families and often have histories of truancy. They typically run away from home after being sexually abused. Once on the street, they face increased risks of being battered or killed. They are also likely to experience drug addiction or psychiatric disorders and contract, and spread, diseases.

"Missing child" is defined in §937.0201(3), F.S. as

> "a person younger than 18 years of age; whose temporary or permanent residence is in, or is believed to be in, this state; whose location has not been determined; and who has been reported as missing to a law enforcement agency."

Runaways fit that definition. §937.021(4)(a), F.S. states that:

> "Upon the filing of a police report that a child is missing by the parent or guardian, the Department of Children and Family Services, a community-based care provider, or a sheriff's office providing investigative services for the department, the law enforcement agency receiving the report shall immediately inform all on-duty law enforcement officers of the missing child report, communicate the report to every other law enforcement agency having jurisdiction in the county, and within two hours after receipt of the report transmit the report for inclusion within the Florida Crime Information Center and the National Crime Information Center databases. A law enforcement agency may not require a reporter to present an order that a child be taken into custody or any other such order before accepting a report that a child is missing."

There is nothing in Chapter 937, F.S. that indicates these steps should not be taken if the child is a runaway. The Interstate Compact on Juveniles applies to runaways and does not treat them differently from other juveniles. Section 409.441, F.S. confirms that law enforcement agencies are to be involved in the process for handling runaway youth. §937.025, F.S. imposes an obligation on government and school employees to "promptly report" any information that could assist law enforcement in locating a child who has been reported as missing, ascertaining the identity of the person who has actual custody of a missing child, or determining whether a missing child is in danger of physical injury or death. All of these statutes together indicate that runaways are simply a subset of missing children, and every effort should be made to find them. Federal law was amended several years ago to require law enforcement agencies to take reports immediately on any missing endangered children under 21, including runaways.

Runaway children should be presumed to be in danger, rather than presumed not to be. According to the National Runaway Switchboard, 75 percent of runaways who remain at large for two or more weeks will become involved in theft, drugs, or pornography, while one out of every three teens on the street will be lured into prostitution and child trafficking within 48 hours of leaving home. Gay or bisexual kids are at even greater risk of becoming involved in prostitution and child trafficking. Other risks that runaways face are malnutrition, psychological disorders, HIV infection and other sexually transmitted diseases, unwanted pregnancies, drug and alcohol abuse, robbery, and sexual and physical assault. Major depression, conduct disorder, and post-traumatic stress are also higher among runaways.

Law enforcement officers should not disregard missing children simply because they may be runaways. The same effort should be made in locating and recovering such children as is devoted to abducted children.

## Florida AMBER Plan

As required by Florida law, the Florida Department of Law Enforcement (FDLE) in conjunction with the Department of Community Affairs and the Florida Association of Broadcasters, Inc., established the statewide Florida AMBER Plan in August 2000. Its purpose is to broadcast critical information about a missing or abducted child, in a timely manner, to the public via radio and television and, more recently, the internet. Persons who see the child or abductor or have knowledge of the abduction can immediately provide information to the investigating law enforcement agency.

To activate the Florida AMBER Plan, five conditions must exist:

1. The child must be under 18 years of age.
2. There must be a clear indication of abduction.
3. The local law enforcement agency of jurisdiction must recommend the activation.
4. There must be a detailed description of child, abductor or the vehicle to broadcast to the public (photo when available).
5. The law enforcement agency's investigation must conclude that the child's life is in danger.

This service is available to every law enforcement agency in Florida, 24 hours a day, and seven days a week. An agency can activate an Amber Alert by calling FDLE Missing Endangered Persons Information Clearinghouse (MEPIC) at 1-888-FL-MISSING (356-4774). FDLE has a reciprocal agreement with the Georgia Bureau of Investigation to activate their plan if needed. An officer may also call FDLE's toll-free clearinghouse number to ask questions or express concerns about the Florida Amber Plan. *(LE049a.3.)*

## Florida Silver Alert Plan

The Florida Chiefs and Sheriffs, Florida Department of Transportation, Florida Department of Elder Affairs, Department of Highway Safety and Motor Vehicles, Florida Highway Patrol, Florida Department of Law Enforcement, and Florida legislators have worked in conjunction with concerned citizens and organizations to develop Florida's Silver Alert Plan.

The statewide Silver Alert is a plan to aid local law enforcement in the rescue or recovery of a missing elderly person who suffers from irreversible deterioration of intellectual faculties. The plan recognizes that the most effective response to a missing senior citizen leverages community resources for the search to augment the investigative response by the local law enforcement agency. The plan further acknowledges that the investigating local law enforcement agency should activate the Silver Alerts because they are in the best position to notify the media and disseminate the information through avenues such as neighborhood telephone alerts and other technologies the agency may have to communicate with its community's citizens.

Local agencies are encouraged to adopt the following standardized criteria and incorporate it into their policies and procedures and to add any other specific community resources available in the event of an activation. Local law enforcement agencies should develop policies and procedures that will work best in their respective jurisdictions to broadcast information about missing endangered persons to the public and the media. As a part of our statewide initiative, the use of A Child is Missing, Inc. and Media Alert are available at no charge to local agencies for Silver Alerts. Additionally, law enforcement may contact the FDLE Missing Endangered Persons Information Clearinghouse to open a case or receive assistance.

In the event that a vehicle is used in the Silver Alert incident, the statewide messaging system may also be activated. This is accomplished by using FDOT's highway dynamic message signs and other highway advisory methods. This Alert will enhance and supplement the local agency response by broadcasting vehicle information about the missing person to motorists and the public.

The standardized criteria for the Florida Silver Alert Plan are as follows:

Missing person must be 60 years or older and there must be a clear indication that the individual has an irreversible deterioration of intellectual faculties (i.e., dementia). This must be verified by law enforcement or;

under extraordinary circumstances when a person age 18 to 59 has irreversible deterioration of intellectual faculties and law enforcement has determined the missing person lacks the capacity to consent, and that the use of dynamic message signs may be the only possible way to rescue the missing person.

In addition to the above criteria, the primary criteria for FDOT/FHP/FDLE dynamic message sign activation (all of which must be met) are the following:

1. Local law enforcement has already activated a local or regional alert by contacting a media outlet in their own and surrounding jurisdictions.
2. The law enforcement agency's investigation must conclude that the disappearance poses a credible threat to the person's welfare and safety.
3. There must be a description of the vehicle, and a tag number to display on the Florida Department of Transportation dynamic message signs.
4. Local law enforcement must verify vehicle and tag information.
5. Local law enforcement agency must have entered the missing person into the Florida Crime Information Center and issued a statewide BOLO to other law enforcement/911 centers.

The activation process will require that the local law enforcement agency contact the Missing Endangered Persons Information Clearinghouse (MEPIC) at 1-888-356-4774. If the criteria are met, the Clearinghouse will contact the FDOT to activate the dynamic message signs.

The following additional resources are available to local law enforcement to aid in the rescue or recovery of cognitively impaired missing persons.

- **Media Alert (813) 282-8612 (voice mail)**—Media Alert is a conduit between the Public Information Officer and television, radio, and newspaper editors to provide important news to the public. This service is provided to local law enforcement agencies free of charge. Media Alert is an internet technology-based system that requires an entry, login, and password code. An assigned person within the agency can log on and enter the information to be broadcast to media outlets. This system also allows for photographs. For access to this system, go to http://www.mediaalert.com, click on the PIO sign up sheet and follow the instructions listed.
- **A Child Is Missing, Inc. (1-888) 875-2246 (http://www.achildismissing.org)**—A Child is Missing, Inc. offers free assistance to law enforcement to aid in the recovery of missing persons (including children, teens, and elderly). It provides immediate neighborhood telephone alerts to the surrounding community. Local law enforcement will contact A Child Is Missing, Inc. with the missing person's information, and a recorded message will be developed and sent to homes and businesses within the requested radius.
- **Florida Department of Elder Affairs (850) 414-2000**—The Florida Department of Elder Affairs can provide an e-mail alert notification through the Aging Services Network, which includes area agencies on aging, community care lead agencies, providers, and volunteers. Local law enforcement can provide the Department of Elder Affairs with the missing persons' flyer or information by e-mailing SilverAlert@elderaffairs.org.
- **Project Lifesaver (http://www.projectlifesaver.org/members/members.aspx?state=FL)**—Project Lifesaver is a plan aiding the victims and families suffering from Alzheimer's disease and related

disorders such as Down's Syndrome and Autism. Project Lifesaver uses state-of-the-art technology, employing wristband transmitters to locate wandering and lost adults and children.

For more information regarding the Florida's Silver Alert Plan, please contact the Missing Endangered Persons Information Clearinghouse at 1-888-356-4774.

## Child Abduction Response Team (CART)

CART is a multi-agency child abduction team that permits law enforcement to make an organized, rapid, and planned response to an abducted child or other missing endangered child cases. CART consists of local, state, and federal law enforcement agencies and private sector partners. They agree to participate and work in conjunction with the FDLE MEPIC to provide personnel and resources to assist in handling missing endangered child cases. CART utilizes the AMBER Alert or the Missing Child Alert when the criteria are met for activation. Criteria for CART activation are a missing, endangered, or abducted child.

The benefits of CART include a multi-agency approach, shared expert resources such as crimes against children investigators, public information officers, and media liaisons, specialized equipment, and most importantly, an organized and prepared rapid response that will help assure the family and community that all resources are being used for the successful rescue and return of the child. CART members include experienced professional investigators, crime intelligence analysts, MEPIC, lead and volunteer coordinators, legal and forensic experts, search and rescue teams, family liaisons, public information officers, and other support personnel.

Rapid response is key to the safe rescue of a child, and the goal of CART is to bring a toolbox full of assets ready to deploy to any location as quickly as possible. CART teams are in operation throughout Florida and they meet at least quarterly for training and preparation. With a single phone call to any of the FDLE Regional Operation Centers, local law enforcement agencies have immediate access to all of the expertise and resources of CART.

The U.S. Department of Justice (DOJ), Office of Justice Programs has adopted CART nationwide to respond quickly to incidents of missing, endangered, and abducted children. When an endangered or abducted child is taken out of state, the FBI will usually spearhead the investigation. An officer should follow his or her agency policy and procedure when contacting the FBI. *(LE174.6.)*

An officer should document missing endangered and abducted child incidents by writing a thorough, complete account of the incident including all actions taken, according to his or her agency policy and procedure. The proper reporting form should be used to log the information into the FCIC/NCIC and MEPIC databases. *(LE049a.12.)*

# UNIT 1 | CRIMES AGAINST PERSONS

## LESSON 8 | Robbery

### Robbery

According to Florida Statute §812.13, a robbery occurs when a suspect takes property from a person by using force, violence, or assault, or by putting the victim in fear, with the intent to permanently or temporarily deprive the victim of his or her right to the property or appropriating the property of the victim to the suspect's own use or to the use of any person not entitled to it. A robbery is a theft plus violence. *(LE513.7.A.)*

**OBJECTIVES**

**LE513.7.A.** Identify the elements of robbery.

**LE513.7.B.** Identify common targets of robbery.

**LE513.7.C.** Identify procedures to follow in a robbery situation.

**LE513.7.D.** Identify items to include in a preliminary robbery report.

Common targets of robberies are homes, retail stores, convenience stores, drunken persons, banks, ATMs, situational victims, senior citizens, drug suspects/participants, and prostitutes. *(LE513.7.B.)*

Many robbery scenes must be completely sealed for thorough processing, such as when a homicide, sexual battery, or other serious injury occurred or the robber was at the scene for an extended period. The scene of any bank robbery must also be sealed pending arrival of the FBI. Procedures an officer should follow upon arrival at a robbery scene include the following:

1. attending to medical needs, if appropriate,
2. securing the scene,
3. requesting that crime scene technicians process the scene,
4. obtaining preliminary statements from witnesses,
5. initiating a BOLO,
6. interviewing witnesses separately,
7. if it was a bank robbery, notifying the FBI *(LE513.7.C.)*

Items in the preliminary robbery report should include a complete description of the suspect and weapons and the manner in which the suspect concealed and displayed the weapons. Officers should attempt to obtain from witnesses the suspect's actions and the exact wording used during the robbery. The report should also include details regarding the suspect's treatment of victims. Finally, if possible, a complete itemized list of property taken, with serial numbers, should be included. *(LE513.7.D.)*

# UNIT 1 | CRIMES AGAINST PERSONS

## LESSON 9 | Sexual Battery, Juvenile Sex Offenders, and Other Sex Crimes

**OBJECTIVES**

**LE145.3.** Request medical personnel provide information, as required, in a sexual battery situation.

**LE513.8.A.** Identify procedures for dealing with victims of sexual battery.

**LE513.8.B.** Define *juvenile sexual offender.*

**LE513.8.C.** Describe lewd and lascivious battery, molestation, conduct, and exhibition.

### Sexual Battery

Historically, sexual battery is one of the most underreported crimes. Victims will sometimes not report a sexual battery to law enforcement because the victim may be embarrassed or may actually have a continuing relationship with the assailant. In Florida, there is no statute of limitations for civil actions relating to sexual battery of a child less than 16 years of age at the time of the offense. A victim may feel that law enforcement may not be able to apprehend the suspect or may fear reprisal by the assailant. Sexual battery victims also fear further victimization during the investigation and in subsequent courtroom proceedings. An officer's attitude during a sexual battery investigation can assist the investigation by being humane, sympathetic, patient, sensitive, letting the victim feel he or she is in control, and reassuring him or her that the officer is there to help and develop facts for legal purposes.

When responding to a sexual battery case, an officer must obtain medical treatment for the victim immediately, and is required by law to provide or arrange for transportation to the appropriate facility. There are special considerations for initiating a medical examination for a juvenile victim of sexual battery. Agency policy and procedure should be followed when arranging for a sexual battery exam, collecting clothing, and notifying a sex crimes investigator. This is also a good time for an officer to contact and coordinate with a victim advocate to calm the victim and encourage him or her to cooperate with the process.

The officer should advise the victim that he or she may contact a certified rape crisis center from which the victim may receive services. The officer is required by law to present the victim a "Victims' Rights Brochure" as per Florida Statute 960.001 and a "Sexual Battery—Victim's Rights and Services" brochure from the Florida Council Against Sexual Violence, as per Florida Statute §794.052.

After determining and locating the crime scene, the officer should secure the scene, if possible. Preliminary information should be obtained from any witnesses. The officer should also initiate a BOLO and secure the crime scene. The victim should be interviewed privately with a victim advocate, if possible. Only medical personnel may perform a physical and sexual battery examination, which may later provide evidence and information to further the investigation. *(LE145.3.)*

The officer should interview the victim privately with the victim advocate. The victim's condition should be documented, including any torn or stained clothing, smeared makeup, disarrayed hair, bruises, scratches, and defense wounds. The victim's emotional state should also be documented. Prior to submitting a final report, the officer should allow the victim to review the final report and provide a statement as to the accuracy of the final report.

An officer should ask the victim the following questions during the interview:

- When did the sexual battery occur?
- Where did the sexual battery occur?
- Exactly what happened?
- Did the assailant use force or a weapon?
- What did the suspect say?
- Is any property missing?
- Were there any witnesses present?

An officer should not ask the victim personal or accusing questions that insinuate willingness or blame on the victim's part, such as his or her prior sexual experiences, whether the victim climaxed, the size of the suspect's penis, what he or she did to bring on the assault, whether he or she will take a polygraph, or whether or not the victim or the suspect enjoyed the assault.

The officer should determine where the crime took place and secure the scene. Preliminary information should be obtained from any witnesses. Should the officer determine the offender is a family member or custodian of a child victim, this is considered child abuse, and the officer should immediately contact DCF. A BOLO should be initiated if necessary. *(LE513.8.A.)*

Community policing can provide awareness of the presence of possible sexual offenders and predators in the officer's area. When searching for a suspect of a sexual assault on a child, the officer should look for the presence of child erotica, pornography, or videos, or the presence of children's toys or computer games when there are no children residing in the home of a sexual offender or predator.

## Juvenile Sex Offenders

Section 39.01(7), F.S. defines an alleged ***juvenile sexual offender*** as a child 12 years of age or younger who is alleged to have committed a violation of sexual battery, prostitution, lewdness, indecent exposure, abuse of a child, obscenity, or any violation of law or delinquent act involving juvenile sexual abuse.

Juvenile sexual abuse is any sexual behavior that occurs without consent, without equality, or because of coercion. "Coercion" means the exploitation of authority or the use of bribes, threats of force, or intimidation to gain cooperation or compliance. "Equality" means two participants operating with the same level of power in a relationship, neither one being controlled or coerced by the other.

Consent is an agreement that includes the following:

- an understanding of what is proposed based on age, maturity, developmental level, functioning, and experience
- knowledge of societal standards for the proposal
- an awareness of potential consequences and alternatives
- the assumption that the person accepts the agreement or disagreement equally

- a voluntary decision
- mental competence

Juvenile sexual offender behavior ranges from non-contact sexual behavior such as making obscene phone calls, exhibitionism, voyeurism, and the showing or taking of lewd photographs to varying degrees of direct sexual contact, such as frottage (the obtaining of sexual pleasure by rubbing the clothed body against that of others, usually strangers in crowded places), fondling, digital penetration, rape, fellatio, sodomy, to various other sexually aggressive acts. *(LE513.8.B.)*

# Other Sex Crimes

***Sexual violence*** as defined in section 784.046(c), F.S. means:

- any one incident of sexual battery, as defined in Chapter 794, F.S.
- a lewd or lascivious act, as defined in Chapter 800, F.S., committed upon or in the presence of a person younger than 16 years old
- sexual performance by a child, and intentionally viewing a sexual performance of a child as described in §827.071, F.S.
- or any other forcible felony in which a sexual act is committed or attempted, regardless of whether criminal charges based on the incident were filed, reduced or dismissed by the State Attorney

Luring or enticing, or attempting to lure or entice, a child under the age of 12 into a structure, dwelling, or conveyance without the consent of the child's parent or legal guardian shall be *prima facie* (upon its face) evidence of intent for something other than a lawful purpose.

Lewd or lascivious battery involves engaging in sexual activity with a person 12 years of age or older but less than 16 years of age; or encouraging, forcing, or enticing any person less than 16 years of age to engage in sadomasochistic abuse, sexual bestiality, prostitution, or any other act involving sexual activity.

Lewd or lascivious molestation occurs when a person intentionally touches in a lewd or lascivious manner the breasts, genitals, genital area, or buttocks, or the clothing covering them, of a person less than 16 years of age, or forces or entices a person less than 16 years of age to so touch the offender.

A person commits lewd or lascivious conduct by intentionally touching a person less than 16 years of age in a lewd or lascivious manner; or soliciting a person under 16 years of age to commit a lewd or lascivious act.

Lewd or lascivious exhibition occurs when a person intentionally masturbates, exposes the genitals in a lewd or lascivious manner, or commits any other sexual act that does not involve actual physical or sexual contact with the victim, including, but not limited to, sadomasochistic abuse, sexual bestiality, or the simulation of any act involving sexual activity in the presence of a victim who is less than 16 years of age. Doing any of these acts live over a computer online service, Internet service, or local bulletin board service is also lewd or lascivious exhibition, if the offender knows or should know or has reason to believe that the transmission is viewed on a computer or television monitor by a victim in Florida who is less than 16 years of age. A minor who uses a computer or any electronic device, such as cell phones, to transmit or distribute the nude photograph or video of another minor commits the offense of sexting, according to §847.0141, F.S. The fact that an undercover operative or law enforcement officer was involved in the detection and investigation is not a defense to a prosecution under this section.

Exposure of sexual organs is the intentional exposure of sexual organs in public, on the private premises of another, or near enough to be visible from private premises, in a vulgar or indecent manner, or being naked in public except in any place provided or set apart for that purpose. Urinating in public should be charged as disorderly conduct rather than exposure of sexual organs. Under no circumstance can a mother violate this section by breastfeeding her baby in public.

According to § 810.14, voyeurism is when someone with lewd, lascivious, or indecent intent secretly observes another person when the other person is located in a dwelling, structure, or conveyance and such location provides a reasonable expectation of privacy. This can also evolve into stalking, loitering, and prowling. *(LE513.8.C.)*

**Section Vocabulary**

*juvenile sexual offender*

*sexual violence*

# UNIT 1 | CRIMES AGAINST PERSONS

## LESSON 10 | Hate Crimes

### Crimes Driven by Hate

A hate crime can be any crime against a person or property that is motivated by prejudice or discrimination. Just as there is no separate offense for domestic violence in Florida, there is no specific offense for a "hate crime." Section 775.085, F.S. imposes stiffer penalties for crimes motivated by or evidencing prejudice or discrimination. A third-degree felony will be punished as a second-degree felony, a second-degree as a first, and so forth.

Statements the suspect makes to the victim and witnesses while committing the crime, graffiti drawn at the scene, as well as other physical evidence found at the scene may establish proof that a crime was motivated by prejudice or discrimination. Evidence may be available to show that the offender deliberately targeted the victim because of the victim's race, color, ancestry, ethnicity, religion, sexual orientation, nationality, age, mental or physical disability, or homeless status.

If evidence at the scene and the facts of the case show that a crime was motivated by prejudice or discrimination, the responding officer must indicate in the report and the arrest affidavit that a hate crime has been committed so that the State Attorney's Office can apply for the appropriate penalty enhancements. *(IN006.1.D.5.)*

**OBJECTIVES**

**IN006.1.D.5.** Apply Florida Statutes regarding hate crimes.

**LE513.9.B.** Identify procedures for dealing with a victim of a hate crime.

## Response to Victims of Hate Crimes

Hate crime victims often react differently from victims of other crimes. The victims realize that they were targeted because of a personal characteristic. The victim may find the officer threatening if he or she is of another national origin or race, especially if the officer belongs to the same race as the perpetrator. The victim may be reluctant to talk if he or she perceives the officer is biased. The victim should be questioned sensitively with the officer remaining discreet about requesting answers from distraught victims. The victim should be asked if he or she knows why he or she was victimized.

Officers who provide the appropriate response to the victim of a hate crime help the entire justice system by encouraging victims to cooperate. The officer also promotes his or her agency's credibility within the communities when victims understand that they can trust officers. When responding to a victim of a hate crime, an officer should remain calm, objective, and professional.

The officer should ask the victim how he or she could help, questioning the victim as to what the individual's needs and wants are. The officer should listen attentively and let the victim vent. At all times, the officer should perform his or her duties professionally and never belittle or make light of a situation. The officer should assure hate crime victims of his or her professional interest in serving justice. *(LE513.9.B.)*

# UNIT 2 | CRIMES AGAINST PROPERTY

## LESSON 2 | Breach of the Peace

**OBJECTIVES**

**LE514.1.A.** Identify procedures for dealing with a loitering and prowling incident.

**LE514.1.B.** Identify the legal distinction between disorderly conduct and disorderly intoxication.

**LE514.1.C.** Define *open house party.*

### Loitering and Prowling

Section 856.021, F.S. states that "it is unlawful for any person to loiter or prowl in a place, at a time, or in a manner not usual for law-abiding individuals, under circumstances that warrant a justifiable and reasonable alarm or immediate concern for the safety of persons or property in the vicinity." If a person takes flight upon appearance of a law enforcement officer, refuses to identify him- or herself, or manifestly endeavors to conceal him- or herself or any object, that person may be loitering or prowling.

The fact that a person is out at odd hours, without exhibiting any other suspicious activity, will not warrant an arrest for loitering or prowling. If a person does not flee, the officer should allow the individual an opportunity to identify him- or herself and explain his or her presence and conduct. A person may not be compelled to explain his or her presence and conduct unless he or she is first properly advised of his rights. Absent probable cause of some other offense, if the person voluntarily explains his or her presence and conduct and the explanation dispels any alarm, the person must be released without charge. Failure to do so may result in dismissal of the case by the court and civil liability for false arrest. The court will also not convict a person of an offense under this section if it appears at trial that the explanation given by the person for his or her presence at the scene was true and, if believed by the officer at the time, would have dispelled any alarm or immediate concern. *(LE514.1.A.)*

### Disorderly Conduct

Section 877.03, F.S. defines breach of the peace and disorderly conduct as conduct that corrupts the public morals, outrages the sense of public decency, or affects the peace and quiet of persons who may witness it. Brawling or fighting in public may constitute a breach of the peace or disorderly conduct. Urinating in public is disorderly conduct, not exposure of sexual organs. Disorderly conduct is not a catchall statute. Unless a suspect's words actually incite a reaction from onlookers or create a danger to others, such as shouting "fire" in a crowded theater, the individual is protected under freedom of speech. A person who curses at others or officers may not be arrested for disorderly conduct. The use of intermediate weapons such as dart-firing stun guns or pepper gas would likewise be inappropriate on a person who is only yelling and cursing at officers or others. Officers must be careful not to rely on this statute when reaching high levels of frustration with subjects. Loud and rowdy subjects should be calmed using verbalization, command presence, and crisis intervention skills. No one can be charged with breaching an officer's peace, whether the officer is on or off duty.

**Section Vocabulary**

*open house party*

## Disorderly Intoxication

Section 856.011, F.S. states that no person in the state shall be intoxicated and endanger the safety of another person or property, and no person in the state shall be intoxicated or drink any alcoholic beverage in a public place or in or upon any public conveyance and cause a public disturbance.

The difference between disorderly conduct and disorderly intoxication is the element of intoxication. Officers should document evidence of intoxication in such cases the same way they would in a DUI investigation, identifying specific indicators of intoxication such as slurred speech, bloodshot eyes, staggered gait, etc. *(LE514.1.B.)*

## Affray

An affray is when two or more persons fight in a public place to the terror of onlookers. In addition, according to §870.01, F.S., a person who riots, incites, or encourages a riot is guilty of an affray.

## Open House Party

An ***open house party*** is a social gathering at a residence and is legal unless minors consuming alcohol or drugs are present. A person with control of a residence where a house party occurs who knows that alcoholic beverages or drugs are in the possession of or are being consumed by a minor at the residence is in violation of Florida Statute §856.015. The person in control of the residence must take reasonable steps to prevent the possession or consumption by minors of alcoholic beverages and drugs. This section does not apply to the use of alcoholic beverages at legally protected religious observances or activities. *(LE514.1.C.)*

# UNIT 2 | CRIMES AGAINST PROPERTY

## LESSON 2 | Burglary and Trespassing

**OBJECTIVES**

**LE514.2.A.** Identify categories of burglars.

**LE514.2.B.** Identify common methods of entry used by burglars.

**LE514.2.** Respond to an incident involving burglary and trespassing.

**LE514.2.C.** Define *burglary tools.*

**LE514.2.D.** Identify the legal requirements for a valid trespass after a warning.

**LE514.2.E.** Identify procedures for responding to an archeological site violation.

### Burglary

There are several different kinds or categories of burglars. Professional burglars commit only a few offenses yearly, have sophisticated knowledge of security systems, and target only residences or businesses with significant assets. Juvenile burglars target schools, their own family or friends, authority figures, and tend to steal age-appropriate items. Juvenile burglars often commit vandalism and may set fires. Drug addicts burglarize vehicles, homes, and businesses, looking for prescription or non-prescription drugs, illegal drugs, and anything of value that can easily be sold for drugs. The impulse burglar is opportunistic, capitalizing on easy targets. Other burglars are driven by their interest in sexual gratification and focus on collecting trophies or mementos such as intimate articles of clothing located in bedrooms or bathrooms and typically leave body fluids or defecate on the scene. *(LE514.2.A.)*

Burglaries are classified according to the type of location entered, such as a dwelling, structure, or conveyance. Penalties are more severe for burglary of a dwelling than for a structure or conveyance. A structure is a building of any kind. A conveyance can be a vehicle, boat, or airplane. Burglars may use several methods of entry, such as entering through unlocked doors and windows or using a hidden key, removing hinge pins, breaking glass, or kicking in the door. Other techniques include prying or spreading a door or window frame, slipping, pulling, or picking the lock, or using a bump key, garage door opener, or electronic decoder for keyless entries. *(LE514.2.B.)*

If during the course of a burglary, the offender commits assault or battery the burglary is punished as a first-degree felony. If the offender enters an occupied dwelling, structure, or conveyance and is armed, or becomes armed in the course of the burglary, he or she commits a first-degree felony. If the offender uses a vehicle as an instrument, other than merely as a getaway vehicle, to assist in committing the burglary, and causes damage to the dwelling, structure, or property in excess of $1,000, the burglary is punished as a first-degree felony. All of these first-degree felonies are punishable by life imprisonment.

Burglary is one of the most frequent crimes that an officer will investigate. Upon arrival at the scene of a burglary incident, the officer should obtain a general statement from the victim and immediately search the scene by conducting a walk-through with the victim. The officer should emphasize to the victim the importance of the preservation of evidence and process the crime scene according to agency policy and procedure.

Officers should determine the entry and exit points the burglar used and note any disturbed areas and possible evidence for processing. The officer should then obtain detailed information from the victim, such as the description of items taken and the timeframe during which the incident may have occurred.

The officer should provide the victim with a case number, the primary officer's name, explain the follow-up procedures, and possibly give some crime prevention advice. The officer must be careful not to minimize the impact this crime may have on the victim by giving examples of more serious burglaries. *(LE514.2.)*

## Associated Crimes

Section 810.06, F.S., prohibits possession of any tool, machine, or implement with intent to use it, or allow it to be used, to commit any burglary or trespass. Burglary tools may include screwdrivers, pliers, wrenches, and pry bars, but can also be anything used to gain entry during a burglary such as a rock or concrete block. *(LE514.2.C.)*

## Trespassing

Trespassing in a dwelling, structure, or conveyance occurs when the suspect, without authorization, willfully enters or remains in any dwelling, structure, or conveyance. Even if the suspect is authorized, licensed, or invited onto the property, if he or she is warned to depart by the owner or lessee of the premises or by a person authorized by the owner, and refuses to do so, the suspect commits the offense of trespassing in a dwelling, structure, or conveyance. If a suspect disregards the notice or communication by posting, fencing, or cultivation, or enters or remains with the intent to commit another offense, he or she commits the offense of trespassing.

A person can be guilty of trespassing on property other than a dwelling, structure, or conveyance if he or she willfully enters or remains on the property. Property can be curtilage, land, or a building immediately adjacent to a dwelling, structure, or conveyance, usually enclosed in some way by fence and/or shrubs, or unenclosed curtilage. Unenclosed curtilage can be land or grounds, and any outbuildings that are directly adjacent to and connected with the dwelling, structure, or conveyance. Unenclosed curtilage is necessary, convenient, and habitually used in connection with that dwelling, and is also defined as property other than a structure or conveyance. If the suspect disregards the notice or communication by posting, fencing, or cultivation, or enters or remains with the intent to commit an offense other than the offense of trespass, he or she commits the offense of trespassing.

Any person who does not have legitimate business on a school campus is trespassing. The suspect is trespassing if he or she has no authorization, license, or invitation to enter or remain upon school property. A student who is currently under suspension or expulsion, who enters or remains on the campus or any other facility owned by the school, also commits a trespass upon the grounds of a school facility.

Trespassing on a designated, posted construction site is a felony, as is trespassing while armed or killing an animal during the trespass. Failure to leave or remaining on the premises after receiving a warning from or in the presence of law enforcement is trespassing. *(LE514.2.D.)*

## Protecting Archaeological Sites

Archeology refers to the study of human cultures from around the world and through time by recovering and examining artifacts, such as graves, buildings, tools, and pottery. Artifacts are objects, or material evidence, removed from the ground the researchers study. As values of artifacts and antiques on commercial and private markets have rapidly escalated, so has looting and vandalism of archaeological sites.

Many jurisdictions include areas of state-owned or state-controlled land, on which archaeological sites are located. The federal government protects these sites under the Archaeological Resources Protection Act

(ARPA, 1979) and the Native American Graves Protection and Repatriation Act (NAGPRA, 1991). Section 267.13(1)(a)-(c), F.S., addresses the protection of archaeological sites under state law.

Altering an archaeological site or artifact by means other than excavation, including removal, destruction, or effacement of property, is a violation of state-controlled land. Other forms of violations of archaeological sites on state-controlled land include excavating, damaging, defacing, altering, or removing property without a permit or counseling, soliciting, or employing others to do so. It is a misdemeanor to walk on an archeological site and remove an object; it is a felony to dig into the site to retrieve an object.

Officers should become familiar with local archaeological sites, the tools and equipment, and persons who normally work at those sites. Archaeologists and researchers commonly use shovels, picks, sifting screens, metal detectors, probing rods, brushes, large buckets, hoses, large shallow containers, and other excavation tools. They mark their working areas with ropes. During regular patrol of these sites, officers can spot unusual and possibly illegal activity. Officers should identify unfamiliar or suspicious persons using equipment at a site at odd hours and request identification, credentials, and permits from suspicious persons.

The officer responding to a call concerning a violation of an archeological site will need to assess the scene to determine if a crime was committed. If the officer believes a crime was committed, he or she should secure and protect the scene, notify a supervisor, and inform local, state, or federal park rangers of the incident and any recovered evidence.

A helpful resource for officers investigating the violation of state archeological lands is the FBI's National Stolen Art File. NSAF is a computerized index of stolen art, antiquities, and cultural property as reported to the FBI by U.S. and international law enforcement agencies. (For more information, officers should visit http://www.fbi.gov/hq/arttheft/artheft.htm). Another source is the LOOT (Listing Of Outlaw Treachery) Clearinghouse. It lists prosecuted cases of looting and vandalism of archaeological resources. The Archaeology Assistance Division of the National Park Service (http://www.cr.nps.gov) maintains this computerized archival database. *(LE514.2.E.)*

**Section Vocabulary**

*burglary tools*

# UNIT 2 | CRIMES AGAINST PROPERTY

## LESSON 3 | Criminal Mischief

**OBJECTIVES**

**LE514.3.A.** Identify the elements of criminal mischief.

**LE514.3.B.** Identify the difference between misdemeanor and felony criminal mischief.

### Elements of Criminal Mischief

Criminal mischief, as outlined in Section 806.13, F.S., is a willful, malicious crime where the offender injures or damages property belonging to another. Injury or damage can include the placement of graffiti or the commission of other acts of vandalism. *(LE514.3.A.)*

### Misdemeanor and Felony Criminal Mischief

Criminal mischief is a second-degree misdemeanor if the property damage is less than $200 and a first-degree misdemeanor if the damage is greater than $200 but less than $1,000. If the value of property damaged totals $1,000 or more, the crime is a third-degree felony. If the offender has one or more prior convictions for criminal mischief, a subsequent offense will be punished as a felony, regardless of the amount of damage.

A person who willfully and maliciously defaces, injures, or damages a sexually violent predator detention or commitment facility is guilty of a third-degree felony. Any person who willfully and maliciously damages any place of worship or religious article is guilty of a third-degree felony if the damage is over $200. Destruction or damage to a public pay telephone with posted warnings that renders the instrument inoperative or illegally opening the body of the telephone is a third-degree felony. Interruption or impairment of a business operation or public communication, transportation, water, gas or power supply, or other public service that costs $1,000 or more in labor and supplies to restore, is a third-degree felony. *(LE514.3.B.)*

# UNIT 2 | CRIMES AGAINST PROPERTY

## LESSON 4 | Defrauding an Innkeeper

### Theft of Services

Ordering and eating a meal in an eating establishment or occupying a room in a public lodging and then refusing to pay is the crime of defrauding an innkeeper or theft of services by failure to pay, under Florida Statute §509.151. Theft of property belonging to a guest of an establishment or theft of property belonging to the establishment by an employee constitutes a felony of the third degree. *(LE514.4.A.)*

The operator of the facility or a law enforcement officer with probable cause may take such a person into custody in a reasonable manner and for a reasonable amount of time for recovering the value of the property for prosecution.

If the operator takes the offender into custody, a law enforcement officer must be called to the scene immediately. When the provisions of this statute are followed, neither the operator nor the officer may be held criminally or civilly liable for false arrest, false imprisonment, or unlawful detention.

If the suspect resists the officer's reasonable efforts to recover property that that officer or the operator believe was stolen, and the suspect is subsequently found guilty of theft of the property, he or she can be charged with resisting apprehension as well, unless the person did not know that the officer was in fact a law enforcement officer. The charge of theft and of resisting apprehension may be tried concurrently. *(LE514.4.)*

**OBJECTIVES**

**LE514.4.A.** Identify the elements of defrauding an innkeeper.

**LE514.4.** Respond to an incident involving defrauding an innkeeper.

# UNIT 2 | CRIMES AGAINST PROPERTY

## LESSON 5 | Fire-related Crimes

**OBJECTIVES**

**LE514.5.A.** Identify the primary responsibility of law enforcement at the scene of a fire.

**LE514.5.** Respond to an incident involving a fire-related crime.

### Arrival at the Scene

If an officer arrives at the scene of an incident and observes a fire, he or she should notify dispatch immediately and request assistance. It is critical to respond quickly to fires, particularly in nursing homes, schools, churches, stores, and apartments. Occupants in the surrounding area may need to evacuate. The officer should contact a supervisor and follow agency procedure when considering evacuations. The primary responsibility of an officer after the arrival of fire personnel is to assist the fire department and the Fire Marshal in their investigation and maintain crowd and traffic control. *(LE514.5.A.)*

Securing the scene at a fire investigation is very important. The investigation of suspicious fires is extremely difficult due to the lack of witnesses to most fires and the fact that much of the evidence is burned. Fire setting is sometimes used as a technique to distract law enforcement authorities' attention away from the location of other crimes and is predominantly a juvenile crime.

Occasionally, officers may respond to a false alarm of a fire. Section 806.101, F.S., states that anyone who, without reasonable cause, makes a false alarm of fire, is guilty of a misdemeanor for the first conviction and a felony for any subsequent convictions.

Officers may also encounter someone who possesses, manufactures, transports, or disposes of a firebomb with intent to willfully and unlawfully cause damage by fire or explosion to a structure or property, in violation of §806.111, F.S. The statute defines a firebomb as a container filled with flammable, combustible liquid or an incendiary chemical mixture, with a wick or other means of causing ignition. This definition does not include commercially manufactured devices used for illumination, heating, or cooking. Local gang activity, organized crime, terrorist activity, and hate crimes are often enacted using firebombs to commit crimes. *(LE514.5.)*

# UNIT 2 | CRIMES AGAINST PROPERTY

## LESSON 6 | Narcotics and Vice Crimes

**OBJECTIVES**

**LE514.6.A.** Identify common reasons why vice activity is rarely reported.

**LE514.6.B.** Identify sources of illicit drug traffic.

**LE514.6.C.** Identify methods used to transport and conceal illicit drugs.

**LE514.6.D.** Identify methods used to investigate vice activity.

**LE514.6.E.** List types of vice crimes.

**LE514.6.F.** Identify the basic characteristics of organized crime operations.

### Narcotics

The primary reason drug activity is under-reported is that the victims of the crimes are also party to illegal activity. The victim must maintain a relationship with the dealer to preserve the source of supply. Often relatives and friends of users are protective or ashamed of them and do not want to get involved. *(LE514.6.A.)*

There are many sources of illicit drugs in the United States. Drugs are smuggled, diverted, and intercepted from legitimate sources; many drugs can be obtained from an elderly person's medicine cabinet. Illegal drugs are also manufactured and cultivated in clandestine laboratories and grow houses. Abuse of prescription drugs is on the rise, and suspects will "doctor shop," abuse pharmaceuticals, steal prescription pads, or deal in gray market drugs in order to meet their needs. *(LE514.6.B.)*

Common methods used to transport drugs include both private and public conveyances and shipments via commercial delivery companies such as UPS, the U.S. Postal Service, and FedEx. Drugs may be concealed in items such as children's toys, or other commodities. Individuals known as mules will conceal drugs on their person, often in balloons hidden in body cavities. *(LE514.6.C.)*

Narcotic investigations may involve undercover operations, use of informants, surveillance, and trash pulls. Patrol officers may be involved as uniformed presence during execution of a search warrant in a narcotics investigation. Other narcotics evidence tasks include field-testing, counting, and weighing seized drugs, sealing and labeling the evidence, transporting it to the lab, and maintaining a properly documented chain of custody during each step. If currency is seized, officers should follow agency procedure for counting and documenting the seizure. Officers must be careful and use personal protective equipment when collecting and handling evidence in narcotics cases.

Drug offenses include trafficking, sale, manufacture or cultivation, and possession. Florida law recognizes different kinds of possession: actual and constructive, and exclusive or joint. The Florida Standard Jury Instructions in Criminal Cases define the terms as follows. To possess means to have personal charge of or exercise the right of ownership, management, or control over the article possessed. Possession may be actual or constructive.

Actual possession means the article is in the hand of or on the person, or the article is in a container in the hand of or on the person, or the article is so close as to be within ready reach and is under the control of the person. Mere proximity to an article is not sufficient to establish control over that thing when the article is not in a place over which the person has control.

Constructive possession means the article is in a place over which the person has control, or in which the person has concealed it. If the article is in a place over which the person does not have control, then the person is not in constructive possession unless the person has control over the article, knowledge that the article is in the person's presence, and knowledge of the illicit nature of the article.

Possession may be joint, that is, two or more persons may jointly have possession of an article, exercising control over it. In that case, each of those persons is considered to be in possession of that article. A person's knowledge of the presence of an article may be inferred only if the person has exclusive possession of the article.

Officers generally do not have to worry about what kind of possession applies in a particular case—that is an issue usually dealt with by a prosecutor. Officers should, however, be aware that a person's presence in a room or building where drugs or other contraband is found does not necessarily mean the person has committed a crime.

## Vice Crimes

Sometimes called "victimless crimes," vice crime activity includes offenses such as prostitution, gambling, alcohol and tobacco violations, and pornography. Vice investigations involve a lot of undercover work and develop information through intelligence; from information gathering, both strategic and tactical, from informants and surveillance.

***Strategic intelligence*** examines crime patterns and crime trends for management use in decision making, resource development, resource allocation, and policy planning. It typically focuses on specific crime types, such as criminal enterprises, drug traffickers, terrorists, or other forms of complex criminality.

***Tactical intelligence*** is used for specific decision making or problem solving to deal with an immediate situation or crisis. It produces information helpful in dealing with specific criminal activity and in identifying the modus operandi of criminals. *(LE514.6.D.)*

## Types of Vice Crimes

**Alcohol and tobacco violations** are vice crimes committed most frequently among people under the age of 21. Open house parties, open containers, disorderly intoxication, and selling alcohol or tobacco to minors are common offenses. Officers may respond to unlicensed establishments selling alcohol, moonshine operations, or places selling alcohol after hours.

**Gambling** offenses officers may encounter include bolita (numbers game popular especially in South Florida), dog or cock fighting, high stakes card games, off track betting, or craps games on the street.

**Child pornography** is illegal to produce, possess, or distribute. Patrol officers are most likely to encounter a pornography case by responding to a call from the film processing department of a retail store. If officers encounter what appears to be child pornography on a computer, they should follow agency policy and procedure for further investigation of the matter. Under no circumstance should officers touch the computer or attempt to find additional images on it. As discussed previously, recovery of computer data involves complex and highly specialized expertise, and officers may inadvertently eliminate or spoil evidence by trying to do it themselves. Officers should remember that sexual offenders and predators who are on probation or parole may not have any pornography in their possession and may be ordered not to have a computer at all.

**Prostitution** is often associated with adult entertainment venues, massage parlors, escort services, and callouts. Street prostitutes tend to be located in particular geographical areas and truck stops. Prostitutes may be victims of human trafficking. *(LE514.6.E.)*

## Section Vocabulary

***strategic intelligence***

***tactical intelligence***

# Organized Crime

There are four basic characteristics of an organized crime operation. The organization has a specific structure, usually hierarchical or paramilitary. The organization has profit continuity; it has both criminal and legitimate businesses. The loss of one source of income will not necessarily eliminate the organization's bottom line. The organization is monopolistic or is a provider of a product or service in a particular market, and rarely shares areas of crime or territory with each other or outside groups. The organization is also insulated, meaning the higher echelon personnel are relatively immune from liability for their criminal behavior. The organizational structure protects such individuals from infiltration by law enforcement and regulatory agencies. The organization will attempt to intimidate or coerce witnesses and even people involved in law enforcement and prosecution.

Organized crime promotes public corruption, street crime, and gang activity and can have a significantly negative impact on the economy. Organized crime is often associated with gambling, loan sharking, narcotics, prostitution, human trafficking, extortion, pornography, white-collar crime, fencing, unions, corruption, numbers games, auto theft, drive-by shootings, adult entertainment, and money laundering.

Some of the methods law enforcement uses to combat organized crime are asset forfeiture, concentration on vice offenses, gathering intelligence, inter-agency cooperation, and prosecution under the Racketeer Influenced and Corrupt Organization (RICO), Florida Statute Chapter 895. *(LE514.6.F.)*

# UNIT 2 | CRIMES AGAINST PROPERTY

## LESSON 7 | Theft and Dealing in Stolen Property

**OBJECTIVES**

**LE514.7.A.** Identify the types of theft victims.

**LE514.7.B.** Differentiate between petit or misdemeanor and grand or felony theft.

**LE514.7.C.** Identify indicators of a stolen vehicle.

**LE514.7.D.** Identify NCIC/FCIC reporting requirements for stolen and recovered property.

**LE514.7.E.** Identify when someone is dealing in stolen property.

### Theft

***Theft*** is defined by Florida Statute §812.014 as knowingly obtaining, using or endeavoring to obtain or use property of another with intent to temporarily or permanently deprive the other person of the use of the property.

The victim in a theft case can provide information helpful to the investigation, such as a thorough description of the property taken including unique characteristics or serial numbers. The victim can also tell the officer the value of the item and the last time and location it was seen. The victim may also know who discovered the item was missing and whether any witnesses were present at the time of the theft.

There are two types of theft victims—businesses and individuals. Theft from individuals may involve pick pocketing, purse snatching, confidence games, auto theft, or taking personal property from homes, businesses, or vehicles.

A business can be a theft victim through shoplifting, embezzlement, skimming from cash registers or petty cash, smash-and-grab attacks, hijacking of delivery trucks or their cargo, quick-change artists or theft of agriculture, services, or construction site materials. ***Retail theft*** involves taking possession of or carrying away merchandise, money, or negotiable instruments; altering or removing a label or price tag; transferring merchandise from one container to another of lower price; or removal of a shopping cart with intent to deprive the merchant of possession, use, benefit, or full retail value. An officer may arrest an individual for retail theft without a warrant even when the offense is not committed in the officer's presence. *(LE514.7.A.)*

If the value of property taken during a retail theft is less than $300, the offense is a misdemeanor. ***Petit theft*** is taking something valued at less than $300. Petit theft is a misdemeanor, but a third conviction for petit theft will be punished as a third-degree felony.

Grand theft involves the theft of anything with a value of $300 or more and other items specified by statute regardless of their value. For example, theft of a will, codicil, or other testamentary instrument, a firearm, motor vehicle, stop sign, or fire extinguisher is grand theft. Motor vehicles are self-propelled vehicles not operated upon rails or a guide-way and do not include bicycles, motorized scooters without a seat, electric personal assistive mobility devices, or mopeds.

Grand theft can also involve theft of any commercially farmed animal or fish, 2,000 or more individual pieces of fruit, items taken from a designated construction site identified by the posting of a sign, and anhydrous ammonia, which is used in methamphetamine production. Theft of property, funds, or assets may be reclassified to a higher degree if the victim was a person 65 years of age or older. *(LE514.7.B.)*

## Motor Vehicle Theft

There are some situations when a person may report a vehicle as stolen when it has in fact been repossessed or taken by another family member. The complainant may just be mistaken about where he or she parked the vehicle. Sometimes during a domestic dispute involving separated or divorced parties, one of the parties may take a vehicle. This may be a civil matter to be resolved by the divorce judge. Officers should look to their agency policy and procedures for dealing with such situations. Officers should exercise caution in cases where the complainant and suspect both claim a right to the vehicle. Sources of information regarding stolen vehicles include used car lot or parking lot operators, repair garages or body shops, insurance companies, service station attendants, and informants.

Vehicles that have broken side and vent windows, a poorly attached license plate, or missing, scratched, or punched door locks may be stolen. The ignition on such vehicles may have been punched out and the steering column may appear damaged. A person in possession of a vehicle in which the ignition or steering wheel locking mechanisms have been bypassed is assumed to know that the vehicle is stolen. During a traffic stop, if an officer encounters a driver who acts jumpy or paranoid, it may be because he or she is driving a stolen vehicle. *(LE514.7.C.)*

If an officer suspects that a vehicle may be stolen, he or she should check the motor or serial number when the suspect is still in the vehicle. The officer should not allow the suspect to reach into the glove compartment or trunk before he or she has legally searched the vehicle. Likewise, the officer should not allow the suspect to enter a building alone to get documents to prove ownership, stroll away, or drive the vehicle to a garage or gas station.

Vehicles can be identified by the license tag number, engine number, vehicle identification number (VIN), hidden number or component part numbers, or other identifying characteristics. The VIN plate on most domestic and foreign cars is on the driver's side dashboard, and can be easily seen through the windshield.

Information about serialized property that is reported stolen should be promptly provided to dispatch so it can be entered into FCIC/NCIC. This is particularly important with stolen vehicles and firearms. Officers should follow agency policy and procedures for FCIC/NCIC notification. The FCIC/NCIC system, the National Insurance Crime Bureau (NICB), and the Driver and Vehicle Information Database (DAVID) are sources of information regarding stolen vehicles. When an officer recovers a stolen vehicle, he or she should promptly notify dispatch so the recovery can be reported to FCIC/NCIC as well as to the owner of the vehicle. *(LE514.7.D.)*

## Dealing in Stolen Property

Dealing in stolen property, also known as fencing, is a second-degree felony in Florida. If the sale price for property is substantially below the fair market value, either the seller or buyer or both may be guilty of dealing in stolen property. People dealing in stolen property sometimes do so under false names. Section 812.022, F.S., states that

### Section Vocabulary

*petit theft*

*retail theft*

*theft*

presenting false identification in connection with leasing property or failing to return leased property within 72 hours of the termination of the lease agreement, without a reasonable explanation, gives rise to an inference that the property was stolen. *(LE514.7.E.)*

# UNIT 2 | CRIMES AGAINST PROPERTY

## LESSON 8 | White Collar Crimes

**OBJECTIVES**

**LE514.8.A.** Identify the elements of fraud.

**LE514.8.B.** Identify two aspects of forgery.

**LE514.8.C.** Identify elements that constitute a worthless check.

**LE514.8.D.** Define *embezzlement.*

**LE514.8.E.** List types of computer crimes.

## Fraud

Officers may encounter confidence games such as the "pigeon drop," the bank examiner swindle, three card Monte, and shell games. Con artists often use a conversational approach, offering something for nothing, thus appealing to the greed or financial hardship of the target. Often the goal is to get the victim to exhibit his or her money physically. Con artists practicing these types of fraudulent games try to make their deals and leave the area quickly. Obtaining information from the victim and passing it on to other officers as soon as possible is critical. Victims can provide information such as the places frequented during contacts with the con artist, description of vehicle that the con artist used, any names used by the con artist during their conversations, and a complete physical description of the con artist. Similar fraudulent transactions are committed by traveling bands of individuals who prey on elderly people by selling driveway sealants or other home repairs that are not done at all after payment is received, or wash off with the first rain.

Other types of fraud include bank kiting, or floating checks between banks, and insurance and telemarketing fraud, which often target the elderly via the phone, mail, or internet. Phishing uses fake web sites that mirror legitimate business sites in order to obtain personal and financial information from unwitting victims. This information is used to steal the identities, bank accounts, or credit availability from the victims. Bankcards may be fraudulently obtained and used through falsified applications, burglary, theft, or robbery. A dishonest store employee can skim a bankcard or retain a card forgotten by a customer. A thief can also solicit a bankcard number by calling unwitting victims or by retrieving information on hotel room key cards. The primary victim and complainant for most bankcard offenses is the issuing bankcard company. Additional victims may include the store or business where the bankcard was fraudulently used and the person whose name was forged on the bankcard, draft, or receipt. The largest growing sector of bankcard fraud is counterfeit credit cards. *(LE514.8.A.)*

# Forgery

According to Florida Statute §831.01 and §831.02, there are two aspects of forgery: forgery and uttering a false instrument. ***Forgery*** is altering, forging, or counterfeiting a public record, certificate, legal document, bill of exchange or promissory note, etc., with intent to injure or defraud someone. ***Uttering*** is knowingly exhibiting or publishing a document to someone or attempting to cash a check by signifying that the check and the endorsement is real. Uttering a false, forged, or altered record, deed, or other instrument with the intent to injure or defraud someone is a third-degree felony under Florida law. The most common types of forgery law enforcement officers encounter are forgery of the signature or endorsement on a check, use of a fictitious name, forgery by alteration, and check washing.

Officers should follow basic investigative procedures in a forgery case. No marks should be made on the documents and they should not be folded, bent, stapled, or attached with paper clips. Officers should place documents in envelopes or clear plastic bags and photograph or photocopy all documents as soon as possible. *(LE514.8.B.)*

# Passing Worthless Checks

A forged check is one that is signed by an unauthorized individual. A worthless check is signed by the account holder, but written on an account in which there are insufficient funds to pay the amount of the check. A worthless check charge requires proof that a suspect issued a check to a payee for goods or services and the issuer of the check knew there was not sufficient money on deposit in the bank to pay the check. If the payee did not know when the check was issued that there were insufficient funds to pay the check, there is no crime. Each State Attorney's Office has specific guidelines and requirements pertaining to prosecution of worthless check cases. Officers should consult their agency procedures when handling these cases. A worthless check offense is a misdemeanor unless the amount of the check was $150 or more, which makes the crime a third-degree felony. *(LE514.8.C.)*

# Embezzlement

A person who wrongfully takes money or other property entrusted to them for safekeeping and uses it for his or her own personal gain is guilty of ***embezzlement***, a form of theft. Embezzlement is a misdemeanor or felony depending upon the value of the property stolen. Certain professions are conducive to embezzlement, such as bail bondsmen, cashiers, bank tellers, clerks, bookkeepers, real estate brokers, investment advisors, treasurers, financial trustees, lawyers, accountants, and public officials.

Many embezzlers intend only to borrow the money temporarily to help them with personal cash shortage and plan eventually to return it. Others feel unfairly compensated or mistreated by their employers and use embezzlement as a means to compensate. Embezzlers sometimes steal to support drug or gambling habits. *(LE514.8.D.)*

**Section Vocabulary**

*embezzlement*

*forgery*

*uttering*

## Computer Crimes

Computers facilitate all sorts of crimes, and new methods to use this technology to commit crime are being devised constantly. E-mail facilitated crimes include phishing, fraud, cyber-stalking, threats, and harassment. Internet fraud is any type of scheme that uses e-mail, web sites, chat rooms, or message boards to solicit victims, conduct fraudulent transactions, or launder the proceeds of fraud. Some of the ever increasing types of internet fraud include the following:

- internet auction fraud
- non-delivery of merchandise or services
- Nigerian scams
- lottery scams
- bankcard fraud
- identity theft
- email scams
- business fraud (get rich quick schemes)
- investment fraud

Identity theft is the unlawful use of a person's identifying information such as a social security number, date of birth, account numbers, etc. to obtain credit, loans, acquire services, establish or take over accounts and commit crimes in the victim's name.

Prohibited computer transmissions of sexual acts live over a computer online service, internet service, or local bulletin board service is also lewd or lascivious exhibition, if the offender knows or should know or has reason to believe that the transmission is viewed on a computer or television monitor by a victim in Florida who is less than 16 years of age. The fact that an undercover operative or law enforcement officer was involved in the detection and investigation is not a defense to a prosecution under this section.

Sexual predators trade child pornography online and use computers to solicit sexual performances by children and lure them into sexual liaisons. Many pedophiles use chatting and e-mail to coordinate traveling to meet child victims. File sharing, peer-to-peer networks, and malware contribute to 99 percent of child porn being shared. Often there are quantities of CDs near the computer of an online sexual offender. *(LE514.8.E.)*

# UNIT 3 | FOLLOW-UP INVESTIGATIONS

## LESSON 1 | Reviewing Initial Information and Pursuing Leads

**OBJECTIVES**

**LE168.1.** Review all notes and reports on preliminary investigations conducted.

**LE168.3.** Continue inquiries begun during the preliminary investigation.

**LE168.9.** Identify how to determine the value and disposition of leads during a follow-up investigation.

**LE168.5.** Interview new contacts, possible witnesses, and informants.

**LE168.6.** Compile complete notes of all possible leads.

### Initiating a Follow-up Investigation

An investigation is the process of making detailed and systematic inquiries and observations about a criminal complaint. The purposes of an investigation are to recreate what happened during an incident, identify and locate the suspect, and develop enough evidence to establish probable cause to make an arrest. In some agencies, this responsibility is assigned to the investigations section. In other agencies, depending on the severity of the crime, responsibility for follow-up investigations may fall to the primary patrol officer dispatched to the call. Regardless of who completes the follow-up investigation, the tools and skills required to complete the investigation are the same. It is unlikely that a recruit will graduate the academy and immediately receive the assignment of investigator. However, some smaller agencies require patrol officers to become familiar with the investigative process.

The preliminary investigation focuses on establishing whether a criminal act has been committed and, if so, what type. From the preliminary incident report, an officer will be able to recreate the initial investigative steps taken at the crime scene. After reviewing the report, a follow-up investigation can include contacting witnesses, victims, and suspects, and writing a capias request or an arrest affidavit.

The state attorney may require additional information in making a filing decision and can request a follow-up investigation. These requests for additional statements or other evidentiary information rests on the initial officer to respond to and provide.

A follow-up investigation gathers information subsequent to the initial report to establish a case. To initiate a follow-up investigation for a previously reported incident, the officer should locate and review the records of the incident. The list of victims, witnesses, and suspects should be compared with the case information to ensure its accuracy, note listed evidence, and determine what may constitute evidence that has not yet been located. The first steps in a follow-up investigation are establishing a case file, reviewing the information gathered during the preliminary investigation, and identifying and pursuing leads. The officer should locate and interview individuals who may have additional information pertinent to the investigation. The information should be factual, relevant to the investigation, and securely documented according to the officer's agency records system.

In some cases, material an officer receives from the preliminary investigation is incomplete. To initiate a follow-up investigation and compile a complete case file, the officer needs to determine how to obtain the missing documentation within his or her agency. Agencies house original reports in a records section staffed by records custodians or technicians. If an officer finds that he or she is missing a report or document from the preliminary investigation, he or she should contact the agency's records section and obtain a copy. *(LE168.1.)*

As the investigation continues, the officer needs to assemble in the case file newly discovered information, determine its relative value, and immediately document its existence by submitting and attaching supplemental reports. The investigative case file is the repository of all information derived from both the preliminary investigation and the follow-up investigation. Investigative case files should be protected and maintained according to agency policy and procedures.

## Surveillance

Conducting surveillance on a subject can continue the information gathering process begun during the preliminary investigation. There are several ways to perform surveillance on a suspect's location. A spot check is not time intensive and the officer can conduct it without drawing undue attention to his or her presence. The officer should conduct a drive-by at the location, behaving as though this is just a part of a normal driving routine, making only two passes by the location without drawing attention.

The officer should park his or her vehicle some distance away in a location that allows an approach to the area on foot in a covert manner. From a concealed position, the officer should conduct the spot checks or set up a fixed location and maintain it. When involved in surveillance, officers must make sure not to enter into an area in which a person has a reasonable expectation of privacy, such as the curtilage surrounding a residence. *(LE168.3.)*

## Leads

The officer needs to determine the disposition and value of additional leads. The disposition of a lead is whether someone has contacted that lead and whether the information obtained is useful to the investigation. Because leads yielding information in support of probable cause for arrest can reconstruct what happened during an incident, they should be pursued first.

During analysis of case documentation, identification of additional leads may occur, some proving more valuable than others. The officer should continue or initiate new inquiries by identifying other sources for the information needed to support the elements of the crime. Agency policy and procedure determines how far the officer can investigate to prove a case. The officer should know the boundaries of the investigation, as most agencies have limited resources. *(LE168.9.)*

## Canvassing

A ***canvass*** is a door-to-door inquiry of all possible sources of information in a given area. This technique may require additional officers depending on the size of the area. Canvassing an area in proximity to the incident or crime scene may yield additional witnesses and possibly even new victims.

The officer should walk the perimeter of the crime scene to identify places where people may have been able to see or hear what happened, which houses have a clear view of the crime scene, and which houses are within hearing distance. The officer should begin by identifying specific locations that could house people who might have additional information about the incident he or she is investigating and make inquiries at each location. The officer should be prepared to conduct individual interviews by approaching each residence or business in the area and knocking on the door to contact the occupants. He or she should ask the occupant to answer a couple of questions and should be courteous, respectful, and friendly to build rapport and obtain cooperation. The officer needs to tell the occupant that he or she is investigating a crime that occurred at a particular time and in a particular place.

The officer should not reveal the details of the crime—names, seriousness, or how the crime was committed. The officer should ask whether the occupant or any other member of the household or business remembers seeing or hearing anything around the time of the crime and document the occupants' identifying information and their response to the questions. The officer should include specific details about what the occupant heard or witnessed and be sure to thank the occupant for his or her cooperation no matter what information the occupant provides.

The officer needs to exercise caution during the canvass, as he or she may actually knock on the suspect's door! An officer needs to be aware of any animals that may be present and should consider the time of day when approaching the occupant, and, if warranted, apologize for the intrusion. *(LE168.5.)*

The officer should document persons contacted, including full legal names, dates of birth, addresses, and telephone numbers. An address is essential to verify that the witness actually lives at the location where the officer made the contact, and is not just a guest. Without the address and phone numbers, the officer will lose time locating the witness again.

The officer should document what witnesses were able to say about the crime; even if a person participating in a canvass reports knowing nothing about the crime, it will be important if the person later claims to have been a witness. *(LE168.6.)*

**Section Vocabulary**

*canvass*

# UNIT 3 | FOLLOW-UP INVESTIGATIONS

## LESSON 2 | Establishing a Suspect's Identity

**OBJECTIVES**

**LE165.1.** Identify known or possible suspects during a follow-up investigation.

**LE165.3.** Identify any possible leads through places frequented, possible acquaintances, friends, or co-workers, and workplace.

**LE165.2.** Study the background, criminal history, and modus operandi of the suspect.

**LE132.8.** Conduct a live or photo lineup.

### Developing Suspects

The officer needs to concentrate on the "who" part of the investigation and establish a suspect's identity through comparing information, evidence, known offenders, possible leads, and intelligence records. When developing suspects, officers should gather intelligence and information to better understand the "why" and "how" of a crime as well. Investigating officers should look at issues such as opportunity, ability, and motivation to identify known or suspected offenders and the type of crime committed, how serious it was, and what means and methods were used to commit the crime. *(LE165.1.)*

An officer can produce leads by visiting a suspect's workplace and other places that he or she frequents, such as clubs, bars, or gyms. By interviewing acquaintances, friends, and family, the officer may learn the suspect's habits, abilities, and places where a suspect may conceal evidence or hide when being sought. *(LE165.3.)*

Other common methods of identifying criminal suspects include confessions, admissions, witness testimony, circumstantial and physical evidence, informant intelligence, and line-up identification (physical and photo). The Department of Corrections (DOC) lists inmates released or the supervision status of former inmates and provides web-based information on all incarcerated and supervised offenders. Records from other agencies, state and county records, and utility company records are good sources of information.

With few exceptions, public records are available to law enforcement. Private records, such as a company's employment records, employees' medical, dental, or financial records, or the records of any private organization, business, or other type, are not necessarily available. A subpoena is necessary to gain access to these private records.

### Modus Operandi

***Modus operandi***, meaning mode of operating or MO, refers to how someone does something, usually repetitive in nature. People are creatures of habit. If something works one time, they tend to think it should work the next time. This thinking often shows up in criminal activity. The same person or group may well have committed similar crimes that exhibit the same or similar MO. The officer should be able to recognize those similarities as important information to the investigative process.

The officer needs to compare past incidents with the current incident, noting actions or features that are the same. He or she should also compare information regarding unsolved crimes to determine what questions may remain unanswered. Be On the Look Outs

(BOLOs) from various incidents including peculiarities of the crimes, known propensities of suspects, and suspects who tend to commit distinctive or specific types of crimes should be reviewed. When comparing modus operandi, the officer should consider the following:

- Does this appear to be a well-planned incident or one committed on the spur of the moment?
- If entry to a building or vehicle is involved, was it forcible, or was a key or lock pick used?
- Were tools used? If so, what kind?
- If this was a crime against a person, what weapon, if any, was used? What verbal commands were given? What was the physical description of the suspect?
- If theft was involved, what and how much was taken?
- What damage was done, and why? Was it malicious damage done to items the burglar could not take away, careless damage done to things that got in the way, or purposeful damage done to gain access to a door or fence?
- What was the motivation for the crime? Profit, revenge, fun, opportunity, hate?
- Were any other resources used in the crime?
- Were any unexplained items left at the scene?
- Were there eyewitness accounts?

Answers to these questions may show purpose. If the thief needs a saw, he or she will take one, or maybe several—one of each kind. If the thief wants items to sell, he or she will take as much as time and transportation will allow. *(LE165.2.)*

## Live or Photo Lineup

The officer needs to follow agency policy and procedure regarding conducting live and photographic lineups. The State Attorney's Office must be notified before any live lineup is conducted if the suspect has been arrested.

For small agencies, the first step in arranging a lineup is conferring with the State Attorney's Office. Larger agencies usually follow established policies and procedures without involvement with the State Attorney's Office except in unusual circumstances. The difference between a photographic and a live lineup is that a live lineup requires a buffer zone between the victim and the lineup participants and the officer must arrange for a video or still photo record. In a photographic lineup, the officer must find photographs of each participant.

When preparing for a photographic lineup, the officer must get a signed, written statement from each victim or witness who will participate in the lineup, including a description of the suspect, and explain the lineup process to the victim or witness. According to §90.603, F.S., the qualities an individual must possess to be a valid witness in identifying a suspect from a lineup are personal knowledge of the crime (he or she saw the suspect clearly enough to identify the suspect's features). The individual must have the ability to accurately either discuss the matter directly or through an interpreter and clearly understand his or her duty to tell the truth. The witness should demonstrate competence, attentiveness, sound state of mind, and a lack of prejudice, according to §90.403, F.S.

The officer will take a photograph or make a video recording of the lineup before or after each witness views the lineup. The officer will ask each witness to view the lineup and make an identification of the subject. He

**Section Vocabulary**

*modus operandi*

or she will record all comments the victim or witness makes during the lineup procedure and will include those comments in the line-up report. The lineup report then becomes evidence and admissible in court. *(LE132.8.)*

# UNIT 3 | FOLLOW-UP INVESTIGATIONS

## LESSON 3 | Gathering Intelligence on Suspects

**OBJECTIVES**

**LE165.5.** Identify how to check with other agencies and public records to discover information, files, and intelligence on known or possible suspects.

**LE165.4.** Identify how to use field contacts and informants during a follow-up investigation.

### Sources of Information

Information the officer receives as the result of a law enforcement position is for criminal justice purposes only. Misuse can result in disciplinary action against the officer. An officer should obtain information from the following resources on a right to know/need to know basis. Although numerous records are available from many different sources, there are two main types of information. Private records of privately owned businesses or organizations, including privately owned utilities, are not open to the public, including law enforcement, and require court orders to acquire information. Public records of government entities and publicly owned utilities are records that, with few exceptions, may be accessed on demand. Public records from federal, state, county, and city databases can provide additional information regarding the suspect's address, employment information, and other essential facts. Agency policy and procedure dictates which databases are available to an officer and how to access them.

Checking for a driver's license is one of the most common ways of locating an individual. The Florida Department of Highway Safety and Motor Vehicles houses the Florida driver's license database, available to all law enforcement officers.

Computer Aided Dispatch (CAD) is a computerized logging system in which every event reported and every instruction given by dispatch is recorded chronologically by date and time. When checking agency records, the officer needs to identify any known aliases of the suspect.

Records pertaining to juvenile arrests and contacts with law enforcement are restricted from the public by Florida law. The statutes do not restrict access to information by criminal justice agencies. However, there may be limits as to how an officer may use the information, depending on the case. It may be helpful to check with school resource officers to obtain information about juvenile offenders.

## Internet

CJNet is a secure internet site used by the Florida criminal justice community as a pathway to FDLE and other online law enforcement agencies. InSite is a web-based application that runs on CJNet. It automatically updates intelligence to notify officers when someone runs an inquiry on an individual. Agency policy and procedures dictate which databases are available to an officer and how to access them.

## Florida Crime Information Center/National Crime Information Center (FCIC/NCIC)

An officer will often call dispatch to get information quickly about a person or persons involved in an incident, a vehicle or its tag, or various property items. A centralized network of databases called the FCIC provides this and other information. The FCIC resides at the Florida Department of Law Enforcement in Tallahassee. The FCIC's major assets are a computerized information system available 24 hours a day, seven days a week, and statewide information on identities of persons and property. In addition to criminal history records, the FCIC contains files that provide statewide data about driver's licenses, wanted and missing persons, stolen guns, vehicles, and other property, domestic violence injunctions, parole statuses, and registered sexual predators and offenders.

The FCIC also links Florida agencies to the NCIC, a network housed in the United States Department of Justice in Clarksburg, West Virginia. The NCIC is a nationwide computerized information system that services criminal justice agencies in the 50 states, the District of Columbia, the Commonwealth of Puerto Rico, the U.S. Virgin Islands, and Canada. The system includes wanted and/or missing persons information, stolen property information, and criminal history information. This linked system makes Florida's information database available to officers in other states and other states' information available to Florida officers. These networks play a critical role in enabling an officer to gather criminal history or stolen property information and deal appropriately with many incidents.

Another major FCIC feature is that it connects to the National Law Enforcement Telecommunications System (NLETS). A message switching system, NLETS runs a high-speed, nationwide communications network. Located in Phoenix, Arizona, NLETS allows for interstate and interagency information exchange. It supports inquiries into out-of-state motor vehicle data files, Canadian criminal histories, aircraft tracking and registration, agency identification information, and out-of-state weather information.

## Requesting a Records Check through the FCIC

Due to the sensitive nature and sheer volume of information included in the FCIC system, law enforcement must follow basic policies on its use when conducting a records check. To request a records check through

FCIC, an officer must provide certain information, which varies depending on the situation and type of information an officer wants to receive back from the database. When requesting a records check, the officer should provide basic information including wanted/missing person identification check, name, date of birth, race, and sex.

When making a request for a stolen property check, an officer should provide basic information only if recovering stolen property, or to identify suspected stolen property. A description of the property, including make, model, manufacturer's name, year of manufacture, and serial number (if the item has one) should be provided. A vehicle/vessel identification check should be conducted by providing the vehicle tag number, identification number (VIN), registration decal number and year, vessel registration number from side of vessel, hull identification number (HIN), and the title number. The reply will describe the vehicle or vessel and include the owner's name and address.

## Matching Information

If FCIC contains data that is the same as or similar to information an officer requests, a list of possible matches appears on the dispatcher's computer screen. Dispatch may ask additional questions to try to narrow the list and make an exact match. The term for an exact match is a "hit."

The officer should confirm the hit before he or she takes action. The dispatcher or teletype operator will contact the agency that entered the record in FCIC to ensure that the person or property the officer inquires about is identical to the person or property the record identifies. This action will also ensure that the report on the wanted person, missing person, or theft is still outstanding. The FCIC system will flag information regarding the possible extradition of a wanted person, return of a missing person, and return of stolen property to its rightful owner. Some agencies have records sections and dispatchers who make criminal history checks. Patrol officers in some smaller departments receive training and certification to perform this work.

## Driver and Vehicle Information Database (DAVID)

In October 2002, the Department of Highway Safety and Motor Vehicles implemented and subsequently enhanced in March 2003 a web-based online inquiry program called DAVID. Users from law enforcement, the judicial system, and various state agencies with statutory authority use DAVID to view driver images and signatures, applications, driving history and vehicle history for motorists, identification documents used by non-citizens, and can also request a driver license re-exam or medical review for a specific driver. DAVID is the first of its kind, providing all information about a motorist (driver/vehicle owner) from one program. Florida Highway Patrol (FHP), in partnership with the Florida Department of Law Enforcement (FDLE), provides DAVID to authorized users via the criminal justice network for enforcement and investigative purposes only.

## FALCON

FALCON, Florida's new Integrated Criminal History System, is a state-of-the-art search/report system that more effectively cross-matches fingerprints and criminal histories; includes photographs (faces, tattoos); searches national and other criminal justice databases; and allows instantaneous updating of criminal justice information systems. FALCON's fast, comprehensive, well-formatted reports offer many benefits to law enforcement, government, and anyone who depends on fast and accurate access to criminal justice information.

## Department of Highway Safety and Motor Vehicles (DHSMV)

This database contains records of vehicles or boats registered in Florida and driver license information. Insurance information is also available through this system. The DHSMV manually processes driver history, which is available during regular business hours. When an officer inquires about a vehicle or vessel registration, DHSMV also checks the FCIC/NCIC database for stolen vehicles or vessels. *(LE165.5.)*

## Field Contacts

Field contacts are a common source of information. A ***field contact*** is any person with whom an officer has contact while on patrol, such as concerned citizens, anonymous callers, confidential informants, and other law enforcement officers. Field contacts are often instrumental in solving a case. When evaluating the statement of a field contact, the officer should consider who the contact is, and what his or her relationship to the victim or suspect may be. A person with an agenda may not always be a good source of accurate information; however, such a person may provide names or other leads worth following.

Individuals who live in homeless camps might provide information as to the identity and whereabouts of a suspect. However, people who work or volunteer for organizations that run homeless shelters are often more reliable sources of information about an individual's location than homeless camps.

Witness information can be helpful; however, the officer needs to evaluate the information carefully. The officer should not depend on an observer for accuracy of details, particularly if time has passed since the incident. Although most people honestly try to help if asked, some witnesses have agendas of their own. A suspect the witness knows may be a friend the witness wants to protect. On the other hand, the suspect may be someone the witness does not like. The witness might like to see the suspect in trouble. Personal attitudes may color witnesses' statements.

## Informants

The use of informants can help the officer complete an investigation and solve a crime. ***Informants*** are persons who furnish police with information about crimes, either from a sense of civic duty or in the expectation of some personal benefit or advantage. Excluded from this category are victims of a crime who openly report a crime to the police. Such persons are complainants rather than informants.

People who may provide information include victims, witnesses, suspects, other police officers, and people with occupations close to the public. Types of informants include mercenary, rival, plea-bargaining, anonymous, self-aggrandizing, false, and fearful. Motivational factors, which may cause an individual to be an informant, include vanity, civic-mindedness, fear, repentance, avoidance of punishment, gratitude, competition, revenge, jealousy, and monetary or other material gain. An officer needs to avoid using entrapment, which can occur when he or she induces or causes a suspect to commit a crime so that the officer may then make an arrest of the suspect.

Rules regarding the treatment of informants include treating them considerately. Officers should follow agency rules concerning confidential informants, especially with regards to Rachel's Law. Officers must be careful about making any promises to informants and must fulfill any ethical promises made and not allow the informant to take charge of any phase of the investigation. In a relationship with an informant, the officer should not compromise his or her law enforcement position, should tell the informant what the officer will,

**Section Vocabulary**

*field contact*

*informant*

and will not do, and what to expect of him or her. The officer must make it very clear that he or she will not condone certain actions that would jeopardize the officer's position. Never accept unauthorized favors or gifts from informants that could provide a basis for blackmail. No informant is important enough to sacrifice an officer's job, reputation, or freedom. An officer should periodically review and evaluate information an informant provides, use reliable information to solve crimes, and always be on the lookout for information that proves to be incorrect.

The officer should follow agency policies and procedures related to the recruitment, control, and use of confidential informants. This includes preserving the safety of the confidential informant, law enforcement, the target, and the public. *(LE165.4.)*

# UNIT 4 | COURT PROCEDURES

## LESSON 1 | Court Procedures

**OBJECTIVES**

**LE365.7.** Comply with department policy regarding the Read or Waive Option after a deposition.

**LE366.1.** Review case notes, reports, photographs, and evidence prior to giving testimony.

**LE366.3.** Discuss the case with appropriate agency personnel and the state attorney in preparation for giving testimony.

**LE366.4.** Check in with prosecutors upon arrival at court and follow instructions.

### First Appearance Hearing

If an arrested suspect is not released from custody by posting bail, he or she must have a hearing before a judge. According to Florida law, the first appearance hearing must occur within 24 hours of arrest. At the first appearance hearing, the judge appoints counsel if the defendant is qualified and desires it. The judge reviews the probable cause affidavit and other information to decide if probable cause exists that the defendant committed the alleged offense. Establishing probable cause is necessary to continue the criminal proceedings. The hearing allows the judge to ask questions to define or address issues, which may not be clear in the affidavit. Usually, a prosecutor is present, and an appointed public defender may attend the hearing.

Officers usually do not need to attend a first appearance hearing. The officer should plan to attend the first appearance hearing only when the state attorney requests his or her appearance and agency policy and procedure permits attendance. The officer should plan to attend when there is a need to clarify or supplement the affidavit or when the officer has information that was not included in the arrest affidavit. Officers may provide any relevant oral testimony that they believe the judge needs to determine if probable cause exists. An officer's agency may allow him or her to attend to ensure the sufficiency of the arrest affidavit. The law allows the judge to determine probable cause initially based on the arrest affidavit the court receives.

The rules of evidence in a first appearance hearing are more relaxed, as opposed to those in a trial to determine guilt or innocence. For example, under the provisions of the Hearsay Rule, in the Evidence Code, Florida Statute §90.802, hearsay is generally not admissible as evidence at a hearing or trial. However, hearsay is admissible at first appearance hearings in determinations of probable cause and bond. The first appearance hearing is not adversarial. Neither the suspect nor the defense attorney may defend the suspect's position or question an officer as a witness. The suspect may exercise the right to defend his or her position later in the court process, usually through pretrial motions to suppress evidence or dismiss the case.

**LE365.6.** Answer each question clearly, completely, and truthfully without volunteering any statement that is not requested.

**LE365.5.** Define "off the record."

**LE366.6.** Identify procedures to follow when the rule of sequestration has been invoked.

**LE366.8.** Identify procedures to follow when providing testimony during a court proceeding.

## Bond and Suppression Hearings

At a first appearance hearing, there may be discussion regarding bond and special conditions of release. A bond hearing can take place prior to a first appearance hearing through pretrial release, during the first appearance hearing, or at a later time. If an officer is familiar with the suspect's history, the officer could influence the judge's decision regarding release by noting concerns on the arrest affidavit or by attending the first appearance hearing. A suppression hearing occurs after the defense, alleging that an officer's improper actions violated their client's rights, files a motion to suppress, or to exclude certain testimony or evidence from trial. This hearing usually occurs before the trial but may occur during it.

## Deposition

Before trial, an officer may receive a subpoena or notice to give a deposition. A ***deposition*** is an official court proceeding in which sworn testimony regarding the facts of the case is provided to one of the attorneys (defense or prosecutor) prior to trial. It is the attorney's chance to assess the case further and document the officer's verbal testimony before a trial or hearing.

An attorney from the State Attorney's Office may be present during the deposition; a judge will not. At a deposition, the attorney asks questions about the case. Responses are recorded and later transcribed and printed. Later, during a criminal trial, the defense can discredit the officer if his or her testimony changes or provides information that differs from the deposition statement. The defense attorney can also plan a defense against any testimony provided that is detrimental to his or her client.

The defense attorney is supposed to ask only questions that are reasonably relevant and material to the case. Section 914.15, F.S., gives law enforcement officers the legal right not to answer personal questions about their spouses, children, residential address, phone number, or any information not related to the case, unless directed by a judge. If asked an improper question, the officer may answer, "Please certify the question." This requires the attorney to present the question to a judge who may decide to order an answer to the question. Often, attorneys will not seek an order for an improper question.

When the deposition ends, the attorney will ask if the officer wishes to read the transcribed or typed deposition or waive the review. It is not advisable to waive the review. Although the officer cannot demand changes, he or she can point out and notify the state and defense attorneys of errors or misstatements. By reviewing and signing a copy of the deposition, the officer has an additional opportunity to refresh his or her memory before testifying at a hearing or trial. *(LE365.7.)*

## Pretrial Meeting

In some circuits, a state attorney will request a pretrial meeting with the arresting officer. Notification may be by telephone or subpoena. Before the meeting, the officer should thoroughly review all the available case documentation, including locating and reading case notes, investigative and violation reports, the victim, witness, and suspect statements, and any supplemental reports such as FCIC/NCIC reports on victims, witnesses, and suspects. Officers should review photographs and other physical evidence as well as case file information from related cases. The officer may discuss the case with appropriate agency personnel, for example, his or her supervisor, watch commander, or crime scene and evidence personnel. The purpose of the pretrial meeting is to give the state attorney an opportunity to clarify facts of the case and deal with any inconsistencies. For example, it is important to know who administered the *Miranda* warning. An officer might be embarrassed to learn in court that every involved officer thought another officer administered the *Miranda* warning, and no one actually did.

The officer should be prepared to discuss the who, what, where, when, how, and why facts of the case, all evidence, and any other information relevant to his or her involvement in and prosecution of the case. The state attorney will ask the officer to relate relevant details and major facts of the case, including the elements of the crime; witness, victim, and suspect statements; information including criminal history (local records, FCIC/NCIC) and past offenses (reported and unreported); information in the offense report and supplemental reports; information in other agency documents such as internal affairs reports, use of force reports, and use of canine reports; if appropriate, type and location of physical evidence; past experience with or knowledge of the defense counsel; and past experience with or knowledge of any witnesses, the victim, or the defendant.

The state attorney must know or have access to everything that the officer knows about the case. If not, the court may suppress evidence and impose sanctions. Officers must be familiar with all issues that could affect successful prosecution. For example, the state attorney may discuss the admissibility of evidence. Chapter 90, F.S. specifically identifies what constitutes ***admissible evidence***. This includes oral testimony. Florida Statute defines admissible evidence as relevant evidence tending to prove or disprove a material fact, with numerous exceptions specified.

The state attorney will also want to know if the officer properly maintained the physical evidence through a legally defensible chain of custody and required documentation. The prosecutor may ask how the evidence pertains to the case, who discovered and collected the evidence, and how the chain of custody was maintained. An officer should identify evidence that supports or does not support facts presented in the arrest affidavit and never enhance facts or manufacture evidence for missing elements of the crime.

The best way to minimize damage is to identify potential weaknesses in the case. To help the prosecutor effectively deal with known problems, the officer should point out his or her errors or those of another officer, any conflicting statements, or problems in documentation of evidence. An officer should leave the pretrial conference confident that he or she has fully informed the state attorney and done his or her best job to help the attorney prepare for trial. Officers have a continuing obligation to keep the prosecutor informed of any developments in the case.

The officer should also know the case well enough to identify its special issues. Special situations may require the officer or the state attorney to make special arrangements. For example, non-English speakers require an interpreter. Some child witnesses require special arrangements, and people with disabilities may need special travel and building accommodations.

## Trial

A trial is the examination of facts and related law presided over by a judge or other magistrate, who has the authority or jurisdiction to hear the matter. It begins with the calling of the parties to be heard, or the selection of a jury. A statement of charges against the defendant is read. Each party is entitled to an opening statement. The prosecution presents the case, followed by the presentation of evidence. The defendant can present a case, followed by a possible rebuttal of evidence, and finish with a final statement. If it is a jury trial, the jury will receive instructions and decide the verdict. If there is no jury, the judge will render judgment.

## Sentencing Hearing

The State Attorney's Office may request that an officer attend a sentencing hearing. At this sentencing hearing, both the defense and the prosecution have an opportunity to present evidence and testimony to recommend an appropriate sentence to the judge. The officer's role is to provide the court a complete picture of the defendant's actions, and the impact on the victim and society.

## Preparing for Testimony

To prepare for a court proceeding, such as a deposition, hearing, or trial, an officer should focus on reports that he or she created and professional activity related to the case. If the role of the officer is the primary officer or investigator, he or she should construct a broad review of all reports, evidence, and information used towards making the decision to arrest and in support of the prosecution. The officer should obtain copies of all case reports for the court proceeding from the records section or bureau or from designated personnel in his or her agency. The officer should review the case file, including all supplemental reports and information on the evidence and chain of custody, and be prepared to answer questions on all relevant facts. *(LE366.1.)*

The officer should discuss the case with the State Attorney's Office to identify and understand areas of weakness relevant to testimony and to clarify any concerns the state attorney may have. The officer should also identify witness information from offense reports, supplemental reports, and statement forms and give it to the State Attorney's Office. Officers can thoroughly prepare for questioning by reviewing the reports or case notes. They should be ready to testify from memory, only using reports for specific details after requesting permission to refer to them. Case documentation can be used to identify correct and credible answers. Officers should also assume that the defense counsel knows everything the officer knows. With full preparation, an officer can meet his or her legal and ethical obligations to give the material facts about a case as the state attorney or defense attorney begins the line of questioning. *(LE366.3.)*

## Giving Testimony

Giving testimony may take place in an attorney's office, in the judge's chambers, or on the witness stand. To provide effective testimony, an officer should follow some general guidelines. If the officer is to appear at a trial or hearing before or after a shift, he or she should look professional, not overdressed, or wearing expensive clothing or excessive jewelry. An officer should remove objects, such as keys and loose change, from his or her person that may cause distractions and turn off beepers, radios, and cellular phones. It is necessary to follow agency policy and procedure regarding appropriate dress for a court appearance. How an officer prepares and presents him- or herself can affect the success of testimony given at a deposition, hearing, or trial.

Checking in with the prosecuting attorney, and following the attorney's instructions gives the officer and the state attorney time to address last-minute concerns. A state attorney usually has a large docket of cases and goes from one case to another every day. He or she may ask the officer to go over relevant details and major facts one more time. Officers should never take a case lightly but always prepare the same way, reviewing case documentation, discussing the case with the state attorney, and following the guidelines for giving effective testimony. *(LE366.4.)*

Before testifying, an officer will take an oath or make an affirmation that the testimony he or she is going to give is the truth. The method is generally the same regardless of where the testimony is given or who administers the oath or affirmation to the officer. Typically, the clerk of the court, a court reporter, the judge, or other designated court personnel will ask the officer to raise his or her right hand and then ask the officer, "Do you swear or affirm to tell the truth and nothing but the truth?" The officer should firmly but not dramatically answer, "I do" while standing or sitting straight and looking at and listening attentively to the person administering the oath. The officer is now sworn to testify truthfully.

The officer should look directly at the judge and listen carefully to the questions asked. When an attorney or judge asks questions, the officer should pause before answering to collect his or her thoughts, make sure the question is understood, and answer accurately, clearly, and completely. If necessary, officers can say they do not understand a question or ask for a question to be clarified or repeated. Officers should never volunteer unsolicited information, only answer the questions asked, and they should never answer with a guess. It is acceptable to say "I don't know," when necessary. The judge may permit an officer to explain why he or she does not know. It is also necessary to resist the urge to fill silence with non-responsive testimony. *(LE365.6.)*

Officers should avoid suggestions or peer pressure to enhance testimony to strengthen a case because officers are subject to perjury laws and may give testimony that contradicts that of another officer. Since a court reporter is documenting what is said, the court can use early testimony to impeach an officer later in the court process. Testifying truthfully and accurately keeps testimony consistent, makes it effective and credible, and keeps officers out of trouble.

The appearance of prejudice destroys credibility, so officers must avoid showing biases and prejudices. They should always use plain, professional terminology, not slang or police jargon. For example, they should not describe an urban community as "the ghetto" or call a government-assisted neighborhood "the projects." It is important to avoid derogatory statements, sarcasm, witty comments, or ridicule, all of which are unprofessional. Officers should, however, be expressive and avoid speaking in monotone, while narrating incidents in chronological order. Use of military time is appropriate, but officers should be prepared to convert times to A.M. or P.M.

It is important for officers to always use good posture, be attentive, and place their hands on their knees or the arms of the chair and never over their mouth. Officers need to convey confidence, not arrogance, or evasion, and avoid fidgeting or showing others signs of nervousness. They should be courteous and use proper titles such as "your Honor," "ma'am," and "sir." They should face the judge while responding to his or her questions and face the jury when responding to the prosecutor or defense counsel. In addition, officers should never address or refer to the defense counsel as a public defender. Doing so can cause a mistrial since it may make the jury and judge aware that the defendant cannot afford other representation.

Just as with a deposition, lawyers may occasionally ask improper questions. Officers may respond to the attorney by asking him or her to certify the question. Officers should maintain the same demeanor for the defense attorney and the state attorney, not change their attitude when responding to opposing counsel's questions just because counsel is an opponent. Occasionally, challenging an officer's credibility is the opposing counsel's job and is usually not personal.

If an officer or his or her close relative experienced abuse, the officer may feel a need to ensure the "proper" prosecution of all abusers. However, it is necessary to avoid allowing personal experiences and beliefs affect the ability to be fair and objective. This principle also applies to cultural, ethnic, and gender issues. Officers should also avoid displaying extraordinary interest in the case. Instead, they should display interest of a professional nature, not a personal one.

The court may record the testimony. All answers to relevant questions are for the record. Do not answer questions "off the record," except at a deposition when requested. ***"Off the record"*** refers to information not recorded in an official document. The officer's job is to provide accurate and complete testimony of the available facts, not steer the case. *(LE365.5.)*

When applicable, a judge might forbid all witnesses from discussing any aspect of a case with anyone but the involved attorneys. Section 90.616, F.S., addresses the ***rule of sequestration***, which states that an officer must follow the judges' orders completely when the rule has been invoked. The officer must not be in the courtroom when other witnesses are giving testimony. Violating the rule of sequestration may mean the judge will penalize or punish the witness. The testimony of the witness could also be stricken from the trial record with the judge instructing the jury to disregard it. The judge could even declare a mistrial. Whether or not the judge invokes the rule, the officer must never communicate with a juror or known potential juror except as directed by the court. If a possible violation of the rule is observed, it should be reported immediately to the courtroom bailiff or presiding judge. *(LE366.6.)*

## Objectionable Questions

Once someone makes an objection, the judge will either sustain or overrule it. Upon hearing an objection, an officer must stop speaking until the judge rules. If the judge sustains the objection, the witness may not answer the question. If the objection is overruled, the witness must answer the question.

There are several types of objectionable questions. One type calls for someone to make a conclusion. Answering this type of question requires officers to make a decision on an issue, which is the job of the jury or judge. (Example: "Based on your knowledge of the facts of this incident, would you say that Mr. and Mrs. Hernandez are just a violent couple?") Irrelevant questions prompt officers to give answers that have no direct relation to or bearing on the facts. (Example: "Officer, are you married?") Some questions go beyond the proper scope of questioning, have nothing to do with the case, and go beyond basic testimony and issues during testimony before cross-examination. (Example: "Do you arrest more men than women?")

## Cross-Examination Tactics

Attorneys may use a variety of tactics during a criminal trial to discredit, misrepresent, or confuse the officer giving testimony. However, officers can be aware of this and go into court with basic techniques to overcome those tactics.

A defense counsel may use condescension to try to give the impression that an officer is inept, unreliable, or lacking confidence.

> **Question:** "You mean to tell this court and jury you have made only one prior arrest. Is it true you had been a sworn officer for only three months when you arrested Mr. Hernandez?"
>
> **Technique:** Convey professionalism, knowledge, and confidence and give firm, decisive answers. If necessary, the state attorney will ask appropriate follow-up questions.

A defense counsel may be belligerent or badger an officer in order to cause him or her to become angry, which can affect logic and calmness and reveal the officer's temperament.

> **Question:** "I have asked this question three different times in three different ways. What do you not understand?"
>
> **Technique:** Officers should pause, stay calm, remember the defense counsel's motive, and speak deliberately.

A defense counsel may fire questions at an officer in quick succession, giving him or her no time to think about or answer the question properly. The attorney hopes to confuse the officer into giving inconsistent answers.

> **Question:** "Did you actually see Mr. Hernandez hit his wife? How do you know what really happened? Where was Mrs. Hernandez in relation to Mr. Hernandez when you first arrived?"
>
> **Technique:** The officer should ask the attorney to repeat the questions one at a time and take time to consider each question one question at a time, while speaking deliberately and remaining calm.

To get as much information as possible and to lull officers into a false sense of security, a defense counsel may try to build rapport to create answers that favor the defense. The defense attorney may also try to lead officers to state that they are experts when that is not the case.

> **Question:** "I did not realize you knew so much about domestic violence. Do you consider yourself an expert on the subject? You should!"
>
> **Technique:** It is necessary to stay alert and control the ego, focus on the facts of the case, and not let the attorney's statements become confusing or distracting.

By mispronouncing an officer's name, forgetting his or her title, or verbally demoting the officer, the opposing attorney implies that the officer is of little consequence. The attorney wants the officer to lose concentration and focus on the error, not the question.

> **Technique:** The first time opposing counsel uses the wrong name, title, or rank, politely correct him or her. If the counsel persists, an officer must ignore the behavior and focus on the question.

The opposing attorney may draw a conclusion, make an assumption, or suggest a response and then ask an officer if the conclusion, assumption, or response is the officer's answer. The goal is to confuse or mislead the officer.

**Question:** "Your entire testimony here today actually points to Mrs. Hernandez as the aggressor, correct?"

**Technique:** Officers should correct factual inaccuracies and avoid allowing the attorney to lead them to incorrect conclusions. By concentrating carefully on the facts and answering the question accurately without expressing opinions, the defense attorney cannot succeed in baiting officers.

Demanding a "yes" or "no" answer to a question that needs explanation prevents the judge or jury from considering pertinent facts and mitigating details.

**Question:** "Did you see the gun in the defendant's hand or not? Yes or no?"

**Technique:** Qualify your answer by saying that you cannot answer, "yes" or "no," then give the facts and details such as saying "I cannot tell you yes or no. All I can tell you is that I saw a small shiny object in the defendant's left hand."

The defense attorney may reverse or rephrase an officer's words to confuse him or her and show the jury that the officer lacks confidence in his or her own statement.

**Question:** "Where did you see them in relation to the car?"

Officer: "They stood toward the front."

**Question:** "So they were standing at the front bumper?"

Officer: "They stood between the tire and front door."

**Question:** "But you just told us they were near the front of the car, right?"

**Technique:** It is necessary to pay attention to what the counsel asks, pause, and avoid agreeing to misstatements. Officers should always listen intently whenever counsel repeats an answer, remember what he or she said, and correct any error counsel made in restating the answer.

A defense attorney may repeat and rephrase questions, hoping officers will give inconsistent or conflicting answers.

**Question:** "Was the defendant riding a green or red bicycle?"

Officer: "It was blue."

**Question:** "Was she riding in the dark?"

Officer: "Yes."

**Question:** "Could it have been green, blue-green, or black?"

Officer: "I already answered that question. It was blue."

**Technique:** Officers should listen carefully to questions and say they have already answered a question if that is the case.

To show inconsistency in the investigation, defense attorneys may compare conflicting answers.

**Question:** "Did you smell alcohol on the defendant's breath?"

Officer: "No, sir."

**Section Vocabulary**

*admissible evidence*

*deposition*

*off the record*

*rule of sequestration*

**Question:** "Have you read the other officer's report on this case?"

Officer: "Yes, I have."

**Question:** "Did you notice that the other report says the defendant reeked of alcohol?"

Officer: "Yes, sir."

Attorney: "Then one of you must be lying, right?"

**Technique:** Officers should remain calm and guard their answers. If they do not have exact information, they should refer to their notes, if permitted, and stay away from absolutes if uncertain.

Some attorneys stare at officers as if they expect them to volunteer more information.

**Technique:** An officer should let the attorney know he or she is finished answering by waiting for the next question. *(LE366.8.)*

# CHAPTER 9

## Traffic Stops



An officer's primary responsibility in making traffic stops is to help increase voluntary compliance with traffic laws and improve driver judgment. The end result of traffic stops should be public education and safer roads.

# UNIT 1 | TRAFFIC LAW

## LESSON 1 | Traffic Law

### OBJECTIVES

**LE092.3.A.** Define a *traffic stop* according to Florida Legal Guidelines.

**LE026.1.C.** Identify important benefits of traffic enforcement.

**LE026.1.A.2.** Identify that F.S. §316 contains criminal and noncriminal traffic violations.

**LE026.1.A.1.** Identify the most common traffic violations.

**LE012.10.** Identify the need to submit the confiscated driver's license to the appropriate driver license office.

**LE012.4.B.3.** Identify the format of the Florida Driver License.

**LE012.4.B.1.** Identify important components of the Florida Driver License.

**LE012.4.B.2.** Identify important components of Florida Vehicle License Plates.

Motor vehicle or traffic stops are among the most frequent activities law enforcement officers perform. According to the Florida Legal Guidelines, a ***traffic stop*** is the lawful, temporary detention of an individual in a vehicle by a law enforcement officer for an investigative purpose *(LE092.3.A.)*. Through traffic enforcement, officers can deter or detect unlawful acts or events requiring law enforcement action. Examples include the following:

- car theft and carjacking
- wanted persons and escaped prisoners
- drivers with suspended licenses
- abused, kidnapped, and runaway children
- illegal weapons
- drug use or trafficking
- minors in possession of alcohol
- impaired drivers under the influence of alcohol or chemical or controlled substances
- criminals fleeing crime scenes
- uninsured motorists *(LE026.1.C.)*

## Traffic Laws

Florida's Uniform Disposition of Traffic Infractions Act (F.S. §318.14) decriminalizes most traffic violations. Some violations are still treated as criminal acts; fleeing or attempting to elude a police officer (F.S. §316.1935); leaving the scene of a crash (F.S. §316.027, §316.061); driving under the influence (F.S. §316.193); reckless driving (F.S. §316.192); making false crash reports (F.S. §316.067); willfully failing or refusing to comply with any lawful order or direction of a police officer or member of a fire department (F.S. §316.072(3)); obstructing an officer attempting to enforce vehicle weight limits (F.S. §316.545(1)); and obstructing traffic for purposes of solicitation (F.S. §316.2045(2)). There are obviously other traffic-related criminal offenses, such as vehicular homicide. These are not violations of F.S. Chapter 316 but violations of other statutes.

All other violations of the F.S. Chapter 316 are deemed infractions, which are noncriminal violations that may be punished by fines, costs, driving school, and community service hours but not by incarceration. Because a traffic-infraction violator may not be jailed, he or she has no right to a trial by jury or court-appointed lawyer.

An infraction can be either a moving or non-moving violation, depending on the statutory definition of the infraction. A criminal violation will be either a misdemeanor or felony. Because a moving violation could result in a crash or injury, a violator pays a higher fine and may have points assessed against his or her driver's license. A non-moving violation does not usually cause a crash or injury, so the fines are reduced. Non-moving violators do not have points assessed against their licenses. Unlawful speed (F.S. §316.183(3)), for example, is a moving violation but having an illegally noisy exhaust system (F.S. §316.272) is a non-moving violation. Other examples of common moving and non-moving violations are listed below. *(LE026.1.A.2.)*

Florida law enforcement officers should be familiar with the traffic laws found in Florida Statute Chapters 316 (Uniform Traffic Control Law), 320 (Motor Vehicle Licenses and Registration) and 322 (Driver's Licenses).

## Examples of Common Traffic Violations within Florida Statutes

### Moving Violations

| | |
|---|---|
| **F.S. §316.074** | Obedience to and required traffic control devices. |
| **F.S. §316.075** | Traffic control signal devices. |
| **F.S. §316.1925** | Careless driving. |
| **F.S. §316.126** | Operation of vehicles and actions of pedestrians on approach of authorized emergency vehicle. |
| **F.S. §316.121** | Vehicles approaching or entering intersections. |
| **F.S. §316.122** | Vehicle turning left. |
| **F.S. §316.183** | Unlawful speed. |
| **F.S. §316.123** | Vehicle entering stop or yield intersection. |
| **F.S. §316.1936** | Possession of open container of alcoholic beverages in vehicles prohibited; penalties. |
| **F.S. §316.613** | Child restraint requirements. |
| **F.S. §316.172** | Traffic to stop for school bus. |
| **F.S. §316.217** | When lighted lamps are required. |

### Non-Moving Violations

| | |
|---|---|
| **F.S. §316.221** | Tail lamps. |
| **F.S. §316.610** | Safety of vehicle. |
| **F.S. §320.07(3)a** | Expiration of registration. |
| **F.S. §316.605** | Licensing of vehicles. |
| **F.S. §316.614** | Safety belt usage. |
| **F.S. §320.131** | Temporary tags. |
| **F.S. §316.224(3)** | Color of clearance lamps, identification lamps, side marker lamps, backup lamps, reflectors, and deceleration lights. |

| | |
|---|---|
| **F.S. §316.2065** | Bicycle regulations. |
| **F.S. §316.1945** | Stopping, standing, or parking prohibited in specified places. |
| **F.S. 316.646(1)** | Security required; proof of security and display thereof; dismissal of cases. |

### *Criminal Traffic Violations*

| | |
|---|---|
| **F.S. §316.193** | Driving under the influence; penalties. |
| **F.S. §322.03** | Drivers must be licensed; penalties. |
| **F.S. §322.16** | License restrictions. |
| **F.S. §322.34(2)(5)** | Driving while license suspended, revoked, canceled, or disqualified. |
| **F.S. §322.32** | Unlawful use of license. |
| **F.S. §316.061** | Crash involving damage to vehicle or property. |
| **F.S. §316.027** | Crash involving death or personal injury. |
| **F.S. §316.192** | Reckless driving. *(LE026.1.A.1.)* |

# The Florida Driver License

According to F.S. §322.15, all persons driving in Florida must possess a valid driver's license from Florida, another state, or entity approved by the state of Florida or the U.S. Government and show it upon demand of a law enforcement officer or authorized representative of the ***Department of Highway Safety and Motor Vehicles (DHSMV)*** (the agency responsible for issuing driver licenses, motor vehicle titles, license plates and vessel registrations as well as overseeing the Florida Highway Patrol). The license may not be faded, altered, mutilated, or defaced. It is unlawful to drive in Florida with a suspended, revoked, cancelled, or disqualified license. The charge may be a moving violation, misdemeanor, or felony depending on the circumstances that exist as per §322.34, F.S. If the driver's license is confiscated due to suspension, mutilation, or revoked or altered data, the officer should attach it to the citation and submit it to the Department of Highway Safety and Motor Vehicles or place it into property as evidence. *(LE012.10.)*

## *Current Formatting*

There are four current versions of the ***Florida Driver License***, which is the license issued to state of Florida residents who pass the DHSMV tests granting them the privilege to drive in Florida. The Florida Driver License includes several different classes. Card types and license classes are identified by color headers:

- **yellow**—Class E Learner's License
- **green**—Class D and E Licenses
- **blue**—Commercial Driver License (CDL)—Classes A, B, and C
- **red (pink)**—Identification Card

In addition, the current version of "Over 21" licenses are formatted horizontally while "Under 21" licenses are vertical. An officer will need to more closely inspect older formats to obtain required information including the expiration date. *(LE012.4.B.3.)*

## *Endorsements/Restrictions/Informational Alerts*

A license ***endorsement*** is a special authorization printed on a Florida Driver License permitting a driver to drive certain types of vehicles or to transport certain types of property or number of passengers. Examples of endorsements include authorization to drive motorcycles, school buses, or combination vehicles with double or triple trailers.

A ***restriction***, printed on a Florida Driver License, may limit a driver from operating certain types of motor vehicles or require that he or she meet certain conditions when driving any motor vehicle. For example, someone who needs corrective lenses may be restricted from driving without them. Another person who is deaf may be required to wear hearing aids when driving. Other restrictions may pertain to equipment required on the vehicle, such as hand controls for a driver who does not have full use of his or her legs.

A Florida Driver License may also include ***informational alerts*** that signal an officer about a person's health condition or public safety status. For example, a diabetic person's license may display "insulin dependant" in red print. If an officer encounters a person who appears to be impaired or in medical distress, he or she must call Emergency Medical Services immediately.

Two other alerts, "§775.21, F.S." for sexual predators and "§943.0435, F.S." for sexual offenders, are displayed in the right hand corner in black. Officers seeing this alert should conduct a field interview and fill out appropriate paperwork as required by agency policy.

Required restrictions and endorsements will be listed on the front of the license. Explanations of the restrictions and endorsements are found on the back of the license. For drivers authorized to operate a motorcycle, the following endorsement will appear on the front of the driver license under the expiration date: **MOTORCYCLE ALSO** or **MOTORCYCLE ONLY.**

## *Classes of Florida Driver Licenses*

Another component of licenses is the notation of the class on the back of the license.

**CLASS A:** required for drivers of trucks or truck combinations with a Gross Vehicle Weight Rating (GVWR) of 26,001 lbs. or more, provided the towed vehicle is more than 10,000 lbs.

**CLASS B:** required for drivers of straight trucks with a Gross Vehicle Weight Rating of 26,001 lbs. or more.

**CLASS C:** required for drivers of vehicles transporting hazardous materials in sufficient amounts to require placards or vehicles designed to transport more than 15 persons (including the driver), and with a Gross Vehicle Weight Rating of less than 26,001 lbs.

**CLASS E:** required for drivers of any non-commercial motor vehicle with a Gross Vehicle Weight Rating less than 26,001 pounds, including passenger cars, 15-passenger

Current version of "Over 21" *Figure 9-1*

Current version of "Under 21" *Figure 9-2*

Valid through year 2015 *Figure 9-3*

Valid through year 2011 *Figure 9-4*

**Section Vocabulary**

*Department of Highway Safety and Motor Vehicles (DHSMV)*

*endorsement*

*Florida Driver's License*

*informational alerts*

*querying (entering, running, vehicle check, records check, wants, warrants check)*

*restriction*

*traffic stop*

(including the driver) vans, trucks or recreational vehicles, and two- or three-wheel motor vehicles 50 cc or less, such as mopeds or small scooters. Farmers and drivers of authorized emergency vehicles who are exempt from obtaining a commercial driver license must obtain a Class E license.

**CLASS E-Learner:** A driver with a Class E Learner license is limited to driving motor vehicles weighing less than 8,000 pounds. In addition, such a driver must be accompanied by a licensed driver 21 years of age or older who occupies the closest seat right of the driver, and the learner may initially drive only between the hours of 6 A.M. and 7 P.M. Three months after issuance of the learner license, the driver may drive from 6 A.M. to 10 P.M. A driver with a learner license may not operate a motorcycle without a motorcycle endorsement. *(LE012.4.B.1.)*

# Florida Vehicle License Plates and Tags

Florida's Department of Highway Safety and Motor Vehicles issues standard and specialized vehicle tags. While the majority of specialized tags are "vanity" plates displaying the owner's nickname or commemorating a college, sports team, or cause, some have specific uses and restrictions. For example, some tags are limited to commercial or government vehicles, while others are assigned based on the owner's status, e.g., state legislator or firefighter. Officers should be familiar with the uses and restrictions of such tags and make sure their use is authorized. In addition, there are specialized tags that require reporting additional prefix characters or descriptions not preprinted on the tag.

When dealing with people, articles, vehicles, licenses/IDs, the following terms, ***querying***, ***entering***, ***running***, ***vehicle check***, ***records check***, ***wants*** and ***warrants check***, are all used synonymously to mean gathering information for law enforcement purposes.

When querying a tag, an officer must make sure to include not only the prefix but a specific description or title of the specialized tag. For example, when running a tag for a wheelchair symbol plate, an officer must include the suffix "WT" *(LE012.4.B.2.)*. A full catalog of specialized tags can be found at the Florida Department Highway Safety and Motor Vehicles web site.

## UNIT 2 | PROFESSIONAL TRAFFIC STOPS AND DISCRIMINATORY PROFILING

# LESSON 1 | Professional Traffic Stops and Discriminatory Profiling

## Discriminatory or Bias-Based Profiling

***Discriminatory*** or ***bias-based profiling*** is the unequal treatment of any person, including stopping, questioning, searching, detaining, or arresting a person, solely or primarily because of the person's race, ethnicity, religion, gender, sexual orientation, or socioeconomic status. This behavior is illegal and will not be tolerated in law enforcement.

Some observers more broadly construe racial profiling to include any law enforcement action—not merely traffic stops—that targets an individual based on a variety of group characteristics other than race. In addition to considering ethnicity, color, national origin, or ancestry, the term is often extended to address groups of individuals defined by gender, sexual orientation, religion, age, occupational status, socioeconomic status, or ability to speak English. (*International Association of Chiefs of Police Bulletin*, September 2006) *(LE026.1.B.1.)*

According to Title 18, Section 242 of the United States Code, anyone who "under color of any law, statute, ordinance, regulation, or custom, willfully subjects any person...to the deprivation of any rights, privileges, or immunities secured or protected by the Constitution or laws...or to different punishments, pains, or penalties, on account of such person being an alien, or by reason of his color, or race...shall be fined under this title or imprisoned for no more than one year, or both, and if bodily injury results...shall be fined under this title or imprisoned for no more than 10 years or both...and if death results...shall be fined under this title, or imprisoned for any term of years or for life or both, or may be sentenced to death." *(LE026.1.B.)*

**OBJECTIVES**

**LE026.1.B.1.** Define *discriminatory* or *bias-based profiling.*

**LE026.1.B.** Identify protections offered by Title 18 of the United States Code and the Fourteenth Amendment.

**LE026.1.B.2.** Identify the perceptions commonly associated with discriminatory profiling.

**LE026.1.C.1.** Identify how an officer's behavior can help minimize tension and maximize the cooperation of citizens during a traffic stop.

**LE026.1.C.2.** Identify the characteristics of a professional traffic stop that may help overcome language and other cultural barriers.

## Equal Protection

The Fourteenth Amendment guarantees every person within the U.S. equal protection under the law. In *Mapp v. Ohio* (1961), the Supreme Court declared that no state can limit this constitutional right; every person is entitled to be treated the same under similar circumstances.

The fact that a person is of a particular racial or ethnic group is not a basis for suspicion of wrongdoing. Suspected violators may be targeted based only on their conduct. It is always wrong, both legally and ethically, to use race, ethnicity, gender, or sexual orientation as the sole basis for a stop. However, an officer may properly focus attention on a person of a particular race or background if the officer has specific suspect information. For example, if a bulletin is issued for an elderly Asian female suspect wearing a red shirt, an officer is justified in stopping elderly Asian females because they fit that specific description.

## Real and Perceived Problems Faced by Minorities

***Minority*** is a less numerous segment of a population that differs from the majority in some characteristics and is often subjected to different treatment. Because of past unequal treatment of racial minorities, most law enforcement agencies across the country now require officers to report racial data on their traffic stops. Various laws and court rulings require this information to detect and eliminate unfair profiling. Whether or not the perception is accurate, minority residents frequently feel unfairly treated by law enforcement officers, particularly with regard to traffic stops. *(LE026.1.B.2.)*

## Minimizing Tension and Maximizing Cooperation

When stopped, traffic violators typically react with embarrassment, anger, fear, and excuses. Tension can be high, but by conducting a proper and professional traffic stop, an officer can minimize negative and potentially unsafe results. This can be done by following established professional agency protocol and by officers doing the following:

- greeting the driver (and passengers) politely, introducing him- or herself and immediately explaining why the stop was made; courts have ruled that persons are entitled to know why they were stopped before any further discussion or requests are made. The officer should describe the violation in terms of what the vehicle, not the driver, was seen doing.
- maintaining a pleasant expression, a calm tone of voice, a non-confrontational interview stance, and command presence, and by using words that convey professionalism and respect
- allowing the driver to talk; law enforcement officers should remain polite and focused, conveying to the driver that he or she is being heard.
- not arguing with the violator; the officer should simply explain his or her observations and the violation, if any. Whether or not a warning or citation is issued, when the officer listens respectfully, many people calm down and accept the situation.
- not lecturing the violator but explaining the seriousness of the violation by mentioning the risk of a crash or other circumstances that heighten the importance of enforcement action
- keeping the detention time as short as possible
- ending the interaction with a "thank you" in a courteous, non-sarcastic manner (especially if the person turns out to be cleared of any wrongdoing)
- providing the citizen with complete name and badge number upon request
- eliminating racially charged stereotypes, racial jokes, and epithets from his or her speech. These increase the likelihood of insensitive behavior or the perception that the officer is biased. *(LE026.1.C.1.)*

During the investigation of the Los Angeles Police Department, following the Rodney King case, investigators downloaded hundreds of racially inappropriate messages that were exchanged on mobile data terminals in Los Angeles Police Department cruisers. The evidence of these incidents of racial discrimination were used against the officers involved in the King case.

When dealing with a particularly disrespectful motorist, officers may be tempted to react arrogantly. A professional law enforcement officer must not let ego or emotion interfere with his or her actions. Law enforcement work is stressful, but officers sworn to uphold the Constitution and laws must consistently heed the laws they are paid to enforce. No circumstances justify an officer acting in an unprofessional or racially discriminatory manner. Florida is becoming increasingly diverse; it is up to individual officers to avoid even the perception of discriminatory profiling in their actions.

**Section Vocabulary**

*discriminatory or bias-based profiling*

*minority*

## Cultural and Language Barriers

Because language barriers can impede an officer's communication ability, an officer making a traffic stop must determine the motorist's ability to understand him or her. For example, many Florida motorists may not understand English. They are concerned about being stopped, what the officer is doing or expects, and what their obligations may be. An officer should consider requesting an interpreter. Hearing impaired drivers also present a challenge, though some can read lips. Writing notes back and forth may be a good communication method in this situation.

To avoid communication barriers, an officer must exhibit professionalism and remember to do the following:

- avoid talking down to anyone or being demeaning
- take his or her time when speaking
- speak clearly
- show respect
- listen carefully and explain fully what is expected and what the officer is doing
- be patient
- refer the motorist, if necessary, to an appropriate source with the department if unable to answer all questions *(LE026.1.C.2.)*

## Building Bridges with the Community

As an officer gains experience in making traffic stops, his or her interaction skills will improve. Sometimes a standardized approach or script minimizes officer/violator conflict and, because it becomes a habit, may assist the officer if testifying in court about interactions with the violator becomes necessary.

When dealing with citizens during traffic stops, an officer's conduct will mean the difference between building a bridge with the community and putting a gap in that bridge. Courteous, professional officers may issue hundreds of citations without generating a citizen complaint, often receiving a verbal "thank you" from the cited motorists. The officer is not being thanked for the citation but for treating the violator with respect, courtesy, and dignity.

# UNIT 3 | UNKNOWN RISK TRAFFIC STOPS

## LESSON 1 | Initiating the Stop

**OBJECTIVES**

**LE026.1.** Identify reasons a vehicle may be stopped during an unknown risk traffic stop.

**LE026.1.D.** Identify traffic conditions that increase the potential for traffic violations during an unknown risk traffic stop.

**LE007.1.A.2.** Identify conditions that would affect traffic flow during an unknown risk traffic stop.

**LE026.1.A.** Identify where to park to observe traffic flow for potential traffic violations during an unknown risk traffic stop.

**LE025.2.** Identify where to position the patrol vehicle so that it can safely re-enter traffic during an unknown risk traffic stop.

**LE026.3.** Identify the need to catch up to the vehicle to be stopped during an unknown risk traffic stop.

**LE279.4.** Identify the need to request backup as required during an unknown risk traffic stop.

**LE026.3.A.** Identify the need to maintain constant observation of a vehicle suspected of a violation.

**LE092.2.** Identify the need to advise communications center of location and description of the vehicle, occupants, and tag number with state of issue during an unknown risk traffic stop.

### Deciding to Make a Traffic Stop

A traffic stop begins the moment an officer observes an event or reason for the stop. An ***unknown risk traffic stop*** refers to a stop in which the identity of the driver is not known. Officers may stop a vehicle if reasonable suspicion exists that a crime was, is being, or is about to be committed, including an observed violation for which a citation may be issued. Other justifications for a traffic stop would be to assist a motorist who is obviously lost or whose vehicle has mechanical trouble, to investigate suspicious behavior, or to investigate a vehicle or occupant matching a BOLO description. *(LE026.1.)*

Upon seeing a violation or other cause for a stop, the officer must decide whether it is necessary, prudent, and safe to stop the vehicle. If the officer is en route to an emergency call or in-progress crime or is transporting a prisoner, stopping a routine traffic violator is not prudent. On the other hand, a reckless driver who is immediately endangering the lives of other motorists and pedestrians may justify a stop, even if the earlier call must be abandoned. Such a decision should be made in consultation with dispatch and, if possible, a supervisor. Agency policy may dictate priority in those situations. If immediately stopping the driver may endanger the officer or other motorists, the officer should not make the stop. Unsafe conditions for a stop include heavy traffic, construction, or roadway conditions that do not allow room to pull over, such as a long bridge.

Officer-driver interaction begins when the officer signals the driver to stop. Once that signal is given, the officer has limited control over where the driver will stop. The officer should initiate the stop in an area that gives the driver a place to stop safely. The officer must also be ready to adjust and react quickly to developments in the situation after the driver stops the vehicle. Any situation could quickly turn a routine traffic stop into a high risk stop. Certain roadway and traffic conditions may increase the potential for particular traffic violations. These include merge areas, intersections, and acceleration lanes. *(LE026.1.D.)*

***Traffic flow*** is the general speed and direction of vehicle or pedestrian movement. Weather conditions, school zones, construction zones, and neighborhood activities may all affect traffic flow, slowing drivers and causing congestion *(LE007.1.A.2.)*. In his or her assigned zone, an officer must be familiar with normal traffic flow, speed limits and where they change, and changes to traffic flow at different times of day.

### Planning the Stop

If working in stationary mode, the officer should choose a safe parking place from which to watch for traffic violations. For example, when using radar or watching an intersection for traffic light violators, the officer should position the patrol vehicle where it does not obstruct traffic flow but can enter the roadway quickly and safely to make a necessary stop *(LE026.1.A.)*. Such safe places include areas with a wide shoulder off the roadway, available parking areas, and areas with an unobstructed sight of violations and oncoming traffic when entering the roadway. *(LE025.2.)*

## Initiating the Stop

### *Step 1:* Maneuver the patrol vehicle through traffic until safely catching up to the violator, and determine at what point to safely make the stop.

The officer's familiarity with area roads is critical to selecting a safe stopping location. Except in emergencies in which a stop must immediately be made, the officer should choose a location where the violator can be stopped out of the flow of traffic, where both the officer and violator can avoid the danger of passing vehicles. Passing traffic is not the only risk—stopping a violator in an area populated by his or her peers may create a volatile and dangerous scene. After deciding to make the stop, the officer should move the patrol vehicle into a position to pursue and catch up to the violator, initiate the stop, and maintain a safe following distance until the violator pulls over. *(LE026.3.)*

The officer should use defensive driving techniques to catch up to the vehicle and follow at a safe distance. All lane changes should be signaled. A well-executed traffic stop should minimally affect normal traffic flow. Other drivers may slow down to see what is going on. This can cause a traffic jam or hazard. An officer may have to follow a vehicle for some time before initiating the stop. If backup is needed, the officer should request another patrol vehicle to help *(LE279.4.)*. When an officer needs backup, he or she may need to follow the violator's vehicle for an extended period before help arrives.

To ensure the correct vehicle is being stopped, the officer should maintain constant visual observation of the vehicle from the time of the violation until the stop is made *(LE026.3.A.)*. The officer should note the vehicle's description, including its type, make, model, year, color, tag number, and state where the tag was issued. The driver's description (glasses, hat, beard, etc.) and any information about passengers should be noted as well as any other vehicle descriptors, such as condition, bumper stickers or decals, dents, or the presence of a toolbox.

### *Step 2:* Notify dispatch of the traffic stop.

Once the decision to stop has been made, the following information must be provided to dispatch:

- the officer's location, such as the street, plus a cross street or a house number; this is crucial on interstate and divided highways. If the situation escalates and the officer is injured or cannot use the radio, dispatch can pinpoint the officer's location.
- the officer's direction of travel: north, south, east, or west
- vehicle tag number and state of issue

**LE025.4.A.** Identify considerations for determining how to locate a safe stopping area to make a traffic stop during an unknown risk traffic stop.

**LE025.4.B.** Identify the need to activate the emergency equipment during an unknown risk traffic stop.

**LE026.2.A.** Identify the Florida Statutes that govern the operation of emergency vehicle lights and siren during an unknown risk traffic stop.

**LE026.2.B.** Identify how to use the emergency lights.

**LE007.3.A.** Identify the need to position the patrol vehicle in line directly behind the suspect vehicle during an unknown risk traffic stop.

**LE026.7.** Identify how to direct the driver on where to stop during an unknown risk traffic stop.

**LE026.7.A.** Identify how to activate the public address system during an unknown risk traffic stop.

- a description of the violator's vehicle
- the number of occupants and descriptions if possible *(LE092.2.)*

Dispatch information is especially important for officer safety. It allows time for a check on the tag before the officer talks to the driver. In addition, if the officer sees the occupants acting suspiciously, he or she may immediately be able to request backup. If the final stop location changes, the officer should update dispatch immediately.

### *Step 3:* Select a safe location to stop.

The following are major considerations when selecting the safest proper location to make the stop:

- lighting
- population
- width of road and shoulder
- traffic congestion
- level of visibility
- presence of hills and curves

The officer should check the width of the road and shoulder to ensure that both the officer and the violator are far enough off the road so other vehicles can pass. This prevents crashes, especially in a congested area where other drivers may not be able to change lanes to give the officer more room. Officers should try to choose a level spot or a slight downgrade. If stopping on an upgrade, a large truck could roll into the patrol vehicle. Additionally, special caution should be taken when conducting stops in areas where children are present, such as school parking lots. Officers should not make a stop on a curve, a ramp, or the crest of a hill, close to an exit ramp, or where road conditions could cause other vehicles to hit the patrol vehicle. *(LE025.4.A.)*

### *Step 4:* Communicate the stop to the violator.

To communicate the stop to the violator, the officer should signal by pulling directly behind the violator's vehicle and, once the area is safe to make a stop, turning on the emergency equipment *(LE025.4.B.)*. Emergency notification equipment includes emergency lights, siren, headlights, PA system, and horn. F.S. §316.216 explains the legal right to use lights and sirens to get the violator's attention during a traffic stop *(LE026.2.A.)*. Several indicators show the violator is aware and anticipating the stop. The violator may look into the rearview mirror and make eye contact with the officer, signal a lane change to pull over, or suddenly slow down.

Officers should use flashing emergency lights cautiously when conducting traffic stops. Each driver reacts differently. Some panic and might stop in the left lane, skid to a stop, or swerve. Others ignore the lights. If this happens, the officer should tap the siren for one or two seconds.

Emergency lighting systems differ among agencies. The light bar is one system, along with ***wig wags***, which are alternating flashes of the vehicle lights, strobe, flashers, and other lights. If the stop occurs at night, the officer should use spotlights for additional lighting.

The patrol vehicle's high beam, spotlight, and takedown lights conceal an officer from the violator's view and are important for officer safety and survival. The officer should activate the patrol vehicle's high beams unless they interfere with oncoming traffic or reflect the violator's rear bumper or another object, restricting the officer's vision. If the patrol vehicle is equipped with them, the officer should activate the takedown lights; the white lights facing forward on the light bar. These illuminate the violator's vehicle's interior and prevent the operator from seeing into the patrol vehicle. *(LE026.2.B.)*

### Step 5: Pull the violator over.

Once the violator acknowledges that the officer has directed him or her to pull over, the following steps should be completed:

1. As the violator changes lanes, follow smoothly.
2. When the officer knows the violator will stop, the officer should unfasten his or her seatbelt while pulling behind the violator's vehicle.
3. The officer will pull the patrol vehicle directly behind the vehicle at a safe distance *(LE007.3.A.)*. A safe distance is far enough behind the violator to react to the situation at hand. The officer must use safety precautions, such as avoiding traffic lanes, watching for pedestrians, and protecting the violator.
4. If uncomfortable with the stopping place, the officer should direct the violator to a safer location using the patrol vehicle's PA system *(LE026.7.)*. The officer might say, "Driver, drive into the parking lot ahead" or "Driver, pull your vehicle farther to the right." The officer should be firm but respectful.

If the officer's PA system does not activate automatically, it must be manually turned on. Once the system is on, the officer can press the button on the side of the microphone and speak into it. It is similar to a Citizen's Band (CB) radio. The system's speakers are usually in the front of the patrol car behind the grille or bumper. The officer's verbal commands should not be as loud as the siren *(LE026.7.A.)*. During the stop, the overhead emergency lights should be left activated to warn oncoming traffic.

**Section Vocabulary**

*traffic flow*

*unknown risk traffic stop*

*wig wags*

# UNIT 3 | UNKNOWN RISK TRAFFIC STOPS

## LESSON 2 | Conducting the Stop

**OBJECTIVES**

**LE012.4.A.** Identify officer safety and survival techniques appropriate for the situation during an unknown risk traffic stop.

**LE026.8.** Identify how to offset the patrol vehicle at the rear of the violator's vehicle after the violator's vehicle stops during an unknown risk traffic stop.

**LE025.4.** Identify how the officer should prepare him- or herself to complete the stop after the officer has positioned the patrol vehicle during an unknown risk traffic stop.

**LE091.8.A.1.** Identify the need to determine the degree of danger involved during an unknown risk traffic stop.

**LE026.9.** Identify how to make contact with the vehicle occupants using proper tactics as demanded by the situation during an unknown risk traffic stop.

**LE026.8.B.** Identify how to make a safe approach to the violator's vehicle during an unknown risk traffic stop.

**LE026.9.A.** Identify the number of additional occupants in the vehicle during an unknown risk traffic stop.

**LE026.8.C.** Identify officer safety techniques in getting the violator to exit the vehicle during an unknown risk traffic stop.

**LE012.4.A.1.** Identify the need to demonstrate a dignified and commanding presence during an unknown risk traffic stop.

**LE026.10.** Identify self as a law enforcement officer.

**LE026.8.D.** Identify the need to maintain a safe distance when talking to a violator during an unknown risk traffic stop.

### *Step 6:* Position the patrol vehicle.

After stopping the violator in a safe location, the officer should position the patrol vehicle a safe distance behind the violator's vehicle. Continued officer safety also involves the following practices:

- ensuring the officer is a safe distance from the roadway
- maintaining a safe reactionary distance between the violator's vehicle and the patrol vehicle
- offsetting and angling the patrol vehicle from the violator's vehicle
- adhering to agency policy and procedure *(LE012.4.A.)*

Because of roadway conditions, traffic, and other environmental factors, each traffic stop is unique. As a general rule, the patrol vehicle should be positioned one and a half to two car lengths behind the violator's vehicle. If the violator stops on the right side of the road, the officer should align the center of the patrol vehicle's hood with the left side taillight of the violator's vehicle. The wheels should be turned outward (toward the road) so the patrol vehicle may be deflected away from the violator's vehicle if the patrol vehicle is struck from behind. This ***offset position*** creates a potential safety corridor where an officer can walk when approaching the violator's vehicle. If the situation escalates, an offset patrol car may also provide cover from potential skipping rounds shot from the violator's vehicle. *(LE026.8.)*

Angling incorporates the offset position with a more dramatic turn of the nose of the vehicle in either direction. If needed, the PA system can be used to verbally direct the violator to move his or her vehicle further to the right to increase officer safety and minimize traffic obstruction.

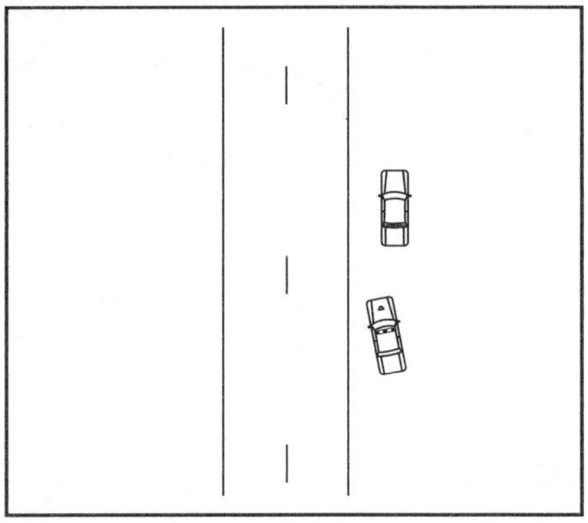

Offset angle positioning on right shoulder of road *figure 9-5*

Sometimes due to environmental conditions, roadway obstacles, or agency policy and procedure, the officer may decide to make a traffic stop on the left side of the roadway.

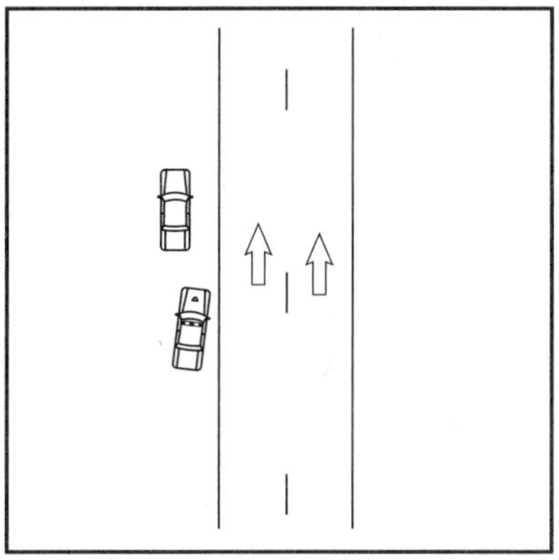

Example 1: *Figure 9-6*
Offset angle positioning on left shoulder of road

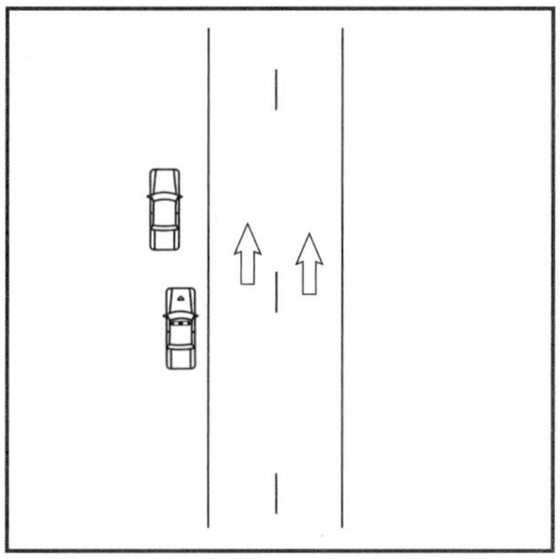

Example 2: *Figure 9-7*
Offset only positioning on left shoulder of road

After making the stop, the officer should be prepared to exit the patrol vehicle quickly. The violator's vehicle and all occupants should be constantly observed. If the officer senses any danger while assessing the situation, he or she should request backup. Upon exiting the patrol vehicle, the officer should make sure his or her equipment belt is free of the seat belt and that the seat belt does not hinder his or her getting out of the vehicle. Emergency lights should be used during a day stop and all lights should be used at night. *(LE025.4.)*

## Backup Vehicle Positions

If the officer has requested backup, the backup officers' vehicle(s) should be parked a safe distance behind the primary patrol vehicle. Depending on the location of the traffic stop and the environmental conditions, the backup vehicle may be offset to the left or right of the primary patrol vehicle. This will enhance the effects of the emergency lighting and create a large safety corridor. The backup officer should approach along the passenger side of the primary officer's vehicle. This will ensure the primary officer is not in crossfire if the situation escalates to the use of deadly force.

Backup officers must limit use of emergency lighting that may blind or silhouette the primary officer. If possible, only rear emergency lighting should be used. (See Figures 9-8 and 9-9 on next page.)

**LE026.12.** Identify the need to explain the reason for the traffic stop during an unknown risk traffic stop.

**LE015.3.** Identify the need to describe the safety violation to the operator.

**LE091.7.** Identify the need to ask the driver for a lawful and reasonable explanation for a law violation during an unknown risk traffic stop.

**LE012.3.B.** Identify how to arrange assistance for the citizen during an unknown risk traffic stop.

**LE012.4.B.** Identify documents to request from the driver during an unknown risk traffic stop.

**LE005.1.A.** Identify the forms of identification that provide the most accurate personal information during an unknown risk traffic stop.

**LE026.5.A.** Identify how to compare a vehicle's registration information to the vehicle's VIN for a match during an unknown risk traffic stop.

**LE279.3.A.** Identify where the driver and occupants should wait during an unknown risk traffic stop.

**LE005.5.** Identify the need to match information received from dispatch with information recorded during an unknown risk traffic stop.

**LE079.10.C.3.** Identify how to determine whether a vehicle is reported stolen through a check of FCIC/NCIC during an unknown risk traffic stop.

**LE091.7.B.** Identify undercover law enforcement officers in the execution of their duties during an unknown risk traffic stop.

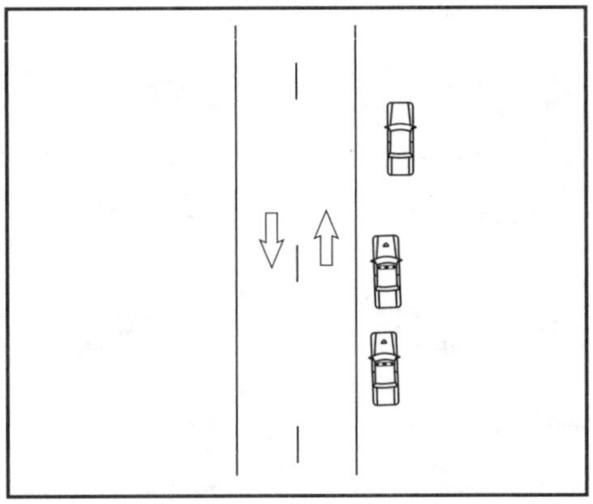

Example 1: Backup positioning *Figure 9-8*

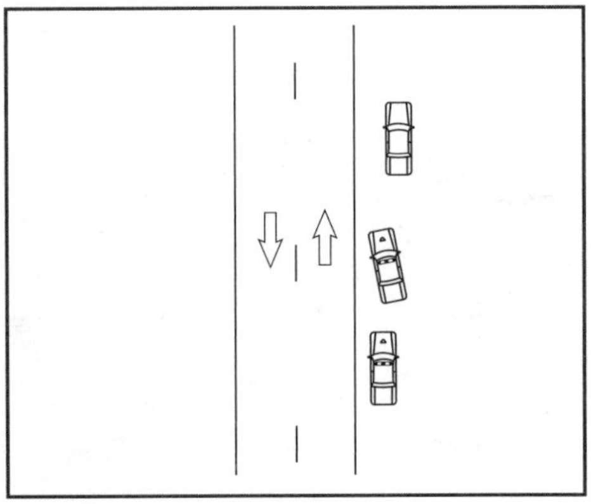

Example 2: Backup positioning *Figure 9-9*

## Step 7: Visual assessment

Before approaching the violator's vehicle, an officer should assess the degree of danger. If any subject attempts to exit the violator's vehicle without being directed to do so by the officer, the officer should immediately order the subject(s) back into the vehicle.

One clue to possible danger is if the occupants are nervously watching the officer. Some activity should be expected as the driver retrieves his or her driver's license, registration, and insurance information from a wallet or glove compartment. Suspicious movements such as moving towards the floorboard or backseat, excessive motion that seems beyond natural curiosity, or rigid, wooden posture (which may indicate occupants who are frightened or poised for action) may all suggest danger. The officer must maintain constant observation.

The officer should check the trunk lock, trunk lid alignment, and, when possible, weight distribution for anything that might suggest the vehicle is stolen.

The following are indications that the license plate may not belong to the vehicle:

- the way the plate is attached (bolts, wire) may suggest the license plate was removed from another vehicle
- age of attachment relative to the plate (i.e., Are there shiny, new bolts on a dirty plate?)
- expired expiration sticker or sticker that looks like it was removed from another plate
- paint or dark film on the license plate
- the presence of dead insects on the tag, suggesting it was the front plate of another vehicle

Officers should also check for a popped trunk lock. This indicates that someone hammered out the keyhole, allowing entry into the trunk without a key. An officer might see a hole in the trunk where the lock should be, which is a common sign of a stolen vehicle. Officers should also note if the trunk lid is fully closed. A subject could hide inside the trunk and surprise an officer. If the trunk lid is unlatched, the officer should push it down when he or she approaches the vehicle. Doing so will lock in anyone hiding inside the trunk.

If the vehicle appears to be heavily weighed down in the rear, the officer should discuss this with the driver. The vehicle could be carrying stolen merchandise, drugs, tools, a person, or a corpse. *(LE091.8.A.1.)*

# Examining the Interior of Vehicle

The officer should look through the rear window into the rear seat, noting the number of occupants, position of the rear seat, and the presence of any contraband or potential weapons.

### *Step 8:* Exiting the Patrol Vehicle

Before exiting the patrol vehicle, the officer should check for oncoming traffic in the rear and side-view mirrors. When exiting his or her patrol vehicle, the officer should securely close the vehicle door so it will not blow open and possibly be struck by a passing vehicle. The officer should close the door quietly and keep the portable radio just loud enough to hear radio traffic. A silent exit from the patrol vehicle gives the officer time to approach the vehicle and assess the situation before the driver reacts.

### *Step 9:* Approaching the Violator's Vehicle

The officer must decide whether to approach the violator's vehicle or call the driver back to the patrol vehicle (called the ***no approach tactic***) to acquire information. In both situations, the officer should exit the patrol vehicle and use available cover from either vehicle. The officer should approach the violator's vehicle cautiously, using all senses to assess the situation. The officer should not fix his or her full attention on any one part of the scene but should scan the vehicle and occupants for suspicious movements and continue to observe both the vehicle and the occupants throughout the stop. If a situation seems dangerous, an officer should request backup and wait for its arrival before taking any further action. *(LE026.9.)*

## Approaching the Violator's Vehicle on the Driver's Side

When approaching the vehicle, the officer should do so cautiously and remain vigilant for dangerous traffic situations. At night, the officer ought to take advantage of light and shadows. Touching the rear of the violator's vehicle ensures the trunk lid/hatch is closed and transfers the officer's fingerprints to the vehicle as evidence of contact. The officer should stay close to the vehicle, stopping at the back edge of the driver's door. At night, only a flashlight should be held in the non-gun hand. The officer needs to remain behind the vehicle's doorpost for cover, assuming an interview stance. *(LE026.8.B.)*

Standing behind the driver's doorpost gives an officer a position of advantage while maintaining a safe distance when talking with the driver. If, when approaching on the violator's side, a passenger is seen in the backseat, the officer should stop at the back of the rear window and instruct the driver to open the window. This requires the driver to turn around to see. The officer should continually watch both the driver and the passengers.

## Approaching the Violator's Vehicle on the Passenger's Side

If the officer decides to approach the violator's vehicle on the passenger side, he or she should begin by walking behind the patrol vehicle to avoid crossing in front of the headlights and betraying his or her location. Approaching on the passenger's side gives the officer extra time to look and listen. The occupants will likely expect the officer to approach on the driver's side, and therefore will not know his or her location. At night, the officer's flashlight should be kept off while approaching the vehicle until contact is made with the driver and other occupants.

An observant officer can see if the driver is concealing something on his or her right side, including a popped ignition, keys in the ignition, a weapon, an alcoholic beverage container, or narcotics. The officer will also notice how many other occupants may be in the vehicle. *(LE026.9.A.)*

*Note:* With a ***popped*** or ***splatted ignition***, the plastic housing around the column's base has been popped open, exposing ignition bars that can be pulled forward to start the car. It also means an ignition key area that has the key portion removed, allowing the ignition bar to be exposed.

If the preliminary visual check reveals a potential threat, the officer should call for backup and assess the situation. If nobody occupies the backseat, the officer should remain behind the front passenger's doorpost for cover, assuming an interview stance to protect his or her firearm side. If passengers occupy the backseat, the officer should stand at the rear of the backseat windows.

## "No Approach": Calling the Driver Back to the Officer's Patrol Vehicle

If the decision is made to call the driver back to the patrol vehicle, the officer should exit the patrol vehicle and assume a safe position, such as behind either the driver's side or passenger's side doorpost, depending on traffic conditions. When moving to a position behind the passenger-side doorpost, the officer should walk behind the vehicle while constantly observing the driver and any passengers. The officer should also keep an eye on passing traffic to avoid being struck by a vehicle. To avoid being silhouetted against the emergency lights, the officer should not walk between the patrol vehicle and the violator's vehicle. The driver may be verbally directed back to the patrol vehicle by using a commanding voice or a PA system. If the driver is looking at the driver directly or through a mirror, the officer may simply motion the driver to come back to the patrol vehicle. As the violator approaches, the officer should be observant, especially of the driver's hands, for any signs of aggression or the presence of a weapon. *(LE026.8.C.)*

### *Step 10:* Interview the driver.

A courteous but commanding presence is the key to effective communication with the vehicle driver. An officer is less likely to encounter resistance if his or her presence is dignified and commanding *(LE012.4.A.1).* An officer should make sure his or her expression, tone of voice, body position, gestures, and words portray professionalism and respect along with sufficient assertiveness. The first thing the officer should do when contacting the driver is identify him- or herself as a law enforcement officer, especially if not in uniform. Many agencies have a specific policy for doing this. *(LE026.10.)*

Observation skills, safe positioning, and safe distancing are important considerations when interviewing the driver or passengers *(LE026.8.D.).* If the situation becomes dangerous or unstable, the officer must increase the distance between him- or herself and the stopped vehicle.

In accordance with agency policy, the officer should courteously explain the reason for the stop and request the required documentation *(LE026.12.).* This could include the officer's observation that the vehicle is in violation of F.S. §316.221, Inoperable Tail Lamps, for instance *(LE015.3.).* The officer should allow the driver to offer an explanation, such as medical difficulties or vehicle malfunctions *(LE091.7.).* If necessary, the officer should contact dispatch to request medical assistance for the driver and, as needed, arrange for a relative or responsible person to remove the vehicle or have it towed. *(LE012.3.B.)*

Drivers in Florida must provide a driver's license, vehicle registration, and proof of insurance upon request per F.S. §322.15, §320.0605, and §316.646 *(LE012.4.B.).* An officer must never accept a wallet from the driver. Instead, the driver should be asked to remove the license from the wallet. This prevents the driver from later accusing an officer of theft. The officer should take the documentation with his or her non-dominant (non-gun) hand. During this process, the officer should observe the interior of the vehicle and activities of the passengers. If an officer is suspicious of a driver's movements, the officer should ask where the driver keeps the documents. By doing this, the officer may predict where the driver's hands will move. If the driver reaches to open the glove compartment or other inside compartment, it should be requested that he or she do so slowly. The officer should pay close attention to both of the driver's hands. The driver could use the reaching hand to distract while going for a weapon or object with the other hand.

The driver is the only occupant compelled to provide documentation unless other occupants are suspected of a crime or violation such as not wearing a seat belt. If identification is needed from occupants, officers should request documents that provide the most accurate personal information such as the following:

- driver's license or state-issued identification card (with picture)
- residence card for non-citizens (green card)
- military ID
- school picture identification
- Social Security card (according to agency policy and procedure) *(LE005.1.A.)*

The officer should verify that the information on the license is current and valid. The information on the registration should be compared to the VIN, make, type, and year of the vehicle *(LE026.5.A.)*. In addition, the officer should confirm the insurance card is current and applicable to that vehicle. The driver and any occupants should be asked to stay in the violator's vehicle or in a designated place within the officer's sight, which makes it more difficult to attack the officer from behind. *(LE279.3.A.)*

After obtaining the required documentation, the officer will safely return to the patrol vehicle and complete FCIC/NCIC Department of Highway Safety and Motor Vehicle checks. Safely returning to the patrol vehicle means never losing sight of the stopped vehicle and the occupants even while running FCIC/NCIC checks.

FCIC/NCIC information can provide an officer with assistance during traffic stops. It can also give useful additional information about the person or vehicle stopped, including wanted persons (entire U.S.), drivers' licenses and vehicle registration (entire U.S. and Canada), missing persons, and juvenile and adult and stolen property (entire U.S.). *(LE005.5.), (LE079.10.C.3.)*

If a hit is confirmed during the check, the officer may arrest the violator and/or impound the vehicle as circumstances and agency policy dictate.

On occasion, when an undercover officer has been stopped for a traffic violation, he or she may or may not present law enforcement identification to the officer who pulled him over. If he or she does offer identification, dispatch can verify his or her employment and official status. In an undercover situation where the officer has no identification or depending on the nature of his assignment, it may be unlikely that the officer will reveal his or her identity to avoid a ticket. Agency policy and procedures should be followed in these situations. *(LE091.7.B.)*

**Section Vocabulary**

*no approach tactic*

*offset position*

*popped or splatted ignition*

# UNIT 3 | UNKNOWN RISK TRAFFIC STOPS

## LESSON 3 | Taking Appropriate Action

**OBJECTIVES**

**LE026.14.** Identify that an officer may issue a citation, or warning, or make an arrest as appropriate during an unknown risk traffic stop.

**LE025.5.A.** Identify how an officer decides whether to issue a citation or a warning during an unknown risk traffic stop.

**LE091.8.A.** Determine the nature of the offense during an unknown risk traffic stop.

**LE026.14.A.1.** Identify appropriate report forms used during an unknown risk traffic stop.

**LE026.14.A.2.** Identify a Uniform Traffic Citation (UTC).

**LE091.6.** Identify the need to explain the nature of the offense during an unknown risk traffic stop.

**LE091.10.A.** Identify the need to give options for handling the citation during an unknown risk traffic stop.

**LE092.6.** Identify the need to explain the violator's responsibility to adhere to traffic laws and local ordinances during an unknown risk traffic stop.

**LE091.9.C.1.** Identify the need to explain that the violator needs to sign the citation during an unknown risk traffic stop.

### Course of Action: Citation, Warning, or Arrest

Officers often use discretion and flexibility in judgment. In the case of traffic violations, officers may issue a warning, or citation, or make an arrest as appropriate *(LE026.14.)*. The law, agency policy, and the circumstances of violation affect the decision. This discretion applies only to traffic violations and misdemeanor offenses, with some exceptions for misdemeanor offenses. Some agencies do not permit officers to issue written warnings. Others do not allow verbal warnings. Individual officers must weigh the offense's seriousness, the road, weather, traffic conditions, and the driver's driving record *(LE025.5.A.)*. It is advisable to document each stop with appropriate, recorded enforcement action, whether it is a citation, a warning, or an arrest.

An officer should write a citation when there is a clear violation which is not satisfactorily excused or justified by the situation, when agency policy supports the writing of the citation, and when the violation affects others (i.e., making drivers swerve or brake suddenly).

Florida law states that all felonies are arrestable offenses. If an officer has probable cause for a felony arrest, he or she must make the arrest. Agency policy dictates proper paperwork that should accompany the arrest. *(LE091.8.A.)*

### Uniform Traffic Citations (UTC)

The Florida Uniform Traffic Citation is designed in four carbon paper parts that are color coded for ease of use and distribution. Each part serves a different purpose. The white copy is submitted to the local clerk of the county court and the blue copy to the Department of Highway Safety and Motor Vehicles. The violator gets the yellow copy, and the officer's agency keeps the pink copy. The issuing officer may add notes to the pink copy to document details of the stop.

The Uniform Traffic Citation is used for traffic offenses covered under Florida Statute Chapters 316, 318, 320, and 322 and is used to collect and store information about traffic enforcement and traffic case adjudication. For traffic offenses, the Uniform Traffic Citation is generally the only report that must be completed. However, individual agencies may require additional reports for particular offenses. *(LE026.14.A.1.)*

The Uniform Traffic Citation is also used for certain non-traffic felony and misdemeanors which can result in suspension or revocation of the offender's driver license. Pursuant to §316.650(10), F.S., a citation must be issued to anyone convicted of any offense that requires mandatory revocation of the driver license.

**LE091.9.E.** Identify the violation for refusal to sign the citation during an unknown risk traffic stop.

**LE091.10.** Identify how to close the interview with the violator during an unknown risk traffic stop.

**LE025.5.B.** Identify whether or not to make an arrest during an unknown risk traffic stop.

Officers are assigned Uniform Traffic Citation books with local jurisdiction court information on the front. Each Uniform Traffic Citation has a preprinted number, and officers must account for each Uniform Traffic Citation assigned to them. If a Uniform Traffic Citation is destroyed or lost before being issued to a violator, the officer to whom that Uniform Traffic Citation was issued must document the circumstances of the destruction or loss. Department of Highway Safety and Motor Vehicles tracks all Uniform Traffic Citation numbers to ensure integrity in citation issuance. It is illegal to "tear up" a citation after it has been issued. F.S. §316.650(8) states "it is unlawful and an act of official misconduct for any traffic enforcement officer or other officer or public employee to dispose of a traffic citation or copies thereof or of the record of the issuance of the same in a manner other than as required."

In addition to the Department of Highway Safety and Motor Vehicle's responsibility to keep accurate records regarding Uniform Traffic Citations, each law enforcement agency must keep records of and account for all citations supplied to them. Each Uniform Traffic Citation book contains two receipts that are used for assigning the book to an officer. Agencies may develop their own procedures for assigning citation books to individual officers and may use these receipts to assist with internal control and record keeping.

Upon receipt of each book, the officer should inspect it to ensure that citations are in correct numeric sequence and that each book contains 25 four-part citations. Sequential numbers assigned to each book should also be inspected to ensure that the numbers on the book are the same as the numbers of the citations contained in the book and listed on the officer's receipt.

Under no circumstances is it permissible for one law enforcement agency to transfer citations to another law enforcement agency. Each Uniform Traffic Citation is recorded in the Department of Highway Safety and Motor Vehicles inventory files as being distributed to a particular agency. When a Uniform Traffic Citation is issued to a violator, the third (blue) copy is sent to Department of Highway Safety and Motor Vehicles where it is compared to the master inventory record. When an officer leaves employment with an agency, his or her Uniform Traffic Citation book(s) shall be turned over to his/her immediate supervisor. Periodically, Department of Highway Safety and Motor Vehicles conducts audits of Uniform Traffic Citation books for accountability purposes pursuant to F.S. §316.650(3)(4)(8). *(LE026.14.A.2.)*

## Distribution of Uniform Traffic Citation—Multiple Copies

The Florida Uniform Traffic Citation form HSMV 75901 contains four copies that are distributed as follows:

**Part One (white)—Complaint—Retained By Court**

This part is designed to serve as a sufficient complaint for both civil and criminal cases, and is used by judges and clerks to indicate court action taken on the reverse side of the form.

**Part Two (blue)—Department of Highway Safety and Motor Vehicles Record—Forward To Uniform Traffic Citation Section, Department of Highway Safety and Motor Vehicles, Tallahassee**

This part is designed for law enforcement agencies to forward to the Uniform Traffic Citation Section in Tallahassee within ten days of issuance to the violator. It is used by the Department of Highway Safety and Motor Vehicles for statistics and accountability purposes.

**Part Three (yellow)—Summons—Defendant's Copy**

This part is reserved for the traffic offender. The reverse side is to be used only to notify individuals charged with traffic infractions (not requiring a court appearance) as to what options they have when answering the offense charged.

**Part Four (pink)—Officer Copy**

Designated for the officer/agency to retain for accountability purposes, to maintain a record of court's action and for officers to make notes for testifying in court. It will be retained for a period of 6 months or until adjudication by the court.

## *Procedures to Complete a Uniform Traffic Citation*

Officers should make sure that a hard divider is used between the sets (four copies) when completing the citation. A ball point pen should be used to ensure that the information is legible on all four copies. (Print all information in black ink.)

Clearly fill-in each data field or "X" the appropriate box based on the requested information at the top of each category. Complete all applicable sections and leave blank any that are not applicable.

The instructions for completing the Uniform Traffic Citation can be found in the DHSMV Uniform Traffic Citations Manual. An officer should review the description and procedures sections in that manual.

The most common reason the Department of Highway Safety and Motor Vehicles returns a Uniform Traffic Citation to the issuing agency is for correction or clarification including illegible handwriting, omitted statute number and sub-section, failure to list a statute corresponding to the description of the violation, failure to check or state violation, or incorrect entry of the violator's date of birth.

# Explaining the Citation

The violator must understand the citation and the violation. The issuing officer must understand Florida traffic violations sufficiently to explain the nature of the offense to someone unfamiliar with the law *(LE091.6.)*. The officer should explain the violator's five options for responding to the citation, which are listed and explained in detail on the back of the violator's (yellow) copy *(LE091.10.A.)*. These options are to pay a civil penalty, elect (request) a hearing in traffic court, or elect to attend and complete a Driver Improvement Course.

The violator may elect to enter a plea of *nolo contendere* (no contest), present a valid driver license, tag, registration, or proper proof of insurance to the Clerk of Court, and pay court costs if charged with any of the following:

- Driver license expired for 4 months or less [F.S. §322.065]
- Tag or registration expired for 6 months or less [F.S. §320.07(3)(a)]

- Failure to display a valid driver license [F.S. §322.15(1)]
- Failure to possess a valid registration [F.S. §320.0605]
- Failure to maintain proof of insurance [F.S. §316.646(1)]

If charged with operating a motor vehicle that is in an unsafe condition or not properly equipped, the violator may elect to provide certified proof of correction of the condition or equipment problem.

Finally, the officer should encourage awareness of the violator's responsibility to obey traffic laws and local ordinances *(LE092.6.)*. By explaining safety issues and the importance of preventing violations, the officer helps the driver understand the law. The driver's documents should be returned with a copy of the warning or citation and any public information pamphlets the department may provide.

On the citation, the officer should point to the section where he or she checked the violation and wrote specifics. If the violator has committed a violation that requires a mandatory hearing listed in §318.19 or any other criminal traffic violation listed in §316, the officer should instruct him or her to sign the Uniform Traffic Citation and explain that signing is not an admission of guilt *(LE091.9.C.1.)*. According to F.S. §318.14(3), refusal to accept and sign a Uniform Traffic Citation requiring a court appearance is a criminal violation that may result in arrest. When confronted with a violator who refuses to sign the officer has an opportunity to use good communication skills to gain compliance from the violator. The officer should tell the violator that refusal to accept and sign the citation might result in arrest. The officer can stress that signing the Uniform Traffic Citation is not an admission of guilt or wavier of rights. If the violator still refuses to sign, the officer should place him or her under arrest and issue another Uniform Traffic Citation for refusal to sign a citation. *(LE091.9.E.)*

Note: Section 316.0083, F.S., permits citations to be made upon photographic or video evidence of an operator failing to come to a complete stop at a steady red signal. Section 318.14(2), F.S., mandates that citations that may be issued upon photographic or video evidence of failure to come to a complete stop at a steady red signal do not have to be signed by the violator, even though they do require the violator to respond or appear in court.

Throughout the traffic stop, the officer should maintain a professional and courteous manner with the driver and passengers. Completing contact with a violator is easiest if the officer clearly explains options for handling the citation. The officer should not argue the merits of the citation with the violator or tell the driver to "Have a nice day," since this could be interpreted as offensive or derogative. *(LE091.10.)*

If the driver expresses a desire to make a complaint against the officer, the officer should politely explain the process for doing so and notify his or her supervisor before the officer's shift ends. A driver who is upset should be allowed time to calm down before resuming driving. Professional courtesy by the officer will help reduce the tension. When the driver is ready to leave, the officer should make sure the driver is able to safely re-enter the traffic stream. The officer should then return to his or her vehicle and clear the stop with the communications center.

During the course of a traffic stop, an officer might be able to develop probable cause if required to justify an arrest of the driver or a passenger. Whether to make a physical arrest or take some other action will depend on the nature of the offense, the severity of the circumstances, and agency policies and procedures. The officer's actions may include the following:

- issuing a criminal Uniform Traffic Citation with mandatory court appearance date
- issuing a Notice to Appear (used for non-traffic offenses)
- arresting for a county or municipal ordinance violation
- arresting for misdemeanor offense (With some exceptions, misdemeanors must be committed in the officer's presence to justify physical arrest.)
- arresting for felony offense (Physical arrest is mandatory for all felonies.) *(LE025.5.B.)*

Once an arrest decision has been made, the officer should call for backup. When the backup officer arrives, the proper method to approach and affect the arrest can be decided. Based on arrest procedures, the officer should handcuff the suspect and place him or her in the patrol vehicle.

# UNIT 4 | HIGH RISK TRAFFIC STOPS

## LESSON 1 | Identifying a High Risk Traffic Stop

**OBJECTIVES**

**LE027.1.** Explain how to identify a suspect vehicle using a BOLO during a high risk traffic stop.

**LE027.1.A.** Identify matching identification points of the observed vehicle with the suspect vehicle description during a high risk traffic stop.

**LE278.3.A.** Identify additional information to give the dispatcher during a high risk traffic stop.

**LE027.5.** Identify how to maintain surveillance until backup arrives during a high risk traffic stop.

### Primary Objectives of the High Risk Traffic Stop

The primary objectives of a high risk traffic stop include an officer being able to recognize a suspect vehicle from a BOLO description, relay what he or she observed properly, stop the suspect vehicle safely, keep him- or herself and the public safe, and apprehend the suspect. To meet these objectives, an officer cannot work alone. He or she must coordinate closely with dispatch and communicate to other officers all pertinent information concerning the suspect vehicle.

### Identifying a Vehicle or Suspect

A traffic stop is never routine. When an officer knows in advance that a vehicle has been reported stolen, was seen in the commission of a felony, or when the driver or an occupant is suspected of a crime in progress or felony, the risk increases, both for the officer and for the public. This is known as a high risk or felony traffic stop. Listening, observing, and communicating are especially critical during these kinds of stops.

To identify the suspect vehicle, the officer must be able to recall its description from a BOLO *(LE027.1.)*. This requires matching identification points, including the observed vehicle's make, model, year, color, and tag number as well as any damage or special markings (unusual features like neon lights, writing on the windows, or bumper stickers) to help confirm the identification. Identifying information also includes driver description, number of occupants in the vehicle, and the vehicle's direction and speed. The officer should look, point by point, at each part of the BOLO to compare his or her observations to the BOLO information. If they match, the officer should then notify dispatch that the vehicle or suspect has been located and request backup. *(LE027.1.A.)*

## Information to be Communicated to Dispatch

As an officer begins the high risk traffic stop process, he or she will give dispatch his or her location, the vehicle's location and travel direction, the vehicle's description (make, model, color, and special identifiers, such as vehicle damage or bumper stickers), the number and description of occupants, the tag number and state, and suspected crimes and weapons. *(LE278.3.A.)*

## Surveillance of Suspect Vehicle While Waiting for Backup

If the information the officer gives dispatch is confirmed, there is probable cause to initiate the stop and backup should then be requested. The officer should follow the suspect vehicle until backup arrives and a safe stopping location is identified. Until backup arrives, the officer should maintain visual surveillance with the suspect vehicle *(LE027.5.)*. As in an unknown risk traffic stop, the officer should maintain a safe distance from the suspect vehicle; this varies based on the speed of travel. Meanwhile, the officer should not activate the emergency equipment *(LE027.5.A.)*. If backup is unavailable from the officer's agency, the officer should request assistance from other agencies *(LE278.5.)*. A high risk stop should only be conducted alone if the suspect's actions force it (for instance, if the suspect stops against the officer's wish).

Not only is the officer required to request and wait for backup before acting, he or she must also maintain radio contact with dispatch and with responding units *(LE027.6.)*. As circumstances change, backup and dispatch must be updated on the suspect vehicle's movement and route, suspect activity, and weapon or contraband information *(LE027.6.A.)*. This is an important role of the primary officer in a traffic stop.

## Maintaining Suspect Vehicle Surveillance and Communication with Dispatch

Throughout the surveillance of the suspect vehicle, the officer should maintain communication with dispatch so the officer's backup knows the primary officer's location *(LE027.4.)*. Without regular updates to dispatch, backup might arrive at the wrong location. This would not only leave the officer without backup but also leave the areas he or she was patrolling without law enforcement presence. Periodically, the primary officer should request the location and estimated time of arrival (ETA) of the backup units to keep from waiting in vain *(LE027.6.B.)*. An accurate ETA allows for planning the best stopping location.

**LE027.5.A.** Identify how to follow the suspect vehicle at a safe distance without activating the emergency equipment during a high risk traffic stop.

**LE278.5.** Identify how to request backup or assistance from other agencies during a high risk traffic stop.

**LE027.6.** Identify how to maintain radio contact with responding units during a high risk traffic stop.

**LE027.6.A.** Identify what information to give to responding backup units during a high risk traffic stop.

**LE027.4.** Identify how to continually update the communications center of the travel route of the vehicle during a high risk traffic stop.

**LE027.6.B.** Identify what information to request from responding backup units during a high risk traffic stop.

# UNIT 4 | HIGH RISK TRAFFIC STOPS

## LESSON 2 | Initiating the High Risk Stop

**OBJECTIVES**

**LE027.7.** Identify the need to locate a safe stopping site during a high risk traffic stop.

**LE027.7.B.** List the characteristics of a safe stopping site during a high risk traffic stop.

**LE027.7.E.** Identify a stopping site that has a line of unobstructed sight during a high risk traffic stop.

**LE027.7.D.** Identify a stopping site that has adequate roadway width to accommodate two patrol vehicles during a high risk traffic stop.

**LE027.7.A.** Identify how to coordinate the stopping site with backup units regarding their arrival time during a high risk traffic stop.

**LE027.9.B.** Identify that the primary officer should direct other units into position as they arrive at the scene during a high risk traffic stop.

**LE027.9.B.1.** Identify how to use the public address system microphone during a high risk traffic stop.

**LE278.2.** List the safety emergency equipment which can be used during a high risk traffic stop.

**LE027.8.** Identify the need to signal the suspect vehicle to pull over to the curb during a high risk traffic stop.

**LE027.8.D.1.** Ensure that emergency lights remain activated during a high risk traffic stop.

### Initiating the High Risk Traffic Stop

The key to safely conducting a high risk traffic stop is an officer's knowledge of his or her work zone. A safe location protects the officer and the public. It is impossible to predict an exact stopping location, but officers should use common sense; every effort should be made not to conduct a high risk stop on active school grounds, at a ball field, or at a busy shopping center.

When backup is near, the primary officer should locate a safe stopping place *(LE027.7.)*. Safety is crucial for the primary officer, the backup officers, and nearby citizens. A safe stopping site is visible to officers and oncoming traffic, away from heavy pedestrian traffic, away from heavy vehicle traffic, and large enough to accommodate backup units, a straight road (versus a curved road), a rural area (versus a business area), and has light traffic *(LE027.7.B.)*. A visible stopping site has an unobstructed view between the suspect vehicle, the patrol units, and oncoming traffic *(LE027.7.E.)*. If the primary officer must make the stop in an area with heavy traffic or two-way traffic, he or she may position an additional patrol vehicle well in front of the traffic stop to block oncoming traffic. For safety, this vehicle should approach from the opposite direction. The primary officer should also choose a site with enough roadway width to accommodate two or more patrol vehicles *(LE027.7.D.)*. If possible, an attempt should be made to stop all vehicular and pedestrian traffic.

### Coordinating the Stop

The primary officer will coordinate a stopping site based on the backup units' ETA *(LE027.7.A.)*. The officer should pick a location that gives all units a chance to reach the officer before the stop is initiated. The primary officer will direct the responding units to positions of backup or control and know what is expected of each position so he or she can communicate that to the responding units and provide directions for the group to work safely and effectively as a team *(LE027.9.B.)*. The primary officer should also set up the PA system and radio so they can be used after the stop is made *(LE027.9.B.1.)*. PA systems vary by model and installation, so an officer should be familiar with his or her vehicle's equipment.

When there is enough backup to initiate the high risk stop, the primary officer should request a secure channel for emergency traffic, and give dispatch the location of the stop, as well as information regarding the occupants' actions and behavior.

### Use of Emergency Equipment

After selecting the stopping location and communicating with dispatch and backup, the primary officer should activate emergency red/blue lights and the siren to initiate the stop *(LE278.2.)*. The suspect vehicle should be signaled to pull over to the curb *(LE027.8.)*. The officer should keep the emergency lights activated throughout the entire stop *(LE027.8.D.1.)*. They may help protect the officer from potential attack by the suspect. Using blinding light for safety is effective day or night *(LE027.8.F.)*. An officer should use the patrol vehicle's takedown lights, high beams, and spotlight during a night stop to illuminate a suspect vehicle's interior.

## Positioning the Patrol Vehicle

In accordance with agency policies and procedures, once the violator's vehicle stops, the primary officer should place the patrol vehicle so the suspect's door can be seen in case it is necessary for the officer to facilitate a quick getaway. The officer should park at a safe stopping distance behind the violator's vehicle. When conducting a high risk traffic stop, the distance behind the violator's vehicle should be increased to provide the officer with more protection. The situation and agency policy will dictate this safe distance. *(LE027.8.C.)*

The primary patrol vehicle should be offset to one side of the violator's vehicle. Agency policy and the situation (terrain, type of intersection, whether it is a highway or street, officer safety) help the officer determine which offset to use. The patrol vehicle should be centered on the suspect vehicle's taillight and slightly angled to provide protection. For example, if offset to the left, the patrol vehicle should be centered on the left taillight of the suspect's vehicle and if to the right, the patrol vehicle should be centered on the right taillight. *(LE027.8.D.)*

### *Backup Positioning*

The high risk traffic stop usually involves multiple backup units. Backup vehicles should be positioned to the right or left of the primary vehicle depending on agency policy, roadway, and environmental conditions. Position vehicles two door widths apart so both vehicle doors can open completely. During a night stop, the backup vehicle's takedown lights, high beams, and spotlight should be focused on the suspect vehicle's passenger side (See Figure 9-10).

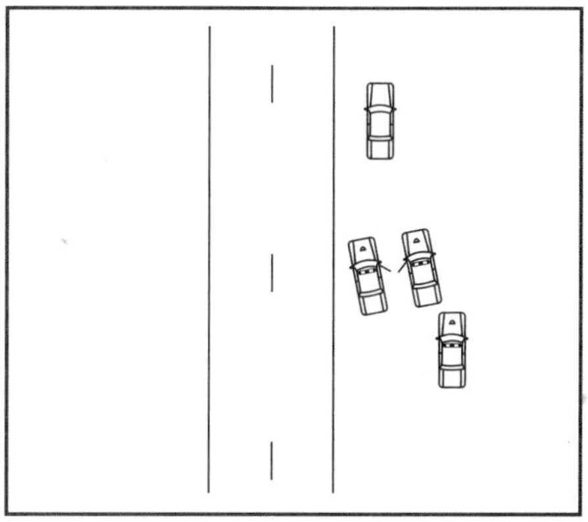

General multiple Backup positioning *Figure 9-10*

**LE027.8.F.** Identify the advantage to the officer of using blinding light, day or night, during a high risk traffic stop.

**LE027.8.C.** Identify the proper distance between the primary patrol vehicle and the suspect's vehicle for the stop during a high risk traffic stop.

**LE027.8.D.** Identify the proper position for the primary patrol vehicle and suspect vehicle during a high risk traffic stop.

**LE027.8.E.** Identify the proper positioning of the backup patrol vehicle in relation to the primary patrol vehicle and suspect vehicle during a high risk traffic stop.

**LE027.9.A.** Identify how to take cover using the patrol vehicles during a high risk traffic stop.

**LE027.9.A.1.** Identify how to take cover from within the vehicle during a high risk traffic stop.

**LE027.9.A.2.** Identify how to take cover from behind the vehicle during a high risk traffic stop.

**LE278.1.** Determine whether or not the pursuit is legal, feasible, necessary, and meets departmental criteria during a high risk traffic stop.

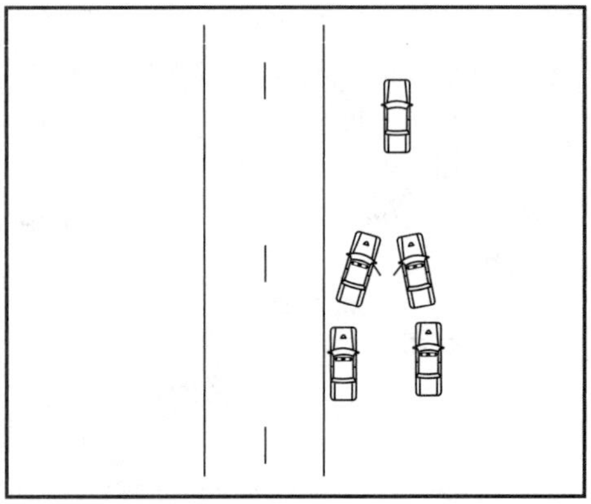

The Wedge *Figure 9-11*
Backup positioning

Some heavily populated areas of the state use a variation of the wedge. In this position, the front of the secondary vehicle is angled closer to the primary vehicle than the rear, creating a V shape with the two patrol vehicles. This formation is used when the stop involves two or more backup officers. The primary officer's employing agency might use other variations.

A third vehicle (or fourth) should be positioned to one side or the rear of the primary vehicle at a slight angle *(LE027.8.E.)*. During a night stop, the control vehicle's takedown lights, high beams, and spotlight should be focused on the suspect vehicle. If other vehicles are available, these officers should assist with securing the occupants, controlling traffic, interviewing, and controlling crowds (See Figure 9-11).

All arriving officers should refrain from leaving their area of cover and approaching the suspect vehicle. The officers should fight the urge to leave cover and rush up to the vehicle.

## Taking Cover Using the Patrol Vehicle

After the suspect vehicle is stopped and all officers' vehicles are properly positioned, the officers must use available cover to increase their safety. The patrol vehicle is the most effective and readily available cover *(LE027.9.A.)*. The officers can remain seated in the vehicle, exit the vehicle, or crouch behind the vehicle's door according to agency policy and procedures *(LE027.9.A.1., LE027.9.A.2.)*. The officers' position is also dictated by the situation at hand. Events are fluid, so flexibility is required.

Once the officers have established proper position, they should draw their firearms and point them at the suspect vehicle with their fingers outside the trigger guard. It is important that officers position themselves in relation to other officers to avoid being caught in a crossfire situation. If the driver pulls away after the stop is initiated, officers should make a second attempt to pull the vehicle over. If the suspect does not stop, an officer must decide whether or not the situation is legal, feasible, and necessary and meets the agency's criteria for pursuit *(LE278.1)*. If the officer's supervisor advises against pursuing or advises the officer to terminate the pursuit at any time, the officer must comply.

# UNIT 4 | HIGH RISK TRAFFIC STOPS

## LESSON 3 | Applying a Tactical Approach and Securing the Vehicle

### Taking Command of the High Risk Traffic Stop

The primary officer assumes command of the high risk traffic stop *(LE027.9.)*. The primary officer will direct all the vehicle's occupants using verbal control, and direct the arriving backup officers *(LE279.2.)*. This verbal control provides order and keeps the suspects from gaining an advantage. *(LE279.2.A.3.)*

### Verbal Commands

Using the PA system, an officer should identify him- or herself as a law enforcement officer, stating his or her name and agency name *(LE027.10.)*. It is imperative to maintain verbal control of suspects when giving voice commands and all attempts should be made to only use the PA system and stay within the cover of the patrol vehicle. *(LE027.11.A.)*

All occupants should be instructed to put their hands up so they are clearly visible. If the vehicle's windows are heavily tinted and the officers cannot see the passengers, the occupants should be told to put their hands outside the window where the officer can see them. *(LE027.11.)*

Specifically, the driver should then be commanded: "Roll down the window slowly with your left hand and then raise your hands again where I can see them" *(LE027.12.F.)*. Next, the driver should be told, "Use your left hand to turn off your engine. Remove and place your keys outside on the roof of your vehicle, open your door from the outside with that same hand, and return your hand above your head" *(LE027.12.D., LE027.12.C.)*. The officer will then direct only the driver to exit, on the driver's side, keeping hands visible and extended above the head while facing away from the officer. *(LE027.12.E.)*

Once outside the vehicle, the driver should be told to step away from the vehicle, stand on the balls of his or her feet, extend arms above head, lift the back of the shirt by the collar, and slowly turn in a complete circle so the officer can see any weapons or obvious bulges from possible weapons. The driver should then be told to stop, facing away from the officer, and listen to commands. If a weapon is seen, the driver must be advised that any movement towards the weapon will be met with appropriate force. The weapon and person must then be safely secured according to agency policy and procedures.

Next, the officer should command the driver to slowly step backward toward the sound of the officer's voice *(LE027.12.G.1.)*. The driver should be told to stop when he or she reaches the rear of the suspect vehicle. If the vehicle is a van or SUV, the driver should

**OBJECTIVES**

**LE027.9.** Identify that the primary officer should assume command of the situation during a high risk traffic stop.

**LE279.2.** Identify that the primary officer will control the suspect and occupants of the vehicle.

**LE279.2.A.3.** Identify the importance of maintaining verbal control of all occupants throughout the stop during a high risk traffic stop.

**LE027.10.** Identify self and agency to the suspect during a high risk traffic stop.

**LE027.11.A.** Identify the need to use the public address system of the patrol vehicle to maintain verbal control of suspects during a high risk traffic stop.

**LE027.11.** Identify how to command the suspect(s) to keep their hands visible during a high risk traffic stop.

**LE027.12.F.** Identify the need to direct the suspect to raise his or her hands and keep them in a visible position.

**LE027.12.D.** Identify the need to direct the suspect to open the driver's door with his or her left hand, using the external door handle during a high risk traffic stop.

**LE027.12.C.** Identify the need to direct the suspect to place ignition keys on top of the vehicle during a high risk traffic stop.

**LE027.12.E.** Identify the need to direct the suspect to exit the vehicle facing away from the law enforcement officers during a high risk traffic stop.

**LE027.12.G.1.** Identify the need to direct the suspect to walk backward toward the sound of the officer's voice during a high risk traffic stop.

**LE027.12.G.** Identify the need to direct the suspect to walk back to a predetermined point for safe securing during a high risk traffic stop.

**LE027.12.I.** Identify that the primary officer should instruct the backup unit to secure the suspect during a high risk traffic stop.

**LE027.12.H.** Identify the need to direct the suspect to assume a position of disadvantage during a high risk traffic stop.

**LE027.12.I.2.** Identify the need to retreat to cover with the suspect during a high risk traffic stop.

**LE279.2.A.2.** Identify the importance of maintaining visual contact with all occupants while conversing with the suspect during a high risk traffic stop.

**LE027.13.** Identify the need to instruct all occupants to exit the vehicle one at a time during a high risk traffic stop.

**LE027.13.1.** Identify how to search a vehicle for hidden occupants during a high risk traffic stop.

**LE280.5.** Identify the need to request backup when searching the vehicle during a high risk traffic stop.

be asked if the back doors are locked and then instructed to take the keys from the roof with the left hand, before he or she is told to begin side-stepping backwards to the center of the vehicle and open the back doors. Next, the primary officer should command the driver to continue backing up until he or she reaches the front of the patrol vehicle(s) or whichever point agency policy dictates *(LE027.12.G.)*. When the driver moves just past the front of the patrol vehicle(s), he or she should be stopped. The arrest team, located at the rear of the arrest vehicle, should begin commanding the driver's movements to search and secure the driver. *(LE027.12.I.)*

## Arrest Team—Procedures

The backup officer should tell the driver to kneel/become prone (position of disadvantage) when the driver reaches the front tires of the backup vehicle *(LE027.12.H.)*. The backup officer should then holster his or her weapon and approach and handcuff the driver. The officer will conduct a cursory pat-down for weapons, secure any weapons, and walk the driver back behind the cover of the backup vehicle to secure, completely search, and interview him or her about occupants and weapons *(LE027.12.I.2.)*. To gather intelligence for officer safety, the interview should concentrate on the presence of any weapons and number of occupants in the vehicle.

Where the driver and occupants are handcuffed may vary. Some agencies handcuff all suspects at the front tires of the backup vehicle, leaving the back of the primary vehicle as a "safe zone," while others take all suspects to the back of the backup vehicle to search and secure. The secured driver should be placed into a patrol vehicle. Once the driver is secured, the backup officer should return to position with his or her weapon drawn until the remaining passengers are removed and the vehicle is checked. When it is reasonable to believe that persons are concealed in the vehicle and concealed persons might present a threat to the officers and other persons, the vehicle must be checked for those persons and the threat reduced. This is an exception to the warrant requirement, and officers must record the facts and circumstances on which they relied for their decision. Officers not involved in the arrest team should stay focused and continually observe the remaining vehicle occupants. *(LE279.2.A.2)*

## Removing Remaining Occupants from the Vehicle

No occupants should be removed from the vehicle until the driver is secured. All occupants will be removed from the vehicle one by one after each is secured. The officer should use the same procedures to remove and secure the occupants as he or she did with the driver. The last occupant exiting the vehicle should leave the door open. *(LE027.13.)*.

When the officer believes that all occupants have been removed from the suspect vehicle and no one can be seen inside, he or she should use a bluff and command any hidden occupants to exit the vehicle. This is a safety technique, often referred to as the ***"plus one" rule*** of safety. When applying the "plus one" rule, the officer should focus on the observed suspects and the "plus one" that may be assumed to be hiding.

## Searching the Vehicle for Hidden Occupants

After the suspects and any occupants are out of the vehicle, the vehicle must be checked for hidden occupants. If there is no response to a bluff, the backup officers should approach the vehicle. While the primary officer continues giving commands, backup officers (if available) should move to the right and left side at the same time using a tactical approach and with their weapons pointed at the vehicle at all times. They should use caution not to bump into the vehicle and alert hidden occupants of their presence.

Maintaining a tactical position, the officer should check the vehicle's interior for occupants. A systematic visual search of the vehicle must be made. After the interior is clear, the officer should retrieve the keys from the roof in order to open the trunk *(LE027.13.1.)*. To clear the trunk, officers should move tactically to the trunk area. The backup officer may retrieve the keys from the roof and move low to the rear of the vehicle and place the key in the trunk's lock. The trunk is unlocked while one officer holds it down to prevent it from opening. After the trunk is unlocked, the officers move back and assume a safe position to cover the vehicle, pointing weapons at the trunk and making sure they are not in a crossfire position. The backup officer should lift the trunk lid. Both officers should then clear the trunk.

If necessary and available, backup officers should be present while conducting a protective sweep of a vehicle. *(LE280.5.)*

When the scene is secured and all is safe, the primary officer should notify dispatch to clear or open the channel and discontinue emergency radio traffic. After the investigation, the suspects are either informed of the charges, arrested, and transported to the agency or jail, or released if they are not the suspect. *(LE027.14.)*

**LE027.14.** Identify the need to inform suspects that they are under arrest during a high risk traffic stop.

**LE027.17.** Identify how to accurately complete the appropriate report(s) during a high risk traffic stop.

## Securing the Vehicle

After an officer has arrested a driver, the officer must decide what to do with the vehicle and any passengers. This decision involves whether the officer has the right to search the vehicle or whether the vehicle should be impounded or used for evidence, or if it meets the requirements for forfeiture. Depending on agency policy, the officer should arrange for removal of the suspect vehicle when the officer arrests the suspect and nobody else can drive the vehicle, when the vehicle is stolen, or when the vehicle must be impounded.

An officer should coordinate with a wrecker to tow the vehicle, inventory the vehicle, remove any personal possessions and items, or collect evidence if the vehicle was stolen or involved in a crime. A vehicle is considered evidence any time it is used in the commission of a crime or in the case of a traffic homicide.

Officers should be aware, however, that inventorying an impounded vehicle may not be used as a pretext to search for criminal evidence.

**Section Vocabulary**

*"plus one" rule*

# Documentation

The appropriate form(s) will be dictated by agency policies and procedure. Reasons for proper documentation include the following:

- Property in the vehicle may be evidence of a crime or personal property that will later be returned to the suspect.
- An officer must maintain a proper chain of evidence as items are secured.
- Correctly documenting property protects the officer from accusations of theft or improper actions.
- Identification of stolen property can help solve other cases.
- Correctly labeling evidence and placing items into the evidence system ensures the chain of evidence is preserved and leads to the successful admission of evidence in trial.
- All property with a serial number must be checked in the FCIC/NCIC database. This ensures that stolen property is identified and seized for safekeeping or evidence.

Proper documentation of the incident—from information at roll call to locating a possible suspect, confirming a warrant, contacting and then arresting the suspect, and seizing evidence—helps lead to a conviction on all charges. *(LE027.17.)*

# CHAPTER 10

## DUI Traffic Stops



Law enforcement officers make numerous traffic stops daily. All too often drivers are impaired by the use of alcohol or drugs, making them a hazard to themselves and other motorists. This chapter will train officers to detect impaired driving, administer field sobriety tests, make arrests when appropriate, and record the evidence of a DUI violation.

# LESSON 1 | Overview of the DUI Problem

**OBJECTIVES**

**LE515.1.** Describe the problem of impaired driving.

**LE515.2** Identify general strategies for solving the problem of impaired driving.

**LE515.3.** Identify keys to an officer's success in deterring impaired driving.

**LE515.4.** Describe how alcohol affects the human body.

**LE515.5.** Define *blood alcohol concentration (BAC).*

**LE515.6.** Define *breath alcohol concentration (BrAC).*

This section, DUI Traffic Stops, has been adapted from the DWI Detection and Standardized Field Sobriety Testing course produced by the National Highway Traffic Safety Administration (NHTSA). It has been modified from a national perspective to be specific for the state of Florida.

*Note:* The NHTSA course uses the term "driving while impaired (DWI)." Florida law uses the term "driving under the influence (DUI)."

## DUI: The Problem

Each year, tens of thousands of people die in traffic crashes. Throughout the nation, alcohol is the major contributor to traffic fatalities. In fact, the number one crime resulting in death in the United States is impaired driving. Some estimates indicate that about 25 percent of America's drivers at least occasionally drive while under the influence, and that offenders actually commit the offense an average of 80 times per year. While driving under the influence (DUI) of alcohol or drugs, impaired drivers are more likely than other drivers to take excessive risks and have slowed reaction times; they are also less likely to wear seatbelts. *(LE515.1.)*

Many factors impair drivers including alcohol, drugs, medical conditions, and mental or physical disabilities. An officer's primary duty in detecting and investigating DUI cases is to remove impaired drivers from the road to ensure public safety.

## DUI: The Solution

DUI is both a societal and law enforcement problem. The ultimate goal is to reduce the number of impaired drivers through prevention, education, and deterrence. Prevention promises the ultimate, lasting solution to the DUI problem, but it will require a substantial amount of time to fully accomplish. Education is an essential component of the solution. Law enforcement must not only enforce the DUI laws but take the time to educate the public through schools, civic groups, special events, etc. Deterrence only offers a partial or limited solution, but it is available right now. Both the public and law enforcement are responsible for working together to accomplish the goal of stopping DUI. *(LE515.2.)*

Behavioral change in individuals is fundamental to prevention. The public should do the following:

- avoid committing DUI, either by avoiding or controlling drinking prior todriving or by selecting alternative transportation
- intervene actively to prevent others from committing DUI (for example, putting into practice the theme "friends don't let friends drive drunk")
- avoid riding with drivers who are impaired

General deterrence is based upon the driving public's fear of being arrested.

- If violators believe there is a good chance they will get caught, some will stop committing the offense at least some of the time.
- Unless there is a real risk of being arrested, there will not be a fear of being arrested.
- Law enforcement must arrest enough violators to convince the public they will be caught if they continue to drive while impaired.

The legal consequences of a DUI conviction include monetary fines, imprisonment, and temporary or permanent loss of driving privileges. The keys to successful deterrence by well-trained law enforcement officers include the following:

- skill at DUI detection
- willingness to arrest every DUI violator who is detected
- support of their agencies *(LE515.3.)*

There are other participants who contribute to the prevention and deterrence of DUI. Legislators pass the laws that law enforcement enforces. Prosecutors prosecute DUI violators, and the judiciary adjudicates fairly and delivers the punishments prescribed by law. The media publicizes the enforcement effort and communicates that the risk is not worth the probable outcome. Each of these elements plays a supportive role in DUI deterrence.

DUI detection is the key to deterrence. Studies show that a practical and realistic increase in DUI enforcement activity will induce a significant degree of general deterrence and a corresponding change in DUI behavior.

## Alcohol and the Human Body

Alcohol is a central nervous system depressant and is the most abused drug in the United States. Alcohol is the active ingredient in beer, wine, whiskey, liquors, etc. Its effect on the body includes loss of fine motor skills, hand/eye coordination, and judgment. Often the person who is affected by alcohol doesn't think that he or she is impaired. ***Absorption*** is the process by which alcohol enters the bloodstream. The absorption rate of alcohol varies based on many factors including the person's weight and gender, whether and how much food he or she has eaten, and the alcohol concentration of the substances being consumed. ***Distribution*** is the process by which alcohol is carried via the bloodstream to the body's tissues and organs. ***Metabolism*** is the biological process by which the body breaks down alcohol into compounds that are more readily eliminated. ***Elimination*** is expelling alcohol from the body through exhaled breath, sweat, tears, saliva, urine, etc. The average alcohol elimination rate of humans is .015 percent per hour. *(LE515.4.)*

## Level of Impairment

How much is too much? Any amount of alcohol will affect a person's ability to drive to some degree. The degree to which the person is affected depends on how much alcohol is consumed, the length of time over which the alcohol is consumed, the gender and physical size of the person, whether or not the person has eaten, and various other factors.

Florida law establishes the ***blood alcohol concentration (BAC)*** or ***breath alcohol concentration (BrAC)*** limit at which an individual is presumed impaired and cannot legally operate a vehicle. Section

## Section Vocabulary

*absorption*

*blood alcohol concentration (BAC)*

*breath alcohol concentration (BrAC)*

*distribution*

*elimination*

*metabolism*

316.193, F.S. establishes that limit as 0.08 BAC. BAC is expressed in terms of grams of alcohol in every 100 milliliters of blood, *(LE515.5.)* and BrAC is expressed as grams of alcohol per 210 liters of breath *(LE515.6.)*. Therefore, 0.08 may refer to the blood alcohol level or the breath alcohol level.

To understand the effects of drinking on blood alcohol concentration, consider the following example: If a 175-pound man drinks two beers or two shots of whiskey within an hour on an empty stomach, his BAC may climb above 0.04. Two more beers can boost him above 0.08. One more can push him over 0.10.

# LESSON 2 | Legal Issues

**OBJECTIVES**

**LE515.7.** Define *driving under the influence (DUI).*

**LE515.8.** Define *actual physical control.*

**LE515.9.** Define *vehicle* per Florida Statutes.

**LE515.10.** Define *Standardized Field Sobriety Tests (SFSTs).*

**LE515.11.** Define *psychophysical tests.*

**LE515.12.** Identify the requirements for *Miranda* warnings during a DUI traffic stop.

**LE515.13.** List the elements of the offense of driving under the influence provided in the Florida Statutes.

An understanding of impaired driving laws that apply in Florida is critical to DUI enforcement.

## Key Terms

***Driving under the influence (DUI)*** refers to a person who is driving, who has driven, or who is in actual physical control of a vehicle while impaired by alcohol or certain substances that adversely affect the auditory, visual, or mental processes. *(LE515.7.)*

A person may be in ***actual physical control*** of a vehicle even though he or she is not actually driving. A person who is physically in, on, or around the vehicle and has the capability to operate the vehicle is legally in actual physical control of the vehicle and can be arrested and prosecuted for DUI *(LE515.8.)*. For example, a person who is asleep or passed out in the front seat of a vehicle with the ignition key in the ignition, in his or her pocket, or on the seat next to him or her is in actual physical control of the vehicle and may be arrested. If the vehicle is inoperable, such a person could not be found to be in actual physical control unless sufficient circumstantial evidence exists that the defendant was driving under the influence when the vehicle became inoperable. Just because a car is made inoperable by a crash that was not witnessed does not mean the driver found passed out behind the wheel is not in actual physical control, since the evidence suggests he or she was driving when the crash occurred.

Florida Statute §316.003(75) defines ***vehicle*** as "every device, in, upon, or by which any person or property is or may be transported or drawn upon a highway, excepting devices used exclusively upon stationary rails or tracks" *(LE515.9.)*. Florida's Third District Court of Appeal held that the term includes bicycles, and a person biking while under the influence of alcohol could be charged with DUI (*State v. Howard*, 510 So.2d 612 (3rd DCA 1987), rev. denied, *Howard v. State*, 520 So.2d 584 (Fla. 1988). Using the logic in the *Howard* opinion, vehicles could also include scooters, ATVs, go-carts, golf carts, etc.

***Within the state*** includes anywhere in Florida, whether on roadways or public or private property. A person may be arrested for DUI even though he or she never drove onto a road or highway.

***Normal faculties*** include the ability to see, hear, walk, talk, judge distances, drive an automobile, make judgments, act in emergencies, and normally perform the mental and physical acts of daily life.

F.S. §316.193 establishes legal presumptions based on the violator's blood alcohol concentration or level. Florida's standard jury instructions give the elements of the crime that the prosecution must prove prior to the subject being convicted. In the case of the crime of DUI, the jury is instructed to presume certain conclusions based on alcohol concentration. If the alcohol concentration was 0.05 or below, the jury must presume the violator was not under the influence of alcoholic beverages to the extent that his or her normal faculties were impaired. If the alcohol concentration was greater than 0.05 but less than 0.08, the jury may not presume any conclusion that the violator was or was not under the influence of alcoholic beverages to the extent that his or her normal faculties were impaired. Such an alcohol concentration may be considered with other competent evidence (i.e., driving pattern, personal contact, and standardized field sobriety tests) in determining whether the person was under the influence of alcoholic beverages to the extent that his or her normal faculties were impaired.

If the alcohol concentration was 0.08 or higher, the jury is instructed to presume that the person was under the influence of alcohol to the extent that his or her normal faculties were impaired. Also, a person could be guilty of driving or being in actual physical control of a motor vehicle with an unlawful alcohol concentration regardless of impairment.

## *Miranda* Requirements

The U.S. Supreme Court has ruled that a law enforcement officer is not required to administer *Miranda* warnings during the course of a traffic stop in which the officer temporarily detains a motorist in order to ask a few brief questions and issue a citation. See *Berkemer v. McCarty*, 468 U.S. 420 (1984). Also, *Miranda* warnings are not typically required prior to administering ***Standardized Field Sobriety Tests (SFSTs)*** (a series of psychophysical tests given to determine impairment) *(LE515.10.)*. ***Psychophysical tests*** describe field sobriety tests that measure a person's ability to perform both mental and physical tasks simultaneously *(LE515.11.)*. An officer should always rely on agency

**LE515.14.** Explain the concept of *implied consent.*

**LE515.15.** Explain when an officer should complete a DUI citation.

**LE515.16.** Describe the offense of DUI Second Refusal.

**LE515.17.** Explain the purpose of requesting a urine test from a DUI subject.

**LE515.18.** Describe the criteria for obtaining a blood test from a DUI subject.

**LE515.19.** Explain the requirements for conducting a DUI investigation on a commercial motor vehicle driver.

**LE515.20.** Explain the procedures for handling a DUI investigation for persons under the age of 21.

policies and procedures in determining when and under what circumstances *Miranda* warnings are administered to DUI subjects. *(LE515.12.)*

# Conviction

Florida law provides the following definition of driving under the influence in section 316.193, F.S.:

> (1) A person is guilty of the offense of driving under the influence and is subject to punishment as provided in subsection (2) if the person is driving or in actual physical control of a vehicle within this state and:
>
> (a) The person is under the influence of alcoholic beverages, any chemical substance set forth in F.S. §877.111, or any substance controlled under chapter 893, when affected to the extent that the person's normal faculties are impaired;
>
> (b) The person has a blood-alcohol level of 0.08 or more grams of alcohol per 100 milliliters of blood; or
>
> (c) The person has a breath-alcohol level of 0.08 or more grams of alcohol per 210 liters of breath. *(LE515.13.)*

In order to arrest someone for a DUI violation, a law enforcement officer must have probable cause to believe that all elements of the offense are present. To convict a person of a DUI violation, it is necessary to show beyond a reasonable doubt that all the elements of the offense were present.

# Implied Consent

Any person who accepts the privilege of driving in Florida has consented to submit to an approved chemical test to determine the alcohol content or the presence of a chemical and/or controlled substance in their breath, blood, or urine once they are lawfully arrested for committing a violation while driving or in actual physical control of a motor vehicle and under the influence of alcoholic beverages. See F.S. §316.1932(1)(a)1.a. Based on this ***implied consent***, Florida law requires that a lawfully arrested driver to take any breath, blood, or urine test requested by a law enforcement officer *(LE515.14.)*. The implied consent warning can be **read** by a law enforcement officer, corrections officer, or certified Breath Test Operator, but it is recommended that a law enforcement officer **read** it to the subject upon refusal of a request to submit as per agency policy and procedures. Figure 10-1 on the following page is an example (Figure 10-1).

# Administering the Breath Test

A permitted Breath Test Operator will administer the breath test. If the results of the test indicate an alcohol concentration of 0.08 or higher, the officer needs to complete a DUI Citation. The results should be written on the citation. If the results are below a 0.08, the officer should complete a Uniform Traffic Citation for the charge of DUI based on the probable cause for the arrest. If the subject refuses to submit to the breath test, an officer should complete a DUI Citation and mark the box for "Refusal." *(LE515.15.)*

Some jail facilities may require medical assistance for extremely impaired subjects. Regardless of the alcohol concentration, an officer's observations may indicate that a person needs immediate medical attention.

**Implied Consent Warning**

I am now requesting that you submit to a lawful test of your BREATH for the purpose of determining the alcoholic content.

I am now requesting that you submit to a lawful test of your BLOOD for the purpose of determining the alcohol content and/or the presence of a chemical and/or controlled substance.

I am now requesting that you submit to a lawful test of your URINE for the purpose of determining the presence of a chemical and/or controlled substance.

***Note:*** *Read only if the subject does not comply with your request.*

I am ________________________________ of the ________________________________________.

If you fail to submit to the test I have requested of you, your privilege to operate a motor vehicle will be suspended for a period of one (1) year for a first refusal, or eighteen (18) months if your privilege has been previously suspended as a result of a refusal to submit to a lawful test of the breath, blood, or urine. Additionally, if you refuse to submit to the test I have requested of you and if your driving privilege has been previously suspended for a prior refusal to submit to a lawful test of your breath, blood, or urine, you will be committing a misdemeanor. Refusal to submit to the test(s) I have requested of you is admissible into evidence in any criminal or administrative proceeding.

Implied consent *Figure 10-1*

## DUI Second or Subsequent Refusal

If a subject is placed under lawful arrest for the offense of DUI, refuses to submit to a lawfully requested test of his or her breath/urine/blood, and refuses to submit to a chemical breath/urine/blood test, the subject commits the offense of DUI Second Refusal per F.S. §316.1939 *(LE515.16.)*. The original refusal information can be verified by checking FCIC/NCIC, DAVID, and/or criminal history. The officer shall place this additional charge on the Probable Cause Affidavit and issue a Uniform Traffic Citation. The charge of a DUI Second (or subsequent) Refusal is a misdemeanor of the first degree.

## DUI Citation

The DUI citation must be completed accurately. This citation is not only a charging document, but is also required to authorize the Department of Highway Safety and Motor Vehicles to suspend the subject's driving privilege. If the subject has an alcohol concentration of 0.08 or above or refuses chemical testing, his or her driver's license is seized and attached to the blue copy of the DUI citation per F.S. Ch. 316. The officer or his or her agency should forward the license and a copy to Department of Highway Safety and Motor Vehicles for an administrative suspension per agency policy.

The DUI Citation is very similar to the Uniform Traffic Citation, except that the DUI Citation is used only for a DUI with an alcohol concentration of 0.08 or higher or when the violator has refused any chemical test after being lawfully arrested. The DUI Citation is filled out in the same manner as a Uniform Traffic Citation, including citing the appropriate violated Florida Statute. However, a DUI citation has additional fields that must be completed regarding the following:

- if the subject refuses
- if the subject is eligible for a permit
- if the subject's license was surrendered
- location of the Department of Highway Safety and Motor Vehicles Hearing Office

## Refusal Affidavit

The State of Florida Refusal Affidavit must be completed in conjunction with a DUI Citation issued for a refusal. The Department of Highway Safety and Motor Vehicles provides refusal affidavits to law enforcement agencies. This form must be completed, notarized, and forwarded to DHSMV as part of the DUI arrest report.

## Urine Test

If a breath test result is below a 0.08 and an officer has probable cause to believe that the subject is impaired by a substance(s) other than alcohol, the officer should request a urine test. The urine test may determine if drugs are in the system and possibly causing the impairment *(LE515.17.)*. If the subject refuses the urine test, the officer must charge him or her with a DUI refusal even if a breath sample was provided. The subject should be requested to submit to all tests (breath and urine) and should be given the Implied Consent Warning for each test refused. The urine sample will be collected according to agency policies and procedures. The officer should write "urine pending" in the Comments section on the issued Uniform Traffic Citation.

## Blood Test

Blood can be requested as long as all of the following criteria are met per F.S. §316.1932(1)(c):

- The subject has been lawfully arrested.
- The individual was under the influence of alcohol or a chemical or controlled substance while driving or in actual physical control of a vehicle.
- The breath test was impractical or impossible to give.
- The subject appeared at a medical facility for treatment.

All blood draws must be conducted at a medical facility as defined by Florida Statutes §316.1932(1)(c). Someone who is unable to have withdrawn their consent (such as an unconscious subject) is deemed to have given consent to the test. All other lawfully arrested subjects should be requested to submit to a blood draw. If they refuse, they should be read the Implied Consent Warning and asked again for a blood sample. The subject need not be under arrest for an officer to request a blood draw under implied consent.

A person suspected of DUI who kills or seriously injures another person is required to submit to a blood test according to F.S. §316.1933.

According to F.S. §316.1932(1)(f)2.a. and F.S. §316.1933(2)(a), only specified personnel are authorized to draw blood. An officer is responsible for ensuring that the blood is drawn according to established procedures. The officer needs to verify the following: the blood kit is not expired, the blood is collected in the appropriate vial, an authorized person collects the blood, and the vial labels contain the subject's name, date, and time the blood was collected as well as the initials of the person drawing the blood. It is a good idea for an officer to initial the label to show that he or she verified the necessary information. If asked to identify the vial in court, seeing his or her own initials could prove beneficial. Due to the serious nature of the DUI offense, the officer must follow agency procedure for obtaining blood. *(LE515.18.)*

### *Commercial Motor Vehicle DUI Investigations*

An officer needs to know that there are certain statutes concerning operating a commercial motor vehicle, as defined in F.S. §322.01(8), while the driver is impaired. See sections 322.61, 322.62, 322.63, 316.1932, and 322.64, F.S.

A person who has any alcohol in his or her body may not drive or be in actual physical control of a commercial motor vehicle in this state. See F.S. §322.62(1). Any driver in violation of this section must be placed out-of-service immediately for a period of 24 hours. An officer should have a responsible party pick up the vehicle or have the vehicle towed, depending on the situation and his or her agency's policy.

If a driver is arrested for a violation of F.S. §316.193 or is in possession of a controlled substance while operating or in actual physical control of a motor vehicle or a commercial motor vehicle, the driver may be subject to the loss of his or her commercial driver license (CDL) for a period of one year. This penalty also applies if the driver refuses to submit to a breath, urine, or blood test to determine alcohol concentration, or if the driver is driving a commercial motor vehicle with an alcohol concentration of 0.04 or higher. Other conditions and penalties may also apply depending on the circumstances.

If an officer suspects a DUI violation, he or she should conduct a DUI investigation utilizing the same process for determining impairment: conduct the SFSTs, follow arrest procedures, administer the chemical or physical tests, and complete documentation. *(LE515.19.)*

## Drivers Under 21 Years of Age (0.02 Violation)

If an officer is involved in a DUI investigation with a driver under the age of 21, the officer should conduct a DUI investigation utilizing the same process for determining impairment: conduct the SFSTs, follow arrest procedures, administer the chemical or physical tests, and complete documentation.

If the DUI investigation does not result in a DUI arrest, but there is evidence that the driver has been consuming alcohol, the officer may request a breath test to determine the driver's alcohol concentration. If the driver's alcohol concentration level is at or above 0.02, or if he or she refuses to submit to a breath test, his or her driver's license will be suspended. The driver is not arrested but is subject to administrative penalties. The officer should take the license and issue a Notice of Suspension. If the driver is issued a Notice of Suspension, then he or she should be released according to agency policies and procedures.*(LE515.20.)*

## Report Forms

The officer must complete many forms to conclude a DUI investigation and/or arrest. The forms vary by agency and may include the following:

- field notes
- implied consent warning
- *Miranda* warning with waiver
- refusal affidavit
- citations (DUI Citation/Uniform Traffic Citation)
- breath test result affidavit
- agency offense incident report(s)
- probable cause affidavit
- alcohol influence report (agency-specific)
- certificate of blood withdrawal

## DUI Case Law Affecting Florida

### Accident Report Privilege

***State v. Cino*, 931 So.2d 164 (Fla. 5th DCA 2006)**—The state was not precluded from using evidence of an officer's observations of defendant's physical traits and demeanor at the scene (during the crash investigation). The state was not precluded from using statements by persons OTHER than the defendant (even if given during the crash investigation). The officer was barred from basing probable cause on statements compelled from the driver (during the crash investigation).

### Accident Report Privilege—Leaving the Scene

***Cummings v. State*, 780 So.2d 149 (Fla. 2nd DCA 2001)**—The accident report privilege does NOT apply when the defendant leaves the scene of the accident.

### Attorney Prior to Administration of a Breath Test

***State v. Burns*, 661 So. 2d 842 (5th DCA 1995)**—Administering a breath test is nothing more than the collection and preservation of physical evidence and DOES NOT constitute crucial confrontation requiring the presence of defense counsel.

### Breath Test Refusal

***Grezlka v. State*, 881 So.2d 633 (Fla. 5th DCA 2004)**—The defendant was not given the entire implied consent warning and the refusal was still admissible. The court went on to clearly state that "nothing in the statute requires exclusion when the statutory warning is not complete." In fact, as long as the defendant was advised of at least one adverse consequence resulting from refusal to submit to the breath test, the refusal was relevant and admissible.

### Good Faith Doctrine

***State v. Geiss* 2011 WL 2097694 (Fla. 5th DCA 2011)**—The court reaffirms the Good Faith Doctrine when officers rely upon an improperly issued search warrant to draw blood from a DUI suspect. The court agreed the warrant statute was improperly used in this case, but the officer relied on it reasonably.

### Cracked Windshield

***Hilton v. State*, 961 So.2d 285 (Fla. 2007)**—The court held that a cracked windshield violates section 316.610 only if it renders the vehicle in "such unsafe condition as to endanger any person or property."

**Defendant Exiting the Vehicle**

***Pennsylvania v. Mimms*, 434 U.S. 106 (1977)**—If the stop is lawful, the officer may order the driver to exit the vehicle for the officer's safety.

**Failure to Maintain Single Lane**

***Yanes v. State*, 877 So.2d 25 (Fla. 5th DCA 2004)**—The court found a violation of failure to maintain a single lane, even when NO ONE was endangered. The defendant deviated from his lane by more than was practicable (three times by one-half the vehicle's width).

**HGN**

***Williams v. State*, 710 So.2d 24 (3rd DCA 1998)**—A properly qualified Drug Recognition Expert (DRE) can give the necessary testimony to permit HGN test results.

***Bowen v. State*, 745 So.2d 1108 (3rd DCA 1999)**—Any qualified and trained officer can give HGN testimony, even if the officer is not a DRE. This determination will be made by the judge.

**Officer Outside of Jurisdiction Makes Arrest**

***State v. Joy*, 637 So.2d 946 (Fla. 3rd DCA 1994)**—An officer can follow a subject into a neighboring community based solely on reasonable suspicion of a traffic infraction and lawfully make a DUI arrest outside the officer's jurisdiction based on the conduct of the defendant in the other jurisdiction.

**Personal Contact**

***Origi v. State*, 912 So.2d 69 (4th DCA 2005)**—The defendant was stopped for speeding, and the officer observed the driver had bloodshot eyes and noticed an odor of alcohol. The court held that this was enough reasonable suspicion to conduct a DUI investigation.

**Refusal of SFSTs**

***State v. Taylor*, 648 So.2d 701 (Fla. 1995)**—The refusal to take SFSTs is admissible in court if the law enforcement officer indicated "adverse consequences" of refusing (i.e., "Your refusal can be used against you in court." "I will base my decision whether or not to arrest you upon all the observations I have made so far, including your refusal." etc.).

**Registered Owner Does Not Have Valid License**

***Smith v. State*, 574 So.2d 300 (Fla. 5th DCA 1991)**—The court held that an officer can stop a vehicle if the officer obtains information that the registered owner does not have a valid license and if the driver of the vehicle matches the general description of the owner on record.

**SFSTs and *Miranda***

***State v. Taylor*, 648 So.2d 701 (Fla.1995)**—For a routine DUI arrest, *Miranda* is NOT required prior to the administration of SFSTs. Custody equals formal arrest. Roadside investigation/questioning does not equal custody.

**SFSTs**

***Meador v. State*, 674 So.2d 826 (4th DCA 1996)**—The Court held that:

"a defendant's ability to perform these simple psychomotor tasks is within a juror's common experiences and understanding. There are objective components of the field sobriety exercises, which

## Section Vocabulary

*actual physical control*

*driving under the influence (DUI)*

*implied consent*

*normal faculties*

*psychophysical tests*

*Standardized Field Sobriety Tests (SFSTs)*

*vehicle*

*within the state*

> are commonly understood and easily determined, such as whether a foot is on a line or not. Jurors do not require any special expertise to interpret performance of these tasks...Thus, evidence of the police officer's observations of the results of defendant's performing the walk-and-turn test, the one-legged stand, the balance test and the finger-to-nose test should be treated no differently than testimony of lay witnesses (officers, in this case) concerning their observations about the driver's conduct and appearance."

**Standard for Traffic Stops**

***Whren v. U.S.*, 517 U.S. 806 (1996)**—The court held that only a reasonable suspicion was required to justify a traffic stop; probable cause was not the threshold requirement.

**Suspected Defendant Was DUI, Ill, or Tired**

***DHSMV v. DeShong*, 603 So.2d 1349 (Fla. 2nd DCA 1992)**—The court held that reasonable suspicion, NOT probable cause, is required to stop a vehicle. The courts have recognized that a legitimate concern for the safety of the motoring public can warrant a brief investigatory stop to determine whether the driver is ill, tired, or DUI.

**Traffic Violations**

***Holland v. State*, 696 So.2d 757 (Fla. 1997)**—As long as the vehicle's observed driving actions constitute a traffic violation, it no longer matters how trivial the violation. An officer is authorized to stop such a vehicle.

**Unusual Operations of Motor Vehicle**

***Bailey v. State*, 319 So.2d 22 (Fla. 1975)**—"Because of the dangers inherent to our modern vehicular mode of life, there is justification for the stopping of a vehicle by a patrolman to determine the reason for its unusual operation." The vehicle in this case was driving well below the speed limit and "weaving not all that bad." As long as an officer can articulate some unusual operation of the vehicle, the officer can conduct a stop to investigate all suspicious possibilities.

**Speed—Lay Opinion**

***State v. Joy*, 637 So.2d 946 (Fla. 3rd DCA 1994)**—An officer's lay opinion of speed is sufficient to support probable cause for a speeding stop.

# LESSON 3 | DUI Detection

## Overview of Detection

***DUI detection*** means the entire process of identifying and gathering evidence to determine whether or not a subject should be arrested for a DUI violation. The detection process begins when the law enforcement officer first suspects that an individual may be driving under the influence and ends when the officer determines that there is or is not sufficient probable cause to arrest the subject for DUI *(LE515.21.)*. Effective DUI enforcers do not leap to the arrest/no arrest decision. Rather, they proceed carefully through a series of intermediate steps, each of which helps to identify the collective evidence.

The typical DUI contact involves three phases:

- **Phase One: Vehicle in motion**—You usually observe the driver operating the vehicle.
- **Phase Two: Personal contact**—After you have stopped the vehicle, there usually is an opportunity to observe and speak with the driver face-to-face.
- **Phase Three: Pre-arrest screening**—You usually administer some formal structured field sobriety tests to the driver to determine impairment.

The DUI detection process does not always include all three phases. Sometimes there are DUI detection contacts in which Phase One is absent, for example, cases in which the driver is passed out behind the wheel of a vehicle that is not in motion. This may also occur at the scene of a traffic crash or when you have responded to a request for motorist assistance. Sometimes there are DUI contacts in which Phase Three never occurs and you would not administer formal tests to the driver. These may occur when the driver is so impaired or injured that he or she cannot perform the tests, or he or she refuses to submit to the tests.

### *Phase One*

The first task in Phase One is to observe the vehicle in operation. Based on this observation, you must decide whether there is reasonable suspicion to command the driver to stop. The second task is to observe the stopping sequence. The following questions may be helpful:

- What is the vehicle doing?
- Do I have grounds to stop the vehicle?
- How does the driver respond to my signal to stop?
- How does the driver handle the vehicle during the stopping sequence? *(LE515.22.)*

**OBJECTIVES**

**LE515.21.** Define *DUI detection.*

**LE515.22.** Explain Phase One in a typical DUI contact.

**LE515.23.** Explain Phase Two in a typical DUI contact.

**LE515.24.** Explain Phase Three in a typical DUI contact.

**LE515.25.** Identify the purpose of field notes in the DUI enforcement process.

**LE515.26.** List types of information that should be included in DUI field notes.

**LE515.22.a.1.** Define *cue.*

**LE515.22.a.** Describe the use of visual cues to detect reasonable suspicion of a possible impaired driver.

**LE515.22.a.2.** Define *divided attention.*

**LE515.22.b.** List observations an officer might make after the command to stop is given to a DUI subject.

**LE515.23.a.** Define *clue.*

**LE515.23.b.** Describe how to use the senses during face-to-face contact to detect clues of impairment.

**LE515.23.c.** Identify medical conditions with clues that may mimic alcohol or drug impairment.

**LE515.23.d.** Identify pre-exit interview techniques that may detect clues of impairment.

**LE515.23.e.** List types of subject behavior observed during the exit sequence that would lead an officer to have reasonable suspicion of impairment.

**LE515.24.a.** Name the three Standardized Field Sobriety Tests used to detect alcohol or drug impairment.

**LE515.24.b.** Define *nystagmus.*

**LE515.24.c.** Define *Horizontal Gaze Nystagmus (HGN).*

**LE515.24.d.** Define *Vertical Gaze Nystagmus (VGN).*

**LE515.24.e.** Identify that nystagmus is a reliable clue of impairment.

**LE515.24.f.** Identify why divided attention tests are effective in detecting impairment.

**LE515.24.g.** List the clues officers may observe in an impaired person during the Walk-and-Turn test.

**LE515.24.h.** List the clues officers may observe in an impaired person during the One-Leg Stand test.

**LE515.24.i.** Explain how to make a decision to arrest a subject for DUI.

## Phase Two

The first task in Phase Two is to observe and interview the driver face-to-face. Based on this observation, you must decide whether there is reasonable suspicion to instruct the driver to step from the vehicle for further investigation. The second task is to observe the driver's exit and walk from the vehicle. Ask yourself the following questions:

- When I approach the vehicle, what do I see?
- When I talk with the driver, what do I hear, see, and smell?
- How does the driver respond to my questions?
- Should I instruct the driver to exit the vehicle?
- How does the driver exit?
- When the driver walks toward the side of the road, what do I see? *(LE515.23.)*

## Phase Three

The task in Phase Three is to administer structured, formal psychophysical tests. This term is used to describe field sobriety tests that measure a person's ability to perform both mental and physical tasks simultaneously. Based on these tests, you must decide whether there is probable cause to arrest the driver for DUI. Ask yourself:

- Should I administer field sobriety tests to the driver?
- How does the driver perform those tests?
- What exactly did the driver do wrong when performing the tests?
- Do I have probable cause to arrest for DUI?

Each of the major decisions can have any one of three different outcomes: Yes—Do it Now, Wait—Look for Additional Evidence, or No—Don't Do It. Consider the following examples:

### Yes—Do It Now

*Phase One:* Yes, there is reasonable suspicion to stop the vehicle.

*Phase Two:* Yes, there is enough reason to suspect subject impairment to justify getting the driver out of the vehicle for further investigation.

*Phase Three:* Yes, there is probable cause to arrest the driver for DUI right now.

### Wait—Look for Additional Evidence

*Phase One:* Don't stop the vehicle yet; keep following and observing it a bit longer.

*Phase Two:* Don't get the driver out of the car yet; keep talking to and observing the driver a bit longer. (This option may be limited if the officer's personal safety is at risk.)

*Phase Three:* Don't arrest the driver yet; administer another field sobriety test before deciding.

### *No—Don't Do It*

*Phase One:* No, there are no grounds for stopping the vehicle.

*Phase Two:* No, there isn't enough evidence of DUI to justify administering field sobriety tests.

*Phase Three:* No, there is not probable cause to believe the driver has committed DUI. *(LE515.24.)*

In each phase of detection, you must determine whether there is sufficient evidence to establish reasonable suspicion necessary to proceed to the next step in the detection process. Your duty is to carry out whatever tasks are appropriate and to make sure that all evidence of DUI is brought to light.

The most successful DUI detectors are those officers who:

- know what to look and listen for
- have the skills to ask the right kinds of questions
- choose and use the right types of tests
- make the correct observations
- are motivated and apply their knowledge and skill whenever they contact someone who may be under the influence

Officers like these are likely to make more arrests and to document the clear, convincing evidence needed to secure convictions.

## Note Taking and Court Testimony

One of the most critical tasks in the DUI enforcement process is the recognition and retention of facts and clues that establish reasonable suspicion to stop, investigate, and subsequently arrest persons suspected of driving or operating a vehicle while impaired. Field notes provide the information necessary for completion of required DUI report forms.

The evidence gathered during the detection process must establish the elements of the violation, and must be documented to support successful prosecution of the violator. This evidence is largely sensory (sight, smell, hearing) in nature, and therefore is extremely short-lived.

Field notes are only as good as the information they contain. Reports must be clearly written and events accurately described if the reports are to have evidentiary value. One persistent problem with DUI incident reports is the use of vague language to describe conditions, events and statements. When vague language is used, reports provide a confused picture of what happened. When clear language is used, reports provide an accurate picture of what happened. Clear and convincing field notes assist the officer in writing a report that provides strong evidence in court. *(LE515.25.)*

Consider the following examples (See Figure 10-2 on the next page).

### *Note Taking Guidelines*

One way to improve the effectiveness of handwritten field notes is to use a structured note taking guide in the detection process. These field notes should assist in documenting those actions which gave you reasonable

| Vague Language | Clear Language |
|---|---|
| *Driver appeared drunk.* | Driver's eyes bloodshot; gaze fixed; hands shaking. Strong odor of alcoholic beverage on driver's breath. |
| *Vehicle stopped in unusual manner or location.* | Vehicle struck or climbed curb; stopped on sidewalk. |
| *Vehicle crossed the center line.* | Vehicle completely crossed the center line into the opposing traffic lane. |

Vague vs. clear language *Figure 10-2*

suspicion to justify further investigation of a suspected DUI incident. During the DUI investigation, the officer should note at least the following:

- basic information describing the subject, the vehicle, the location, and the date and time the incident occurred
- brief descriptions of the vehicle in motion (Detection Phase One), including initial observation of the vehicle and observation of the stopping sequence
- brief descriptions of the personal contact with the subject (Detection Phase Two), including observations of the driver such as the subject's manner of speech (including admissions), attitude, clothing, etc. Any physical evidence collected should also be noted in this section.
- the results of all field sobriety tests that were administered
- any other pertinent evidence specific to the incident *(LE515.26.)*

Since this is a note taking guide and space is limited, you will have to develop your own shorthand system. Your notes should be as descriptive as possible and should create mental pictures of the facts, circumstances, or events being described. Whenever possible, complete the DUI field notes before you leave the site of the arrest. You will use these notes to refresh your memory, write the arrest report, and testify in court.

Field notes may be subpoenaed as evidence in court. It is important that any shorthand system you use be describable, usable, complete, and consistent.

## Courtroom Testimony

Testimonial evidence in DUI cases establishes that the accused was in fact the driver and was impaired at the time of the violation. The arresting officer must be fully prepared to testify in court on any case. Even when scientific evidence is available, supportive testimonial evidence will be required to permit introduction of that scientific evidence in court.

Refer to the section on Court Procedures in Chapter 8, Criminal Investigations, for a review of preparing for and giving testimony.

In court, your testimony should cover each phase of the DUI incident:

- initial observation of the vehicle and driver
- reinforcing cues or actions observed while stopping the vehicle
- statements and other evidence obtained during your initial face-to-face contact with the driver
- sobriety tests administered to the driver
- arrest procedures
- subject's actions and statements before, during, and after the arrest
- procedures used during the chemical test, including rights and legal requirements
- the administration and results of the chemical test(s), if you were also the testing officer
- interview of the subject

## Phase One: Vehicle in Motion

The first task, observing the vehicle in motion, begins when you first notice the vehicle and its driver. Your attention may be drawn to the vehicle by such things as a moving traffic violation, an equipment violation, an expired registration, unusual driving actions such as weaving within a lane or moving at slower than normal speed, or evidence of drinking or drugs in the vehicle.

If this initial observation discloses vehicle maneuvers or human behaviors that may be associated with impairment, you may develop an initial suspicion of DUI.

Based upon this initial observation of the vehicle in motion, you must decide whether there is reasonable suspicion to stop the vehicle. At this point you have three choices: stop the vehicle, continue to observe the vehicle, or take no action.

### *Initial Observations: Visual Cues to DUI*

The common effects of alcohol on the driver's mental and physical faculties lead to predictable driving violations and vehicle operating characteristics. These include:

- slowed reactions
- impaired judgment as evidenced by a willingness to take risks
- impaired vision
- poor coordination (See Figure 10-3)

The National Highway Traffic Safety Administration (NHTSA) sponsored research to identify the most common and reliable initial indicators of DUI. This research identified 24 cues, each with a high probability that the driver exhibiting the cue is impaired. A ***cue*** is a reminder, prompt or a signal to do something, i.e., take enforcement action or observe the vehicle more closely. *(LE515.22.a.1.)*

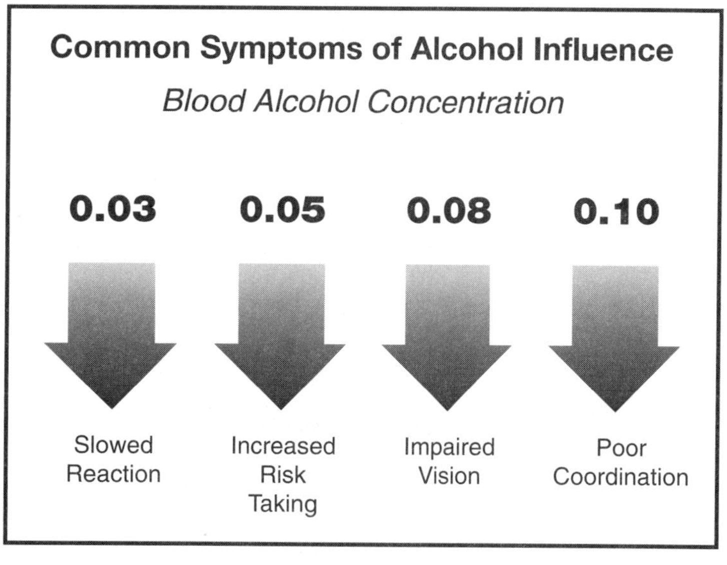


Common symptoms of alcohol influence *Figure 10-3*

The following are 24 cues which law enforcement officers may use to detect nighttime impaired drivers. The cues were developed from a list of more than 100 driving cues that have been found to predict alcohol concentrations of 0.08 or greater.

## *Visual Cue Descriptions*

### *1. Problems Maintaining Proper Lane Position*

**Weaving**—Weaving occurs when the vehicle alternately moves toward one side of the roadway and then the other, creating a zigzag course. The pattern of lateral movement is relatively regular as one steering correction is closely followed by another.

**Weaving Across Lane Lines**—Extreme cases of weaving occur when the vehicle's wheels cross the lane lines before correction is made.

**Straddling a Lane Line**—The vehicle is moving straight ahead with the center or lane marker between the left-hand and right-hand wheels.

**Swerving**—A swerve is an abrupt turn away from a generally straight course. Swerving might occur after a period of drifting when the driver discovers the approach of traffic in an oncoming lane or discovers that the vehicle is going off the road. It may also occur as an abrupt turn is executed to return the vehicle to the traffic lane.

**Turning with Wide Radius**—During a turn, the radius defined by the distance between the turning vehicle and the center of the turn is greater than normal. The vehicle may drive wide in a curve.

**Drifting**—Drifting is a straight-line movement of the vehicle at a slight angle to the roadway. As the driver approaches a marker or boundary (lane marker, center line, edge of the roadway), the direction of drift might change. Drifting can occur within a single lane, across lanes, across the center line, or onto the shoulder.

**Almost Striking Object or Vehicle**—The observed vehicle almost strikes a stationary object or another moving vehicle.

### *2. Speed and Braking Problems*

**Stopping Problems**—Stopping problems may include stopping abruptly or too far from a curb, at an inappropriate angle, too short or beyond the intersection limit line, or with a jerking motion.

**Accelerating or Decelerating Rapidly**—This cue encompasses any acceleration or deceleration that is significantly more rapid than that required by the traffic conditions. Rapid acceleration might be accompanied by breaking traction; rapid deceleration might be accompanied by an abrupt stop.

**Varying Speed**—A driver may alternate between speeding up and slowing down.

**Slow Speed**—The observed vehicle is traveling at a speed that is 10 mph or more below the speed limit.

### *3. Vigilance Problems*

**Driving in Opposing Lanes or Wrong Way on a One-way Street**—The vehicle is heading into opposing or crossing traffic by driving in the opposing lane, backing into traffic, failing to yield the right-of-way, or driving the wrong way on a one-way street.

**Slow Response to Traffic Signals**—The observed vehicle exhibits a longer than normal response to a change in traffic signal.

**Slow or Failure to Respond to Officer's Signals**—The driver is unusually slow to respond to an officer's lights, siren, or hand signals.

**Stopping in Lane for No Apparent Reason**—The critical element in this cue is that there is no observable justification for the vehicle to stop in the traffic lane.

**Driving Without Headlights**—The observed vehicle is being driven without headlights during a period of the day when headlights are required.

**Failure to Signal or Signal Inconsistent with Action**—This cue occurs when inconsistencies are observed such as failing to signal a turn or lane change, signaling opposite to the turn or lane change executed, signaling constantly with no accompanying driving action, and driving with four-way hazard flashers on.

## *4. Judgment Problems*

**Following Too Closely**—The vehicle is following another vehicle while not maintaining the legal minimum separation.

**Improper or Unsafe Lane Change**—The driver takes risks or endangers others by frequently or abruptly changing lanes without regard to other motorists.

**Illegal or Improper Turn**—The driver executes any turn that is abnormally abrupt or illegal such as turning with excessive speed, turning sharply from the wrong lane, or making an illegal U-turn.

**Driving on Other than Designated Roadway**—The driver maneuvers onto an area other than the designated roadway. Examples include driving at the edge of the roadway, on the shoulder, off the roadway entirely, or straight through turn-only lanes or areas.

**Stopping Inappropriately in Response to an Officer**—The vehicle stops in an inappropriate location such as a prohibited zone, crosswalk, intersection, or sidewalk, or under inappropriate conditions such as a green or flashing yellow traffic signal.

**Inappropriate or Unusual Behavior**—The driver or occupants display inappropriate or unusual behavior such as throwing objects from the vehicle, drinking in the vehicle, or urinating on the roadside.

**Appearing to Be Impaired**—This cue is actually one or more indicators related to the personal behavior or appearance of the driver. Examples of specific indicators might include eye fixation, tightly gripping the steering wheel, slouching in the seat, gesturing erratically or obscenely, face close to the windshield, or driver's head protruding from the vehicle.

## *5. Post Stop Cues*

An officer may observe any of the following behaviors in the driver after he or she stops the vehicle:

- difficulty with motor vehicle controls
- difficulty exiting the vehicle
- fumbling with driver's license or paperwork
- repeating questions or comments
- swaying, unsteady, or balance problems

- leaning on the vehicle or other object
- slurred speech
- slow to respond to officer/officer must repeat questions
- provides incorrect information, changes answers
- odor of alcoholic beverage from the driver

### *6. Visual Detection of DUI Motorcyclists*

NHTSA has also developed research identifying driving impairment cues for motorcyclists.

*Excellent Cues* (50% or greater probability that the driver is impaired)

- drifting during turn or curve
- trouble with dismount
- trouble with balance at a stop
- turning problems (e.g., unsteady, sudden corrections, late braking, improper lean angle)
- inattentive to surroundings
- inappropriate or unusual behavior (e.g., carrying or dropping object, urinating at roadside, disorderly conduct)
- weaving

*Good Cues* (30 to 50% probability that the driver is impaired)

- erratic movements while going straight
- operating without lights at night
- recklessness
- following too closely
- running stop light or sign
- evasion
- going the wrong way *(LE515.22.a.)*

## Divided Attention

Safe driving demands the ability to divide attention among these various tasks. ***Divided attention*** simply means the ability to concentrate on two or more things at the same time *(LE515.22.a.2.)*. Under the influence of alcohol and/or other drugs, a driver's ability to divide attention is impaired. As a result, the impaired driver tends to concentrate on only the most important or critical parts of driving and disregard the less important parts, often creating unexpected or dangerous situations for other drivers. An impaired driver may have difficulty in steering, controlling the accelerator, signaling, and making decisions (whether to stop, turn, speed up, slow down).

## *The Stopping Sequence*

The second task during Phase One of the detection process involves observation. These observations reinforce the suspicion of DUI during the stopping sequence. After the command to stop is given, the impaired driver may exhibit additional important evidence of DUI. These observations may include the following:

- an attempt to flee
- no response
- slow response
- an abrupt swerve
- sudden stop
- striking the curb or another object

Some of these cues are exhibited because the stop command places additional demands on the driver's ability to divide attention. The signal to stop creates a new situation with which the driver must cope. Officers must be able to recognize evidence of impairment and describe that evidence clearly and convincingly. *(LE515.22.b.)*

# Phase Two: Personal Contact

DUI Detection Phase Two comprises two major evidence gathering tasks and one major decision. The first task is to approach, observe, and interview the driver while he or she is still in the vehicle to note any evidence of impairment. During this face-to-face contact, you may employ some interviewing techniques to gain additional information to evaluate whether or not the driver may be impaired. After this evaluation, you must decide whether to ask the driver to exit the vehicle for further field sobriety testing. In some jurisdictions, departmental policy may dictate that all drivers stopped on suspicion of DUI be instructed to exit. As the driver exits the vehicle, observe the manner in which he or she exits to note any additional evidence of impairment.

Remember, you may initiate Phase Two without Phase One. This may occur, for example, if the driver is passed out at the wheel or when you have responded to the scene of a crash.

The first task of Phase Two, observation and interview of the driver, begins as soon as the subject vehicle and the patrol vehicle have come to complete stops. It continues through your approach to the subject vehicle and involves all conversation between you and the driver prior to the driver's exit from the vehicle. In some cases, your initial face-to-face contact with the driver may provide the first indications that the driver is impaired. For example, you stop a vehicle for an equipment violation and only see indicators of impairment as you interview the driver.

Face-to-face observation and interview of the driver allow you to use three senses to gather evidence of alcohol and other drug influence: sight, hearing, and smell.

### *Sight*

There are a number of things you might see during the interview that would be describable clues or evidence of alcohol and other drug influence. A ***clue*** is something that leads to the solution of a problem, such as a fingerprint or DNA evidence. In a DUI investigation, this includes using the three senses to note observable facts that are used as potential evidence of alcohol and other drug influence. Clues are also the behaviors observed during the performance of the standardized field sobriety tests *(LE515.23.a.)*. Some specific DUI clues related to sight include:

- bloodshot eyes
- soiled clothing
- fumbling fingers
- alcohol containers
- drugs or drug paraphernalia
- bruises, bumps, or scratches
- unusual actions

### *Hearing*

Among the things you might hear during the interview that would be describable clues or evidence of alcohol and other drug influence include:

- slurred speech
- admission of drinking
- inconsistent responses
- abusive language
- unusual statements

### *Smell*

There are things you might smell during the interview that would be describable clues or evidence of alcohol and other drug influence. Typically these include the following examples:

- alcoholic beverages
- marijuana
- cover up odors like breath sprays
- body odors *(LE515.23.b.)*

## Medical Conditions that Mimic Impairment

Certain medical conditions may mimic drug- or alcohol-induced impairment. The officer should check for medical restrictions on the driver's license and look for a medic alert ID bracelet to determine if a medical problem might be the cause of the suspicious driving. Some of the causes of abnormal behavior may include medical conditions such as epilepsy, diabetes, injury to the head, or cognitive problems (dementia or Alzheimer's).

Officers should follow their department's policies and procedures for handling these cases. If the officer does not suspect a medical condition, and other signs of drug- or alcohol-impairment are present, he or she should continue with the DUI investigative process. *(LE515.23.c.)*

## Pre-Exit Interview Techniques

During the face-to-face observation and interview stage, you may use a number of techniques while the driver is still behind the wheel. Most of these techniques apply the concept of divided attention. They require the driver to concentrate on two or more things at the same time. They include both questioning techniques and psychophysical tasks.

*Note:* These techniques are not as reliable as the Standardized Field Sobriety Tests but they can still be useful for obtaining evidence of impairment. **These techniques do not replace the Standardized Field Sobriety Tests.**

The questions you ask and the way in which you ask them can constitute simple divided attention tasks. Three techniques are particularly pertinent:

- asking for two things in one request
- asking interrupting or distracting questions
- asking unusual questions

An example of the first technique, asking for two things in one request, is requesting that the driver produce both the driver's license and the vehicle registration. Possible evidence of impairment may come to light as the driver responds to this dual request. Be alert for the driver who:

- forgets to produce both documents
- produces documents other than the ones requested
- fails to see the license, registration, or both while searching through wallet or purse
- fumbles or drops wallet, purse, license, or registration
- is unable to retrieve documents using fingertips

The second technique, asking interrupting or distracting questions, forces the driver to divide attention between searching for the license or registration and answering a new question. While the driver is responding to the request for license, registration, or both, you ask an unrelated question like, "Without looking at your watch, what time is it right now?" Possible evidence of impairment may be disclosed by the interrupting or distracting question. Be alert for the driver who:

- ignores the question and concentrates only on the license or registration search
- stops searching to answer question, then forgets to resume the search after answering the question
- supplies a grossly incorrect answer to the question

The third technique, asking unusual questions, is employed after you have obtained the driver's license and registration. Using this technique, you seek verifying information through unusual questions. Unusual questions require the driver to process information; this can be especially difficult when the driver does not expect to have to process information. For example, a driver may respond to the question about the middle name by giving a first name.

## Additional Pre-Exit Tests

If an officer needs additional evidence, the following additional tests may be used for pre-exit testing. These should only be employed in compliance with agency policies and procedures. In addition, you should know if there are any judicial restraints in reference to these tests.

### *Alphabet*

This technique requires the subject to recite a part of the alphabet. You instruct the subject to recite the alphabet beginning with a letter other than A and stopping at a letter other than Z. For example, you might say to a driver, "Recite the alphabet, beginning with the letter E as in Edward and stopping with the letter P as in Paul." This divides the driver's attention because the driver must concentrate to begin at an unusual starting point and recall where to stop.

### *Count Down*

This technique requires the subject to count out loud 15 or more numbers in reverse sequence. For example, you might request a driver to, "Count out loud backwards, starting with the number 68 and ending with the number 53." This, too, divides attention because the driver must continuously concentrate to count backwards while trying to recall where to stop. Avoid starting and stopping numbers that end in 0 or 5 because these numbers are too easy to recall. For example, do not request the driver to count backwards from 65 to 50. Instead, ask the driver to count backwards from 64 to 49.

### *Finger Count*

In this technique, the subject is asked to touch the tip of the thumb in turn to the tip of each finger on the same hand while simultaneously counting up one, two, three, four; then to reverse direction on the fingers while simultaneously counting down four, three, two, one. Note whether or not the subject is able to perform the divided attention task. *(LE515.23.d.)*

## The Exit Sequence

You may have already developed reasonable suspicion that the driver is impaired before instructing the driver to step from the vehicle. Even though that suspicion may be very strong, probable cause is required to make a DUI arrest. *Note:* You should keep driver and officer safety in mind at all times. Safety considerations take precedence over all other considerations.

In addition to the driver's behavior during the Pre-exit Interview, the manner in which the driver steps and walks from the vehicle and actions or behavior during the exit sequence may provide important evidence of impairment. Be alert to the driver who:

- shows angry or unusual reactions
- cannot follow instructions
- cannot open the door
- leaves the vehicle in gear
- climbs out of vehicle
- leans against vehicle
- keeps hands on vehicle for balance *(LE515.23.e.)*

If a subject exhibits observable signs of alcohol or drug impairment, the officer should proceed to Phase Three and conduct the Standardized Field Sobriety Tests.

## *Selecting a Safe Location*

When practical, the officer should select a safe area with a reasonably level surface that is well-lit and away from traffic to administer the tests. After exiting the vehicle, the officer should assist the driver in moving to a safe area away from traffic. At night, the officer should use lights to illuminate the location, and if possible, minimize distracting lights.

# Phase Three: Pre-Arrest Screening

The task in Phase Three is to administer three scientifically validated psychophysical (field) sobriety tests: Horizontal Gaze Nystagmus, Walk-and-Turn, and One-Leg Stand *(LE515.24.a.)*. Based on these tests and on all other evidence from Phase One and Two, you must decide whether there is sufficient probable cause to arrest the driver for DUI. The entire detection process culminates in the arrest/no arrest decision.

## *Horizontal Gaze Nystagmus*

***Nystagmus*** means an involuntary jerking of the eyes *(LE515.24.b.)*. ***Horizontal Gaze Nystagmus (HGN)*** refers to an involuntary jerking occurring as the eyes gaze toward the side. In addition to being involuntary, the person experiencing nystagmus is usually unaware that the jerking is happening *(LE515.24.c.)*. Involuntary jerking of the eyes becomes readily noticeable when a person is impaired by alcohol and certain drugs. As a person's alcohol concentration increases, the eyes will begin to jerk sooner as they move to the side.

Horizontal Gaze Nystagmus is the most reliable field sobriety test, particularly when used in combination with the divided attention tests. In administering the HGN test, the officer has the subject follow the motion of a small stimulus with the eyes only. The stimulus may be the tip of a pen or penlight, an eraser on a pencil, or a finger tip, whichever contrasts with the background.

When the HGN test is administered, always begin with subject's left eye. Each eye is examined for three specific clues.

1. As the eye moves from side to side, does it move smoothly or does it jerk noticeably? As people become impaired by alcohol, their eyes exhibit a lack of smooth pursuit as they move from side to side.
2. When the eye moves as far to the side as possible and is kept at that position for several seconds, does it jerk distinctly? Distinct and sustained nystagmus at maximum deviation is another clue of impairment. ***Maximum deviation*** occurs when the gaze of the eye has moved as far as it can go toward the shoulder, and no white is visible at the outside of the eye.
3. As the eye moves toward the side, does it start to jerk prior to a 45-degree angle? Onset of nystagmus prior to 45 degrees is another clue of impairment.

As a person's alcohol concentration increases, it is more likely these clues will appear. The maximum number of clues that may appear in one eye is three. The maximum total number for any subject is six. The research shows that if four or more clues are evident, it is likely that the subject's alcohol concentration is above 0.10. This research has been shown to be accurate 77 percent of the time.

## *Vertical Gaze Nystagmus*

***Vertical Gaze Nystagmus (VGN)*** is an involuntary jerking of the eyes (up and down) which occurs when the eyes gaze upward at maximum elevation *(LE515.24.d.)*. Field experience has indicated that the presence of Vertical Gaze Nystagmus when accompanied with HGN is a reliable indicator of the use of high doses of alcohol or certain other drugs. *(LE515.24.e.)*

## Psychophysical Tests

Psychophysical tests are methods of assessing a subject's mental and physical impairment. These tests focus on the abilities needed for safe driving: balance, coordination, information processing, and so on. The most significant psychophysical tests are the two scientifically validated divided attention tests that you administer roadside: Walk-and-Turn and One-Leg Stand.

Driving is a complex divided attention task. In order to operate a vehicle safely, drivers must simultaneously control steering, acceleration, and braking; react appropriately to a constantly changing environment; and perform many other tasks. Alcohol and other drugs reduce a person's ability to divide attention. Impaired drivers often ignore the less critical tasks of driving in order to focus their impaired attention on the more critical tasks. For example, a driver may ignore a traffic signal and focus instead on speed control.

Even when impaired, many people can handle a single, focused attention task fairly well. Field sobriety tests that simulate the divided attention characteristics exercise the same mental and physical capabilities that a person needs to drive safely:

- information processing
- short-term memory
- judgment and decision making
- balance
- steady, sure reactions
- clear vision
- small muscle control
- coordination of limbs

Any test that requires a person to demonstrate two or more of these capabilities simultaneously must be reasonably simple for the average person to perform when sober. Tests that are difficult for a sober subject to perform have little or no evidentiary value. Two validated divided attention field sobriety tests, the Walk-and-Turn and the One-Leg Stand, have proven accurate and effective in DUI detection because they require the subject to concentrate and perform mental and physical tasks at the same time. *(LE515.24.f.)*

### Walk-and-Turn

Walk-and-Turn is a test that has been validated through extensive research by NHTSA. This divided attention test consists of two stages: Instructions Stage and Walking Stage.

In the Instructions Stage, the subject must stand with feet in heel-to-toe position, keep arms at sides, and listen to the instructions. The Instructions Stage divides the subject's attention between a balancing task (standing while maintaining the heel-to-toe position) and an information processing task (listening to and remembering instructions).

In the Walking Stage the subject takes nine heel-to-toe steps, turns in a prescribed manner, and takes nine heel-to-toe steps back, while counting the steps out loud and watching his or her feet. During the turn, the subject keeps the front foot on the line, turns in a prescribed manner, and uses the other foot to take several small steps to complete the turn. The Walking Stage divides the subject's attention among a balancing task (walking heel-to-toe and turning); a small muscle control task (counting out loud), and a short-term memory task (recalling the number of steps and the turning instructions).

The Walk-and-Turn test is administered and interpreted in a standardized manner (the same way every time). Officers administering the Walk-and-Turn test observe the subject's performance for eight clues:

- can't balance during instructions
- starts too soon
- stops while walking
- does not touch heel-to-toe
- steps off line
- uses arms to balance
- loses balance on turn or turns incorrectly
- takes the wrong number of steps

The officer should terminate the Walk-and-Turn test if the subject is in danger of falling or otherwise cannot complete the test.

Research shows that if a subject exhibits two or more of the clues or cannot complete the test, the subject's alcohol concentration is likely to be above 0.10. This research has been shown to be accurate 68 percent of the time. *(LE515.24.g.)*

## *One-Leg Stand*

The One-Leg Stand test also has been validated through NHTSA research. This divided attention test consists of two stages: Instructions Stage, and Balance and Counting Stage.

In the Instructions Stage, the subject must stand with feet together, keep arms at sides, and listen to instructions. This divides the subject's attention between a balancing task (maintaining a stance) and an information processing task (listening to and remembering instructions). In the Balance and Counting Stage, the subject must raise either leg with the foot approximately six inches off the ground, keeping the raised foot parallel to the ground. While looking at the elevated foot, the subject counts out loud in the following manner: "one thousand and one," "one thousand and two," "one thousand and three" until told to stop. This divides the subject's attention between balancing (standing on one foot) and small muscle control (counting out loud).

The One-Leg Stand will be timed for 30 seconds. Research has shown that many impaired subjects are able to stand on one leg for up to 25 seconds, but few can do so for 30 seconds.

One-Leg Stand is also administered and interpreted in a standardized manner. Officers carefully observe the subject's performance and look for four specific clues:

- sways while balancing
- uses arms to balance

**Section Vocabulary**

*clue*

*cue*

*divided attention*

*DUI detection*

*Horizontal Gaze Nystagmus (HGN)*

*maximum deviation*

*nystagmus*

*Vertical Gaze Nystagmus (VGN)*

- hops
- puts foot down

The officer should terminate the One-Leg Stand test if the subject is in danger of falling or otherwise cannot complete the test.

Research shows that, when the subject displays two or more clues or is unable to complete the test, the alcohol concentration is probably above 0.10. This criterion has been shown to be accurate 65 percent of the time. *(LE515.24.h.)*

# The Arrest Decision

The decision whether to arrest the subject is the culmination of all the evidence accumulated during the DUI detection process.

## Phase One: Vehicle in Motion

- initial observation of vehicle in motion
- observation of the stop

## Phase Two: Personal Contact

- face-to-face observation and interview
- observation of the exit

## Phase Three: Pre-Arrest Screening

- SFSTs

If all of the evidence taken together establishes probable cause to believe that DUI has been committed, you should arrest the subject for DUI. Any reduction of DUI to a lesser charge is the responsibility of the prosecutor or judge. *(LE515.24.i.)*

*Note:* Portable breath test devices may not be used for DUI arrests. They may be used for violations such as drivers under 21 years of age (0.02 violation) or commercial motor vehicle enforcement when there is insufficient evidence of DUI.

# LESSON 4 | Standardized Field Sobriety Tests

## Research and Development of SFSTs

For many years law enforcement officers have utilized field sobriety tests to determine the impairment of a person's driving due to alcohol influence. The performance of the person on those field sobriety tests was used by the officer to develop probable cause for arrest and as evidence in court. A wide variety of field sobriety tests existed and there was a need to develop a battery of standardized valid tests.

Beginning in late 1975, extensive scientific research studies were sponsored by NHTSA through a contract with the Southern California Research Institute (SCRI) to determine which roadside field sobriety tests were the most accurate. SCRI published the following three reports:

- California: 1977 (Lab)
- California: 1981 (Lab and Field)
- Maryland, District of Columbia, Virginia, North Carolina, 1983 (Field)

SCRI traveled to law enforcement agencies throughout the United States to select the most commonly used field sobriety tests. Six tests were used in the initial stages of this study.

Laboratory research indicated that three of these tests, when administered in a standardized manner, were a highly accurate and reliable battery of tests for distinguishing alcohol concentration above 0.10:

- Horizontal Gaze Nystagmus (HGN)
- Walk-and-Turn (WAT)
- One-Leg Stand (OLS)

NHTSA analyzed the laboratory test data and found:

- HGN, by itself, was 77% accurate.
- WAT, by itself, was 68% accurate.
- OLS, by itself, was 65% accurate.
- By combining HGN and WAT, an 80% accuracy can be achieved.

The final phase of this study was conducted as a field validation.

- Standardized, practical, and effective procedures were developed.
- The tests were determined to discriminate between impaired and unimpaired drivers in the field, as well as in the laboratory.

The three standardized tests were found to be highly reliable in identifying subjects whose alcohol concentrations were above 0.10. The results of the study unmistakably validated the SFSTs.

**OBJECTIVES**

**LE515.27.** Describe the reliability of the Standardized Field Sobriety Tests based on NHTSA research.

**LE515.28.** List the three categories of nystagmus.

**LE515.29.** Identify the three clues that point to impairment through the Horizontal Gaze Nystagmus test.

**LE515.30.** Explain the procedures for Horizontal Gaze Nystagmus testing.

**LE515.30.a.** Identify how to interpret the Horizontal Gaze Nystagmus test.

**LE515.31.a.** Identify what the presence of Vertical Gaze Nystagmus may indicate about impairment.

**LE515.31.** Explain the procedures for the Vertical Gaze Nystagmus test.

**LE515.32.** Explain the procedures for the Walk-and-Turn test.

**LE515.32.a.** Identify how to interpret the Walk-and-Turn test.

**LE515.33.** Explain the procedures for the One-Leg Stand test.

**LE515.33.a.** Identify how to interpret the One-Leg Stand test.

**LE515.34.** Explain the note taking procedures necessary when administering the Standardized Field Sobriety Tests.

## *SFST Validation Studies*

Three SFST validation studies were undertaken between 1995 and 1998:

- Colorado—1995
- Florida—1997
- San Diego—1998

The Colorado SFST validation study was the first full field study that utilized law enforcement personnel experienced in the use of SFSTs.

- The initial study utilized only a few experienced officers in DUI enforcement in both a laboratory setting and field setting.
- Correct arrest decisions were made 93 percent of the time based on the three-test battery (HGN, WAT, OLS). These results were substantially higher than the initial study results.

The Florida SFST field validation study was undertaken in order to answer the question of whether SFSTs are valid and reliable indices of the presence of alcohol when used under present day traffic and law enforcement conditions.

- Correct decisions to arrest were made 95 percent of the time based on the three-test battery (HGN, WAT, OLS).
- The study showed that the SFST three-test battery is the only scientifically validated and reliable method for discriminating between impaired and unimpaired drivers.

The San Diego SFST validation field study was undertaken because of the nationwide trend towards lowering the alcohol concentration limits to 0.08. The question to be answered was "Does SFST discriminate at alcohol concentration below 0.10?"

- Correct arrest decisions were made 91 percent of the time based on the three-test battery (HGN, WAT, OLS) at the 0.08 level and above.
- The results of this study provided clear evidence of the validity of the three-test battery to support arrest decisions at, above, or below 0.08. It strongly suggests that the SFSTs also accurately discriminates alcohol concentration at 0.04 and above. *(LE515.27.)*

# Overview of Nystagmus

Recall that nystagmus is defined as an involuntary jerking of the eyes, which can be caused by the use of alcohol and certain other drugs. There are three general categories of nystagmus:

1. ***Vestibular Nystagmus*** is an involuntary jerking of the eyes caused by movement or action to the vestibular (inner ear) system. Types of vestibular nystagmus include the following:
   - Rotational Nystagmus occurs when the person is spun around or rotated rapidly causing the fluid in the inner ear to be disturbed. If it were possible to observe the eyes of a rotating person, they would be seen to jerk noticeably.
   - Post Rotational Nystagmus is closely related to rotational nystagmus. When the person stops spinning, the fluid in the inner ear remains disturbed for a short period of time and the eyes continue to jerk.

- Caloric Nystagmus occurs when fluid motion in the canals of the vestibular system is stimulated by temperature as by putting warm water in one ear and cold in the other.
- Positional Alcohol Nystagmus (PAN) occurs when a foreign fluid, such as alcohol, that alters the specific gravity of the blood is in unequal concentrations in the blood and the vestibular system.

2. ***Neurological Nystagmus*** is an involuntary jerking of the eyes caused by a disruption of the central nervous system. Some common examples include the following:
    - Optokinetic Nystagmus occurs when the eyes fixate on an object that suddenly moves out of sight, or when the eyes watch sharply contrasting moving images. Examples of optokinetic nystagmus include watching rotating lights or rapidly moving traffic in close proximity. The Horizontal Gaze Nystagmus test will not be influenced by optokinetic nystagmus when administered properly.
    - Physiological Nystagmus is a natural nystagmus that keeps the sensory cells of the eye from tiring. It is the most common type of nystagmus. It happens to all of us, all the time. This type of nystagmus produces extremely minor tremors or jerks of the eyes. These tremors are generally too small to be seen with the naked eye. Physiological nystagmus will have no impact on the HGN test because its tremors are generally invisible.
    - Gaze Nystagmus occurs as the eyes are focused on a stimulus and move from the center position. Gaze nystagmus is separated into three types:
        1. Horizontal Gaze Nystagmus occurs as the eyes move to the side. It is the observation of the eyes for Horizontal Gaze Nystagmus that provides the first and most accurate test in the Standardized Field Sobriety Test battery. Although this type of nystagmus is most accurate for determining alcohol impairment, its presence may also indicate use of certain other drugs.
        2. Vertical Gaze Nystagmus is an involuntary jerking of the eyes (up and down) which occurs when the eyes gaze upward at maximum elevation. The presence of this type of nystagmus is associated with high doses of alcohol for that individual and certain other drugs. The drugs that cause Vertical Gaze Nystagmus are the same ones that cause Horizontal Gaze Nystagmus.

        *Note:* There is no drug that will cause Vertical Gaze Nystagmus that does not also cause Horizontal Gaze Nystagmus. If Vertical Gaze Nystagmus is present and Horizontal Gaze Nystagmus is not, it could be a medical condition.

        3. Resting Nystagmus is an involuntary jerking of the eyes as they look straight ahead. Its presence usually indicates a pathological condition or high doses of a dissociative anesthetic drug such as PCP. If detected, take precautions.

3. ***Pathological Nystagmus*** is an involuntary jerking of the eyes which can occur as a result of brain tumors, other brain damage, or some diseases of the inner ear. These pathological disorders occur in very few people and in even fewer drivers. *(LE515.28.)*

## Medical Impairment

The examinations that an officer can conduct to assess possible medical impairment include the following:

- pupil size
- resting nystagmus
- tracking ability

Prior to administration of HGN, the eyes are examined for medical impairment. If the pupils are noticeably unequal in size, if the eyes are jerking as the subject looks straight ahead (resting nystagmus), or if the eyes do not track together, the chance of a medical disorder or injury causing the nystagmus is present.

# Procedures for Detecting Nystagmus

Recall that Horizontal Gaze Nystagmus is an involuntary jerking of the eyes occurring as the eyes gaze toward the side. Some jerking may be seen if the eyes are moved far enough to the side. The roadside test to detect HGN includes three clues:

- **Lack of smooth pursuit**—The officer can observe the eyes jerk or bounce as the eyes follow a smoothly moving stimulus, such as a pencil or penlight. In contrast, the eyes of an unimpaired person will follow smoothly like a marble rolling across a smooth pane of glass.
- **Distinct and sustained nystagmus at maximum deviation**—This will be evident when the eye is held at maximum deviation for a minimum of four seconds. Some people exhibit slight jerking of the eye at maximum deviation even when unimpaired, but this will not be evident or sustained for more than a few seconds. When impaired by alcohol, the jerking will be more pronounced, sustained for more than four seconds, and easily observable.
- **Onset of nystagmus prior to 45-degrees**—If the point at which the eye is first seen jerking begins prior to 45 degrees, it is evident that the person has a BAC above 0.08. *(LE515.29.)*

The higher the degree of impairment, the sooner the nystagmus will be observable.

## *Procedures of Horizontal Gaze Nystagmus Testing*

During the administration of HGN testing, an officer should keep his or her weapon away from the subject for officer safety. First, if the subject is wearing eyeglasses, the officer should request the subject remove them. The subject should then be given the following verbal instructions from a safe position:

"I am going to check your eyes."

"Keep your head still, and follow this stimulus with your eyes only."

"Keep following the stimulus with your eyes until I tell you to stop."

The stimulus should be positioned approximately 12–15 inches from the subject's nose and slightly above eye level. The officer should check to see that both pupils are equal in size (unequal size may indicate a head injury). Resting nystagmus may be observed at this time. An officer should check that the eyes can track together by moving the stimulus smoothly across the subject's entire field of vision. If the eyes don't track together, it could indicate a possible medical disorder, injury, or blindness.

The officer should check the subject's left eye by moving the stimulus to the right. The stimulus should be moved smoothly at a speed that requires approximately two seconds to bring the subject's eye as far to the side as it can go. While moving the stimulus, the officer should look at the subject's eye and determine whether it is able to pursue smoothly. Next, the officer moves the stimulus all the way to the left, back across the subject's face, checking if the right eye pursues smoothly. Movement of the stimulus should take approximately two seconds out and two seconds back for each eye. The procedure is then repeated.

After checking both eyes for lack of smooth pursuit, the officer should check the eyes for distinct and sustained nystagmus at maximum deviation, beginning with the subject's left eye. To do this, the officer simply moves the object to the subject's left side until the gaze of the eye has gone as far to the side as possible. Usually, no white will be showing in the corner of the eye at maximum deviation. The eye should be held at that position for a minimum of four seconds, with the officer observing the eye for distinct and sustained nystagmus. The stimulus should be moved all the way across the subject's face to check the right eye, holding that position for a minimum of four seconds. The procedure is then repeated. *Note:* Fatigue nystagmus is a type of nystagmus that may begin if a subject's eyes are held at maximum deviation for more than 30 seconds.

**Procedures of Horizontal Gaze Nystagmus Testing**

1. Check for eyeglasses
2. Verbal instructions
3. Position stimulus *(12–15 inches)*
4. Equal pupil size and resting nystagmus
5. Tracking
6. Lack of smooth pursuit
7. Distinct and sustained nystagmus at maximum deviation
8. Onset of nystagmus prior to 45°
9. Total the clues
10. Check for vertical gaze nystagmus

Procedures of horizontal gaze nystagmus testing *Figure 10-4*

It is important to know how to estimate a 45-degree angle (see Figure 10-5). This is a critical factor in indicator three. For practice, a 45-degree template can be prepared by making a 15" square cardboard and connecting its opposite corners with a diagonal line.

To use this device, the officer holds it up so that the person's nose is above the diagonal line. It should be made certain that one edge of the template is centered on the nose and perpendicular to (at right angles to) the face. The person should then be required to follow a penlight or some other object until the subject is looking down the 45-degree diagonal. The position of the eye should be noted. With practice, the officer should be able to recognize this angle without using the template.

Next, the officer checks for onset of nystagmus prior to 45 degrees. This is done by moving the stimulus towards the right (subject's left eye) at a speed that would take approximately four seconds for the stimulus to reach the edge of the subject's shoulder. The eye should be carefully observed for any sign of jerking. When jerking is seen, the officer should stop and verify that it continues. Now, the stimulus is moved to the left (subject's right eye) at a speed that would take approximately four seconds for the stimulus to reach the edge of the subject's shoulder. The eye should again be carefully observed for any sign of jerking. When jerking is seen, the officer should stop and verify that it continues. The procedure is then repeated. It is important to use the full four seconds when checking for onset of nystagmus. If moving the stimulus too fast, the officer may go past the point of onset or miss it altogether.

If the subject's eyes start jerking before they reach 45 degrees, the officer should check to see that some white of the eye is still showing on the side closest to the ear. If no white of the eye is showing, either the officer has taken the eye too far to the side (more than 45 degrees) or the person has unusual eyes that will not deviate very far to the side.

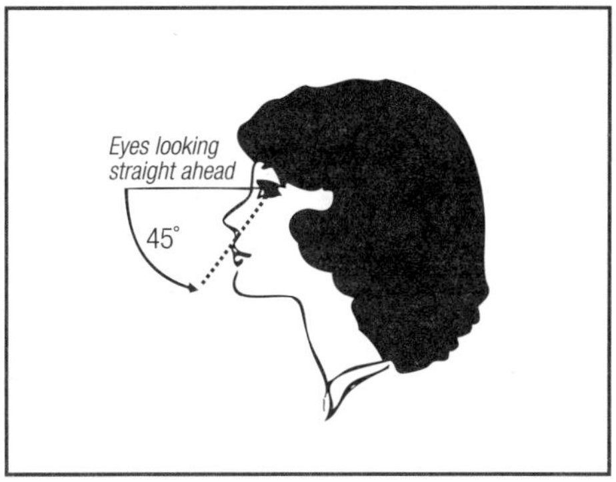


45 degree angle *Figure 10-5*

*Note:* Nystagmus may be due to causes other than alcohol. These other causes include seizure medications and some other drugs. A large disparity between the performance of the right and left eye may indicate a medical condition. *(LE515.30.)*

### HGN Test Interpretation

There are three possible clues that may appear in each eye for a total of six indicators:

- **Lack of smooth pursuit**—The eye cannot follow a moving object smoothly.
- **Distinct and sustained nystagmus at maximum deviation**—Nystagmus is continuous and clearly visible for a minimum of four seconds.
- The angle of onset of nystagmus is prior to 45 degrees.

Based on the research, if an officer observes four or more clues it is likely that the subject's alcohol concentration is above 0.10. Using this criterion, officers will be able to classify about 77% of subjects accurately. This was determined during laboratory and field testing and helps an officer weigh the various field sobriety tests in this battery as he or she makes an arrest decision. *(LE515.30.a.)*

## *Procedures of Vertical Gaze Nystagmus Testing*

During the Vertical Gaze Nystagmus test, an officer should look for jerking as the eyes move up and are held for approximately four seconds at maximum elevation as a clue to impairment. As with HGN, Vertical Gaze Nystagmus can also be observed directly and does not require special equipment. The officer will need a contrasting stimulus for the subject to follow with his or her eyes. This can be the tip of an index finger, penlight, or pen. The stimulus used should be held slightly above eye level, so that the eyes are wide open when the subject looks directly at it. It should be held approximately 12–15 inches in front of the nose. An officer needs to remain aware of his or her position in relation to the subject at all times. The presence of VGN is associated with high doses of alcohol for that individual and certain other drugs. *(LE515.31.a.)*

1. Position a stimulus (pen, penlight, index finger, etc.) horizontally about 12–15 inches in front of the subject's nose.
2. Instruct the subject to hold his or her head still and follow the object with the eyes only.
3. Raise the object until the subject's eyes are elevated as far as possible.
4. Hold for approximately four seconds.
5. Watch closely for evidence of jerking. *(LE515.31.)*

# Procedures for Walk-and-Turn Testing

## *Instructions Stage: Initial Positioning and Verbal Instructions*

For standardization in the performance of this test, have the subject assume the heel-to-toe stance by giving the following verbal instructions accompanied by demonstrations:

1. "Place your left foot on the line" (real or imaginary). Demonstrate.
2. "Place your right foot on the line ahead of your left foot with the heel of your right foot against the toe of your left foot." Demonstrate.

3. "Place your arms down at your sides." Demonstrate.
4. "Maintain this position until I have completed the instructions. Do not start to walk until told to do so."
5. "Do you understand the instructions so far?" Make sure the subject indicates understanding.

## *Walking Stage: Demonstrations and Instructions*

Explain the test requirements using the following verbal instructions accompanied by demonstrations:

1. "When I tell you to start, take nine heel-to-toe steps, turn, and take nine heel-to-toe steps back." Demonstrate three heel-to-toe steps.
2. "When you turn, keep your front foot on the line, and turn by taking a series of small steps with the other foot, like this." Demonstrate.
3. "While you are walking, keep your arms at your sides, watch your feet at all times, and count your steps out loud."
4. "Once you start walking, don't stop until you have completed the test."
5. "Do you understand the instructions?" Make sure the subject understands.
6. "Begin and count your first step from the heel-to-toe position as 'One.'" *(LE515.32.)*

## *Test Interpretation*

An officer may observe a number of different behaviors when a subject performs this test. Research demonstrates that the behaviors listed below are likely to be observed in someone with a BAC above 0.10. Officers will look for the following clues each time this test is given:

- **Cannot keep balance while listening to the instructions**—Two tasks are required at the beginning of this test. The subject must balance heel-to-toe on the line, and at the same time, listen carefully to the instructions. Typically, the person who is impaired can do only one of these things. The subject may listen to the instructions but not keep balance. Record this clue if the subject does not maintain the heel-to-toe position throughout the instructions. The feet must actually break apart. Do not record this clue if the subject sways or uses the arms to balance but maintains the heel-to-toe position.
- **Starts before the instructions are finished**—The impaired person may also keep balance but not listen to the instructions. Since you specifically instructed the subject not to start walking "until I tell you to begin," record this clue if the subject does not wait.
- **Stops while walking**—The subject pauses for several seconds. Do not record this clue if the subject is merely walking slowly.
- **Does not touch heel-to-toe**—The subject leaves a space of more than one-half inch between the heel and toe on any step.
- **Steps off the line**—The subject steps so that one foot is entirely off the line.
- **Uses arms to balance**—The subject raises one or both arms more than six inches from the sides in order to maintain balance during the walking stage.
- **Improper turn**—The subject removes the front foot from the line while turning. Also record this clue if the subject has not followed directions as demonstrated, i.e., spins or pivots around.
- **Incorrect number of steps**—Record this clue if the subject takes more or fewer than nine steps in either direction.

*Note:* If the subject can't do the test, record observed clues, and document the reason for not completing the test, e.g. subject's safety.

If the subject has difficulty with the test (for example, steps off the line), continue from that point, not from the beginning. This test may lose its sensitivity if it is repeated several times.

Observe the subject from a safe distance and limit movement which may distract the subject during the test. Always consider officer safety.

Based on research, if the subject exhibits two or more clues on this test or fails to complete it, classify the subject's alcohol concentration as above 0.10. Using this criterion, officers will be able to accurately classify 68 percent of subjects. *(LE515.32.a.)*

### Test Conditions

The Walk-and-Turn test should be conducted on a reasonably dry, hard, level, non-slippery surface. There should be sufficient room for a subject to complete nine heel-to-toe steps. *Note:* Field validation studies have indicated that varying environmental conditions have not affected a subject's ability to perform this test.

Individuals over 65 years of age or those with back, leg, or inner ear problems may have difficulty performing this test. Individuals wearing heels more than two inches high should be given the opportunity to remove their shoes.

## Combined Interpretation of Horizontal Gaze Nystagmus and Walk-and-Turn Tests

Based on research, subjects who display a combination of four or more clues of HGN and two or more clues of Walk-and-Turn can be accurately classified as above 0.10 alcohol concentration about 80 percent of the time.

## Procedures for One-Leg Stand Testing

### Instructions Stage: Initial Positioning and Verbal Instructions

Initiate the test by giving the following verbal instructions, accompanied by demonstrations.

- "Please stand with your feet together and your arms down at the sides, like this." Demonstrate.
- "Do not start to perform the test until I tell you to do so."
- "Do you understand the instructions so far?" Make sure the subject indicates understanding.

### Balance and Counting Stage: Demonstrations and Instructions

Explain the test requirements using the following verbal instructions accompanied by demonstrations:

- "When I tell you to start, raise either leg with the foot approximately six inches off the ground, keeping your raised foot parallel to the ground." Demonstrate the one-leg stance.
- "You must keep both legs straight with arms at your side."

- "While holding that position, count out loud in the following manner: 'one thousand and one, one thousand and two, one thousand and three,' until told to stop." Demonstrate a count. (Do not look at your foot when conducting the demonstration.) Be aware of officer safety.
- "Keep your arms at your sides at all times and keep watching the raised foot."
- "Do you understand?" Make sure the subject indicates understanding.
- "Go ahead and perform the test." The test should be timed for 30 seconds.

Observe the subject from a safe distance. If the subject puts the foot down, give instructions to pick the foot up again and continue counting from that point. Terminate the test after 30 seconds. *(LE515.33.)*

## Test Interpretation

Research found the following behaviors are the most likely to be observed in someone with an alcohol concentration above 0.10. Officers will look for the following clues each time the One-Leg Stand test is administered.

- **Sways**—The subject sways side-to-side or back-and-forth while balancing.
- **Uses arms for balance**—The subject uses his or her arms six or more inches from the side of the body in order to maintain balance.
- **Hops**—The subject is able to keep one foot off the ground but hops to maintain balance.
- **Puts foot down**—The subject puts the raised foot down one or more times during the 30-second count.

*Note:* If the subject can't do the test, record observed clues and document the reason for not completing the test.

Time is critical in this test. Research has shown a person with an alcohol concentration above 0.10 can maintain balance for up to 25 seconds, but seldom as long as 30. Research indicates that if an individual shows two or more clues or fails to complete the One-Leg Stand, there is a good chance the alcohol concentration is above 0.10. Using that criterion, officers will accurately classify 65 percent of the people they test as to whether their alcohol concentration is above 0.10. *(LE515.33.a.)*

Observe the subject from a safe distance and limit movement which may distract the subject during the test. Always consider officer safety.

## Test Conditions

One-Leg Stand requires a reasonably dry, hard, level, and non-slippery surface. The subject's safety should be considered at all times.

Individuals over 65 years of age, those with back, leg, or inner ear problems, or those who are overweight by 50 or more pounds may have difficulty performing this test. Individuals wearing heels more than two inches high should be given the opportunity to remove their shoes.

# Taking Field Notes on Subjects' Performance of Field Sobriety Tests

For purposes of the arrest report and courtroom testimony, it is not enough to record the total number of clues on the three tests. The number of clues is important to the officer in the field because it helps determine whether there is probable cause to arrest. To convict the subject, more descriptive evidence is needed.

The officer must be able to describe how the subject performed on the tests, and exactly what the subject did. The DUI Field Notes sample form is designed to help you develop a clear description of the subject's performance on the tests.

## *Taking Field Notes on the Eye Procedures*

First, have subject remove glasses. In the Medical Assessment section:

- Check "Yes" or "No" box for equal pupil size.
- Check "Yes" or "No" box for equal tracking.

In the Other section, record any facts, circumstances, conditions, or observations that may be relevant to this procedure (i.e., resting nystagmus).

Complete the entire test for both eyes, writing "yes" or "no" for each nystagmus clue.

- Write "yes" if the clue is present.
- Write "no" if the clue is not present.

In the Other section, record any facts, circumstances, conditions, or observations that may be relevant to this test.

Examples of additional evidence of impairment emerging during nystagmus test include the following:

- subject unable to keep head still
- subject swaying noticeably
- subject utters incriminating statements

Examples of conditions that may interfere with subject's performance of the Horizontal Gaze Nystagmus test include the following:

- wind, dust, etc. irritating subject's eyes
- visual or other distractions impeding the test

## *Taking Field Notes on Walk-and-Turn Testing*

The first two clues, <u>cannot keep balance</u> and <u>starts too soon</u> apply only during the instructions stage of the test. Record the number of times each of those clues appear. For example, if the subject's feet <u>break apart</u> from the heel-to-toe stance twice during the instructions stage, write "2" in the box alongside the <u>cannot keep balance</u> clue. Similarly, if the subject <u>starts too soon</u>, write "1" in that box. *Note:* <u>Actual steps taken</u> is for scoring purposes only. Wrong number of steps is the validated clue.

Don't leave boxes blank. If a particular clue never shows up, write "0" in the corresponding box.

Record the next five clues separately for the walk down the line, and then up the line.

A. If a subject stops walking, record it by drawing a vertical line across the toe of the step at which the stop occurred. Do this for the first and the second nine steps. Place the letter "S" at bottom of the vertical line to indicate where the subject stops walking.

B. If a subject fails to touch heel-to-toe, record how many times this happens. Draw a vertical line across the toe of the step where the miss occurred. Place the letter "M" at the top of the vertical line to indicate missed heel-to-toe.

C. If a subject steps off the line while walking, record it by drawing a line from the appropriate foot print at an angle in the direction where the foot stepped. Do it for each of the nine steps.

D. If a subject uses his or her arms to balance, give some indication of how often or how long this happens.

- *Example:* subject raised arms from sides three times. Place a check for each occurrence in appropriate box.
- *Example:* subject held arms away from sides during steps 3 through 7. Place a check for each occurrence in appropriate box.
- *Example:* subject flapped arms continuously. Make a note.

E. Record the actual number of steps taken by the subject in each direction.

For the next point, improper turn, record a description of the turn.

If you note that the subject cannot perform test, indicate specifically why you did so.

- *Example:* stepped off line three times on steps 2, 4, and 6
- *Example:* staggered six steps to the right, nearly fell
- *Example:* fear of injury

At the end of the test, examine each factor and determine how many clues have been recorded. Remember, each clue may appear several times, but still only constitutes one clue.

In the Other section, record any facts, circumstances, conditions, or observations that may be relevant to this test.

Examples of additional evidence of impairment during Walk-and-Turn test:

- subject verbally miscounts steps
- subject utters incriminating statements

Examples of conditions that may interfere with subject's performance of the Walk-and-Turn test:

- wind/weather conditions
- subject's age, weight
- subject's footwear

**Section Vocabulary**

*Neurological Nystagmus*

*Pathological Nystagmus*

*Vestibular Nystagmus*

## Taking Field Notes on the Combined Interpretation of Nystagmus and Walk-and-Turn

By combining four or more clues of HGN with two or more clues of the WAT test, subjects can be correctly classified as above 0.10 alcohol concentration 80 percent of the time.

## Taking Field Notes on One-Leg Stand Testing

By recording when things happen as well as what happens, an officer will be able to prepare a more descriptive arrest report.

Place check marks in or near the small boxes to indicate how many times you observed each of the clues. Do this separately for the test on the left leg (L) or on the right leg (R).

In addition, if the subject puts the foot down during the test, record when it happened. Write the count on the form. For example, when standing on the left leg, write, "The subject lowered the right foot at a count of 'one thousand and thirteen' and again at 'one thousand and twenty.'" Also pay attention to the subject's general appearance and behavior while the test is being performed.

At the end of the test, examine each factor and determine how many distinct clues have appeared. Remember, each clue may appear several times, but still only constitutes one clue.

It is necessary to emphasize this validation applies only when:

- The tests are administered in the prescribed, standardized manner.
- The standardized clues are used to assess the subject's performance.
- The standardized criteria are employed to interpret that performance.

If any one of the standardized field sobriety test elements is changed, the validity may be compromised. *(LE515.34.)*

# LESSON 5 | Drug-Impaired Driving

## Drug Impairment

Law enforcement officers encounter not only drivers driving under the influence of alcohol, but also those who may be impaired due to the use of legal or illegal drugs. The best available data suggest that tens of millions of Americans routinely use drugs other than alcohol and some of these people sometimes drive when they are under the influence of those drugs.

Some drug-impaired drivers look and act very much like alcohol-impaired drivers. Others look and act very differently. All of them are dangerous to themselves and to everyone else on the road. *(LE515.36.)*

A ***drug*** is any substance that, when taken into the human body, can impair the ability of the person to operate a vehicle safely *(LE515.37.a.)*. There are seven broad categories of drugs that may impair drivers. These drugs are classified by category based on the observable signs and symptoms they produce.

**Central Nervous System Depressants**—This category includes a large number of different drugs, all of which slow down the operation of the brain and other parts of the central nervous system (CNS). Examples include alcohol, Valium, Xanax, and Soma.

**Central Nervous System Stimulants**—This category of drugs acts quite differently from depressants. Central nervous system stimulants impair drivers by speeding up or overstimulating the brain. Cocaine and methamphetamine are examples of CNS stimulants.

**Hallucinogens**—This category includes both natural substances and synthetic chemicals. All hallucinogens impair the user's ability to perceive the world as it really is. Peyote and psychedelic mushrooms are naturally occurring hallucinogens. LSD and ecstasy are examples of synthetic hallucinogens.

**Dissociative Anesthetics**—This category consists of the drug PCP and its various analogs (chemical cousins). Originally developed for use as an anesthetic, PCP is a powerful drug that may act like a depressant, stimulant, and hallucinogen. Another dissociative anesthetic, dextromethorphan (DXM), is found in many over-the-counter medications like Coricidin Cough and Cold.

**Narcotic Analgesics**—This category includes the natural derivatives of opium, such as morphine, heroin, codeine, and others. The category also includes many synthetic drugs, such as Demerol, methadone, and others. All narcotic analgesics are designed to relieve pain and are likely to produce addiction. A ***narcotic*** is a substance that induces sleep (narcosis). An ***analgesic*** is a pain-relieving drug.

**OBJECTIVES**

**LE515.36.** Describe the problem of drug-impaired drivers.

**LE515.37.a.** Define *drug* as it pertains to driving impairment.

**LE515.37.** List the seven categories of drugs that may impair drivers.

**LE515.38.** Describe the five eye examinations that are helpful in detecting drug influence.

**LE515.39.a.** Define *polydrug use*.

**LE515.39.** Describe the problem of polydrug use.

**LE515.39.b.** Explain the possible effects of polydrug use.

**LE515.39.c.** List indicators that may suggest an impaired driver is under the influence of medication.

**Inhalants**—This category includes many familiar household materials such as paint, glue, aerosol sprays, etc. None of these substances is manufactured for use as a drug. However, they produce fumes that can cause significant impairment. Inhalants such as nitrous oxide and chloroform are intended for medical use.

**Cannabis**—This is the category that includes marijuana and hashish, as well as synthetic compounds such as Marinol. Marijuana and other cannabis products impair the attention process. The ability to perform divided attention tests diminishes under the influence of cannabis. *(LE515.37.)*

## Eye Examinations: Important Clues of Drug Influence

A subject's eyes often disclose some important, easy-to-observe indicators of drug influence or medical impairment. Five eye examinations are especially helpful:

- pupil size
- resting nystagmus
- tracking ability
- horizontal gaze nystagmus
- vertical gaze nystagmus

Pupil size is an important indicator of the use of certain categories of drugs. The size of a person's pupils changes naturally in response to various light conditions. Usually, the diameter of the pupils constricts in bright light and dilates in darkness. If the two pupils are noticeably different in size, the subject may be suffering from an injury or medical condition or have an artificial eye.

Subjects under the influence of narcotic analgesics generally have constricted pupils. Subjects under the influence of CNS stimulants, hallucinogens, or cannabis generally have dilated pupils. Pupil size remains within the normal range with the use of most CNS depressants, dissociative anesthetics, and inhalants.

A precise measurement of pupil size is not necessary. Estimating whether the pupils are of equal size, noticeably smaller, normal, or noticeably larger is sufficient for this evaluation.

Resting nystagmus is the jerking of the eyes as the eyes look straight ahead. This condition, though not frequently seen, usually indicates a pathological disorder or high doses of a drug such as PCP.

*Note:* Resting nystagmus may also be a medical problem. Although this observation is an important medical assessment, it is NOT an HGN administrative procedure step.

Tracking ability is the ability of the eyes to track together when the subject attempts to follow an object moving side-to-side. The test of tracking ability is conducted in the same manner as the check for lack of smooth pursuit in the horizontal gaze nystagmus test. The possibility of a medical condition or injury exists if the two eyes do not track together, for example, if one eye has full range of motion, but the other moves only slightly or not at all.

Horizontal gaze nystagmus generally occurs when the subject is under the influence of one or more drugs in the CNS depressant, inhalant, or dissociative anesthetic categories.

Vertical gaze nystagmus usually occurs with the use of dissociative anesthetics and may occur with relatively high doses of CNS depressants or inhalants for that individual. *(LE515.38.)*

The drug categories and their impairment effects are summarized in Figure 10-6, below and on the following page.

| Signs/Symptoms | CNS Depressants | CNS Stimulants | Hallucinogens |
|---|---|---|---|
| **Action** | slow brain operation, depress the heartbeat, lower blood pressure, respiration and other processes controlled by the brain | accelerate the heart rate and respiration, elevate the blood pressure and speed up or over-stimulate other processes of the body | distorted reality, hallucinations, affect sensations, thinking, self-awareness, and emotions |
| **General Indicators** | drunken behavior, uncoordinated, drowsy, sluggish, disoriented, thick slurred speech | restlessness, talkative, excited, euphoria, exaggerated reflexes, loss of appetite, grinding teeth, redness to nasal area, body tremors | hallucinations, dazed, body tremors, uncoordinated, perspiring, disoriented, paranoid, difficulty speaking, nausea |
| **Eye Indicators HGN** | present | not present | not present |
| **Eye Indicators VGN** | may be present | not present | not present |
| **Pupil Size** | normal (except methaqualone and Soma cause dilation) | dilated | dilated |
| **Examples** | alcohol, Rohypnol, tranquilizers (Valium, Xanax), barbiturates, muscle relaxers | cocaine, amphetamines, methamphetamines | peyote, psilocybin, LSD, MDA, MDMA (ecstasy) |

Drug categories and effects (Table 1 of 2) *Figure 10-6*

| Dissociative Anesthetics | Narcotic Analgesics | Inhalants | Cannabis |
|---|---|---|---|
| powerful anesthetic, causes bizarre and sometimes violent behavior | relieve pain, produce withdrawal symptoms | block the passage of oxygen to the brain | impair the attention process, inability to perform divided attention tasks |
| perspiring, repetitive speech, confused, possibly violent and combative, blank stare, incomplete verbal responses, muscle rigidity | "on the nod," droopy eyelids, depressed reflexes, dry mouth, facial itching, low raspy speech, fresh puncture marks | disorientation, confusion, slurred speech, possible nausea, possible residue of substance on face, hands, clothing | reddening of conjunctivae, body tremors, marijuana odor, disoriented, relaxed inhibitions, difficulty in dividing attention |
| present | not present | present | not present |
| present | not present | may be present | not present |
| normal | constricted | normal | dilated (may be normal) |
| PCP, Ketamine, dextromethorphan | morphine, heroin, codeine, fentanyl, Demerol, methadone, Oxycontin | glue, paint, gasoline, hair sprays, insecticides, nitrous oxide, ether, chloroform | marijuana, hashish, hash oil, Marinol, dronabinol |

**Drug categories and effects (Table 2 of 2)** *Figure 10-6*

## Drug Combinations

Officers may encounter subjects who are impaired by a combination of drugs or who use alcohol to mask illegal drug use. ***Polydrug use*** is using drugs from two or more drug categories simultaneously. Examples include drinking alcohol while smoking marijuana, sprinkling PCP on marijuana joints, or injecting heroin laced with cocaine ("speedball"). Such combinations often increase impairment. Impairment could also occur unintentionally through the use of alcohol and prescription medication *(LE515.39.a., LE515.39.).*

Polydrug use may produce the following effects:

**Null**—Neither drug has an effect on the indicator. For example, neither a CNS Stimulant nor a Narcotic Analgesic will cause HGN; therefore, HGN will not be present.

**Overlapping**—One drug affects some indicator of impairment, and the other drug has no effect whatsoever on that indicator. For example, alcohol will cause HGN, but marijuana will not cause HGN. Therefore, HGN will be present.

**Additive**—Drugs from two categories both affect some indicator in the same way and, in combination, these effects reinforce each other. For example, CNS Stimulants and Hallucinogens both cause pupil dilation; therefore, pupils will be dilated.

**Antagonistic**—Drugs from two categories may produce some effects that are exactly opposite, but in combination, the effects are difficult to predict. For example, cocaine dilates the pupils, and heroin constricts the pupils. The eyes may be dilated, constricted, or normal. *(LE515.39.b.)*

**Section Vocabulary**

***analgesic***

***drug***

***narcotic***

***polydrug use***

## Medication Effects

Some indicators suggest that an impaired driver may be under the influence of medication or affected by a medical condition. One is the absence of the odor of alcoholic beverages. The driver may be wearing a medical alert bracelet or have a medical alert information card. Prescription bottles, leftover pills, or drug paraphernalia may be in the driver's possession or in the vehicle. The driver (or a passenger) may volunteer information regarding use of medication. The driver's license may indicate insulin dependence. When a person's sugar level is too high, his or her breath could emit an odor similar to that of an alcoholic beverage. The driver may also have a comprehension or awareness problem.

If one or more indicators are present, the driver may be in legal possession of prescription medication. However, if the effects of the prescribed medication impair the driver's ability to drive, the driver should be treated the same as someone impaired by illegal drugs or alcohol. If the officer determines that there are indicators of impairment, he or she should administer the SFSTs. *(LE515.39.c.)*

Officers should become familiar with their agency's policies and procedures for handling drug- or medically-impaired subjects.

# LESSON 6 | Report Writing

**OBJECTIVES**

**LE515.40.** Describe the responsibility of officers in preparing written reports for DUI violations.

**LE515.41.** Name the basic elements of DUI investigation to include in a DUI Arrest Report.

**LE515.41.a.** List the parts of a comprehensive narrative in a DUI Arrest Report.

The successful prosecution of a DUI case is dependent on the officer's ability to organize and present all relevant evidence of each element of the DUI violation. The officer must keep in mind that virtually all of this evidence must be compiled during the three phases of detection—vehicle in motion, personal contact, and pre-arrest screening. The officer must be able to establish the level of impairment at the time that the violation occurred; therefore, observations are of critical importance. Subsequent evidence of impairment, such as the evidential chemical test result(s) and the evidence gathered during a drug evaluation, will be admissible only when a proper arrest has been made. The efforts expended in detecting, apprehending, investigating, and testing/evaluating the DUI violator will be of little value if there is not sufficient evidence to prove every element of the violation.

Accordingly, if the evidence is not presented clearly and convincingly in court, the case may be lost, no matter how good that evidence may be. Therefore, it is essential that officers develop the ability to write a clear and concise report describing their observations and results of their investigation for presentation to the prosecutor. *(LE515.40.)*

## Processing Stage

The processing of an arrested subject is the bridge between the arrest and conviction of a DUI offender. During the processing stage, all evidence gathered during the detection phases is organized to ensure that it will be available and admissible in court. Additional evidence may also be obtained during the processing stage subsequent to arrest. It is important that proper procedures be followed during this stage; otherwise, important evidence might be ruled inadmissible.

The processing stage begins with the arrest of the offender and ends when the offender is incarcerated or released to a responsible third party (depending on jurisdiction).

## Preparing the DUI Offense/Arrest Report

Successful prosecution depends on the clarity and completeness with which the arresting officer's observations are presented. The arresting officer must articulate in writing each element of the offense to establish probable cause that the subject was under the influence.

Chemical test evidence and additional evidence gathered subsequent to the arrest may be suppressed if the arresting officer does not adequately establish probable cause for the arrest prior to the chemical test.

Trials are often held many months after the defendant's arrest. A clear, concise report and the accompanying documentation will enable the officer to recall those details and present them through convincing direct testimony in court.

The DUI report should establish the following elements for the arrest:

- The accused was the operator or in actual physical control of the vehicle.
- There was reasonable suspicion for stopping/contacting the accused.
- There was probable cause to believe the accused was impaired.
- Proper arrest procedures were followed.
- Proper procedure was followed with regards to the rights of the accused.
- Subsequent observation and interview of the accused provided additional evidence relevant to the alleged offense.
- There was a proper request for the accused to submit to the chemical test and what the results of that test indicated. *(LE515.41.)*

# Narrative of the DUI Arrest Report

The narrative offense/arrest report should be organized around the total sequence of events, beginning at the first observation of the offender, continuing through the arrest, and ending with the incarceration or release of the subject. The following is a suggested report format:

## *PHASE ONE: Vehicle in Motion*

### *Initial Observations*

- First observations of the offender and his or her actions
- Factors that drew officer's attention
- Time and location of first observations

### *Vehicle Stop*

- Subject's unusual actions taken
- Offender's response to the stop command
- Method(s) officer used to signal the stop command
- The fashion in which the offender stopped the vehicle

## *PHASE TWO: Personal Contact*

### *Face-to-Face Contact*

- Offender's personal appearance
- Condition of eyes, speech, etc.
- Names, contact information, seating locations of passengers
- Unusual actions taken
- Unusual statements made
- What officer saw, heard, and smelled

### *Operation/Actual Physical Control*

- Establish offender as the operator

### *Exit from Vehicle*

- Unusual actions, occurrences

## ***PHASE THREE: Pre-Arrest Screening***

- Standardized Field Sobriety Tests
- Physical performance
- Mental performance

### *The Arrest*

## ***POST ARREST: Breath Testing and Processing***

### *Disposition/Location of Vehicle and Keys*

### *Disposition of Passengers and Property*

### *Transport of Offender*

- Departure time
- Arrival time
- Subject statements

### *Evidential Tests/Implied Consent*

- What tests were administered
- Who administered the tests
- Test results

### *Subject Interview*

- *Miranda* warning
- Post-*Miranda* questioning

### *Statements of Witnesses*

### *Citations*

- Charges issued
- When issued

### *Incarceration or Release*

- Time
- Place
- If released, to whom

## *Additional Chemical Tests*

- Types of test
- Time taken
- Where taken
- By whom administered *(LE515.41.a.)*

# CHAPTER 11

## Traffic Crash Investigations



A ***traffic crash*** is a collision involving one or more vehicles, which causes property damage, personal injury, or death, and which is the result of an unintentional act. The terms "unintentional" and "causes property damage, personal injury, or death" are important elements in the definition. If the act that causes damage or injury is intentional then it would not be a crash but a crime, such as aggravated battery or murder, depending on the elements of the incident. The majority of traffic crashes do not involve criminal activity. However, an officer should treat each traffic crash as a crime scene.

Law enforcement officers conduct traffic crash investigations by following a step-by-step approach which encompasses the initial response to the scene, scene assessment and protection, identifying and analyzing information gathered from witnesses, evaluating physical evidence, thoroughly investigating and documenting the crash, and concluding with the appropriate law enforcement action.

# UNIT 1 | ASSESSING AND SECURING THE SCENE

## LESSON 1 | Responding to and Assessing the Scene

**OBJECTIVES**

**LE082.2.D.** Identify the Florida Statutes relating to uniform traffic control when conducting a traffic crash investigation.

**LE078.1.D.** Identify the traffic crash management process.

**LE079.1.** Arrive safely at a traffic crash scene.

**LE078.5.A.** Assess the scene of a traffic crash incident.

**LE083.1.** Identify any dangers or hazards at the traffic crash scene.

**LE295.3.C.2.** Identify the Department of Transportation's hazardous material identification placard information from placard symbols found in the DOT ERG book of hazardous materials identification.

**LE083.4.** Assess requirements for additional aid for a vehicle crash, identifying situations that require assistance.

**LE083.5.** Request assistance needed in a traffic crash situation.

**LE082.1.** Locate vehicle or property damaged in the crash upon arrival at the traffic crash scene.

**LE080.2.A.8.** Define *first harmful event.*

**LE078.6.B.1.** Identify conditions for transferring jurisdiction in a situation involving a traffic crash scene with multi-jurisdictional boundaries.

### Terms and Definitions

Florida Statute §316.003 identifies terms and definitions related to state uniform traffic control including roadway, vehicle, and sign descriptions that an officer will use in documenting a traffic crash incident. It is through the accurate recording of observations and applying the corresponding statute in violation that an officer will be able to successfully defend his or her investigation in court. The terms listed below are routinely used by patrol officers in traffic crash investigations.

*vehicle* [§316.003(75), F.S.]—every device in, upon, or by which any person or property is or may be transported or drawn upon a highway, excepting devices used exclusively upon stationary rails or tracks

*motor vehicle* [§316.003(21), F.S.]—any self-propelled vehicle not operated upon rails or guideway, but not including any bicycle, motorized scooter, electric personal assistive mobility device, or moped

*tri-vehicle* [§316.003(88), F.S.]—an enclosed three-wheeled passenger vehicle designed to operate with three wheels, with a minimum unladen weight of 900 pounds, and a single enclosed occupant compartment capable of a speed greater than 60 miles per hour

*motorcycle* [§322.01(22), F.S.]—a motor vehicle powered by a motor with a displacement of more than 50 cubic centimeters, having a seat or saddle for the rider, and designed to travel on not more than three wheels in contact with the ground, but excluding a tractor, tricycle or moped

*pedestrian* [§316.003(28), F.S.]—any person afoot

*laned highway* [§316.003(18), F.S.]—a highway the roadway of which is divided into two or more clearly marked lanes for vehicular traffic

*limited access facility* [§316.003(19), F.S.]—a street or highway especially designed for through traffic and over, from, or to which owners or occupants of abutting land or other persons have no right or easement, or only a limited right or easement, of access, light, air, or view by reason of the fact that their property abuts upon such limited access facility or for any other reason; such highways or streets may be parkways from which trucks, buses, and other commercial vehicles are excluded; or they may be freeways open to use by all customary forms of street and highway traffic.

*private road or driveway* [§316.003(33), F.S.]—except as otherwise provided in paragraph (53)(b), any privately owned way or place used for vehicular travel by the owner and those having express or implied permission from the owner, but not by other persons *state road* [§316.003(50), F.S.]—any highway designated as a state-maintained road by the Department of Transportation

*roadway* [§316.003(42), F.S.]—that portion of a highway improved, designed, or ordinarily used for vehicular travel, exclusive of the berm or shoulder; in the event a highway includes two or more separate roadways, the term roadway as used herein refers to any such roadway separately, but not to all such roadways collectively.

*street or highway* [§316.003(53), F.S.]

(a) the entire width between the boundary lines of every way or place of whatever nature when any part thereof is open to the use of the public for purposes of vehicular traffic;

(b) the entire width between the boundary lines of any privately owned way or place used for vehicular travel by the owner and those having express or implied permission from the owner, but not by other persons, or any limited access road owned or controlled by a special district, whenever, by written agreement entered into under section §316.006(2)(b) or (3)(b), a county or municipality exercises traffic control jurisdiction over said way or place;

(c) any area, such as a runway, taxiway, ramp, clear zone, or parking lot, within the boundary of any airport owned by the state, a county, a municipality, or a political subdivision, which area is used for vehicular traffic but which is not open for vehicular operation by the general public; or

(d) any way or place used for vehicular traffic on a controlled access basis within a mobile home park recreation district which has been created under section §418.30, F.S., and the recreational facilities of which district are open to the general public

*intersection* [§316.003(17), F.S.]

(a) the area embraced within the prolongation or connection of the lateral curblines; or, if none, then the lateral boundary lines of the roadways of two highways which join one another at, or approximately at, right angles; or the area within which vehicles traveling upon different highways joining at any other angle may come in conflict

(b) where a highway includes two roadways 30 feet or more apart, then every crossing of each roadway of such divided highway by an intersecting highway shall be regarded as a separate intersection; in the event such intersecting highway also includes two roadways 30 feet or more apart, then every crossing of two roadways of such highways shall be regarded as a separate intersection.

*crosswalk* [§316.003(6), F.S.]

(a) that part of a roadway at an intersection included within the connections of the lateral lines of the sidewalks on opposite sides of the highway, measured from the curbs or, in the absence of curbs, from the edges of the traversable roadway

(b) any portion of a roadway at an intersection or elsewhere distinctly indicated for pedestrian crossing by lines or other markings on the surface

**LE079.10.C.1.** Identify if a vehicle was involved in a crime.

**LE017.2.** Request medical and/or fire assistance for a vehicle fire, if appropriate.

**LE017.3.** Extinguish a vehicle fire with current fire extinguisher equipment, if feasible.

**LE017.6.** Complete an incident report for a vehicle fire.

**LE017.1.** Determine if it is necessary to evacuate persons from the area of a vehicle on fire.

*sidewalk* [§316.003(47), F.S.]—that portion of a street between the curbline, or the lateral line, of a roadway and the adjacent property lines, intended for use by pedestrians

*bicycle path* [§316.003(63), F.S.]—any road, path, or way that is open to bicycle travel, which road, path, or way is physically separated from motorized vehicular traffic by an open space or by a barrier and is located either within the highway right-of-way or within an independent right-of-way

*Ronshay Dugans Act* [§683.332, F.S.]—Research shows fatigue or drowsiness to be as much of an impairment and as dangerous as alcohol while operating a motor vehicle. The DHSMV and DOT will educate the law enforcement community and public about the relationship between fatigue and driving performance during the Drowsy Driving Prevention Week every first week of September.

*Ashley Nicole Valdes Act* [§316.027(1)(b), F.S.]—The driver of any vehicle involved in a traffic crash occurring on public or private property that results in the death of any person must immediately stop the vehicle at the scene of the crash, or as close thereto as possible, and must remain at the scene of the crash until he or she has fulfilled the requirements of §. 316.062. Any person who willfully violates this paragraph commits a felony of the first degree, punishable as provided in §. 775.082, §. 775.083, or §. 775.084.

Definitions relating to injuries that may be incurred by an individual in a traffic crash incident include the following:

*serious bodily injury* [§316.1933(1)(b), F.S.]—an injury to any person, including the driver, which consists of a physical condition that creates a substantial risk of death, serious personal disfigurement, or protracted loss or impairment of the function of any bodily member or organ

*fatal injury*—an injury resulting in an individual's death within a 30 day period after the traffic crash accident

*incapacitating injury*—visible/non-visible signs of injury, such as a bleeding wound or distorted member, usually requiring hospitalization and transport to a medical facility

*non-incapacitating injury*—visible/non-visible signs of injury or complaint of injury, not requiring transport from the scene

The Florida Statutes on the following page (Figure 10-1) are important for an officer to understand when conducting a traffic crash investigation.

## Crash Management

Officer safety and the protection of traffic crash victims depend on an officer's safe arrival at the scene. If a crash scene involves fire, hazardous materials, or chemicals, it can quickly become out of control. Parking the patrol vehicle safely and rapidly and accurately assessing the crash scene as well as requesting necessary assistance, prevents further injuries. An officer must take control of a traffic crash situation and conduct the resulting investigation quickly and efficiently. This process is usually referred to as ***crash management***, which is law enforcement's responsibility to control and normalize a traffic crash scene. *(LE078.1.D.)*

| | |
|---|---|
| **316.027** | Crash involving death or personal injuries. |
| **316.061** | Crashes involving damage to vehicle or property. |
| **316.062** | Duty to give information and render aid. |
| **316.063** | Duty upon damaging unattended vehicle or other property. |
| **316.064** | When driver unable to report. |
| **316.065** | Crashes; reports; penalties. |
| **316.066** | Written reports of crashes. |
| **316.067** | False reports. |
| **316.068** | Crash report forms. |
| **316.070** | Exchange of information at scene of crash. |
| **316.193** | Driving under the influence; penalties. |
| **316.1932** | Tests for alcohol, chemical substances, or controlled substances; implied consent; refusal. |
| **316.1933** | Blood test for impairment or intoxication in cases of death or serious bodily injury; right to use reasonable force. |

Florida Statutes regarding traffic crash investigations *Figure 10-1*
*(LE082.2.D.)*

The crash management process involves the following steps:

**Step 1**—Respond to the traffic crash scene safely.

**Step 2**—Assess the scene of the crash.

**Step 3**—Secure a safe work environment at the crash scene.

**Step 4**—Provide emergency assistance to injured persons if necessary.

**Step 5**—Obtain pertinent information.

**Step 6**—Investigate the crash to determine the cause.

**Step 7**—Document the crash.

**Step 8**—Return the scene to normal as quickly as possible.

**Step 9**—Conclude enforcement action.

An officer begins the traffic crash management process as he or she approaches the scene.

### *Step 1:* Respond to the traffic crash scene safely.

After receiving the call, the officer should obtain as much information as possible about the crash location (e.g., street names, address, mile marker, etc.). It is important to respond to the scene safely in accordance with agency policy and state statutes. An officer cannot assist others if he or she becomes a victim of a second crash. Officers must consider the legal liability risks for their agency and themselves created by their response to a crash scene. *(LE079.1.)*

### Step 2: Assess the scene of the crash.

Many different factors will aid in an officer's scene assessment. Upon approaching the traffic crash scene, an officer should view it from a distance to determine its type and extent *(LE078.5.A.)*. The officer must be aware of the possible dangers and hazards that he or she may encounter at the crash site. Several potential dangers include fire, fluids on the ground, clouds of gases or smoke, or people running away, falling down, or lying injured in the roadway. The officer must be aware of hazards such as additional crashes, hazardous materials, and electrocution from downed wires, flooding, or cave-ins from damaged retaining walls. Crash debris poses additional threats to both vehicle and pedestrian traffic; pieces of metal or glass that could puncture a tire or be struck by a passing vehicle could be hurled, striking other vehicles, pedestrians, or emergency responders. Large parts from the crashed vehicles could make motorists swerve to avoid running into the debris and cause additional crashes. *(LE083.1.)*

During an officer's scene assessment, he or she may discover that a commercial motor vehicle is involved in the traffic crash. Before approaching the scene, the officer should determine if the vehicle's contents are hazardous. The officer should locate the placard on the vehicle and refer to the Department of Transportation's Emergency Response Guide (ERG) to verify the contents *(LE295.3.C.2.)*. If the contents are hazardous, an officer should follow agency policy regarding handling procedures.

Once an officer has determined that it is safe to move closer to the scene, the officer should assess where to park his or her vehicle and what assistance to request. Although officers know how to perform first aid, direct traffic, and interview witnesses, they cannot do all of this at the same time. The officer must decide which additional units, if any, are needed, such as the fire department, Emergency Medical Services (EMS), Department of Transportation (DOT) Motor Carrier Compliance, or hazardous materials (HAZMAT) team *(LE083.4.)*. The officer will radio dispatch to arrange additional assistance and request that dispatch advise the responding units of any unusual details that they should be aware of before arrival. Such information should include details and conditions regarding hazards or dangers that may affect a responding unit. *(LE083.5.)*

By locating the vehicles and property damaged in the incident, an officer should be able to conclude the parameters of the actual crash scene. By examining the marks and debris left by the vehicles, he or she can determine the path of the vehicles. Property that was in the path of the vehicles may show signs of damage from the crash. Witnesses and involved persons may inform the officer of property damaged by the crash, vehicles that were involved and may have left the scene, or other involved vehicles not immediately obvious during the initial scene assessment. An officer must identify and protect any fragile, trace, and time sensitive evidence because it may be transitory and should be photographed or gathered as soon as possible. *(LE082.1.)*

## Determining Jurisdiction

The crash scene should be handled by the jurisdiction where the ***first harmful event*** or the first damage-producing event in a traffic crash occurred. It determines the exact time, location, and type of crash. An officer can calculate the ***area of collision (AOC)*** by determining the location of the first harmful event. The AOC may be indicated by crash debris, fixed property damage, broken glass, gouge marks, and scrape marks. *(LE080.2.A.8.)*

When the responding officer's jurisdiction is the AOC of the crash, the officer should maintain jurisdiction and continue the crash investigation. Otherwise, the appropriate jurisdiction should be notified. The initial responding officer should remain on the scene to protect the public and the traffic crash scene until the appropriate agency officer arrives. The responding officer may remain at the traffic crash scene to assist with the investigation or provide traffic control depending upon his or her agency policy. Individual agencies may have policies that govern how to handle a crash scene with multi-jurisdictional boundaries. If so, officers should follow their agency policy. When jurisdiction cannot be determined, the Florida Highway Patrol may be called since they have statewide jurisdiction. *(LE078.6.B.1.)*

## Unique Traffic Crash Situations

Some traffic crash incidents warrant special consideration. If one of the vehicles involved has left the scene, the crash may be categorized as a hit-and-run. The officer should ask witnesses at the scene for a description of the vehicle and contact dispatch to send out a BOLO alert.

At times a traffic crash will involve only a single vehicle. An officer will want to look closely at the cause of the crash, as single vehicle crashes tend to be related to driver error or condition. Before a person can be successfully prosecuted for a criminal offense that resulted in a single-vehicle crash, the officer must search for evidence that places the driver behind the wheel at the time of the crash. Such evidence includes skin and blood found on deployed airbags, bruises or scratches on an injured person's head that are consistent with damage to the windshield, and/or fingerprints on the steering wheel or the keys in the ignition. This is a legal search under the *Carroll* Doctrine, which permits officers to search a vehicle if the officer has probable cause to believe that the vehicle contains evidence of a crime. The officer is permitted by law to search any part of the vehicle that may contain evidence of the suspected crime for which the arrest has been made.

Traffic crash situations may require specialized assistance from the law enforcement community. If a traffic crash results in life-threatening injuries or in the death of a person injured as a direct result of the crash, the vehicles are considered evidence and must not be removed from their final resting places. The responding officer must protect the scene and notify his or her supervisor and request a traffic homicide investigator and other personnel such as the crime scene unit and a victim advocate to assist.

In addition to traffic homicide investigators, some agencies have specialized officers for working with DUI drivers. The decision to use these officers may be dictated by departmental policy or by their availability. *(LE079.10.C.1.)*

## Fire Management

Officers should request assistance for extensive vehicle fires *(LE017.2.)*. If the fire is small enough and appropriate for the type of fire extinguisher in the patrol vehicle, the officer should extinguish the flames. The fire should never be allowed to get between an officer and his or her means of escape. An officer should always attack the fire with the wind to his or her back; he should never turn away from it. Backing away from the fire lets the officer maintain visual awareness of the fire. While waiting for assistance, an officer should keep a watchful eye on the extinguished fire to ensure there is no remaining fire threat *(LE017.3.)*. An officer must be careful to not overlook crash damage that can be camouflaged by fire damage. He or she should note observations of the crash damage on the incident report. *(LE017.6.)*

## Section Vocabulary

*area of collision (AOC)*

*crash management*

*first harmful event*

*traffic crash*

An officer must decide if passengers in the vehicle can be removed safely given the officer's training and available equipment. People should be evacuated 20 to 25 feet away from a small vehicle fire if there are no other hazards present. If other hazards, such as toxic fumes or the risk that the fire could reach gas tanks, are present, the Emergency Response Guide (ERG) recommends a minimum evacuation of 80 to 160 feet in all directions. (See the ERG for additional information.)

To conduct the evacuation, an officer should use verbal commands and hand signals to direct all persons away from the fire toward a safe location. If a large number of people are present, an officer may need to use the patrol vehicle's public address system to direct observers away from the scene. When deciding on a safe location, an officer must consider the location, buildings in the area, the amount of traffic, and the weather. If there is any breeze, people should be directed upwind. *(LE017.1.)*

# UNIT 1 | ASSESSING AND SECURING THE SCENE

## LESSON 2 | Protecting the Scene

### *Step 3:* Secure a safe work environment at the crash scene.

Traffic crashes attract motorists' attention and cause gawking or "rubbernecking," which slows the traffic flow. This can be a hazard since drivers' attention is focused on the crash scene and not on driving around the crash. Many secondary crashes happen because of this lack of attention. Nighttime crash scenes compound this hazard because vision is already limited, and the lights from the patrol vehicle and flares distract drivers' attention and obscure their vision. People with night vision difficulties have trouble adjusting from the bright lights around the crash scene to normal lighting from headlights or streetlights. Effective traffic control can help reduce the chance of additional crashes.

Traffic conditions, whether during the day or night, can sometimes make the crash scene difficult to see. Conditions due to heavy traffic, speed limits, or movement on and off the roadway can reduce vision. Traffic conditions affected by buildings, signs, curves, hills, trees, rain, smoke, and fog will also impact driver vision. Low light conditions add to the visibility problems of motorists approaching a crash scene. The number of emergency vehicle lights can confuse and cause some drivers to not see what is going on in front of them. Whenever possible, officers should work facing oncoming traffic, so they will see hazardous situations as they develop. *(LE023.5.A.)*

The patrol vehicle is the primary tool to control traffic and warn motorists of the hazards at a traffic crash scene. When positioning the patrol vehicle, an officer should locate a safe location that can be clearly seen by oncoming vehicles, is away from hazards or threats at the scene, and redirects the flow of traffic around the crash and injured people while maintaining officer safety. A properly placed patrol vehicle will allow drivers time to slow down before coming upon the crash scene. Although this is only the first step in protecting the crash scene, it is instrumental in preventing additional crashes. Officers should follow departmental policies when parking their vehicles.

The emergency lighting on an officer's parked patrol vehicle can help to warn oncoming traffic. These lights can be seen from long distances and are universally recognized as a caution or alert. The emergency lights should be used throughout the traffic crash investigation. An officer should place the headlights on low beam so as not to blind drivers approaching the scene from the opposite direction, unless agency policy directs otherwise. *(LE079.2.)*

**OBJECTIVES**

**LE023.5.A.** Identify the traffic conditions at a traffic crash incident.

**LE079.2.** Protect a traffic crash scene by properly positioning a patrol vehicle.

**LE079.2.B.** Preserve a traffic crash scene.

**LE104.4.** Position a patrol vehicle and/or warning devices to route traffic around a traffic crash incident.

**LE029.4.** Set out flares, barricades, or other warning devices with caution to direct traffic away from damage or hazard on a roadway.

**LE023.4.** Identify the need to wear a safety vest and gloves when conducting a traffic crash investigation.

**LE029.5.** Re-route traffic from a traffic crash scene immediately upon setting up warning devices.

**LE079.10.F.** Inventory the contents of a vehicle to be towed from a traffic crash incident.

**LE079.4.** Call for medical assistance for victims of a traffic crash incident, if necessary.

## Preserving the Scene

In addition to protecting the scene for safety reasons, an officer must preserve the scene for investigative purposes, such as a fatality or serious injury crash when traffic homicide is requested to respond, or hit-and-run crashes. The scenes of traffic crashes involving government vehicles or vehicles used in a crime must also be preserved for further investigation. Care should be taken to avoid parking on any evidence such as skid marks, debris, or fluids from the crash. Nothing should be touched or moved at the traffic crash scene. The exception is injured parties.

If the injured are treated (or there are no injuries) and the vehicles are drivable, and if there is no specialty investigator en route to investigate the crash, the officer should consider moving the vehicles off the roadway. How this is accomplished may be dictated by agency policy. Sections 316.027(3) and 316.061(2), F.S., require drivers of vehicles involved in crashes to move their vehicles "so as not to obstruct the regular flow of traffic." If the crash is major and vehicles are moved off the road, all debris and vehicle parts (glass, plastic) must be removed from the road after they have been photographed and their placement noted in field notes.

If injuries or death resulted from the crash, the vehicles should not be moved until after the traffic homicide investigator assesses the scene and documents the evidence or until otherwise directed. The final resting position of the vehicles is a very important part of the traffic homicide investigation. *(LE079.2.B.)*

## Warning Devices

Although the patrol vehicle is the first available equipment to use in protecting the crash scene, tools such as traffic cones, flares, and other warning devices serve to alert and direct passing motorists while protecting the scene. Traffic cones, barricades, and posts are useful items for assisting traffic direction at a crash scene due to their size and visibility. Individual agency policies and procedures may limit the equipment available to officers and require outside resources such as the city or county road department to provide any necessary barricades, cones, or flares.

Flares, also referred to as fuses, are small and easily used warning devices that may be stored in cases in the patrol vehicle trunk. When at a scene, an officer can retrieve the number of flares necessary to protect the scene while obtaining other equipment from his or her trunk. Flares not only work at night as an effective warning but are also visible to motorists during the day. *(LE104.4.)*

### *Placement of Warning Devices*

An officer's first step in placing warning devices is to assess the scene and determine what type of warning devices to use, where they should be placed, how many will be required to complete the protection, and the safe distance required to prevent further damage or injury.

Flares should be placed away from combustible materials. Before using flares, an officer must make sure there are no flammable items, liquids, or chemicals that may react to any flame involved in the crash. Such leaks at the crash scene and the use of flares could result in a catastrophe. In drought areas of Florida, wildfires could break out if the flare comes into contact with the dry, highly flammable grass on the side of the road. Placement and use of these devices is also weather-dependent. If it is windy, people should be directed upwind from hazards. If rain creates a wash of hazardous materials, traffic should be directed around the contaminated areas.

A safe distance for hazardous materials is determined by the type of hazardous material involved (see ERG). Safe distance for damage and debris is determined by the amount of space required for people involved in the crash to get out of the vehicles safely, for any emergency vehicles to get to the injured people or damaged vehicles, and for the officer to investigate the crash and crash evidence. For that reason, the "extent of the scene" at the crash site is the area between the first signs of evidence of crash avoidance or damage to vehicles or property and the final resting places of vehicles, property, and debris, including the immediate surrounding area for access to the scene.

The number of warning devices an officer will have to use is dependent on the size of the area to be protected, which is determined by the distance between the first evidence (usually skid marks) to the final resting position of vehicles and debris from the crash. The size is also affected by the number of traffic lanes affected and the normal speed of travel on the roadway. Selecting the location for the warning devices includes deciding how far away to begin placement as well as the pattern to use in placement. To determine how far away from the crash to place the cones or flares, an officer must first consider how fast traffic is moving. The impact of reaction time on stopping should also be considered when looking at how much distance to place between the first warning device for oncoming traffic and the scene. Drivers must have time to react. This means that the faster the traffic is moving, the further away from the scene the officer will have to place warnings. Posting an officer at the scene's access point is also a good technique for preventing further crashes. Environmental conditions also affect the placement and number of traffic warning devices. *(LE029.4.)*

## Personal Clothing Visibility

It is extremely important that officers directing traffic or investigating the crash are visible to oncoming traffic. A flashlight, wand attachment, orange or reflective gloves, and reflective hat bands are tools for making officers more visible. A reflective traffic vest is highly recommended. The vest should be worn over the uniform without restricting access to the gun belt. Some agencies have policies requiring the use of reflective clothing when working a crash. Failure to follow this policy could affect an officer's workers' compensation coverage in case of an injury on the job. *(LE023.4.)*

## Directing Traffic Around the Crash Scene

The responding officer may have to direct traffic around the scene until assistance arrives. Traffic direction is a basic skill for all officers. When using cones or flares to establish traffic control patterns, the key is to remember how it looks to oncoming motorists. Officers must carefully place flares and cones in a clear pattern that directs motorists where they should go and away from where they should not. It is sometimes a good idea to observe the setup from the vantage point of oncoming traffic to see how it looks to approaching motorists. Officers should also use warning devices to clear a path for emergency vehicles and tow trucks and be aware of all surroundings, evidence, and behaviors of all road users. An officer may have to re-position the patrol vehicle after stabilizing any emergency and assessing the protection necessary to keep the scene safe.

When there is no safe way to protect motorists as they go around damage, evidence, or a hazardous material, a roadblock must be used to block off the road and re-route traffic through the safest and shortest route back to the original road. Traffic should be re-routed using a route, street, or road that avoids residential areas, schools, and playgrounds when possible. The purpose of the roadblock is to prevent injury or damage to motorists and protect the road or crash scene from further damage or contamination.

When investigating a traffic crash that blocks or damages the roadway, it is necessary to notify both dispatch and a supervisor of the obstruction and roadblock location and request assistance to temporarily re-route

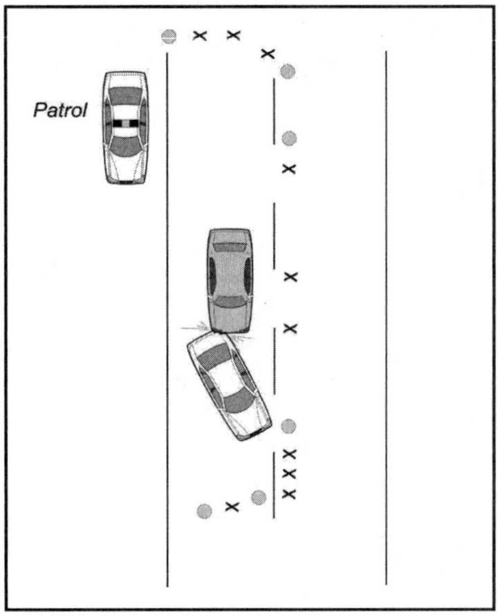


Traffic cones or flares *Figure 10-2a*

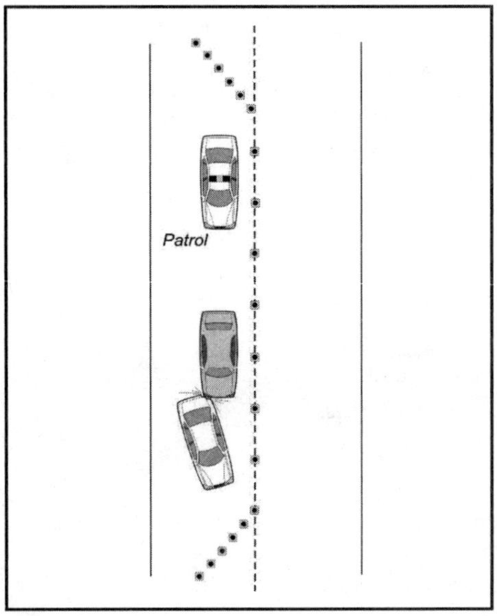


Traffic cones or flares *Figure 10-2b*

traffic. Dispatch should be advised immediately so that information can be relayed to the public and to other affected jurisdictions regarding the nature of damage and the anticipated time required to remove or repair the damage or obstructions and clear the roadway of debris. The responding officer should coordinate with other jurisdictional agencies such as Florida Highway Patrol and city or county law enforcement agencies as appropriate and notify agencies responsible for blocking, repairing or cleaning up the roadway. Typically, those agencies include state or county departments of transportation, the local public works department, specialized cleanup companies, or Environmental Protection Agency or Department of Environmental Protection. *(LE029.5.)*

Look at Figures 10-2a and 10-2b for examples of a traffic crash scene. There are two disabled vehicles involved in a crash on a two-lane road. In Figure 10-2a, used by most Florida law enforcement agencies, the officer parks the patrol vehicle in the roadway so as to block oncoming traffic from the crash scene, and places flares or cones. Figure 10-2b depicts how officers of some Florida agencies place flares or cones in a pattern around the crash scene to redirect the traffic. Both patterns help to draw attention to the cones or flares and indicate to oncoming drivers to drive around the scene. Another alternative would be to place the patrol vehicle with the emergency lights activated on the roadway as a physical barrier to protect the scene, especially when flares and cones are not available.

## Theft-Prevention Measures

If a vehicle crash exposes occupants' property such as a purse, suitcase, or briefcase that could be taken by observers, an officer must take action to secure those items. If there are uninjured vehicle occupants, the property may be given to them or secured in the occupants' vehicle trunk or passenger compartment. If the property cannot be secured in this manner, it should be secured in the patrol vehicle, and a Property Receipt form completed as required by agency policy. If any of the vehicles involved in a crash is to be towed, the officer should document on the tow receipt any property left in the crashed vehicle, such as clothing, CDs, cell phones, laptops, etc. *(LE079.10.F.)*

### *Step 4:* Provide emergency assistance to injured persons, if necessary.

During the initial call reporting the crash, dispatch should ask if there are any injured victims at the scene. If there are, EMS will be dispatched and may arrive at the scene before an officer does. If EMS is not present when the first officer arrives, that officer is responsible for making sure EMS is en route and rendering aid to injured victims until EMS arrives.

The officer should locate all people involved in the crash and ask if they have any injuries resulting from the crash. It is common for people involved to be emotionally upset regardless of how minor the crash may be. The officer needs to quickly determine if anyone is physically hurt while remaining calm and sympathetic to a person's emotional state and concern about vehicle damage. *(LE079.4.)*

# UNIT 2 | INVESTIGATING THE CRASH

## LESSON 1 | Obtaining Pertinent Information

### Beginning the Investigation

Once an officer has secured the scene, aided the injured, and set up traffic direction, it is time to begin the traffic crash investigation. To determine how to investigate a traffic crash, officers must understand the three phases of a traffic crash: pre-collision, at-collision, and post-collision.

In the pre-collision phase, the earliest possible time the driver could have become aware of a potential danger or hazard is called the ***point of possible perception.*** The ***point of perception*** is anything detected by the driver through one of the five senses that makes him or her aware of a potential danger or hazard. The ***start of evasive action*** is any action the driver takes that alters the speed or direction of the vehicle, such as applying the brakes or turning the steering wheel. The ***reaction time*** is the length of time from when a person perceives a given situation as a hazard to when he or she reacts to his or her perception. The ***point of no escape*** is the point in time when the crash is inevitable, no matter what evasive actions the drivers may attempt. ***Encroachment*** occurs when two objects begin to enter the same space at the same time.

In the at-collision phase, the first harmful event is the point of initial impact or contact, as discussed previously. Usually this point is when the first injury or damage occurs. Information regarding the first harmful event is crucial to the investigation and must be obtained and documented on the officer's traffic crash diagram report.

In the post-collision phase, ***maximum engagement*** is the point at which the vehicles or other objects are crushed together to the greatest extent. ***Disengagement*** is the point when the vehicles separate, either naturally or artificially. Often, a second impact, known as re-engagement, occurs in chain reaction collisions or when one vehicle glances off another into the path of a third driver. ***Final rest*** is the point when all activity from the crash comes to a halt. *(LE080.1.G.)*

***Step 5:*** **Obtain pertinent information.**

### Identifying Drivers, Passengers, and Witnesses

When gathering information on the traffic crash, the officer must locate, separate, and interview the witnesses and other involved parties. Passengers and witnesses usually provide more accurate and reliable information about the events that took place prior to and during the crash than the drivers. Drivers tend to rationalize crashes by claiming their vehicles failed. Witnesses to the crash who are not involved with a vehicle or damaged property are considered independent witnesses and are more likely to be objective than the involved parties.

**OBJECTIVES**

**LE080.1.G.** Identify the three phases of a traffic crash incident.

**LE079.4.B.** Identify all involved parties in a traffic crash incident.

**LE079.5.** Obtain the driver's license, registration, and proof of insurance from the operator(s) involved in a traffic crash incident.

**LE079.6.D.** Obtain statements from all witnesses at the scene of a traffic crash incident.

**LE079.6.** Obtain written statements from witnesses, operators, and victims involved in a traffic crash incident.

**LE082.1.C.** Identify the owner of vehicle damaged during a traffic crash incident.

**LE090.5.** Relay facts of property damaged in a traffic crash incident to the owner.

**LE090.6.** Advise owner(s) of appropriate actions to take to safeguard property damaged in a traffic crash incident.

**LE079.4.B.1.** Identify signs of driver impairment while interviewing the driver involved in a traffic crash incident.

**LE079.4.B.2.** Define crash privilege when investigating a traffic crash incident

**LE079.4.B.3.** Identify the changing of the hats procedure when investigating a traffic crash incident.

The officer should first find out who the drivers were and ask them to provide their drivers' licenses, vehicle registrations, and insurance information. The officer should verify each driver's identity, and check for outstanding warrants by calling in the license information to dispatch *(LE079.4.B.)*. If a driver does not have a valid driver's license, the officer should cite him or her for a violation of §322.03(1), F.S. Pursuant to F.S. §322.03, a person may not drive any motor vehicle upon a highway in this state unless such person has a valid driver's license.

F.S. §322.15 requires every licensee, when driving a motor vehicle, to carry his or her license and exhibit it upon the demand of a law enforcement officer. An identification card issued by the Department of Highway Safety and Motor Vehicles is NOT a driver's license, but is only a form of identification provided by the DHSMV as a service to non-drivers who require photo identification. Because it resembles a driver's license, some may confuse it for one.

If a driver cannot produce a valid driver's license, the officer should request another form of photographic identification, military identification, or reliable personal confirmation and imprint the driver's fingerprint on the citation issued for the violation. If the individual does not have a valid driver's license, the officer cannot allow him or her to operate a motor vehicle. If a driver is licensed, but does not have the license in his or her possession, the officer should issue a citation for failure to carry and exhibit the license upon demand in violation of F.S. §322.15.

Florida law requires the reporting of certain information when a traffic crash occurs. Florida Statutes §316.061, §316.062, §316.063, and §316.066 provide the requirements for the reporting of information and exactly what information must be provided and under what circumstances:

1. The driver of any vehicle involved in a crash resulting in damage to a vehicle or property must immediately stop and remain at the scene.
2. Drivers must exchange information including name, address, and registration number of vehicle, and upon request, drivers' license information.
3. Drivers must render reasonable assistance to any injured persons including taking them or arranging for their transportation to a health care provider for medical treatment if it appears that treatment is needed or the injured person requests such transportation.
4. A driver of a vehicle that collides with an unattended vehicle or other property must immediately stop and leave a written notice with all of the driver's information in a conspicuous place on the unattended vehicle or property. The driver must then notify the nearest law enforcement agency of the crash without unnecessary delay.
5. The law enforcement officer at the scene of the crash required to be reported in accordance with the provisions of §316.066 shall instruct the driver of each vehicle involved in the crash to report the following to all other parties suffering injury or property damage as an apparent result of the crash:
   a. the name and address of the owner and the driver of the vehicle,
   b. the license number of the vehicle, and the name of the liability insurance carrier for the vehicle. *(LE079.5.)*

## Obtaining Statements

The traffic crash investigative stage begins with obtaining statements from witnesses and collecting physical evidence. Statements should be obtained from all people at the scene with knowledge of the crash: the involved drivers, passengers, pedestrians, passing drivers, and their passengers. Physical evidence can be obtained from the vehicles, condition of and marks on the highway, traffic videos, property damage such as tree gouges or flattened mailboxes, and debris.

Sometimes, witness accounts are all a traffic crash investigator can rely on when determining what occurred. Officers must accurately document witness statements from all involved parties in order to properly cite violators and determine the cause of the crash for the report. Officers must take care to distinguish between actual witnesses, bystanders with opinions based on the final rest of the vehicles, and those who may have heard but not seen the crash.

Officers should remember that a witness is not legally obligated to give any information or provide a statement about the crash. Likewise, passengers are not required to give statements, because they were not driving any of the involved vehicles. Officers should impress upon passengers and witnesses that their help, although voluntary, is important and appreciated.

An officer must assess each witness' ability to understand the request for a statement and should note any indications of impairment caused by injury, dementia, mental retardation, intoxication, medication or any other cause that could affect the witness' comprehension and memory, as per §316.064, F.S. *(LE079.6.D.)*

## Interviewing at a Traffic Crash Scene

The officer should locate places for the drivers, passengers, and witnesses to stand or sit which are safe and visible to the officer while he or she interviews others or examines the scene. Factors to consider in selecting a safe location include being away from oncoming traffic, being protected from environmental conditions, and being out of the path of emergency vehicles at the scene. Just as when investigating any matter, if possible, witnesses should be separated to prevent them from influencing each other's statements or recollection. Officers should be aware that the witnesses may have already talked with each other while waiting for law enforcement. Separating witnesses may occasionally be inadvisable, especially when dealing with injured family members. Officers should encourage witnesses not to discuss what happened until after their statements are taken.

When deciding the order of interviews, the officer should remember that independent witnesses remain because of their own free will and their good intentions to help. They should not be kept at the scene any longer than is really required to obtain their statements and information. Therefore, it is important to get their information and statements first.

The drivers of the vehicles are required by law to stay at the scene and report the information. Of course, if injured drivers are being taken from the scene to a hospital, the officer should get their information first, and then conduct a follow-up interview.

Officers can ask questions such as, "Can anyone give me information about the crash?" and "Can anyone tell me how this person was hurt?"

An officer should interview all witnesses, drivers, and passengers separately and compare their stories to try to resolve conflicting information about what happened. Any discrepancies should be handled by asking questions to help determine the reliability of the information. Some witnesses will have had a better vantage point to see the crash than others. As the officer begins each interview, he or she should record the contact information for each witness.

To help witnesses recall specific events and details of the crash, the officer should interview them near where they were at the time of the crash, if possible. For interviews conducted after the scene is cleared, this may mean meeting the witness at the crash site for the interview, rather than at the witness' home or workplace. During the interview, the officer should help the witness focus on what he or she actually saw, not on what others said that they saw.

When an officer interviews witnesses, it is best to ask open-ended questions. Even though a person may not have witnessed the pre-crash events, he or she may have valuable information to contribute to the officer's investigation. The interviewing officer should listen to what the witnesses have to say and decide on the value of the information after all of the facts are gathered. When interviewing passengers, an officer should determine the passengers' relationships to the driver to identify potential biases.

## Written Statements

An officer may need to delay interviews to document or collect physical evidence or because an interviewee was injured in the crash and was taken to a hospital. When interviews must be delayed, the officer should consider asking drivers, passengers, and witnesses to provide written statements about the crash.

Having witnesses write statements about what they saw and heard allows an officer to obtain valuable information while performing other necessary tasks. Written statements also help collect more accurate information by prompting people to record their information as soon as possible after the crash, rather than allowing the passage of time to dull or warp their recollection.

Written statements should include the witness' full legal name, physical address (no P.O. boxes), and telephone numbers. Statements should also include an account of the witness' recollection of the crash sights and sounds, and observed actions of the involved parties. The witness should sign and date the statement as well.

If there are a number of people who witnessed the traffic crash, such as passengers on a bus, the officer should list personal information for each person, seating positions, and other information, and get statements from each person. The officer should request assistance of other officers in obtaining statements from the witnesses. *(LE079.6.)*

## Crashes Involving an Unattended Vehicle or Property Damage

If the owner of an unattended crash-damaged vehicle cannot be identified from people at the scene, dispatch should be able to identify the registered owner of a vehicle through the vehicle tag number. Once the owner's contact information is located, dispatch should call the owner and notify him or her of the damage. *(LE082.1.C.)*

If property other than a vehicle is damaged in a crash, such as a structure, billboard, or mailbox, the owner of the damaged property should be notified in person, if possible, or dispatch should call the owner. If the owner's identity is unknown, nearby occupants may be able to provide his or her name and contact information. If not, the officer should ask the dispatcher to try to identify the owner of the structure through property tax or utility records *(LE090.5.)*. If a security breach results from the crash, the owner should be advised to take action to safeguard the property. The officer may need to stay at the scene until the property is secured, as provided by agency policy. *(LE090.6.)*

## Driver Impairment

An officer must be alert to evidence and indicators of driver impairment from drugs, fatigue, alcohol, or health problems like diabetes. If a driver's mental or physical condition impairs his or her ability to operate a vehicle, the officer must document that condition in the crash report and mark the appropriate box to have the driver evaluated. Such a driver must not be allowed to operate a vehicle; rather, the officer must make appropriate arrangements for the impaired driver and the vehicle. *(LE079.4.B.1.)*

## DUI Investigations

If an officer sees indicators of impairment, a criminal investigation for Driving Under the Influence (DUI) should be done. Florida law provides drivers with a legal privilege regarding information given during a crash investigation. This means that drivers do not have the right to refuse to answer questions about a crash, since nothing they say to the investigating officer can be used against them in court. This "crash privilege" exists so that drivers will give full information required to complete a crash investigation without fear of self-incrimination as per §316.062(3), F.S. The privilege applies to any crash from a simple fender-bender to one involving criminal conduct, such as driving with a suspended license or leaving the scene of an accident. *(LE079.4.B.2.)*

If an officer investigating a crash has reason to believe that one of the drivers was driving under the influence, the officer must separate the crash investigation from the criminal (DUI) investigation. The officer must specifically tell the suspect driver that a criminal DUI investigation is beginning. This changing of the hats, or going from a crash investigator to a criminal investigator means the crash privilege no longer applies. Anything the driver says during the criminal investigation may be used in court against the driver. That means that if the driver is not free to go, the officer must read the *Miranda* warnings before asking questions that call for potentially incriminating answers. Obviously, if the officer suspects DUI, the suspected driver is not going to be free to go, so any interrogation will require *Miranda*. Questions that may be asked without *Miranda* will likely be asked and answered during the crash investigation, such as the driver's name, direction of travel, and speed before the crash. *(LE079.4.B.3.)*

Officers cannot use the suspected driver's admission that he or she was driving one of the cars involved in the crash in the DUI case unless there is other evidence to put the suspect behind the wheel. The prosecutor must be able to prove two things to obtain a conviction: that a crime was committed and that the defendant committed it. This is referred to as the ***corpus delicti*** of the offense.

Usually, other people are available at a crash scene that can establish that the suspected driver was behind the wheel. These are referred to as "wheel witnesses." In a single car crash, late at night on a sparsely traveled road, there may be no wheel witness, and when the officer arrives, the driver may be outside of the vehicle. Such crashes usually involve a tree, utility pole, or bridge abutment. In that case, the officer must find physical

## Section Vocabulary

*corpus delicti*

*disengagement*

*encroachment*

*final rest*

*maximum engagement*

*point of no escape*

*point of perception*

*point of possible perception*

*reaction time*

*start of evasive action*

evidence that will place the suspect behind the wheel, such as fingerprints, the vehicle's keys in the suspect's pocket or airbag dust on the suspect's clothing and skin. The facts that the vehicle is registered to the person sitting outside, that no one else is around, and that the person has injuries consistent with damage to the interior of the vehicle will be sufficient to prove he or she was behind the wheel when the crash occurred. Of course, if the suspect admits after *Miranda* that he or she was driving the vehicle, that admission can be used in court to establish the *corpus delicti.*

With evidence that the suspect driver was behind the wheel, a DUI investigation with Standardized Field Sobriety Tests (SFSTs) can begin. As discussed previously, if the suspect driver is arrested for DUI, the officer should request the suspect driver to submit to a breath test. A person MUST be under arrest in order to be offered a breath test. If the subject refuses to submit to the breath test, Florida's Implied Consent Warning must be read. In this case, a DUI citation and a refusal affidavit must be completed, and the individual's driver's license should be confiscated. If a physical arrest cannot be made due to the DUI driver's incapacitating injuries, a legal blood sample can be drawn at the hospital for laboratory testing. The physical arrest of the driver can be made after blood test results are received.

At a crash where there is serious bodily injury or death, the same rules apply. The only difference is that Florida Statute §316.1933(1)(a) provides that reasonable force may be used to take a blood sample from a driver involved in such a serious crash. There is NO refusal right or implied consent issue in crashes resulting in serious bodily injury or death of another driver, passenger, or pedestrian. The suspected DUI driver does NOT have to be under arrest to be required to submit to a blood draw. If the suspect driver is not injured, the investigating officer should administer whatever Standardized Field Sobriety Tests the driver can demonstrate. If the officer has SUBSTANTIAL physical evidence that the person was under the influence at the time of the crash based on observations and the results of the SFST, the subject may be arrested and booked on a DUI charge, pending the blood test results. An officer must be familiar with the local state attorney's office guidelines and agency policy before making such an arrest decision.

# UNIT 2 | INVESTIGATING THE CRASH

## LESSON 2 | Determining Point of Occurrence and Taking Measurements

***Step 6:*** **Investigate the crash to determine the cause.**

### Collecting Evidence

Sometimes, it is not easy to identify evidence consisting of roadway marks, debris, or vehicle damage, or correctly interpret what is seen. The roadway may already have damage, skid marks, and debris from other incidents. The involved vehicles may have pre-existing damage or may have been moved to the side of the road to allow traffic flow to continue.

Temporary and short-lived evidence should be identified and measured first. Temporary evidence, such as squeegee marks, lasts only a few minutes. Short-lived evidence lasts several hours or days. The officer should measure the temporary and short-lived evidence immediately after photographing it. Permanent items should be measured as soon as possible. Some examples of short-lived evidence at a crash scene include the following:

- tire prints
- skid-mark smears
- furrows
- puddles (e.g., gasoline, oil, and water)
- vehicle debris
- vehicle position in a roadway
- vehicle position off a roadway
- position of injured or deceased people

Roadway dimensions, sight distances, grade or slope, locations of traffic-control devices, and distances between landmarks are examples of evidence at a crash that would last longer than a few days. *(LE078.8.)*

### Identifying the Impact Area on the Vehicle

To identify the area of collision (AOC), a natural place to start is by examining the damage to the vehicles. Vehicle damage falls into three types: contact, induced, and pre-existing. An officer must be able to differentiate between these types of damage to correctly identify the AOC.

***Contact damage*** is damage to a vehicle resulting from the direct pressure of any object in a collision or rollover. It usually appears as scrape marks or striations on the body of the vehicle, material rub-off, such as paint from the other vehicle (called paint transfer), rubber, or tree bark, or as a puncture to or imprint on a bumper, guard rail, or other fixed object. ***Induced damage*** is damage to a vehicle other than contact

**OBJECTIVES**

**LE078.8.** Identify what evidence must be collected at a traffic crash scene.

**LE080.1.** Locate the area of damage on a vehicle involved in a traffic crash.

**LE080.2.** Examine the traffic crash scene for area of collision (AOC).

**LE079.13.** Select which events reported from interviews at a vehicle crash were crucially related to the crash, including road conditions at time of the crash.

**LE080.5.** Verify the AOC based on physical evidence and witness and participant statements.

**LE079.9.** Take photographs of vehicles involved in a traffic crash, if necessary.

**LE079.12.** Measure skid marks and other measurements pertinent to the incident at the crash scene, identifying tools and methods of measurement to use.

**LE079.12.E.** Identify how to determine vehicle speed from skid mark measurements.

**LE079.8.B.** Identify how to sketch a diagram of a traffic crash.

or other fixed object. ***Induced damage*** is damage to a vehicle other than contact damage, often occurring as bending, breaking, crumpling, and distortion of the vehicle. The twisting or buckling of the metal of a vehicle without direct contact is another example. ***Pre-existing damage*** is damage that existed before the crash. This is usually identifiable as damage that does not fit the pattern of the crash or damage that appears rusted, dirty, or weathered.

The impact area on a vehicle can be identified by looking at the contact damage. An officer can then determine what part of the vehicle was first contacted and damaged by another vehicle or object. Sometimes, the officer can determine the AOC by looking at how the damage "flows" or the direction of the damage on the vehicle and going backwards to the first appearance of damage. This process helps determine the area on each vehicle that was damaged by the crash. An officer should reach a conclusion about each vehicle's actions based on the physical evidence as well as statements from the drivers, passengers, and witnesses. Contact damage should be consistent with other physical evidence, statements from persons involved, and independent witnesses. *(LE080.1.)*

## Assessment of Area of Collision

Evidence found at a crash site can assist the investigating officer in locating the area of impact on the roadway. Crash evidence could include marks on the roadway made by the vehicle during the crash, such as gouges, scrapes, liquid runoffs and pools, and debris. An officer should look at how each type of evidence can help determine the AOC.

A ***gouge*** is a cut into the surface of the roadway where the road surface material has been removed by a metal part from the vehicle. These are usually deep enough to feel with the fingers. An example is when a bolt on the underside of a vehicle cuts into the pavement, leaving a trench or gouge in the road surface at the area of impact. This can be considered property damage other than the vehicle damage in the crash report.

A ***scrape*** is a broad area of a hard surface covered with many scratches, striations, or streak marks made without great pressure by a sliding metal part. Scrapes occur between the area of impact and the point of the vehicle's final rest.

***Runoff*** is a liquid pool, fluid trail, or line of flow from fluids escaping from a vehicle as a result of impact. Quite often during hard impacts, radiators, hoses, and brake lines can burst. When this occurs, the liquid will run out of the vehicle onto the roadway. Often, these liquids will leave a trail from near impact to final rest. While not pinpointing the exact location of the AOC, runoff does give the general location.

***Debris*** is loose material strewn about the road as the result of a traffic collision and can be composed of dirt, liquids, vehicle parts, and other materials from the involved vehicles. Looking at the scene for debris on the roadway may help to indicate the AOC. Finding where the debris first starts may help to locate the area where impact initially happened.

Officers can try matching the damage on the vehicles involved to the debris found on the scene. For example, the crash vehicle's rear reflectors are red. If there are yellow reflector pieces lying on the ground, officers can deduce that they could not have come from the crash vehicle. Glass that has been on the roadway for some time has a tendency to become rounded on the edges. New glass, on the other hand, has sharp, well-defined edges.

Locating parts of a vehicle such as bumpers, metal frames around headlights, radiator grills, etc., also indicates the location of the vehicles upon impact and the direction they were traveling. Vehicle parts continue to move in the direction of the force of the impact until stopped by an object or the resistance of the roadway surface.

All vehicles tend to accumulate road grime, grease, dust, or other foreign matter and dirt on their undercarriages. The forces involved in collisions cause this debris to become dislodged from the undercarriage and the debris falls downward and in the direction of the force. To find the debris, officers can examine the probable paths of the vehicles based on witness statements and physical evidence present at the scene.

The final information an officer will use in determining the AOC is ***vehicle dynamics***, which is the movement of vehicles during and after collision. Basic physics teaches that an object in motion continues to remain in motion until acted upon by an external force. In a crash investigation, that external force is normally another moving vehicle or a stationary object such as a tree or building. These principles will either support the statements of the drivers, passengers, and witnesses and the physical evidence at the scene or will indicate that there may have been other factors involved in the crash.

At a four-way intersection divided into quadrants where a vehicle traveling east is struck by a vehicle traveling north, based on the laws of physics, officers can expect the two vehicles to travel into the northeast quadrant (Example 1). The actual result will be dependent upon several factors: size, weight and speed. Likewise, if a vehicle is traveling south, and the other is traveling west, the two vehicles can be expected to come to rest in the southwest quadrant (Example 2). A vehicle traveling east striking a second one traveling south would likely result in final rest in the southeast quadrant (Example 3). If one of the vehicles involved in the collision is traveling north and the other traveling west, then the final rest will be in the northwest quadrant (Example 4).

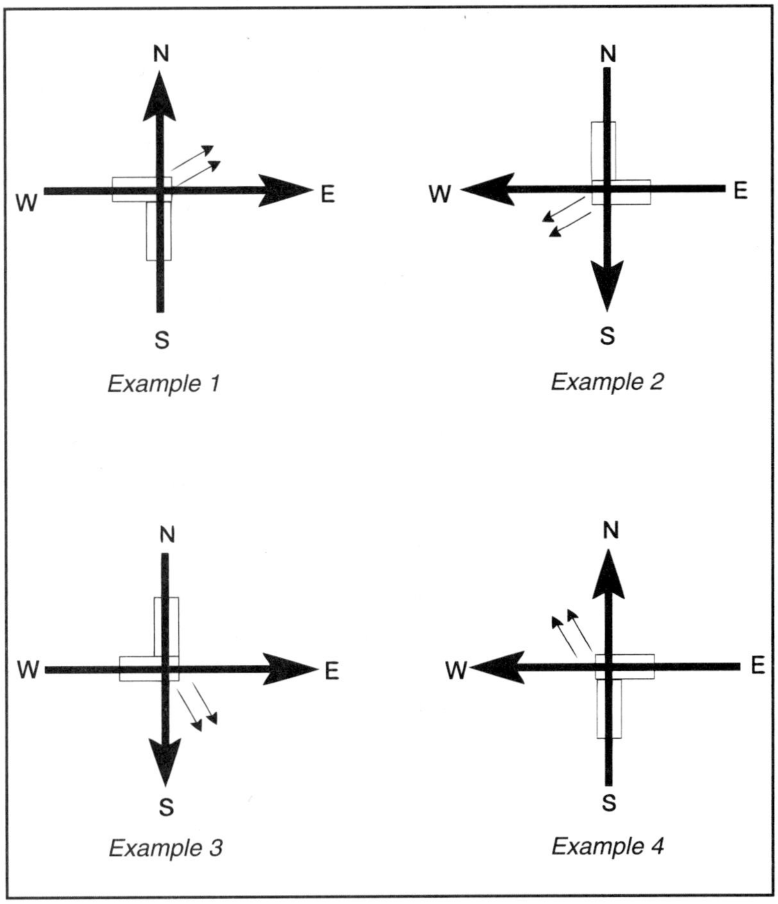

Vehicle dynamics *Figure 10-3*

By understanding the concept of vehicle dynamics, an officer will be able to evaluate the travel patterns of vehicles involved in a traffic crash. For example, if one driver claims he was driving west and the other driver claims he was driving north, and both vehicles came to a final rest in the northeast quadrant after an uncontrolled skid, then we know that one of the vehicles had to be traveling east. Careful examination of the crash scene should corroborate this data.

Items that were struck and moved should be identified. Although this evidence does not fall into any of the previous categories of evidence found on the roadway, this type of damage may also help to determine the AOC by showing the path a vehicle followed either prior to or after the crash. It may also help explain damage to the vehicles. The officer should look for objects or items located at the scene which may have been moved from their original location. These items may be located in a position that is not consistent with the original direction of the vehicles or with the direction of force.

The terms ***surface marks*** or ***marks*** include a number of types of surface marks a vehicle can leave. Each of these provides specific information to the investigator and should be identified and measured for the traffic crash report. Each mark should be labeled as to which vehicle it came from and from which tire on the vehicle. By applying a math formula to the skid mark measurement, an officer can obtain the minimum speed a vehicle was traveling when the skid occurred.

A ***skid mark*** is the black mark left by a tire sliding while not free to rotate. "Skid marks tend to be straight, although they can exhibit some curvature due to asymmetrical braking (not all brake pads locking simultaneously) or due to the crown of the road. These factors can make the vehicle depart from a straight-ahead path. Front tire skid marks tend to be darker than rear tire marks (officers should remember that when braking, weight shifts toward the front of the vehicle) and the outside edges of the mark may be darker than the inside area, due to over deflection of the tire (weight shift, again). The tire grooves are generally visible and easy to see in a skid mark. Rear tire skid marks tend to be even in appearance, that is, no dark outside edges." (Martinez, 1994)

Skid marks generally indicate the beginning of the braking of a vehicle. It is only generally the beginning because a vehicle braking hard will actually start to cease tire rotation before skid marks begin. This beginning point of braking leaves a discoloration on the roadway that is called an ***incipient skid mark***. The beginning of this part of the skid is called the skid mark loading point. The skid mark loading point is the start of the skid mark that should be measured. This is hard to see unless the skid mark is closely observed. It is also temporary and will no longer be visible 15 to 20 minutes after the marks are made.

***Intermittent skid marks*** are a series of skid marks with long gaps (30' or more) between heavy skid marks. This pattern is caused by rapidly applying and releasing the brakes. ***Skip skid marks*** are a series of skid marks usually short in length with irregular intervals between the skid marks. This pattern appears when a vehicle has a sudden load shift while braking hard. The weight shift causes a bouncing, which results in the skip skid mark. This is more typical of vehicles with trailers. A car skidding on a bumpy road also makes this mark. An ***offset mark*** is a skid mark indicating an abrupt change of direction of a tire due to collision forces. The only item of evidence that pinpoints the exact AOC on the roadway is offset skid marks. The offset skid mark is the direct result of the movement of the vehicle by the force of collision and occurs at the moment of collision.

***Anti-lock Braking System (ABS) scuff marks*** are the pattern left by a vehicle with anti-lock brakes when a driver brakes hard. These marks do not resemble the solid skid marks. The function of the ABS is to prevent the wheels from locking by rapidly applying and releasing the brake and thereby allowing the driver to remain in control of the steering. Vehicles equipped with ABS may leave faint, intermittent, visible skid marks. These are also limited in time and will no longer be visible 15 to 20 minutes after the marks are made.

A ***squeegee mark*** is a strip of dry pavement remaining after a vehicle skids on a wet roadway. The locked tire acts similar to a window squeegee in removing water from the skid path. Due to the way that these marks are made, they are transitory and thus temporary evidence.

A ***furrow mark*** is a type of trench dug by locked tires when driven on a softer surface such as gravel, sand, or dirt. The furrow is shallow at the beginning of the skid and deepens with a piling of the surface material in front of the tire at the place where the vehicle finally rests.

A ***scuff*** or ***yaw mark*** occurs when a vehicle loses tire traction in a turn or curve as a result of entering a curve too fast or over steering and slides off the curve. The tires in this case continue rotating but slide sideways at the same time. The centrifugal force of the curve causes the sideways motion of the vehicle. Marks are left from the tires slipping across the roadway once the adhesion limit of the tires is exceeded. The tires produce a screeching sound and leave rubber marks on the roadway. The scuff or yaw marks may be evidence of when the driver began to lose control of the vehicle. They will always be curved and will show a sideways striping or striation from the side motion of the tires.

An ***acceleration scuff mark*** results from rapid acceleration, usually from a stop, causing the tires to produce a dark tire mark that gradually fades. A ***tire print*** is a mark left by a tire that is rolling over a soft material such as sand, dirt, or a liquid such as oil on a hard surface and leaves an identifiable pattern matching the tread of the tire. *(LE080.2.)*

## Determining How the Crash Occurred

Determining the AOC involves examining the scene of the crash and the surrounding areas for marks, debris, and damage. The force of the crash may cause vehicle parts to travel great distances, involve damage to objects near the roadway, and leave trails of evidence along the paths of the vehicles. All of the items of evidence found on the crash scene, when viewed as a whole, should provide a fairly accurate location of the AOC or area of impact on the road surface. If no offset skid marks are located, the area of impact will usually be accurate within two-to-three feet.

The statements from passengers and witnesses provide additional information about the behavior of the drivers in the crash situation and what each person believed was the cause of the crash. If the drivers who were not paying attention were under the influence of a drug or alcohol or texting or if the vehicles were having mechanical problems, this probably would be considered by the officer as contributing to the cause by the time the interviews were completed. In field notes and for later use in preparing the report, the officer should note the drivers' conditions or pre-crash events that may have contributed to the crash.

An officer will analyze the information obtained to determine if the condition of a vehicle contributed to the cause of the crash. Observations of the vehicle, physical evidence, and statements from drivers, passengers, and witnesses are compared for consistency. The officer should be sure to list any conditions of the road, weather, or vehicle observed or reported by involved persons in field notes for use in preparing the traffic crash report. For example, if the driver says that it was because of foggy weather or the brakes failed to function or the slippery road condition that he ran into the back of the vehicle, an officer should compare this statement to other statements he or she obtained. Did passengers or witnesses hear the screech of braking by the vehicle and skidding prior to impact? Their statements should be compared to the physical evidence. Was the road slippery at the time of the crash? Were there skid marks left by the vehicle prior to the AOC? Do the brake lights come on when the pedal is pressed? If the witnesses and physical evidence both indicate that the vehicle was braking, the brakes did not fail. *(LE079.13.)*

The next question in an officer's analysis is "Why did the crash occur?" This is the point at which the officer establishes what or who he or she believes is responsible for the crash. To make this decision, all of the events

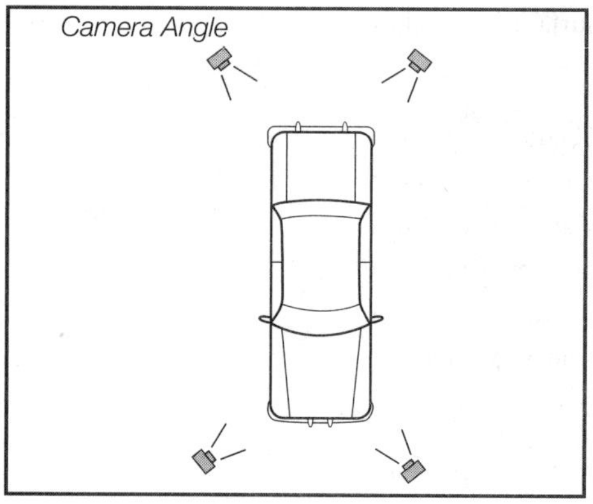


Photographing from the "four corners" *Figure 10-4*

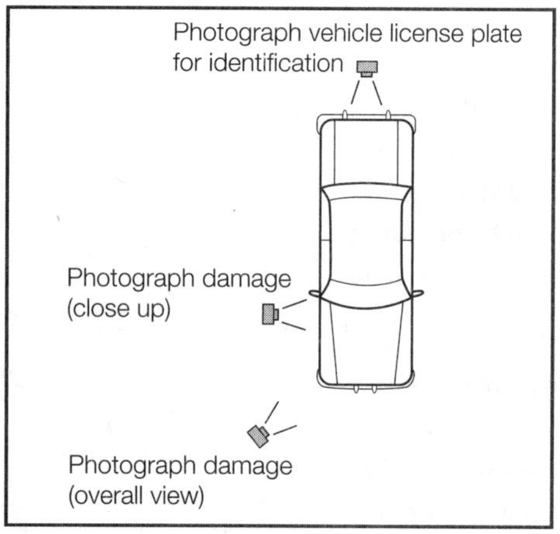


Photographing a vehicle and damage *Figure 10-5*

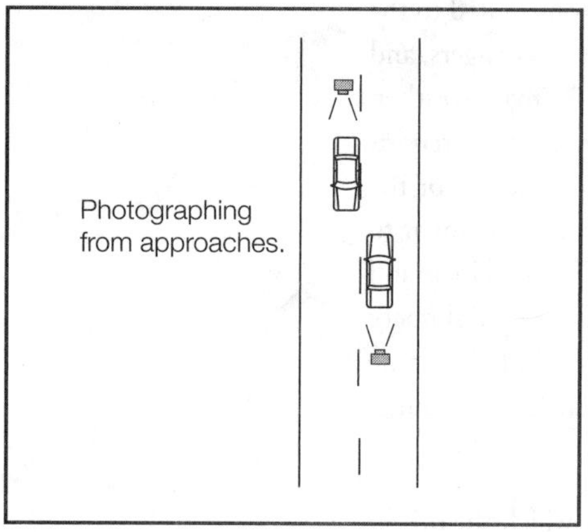


Photographing from approaches *Figure 10-6*

reported during interviews and supported by the evidence should be considered. Then the events which were crucially related to the crash should be selected.

From the events related to the crash, the officer must determine which of these events is the first event or primary factor that caused the crash. The primary factor, more accurately described as the ***primary collision factor***, is where the first injury element or driving action occurs and describes the main or primary cause of the crash. The first event, more accurately described as the first harmful event, is defined as where the first injury or damage occurs. The first harmful event determines the time, place, and type of crash. *(LE080.5.)*

## Documenting Markings and Measurements

After examining the scene for evidence and identifying what is crucial to the investigation, the officer must document the evidence in field notes and photographs. The best way to preserve evidence found at the crash scene is with a combination of photographs, measurements, and paint. To mark and take measurements properly at the crash scene, precautions should be taken to ensure the safety of all parties. For example, one officer should be posted to control traffic while another officer photographs, marks, and takes the measurements. After the decision is made on what items to mark and record in the collision diagram, the issue of how many marks or spots are on the road surface must be addressed. Evidence should be photographed before and after marking.

Generally, law enforcement agencies issue common spray paint or lumber crayons to their officers for marking purposes. Bright orange or yellow paint is the most common color as it is easily visible and located for subsequent measuring. With paint, less is usually best. There is no need to deface the roadway with colorful "art." A simple paint dot to locate an item is sufficient. Paint, however, is of little use on unpaved or dirt roadways.

## Photographing the Crash Scene

Photographs are a necessary and important part of the crash scene because they record the scene's physical condition, supplement other documentation, help to reconstruct the crash, and aid the officer in drawing conclusions about the crash. Photographs also serve as evidence to prosecute traffic violators and document the amount of damage. The officer should record the date and time pictures were taken and who took them. He or she should also photograph the crash scene immediately after the emergency is under control but before the vehicles have been moved and the road surface has been disturbed with crayon or paint-measurement marks.

When photographing a traffic crash scene, an officer should photograph all relevant evidence. The scene and the vehicles should be photographed from several angles. When photographing vehicle damage, an officer should, at a minimum, take pictures from all four corners of the vehicle and of the entire scene from all four compass points. The officer should also take pictures of drivers' and pedestrians' approach paths from their points of view as well as the AOC and damage on all vehicles involved.

The extent to which an officer will be required to photograph the evidence in a traffic crash investigation is established by agency policy and is largely dependent upon the severity of injuries resulting from the crash. A great variation exists among law enforcement agencies regarding taking photos. *(LE079.9.)*

## Measurements

Once the crash scene is photographed, an officer should take measurements to document distances and locations and size of evidence. In general, officers should take relevant measurements of all crash scenes. Crash-scene measurements serve to precisely locate significant objects in the crash, accurately document the events of a crash, and facilitate accurate testimony in corresponding court cases. Instruments that can be used to measure evidence include rolling measuring wheels, fiberglass and steel measuring tapes of various lengths, and laser measuring devices.

The following list describes evidence that should be measured, but it is not all inclusive:

- area of collision
- final rest positions of vehicles and bodies—this includes cars, trucks, bicycles, pedestrians, etc.
- tire marks on pavement and surrounding terrain if they are related to the collision—skid marks, scuff marks, or tire prints
- gouges and scratches on the road surface
- debris of any type such as undercarriage, vehicle parts, or liquids
- any items which were scarred or marked as a result of the collision

## Measuring Skid Marks

Skid marks to measure include plain skid marks, the incipient skid, offset skids, skip skids, and intermittent skids. If an officer works in an area where there are pre-existing skid marks, he or she may want to measure the width of the skid mark to make sure that he or she is looking at the correct marks. "When skid marks are not continuous but are intermittent, they may have been made by a vehicle bouncing along on the roadway. In this situation the length of the skid mark and the length of the space between them is uniform and consistent, and less than 3 to 4 feet apart. This condition can result when the wheel strikes a pothole, or bump on the roadway, which starts the vehicle bouncing." (Martinez, 1994)

The ***incipient skid*** or ***impending skid*** is the portion of the skid mark that represents the most efficient braking of the wheel. This is also the type of skid mark left by ABS. The incipient skid is included in the measurement of any skid mark.

In the case of an offset mark, the skid should be measured in two parts with the two lengths recorded separately. The distances that should be recorded and labeled include a) the distance from beginning to the offset beginning and b) the offset beginning to the end of the skid. To prepare to measure skid marks, an officer must locate the beginning and the end of each skid mark made by each wheel and all gaps in between, including the incipient skid mark area. It is important to be sure to distinguish tire imprints from skid marks.

The procedures for measuring skid marks include determining how many wheels were skidding and the beginning and ending of each skid mark. Each skid mark should be identified by the wheel that made it. For example, the label FR may be used to denote the front right wheel. Numbered markers should be placed at the specific locations from which or to which measurements are made. The beginning and end of each skid mark should be noted with a numbered marker, crayon, paint, or some other marking object. Photographs are then taken with markers in place.

Each skid should be measured individually. When the skid mark has a gap of 30 feet or more, such as an intermittent skid, the officer should count the skid mark as two skid marks. Each surface should be measured and recorded separately. The total skidding distance is the sum of the separate skid parts. Finally, the officer should record the locations and lengths of all skid marks in a field sketch.

Common mistakes or issues that can affect accurate measurements are the type of surfaces the skid marks are made on, the incorrect identification of the beginning of a skid mark, and the inclusion of gaps in the skid measurement. *(LE079.12.)*

## Determining Minimum Speed from Skid Marks

A common crash cause is excessive speed. An officer may be able to determine this if the vehicles left skid marks at the scene. By accurately measuring the skid marks and applying the minimum speed from the skid formula ($S=\sqrt{30df}$), the officer can determine the minimum speed that a vehicle was traveling to leave the skid marks. This and other proven mathematical formulas used in traffic crash investigations are accepted as valid in court.

***Minimum speed*** is defined as the slowest speed the vehicle could have been traveling to leave the skid marks on that roadway surface. To determine the minimum speed of a vehicle, certain information is needed. The first necessary item is the coefficient of friction.

The ***drag factor*** or ***coefficient of friction*** is a measure of the friction generated between a vehicle tire and the road surface. It is referred to as "*f*" in the formula used to determine the minimum speed of the vehicle leaving the skid marks. Drag Factor does not include other issues that might have affected the rate of deceleration, such as atypical braking, mechanical delay, spin-down in the braking, grade of the roadway, or slowing with an ABS equipped car.

The most recent definition of ***mechanical delay*** refers to the phase of brake application beginning with pedal depression and ending with any resulting change in wheel rotational velocity. The vehicle does not appreciably slow during this phase that lasts only about a tenth of a second. No tire marks are created during mechanical delay.

***Spin-down*** begins at the end of mechanical delay and ends when the total four-wheel lockup or skid begins. This phase can last about three-tenths of a second and results in tire marks ranging from light to dark in appearance. The beginning of spin-down can be seen at the beginning of the skid as a shadow, a faint or light mark produced as the wheels begin slowing and just prior to full lock. This is also known as incipient or impending skid. *(LE079.12.E.)*

# Prepare a Rough Field Sketch of the Crash Scene

A ***sketch*** is a hand-generated drawing of the scene as an officer perceives it on arrival. This is a rough drawing and is not made to scale. The sketch uses simple symbols to indicate details of the crash. This is usually part of an officer's field notes, and its purpose is to provide information concerning the crash that will help create the crash scene diagram. The detail of the field sketch will depend on the seriousness of the crash or the amount

The principles of sketching a crash scene are the same as with other investigations. The differences in creating the crash-scene sketch are the types of objects an officer will typically be sketching (roads and vehicles, traffic signals, signs, etc.) and what must be included in the sketch to cover the minimum information necessary for the investigation. The officer should look more closely at what he or she will sketch and the minimum information to include, remembering to add the date and time that measurements were taken.

It is not important what symbols are chosen to use in the sketch. However, whatever symbols an officer uses should be used consistently in all of his or her sketches. This will prevent the officer from misinterpreting a symbol or forgetting what something means and will make the officer more confident in describing his or her investigative methods should he or she ever be called upon to depose or testify in court.

The sketch should include only significant factual, observable items, not opinions or conclusions because the field sketch may be made available with other crash records for court presentation. When making a field sketch, all relevant evidence and measurements should be clearly indicated in the sketch. The field sketch should be consistent with photographs if photographs were taken. The field sketch should be available with other crash records for court presentation. *(LE079.8.B.)*

## Additional Investigative Resources

If the investigation reveals that additional resources are needed, the officer should (according to agency policy) contact the appropriate entity, such as Traffic Homicide Investigative Unit, DOT Motor Carrier Compliance if a commercial motor vehicle is involved, local or state traffic engineering, or crime scene or tech services.

### Section Vocabulary

*ABS scuff marks*

*acceleration scuff marks*

*contact damage*

*debris*

*drag factor (coefficient of friction)*

*furrow mark*

*gouge*

*incipient skid mark*

*induced damage*

*intermittent skid marks*

*mechanical delay*

*minimum speed*

*offset mark*

*pre-existing damage*

*primary collision factor*

*runoff*

*scrape*

*scuff or yaw mark (critical speed mark)*

*sketch*

*skid mark*

*skip skid mark*

*spin-down*

*squeegee mark*

*surface marks*

*tire print*

*vehicle dynamics*

# UNIT 3 I DOCUMENTING THE CRASH

## LESSON 1 I Completing the Crash Report

**OBJECTIVES**

**LE008.3.** Explain the use of exchange of information forms to drivers involved in a traffic crash incident.

**LE082.2.A.** Identify the appropriate crash report forms.

**LE008.1.B.** Identify the statutory requirements for the exchange of information.

**LE082.2.** Complete the appropriate crash report form.

**LE079.16.** Describe the key events of a traffic crash on Florida Traffic Crash Report forms.

**LE012.9.** Order driver's examination retest according to Florida Statute 322.221, if the operator requires license retesting for mental or medical reasons.

**LE012.9.C.** Identify the Florida Statute requirement to report an individual's disability to drive.

**LE079.8.** Record vehicle damage using available charts and information.

***Step 7:*** **Document the crash.**

### Traffic Crash Report Forms

All law enforcement traffic crash reports should include enough information to allow others to reconstruct the crash scene at a later date. A crash report form is a convenient and standardized means for storing crash-related information. The traffic crash report has many uses. Some of these include recording facts into permanent record, providing a source for officer evaluation, providing statistical data, and providing reference material.

An officer can gather the information needed to complete the crash report form by observing the physical conditions and evidence at the scene. The officer can inspect the drivers' licenses, vehicle registration/license plate, and proof of insurance. Finally, the officer can interview the drivers, pedestrians, passengers, and witnesses. Law enforcement officers in Florida use and complete the ***Florida Traffic Crash Report*** form for traffic crashes. This form combined the three formerly separate Long, Short, and Update forms into one comprehensive form—HSMV 90010S. They also use and complete HSMV 90011S—Driver Report of Traffic Crash/Driver Exchange of Information Form.

Long Form (HSMV 90010S) includes a narrative, diagram, and any other necessary update reports. When using the HSMV 90010S as the Long Form, the reporting officer should check the box marked "Long Form" in the upper left corner and fill out the entire form. As a Long Form, the HSMV 90010S is required for crashes that involve death or personal injury, leaving the crash scene involving damage to attended vehicles or property (§316.061(1)), driving while under the influence (F.S. §316.193), and any crash involving a criminal violation. In this case, every law enforcement officer who in the regular course of duty investigates a motor vehicle crash is required to use, complete, and submit the Florida Traffic Crash Report Long Form (HSMV 90010S) to DHSMV within ten days after completing the crash investigation. The DHSMV will continue to be the official records custodian for completed Long Form crash reports and is responsible for all applicable records retention requirements.

Short Form Report (HSMV 90010S) is used to report other types of traffic crashes that do not warrant the use of the Long Form. When the HSMV 90010S form is used as a Short Form report, the reporting officer should check the box marked "Short Form" in the upper left corner and fill out only the shaded areas. F.S. §316.066 requires each law enforcement agency to maintain and be responsible for compliance with all applicable record retention requirements for completed Short Form crash reports at their agency and no longer submit them to the DHSMV. The DHSMV will no longer be the official records custodian for completed Short Form crash reports. However, law enforcement agencies that submit crash reports electronically to the DHSMV may continue to submit completed Short Form crash reports to the department, but such law enforcement agencies will be designated as the official records custodian and must comply with all applicable record retention requirements for their respective agencies.

Update Form Report (HSMV 90010S) is used to update, upgrade, or continue information previously recorded on a Florida Traffic Crash Report form (HSMV 90010S). When the HSMV 90010S form is used as an Update Form report, the reporting officer should check the box marked "Update Form" in the upper left corner and fill out only the appropriate updates, upgrades, or continuation information. The update, upgrade, or continuation information must be entered in the appropriate field(s) in the form. Also, all open investigations must be updated every 30 days until the investigation is closed.

An officer will use the form as a continuation report when he or she needs additional space to complete or update the original traffic crash report. The form contains additional sections for vehicles, pedestrians, witnesses, passengers, additional property damage, additional violations, and the traffic crash narrative. Examples of new or updated information may include Blood Alcohol Content (BAC) results, insurance information, any injury status change or hit and run follow-up information, and corrections to the original report after it was submitted to the DHSMV.

Because the HSMV 90010S form allows for multiple uses, it may initially be confusing to determine when to complete a Long, Short, or Update Form. In all situations, the officer will complete the appropriate sections of the form based on the statutory requirements and the number of vehicles involved, proof of insurance, pedestrians, passengers, and witnesses that must be reported.

HSMV 90011S may be used for three purposes—Law Enforcement (Optional) Short Form Report, Driver Report of Traffic Crash, or Driver Exchange of Information between the parties involved in a traffic crash. When used by law enforcement as an optional Short Form Report, it will not replace the Short Form feature of HSMV 90010S, but provides a secondary choice depending on agency needs. The appropriate box on the upper left corner of the form should be checked to indicate the form's intended use.

The officer should explain to the drivers involved in the crash that it is required by state law that they complete the driver exchange information form and then give a form to each driver to complete. Communicating in a professional manner, the officer should explain to the drivers how to complete the form, including what fields to complete, to print legibly, to use a black ballpoint pen, and where to sign the form. It is the officer's responsibility to check the form to make sure that it has all required information correctly completed and has any corrections made by the drivers pursuant to F.S.§316.070. Each driver signs and dates the form that he or she completes. The officer should place an "X" in the box at the top that identifies the type of report. An "X" should also be placed in the box at the bottom of Sheet 1 that states, "You must read and comply with the instructions on the back of this form." A copy of the completed form is given to each driver. *(LE008.3.)*

On some occasions, an officer may find that a driver cannot adequately read or complete the form due to language or physical limitations. The officer may complete the form for the driver and have him or her sign the form.

The officer may attach a copy of the completed HSMV 90011S form to the Long Form report. If, however, the form is not used to exchange drivers' information, then the officer must provide each driver and/or non-motorist with the other party's driver and vehicle information.

The above forms provide a standardized means for recording traffic crash-related information. Most of the information learned through the investigation of the scene will be recorded on the report forms, standardized blocks, narrative, and crash diagram portions of the report. *(LE082.2.A.)*

The DHSMV creates and publishes the Florida Traffic Crash Report forms. It is necessary to always use the most current version. The instructions for completing the forms can be found in the DHSMV Manual, *Instructions for Completing the Florida Uniform Traffic Crash Report Forms.* These forms and their completion instruction manuals are available from the Department of Highway Safety and Motor Vehicles website at http://www.flhsmv.gov/courts/.

Samples of the forms can be printed from the DHSMV website or ordered directly from DHSMV. An officer should review the statutes sections that are referenced within the manuals.

## Requirements for Driver Exchange of Information

Exchanging driver information is important, not only because the law requires it, but also because it serves the purpose of providing insurance companies with the necessary information to process claims for damage.

Florida Statutes require a driver of a motor vehicle involved in a traffic crash involving death of a person (§316.027), personal injuries, or damage to a vehicle or property (§316.061) to stop at the scene (or as close thereto as possible). The driver must remain at the scene of the crash until he or she has fulfilled the requirements of § 316.062. A person who is arrested for fleeing the scene of a traffic crash and who has previously been convicted of a violation of §316.027, §316.061, §316.191, or §316.193, or a felony violation of §322.34, shall be held in custody until brought before the court for admittance to bail in accordance with chapter 903. Any person who willfully flees the scene of a crash commits a felony of the first degree, punishable as provided in §775.082, §775.083, or §775.084.

Florida Statutes §316.062 states the information that must be exchanged. The driver of the vehicle must give his or her name, address, and the registration number of the vehicle he or she is driving and exhibit his or her driver's license or permit to any person injured at the crash or to any police officer. If an officer is not present, the driver is obligated to provide this information to the nearest police authority by completing HSMV 90011S and checking the box marked "Driver Report of Traffic Crash" in the upper left corner of the form. Failure to provide the required information violates §316.062, F.S.

If the driver does not own the vehicle, F.S. §316.066(3)(c) provides that each person involved in the crash must provide proof of insurance, whether or not he or she is the owner. The officer will use F.S. §316.066(3)(c) when completing a citation for a driver involved in a traffic crash who is not the owner of the vehicle and cannot provide proof of insurance.

Based on F.S. §320.0605, an operator of a vehicle must possess and present upon demand of a law enforcement officer a certificate of registration (or an alternative stated in the statute) for the vehicle he or she operates, except during the first 30 days after purchase of a replacement vehicle. This includes the registration certificate or official copy, copy of rental or lease agreement, replacement vehicle registration, internet electronic renewal temporary receipt, or cab card issued under the International Registration Plan. If an operator violates this statute or has questions about the certification requirement, the on-scene officer should explain this statute to the operator.

The registration is considered current if it reflects the information for the vehicle being driven by the driver and if the effective dates include the period in which the crash occurred. For example, in Florida, a certificate of registration is issued with each renewal of the registration license tag and reflects the period of one year from the birth date of the owner or from January 1 for vehicles registered under §320.08, F.S.

Florida Statute §316.066(1)(d) requires that "the driver of a vehicle which is in any manner involved in a crash resulting in bodily injury to or death of any person or total damage to all property to an apparent extent of $500 shall, within 10 days after the crash, forward a written report of such crash to the department," unless the investigating officer has made a written report of the crash. The on-scene officer should explain the use, purpose, and requirements for the exchange of information to the vehicle operators. The entity receiving the report may require witnesses of a crash to render reports and may require any driver involved in the crash to file supplemental written reports.

When an officer is required to complete a written crash report based on statute or agency policy, the drivers must provide the information necessary to complete the driver's information portion of the report form. The reporting officer completes the law enforcement Short Form report and gives each driver a copy of the report. If the Long Form report must also be completed, the officer should explain to the drivers that they may obtain a copy of the completed report by contacting the officer's agency. If a written report is not required for the crash, an officer should give each party involved in the traffic crash a Driver Report of Traffic Crash form (HSMV 90011S) to complete and instruct each party to mail a copy of the completed form to DHSMV. *(LE008.1.B.)*

## Required Entries for Long and Short Form Reports

When completing the HSMV 90010S as a Long Form report, the reporting officer must fill out all fields on the HSMV 90010S with the required information. Most of the values needed to complete the event section of this form are displayed next to the data fields. The remaining data fields are completed based on the information requested at the top of each category. If not applicable, leave blank. *(LE082.2.)*

When the HSMV 90010S form is used as a Short Form report, additional data beyond the mandated shaded areas may be entered by the reporting officer if required by the reporting officer's agency. Once the form is completed, the report is separated and a copy given to each driver for insurance purposes. The report, if completed electronically, should be sent to the DHSMV after the investigating officer's agency review and approval and should also be retained by the agency. Agencies are the official custodians of Short Form reports despite sending them electronically to the DHSMV.

If a citation is written, the officer should fill out the report completely in case he or she has to give a deposition or testify in court.

An officer should refer to the Instructions for Completing the Florida Uniform Traffic Crash Report Forms to identify additional required information. The officer must number the pages starting with the front of the Long Form, HSMV 90010S, "page 1 of ___". The forms are then placed in numerical order and the number of pages counted. The page numbering for the Update Report continues from the initial report. For example, if the initial report was six pages long, the Update Report begins with page seven. Each page of the report is numbered in the spaces provided on the form.

Reports are fairly easy to complete, but errors do sometimes occur. Some of the most common errors that occur on crash report forms include using military time as opposed to the 12-hour clock system, not putting the HSMV Crash Report Number in the proper box or narrative/diagram page, and incorrectly counting the number of road lanes; all road lanes must be counted, not just travel road lanes. Other common mistakes include leaving blanks when information is unknown. "UK" for "unknown" must be entered in boxes when information is not known, with an exception: if the motor carrier's current address is not known, the officer should spell out "unknown." Other mistakes include a failure to correctly indicate if the vehicle owner is the driver—an officer should check the appropriate box and write "same as driver." Also the officer must not fail to enter the correct required endorsement for the vehicle being operated by the driver. An officer must not leave test results for Blood Alcohol Content (BAC) blank—if test results for BAC are not known at the time the report is completed, "UK" should be entered; failing to update BAC testing information when results become known is a serious error. Other common mistakes include incorrectly entering the number for the appropriate sex identifier, or failure to enter the appropriate identifier number for the cause of the crash.*(LE079.16.)*

## The Florida Uniform Traffic Crash Report Form—Narrative and Diagram Sections

The narrative and diagram portions of the HSMV 90010S form must be completed to go with the Long Form report.

The narrative section should include a description of all key events in the crash including the pre-collision, actual collision, and post-collision phases. If an officer determines that a driver re-examination should be conducted, he or she should include the explanation in the narrative for the request to be accepted. Spaces are also provided for recording injury treatment information, investigation information, and reporting officer and department identification.

The section below the narrative is used to record information about any additional passengers involved in the crash. If there are no additional passengers, a diagonal line is drawn through the section. Space is also provided for additional violations/citations to be recorded. If there are no additional citations, an officer should leave blank each box that is not used.

The diagram section is used to sketch the traffic crash incident, accurately show the vehicle positions after the crash, and reflect the information contained in the narrative section.

There are spaces on the front page of the HSMV 90010S to record the witnesses to a crash and their addresses. If more than two witnesses are present, the additional names are recorded on the narrative or diagram sections.

## Driver Retesting

If the officer determines that the questionable driving ability of one of the drivers caused or contributed to the crash, the officer may request a mandatory retesting of the licensed driver by checking the "Recommend Re-exam" block in the driver's section. A new feature in the Driver and Vehicle Information Database (DAVID) allows officers to easily request a driver license re-examination or medical review for a specific driver. This feature is accessed by clicking on the Report Driver for Medical Review or Re-exam button from the Individual Summary page. This action will pre-populate the driver's personal information on the form. The officer will then verify the information, select the reason(s) for this request, provide a short narrative explaining the reason for the retest, and confirm his or her contact information to enable DHSMV to undertake the retesting. This narrative explanation and officer's signature on the traffic crash report serve as a report to DHSMV that the driving ability of the driver indicated on the report is questionable and should be re-examined by that department. The traffic crash report must be forwarded to DHSMV through the officer's agency in order for the re-examination to be initiated.

In such a situation, an officer should check the statute regarding the re-examination of licensed drivers in the statute book and read the actual provisions of the law. It can be found in §322.221(1) F.S. This section describes how the crash report information gives the DHSMV the authority to require a re-examination of a driver. *(LE012.9.)*

## Medical Reporting Form

Section 322.126 (2), (3), Florida Statutes, provides that "Any physician, person, or agency having knowledge of any licensed driver's or applicant's mental or physical disability to drive...is authorized to report such knowledge to the Department of Highway Safety and Motor Vehicles." The form is available online at the Department of Highway Safety and Motor Vehicles website: http://www.hsmv.state.fl.us/html/forms.html. The form should be completed and forwarded to DHSMV along with the crash report. *(LE012.9.C.)*

## Diagramming the Crash

The final step in documenting the traffic crash investigation is the completion of the diagram of the crash for the report. This involves carefully preparing a proportional drawing of the field sketch and notes using a traffic crash template. The finished diagram should appear professional in nature. Vehicle sizes should adequately conform to roadway sizes. The final diagram should be prepared in ink with all appropriate entries, measurements, and a legend of symbols. The diagram is the finished product showing what occurred during the crash. The traffic crash template is used to complete the crash diagram. The final report should include all the information necessary to the diagram.

All drawings should include the compass direction for North. The preferred method is to use the top of the page for North; the diagram page of the uniform crash report provides a circle in the upper right-hand corner of the diagram for this notation.

The following information should be shown on a crash diagram:

- location of crash (road names)
- roadway width of each lane and roadway markings
- North directional arrow being placed upward or to the right when looking at the page
- any physical evidence on the roadway (skid marks, ruts, holes, standing water, etc.)
- each vehicle's position prior to, at, and post-crash. This would include where the vehicle was located at final rest upon the officer's arrival on the scene even if the vehicle was moved.
- traffic conditions in effect
- fixed objects, road defects, other physical factors present
- road obstructions
- possible view obstructions
- traffic control devices such as signs, lights, lane markings, etc.
- labels or a legend of any symbols used in the diagram

Measurements that should be included in the crash diagram include those of skid mark length and roadway as well as the positioning of any pedestrian victims or victims thrown clear of their vehicles and the area of collision.

## Using the Traffic Diagram Template to Create the Diagram

The Traffic Crash Template was designed specifically for law enforcement to make diagramming crash and incident scenes easier and more accurate. It is the primary tool for completing a professional-looking crash diagram, and it can be used when making a field sketch. The template provides a number of scales of measure, angles, curves, straight edges, and cut-outs to aid in the diagramming of the scene.

In addition to aids for drawing the diagram, some templates provide a nomograph (a set of distance, speed, and drag factor scales) that helps determine vehicle speed based on skid marks without using the math formula. The template instructions provide directions for how to use the template for this purpose.

Most templates provide a way to show diagrams to scale such as 1 inch to 1 foot on the diagram or a 1:12 ratio. Some include multiple scales for sizing purposes. For example, a large scene would require a smaller scale in order to have the diagram displayed on a single page. For the larger crash scene, an officer would use a scale of 1 inch to 20 feet or a 1:240 ratio. The larger scale is preferred because it shows details better and is easier to see. Unless the scene is too large to diagram at that ratio using a single diagram page, an officer should use the larger scale.

Every diagram uses symbols for the crash scene. The cut-outs on the template are designed to make the symbols easy and quick to draw. The most common symbols used are cars, trucks, trailers, motorcycles, pedestrians, signs, traffic signals and lights, buildings, camera directions, and directional arrows. The crash scene should be diagrammed using the "bird's eye" view, like when sketching a crime scene. Only relevant items should be included so the diagram will be easier to read. The area of importance should be centered on the diagram form.

First, the officer should locate the center of the diagram form and that will be the approximate center of the AOC. Then the officer should draw the roadway. The template gives a straight edge to draw lines. The roadway involved in the crash should be depicted by diagramming all lanes, labeling turn lanes, bike lanes, and the median. The officer will then insert the vehicles, pedestrians, and any other pertinent information as needed. Officers should remember that in the diagram they have to include the position of the vehicles prior to the crash, at the point of impact, and at final rest. An officer should start with the final rest and work backwards. (See Figure 10-7.)

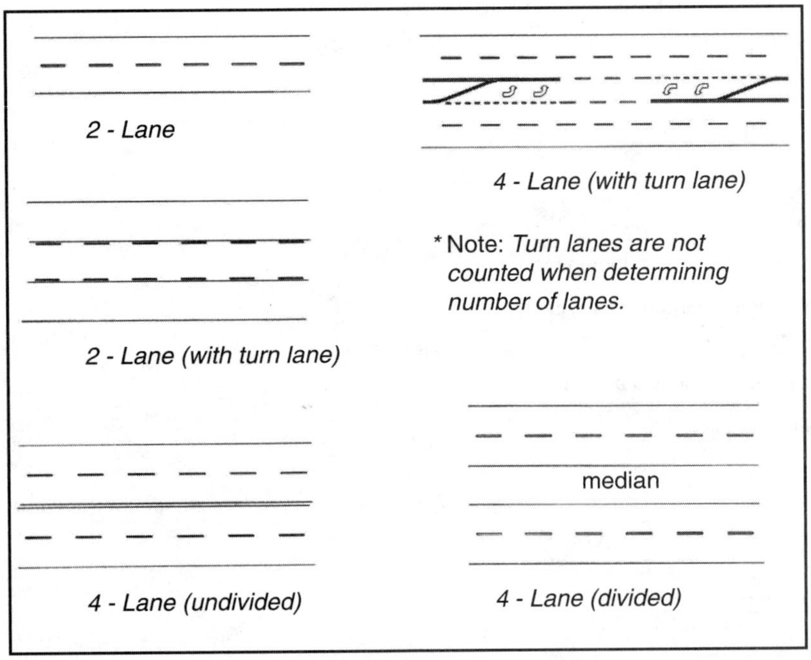


*Figure 10-7*

Next, the officer should draw the position of the vehicles prior to the crash. Each vehicle will carry a directional arrow to indicate the front of the vehicle and the number assigned to it for this report. The front of each vehicle should be indicated with a directional arrow and a number in a circle. The vehicle that caused the crash is numbered 1, and each subsequent vehicle involved is numbered in its order of involvement. To show the direction of movement of the vehicles prior to the crash, the officer can draw solid directional arrows behind the vehicles to demonstrate where the vehicles came from to the AOC. To draw the vehicle movement after impact to place of final rest, the officer should use a directional arrow with dashes for the line.

The remaining entries are the labels for the roadway names, grade of the roadway, lane and roadway measurements, and directional arrow. There is a symbol on the template for the directional arrow. The grade and measurements are printed in neat block print. Standard abbreviations for degree of grade (°), feet (') and inches (") should be used.

If a crash has debris or there is extensive damage to the vehicles or to property, the vehicle damage, debris, or other details should be drawn freehand. The suggested symbols for freehand drawings provided with the template may be used for these entries on the diagram. *(LE079.8.)*

Once the scene has been assessed and assistance requested, officers should focus on normalizing the crash scene, remembering that law enforcement's responsibility in crash management is to control and normalize the traffic crash scene.

**Section Vocabulary**

*Florida Traffic Crash Report*

# UNIT 4 | RETURNING THE SCENE TO NORMAL

## LESSON 1 | Returning the Scene to Normal

**OBJECTIVES**

**LE079.10.H.** Ensure that the wrecker driver or officer removes all hazardous debris resulting from the traffic crash from the roadway.

**LE079.13.D.** Identify violations of traffic laws.

**LE023.8.** Remove all temporary traffic warning devices.

**LE082.3.** Complete the crash report.

**LE090.8.** Remain at the scene if property damage poses safety or security risk(s) until notified person arrives or until other security arrangements are made.

***Step 8:*** **Return the scene to normal as quickly as possible.**

### Clearing the Scene

The final step in crash management is clearing the scene. An officer's responsibility for the crash scene is concluded once all the debris and hazards are removed. Returning the scene to normal could involve simply moving the vehicles off the roadway when possible, requesting a tow for vehicles that cannot be moved, or redirecting traffic around the crash or along an alternate route. If the crash scene includes debris from vehicles and a wrecker is involved in removing the vehicle, the wrecker driver should remove it from the roadway.

If part of the crash assistance involves a HAZMAT team, responsibility for the hazardous materials falls to that team. If HAZMAT is not involved, the services of a cleanup team for hazardous materials may be required. Individual agency policy should be consulted regarding obtaining this service. *(LE079.10.H.)*

***Step 9:*** **Conclude enforcement action.**

### Taking Law-Enforcement Action

After the officer concludes the crash investigation, there may be additional necessary law enforcement action to be taken. Florida Statute §316.640 authorizes officers to conduct traffic crash investigations and issue citations under chapters 316, 319, 320, and 322. Once an officer determines how and why a crash occurred, he or she may identify violations and issue traffic citations accordingly. Some agencies require an officer to issue a citation if the officer is able to determine a violation was committed; specific agency policy should be consulted regarding this requirement.

Three types of traffic violations are found in crash situations. A ***contributing traffic violation*** is a direct cause or contribution to the crash itself, such as a vehicle running a red light and striking another vehicle. A ***non-contributing traffic violation*** has no direct bearing on the cause of the crash, but is discovered during the crash investigation. Examples include expired tag or seat belt violations. A ***non-traffic violation*** is generally a criminal offense discovered during the crash investigation. An example would be a quantity of cocaine discovered by an officer while inventorying one of the wrecked vehicles.

In most traffic crashes, at least one driver committed one or more contributing traffic violations. Surprisingly few crashes are caused by vehicle defects. Most are the result of driver error. In such cases, together with the traffic crash report, the officer will complete a Uniform Traffic Citation (UTC) for each apparent violation at the end of the investigation. Both drivers in a two-car crash may have committed violations and should be cited accordingly. The officer should identify the specific violations and note the relevant statute on the UTC. In addition to uncovering the primary violation, the officer is responsible for detecting other violations and taking the appropriate law enforcement action for each offense. A separate citation must be completed for each violation.

F.S. §318.14(2) states that an officer must certify that a UTC was delivered to the person cited when a violator's signature is not required. It states:

> "Except as provided in ss. §316.1001(2) and §316.0083, any person cited for a violation requiring a mandatory hearing listed in §318.19 or any other criminal traffic violation listed in chapter 316 must sign and accept a citation indicating a promise to appear. The officer may indicate on the traffic citation the time and location of the scheduled hearing and must indicate the applicable civil penalty established in §318.18. For all other infractions under this section, except for infractions listed under §316.001, the officer must certify by electronic, electronic facsimile, or written signature that the citation was delivered to the person cited. This citation is prima facie evidence that the person cited was served with the citation."

A violator must sign a traffic citation only when the citation is issued for a criminal traffic violation or a traffic violation that requires a mandatory hearing. Included in some citations that require mandatory hearings are the following:

- a violation which results in a crash that causes the death of another
- a violation which results in a crash that causes serious bodily injury of another

Possible traffic violations officers should consider when determining the contributing causes of the traffic crash include driving too fast for conditions, failing to yield the right-of-way, failing to keep a safe distance, driving left of center, making an improper turn, overtaking improperly, driving with improper lights or defective braking or steering, ignoring a traffic control device, and driving under the influence of drugs or alcohol. *(LE079.13.D.)*

If the death of a person occurs and an agency has in its possession a photograph, video, or audio recording that depicts or records the killing, such records are confidential and exempt from §119.07(1) F.S. and s. 24(a)(1) of the State Constitution. However, surviving parents, spouse, adult child, or designated and authorized agent, local, state, or federal agents in furtherance of their official duties shall have access to such records. Refusal by the custodian agency to comply may subject the agency to criminal and administrative penalties.

## Terminating the Crash Investigation

Before leaving the scene, an officer must take all necessary law-enforcement actions and issue all appropriate citations. The officer should verify that all forms have been completed, copies distributed to the appropriate individuals, and all personal documents (e.g., drivers' licenses, insurance cards and registrations) returned to drivers. The officer should also check that all equipment (e.g., tape measure, blanket, flashlight, cones, barricades, and identifying markers) has been returned to the patrol vehicle *(LE023.8.)*. The officer must then verify that the roadway is safe for traffic and that all flares, vehicle parts, or debris have been cleared from the roadway. Finally, the officer will complete the crash report *(LE082.3.)*. If safety or security risks remain, an officer must stay at the scene until the danger is removed or other security arrangements are made. If the officer made an arrest, he or she must arrange for backup to remain at the scene. *(LE090.8.)*

## Section Vocabulary

*contributing traffic violation*

*non-contributing traffic violation*

*non-traffic violation*

For the crash investigator, there are many overlapping and pressing responsibilities at the scene of a crash. Officers have an obligation to secure the scene, tend to injuries, maintain traffic flow, and investigate the crash according to state law. With time, officers will gain the experience and skills required for efficiently and thoroughly investigating a crash with professionalism.

# GLOSSARY

## A

**abandoned vehicle:** a vehicle without a driver or person in charge of the vehicle which could be a disabled vehicle, improperly parked vehicle, or a potential crime scene (Patrol 1)

**ABS scuff marks:** the pattern left by a vehicle with anti-lock brakes that results from hard braking (Traffic Crash)

**absorption:** the process by which alcohol enters the bloodstream (DUI Traffic Stops)

**abuse of a disabled adult or elderly person:** any willful or threatened act by a caregiver that significantly impairs or is likely to impair a vulnerable adult's physical, mental, or emotional health significantly (Criminal Investigations)

**acceleration scuff marks:** dark marks, resulting from rapid acceleration, that gradually fade (Traffic Crash)

**accessory:** a person who aids or contributes in committing or concealing a crime (Legal)

**accessory after the fact:** an offense in which a person assists an offender while having knowledge that the felony is being or has been committed F.S. 777.03 (Legal)

**accumulative stress:** the stress that results from numerous sources over time (Patrol 1)

**acting within the scope of employment:** the reasonable and foreseeable activities that an employee engages in while carrying out the employer's business (Legal)

**actual physical control:** being physically in or on the vehicle and having the capability to operate the vehicle (DUI Traffic Stops)

**acute stress:** a type of stress that is short-lived and severe (Patrol 1)

**addiction:** a physical and/or psychological dependence on a substance (Human Issues)

**admissibility of evidence:** the legal requirements that must be met before a jury is allowed to see or hear evidence (Legal)

**admissible evidence:** relevant evidence tending to prove or disprove a material fact, with numerous exceptions specified (Criminal Investigations)

**affirmation:** a solemn and formal declaration or assertion in place of an oath (Communications)

**aggravated child abuse:** a first-degree felony that occurs when a person either commits aggravated battery on a child; tortures, maliciously punishes, or cages a child; or knowingly or willfully abuses a child, and in so doing, causes great bodily harm, permanent disability, or permanent disfigurement to the child (Criminal Investigations)

**alibi:** a suspect or defendant's claim that he or she was not present when the alleged act was committed (Legal)

**alphanumeric code:** a system that combines letters and numbers that may include officer call signs or auto tags (Communications)

**Americans with Disabilities Act (ADA):** the federal civil rights law that protects individuals with disabilities (Human Issues)

**analgesic:** a pain-relieving drug (DUI Traffic Stops)

**area of collision (AOC):** the location of the first harmful event, or the first damage-producing event in a traffic crash (Traffic Crash)

**arrest:** to legally deprive a person of liberty or freedom to go as he or she chooses; to take a person into custody to be held to answer for a crime (Legal)

**arrest affidavit:** a charging document that states the probable cause for the arrest (Patrol 1)

**arrest warrant:** a court order authorizing law enforcement to take the individual named on the warrant into custody (Legal)

**assumption:** a notion, statement, or belief about a person, group, or event that may or may not be factual (Communications)

**attempt:** committing an act, beyond thinking or speaking, towards carrying out a crime; a situation in which a person would have committed a crime except that he or she failed or was prevented from doing so by an outside occurrence or person (Legal)

**autism:** a developmental disability that occurs in early childhood and continues throughout adulthood which may result in difficulties with learning, communication, and social interaction (Human Issues)

## B

**Baker Act:** a law that provides access for mentally ill persons to emergency services and temporary detention for evaluation and voluntary or involuntary short-term community inpatient treatment (Human Issues)

**bias/prejudice:** a strong, negative belief or feeling about a person, group, or subject that is formed without reviewing all available facts or information (Legal)

**bird's-eye-view:** a depiction of a crime scene sketched as if looking down from above the scene (Crime Scene Investigations)

**blindness:** a functional loss of vision (Human Issues)

**blood alcohol concentration (BAC):** the limit at which an individual is presumed impaired and cannot legally operate a vehicle; BAC is expressed in terms of grams of alcohol in every 100 milliliters (DUI Traffic Stops)

**BOLO:** an acronym that stands for Be On the Look Out (Patrol 1)

**breach of duty:** a failure of the defendant to act in a reasonable manner (Legal)

**breath alcohol concentration (BrAC):** the limit at which an individual is presumed impaired and cannot legally operate a vehicle; BrAC is expressed as grams of alcohol per 210 liters of breath (DUI Traffic Stops)

**bribery:** to give, offer, or promise a benefit or gift to a person in order to influence that person to a certain course of action. F.S. §838.015 (Introduction to Law Enforcement)

**burglary tools:** any tool, machine, or implement with the intent to use, or allow it to be used, to commit any burglary or trespass such as screwdrivers, pliers, wrenches, and pry bars (Criminal Investigations)

## C

**canvass:** a door-to-door inquiry of all possible sources of information for a given area (Criminal Investigations)

**caregiver:** a person, such as a relative, court-appointed or voluntary guardian, adult household member, neighbor, health care provider, or employee or volunteer of facilities, who has been entrusted with or has assumed responsibility for the care or the property of a disabled adult or elderly person (Criminal Investigations)

**case law:** the body of law that is formed by the decisions of the court system (Legal)

**CBRNE:** an acronym that stands for Chemical Biological Radiological Nuclear Explosives (Patrol 2)

**certified:** sworn, as in a certified police officer (Introduction to Law Enforcement)

**chain of command:** the order of authority within an organization (Introduction to Law Enforcement)

**chain of custody:** the documentation of who came into contact with the evidence, as well as when, why, and what changes, if any, were made to the evidence (Crime Scene Investigations)

**child abuse:** the intentional infliction of physical or mental injury upon a child (Criminal Investigations)

**child, juvenile, or youth:** any unmarried person under the age of 18 who has not been emancipated by order of the court and who has been found or alleged to be dependent, in need of services, or from a family in need of services; or any married or unmarried person who is charged with a violation of law occurring prior to the time that person reached the age of 18 years. F.S. §985.03(6) (Legal)

**child neglect:** occurs when a caregiver fails or omits to provide child with the care, supervision, and services necessary to maintain the child's physical and mental health (Criminal Investigations)

**chronic stress:** a type of stress that continues for a long period (Patrol 1)

**circumstantial or indirect evidence:** any evidence that requires an inference or presumption to establish a fact (Legal)

**civil law:** the area of law that allows individuals to resolve their disputes through legal action (Legal)

**civil liability:** the legal action a person takes to resolve a dispute with another person (Legal)

**civil rights violation:** an unlawful interference with the fundamental rights of another inhabitant of the United States (Legal)

**clue:** something that leads to the solution of a problem, such as a fingerprint or DNA evidence; the behaviors observed during the performance of the Standardized Field Sobriety Tests (DUI Traffic Stops)

**color of law:** when an officer acts or purports to act in the performance of official duties under any law, ordinance, or regulation (Legal)

**command presence:** the bearing of one who commands or influences others which encompasses professional appearance, demeanor, poise, and attitude (Communications)

**communication:** the exchange of thoughts or messages, verbally and nonverbally, through signals or writing (Communications)

**community:** the people and locations comprising the neighborhoods, institutional settings, and workplaces in which an officer lives or works (Communications)

**community control (house arrest):** community supervision in which a person is closely monitored and is more restrictive than probation or parole (Introduction to Law Enforcement)

**compensatory damages:** court awards designed to compensate for the actual property damage, harm, or injury the plaintiff suffers (Legal)

**complainant:** the person who reports the crime or alleges that a crime has been committed (Communications) (Crime Scene Investigations)

**concealment:** an object or group of objects that creates a visual barrier between an officer and a threat but may not stop a projectile (Patrol 1)

**conflict of interest:** the actions and situations that could conflict with official responsibilities (Introduction to Law Enforcement)

**consensual encounter:** when an officer comes into voluntary contact with a citizen under circumstances in which a reasonable person would feel free to disregard the police and go about his or her business (Legal)

**consent:** intelligent, knowing, and voluntary consent that does not induce coerced submission; a legal defense that claims that the acts in question were committed with the victim's consent and permission (Legal)

**conspiracy:** a situation in which the offender agreed, conspired, combined, or confederated with the person(s) alleged to cause a crime to be committed. F.S.§777.04(3) (Legal)

**constitutional law:** the standards set forth in the Constitution and decisions and interpretations of the Constitution handed down by U.S. District and Supreme Courts (Legal)

**contact damage:** any damage to a vehicle resulting from the direct pressure of any object in a collision or rollover (Traffic Crash)

**contact officer:** the primary officer on a call (Patrol 1)

**contraband:** anything that is illegal to possess (Legal)

**contributing traffic violation:** the direct cause or contribution to a crash (Traffic Crash)

**conveyance:** a motor vehicle, vessel, ship, aircraft, railroad vehicle or car, trailer, or sleeping car (Legal)

***corpus delicti*:** a Latin term meaning the "body of the offense" describing the legal principle that claims it must be proven that a crime has occurred before a person can be convicted of committing that crime (Legal) (Traffic Crash)

**corrections:** the part of the legal system responsible for enforcing punishments outlined by the court system (Introduction to Law Enforcement)

**court system:** the part of the legal system responsible for the interpretation of laws (Introduction to Law Enforcement)

**courtesy:** behavior that involves showing consideration, respect, and cooperation when interacting with others (Communications)

**cover:** anything that creates a bullet-resistant barrier between an officer and a threat (Patrol 1)

**cover officer:** the backup officer who is strictly responsible for officer safety concerns at a scene (Patrol 1)

**crash management:** law enforcement's responsibility to control and normalize a traffic crash scene (Traffic Crash)

**crash privilege:** the legal right of a driver to answer questions about a traffic crash and to give full information required to complete a crash investigation without fear of self-incrimination (Traffic Crash)

**crime:** an improper act (Legal)

**criminal justice:** the structures, functions, and decision-making processes of agencies that deal with the management and control of crime and criminal offenders (Introduction to Law Enforcement)

**criminal law:** the part of statutory law that defines unacceptable behaviors and government prosecution of those who commit them (Legal)

**criminal liability:** the liability incurred when an officer is found guilty of committing a crime and is sentenced to incarceration or other penalties (Legal)

**criminal negligence:** the liability that occurs when a person breaches a duty to conform to a particular standard of conduct with others (Legal)

**criminal street gang:** "a formal or informal ongoing organization, association, or group that has as one of its primary activities the commission of criminal or delinquent acts, and that consists of three or more persons who have a common name or common identifying signs, colors, or symbols and have two or more members who, individually or collectively, engage in or have engaged in a pattern of criminal street gang activity." F.S.§874.03 (Patrol 2)

**crisis:** an event that significantly alters or threatens to alter a person's life or a situation, usually in a negative way; a crucial period in which a significant change seems inevitable (Human Issues)

**cue:** a reminder or prompting as a signal to do something, i.e., take enforcement action or observe the vehicle more closely (DUI Traffic Stops)

**culpable negligence:** consciously doing an act or following a course of conduct that the person must have known or reasonably should have known was likely to cause death or great bodily injury (Legal)

**curtilage:** the enclosed space of ground and the outbuildings immediately surrounding a structure (Legal)

**custody:** the suspect is deprived of freedom in a significant way (Legal)

**cyber-stalk:** to communicate words, images, or language through the use of electronic mail or electronic communication to a specific person, causing substantial emotional distress to that person and serving no legitimate purpose (Legal)

# D

**deadly force:** force that is likely to cause great bodily harm or death (Legal)

**deafness:** a hearing loss of such severity that the individual must rely on visual communication, such as writing, gestures, sign language, and lip-reading (Human Issues)

**debris:** the loose material that is strewn about the area as the result of a traffic collision (Traffic Crash)

**defense of property:** a common legal term describing a person's authority to take reasonable steps, including the use of force (except deadly force) to the extent that a person reasonably believes that it is necessary to protect his or her possessions from trespass or theft or to terminate these acts (Legal)

**delayed stress:** any stress that lies buried for a period and then resurfaces (Patrol 1)

**delegation of authority:** when a person with authority grants power to another person (Introduction to Law Enforcement)

**delusion:** a firmly held but false belief that is retained despite logical proof to the contrary (Human Issues)

**dementia:** an intellectual deterioration or an organic, progressive mental disorder characterized by a loss of memory, the impairment of judgment and abstract thinking, and changes in personality (Human Issues)

**Department of Highway Safety and Motor Vehicles (DHSMV):** the Florida agency responsible for issuing driver licenses, motor vehicle titles, license plates, and vessel registrations, and for overseeing the Florida Highway Patrol (Traffic Stops)

**deposition:** an official court proceeding in which sworn testimony regarding the case facts is provided to the defense or prosecuting attorney prior to trial (Criminal Investigations)

**detoxification:** the process that brings a physically or psychologically dependent person to a substance-free state (Human Issues)

**direct evidence:** evidence which proves a fact without an inference or presumption and which, if true, conclusively establishes that fact (Legal)

**direct liability:** a liability which arises in cases where the officer committed an intentional or negligent tort in violation of the employing agency's orders or policies (Legal)

**disabled adult:** a person 18 years of age or older who suffers from a condition of physical or mental incapacitation due to a developmental disability, organic brain damage, or mental illness, or who has one or more physical or mental limitations that restrict the person's ability to perform the normal activities of daily living (Criminal Investigations)

**discrimination:** actions a person takes to deprive another individual or group of a right because of prejudice involving color, national origin, race, religion, or sex (Introduction to Law Enforcement) (Communications)

**discriminatory profiling or bias-based profiling:** unequal treatment of any person including stopping, questioning, searching, detaining, or arresting based solely or primarily because of discrimination (Traffic Stops)

**disengagement:** the point at which the vehicles in a traffic crash separate, either naturally or artificially (Traffic Crash)

**distribution:** the process by which the bloodstream carries alcohol to the body's tissues and organs (DUI Traffic Stops)

**divided attention:** the ability to concentrate on two or more things at the same time (DUI Traffic Stops)

**documentary evidence:** anything written or printed which is offered to prove or disprove a fact (Legal)

**domestic violence:** not a specific crime but actions that include any assault, aggravated assault, battery, aggravated battery, sexual assault, sexual battery, stalking, aggravated stalking, kidnapping, false imprisonment, or any criminal offense resulting in physical injury or death of one family or household member by another (Legal) (Criminal Investigations)

**drag factor (coefficient of friction):** a measure of the friction generated between a vehicle tire and the road surface (Traffic Crash)

**driving under the influence (DUI):** operating a vehicle while impaired by use of alcohol or drugs (DUI Traffic Stops)

**drug:** any substance that, when taken into the human body, can impair ability of a person to operate a vehicle safely (DUI Traffic Stops)

**due process clause:** a part of the Fourteenth Amendment that expands the restrictions the Bill of Rights places on the federal government to state and local governments and states, "No state shall make or enforce any law which shall abridge the privileges and immunities of citizens of the United States; nor shall any State deprive any person of life, liberty or property, without due process of law; nor deny any person within its jurisdiction of the equal protection of the laws." (Legal)

**DUI detection:** the entire process of identifying and gathering evidence to determine whether or not a subject should be arrested for a DUI violation (DUI Traffic Stops)

**duress or coercion:** a defense that requires the person committing the act to reasonably believe that the only way to avoid death or great bodily harm to self or a third party is to commit the crime (Legal)

# E

**elderly person:** a person 60 years of age or older who suffers from the infirmities of aging as manifested by advanced age or organic brain damage, or other physical, mental, or emotional dysfunction, to the extent that the ability of the person to provide adequately for his or her own care or protection is impaired (Criminal Investigations)

**elimination:** a process by which alcohol is expelled from the body which includes breath, sweat, tears, and saliva (DUI Traffic Stops)

**elimination prints:** the physical evidence that allows a fingerprint analyst to distinguish between prints belonging to the victim or witness and possible suspects (Crime Scene Investigations)

**embezzlement:** an act of theft in which a person wrongfully takes money or other property entrusted to him or her for safekeeping and uses it for his or her own personal gain (Criminal Investigations)

**emergency doctrine:** a defense against liability that allows an officer to react instinctively to sudden peril without being held to the same legal standard of care as he would have been had there been time to reflect upon the circumstances (Legal)

**Emergency Response Guidebook (ERG):** a resource to guide a first responder's initial actions to a HAZMAT incident including the identification of hazardous materials, areas of personal protection, and initial safety plan (Patrol 2)

**encroachment:** when two objects begin to enter the same space at the same time (Traffic Crash)

**endorsement:** a special authorization printed on a Florida Driver License permitting a driver to drive certain types of vehicles or to transport certain types of property or a certain number of passengers (Traffic Stops)

**entrapment:** when a law enforcement officer induces or causes a suspect to commit a crime so that the officer may then arrest the suspect; can be used as a legal defense (Legal) (Criminal Investigations)

**ethical behavior:** principled, value-based decision making (Introduction to Law Enforcement)

**ethical principles:** any rules of conduct derived from ethical values (Introduction to Law Enforcement)

**ethics:** the standards of conduct based on moral duties and virtues that are derived from the principles of right and wrong (Introduction to Law Enforcement)

**evidence:** anything presented in a court of law to prove or disprove the validity of information (Legal)

**exclusionary rule:** a rule which states that evidence obtained illegally by law enforcement will not be admissible at trial (Legal)

**exigent circumstances:** certain emergencies, such as evidence destruction, an emergency scene, or fresh pursuit that justify a warrantless entry (Legal)

**explosives:** the materials or devices designed to release energy very rapidly (Patrol 2)

**exploitation of a disabled adult or elderly person:** when someone knowingly, by deception or intimidation, obtains or uses a disabled adult's or elderly person's funds, assets, or property (Criminal Investigations)

**extremist group:** any formal or informal association of individuals acting in concert or independently to advocate violence and/or the illegal disruption of the lawful activities of others; it can be domestic or international (Patrol 2)

## F

**family or household member:** spouses, former spouses, people related by blood or marriage, people who reside together or who have resided together in the past in the same dwelling unit, and people who are parents of a common child (Legal)

**FCIC/NCIC:** a computer system that provides information about criminal incidents, people, vehicles, and property (Communications)

**fellow officer rule:** a rule that involves relying on the collective knowledge of other officers in taking law enforcement action (Legal)

**felony:** a criminal offense committed within a state in which the maximum penalty is death or incarceration in a state correctional facility for a period exceeding one year (Legal)

**field contact:** any person with whom an officer has contact while on patrol, such as concerned citizens, anonymous callers, confidential informants, and other law enforcement officers (Criminal Investigations)

**field sobriety exercise:** the psychophysical exercises given to determine chemical impairment (Traffic Stops)

**fight or flight response:** the body's preparation to either fight a threat or flee the situation (Patrol 1)

**final rest:** the point when all activity from the traffic crash comes to a halt (Traffic Crash)

**first harmful event:** the first damage-producing event in a traffic crash. It determines the exact time, location, and type of crash (Traffic Crash)

**Florida driver license (FDL):** a permit granting the privilege to drive to a Florida resident who passes the DHSMV test (Traffic Stops)

**Florida Traffic Crash Report form (HSMV 90010S):** a set of forms provided by the Florida Department of Highway Safety and Motor Vehicles that combined previous separate Long, Short, and Update traffic crash report forms into one comprehensive form and used to record pertinent information, narrative, and diagram regarding traffic crash incident. (Traffic Crash)

**forfeiture:** a civil proceeding in which the law enforcement agency asks the court to transfer ownership of property from the defendant to the government (Legal)

**forgery:** altering, forging, or counterfeiting a public record, certificate, legal document, bill of exchange or promissory note, etc., with the intent to injure or defraud someone (Criminal Investigations)

**fresh pursuit:** a legal doctrine that permits a law enforcement officer to arrest a fleeing suspect who crosses jurisdictional lines (Legal)

**fruits of a crime:** the objects obtained by the defendant as a result of committing a crime (Legal)

**furrow mark:** a trench dug by locked tires when a car is driven on a soft surface such as gravel, sand, or dirt (Traffic Crash)

## G

**gases:** flammable, non-flammable, poisonous, or corrosive materials stored in containers under pressure (Patrol 2)

**general intent:** an offender's intention to make the bodily movement which becomes the act to commit a criminal offense (Legal)

**gouge:** occurs when a metal vehicle part cuts into and removes the road surface (Traffic Crash)

**grand theft:** the theft of anything with a value of $300 or more or theft of a will, codicil or other testamentary instrument, a firearm, motor vehicle, stop sign, or fire extinguisher (Criminal Investigations)

**gratuity:** anything of value intended to benefit the giver more than the receiver; something given to a person because of that person's position or authority (Introduction to Law Enforcement)

**grid search pattern:** a variation of the strip/line search pattern that is often used indoors and which overlaps a series of lanes in a cross pattern, making the search more methodical and thorough (Crime Scene Investigations)

## H

**hallucination:** any sensory perceptions in which a person can see, hear, smell, taste, or feel something that is not there (Human Issues)

**harass:** when a person engages in conduct that causes substantial emotional distress in a person and serves no legitimate purpose (Legal)

**hard of hearing:** a loss of hearing, but not to the extent that an individual must rely on visual communication (Human Issues)

**hazardous material (HAZMAT):** a substance that may cause harm, serious injury, or death to humans and animals, or harm the environment (Patrol 2)

**hearing impairment:** any degree of hearing loss (Human Issues)

**hearsay:** a statement that is made out of court by someone not testifying at a trial or hearing which offers evidence to prove or disprove the truth of the matter asserted (Legal)

**hit:** an exact match in a database (Communications)

**Horizontal Gaze Nystagmus (HGN):** an involuntary jerking of the eyes as they move to the side (DUI Traffic Stops)

**hostile work environment:** a work situation in which lewd jokes or offensive habits are acceptable (Introduction to Law Enforcement)

**human trafficking:** transporting, soliciting, recruiting, harboring, providing, or obtaining another person for transport (Legal)

# I

**impairment:** a physical, mental, or psychological disorder affecting one or more body systems (Human Issues)

**implied consent:** the fact that any person who accepts the privilege of driving in Florida has consented to submit to an approved chemical test to determine the alcohol content or the presence of a chemical and/or controlled substance in their breath, blood, or urine (DUI Traffic Stops)

**improper or misused words:** words that are often confusing, such as words that sound the same but are spelled differently (there/their/they're) or words that sound similar but have different meanings (advise/advice or accept/except) (Communications)

**incipient skid mark or impending skid mark:** a portion of the skid mark that represents the most efficient braking of the wheel (Traffic Crash)

**indirect evidence:** any evidence that requires an inference or presumption to establish a fact (Legal)

**induced damage:** damage to a vehicle other than contact damage, often occurring as bending, breaking, crumpling, and distortion of the vehicle (Traffic Crash)

**informant:** a person who provides information in confidence about crimes, either from a sense of civic duty or in the expectation of some personal benefit or advantage, and whose identity is normally not disclosed until required by law (Communications) (Criminal Investigations)

**informational alert:** wording printed on a Florida driver license that signals an officer about a person's health condition or public safety status (Traffic Stops)

**insanity:** any mental disorder so severe that it prevents a person from having legal capacity and excuses that person from criminal or civil responsibility (Legal)

**instrumentalities (of crime):** the items used by the defendant to commit the crime (Legal)

**insubordination:** a failure to follow orders from superiors in the chain of command (Introduction to Law Enforcement)

**intent:** when a person purposely does what the law declares to be a crime (Legal)

**interference with custody:** knowingly or recklessly taking or enticing any child under the age of 18 years from the custody of its parent, guardian, or other lawful custodian. F.S. §787.03. (Criminal Investigations)

**intermittent skid marks:** a series of skid marks with long gaps (30 feet or more) between heavy skid marks (Traffic Crash)

**intoxication:** a legal defense in limited circumstances when it negates an essential element of the crime, such as the ability to form criminal intent in the commission of certain offenses (Legal)

**investigation:** a process that involves making detailed and systematic inquiries or observations that begins upon the officer's arrival at the scene of a reported crime, and usually ends with him or her filing the initial report or turning the matter over to a detective or investigator (Crime Scene Investigations)

**investigative stop:** a stop that may be made only if an officer has reasonable suspicion that the person stopped was committing, is committing, or is about to commit a law violation; also known as a *Terry* stop (Legal)

# J

**jargon:** the technical vocabulary of a particular profession that has meaning specific to people who work in that field (Communications)

**jurisdiction:** the types of cases in which the court can make decisions (Introduction to Law Enforcement)

**justifiable use of force:** any force a person may legally use to defend against the use of force by another. Chapter 776, F.S. (Legal)

**juvenile:** an unmarried person under the age of 18 who has not been emancipated by order of the court and who has been found or alleged to be dependent, in need of services, or from a family in need of services; any married or unmarried person who is charged with a violation of law occurring prior to the time that person reached the age of 18 (Legal)

**juvenile sexual offender:** a child 12 years of age or younger who is alleged to have committed a violation of sexual battery, prostitution, lewdness, indecent exposure, abuse of a child, obscenity, or any violation of law or delinquent act involving juvenile sexual abuse (Legal) (Criminal Investigations)

# L

**latent prints:** a type of fingerprint that is invisible to the naked eye and is the most common evidence found at crime scenes. Latent prints result from body residues left behind when the friction ridges of the hands or feet make contact with a surface (Crime Scene Investigations)

**lateral communication:** the communication in an organization that travels across employees on the same level within the chain of command (Introduction to Law Enforcement)

**law enforcement:** the part of the criminal justice system responsible for the enforcement of and maintaining civil order (Introduction to Law Enforcement)

**lip-reading:** a form of visual communication sometimes used by persons who lose their hearing after language development (Human Issues)

**live lineup:** the presentation of a number of individuals, which may include a known suspect, to a victim or witness in a nonsuggestive manner for the purpose of identification (Legal)

# M

**major life activities:** caring for oneself, performing manual tasks, walking, seeing, hearing, speaking, breathing, learning, and working (Human Issues)

**maliciously:** wrongfully, intentionally, and without legal justification or excuse (Criminal Investigations)

**Marchman Act:** a law that provides substance abusers with access to emergency services and temporary detention for evaluation and treatment (Human Issues)

**maximum engagement:** the point at which the vehicles or other objects in a traffic crash are crushed together to the greatest extent (Traffic Crash)

**maximum deviation:** the condition where the gaze of the eye has moved as far as it can go towards the shoulder and no white is visible at the outside of the eye (DUI Traffic Stops)

**mechanical delay:** the phase of brake application beginning with pedal depression and ending with any resulting change in wheel rotational velocity (Traffic Crash)

**mental illness:** an impairment of the mental or emotional processes that exercises conscious control of actions or of the ability to perceive or understand reality that substantially interferes with a person's ability to meet the ordinary demands of living (Human Issues)

**mental incompetence:** a legal defense which recognizes that a criminal defendant will be judged on his or her present ability to assist counsel by participating in the criminal defense (Legal)

**mental retardation:** a diagnosis of a person with significantly sub-average general intellectual functioning, existing concurrently with deficits in adaptive behavior, which occurs prior to age 18 (Human Issues)

**mere suspicion:** a hunch or gut feeling based on law enforcement training and knowledge but is not an acceptable justification for interfering with someone's rights (Legal)

**metabolism:** the biological process by which the body breaks down substances into compounds that are more readily excreted (DUI Traffic Stops)

**minimal encouragers:** the brief statements made during an interview which indicate that the officer hears what the person is saying and is inclined to hear more (Communications)

**minimum speed:** the slowest speed a vehicle can travel to leave skid marks on the roadway surface (Traffic Crash)

**minority:** the less numerous segment of a population that differs from the majority and is often subjected to differential treatment (Traffic Stops)

**mirroring:** a technique in which the interviewer acts as if he or she looks in a mirror and sees him- or herself as the interviewee (Communications)

**misdemeanor:** a criminal offense committed within a state where the maximum penalty is incarceration in a county jail for up to one year (Legal)

**mistake or ignorance of fact:** a legal defense that is used when the accused does not possess the mental state required to commit a criminal offense because of a reasonably mistaken belief about the facts relating to the circumstances; not to be confused with diminished mental capacity or insanity (Legal)

**Mobile Data Terminal (MDT):** the laptop computers installed in a patrol vehicle and used by the officer to access information regarding criminal records, driving history, and agency records as well as to write and submit electronic/paperless reports to the supervisor (Communications)

**mobility impairment:** a functional limitation that affects one or more of a person's limbs (Human Issues)

***modus operandi***: a Latin term meaning "the mode of operating" or MO and referring to how someone does something which is usually repetitive in nature (Criminal Investigations)

## N

**narcotic:** a substance that induces sleep (DUI Traffic Stops)

**narrative:** the paragraphs in a police report containing specific details and pertinent information about an incident and the elements of the crime (Communications)

**negligence:** a failure to use due or reasonable care in a situation that results in harm to another (Legal)

**Neurological Nystagmus:** an involuntary jerking of the eyes caused by a disruption of the central nervous system (DUI Traffic Stops)

**no approach tactic:** used in traffic stops in which the officer calls the driver to the patrol vehicle to acquire information instead of approaching the vehicle directly (Traffic Stops)

**no retreat law:** a section of the Florida Statues that says an individual has "no duty to retreat when faced with imminent harm," "has the right to stand his or her ground," and may "meet force with force, including deadly force when he reasonably believes it is necessary to do so to prevent death or great bodily harm." F.S. §776.013 (Legal)

**non-contributing traffic violation:** a traffic violation that has no bearing on the cause of the crash (Traffic Crash)

**noncriminal violation:** an offense, also known as a civil infraction, for which the only penalty may be a fine, forfeiture, or other civil penalty (Legal)

**noncustodial interview:** an interview in which the person is not under arrest and a reasonable person would believe that he or she is free to leave at any time during the interview (Legal)

**non-traffic violation:** a violation that has nothing to do with traffic or the traffic crash (Traffic Crash)

**nonverbal communication:** the messages sent by body language, posture, muscle tension, facial expression, and response time (Communications)

**normal faculties:** the ability to see, hear, walk, talk, judge distances, drive an automobile, make judgments, act in emergencies, and normally perform the mental and physical acts of daily life (DUI Traffic Stops)

**notice to appear:** in misdemeanor or ordinance violations, the option for an offender to be released at the scene provided he or she signs a notice promising to appear in court (Legal)

**nuclear weapon:** a weapon that derives its destructive power from an uncontrolled nuclear reaction (Patrol 2)

**nystagmus:** an involuntary jerking of the eyes (DUI Traffic Stops)

## O

**oath:** a promise to tell the truth regarding an incident or occurrence (Communications)

**observation:** accurately noting what is presented to the five senses by keeping in view, noticing, or giving attention to persons, things, or circumstances (Patrol 1)

**offense:** a criminal or noncriminal act punishable by law (Legal)

**offset mark:** a skid mark indicating an abrupt change of direction of a tire due to collision forces (Traffic Crash)

**offset position:** a traffic stop position where the wheels of the police officer's vehicle should be turned outward (toward the road) so the patrol vehicle may be deflected away from the violator's vehicle if the patrol vehicle is struck from behind; this position creates a potential safety corridor where an officer can walk when approaching the violator's vehicle (Traffic Stops)

**off the record:** information not recorded in an official document during a court proceeding (Criminal Investigations)

**omission:** when an officer neglects to perform what the law or duty requires (Legal)

**open house party:** a social gathering at a residence that is legal unless minors are consuming alcohol or drugs are present (Criminal Investigations)

**ordinance:** any locally applied law; statute enacted by a municipal (city) or county government (Legal)

**overdose:** the accidental or intentional use of a dangerously large amount of a substance (Human Issues)

## P

**park:** the standing of a vehicle, whether occupied or not, otherwise than temporarily for the purpose of and while actually engaged in loading or unloading merchandise or passengers (Patrol 1)

**parole:** the release of an inmate from a correctional institution prior to the conclusion of the inmate's court-imposed sentence (Introduction to Law Enforcement)

**partial sight:** the loss of visual acuity in which objects look dim or out of focus (Human Issues)

**patent prints:** fingerprints that are visible to the naked eye and are transferred from the friction ridges on fingers by a foreign substance (not a body residue) like blood, paint, or dirt (Crime Scene Investigations)

**Pathological Nystagmus:** an involuntary jerking of the eyes which can occur as a result of brain tumors, other brain damage, or some diseases of the inner ear (DUI Traffic Stops)

**perception:** an impression in a person's mind of an individual, people, or events based on experiences, biases, beliefs, assumptions, and observations; the process of organizing and attaching meaning to sensations, so that they can be interpreted (Communications) (Patrol 1)

**perimeter:** the area surrounding the site of an incident that may be cordoned off to prevent unauthorized personnel from leaving or entering the area (Patrol 1)

**perjury:** a false statement made under oath which the person speaking does not believe to be true (Introduction to Law Enforcement)

**personality disorder:** a lifelong pattern of maladaptive behavior that interferes with daily living (Human Issues)

**personal values:** individual convictions about what is right and wrong based on religious beliefs, cultural roots, family background, personal experiences, laws, organizational values, professional norms, and political habits (Introduction to Law Enforcement)

**petit theft:** taking something valued at less than $300 (Criminal Investigations)

**phonetic-alpha code:** a system of code words for identifying letters in voice communication (Communications)

**photo array:** a presentation of a series of photographs in a non-suggestive manner to a victim or witness in order to identify a suspect (Legal)

**physical dependence:** a state in which the body becomes accustomed to a substance and needs that substance to function normally (Human Issues)

**physical or real evidence:** actual objects which may be offered to prove facts about a case (Legal)

**pie/wheel search pattern:** a search pattern often used at extremely large search areas that entails dividing the area into a number of pie-shaped sections, which are usually searched using the strip/line search pattern (Crime Scene Investigations)

**plastic prints:** any molded or imbedded fingerprints made by touching a surface that is impressionable, or when the fingers or hand is coated with a foreign substance (Crime Scene Investigations)

**plus one rule:** a bluff safety technique in which an officer, after the suspect(s) and occupant(s) are out of the vehicle, checks for another hidden occupant (Traffic Stops)

**point of no escape:** the point in time when the crash is inevitable, no matter what evasive actions the drivers may attempt (Traffic Crash)

**point of possible perception:** the earliest possible time the driver could have become aware of a potential danger or hazard (Traffic Crash)

**point of perception:** anything directed through one of the five senses that makes the driver aware of a potential danger or hazard (Traffic Crash)

**polydrug use:** when a person uses two or more drug categories simultaneously (DUI Traffic Stops)

**popped or splatted ignition:** the plastic housing around the column's base that has been popped open, exposing the ignition bars that can be pulled forward to start the car; the key portion of the ignition key area has been removed, exposing the ignition bar (Traffic Stops)

**post-traumatic stress disorder (PTSD):** a psychological reaction that occurs after experiencing a highly stressful event (Patrol 1)

**pre-existing damage:** any damage to a vehicle that was present before the crash (Traffic Crash)

**prejudice:** the pre-judging of people who are different from an individual (Communications)

**pretext stop:** a stop made by an officer on the basis of a traffic infraction when there is not enough information for reasonable suspicion to make the stop but for the objective purpose of looking inside the vehicle for evidence of criminal activity (Legal)

***prima facia*** or ***per se***: something that is apparent on its face and is considered less than obvious, but more than mere suspicion (Traffic Stops)

**primary collision factor:** the one element or action which describes the primary cause of a crash (Traffic Crash)

**principal in the first degree:** a defendent who helped another person commit or attempt to commit a crime and whose actions must be treated as if he or she had done all the things the other person did (Legal)

**private property:** the property that belongs to an individual and is not open to the public and where the person occupying that property has an expectation of privacy (Crime Scene Investigations)

**probable cause:** a fair probability or reasonable grounds to believe that a crime was committed, based on the totality of circumstances (Legal) (Patrol 1)

**probable cause affidavit:** a sworn, written statement by a law enforcement officer establishing certain facts and circumstances to justify an arrest (Legal)

**probation:** a sentence placing a person under the supervision of a probation officer for a specified length of time instead of in confinement (Introduction to Law Enforcement)

**professionalism:** a behavior that follows the prescribed Law Enforcement Code of Ethics, which demonstrates good character and is marked by pride in self and career (Introduction to Law Enforcement)

**proof beyond a reasonable doubt:** the presentation of evidence sufficient to prove the guilt of each element of the crime beyond a reasonable doubt (Legal)

**protective action distance:** the distance that people should stay from a hazardous spill (Patrol 2)

**proximate cause:** a link between the breach of duty and the harm caused (Legal)

**psychological dependence:** a mental condition caused by repeated use of a drug that causes the user to crave the substance (Human Issues)

**psychophysical tests:** field sobriety tests that measure a person's ability to perform both mental and physical tasks simultaneously (DUI Traffic Stops)

**public property:** any property designated for public use and enjoyment that is open to the public (Crime Scene Investigations)

**punitive damages:** damages awarded in addition to actual damages when the defendant acted with recklessness, malice, or deceit (Legal)

# Q

**qualified immunity:** a defense which protects government officials from liability for civil damages insofar as their conduct does not violate clearly established statutory or constitutional rights of which a reasonable person would have known (Legal)

**querying:** gathering information for law enforcement purposes (also includes entering, running, vehicle check, records check, wants and warrants check) (Traffic Stops)

***quid pro quo*:** a Latin term meaning "something for something in return" (Introduction to Law Enforcement)

# R

**radio protocol:** procedures for properly constructing and transmitting messages (Communications)

**reaction time:** the length of time from when a person perceives a given situation as a hazard to when he or she reacts to his or her perception (Traffic Crash)

**reasonable suspicion:** the level of justification needed to support a legal stop or investigative detention where an officer can articulate the facts that support a suspicion of a law violation (Legal)

**receiver:** a person who receives a message (Communications)

**report:** a written document prepared by a law enforcement officer that gives information about an event, situation, or person encountered by the officer (Communications)

**restriction:** the language printed on a Florida driver license that may limit a driver from operating certain types of motor vehicles or require that he or she meets certain conditions when driving any motor vehicle (Traffic Stops)

**retail theft:** taking possession of or carrying away of merchandise, money, or negotiable instruments; altering or removing a label or price tag; transferring merchandise from one container to another of lower price; or removing a shopping cart with intent to deprive the merchant of possession, use, benefit or full retail value (Criminal Investigations)

**roll call:** a brief informational meeting that officers attend before starting a shift (Patrol 1)

**rule of sequestration:** a judge's order during a court proceeding that forbids all witnesses from discussing any aspect of a case with anyone but the involved attorneys (Criminal Investigations)

**runoff:** a fluid trail or pool of fluids escaping from a vehicle as a result of impact (Traffic Crash)

## S

**scrape:** a broad area of a hard surface covered with many scratches, striations, or streak marks made without great pressure by a sliding metal part (Traffic Crash)

**scuff/yaw mark (critical speed mark):** a mark caused by the tires of a vehicle that negotiates a curve too fast and slides off the curve (Traffic Crash)

**search:** any government intrusion into a place in which a person has a reasonable expectation of privacy (Legal)

**search warrant:** a court order that authorizes law enforcement to conduct a search and seizure (Legal)

**SECURE:** an acronym for Safety, Ethics, Community, Understanding, Response, and Evaluation; the model used to enhance an officer's problem-solving capabilities (Patrol 1)

**self-defense:** a common legal term that describes the justifiable use of force that is necessary to protect oneself (Legal)

**self-help repossession:** the process where a creditor may take possession of the collateral after default without a court order, if the repossession can be done without breach of the peace (Legal)

**seizure:** an act that occurs when the government affects a person's right to have or control his or her property, usually by taking that property (Legal)

**self-knowledge:** an awareness of one's inner nature, feelings, abilities, and limitations (Communications)

**self-talk:** a continual internal monologue in which an individual narrates events that are occurring (Communications)

**sender:** the person who sends a message to a receiver (Communications)

**sentence:** a group of words that contains a subject and a verb and expresses a complete thought (Communications)

**sentence fragment:** a group of words that lacks a subject or verb or fails to express a complete thought (Communications)

**sexual battery:** the oral, anal, or vaginal penetration by or union with the sexual organ of another; anal or vaginal penetration of another by any other object (Legal)

**sexual harassment:** unwelcome sexual advances, requests for sexual favors, and other verbal or physical conduct of a sexual nature (Introduction to Law Enforcement)

**sexual violence:** defined in F.S. §784.046(c) and means any one incident of sexual battery as defined in F.S. Ch. 794;

- a lewd or lascivious act, as defined in F.S. Ch. 800, committed upon or in the presence of a person younger than 16 years old
- luring or enticing a child, as described in F.S. Ch. 787
- sexual performance by a child, as described in F.S. §827.071
- or any other forcible felony in which a sexual act is committed or attempted, regardless of whether criminal charges based on the incident were filed, reduced or dismissed by the State Attorney (Criminal Investigations)

**show-up:** a one-on-one identification of a suspect in the field by a victim or witness orchestrated by a law enforcement officer a short time after the commission of an offense (Legal)

**sign-language interpreter:** a person who can both receive and express information and interpret it effectively, accurately, and impartially (Human Issues)

**signals:** a system of communication that uses the word "signal" to precede numbers (Communications)

**sketch:** a hand-drawn picture of the crash scene as an officer perceives it upon arrival (Traffic Crash)

**skid mark:** a black mark left by a tire that slides and cannot rotate (Traffic Crash)

**skip-skid marks:** a series of skid marks usually short in length with irregular intervals between them (Traffic Crash)

**slang:** informal, nonstandard words often characterized by regional or specific group usage (Communications)

**smuggling:** an offense against the integrity of the United States borders (Criminal Investigations)

**solicitation:** an offense in which a person commands, encourages, hires, or requests another person to engage in specific conduct which would constitute the commission of an offense or an attempt (Legal)

**sovereign immunity:** a legal concept derived from the common law idea that the king and his agents can do no wrong, which is applied to employees or agents of a governmental entity, or to the governmental entity as an organization, to preclude the award of damages in a civil lawsuit (Legal)

**specific intent:** a special mental element of intention to cause a particular result, which is required over and above any mental state required for the offender to commit the act (Legal)

**speech impairment:** a physiological condition that causes difficulty in producing sound or understanding language, including reading and writing (Human Issues)

**spin-down:** begins at the end of mechanical delay and ends when the total four-wheel lockup or skid begins (Traffic Crash)

**spiral search pattern:** a search pattern often used outside by one person in which the searcher begins at a certain point and walks in increasingly larger circles to the outmost boundary of the search area (Crime Scene Investigations)

**squeegee mark:** the strip of dry pavement left after a vehicle skids on a wet roadway (Traffic Crash)

**stand:** the halting of a vehicle, whether occupied or not, otherwise than temporarily, for the purpose of, and while actually engaged in, receiving or discharging passengers (Patrol 1)

**standard of care:** the level of competency expected or required during the performance of a service or a duty (Patrol 2)

**Standardized Field Sobriety Tests (SFST):** the psychophysical tests given to determine impairment (DUI Traffic Stops)

**start of evasive action:** any action the driver takes that alters the speed or direction of the vehicle, such as applying the brakes or turning the steering wheel (Traffic Crash)

**statement:** a permanent, verbal, or written record of a person's account of an incident or occurrence that may or may not be made under oath (Communications)

**statute of limitations:** a law that bars the state from prosecuting an individual after a certain period of time has elapsed since the criminal act occurred (Legal)

**statutory law:** the written laws enacted by Congress, state legislatures, or local governing authorities in response to a perceived need to clarify the function of government (Legal)

**stereotyping:** the labeling of people either positively or negatively based on generalizations about their gender, race, ethnicity, religion, or other characteristic (Communications)

**stop:** when prohibited, any halting, even momentarily, of a vehicle, whether occupied or not, except when necessary to avoid conflict with other traffic or to comply with the directions of a law enforcement officer or traffic control sign or signal (Patrol 1)

**strategic intelligence:** examines crime patterns and crime trends for management use in decision making, resource development, resource allocation, and policy planning; typically focuses on specific crime types (Criminal Investigations)

**stress:** the physical or emotional reactions to an event or situation (Patrol 1)

**stressors:** the factors which may cause stress (Patrol 1)

**strip/line search pattern:** a search pattern often used outside by several people in which the search area is divided into lanes that are searched by one or more people in both directions until the entire area has been examined (Crime Scene Investigations)

**structure:** any building of any kind, either temporary or permanent, which has a roof over it, and the enclosed space of ground and outbuildings immediately surrounding that structure (Legal)

**substance abuse:** the continued use of a substance for non-medical reasons despite the knowledge that the substance causes adverse effects on an individual's social life, occupational life, and psychological or physical health (Human Issues)

**substance dependence:** continued substance use due to an uncontrollable physical or psychological craving for that substance (Human Issues)

**substance use:** the legal, illegal, therapeutic, or recreational intake of a substance that alters physical or mental function (Human Issues)

**substantial limitation:** a situation in which major life activities are restricted in the manner, condition, or duration in which they are performed in comparison with most people (Human Issues)

**surface marks:** the marks a vehicle can leave on roadways (Traffic Crash)

**suspect:** a person believed to have committed a crime or offense (Legal) (Crime Scene Investigations)

**suspected perpetrator:** a person believed to have committed a crime or offense (Legal)

## T

**tactical intelligence:** used for specific decision making or problem solving to deal with an immediate situation or crisis (Criminal Investigations)

**ten or numeric code:** a system that uses the number "10" to precede other numbers that represent specific activities (Communications)

**testimonial evidence:** evidence comprised of the statements solicited from witnesses on the stand (Legal)

**theft:** knowingly obtaining, using or endeavoring to obtain or use property of another with the intent to temporarily or permanently deprive the other person of the use of the property (Criminal Investigations)

**tire print:** the mark left by a tire that rolls over a soft material, such as sand, dirt, or a liquid, such as oil that is distributed over a hard surface, leaving an identifiable pattern matching the tread of the tire (Traffic Crash)

**tolerance:** the physical resistance to effects of a substance that causes a user to need a larger amount of it to experience the desired effect (Human Issues)

**tort:** an improper act in civil law (Legal)

**totality of circumstances:** a court review of all factors known to the officer at the time of the incident (Legal)

**traffic crash:** a collision involving one or more vehicles, which causes personal injury, property damage, or death, and which is the result of an unintentional act (Traffic Crash)

**traffic flow:** the general speed and direction of vehicle or pedestrian movement (Traffic Stops)

**traffic stop:** the temporary detention of an individual in a vehicle by an officer for an investigative purpose (Traffic Stops)

**trafficking:** an offense against a person for the purposes of subjection to involuntary servitude, peonage, debt bondage, slavery, or commercial sex (Criminal Investigations)

**transferred intent:** the intent that is present when an intentional act harms an unintended second victim (Legal)

**triangulation:** the method employed in crime-scene sketching using measurements made from at least two fixed objects to form a triangle (Crime Scene Investigations)

## U

**uttering:** knowingly exhibiting or publishing a document to someone or attempting to cash a check by signifying that the check and the endorsement is real (Criminal Investigations)

## V

**values:** the principles, standards, or qualities considered worthwhile or desirable; the core beliefs or desires that guide or motivate attitudes and actions (Introduction to Law Enforcement)

**vehicle:** every device in, upon, or by which any person or property may be transported or drawn upon a highway, excepting devices used exclusively upon stationary rails or tracks (DUI Traffic Stops)

**vehicle dynamics:** the movement of the vehicle during and after collision (Traffic Crash)

**verbal communication:** communication through spoken words (Communications)

**vertical communication:** the information that flows down through the supervision level to the lowest levels of the organization (Introduction to Law Enforcement)

**Vertical Gaze Nystagmus (VGN):** the involuntary jerking of the eyes as they move upward are held at maximum deviation (DUI Traffic Stops)

**Vestibular Nystagmus:** an involuntary jerking of the eyes caused by movement or action to the vestibular (inner ear) system (DUI Traffic Stops)

**vicarious liability:** when a person or entity is held liable for the negligent actions of another person, even though the first person or entity was not directly responsible for the injury (Legal)

**victim:** a person harmed by a crime (Crime Scene Investigations) (Legal)

**voluntary examination:** a decision by an individual to voluntarily seek psychiatric evaluation for symptoms that may be due to a mental illness (Human Issues)

**vulnerable adult:** a person 18 years of age or older whose ability to perform the normal activities of daily living or to provide for his or her own care or protection is impaired due to a mental, emotional, sensory, long-term physical, or developmental disability or dysfunction, brain damage, or the infirmities of aging (Criminal Investigations)

## W

**wig wags:** the alternating flashes of the vehicle lights, strobe, flashers, and other lights (Traffic Stops)

**withdrawal:** the physical and mental symptoms experienced by an addicted individual who stops using the addictive substance (Human Issues)

**within the state:** anywhere in Florida, whether on roadways, or public or private property (DUI Traffic Stops)

**witness:** a person who has information about some element of a crime or about evidence or documents related to a crime and who may have heard statements or observed events before, during, or after a crime; a person who sees, knows, or vouches for something and makes a sworn statement about that information (Legal) (Crime Scene Investigations)

**writ of replevin:** a court order to recover property that is in the wrongful possession of another (Legal)

## Z

**zone/quadrant search pattern:** a search pattern often used for an area that is large or outdoors in which the area is divided into four different sections and searched using an alternative search pattern (Crime Scene Investigations)

# COURT CASE INDEX

# INDEX

# D

# E



# F

# G



# H



# I

# J



# K



# L



# M

# S



# T

# U



# V

# W



# Y

# REFERENCES

## Chapter 1 Introduction to Law Enforcement

Florida Department of Law Enforcement. *FDLE Professional Compliance Bulletin.* Retrieved from: http://www.fdle.state.fl.us

International Association of Chiefs of Police. *Law Enforcement Code of Ethics.* Retrieved from: http://www.theiacp.org/

## Chapter 3 Communications

Cheatham, T.F., Erickson, K.V., and Dyson, F. *The Police Officer's Guide to Better Communication.* (1984). New York: Scott Foresman Trade.

## Chapter 4 Human Issues

Williams, John. *Dope 101.* (June, 2005). Los Angeles County Sheriff's Department.

## Chapter 5 Patrol 1

Goldstein, H. *Problem-oriented Policing.* (1990). New York: McGraw Hill.

## Chapter 6 Patrol 2

*Emergency Response Guidebook.* (2008). Retrieved from: http://hazmat.dot.gov/pubs/erg/gydebook.htm

## Chapter 7 Crime Scene Investigations

Holtz, Larry E. *Contemporary Criminal Procedure: Court Decisions for Law Enforcement.* (7th ed). (2001). Longwood, FL: Gould Publications.

*Florida Crimes, Motor Vehicles, and Related Laws with Criminal Jury Instruction.* (2005). Longwood, FL: Gould Publications.

LeBlanc, F. *Law Enforcement and Victim Sensitivity.* (1996). Broward County Sherriff's Office: Broward County, FL.

## Chapter 8 Criminal Investigations

*Cone of Knowledge* [Brochure]. (2004). Glynco, GA: Federal Law Enforcement Training Center.

Krupinski, Eve and Weikel, Dana. *Death from Child Abuse…and No One Heard.* (2002). Gulfport, FL: Currier Davis Publishing.

LeBlanc, Frank. *Law Enforcement and Victim Sensitivity.* (1996). Broward County Sherriff's Office: Broward County, FL.

Florida Department of Children and Families. (2006). http://www.myflorida.com/cf_web/

*Florida Responds to Human Trafficking.* (2003). Florida State University, Center for the Advancement of Human Rights. Retrieved from: http://www.humantrafficking.org/publications/250

*Human Trafficking in the United States: Promoting Law Enforcement Awareness.* (2005). Bureau of Justice, in collaboration with the Institute for Intergovernmental Research.

*"Interviewing Techniques."* (June 2007). Florida Juvenile Handbook. Tallahassee, FL: Florida Department of Law Enforcement, Florida Department of Juvenile Justice, Florida Department of Children and Families. Retrieved from: http://www.childnetswfl.org/UserFiles/File/Florida%20Juvenile%20Handbook%202007.pdf

Department of Juvenile Justice, Florida Department of Children and Families. (2000). Tallahassee, FL.

*Introduction to Human Trafficking.* (2005). St. Petersburg College, FL: Florida Regional Community Policing Institute.

*Notice of legal rights and remedies* [Brochure]. (2003). Tallahassee, FL: Criminal Justice Standards & Training Commission, Florida Department of Law Enforcement.

*Report on Activities to Combat Human Trafficking, Fiscal Years 2001–2005.* U. S. Department of Justice, Civil Rights Division.

*The ten commandments of communicating with people with disabilities* [Handout]. Adapted from many sources and updated by Irene M. Ward and Associates. Washington, DC: United Cerebral Palsy Association.

## **Chapter 10** DUI Traffic Stops

*Institute of Police Technology and Management (IPTM). DWI Detection and Standardized Field Sobriety Testing Manual.* Retrieved from: http://www.iptm.org, National Highway Traffic Safety Administration (NHTSA), United States Department of Transportation (DOT).

National Highway Traffic Safety Administration (NHTSA), United States Department of Transportation (DOT). *Drugs that Impair Driving.* (2006). Washington, DC: National Highway Traffic Safety Administration (NHTSA), United States Department of Transportation (DOT).

## **Chapter 11** Traffic Crash Investigations

Conklin, A.G. *Equations for the Traffic Crash Reconstructionist.*

Cloutier, Michel & Cushmac, George. *U.S. Department of Transportation Emergency Response Guide.* (2004). Washington, DC: U.S. Department of Transportation.

Florida Department of Highway Safety & Motor Vehicles. *Florida Uniform Traffic Citations.* (2009). Tallahassee, FL: Florida Department of Highway Safety & Motor Vehicles.

Florida Department of Highway Safety & Motor Vehicles. *Instructions For Completing the Florida Uniform Traffic Crash Report Forms (HSMV 90010S).* (July 2010). Tallahassee, FL: Florida Department of Highway Safety & Motor Vehicles.

Florida Department of Highway Safety & Motor Vehicles. *Florida Department of Highway Safety & Motor Vehicles Traffic Crash Report Forms.* (2008). Tallahassee, FL: Florida Department of Highway Safety & Motor Vehicles.

*Police One.* (2007). San Francisco, California: Praetorian Group, Inc.

Martinez, Luis. *Accident Investigation Manual for Patrol Officers.* (1994). (2nd ed.). Retrieved from: http://www.tarorigin.com/art/Lmartinez/

U.S. Department of Transportation Federal Highway Administration. *National Stop on Red Week.* (2007). Washington, DC: U.S. Department of Transportation Federal Highway Administration.

Rivers, R.W. *Institute of Police Technology and Management Training and Reference Manual for Traffic Accident Investigation.* (1997). (2nd ed.). Jacksonville, FL: University of North Florida.

# NOTES

# NOTES

# NOTES

# NOTES

# NOTES

# NOTES